D1029282

THE A. F. OF L.
IN THE TIME OF GOMPERS

SYRACUSE UNIVERSITY
LIBRARY

THE A.F. OF L.
IN THE TIME OF GOMPERS

by PHILIP TAFT
Professor of Economics, Brown University

HARPER & BROTHERS, PUBLISHERS, NEW YORK

THE A. F. OF L. IN THE TIME OF GOMPERS

Copyright © 1957 by Philip Taft

Printed in the United States of America

All rights in this book are reserved. No part of the book may be used or reproduced in any manner whatsoever without written permission except in the case of brief quotations embodied in critical articles and reviews. For information address Harper & Brothers, 49 East 33rd Street, New York 16, N. Y.

FIRST EDITION

D-G

Library of Congress catalog card number: 57-6741

33 A 88
TV24a
HD
8055
A5
T3
1957

M 5N57

10557 SUS (Econ)

to
Selig and Isabelle
Silverman

Contents

Preface

THIS work would not have been possible without the cooperation of the Executive Council of the American Federation of Labor, particularly President George Meany, Secretary-Treasurer William F. Schnitzler, and Mr. Boris Shiskin, who gave me their constant encouragement and aid at all stages of the study. The late Matthew Woll and Mr. David Dubinsky were also of help. A number of libraries made materials and documents available. The manuscript division of the Library of Congress enabled me to examine the papers of John P. Frey; the New York Public Library made available its valuable collection of labor newspapers and documents as well as the manuscript material of Frank P. Walsh and the National Civic Federation. Mr. Edward DeRoma and Dr. Robert Hill, the latter in charge of the manuscript division, were especially helpful. Miss Margaret F. Brickett and her staff of the U. S. Department of Labor made available files of old labor papers and Mr. John H. Berthel allowed me the use of the labor collection of the Johns Hopkins University, and Miss Margaret E. Lough and Miss Angela Lavarello were extremely helpful in making the labor material available. Mr. Leonard Rapport of the National Archives aided me with advice on using the labor collection in that division. Father Henry J. Browne of Catholic University was helpful both as an adviser in general and as a guide through the Powderly and Mitchell papers. Woodruff Randolph, president of the International Typographical Union, generously allowed me the use of old records of his unions. Mrs. Eloise Giles of the Library of the A. F. of L. was helpful. To the heads and staff of the above I express my sincere thanks for their aid and many kindnesses.

A number of friends and colleagues helped with advice on all or some parts of this study. Mr. and Mrs. Harry Lang furnished information which could not be obtained from mere documentary sources. Dr. John Sessions and Harry Crone of the International Ladies Garment Workers Union read much of the material. Mrs. Nora Piore gave me the benefit of her wide knowledge of American labor, and Jack Barbash's extensive knowledge and deep understanding of labor and social movements were freely placed at my disposal. I was fortunate in obtaining the insights of Mother Marguerite Green of the Convent of the Sacred Heart on a number of vital issues, and Matty Burry's help.

For many kindnesses and continuous help, I must express my sincere gratitude to the entire staff of the American Federation of Labor, who, while continually harrassed by my demands, were always tolerant and invariably helpful. Miss Martha Ford helped me decipher many of the old letters and guided me through documents and correspondence; Logan Kimmel supplied correspondence, and Bernard Green made it easier for me to carry on my work. Mr. Courtland Szell and his staff were always kind. George Brown helped on more than one occasion. The research department was of special aid, especially Seymour Brandwein and Nancy Pratt. Peter Henle, the associate head of this Department, read the first draft of the material, and his comments made it much easier for me to knit it together into meaningful patterns. Philip Pearl's suggestions were of help, but even more his kindness is gratefully acknowledged. To all of the staff members, individually and collectively, I wish to express my sincere gratitude.

There are a large number of studies from which I profited. Space compels me to limit my mention to Dr. Louis Lorwin's *American Federation of Labor,* a pioneer work for which all who write on the topic must be grateful.

In closing, I must note the aid of the late Arthur Elder. It is difficult for me to describe in a short space the debt I personally owe to this devoted servant of the labor movement. Convinced of the need for this work, he gave his time and energy so as to bring it into being. He asked for nothing, not even the meager recognition of mention in a Preface. Without his unselfish efforts this work would never have been started, and whatever merit my study may have, it is, in part at least, due to Arthur Elder's unselfish aid and devotion.

PHILIP TAFT

Introduction

A STUDY of the American Federation of Labor can be undertaken from two general points of view. In a limited sense, the A. F. of L. is nothing more than its constituent national, international, federal, and trade unions. Although there have been wide differences in outlook among them, these units have exercised a predominating influence upon policy.

More important, however, is the American Federation of Labor as a distinct entity, separate from its individual components. This study examines the evolution of policy and programs within the Federation and seeks to describe the problems, conflicts, and activities of the A. F. of L. as an independent institution and the spokesman for the major segment of the organized workers of the United States and Canada. Without authority or pretensions, the A. F. of L. was nevertheless able to become a driving force in providing assistance and leadership to the workers of the North American continent.

For many purposes, the rise of the American Federation of Labor can be dated from 1886. Its immediate predecessor, the Federation of Organized Trades and Labor Unions, made only a slight contribution to the subsequent policies and practices of the A. F. of L. As one examines the record, it appears evident that only if the principle of trade autonomy had been accepted could a federation of trade unions have been established. Yet the A. F. of L., if it were to be more than an annual meeting of delegates, had to be clothed with some purpose and authority. Consequently, it was given the responsibility for organizing the unorganized, although not the resources with which to carry out this objective.

The organizing activities of the Federation and the problems which they encountered and generated have been examined in some detail. Instead of laxity and lack of interest by the Federation and its officers, there is evidence that they always were debarred from more vigorous activity by the refusal of the affiliates to furnish the financial resources needed for such campaigns. Yet, as noted in Chapters II and VII, in its early years the Federation was active in organizing. Not only did it play a leading part in unifying regional and national organizations, but the A. F. of L. early became the center for disseminating information among trade unionists, bringing active union workers together, and mobilizing aid for the untried, inexperienced mass of newly-organized workers and their organizations. It carried on substantial organizing activity which was gradually absorbed by the affiliated unions as the latter grew in power. In an age when the trade unions were weak and dispersed, even the limited financial aid of the A. F. of L. was of great importance.

Another function performed by the A. F. of L. was to unify competing organizations occupying the same jurisdiction. Persistent efforts were made by leaders of the Federation in this direction, and they frequently succeeded where direct negotiations between competing unions had failed. The leaders of the Federation, although as sensitive as other men, did not feel their own prestige involved and were therefore ready to accept rebuffs which the leaders of the separate unions would not themselves have tolerated. Moreover, they were able to initiate and reinitiate efforts toward unity of a craft or trade, suggest compromises, and aid in the working out of agreements. While some of those directly involved might be reluctant to initiate such meetings, the Federation regarded these efforts as an integral part of its duties.

The labor movement, as represented by the A. F. of L., was from the beginning made up of organizations of unequal strength. Some, like the International Typographical and International Molders' Unions, were able to meet all their financial needs. Others insisted that the A. F. of L. provide financial support. There was no way in which the resources of affiliates could be mobilized, and the heads of the Federation believed for many years that the labor movement would profit if some system of mutual aid under the aegis of the Federation could be devised. In contrast, the leaders of a majority of unions saw in such a policy a possible threat to their independence, and therefore withheld their consent from a number of arrangements which would have enabled the Federation to mobilize a defense or organizing fund. The A. F. of L. was forced to depend upon the occasional assessment to raise funds for a distressed or needy affiliate. Even this kind of occasional levy at times aroused protests from some unions.

The aid so mobilized was often of great importance to organizations engaged in contests with employers or with difficult problems which could not be met with their own resources. Whatever aid was given in many instances would not have been forthcoming without the endorsement and support of the A. F. of L. The pleas for assistance directed at the Federation were often numerous; some selection among the various claimants had to be made, for if the pleas of the Federation became too numerous, they might not have been answered even on the scale to which they usually were. Even so, the record shows that locals and internationals frequently protested the constant stream of importunities directed at them by sister organizations in need of financial support. Unless the Federation was ready to screen the applicants and appeal only for those whose need was greatest or most pressing, or whose cause was

most important to the general labor movement, its appeals on behalf of
affiliates might have brought forth only a meager response.⌉Refusal to
sponsor all appeals was sometimes interpreted as indifference or cal-
lousness to the struggles of a beleaguered group of workers, but the
A. F. of L. had to make the choice between destroying its effectiveness in
this area or limiting its endorsement to appeals for funds for those causes
which appeared to be most deserving at the time.⌉

The Federation was not, even at the beginning, without influence. On
issues such as shorter hours, dealt with in Chapter IX, the Federation
could lead and inspire. On other issues, its views and actions might be
criticized by a section of its member-unions. On the other hand, as the
representative of the general labor movement rather than of a specific
group of workers, the Federation was alert to the need for devising
policies which would make it easier to marshal the workers remaining
outside the unions into the organized ranks of labor. In this area, as in
many others, the heads of the Federation could only plead or scold,
for they lacked the authority or power to impose their will. Where differences over internal questions developed between the heads of the Federation and some of its affiliates, the A. F. of L. could not make them
subjects of public argument. At times such differences, especially when
they involved matters that came before conventions, might not be kept
out of the public domain, but the heads of the Federation were always
averse to airing publicly dissension over internal policy. Usually the
heads of the Federation offered their advice, and attempted to persuade.
There was, however, no way for them to enforce their will if they met
with refusal. Differences over political tactics or ultimate aims were
not regarded in the same fashion. These issues could be and were
frequently and acrimoniously debated on the floor of conventions.

Thus the heads of the Federation were not completely lacking in
power, though there existed no basis for it in the constitution of the
organization. [Almost from the beginning Gompers assumed the role
of active statesman, and although he was only thirty-six years old there
was no serious objection to his role. His opponents as well as supporters
frequently called on him for advice and aid. Perhaps better than any
man, Gompers knew the sources of his strength and the limits of his
power. He was the unofficial ambassador to the non-labor world. It was
his task to offer the views of the A. F. of L. upon a multitude of issues and
to become recognized as the official spokesman for all labor. Such an office,
despite its limitations, conferred much prestige and a measure of power.
Moreover, unions were frequently placed in a position where they needed
the moral, financial, and political support of the entire labor movement,
and the heads of the Federation were the only ones who could muster
such aid.⌉The need of the unions for some agency which might settle

or conciliate differences among them was another source of the Federation's power. While technically the Federation had no right to intervene or even to offer its services, the unions were satisfied with, and sometimes anxious for, some forum for the settling of inevitable differences arising among affiliated organizations.

Such power had to be exercised with restraint, for otherwise it would have ceased to be effective. Gompers and other members of the Executive Council sometimes sought to suggest a given policy, or voiced opposition toward others. In some instances the advice would be heeded, in others rejected. The Federation would sometimes be compelled to side with a union in an internal dispute over policy that the heads of the Federation might themselves hold questionable. Yet an examination of the problem in Chapter XI indicates that against the wishes of the affiliated union, the A. F. of L. was generally powerless to intervene. A number of instances described illustrate this view.

[Moreover, the A. F. of L. was occasionally forced, despite the reluctance of its active officers, to intervene on the side of an affiliate engaged in a controversy with some of its members or with their locals even when the heads of the Federation believed that the members or the locals, rather than the officers of the affiliate, had right on their side. Such intervention was always a difficult choice, but one the heads of the Federation had to make if they wanted the A. F. of L. to continue to be effective.] The affiliated unions would not allow a tutelary power to direct and regulate their conduct and insisted that central organizations under direct control of the A. F. of L.—city centrals and state federations—refrain from supporting insurgents within their unions.

The adjudication of one internal issue, jurisdictional boundaries, was forced upon the A. F. of L. by its affiliates. Not only were the heads of the A. F. of L unenthusiastic about the attempts of the affiliates to saddle them with the responsibility for settling conflicting jurisdictional claims, but, as is noted in Chapter XII, they regarded jurisdictional controversies among unions as a harmful and unfavorable development. Despite the insistence of many of the affiliates that they were sovereign in their own jurisdictions and that they alone had the authority to decide their limits, these disputes were continually brought to the floor of the A. F. of L. conventions. Considering the absence of power and the frequent unwillingness of affiliates to accept unfavorable decisions, the contribution of the A. F. of L. to the allaying of jurisdictional differences cannot be minimized.

On this issue, as on many others, the Federation was not always consistent, but inconsistency was forced upon it by the exigencies of particular situations. [The Federation was more concerned with eliminating division and conflict than in devising a consistent policy] which, because

of constantly changing circumstances and problems, could not be enforced. Nor were the heads of the Federation oblivious to the need for
allowing violations of the jurisdictional rights of their affiliates under
some circumstances. The evidence reveals that they were aware of the
need of some sacrifice of jurisdictional rights in various industries, so
that the workers could be effectively organized by one "predominant"
union. For the heads of the Federation the jurisdictional question, like
all others, could be regarded only as a practical matter. Consequently,
they were able to devise a working compromise in the coal mining
industry.

Contrary to the general impression, the heads of the Federation were
not, on principle, either in favor of or opposed to industrial organization,
or to the organization of the unskilled. The Federation did not have
the financial resources to conduct large-scale organizing drives, but there
was never any view expressed that the semiskilled and unskilled could not
be marshaled into unions. [Because he believed that an increase in contributions would militate against the organizing of the unskilled, Gompers
opposed an increase in the per capita tax of the federal labor unions, although he was a strong believer in high dues and per capita tax payments.] Gompers was convinced that all workers were ultimately orga-
nizable, and his opposition to government intervention was in part
founded on the belief that eventually all workers would find their way
into a labor organization, and would thereby be able to solve their own
problems without the aid of a government bureaucracy which he regarded as evil on other grounds.

The structure of the affiliates was a problem almost from the beginning.
The heads of the A. F. of L. approached this issue as a practical matter
which had to be worked out in accordance with the needs, pressures, and
power relations of the affiliates. [At the beginning the majority of affiliates
were craft organizations, but some were industrial in their arrangement
and others exercised jurisdiction over more than one kind of workers.
The leaders of the Federation would have preferred that the affiliates
follow a broad and tolerant policy and that functioning unions, irrespective of their structure, not be disturbed. However, the affiliates whose
jurisdictions were invaded by other unions would not accept such a
liberal policy, and the Federation had no means of overruling these
opponents.]

[Industrial organization was in the early years a problem in two industries—coal mining and brewing. In the former, the A. F. of L. was able
to work out an arrangement which recognized the *de facto* situation,
the right of the United Mine Workers of America to organize all workers
in and around the mines. In the brewing industry, however, no such
compromise was acceptable to the craft unions, which were on much

stronger ground than in the coal industry. Industrial organization as a doctrine was opposed because the heads of the A. F. of L., from their experience with the settlement of jurisdictional disputes, well knew that the passage of a resolution by the convention could in no sense compel affiliates to revise their structure or surrender parts of their jurisdiction to other unions. Endorsement of such proposals would only have aroused the fears and suspicions of a number of unions and would not have contributed in any manner to the solution of the problem.⎤

Jurisdictional problems and the existence of several unions in a plant posed the necessity of cooperation among closely related organizations. ⎡The American Federation of Labor favored cooperation among unions on a local scale, and among international unions under the aegis of the Federation.⎦ However, when such cooperation developed in the building construction industry independently of the A. F. of L., the latter feared its position might be threatened by a rival central organization. In the end the departmental form was devised, and unions within some departments complained of the attempts of the latter to subvert their rights. The fear of the A. F. of L. that a competing power within the trade union movement might be established was not realized, in part because of the unwillingness of some large unions to accord the departments more than limited authority.

⎡Internal problems, its relations with the constituent unions, and the balance of their power within the Federation were of overriding concern to the A. F. of L. during its formative years.⎦Attitudes on public questions and on tactics to be pursued in achieving non-trade-union goals had to be defined, and those inevitably aroused sharp differences within the ranks. As can be noted in the first several chapters, radical influences were of some importance within the trade union movement, but socialism was not the only radical doctrine then seeking the suffrage of the worker and his organization. Anarchism also had a following within the ranks of labor, and the adherents of this view were as anxious to avoid political entanglements as the "pure" trade unionists. It is difficult to weigh the influence of the anarchists in the development of a bias against an independent political party within the A. F. of L. That they played a role there can be no doubt. One of the early officers of the A. F. of L. was a believer in this persuasion. In a sense the debates on abstract questions had an air of unreality, for the A. F. of L. could not bind any of its affiliates to a particular view. Yet endorsement of a program by the Federation might have given it support and stature it would not otherwise have achieved.

In any event the trade unionists, who were anxious to concentrate their main effort upon organization on the economic level, carried the day. They were also able to limit the political activities of the Federation to a few specific demands, which were later enlarged. The dominant group in the Federation wanted to concentrate the efforts and resources of the trade unions upon organizing on the economic front, and limit their political activity. Their views were influenced by suspicion of both government and centralized power, as well as by their reading of the history and the temper of American society.

[Emphasis upon immediate demands by the trade unions is not peculiar to those established in the United States. In a sense, the primary interest of a free trade union must be directed toward such ends. There need, however, be no necessary conflict between typically trade union behavior and the endorsement of socialism or other collectivist doctrines. Certainly the economic organizations of labor in England and the Scandinavian countries, which espouse socialism, fall in the category of unions as much as those in the United States. In contrast to the unions of the former two countries, those in the United States and Canada did not embrace socialism or a similar doctrine. While it is difficult to give precise weight to the various forces that influenced the distinctive development of the unions of the North American continent, the efforts and arguments of the leaders of the Federation must be regarded as of great significance. Socialists did not always dominate the trade union movement of England, and there was some opposition to their hegemony within the early trade union movement of Sweden; yet the ideological direction of the labor movement of the United States and Canada was different from that of these European countries. In England, as in Sweden, Socialist doctrine has become the accepted view among unionists, even though it might not always have a predominating influence upon day-to-day union policy. In the United States, in contrast, this view has steadily lost ground and its direct influence is today almost gone.]

It cannot be argued that the Socialists, between the founding of the A. F. of L. and the mid-1920's, lacked either devotion to the cause of labor or adroit and effective leadership. A number of international unions, some of them important ones, were dominated by followers of this creed, and other unions contained active and significant minorities who were allied to the Socialist cause. One might also recognize that the soil of the United States was not as fertile for the diffusion of Socialist influence as other parts of the world. The absence of feudalism in America, the *Hartz* greater class mobility, higher standards of living, the existence of the right of the franchise for all male citizens, as well as the greater social democracy, proved greater handicaps to the spread of Socialist ideas in the United States than in the older world.

Against these positive elements, one must recognize the fierce and bitter character of American industrial warfare, the intransigence of the American industrialist when facing the union, and the demand of many

industries in the period from the end of the Civil War to the mid-1930's
for absolute domination over the terms of employment without any in-
trusion or recognition of the union. Yet, despite the bitter and often brutal
character of American industrial warfare, the American worker failed
to respond to the collectivist appeal based upon a class struggle doctrine.
While the American workers' response to socialism was influenced by
many forces, the contribution of the A. F. of L. should not be underestimated. It insisted that trade unionism, through collective bargaining and
control over conditions of employment, could be the most effective means
for rectifying injustice and inequity. Undoubtedly the rejection of socialism by the dominant wing in the Federation was influenced by its experience and appreciation of the American social and political scene;
but by throwing its influence against the endorsement of collectivist
philosophies, the Federation, with its insistence upon immediate job
control and concessions, greatly contributed to the development of the
specific outlook of American labor and its unions.

Rejection of collectivist ideas did not mean that the A. F. of L. was
without a philosophy. Not as elaborate or as full-bodied as the philosophies of anarchism and socialism, the A. F. of L. held that workers could
improve their economic position and enlarge their freedoms through
organized trade union action and the establishment of systems of collective
bargaining or industrial government. Side by side with the reliance upon
the organized effort of the workers themselves and the belief in the possibility of cooperation with the employer through systems of industrial
government was the fear of the state and collectivism as possible new
sources for oppression of the individual worker.

The differences in political and social outlook among trade unionists
affected their attitudes toward a number of issues. Not only were there
deep differences over socialism and independent political action, but
conflict also existed over the role of government in economic affairs, and
the extent to which labor and other types of welfare legislation were to
be supported. The dominant group in the Federation started with a philosophical bias against reliance upon government for correction of economic
ills. It was a remarkable development that leaders with limited human
and financial resources, fighting to establish trade unions, would seek to
avoid a too close dependence upon political activity. Moreover, some
of the leaders, as already noted, had a deep suspicion of government, and
the trade union movement represented for them a means whereby problems could be solved without the intervention of government. They
wanted the workers to develop an independent source of power so that
they would not be compelled to rely upon a government agency for
improvement in their economic condition. Their initial suspicion was
later reinforced by the experience with government of many labor organi-

zations and workers during industrial disputes.

The extreme to which this view was carried by Gompers and his close co-workers aroused strong and growing opposition among Socialist and other trade unionists. Some evidence will be found in the study that in the period immediately before and after World War I, this extreme view was no longer acceptable to a majority of A. F. of L. members and their unions. However, the defeats of labor in the early 1920's led a majority to return to the earlier intellectual position. The leaders of the Federation in the early years visualized control of the job and collective bargaining as the means for improving the position of the majority of workers. They were willing to support legislation, but only for workers whose bargaining position was inferior to that of the majority. In pursuance of the policy of promoting collective bargaining, these leaders were not averse to meeting with heads of business on a friendly basis. This policy, epitomized by the friendship and cooperation with the National Civic Federation, aroused strong opposition in some quarters. As indicated in Chapter XIV, the heads of the A. F. of L. were under no illusion about the advantages to be gained from their relationship to the Civic Federation, but they saw no reason for forfeiting an opportunity to gain even minor concessions.

World War I presented both a challenge and an opportunity. Several of the more conservative leaders complained that the heads of the Federation were too closely tied to the Federal government. On the other hand, the increases in membership and the friendly attitude of government toward labor unions during this period tended to undermine the ideological basis of the opposition to government intervention in economic affairs. In this period the older leadership faced its most serious challenge from within. The defeats of the labor movement in the postwar period removed the edge from this opposition.

The A. F. of L. always fought for the complete extension of civil rights, and throughout its history protested against persecution of minorities and political dissidents. Beginning in the 1890's, it favored a restrictive immigration policy, but its views were influenced by economic and not racial considerations. Within this country, it fought against any restrictions upon foreign workers, whom it sought to protect against discrimination. It opposed efforts to place foreigners under special restrictions, suggested after World War I. Like its affiliates, the Federation always showed more hostility to Oriental immigration than to the influx from European countries. Opposition to Orientals was not based upon racial grounds, but upon the effect the arrival of large numbers would have on the supply of labor.

The A. F. of L. was usually ahead of its affiliates in its desire to establish closer relations with the trade union movements of other countries, and [t hoped the trade union movements of different countries would cooperate in common enterprises and help to abolish war.]Even when it failed to maintain formal relations with the labor movements of Europe, it rallied to appeals for aid from workers' organizations of these countries.

[The period covered in this volume was not one of uninterrupted progress. It was one in which the A. F. of L. was firmly established, but also one in which it suffered serious reverses.]Labor depended upon limited resources, government was usually hostile, and the activities of the trade unions were frequently circumscribed. It was a time in which the views we associate with the American Federation of Labor were hammered out in countless and often acrimonious controversies; it was a period in which the American Federation of Labor took firm root. While it was sometimes defeated and its numbers reduced, it remained nevertheless the indestructible rallying center for the workers of the United States and Canada.]

I

The Beginnings

[THE A. F. of L. came into existence as a result of the desire of many unions to band together to form a trade national union center or federation which, while enabling them to cooperate on many issues, would yet possess only limited power over the affiliates. The twice-born A. F. of L. —in 1881 and 1886—was the culmination of a series of efforts going back to the 1820's to establish a viable center for labor organizations.]

FIRST LABOR MOVEMENT

The Mechanics Union of Trade Associations, established in Philadelphia in 1827, marked the beginning of interunion cooperation or what has since been described as a "labor movement." Local in character, this federation was organized on the basis of a common interest of all workers, such as absence of adequate public schools, the requirement of militia service, and imprisonment for debt.

In the next decade, a labor movement which stretched beyond the local area was established. At the invitation of the General Trades Union of New York and its vicinity, thirty delegates from labor centers in six cities—Boston, Brooklyn, New York, Newark, Philadelphia, and Poughkeepsie—met in New York City in August 1834 and formed the National Trades Union. Ely Moore, a New York printer, was elected president and William English, a Philadelphia shoemaker, secretary. [It was a loose and impermanent arrangement, significant only in that it was the first attempt of organized workers to build a national labor federation. The National Trades Union lasted for three years, failing to survive the depression of 1837.]

There was not much experimenting with forms of labor organization in the 1840's. Conditions were not hospitable to the survival of, much less the expansion of trade unions. [The 1850's witnessed a new departure, the establishment of regional and national organizations by single trades.] The extension of interest from the locality to the region and nation was in response to both technical and market changes which were beginning to make themselves felt. It was now possible for products manufactured in different places to compete with each other. Inevitably, union men found themselves faced by the competition of the products of unorga-

1

nized workers, and [only the expansion of their organizations beyond their own localities could effectively ward off this competitive threat.]

Another source of anxiety for the organized craftsmen was the migration of out-of-town journeymen who had not completed their full apprenticeship, and who frequently ignored local standards and scales. At times, organized workers were subjected to the pressure of a combination of employers, a pressure which in turn tended to encourage organization of workers of kindred trades in a number of localities to resist the now more powerful masters. Again regional and national organization of labor in a trade was stimulated by technical change which exposed the industry to an invasion of unskilled or "green hands."[1]

NATIONAL UNION

The 1850's saw the emergence of a new type of trade union. The first national union, the National Typographical Union, was established in 1852, and five other national organizations were formed in the decade. Even at the beginning, these organizations showed a tendency to espouse more limited and "narrow" policies. Meeting for a first time in a national assembly in 1850, the Journeymen Printers of the United States attributed the power of the employer to dominate labor to the rise in the size of the labor force. To eliminate disparity in bargaining, the first declaration advised that the establishment of a national union was necessary. The objectives of this national movement were defined as first the

. . . regulation and adjustment of the different scales of prices, so as not to conflict with each other, second giving traveling certificates to the members in good standing, to be legal for one year, which shall recommend holders thereof to assistance and traveling expenses from the Union, in any city or town they cannot obtain work.[2]

In addition, the names of "rats or other unworthy members of the trade and a description of these persons" were to be sent to subordinate unions. The locals were allowed to call for assistance in case of need. The convention also urged a limitation on the training of apprentices, and opposed the awarding of state printing to the lowest bidder.

In 1852, when the Journeymen Printers became the National Typographical Union, it placed the abolition of Sunday labor at the top of its demands. At the second convention the objective of the organization was defined as the securing of "a just remuneration for our labor."[3] As one examines the questions that came before this pioneer trade union in the first years of its existence, it becomes clear that the principal sessions of the early conventions were almost entirely given over to questions affecting the job. Thus the sixth convention of the union, in addition to discussing apprenticeship, a perennial topic, considered methods for

regulating traveling journeymen; urged subordinate unions to divide
the available work equitably so as to avoid dissension in the ranks; and
requested locals "to adopt some conciliatory method of making important
changes in their scale of prices."[4]

It is obvious that what has since been described as "business unionism"
had already been discovered or devised by the early members of the
printers' organization. This concentration on job problems does not
necessarily mean that printers were not concerned about other issues,
and that politics and both producers' and consumers' cooperation had no
place in their thinking. However, the early national unions seem more
interested in devising common programs of immediate economic demands
and of policies to effectuate them than in elaborating basic plans for
social reorganization. Even when the interests of trades other than printing are considered, the National Typographical Union limited its vision
to improvements on the job. At its convention in 1864 it recommended
to its locals of "different cities and towns the immediate initiation of
such steps as will secure the formation of trades unions, for the mutual
protection and support of the working men of all trades."[5]

While the printers were in advance of most crafts in the forming of
trade unions and in developing what might be called, "pure" trade union
policies, they were by no means the only group which showed a tendency
in this direction. The twenty-six delegates who organized the Carpenters'
and Joiners' National Union in 1865 defined the purpose of their national
organization as the "better protection of our trade, for the benefits to be
derived from having a national traveling card and password so that our
enrolled members may receive aid in case of need."

The carpenters were conscious that they were not innovators, for the
leaders in this endeavor advised the delegates to "model our plan of action
after some trade that has organized successfully." Members were told
that demands ought to be "well timed, prudent and reasonable." Even
more interesting were the views on the calling of strikes. The head of
the union suggested that strikes should only be called when approved
by two-thirds of the members in good standing. The creation of a national
fund was recommended:

. . . eventually to be available in case of strikes or other exigencies. . . . In that
case the National Union would amount to something; its utility would then be
palpable to the dullest comprehension. It would then be considered a vital
necessity, and not as now, a conventional abstraction, that may or may not be
useful.[6]

The desirability of national unions establishing a fund for the mutual
support of locals in the craft was first generally recognized in the 1860's.
Establishment of such funds meant a diminution in the powers of the

locals and an added expense upon the members—factors which undoubtedly strengthened the local opposition to such measures. President John
Oberly of the National Typographical Union urged that the establishment of a national fund would increase rather than diminish the power of
the subordinate locals. In discussing the functions of the national organization, Oberly described it as the legislative body with authority to
determine the usages and customs of the trade, the tribunal with authority
to decide differences between members of a local and the local officers,
or between locals, and the "organization that will be effective in maintaining the wages of printers at a reasonable rate."[7]

The national union, because of lack of funds, was not effectively aiding
subordinate locals to enforce a just scale of prices for the labor of members. The proposal for setting up a national fund by levying an annual tax
of fifty cents per member gained almost unanimous support of the delegates at the convention of 1867. It was passed by a vote of forty-seven
to three, yet in the end the opposition of several influential locals was
sufficient to deter President Oberly from putting the plan into effect. At
the next reunion he pointed to the loss of several strikes whose failure
he traced "to lack of funds to sustain them."[8]

The desirability of a national defense fund for effectively carrying on
the work of the union was recognized by leaders in crafts other than
printing. In his report to the seventh annual convention of the Bricklayers'
National Union in 1872, President Merideth Moore stressed the desirability of building a healthy treasury, and in the preceding year had
urged the adoption of "some benevolent feature, so as to combine benevolence with protection."[9]

OPPOSITION TO RADICAL DOCTRINES

While the trade unions were seeking to rally the members of their crafts
around a program of job improvements, individuals and organizations,
interested in broader and perhaps more fundamental reforms, were also
appealing for labor support. Many trade union officers did not take
kindly to such appeals, and union spokesmen occasionally denounced
the attempts to lure the workers into such "questionable" enterprises. In
the opinion of one trade union editor, labor had "suffered exceedingly
from their quackery and preposterous visionary ranting."[10] In the same
spirit President Bodwell of the International Typographical Union warned
against false doctrines and violence. He believed that radicals:

. . . [by] their vociferous assertions that they represent the laboring classes of
America . . . have been the means of retarding greatly the legitimate and
thorough organization of workingmen. . . . The workingmen desire no division
of property and overthrow of the social structure. . . . What workingmen desire

is that they shall have the same right to form associations for the protection and advancement of their interests that businessmen of all professions have . . . to have the opportunity to earn honestly enough pay to enable them to keep themselves and their families decently, to educate them, to put something by for sickness or old age. And this they propose to accomplish, without interfering with the rights of others, in a perfectly legitimate manner, through organization. I am not only certain that printers have no sympathy with these communist cut-throats, but I am also certain that no good is wished them by trades-unions generally.[11]

From a somewhat different side, the same criticism appears in the *Iron Molders' Journal*, which observed that the attempt to organize "labor as a whole" was a failure, while the trade unions, in contrast, had done reasonably well. "Trade unions look only to the organization of trades—each trade union to its own particular trade—and the only question they deal with are [sic] the hours and wages of labor."[12]

On the whole the national unions shied away, almost from the beginning, from radical reform movements, although some officers and members favored such programs. At the same time, the national unions were conscious of the need for a trade union federation which would limit its membership to trade and labor organizations and bar reform groups and political parties from affiliation. This did not necessarily imply hostility to reform, monetary or governmental, but it represented a recognition that trade unions had special problems which only they themselves could solve. As early as 1872, the *Coopers' Journal* advocated

. . . more solidarity between the several national and international organizations . . . we want a fraternity of trades of mechanics of all branches of industry; we want a movement that will generalize and combine the acts and movements of the various trades and direct them to the accomplishment of a common purpose; in a word, we want a national trades assembly, or a combination of all the disconnected trade organizations in the country; a central medium of communication and cooperation between the several labor associations that are now isolated. We unhesitatingly declare that a national trades assembly is essentially and absolutely necessary to the success of the labor movement on this continent.[13]

This organization favored a "narrow" trade union federation, and not a reform party. In fact, the leaders of the Coopers' Union regarded labor reform parties as "ephemeral and transitory as summer dew." In their opinion, the "elements of the labor movement are too diverse" for the establishment of a labor political party. On the other hand, the "same argument which clearly establishes the immeasurable advantages of combination when applied to a single trade or branch of industry, is equally cogent and conclusive that a combination of all trades would enhance these advantages incomprehensibly."[14]

SEEKING A TRADE UNION FEDERATION

There were, at the time, other advantages of a trade union federation divorced from political and reform parties. Based upon the recognition of the particularistic interests of trade unions, leaders of organized labor were seeking a means by which their organizations could cooperate on common problems. During 1873, for example, the heads of several international unions almost simultaneously approved of the need for a trade union federation. Writing to William Saffin, the head of the International Typographical Union, the president of the Iron Molders' International Union, informed him that:

Many of the discreet and thoughtful men in the trade union movement, have canvassed the advisability of forming a national trades assembly or industrial congress, and have decided that such an association must be entirely free from political influences, and composed of delegates from *bona fide* trade and labor unions. The cooperation of this body is solicited, and I deem it respectful and proper to call your attention to the subject.[15]

The depression of 1873 put an end to the plans for a wider federation of trade unions, and prevented any action on plans already formulated; but by 1874-1875 trade unions had recovered some of their strength, and they again turned to the possibility of forming a federation. The enthusiasm of the Molders' Union for a federation of trade unions was still qualified by its suspicion of all inclusive movements of labor. In its view

Every effort to unite labor has been as grand a fizzle as the conception was grand. We are referring to labor as a whole, not to the efforts to organize trade unions. Trade unions look only to the organizations of trades—each trade union to its own particular trade—and the only questions they deal with are hours and wages of labor.[16]

The leaders of the Molders' Union also thought the Pittsburgh convention of labor and social reformers, in April 1876, lacking in practical results. The gathering found the trade unions not directly represented. A contest for control between the Socialists and the advocates of cheap money (or greenbackers) took place, with the latter gaining the victory. The convention endorsed a scheme for the issuance of inconvertible bonds and paper money. A protective tariff for protecting American labor, cooperation for trading and manufacturing, abrogation of the Burlingame treaty with China, and a liberal policy of internal improvements were also proposed.

The difficulty of such attempts to unify all groups that claimed to represent labor lay both in a conflict of views and a failure to define a policy. According to the Molders' Union "a national council of all labor must be as a national or union of a particular labor."[17] In other words, a central labor federation could only be effective if it were made up of workers organized in specific trades.

[The Molders' Union was not the only trade union thinking in terms of wider labor unity. In 1878 the president of the Amalgamated Association of Iron and Steel Workers, at the orders of the convention of his union, called for a meeting of representatives of International Unions to organize a central federation. In response to this suggestion the Molders' Union authorized its president to meet with representatives from other trades for the purpose of setting up a federation of trades unions. However, no action was to bind the Molders' Union until the plan was approved by a majority of the local organizations.[18] Nothing came of this attempt, and the initiative in this endeavor was taken over by the International Typographical Union. Its convention in 1879, the Twenty-Seventh Session voted "to open a correspondence with the different International Labor Unions of North America with a view of forming International Amalgamated Union. The corresponding secretary was directed to lay such correspondence before the next annual convention."[19]]

A number of International Unions were then requested by the International Typographical Union to give their views on the feasibility of forming a federation of trades organizations. Only the Cigar Makers' International Union showed an interest in this project, but even this organization failed to elect a delegate to attend a conference for considering the matter. [Although the response was not favorable, the International Typographical Union refused to be discouraged. At its convention in 1880, a Special Committee on the Amalgamation of International Trades Unions was elected. Among its members were Lyman A. Brant and W. H. Foster, two men who later were to play an important role in the forming of the subsequent trade union federation. The convention also instructed its corresponding secretary to invite the national and international trades unions and trades assemblies in the United States and Canada to send delegates to a convention to organize a Continental Federation of Trades. The projected federation was to "meet annually at such time and in such place as may be chosen by a majority of the delegates at any regular session of the federation."[20]]

[The purpose of the federation was to discuss and examine all issues "affecting the interests of the working classes which cannot be acted upon in special trade or labor unions, and to concentrate labor as to enable it to successfully compete with concentrated capital." Other purposes, given in the call, were to encourage branches of industry to organize unions, help in adjusting disputes between labor and capital, promote labor legislation, and encourage producers' and consumers' cooperation. The federation was "to propagate strictly trades unions doctrines wherever possible; disseminate arguments in their favor, and generally to elevate unionism and obtain for it the respect and recognition to which it is entitled at the hands of employers, legislators and the general public."]

TOWARD FEDERATION

In 1881, Lyman Brant, the corresponding Secretary of the ITU, upon whom fell the burden of getting the federation started, again reported failure. Three encouraging replies were received,[21] but of the three, only the Cigar Makers' Union committed itself by resolution to the idea of a federation, and even this organization again failed to appoint delegates to the projected conference.

Yet neither Brant nor [William Atkinson,] the head of the International Typographical Union, was inclined to give up the effort. The latter was of the opinion "that the subject is one of such importance that we can afford to suffer in patience numerous failures, if as an ultimate result, the mechanics of the United States and Canada can be brought into closer common organization for the common good." Consequently, he urged the convention of 1881 to continue the effort so that "action shall be taken at this session which will render it impossible for international bodies holding sessions during the coming year to overlook this subject."[22] Upon the recommendation of its president—and the urging of Brant— the convention decided to redouble its efforts to win the support of the International Unions for the establishment of a federation of trades.

TERRE HAUTE MEETING

Under authority given him by the convention of his organization, Brant called a conference of trade unions at Terre Haute, Indiana, on August 2, 1881. Twenty-one delegates from thirteen unions in eight cities were present.[23]

The convention was opened by E. F. Pagette, the secretary of the Amalgamated Labor Union of Terre Haute, the convention city. He also served as temporary secretary.[24] The committee on plan of organization reported that "in view of the small attendance of delegates . . . we deem it inexpedient for this body to take steps looking to the framing of a constitution and by-laws for the government of a national Amalgamated Labor Union."[25] Instead, the committee recommended the issuance of a "call for a national labor congress," for Pittsburgh on November 15, 1881.

CALL FOR A MEETING OF LABOR

The call declared that

[The time has now arrived for a more perfect combination of Labor—one that will concentrate our forces as to more successfully cope with concentrated capital. We have numberless trades unions, trades assemblies or councils, and various other local, national and international labor unions, all engaged in the noble task of elevating and improving the condition of the working classes. But, great as has been the work done by these bodies, there is vastly more that can be done by a combination of all these organizations in a federation of trades.]

The call pointed to the annual congresses of labor in Britain and France, and the significant work accomplished by these bodies. Only a general federation of labor could, in the opinion of the committee, promote "the general interest of the industrial classes. There we can discuss and examine all questions affecting the national interest of each and every trade, and by a combination of forces secure that justice which isolated and separated trade and labor unions can never fully command."

[The conference urged the establishment of a "Congressional Labor Committee, after the manner of the Parliamentary Committee of Trades Unions in England . . . to urge and advance legislation at Washington on all such measures, and report to the various trades." The meeting in Terre Haute had simple aims, for in addition to setting up a committee to lobby for labor legislation before Congress, it believed that

An annual congress of trades unions could organize a systematic agitation to propagate trades union principles, and to impress the necessity of protective trade and labor organizations, and to encourage the formation of such unions and their amalgamation in trades assemblies. Thus we could elevate trades unionism and obtain for the working classes that respect for their rights, and that reward for their services, to which they are justly entitled.[26]]

The declaration was signed by nine of the delegates present.[27] The call was also endorsed by several leaders of labor who were not present at the Terre Haute meeting.[28] A committee of arrangements was named,[29] and Mark W. Moore,[30] who represented Typographical Union No. 76 of Terre Haute, was appointed secretary. Moore got in touch with unions and prominent union men. He found considerable sentiment for the Terre Haute plan.

At the outset he advanced his own money to pay for postage and other incidental expenses, and then appealed for funds to finance the Pittsburgh conference. One hundred and seventy-four dollars was donated by local unions, and all but twenty dollars was spent in preparing for the meeting. Moore, like the other sponsors, hoped

. . . to form a Federation of Trade Unionists—the fraternity of toil, of enterprise and invention. The character is to be international. The objects to be promoted by this meeting, its designs and its influences, are to be far-reaching as the abodes of civilized men. Let your action be cool, deliberate, and not too

S. U. Libraries

over-reformatory. Grasp one idea, viz., less hours and better pay, and carry it into all your work as the first principle.[31]

⌊The plan of the trade unions to establish a federation aroused the suspicion of Terrence V. Powderly, the Grand Master Workman of the Knights of Labor, whose organization was not specifically invited. He believed that another organization of labor was unnecessary, there being in his opinion "plenty of labor societies in the country." Powderly believed that if the Terre Haute sponsors of the call for a labor federation knew "of the existence of the Knights of Labor" and that "it represented every principle they advocated . . . the authors of the move are not sincere"; on the other hand, if they were unaware of the objectives of the Knights of Labor, then it was a "good move, and in either case we should capture it at the Pittsburgh convention next month. Be there if you can."[32]⌋

Pittsburgh Meeting

Undoubtedly the fear of the leaders of the Knights of Labor that a rival federation would be established, one that might threaten the dominance of their organization, accounts for the large turnout of delegates from Knights of Labor assemblies at the Pittsburgh convention which opened on November 15, 1881. Of the one hundred and eight delegates reported by the credentials committee, fifty came from the Knights of Labor, and the remaining fifty-eight were from trade unions and central labor councils. Clearly, the trade union element was strongly represented. The leading trade union of the time, the International Typographical Union, had sixteen of its members among the delegates, five of whom served as members of the twelve-man committee on Platform and Principles, with Samuel Leffingwell, a leading member of this union, serving as chairman. While there were delegates from fourteen states, among them one from California and eight from New York, sixty-eight delegates came from Pennsylvania, with a large number from the area around Pittsburgh.[33]

John Jarrett, the president of the Amalgamated Association of Iron and Steel Workers of the United States and Canada, was elected temporary chairman. While the committee on credentials was preparing its report, several delegates, including⌊Samuel Gompers from the Cigar Makers' International Union,⌉delivered speeches. He informed the delegates that he had come to Pittsburgh, "not to air his opinions, but to work, not to build a bubble, but to lay the foundations for that superstructure that would be solid, and that would be a true federation of trade unions." He was for progressing slowly, and wanted the "organization to be a workingmen's organization."[34]

On the second day, Gompers again took the floor, this time to answer charges appearing in the local press that he was in league with Socialist elements who were seeking to capture the convention. It appeared that the charges had been inspired by some of the delegates in an effort to prevent the election of Gompers as permanent president of the prospective organization. Gompers denied the accusation, which led one of the Western delegates, Michael F. Walsh, to disclaim its authorship.[35] Walsh assured the convention that he was first aware of the charges against Gompers when he read them in the newspapers.

[Whatever may have been the origin and purpose of the charges, they apparently hurt Gompers' chances of becoming chairman of the convention. The majority of the commitee on permanent organization presented Gompers' name for the post. A minority recommended Richard Powers, the head of the Lake Seamen's Union, who had been present at the Terre Haute meeting. John Jarrett of the Amalgamated Association of Iron and Steel Workers of America, one of the great organizations of labor at the time, was then nominated from the floor. Thereupon both Gompers and Powers withdrew and Jarrett was chosen.]

Greetings were sent to Henry Broadhurst and the Parliamentary Committee of the British Trade Union Congress. The suggested name of the organization was then placed before the delegates. Gompers, who had been appointed chairman of the committee on the plan of organization, suggested the new federation be called "The Federation of Trades Unions of the United States of America and Canada." This touched off a debate, several delegates objecting to the implied restriction of the organization to craftsmen or tradesmen. It was argued that, because the new organization would recognize "neither creed, color, nor nationality," the name should read "Trades and Labor Unions." Richard Powers, however, defended the original version, for he believed "it will keep out of the Federation political labor bodies." However, his views were not accepted, and the name ["Federation of Trades and Labor Unions of the United States and Canada" was voted.]

[The sponsors voted to give the national and international unions a dominating position. These organizations were allowed a form of proportional representation.[36] On the other hand, trades councils, irrespective of size, were allowed only one delegate.]

The committee on platform submitted a preamble which was adopted without discussion. Couched in the standard language of the time, the preamble reads more like a trade union document than a statement of reformers:

Whereas, a struggle is going on in the nations of the civilized world between the oppressors and oppressed of all countries, a struggle between capital and labor, which must grow in intensity from year to year and work disastrous results to the toiling millions of all nations if not combined for mutual protection and benefit. The history of the wage-workers of all countries is but the history of constant struggle and misery engendered by ignorance and disunion; whereas the history of the non-producers of all ages proves that a minority, thoroughly organized, may work wonders for good or evil. It behooves the representatives of the workers of North America, in Congress assembled, to adopt such measures and disseminate such principles among the people of our country as will unite them for all time to come, to secure the recognition of the rights to which they are justly entitled. Conforming to the old adage, "in union there is strength," the formation of a Federation embracing every trade and labor organization in North America, a union founded upon a basis as broad as the land we live in, is our only hope. The past history of Trades Unions proves that small organizations, well conducted, have accomplished great good, but their efforts have not been of that lasting character which a thorough unification of all the different branches of industrial workers is bound to secure.

[The convention urged the adoption of laws for the incorporation of trade unions and similar labor organizations, the limitation of child labor (although one delegate regarded such legislation as an interference with individual rights), uniform apprentice laws, an enforceable eight-hour work day, the outlawing of the truck system of wage payment and a requirement that payment of wages be made in lawful money, and the adoption of a mechanic's lien law. Differences arose over the tariff, and John Jarrett, speaking for the Iron and Steel Union, demanded that the convention endorse protection even though several delegates held the issue foreign to the purposes of the convention. In the end, a resolution demanding "laws as shall give to every American industry full protection from the cheap labor of foreign countries" was endorsed.]

Many of the resolutions dealt with topics that all labor could endorse. The importation of contract laborers was opposed. A California delegate, Charles F. Burgman, offered a much harsher resolution against Chinese immigration. Arguing that the experience of white labor on the Pacific Coast demonstrated that the "presence of Chinese, and their competition with free white labor is one of the greatest evils with which any country can be afflicted," the resolution called upon Congress to prohibit absolutely the immigration of Chinese into the United States. Only one delegate— Sherman Cummin, a printer from Massachusetts—protested against the proposal. He doubted whether the Chinese could swallow up the United States, pointed to their high civilization, and urged that they be granted the same rights of entry as other foreigners. His was a lone voice, and the proposal was enacted with one dissenting vote, presumably Cummin's.

Several resolutions were enacted urging the organization of workers in several crafts, and advising workers so organized to join together into a national union.

W. H. Foster, a printer, was elected secretary, on the third ballot, defeating Gompers. A Legislative Committee was appointed, charged with managing the Federation.[37]

In order that the Legislative Committee should not be entirely without funds with which to commence their duties, the Chair called for voluntary contributions, which were paid in by the delegates to the amount of $53.60. Mr. M. L. Crawford handed over $2.50 which had been paid to him in his capacity of Secretary of the Congress, making a total of $56.10.[38]

It was not a sum which would allow for great or extensive activities.

FEDERATION OF ORGANIZED TRADES AND LABOR UNIONS

The first year of the Federation was far from auspicious. It received endorsements, but few organizations were sufficiently enthusiastic to help the new movement by providing the "necessary funds wherewith to meet the expenses incident to our trust."[39] The cost of printing the *Proceedings* exhausted its meager resources. No activity was carried on by the Legislative Committee, which held no meetings. On the basis of the first year's experience, one might wonder why the organization continued to exist. Certainly it was little more than a hollow shell.

[The second convention at Cleveland was attended by only a handful of delegates, a mere 19 as against 108 who had been present in Pittsburgh the year before.] Seven represented national and international unions, and nine, central bodies.[40] In part, the difference in the number can be attributed to the absence of many representatives from the Knights of Labor at Cleveland. Yet this is only part of the explanation. The trade unions were far from enthusiastic about the new venture, and the Iron and Steel Workers', Iron Molders', Bricklayers', Glass Bottle Blowers', and Stone Cutters' were unrepresented. Lyman A. Brant, a delegate to the Pittsburgh meeting from the International Typographical Union and one of the leading proponents of a trade union federation, was forced to conclude that the "results of the Pittsburgh congress have, perhaps, not been so plainly marked as those which may be reasonably expected to follow from the assembling of industrial congresses."[41] Brant also objected to the Federation's financing methods, and suggested that each delegate to future conventions contribute a "small fixed sum," and that added amounts, whenever needed, could be contributed by unions on a voluntary basis. Many unions nominally favoring a federation of trades were not yet ready for the steps that would help transform the vision into reality. [The original sponsors at Terre Haute envisaged an organization "with a few simple rules and no salaried officers," which in fact meant that the Federation could never mobilize the resources necessary for conducting organizing drives or for aiding affiliated groups.] Although the promotion of legislation was one of the primary purposes of the new movement, the organization made no impression on the political scene. When the secretary asked the Speaker of the House of Representatives to consider the appointment of several members favorable to labor to the Committee on Education and Labor, he was not even given the courtesy of an answer.

The second convention considered a number of resolutions, and the staple legislative labor demands of the time were endorsed. But two actions of the convention are of more than general interest: the revocation of the endorsement of the protective tariff previously adopted by the Pittsburgh convention, with the substitution instead of labor's approval of free trade; and the support of the eight-hour work day. Only one delegate, W. H. Foster, opposed free trade.

The removal of the plank favoring protection led the Amalgamated Association of Iron and Steel Workers to instruct its president that it could not affiliate with the Federation as the "Amalgamated Association of Iron and Steel Workers is heartily in favor of tariff laws, especially on iron and steel manufactures thereof." However, the head of the Amalgamated was certain that his union would go "hand in hand" with the Federation when "your very censure on our tariff laws" was withdrawn. Frank Foster, the secretary of the Federation in 1883 and the author of the free trade resolution, assured the Amalgamated Association that the Federation did not censure the views of those favoring the tariff, but desired to remain neutral on this question.[42] The Amalgamated withdrew and did not reaffiliate for several years.

Gompers objected to the endorsement of the eight-hour day "on the ground that he did not think the majority of his constituents were ready for the practical endorsement of the measure." It was nevertheless adopted without any votes being cast in opposition.

Another change made at Cleveland was in the method of representation. At the first convention, provision was made for national and international unions and trades assemblies to be represented. The second convention amended this provision to allow for representation by district assemblies of the Knights of Labor. This proposal was opposed by Gompers, who objected to construing local trade unions, as used in the report on representation, to "mean local assemblies of the Knights of Labor." Gompers' views were, however, rejected. The sparse attendance at the second convention may have influenced the delegates to open the doors a bit wider and admit assemblies of the Knights of Labor, which the trade unionists did not at first wish to include. The convention of 1882 elected Gompers, Robert Howard of the National Mule Spinners' Association, Gabriel Edmonston of the District of Columbia Federation of Labor, and Richard Powers of the Lake Seamen's Union as the Legis-

lative Committee.] W. H. Foster was again chosen secretary of the
Federation and a member of the Legislative Committee. [At its first
session, the Legislative Committee elected Gompers chairman.]

From the report of the organization's activity in the period between
the second and third conventions, it would appear that the Federation
was gaining increasing support. The receipts of $726.14, while scarcely
an amount with which to build a national labor movement, was almost
two and one-half times the income of $292.10 of the preceding period.
The increased receipts largely came from the per capita payments made
by several international unions, in itself a very favorable development.
Only two internationals, the Lake Seamen's Union and the Granite
Cutters' National Union, had each paid sixty dollars per capita in the
first year.

In the second year, however, in addition to the latter two unions, the
International Typographical Union, Cigar Makers' International Union,
the Brotherhood of Carpenters and Joiners of America, Amalgamated
Society of Engineers, and the National Mule Spinners' Union, all made
some contributions to the Federation. As a matter of fact, the per capita
of $211.53 of the International Typographical Union, added to the
$129.10 of the International Cigar Makers' Union, were greater than the
total amount collected by the Federation in the first year of activity.

There were more delegates present at the third convention in 1883,
but the Legislative Committee had little of importance to report. Actually
the Federation was conducting virtually no activity and its annual meetings were, perhaps, the only signs of life. [At the third convention
Gompers was chosen the presiding officer of the sessions; P. H. Logan, a
printer from Chicago, was elected president; and the executive committee was enlarged to include, in addition to the president, a secretary, a
treasurer, and six vice-presidents, one of whom was Gompers.]

The convention acted on several issues. A proposal to send committees
presenting the point of view of labor to the conventions of the two
political parties was defeated. The establishment of a postal telegraph
system by the federal government was supported by a vote of sixteen
to eight.

Other than these resolutions, little business was transacted at this
convention. The International Typographical Union was perhaps, at
this stage, the chief supporter of the Federation. [President George
Clark of the ITU, despite the poor performance of the Federation, was
pleased to be able to announce to the convention of his union in 1883,
that "after many delays, and repeated failures, the project for a Federation of the Trades of the United States and Canada has passed the primary
stage of existence and taken its place among the organizations of the
time."[43]]Few unions were as sympathetically inclined or as willing to

cooperate as the printers' organization. [Of the twenty-five delegates to the fourth convention in 1884, ten were members of the International Typographical Union, three typographers representing the International, and the other seven representing locals and central bodies.]

[The fourth convention reflected a decline in interest by important international unions. Only two, the International Typographical Union and the Cigar Makers' International Union, donated forty dollars apiece; several other international unions contributed smaller sums, with total receipts during the preceding fiscal year amounting to only $336.22. Lack of interest and insufficient funds, as well as the failure to develop a well-defined plan, were the chief reasons for the virtual absence of any significant activity by the Federation.]

Reporting to the convention of 1884, Secretary Frank K. Foster declared: "The lack of funds has seriously crippled the work of the Federation, and this, coupled with an organization lacking cohesiveness, has allowed small scope for effective expenditure of effort."[44] Secretary Foster was, however, convinced that "in a Federation of Trades lies the key to the solution of the labor problem." One of the leading trade unionists of the time, he recognized the need for a closer alliance of trade unions; he realized, however, that the Federation as then constituted was not the instrument through which this objective could be achieved. He was hopeful that unity could be achieved, but only "among the genuine unions." Foster suggested that "aggressive and constant work is needed to build up the Federation. A secretary who can devote at least half, if possible the whole, of his time to it is a necessity."

In addition to the resolutions on the usual questions that came before labor assemblies, the convention of 1884 considered one introduced by Gabriel Edmonston, a leading member of the Brotherhood of Carpenters and Joiners of America, on the eight-hour work day. Approval of this proposal helped to set in motion a movement which stimulated interest within trade unions and offered to workers a common cause and purpose. [The resolution decreed "that eight-hours shall constitute a legal day's labor from and after May 1, 1886, and that we recommend to labor organizations throughout this jurisdiction that they so direct their laws as to conform to this resolution by the time named.[45]]

The resolution was adopted by a vote of 23 to 2, but it was in fact merely an expression of opinion. Although the Federation had neither the authority nor the prestige to initiate a movement involving the trade unions, the enactment of this resolution had the result of starting a substantial campaign and widespread action for the reduction of the hours of labor.

[In retrospect, it is difficult to explain the influence of the resolution; the Federation had little prestige among the international unions, and scarcely any support. The answer would appear to lie in a deeply and widely held desire for shorter hours. The setting aside of a specific day for the inauguration of this policy inspired a chain activity, and gave the shorter-hour movement unity and cohesion. The convention instructed the Legislative Committee to invite the cooperation of the Knights of Labor in this campaign, but the latter were unwilling to become involved in what it regarded as a dubious venture.]

Frank K. Foster retired as secretary and was replaced by Gabriel Edmonston, the sponsor of the eight-hour resolution. Edmonston had no intention of accepting a "position and sit-down to enjoy honors. I take it as a kindly act, to suggest how I may best perform my duty to those who have a right to command me."[46] In addition to Edmonston, the convention elected W. W. McClelland of the Amalgamated Society of Engineers as chairman, Robert Howard as secretary, and five other vice-presidents to complete the Legislative Committee. McClelland did not serve out his term, and resigned his office soon after the adjournment of the convention.

[The fifth convention of the Federation of Organized Trades and Labor Unions, held in Washington in 1885, clearly demonstrated that the organization was still unable to arouse enthusiasm or a large following among the trade unionists of the United States. Only twelve organizations, represented by twenty-one delegates, were present at the Washington session. Edmonston had little to report, although he himself had, with the aid of several Washington labor men, testified before Congressional committees on bills affecting labor. He had also intervened for the workers employed at a government arsenal in Springfield, Massachusetts,[47] with the Secretary of the Interior on behalf of payment for a holiday not worked.]

Aside from these minor efforts, the report of the secretary showed virtually no trade union activity by the Federation. It is, therefore, interesting that the International Typographical Union, a model labor organization of that time, continued to be the chief financial supporter of the Federation. Its contribution of over one hundred and eighty-three dollars provided nearly a third of the total income of $584.03 during this period. All other international unions donated amounts far below the sum of the Printers' Union, the sixty dollars from the Cigar Makers' International Union being the next highest.

The convention again considered the movement for the eight-hour work day, which two preceding meetings had endorsed. Another resolution approved the label of the Cigar Makers' International, a union which had supported the Federation from its inception and which was now engaged in a dispute with a dual organization, the Cigar Makers' Progressive Union. [Gompers was elected president of the Federation, and the Federation's first secretary, W. H. Foster, was unanimously returned to the office he had previously held.]

REFERENCES

1. John R. Commons and Associates, *History of Labor in the United States* (New York: The Macmillan Company, 1936), II, pp. 43-48; *The Labor Movement: the Problem of To-Day* (Boston: A. M. Bridgman and Co., 1887), pp. 271-272.

2. *Proceedings of the National Convention of the Journeymen Printers,* 1850, pp. 6-7, 14.

3. *Second National Convention of Journeymen Printers of the United States,* 1851, p. 6: *The Third National Convention of Journeymen Printers of the United States,* 1852, p. 19; *Proceedings of Second Session of National Typographical Union,* 1853, pp. 19-20.

4. *Proceedings of the Sixth Session of the National Typographical Union,* 1857, p. 31.

5. *Thirteenth Annual Session of the National Typographical Union,* 1865, p. 57.

6. *Proceedings of the Carpenters' and Joiners' National Union and its First Annual Session,* 1865, pp. 12, 27; *Proceedings of the Carpenters' and Joiners' National Union and its Second Annual Session,* 1866, pp. 8, 24, 27.

7. *Fifteenth Annual Session of the National Typographical Union,* 1867, p. 7. See also Lloyd Ulman, *The Rise of the National Trade Union* (Cambridge, Mass.: Harvard University Press, 1955), pp. 155-173.

8. *Report of the Proceedings of the Sixteenth Annual Session of the National Typographical Union,* 1868, p. 5.

9. Quote from *Sixth Annual Report of Bricklayers' National Union,* 1871, p. 15; See also *Seventh Annual Session of Bricklayers' National Union,* 1872, p. 7.

10. *Coopers' Journal,* October 1872, p. 598.

11. *Twenty-sixth Annual Session of the International Typographical Union,* 1878, p. 19.

12. *Iron Molders' Journal,* March 10, 1876, p. 609.

13. *Coopers' Journal,* February 1872, p. 599.

14. *Ibid.,* October 1872, p. 599.

15. *Twenty-first Annual Session of the International Typographical Union,* p. 13; *Iron Molders' Journal,* August 31, 1873, p. 65.

16. *Iron Molders' Journal,* March 10, 1876, p. 609. *Proceedings of the Thirteenth Annual Session of the Iron Molders' Union,* 1876, pp. 5-7.

17. *Ibid.,* May 10, 1878, p. 677.

18. *Iron Molders' Journal,* August 10, 1878, pp. 6-7; November 10, 1878, p. 15; *Fourteenth Session of the Iron Molders' Union of North America,* 1878, p. 35.

19. *Twenty-Seventh Annual Session of the International Typographical Union,* pp. 39-40.

20. *Twenty-Eighth Annual Session of the International Typographical Union*, 1880, p. 61.

21. From Adolph Strasser, the head of Cigar Makers' International Union, P. M. Arthur of the Brotherhood of Locomotive Engineers, and Paul Fitzpatrick of the Iron Molders' Union of North America.

22. *Twenty-Ninth Annual Session of the International Typographical Union*, 1881, pp. 26-27.

23. P. J. McGuire, St. Louis Trades Assembly; Richard Powers, Lake Seamen's Union; Mark L. Crawford, Chicago International Typographical Union No. 16; Thomas Thompson, Dayton, Ohio, Iron Molders' Union No. 181; James Pierce and Simon Neale, Terre Haute Coopers' Union No. 16; George W. Osborne, Springfield, Ohio, Iron Molders' Union; Mark W. Moore, Terre Haute Typographical Union No. 76; John E. Coughlin, president of National Tanners' and Curriers' Union, who represented Chicago Trades Assembly; Samuel L. Leffingwell, Indianapolis Trades Assembly; F. M. Light, Coopers Union No. 16, Terre Haute; W. C. Pollner, Cleveland Trades Assembly; Lyman A. Brant, Detroit International Typographical Union No. 18; J. R. Backus, E. P. Pagette, Moses Crapo, John Rupe, Jr., and N. A. Murphy, Terre Haute Amalgamated Labor Union; and John Toit, James Herring, and Michael Howard of Terre Haute Iron Molders' Union.

24. J. R. Backus, of the Amalgamated Labor Union of Terre Haute, served as temporary chairman, and after the convention was permanently organized J. E. Coughlin, of Chicago, and W. C. Pollner of Cleveland were chosen as chairman and secretary respectively.

25. *Terre Haute Press*, August 3, 1881.

26. The report and call and declaration appeared in the *Terre Haute Press*, August 3, 1881; see also *Report of the First Annual Convention of the Federation of Organized Trades and Labor Unions of the United States and Canada*, 1881, p. 7.

27. Coughlin, Richard Powers of the Lake Seamen's Union; Brant, P. J. McGuire, Pollner, and Backus; Thomas Thompson of the Dayton Iron Molders' Union; George Osborn, Iron Molders' Union of Springfield, Ohio; and Samuel Leffingwell of the Indianapolis Trades Assembly.

28. These were Paul Fitzpatrick, president of the Iron Molders' Union; George Clark, president of the International Typographical Union, John Kinnear, president of the Central Trades and Labor Assembly of Boston; and George Rodgers, president of Chicago Trades Assembly.

29. Chairman Brant, Pollner, Mark L. Crawford of the Chicago Trades Assembly, and P. J. McGuire.

30. According to Commons, *op. cit.*, II, p. 319. "Moore apparently represented the insurgent Knights of Labor." This is scarcely likely, as he was an active member of the International Typographical Union, largely responsible for the Terre Haute meeting. The assumption that he belonged to the insurgent Knights of Labor was based upon his closing words in his report: "Agitate! Educate! Consolidate!" Labor men were, however, fond of such slogans. Moore was, in 1881, corresponding secretary and treasurer of his local.

31. *Report of the First Annual Convention of the Federation of Organized Trades and Labor Unions of the United States and Canada*, 1881, pp. 14-15.

32. Quotations are from the letter of Terrence V. Powderly to A. M. Owens, October 22, 1881, in the archives of Catholic University. Letters from Powderly are in the Catholic University archives.

33. *The International Typographical Union Presents the Record of the Formation of the American Federation of Labor* (Indianapolis: International Typographical Union, 1951), pp. 12-13.

34. Quotation is from the *Pittsburgh Gazette*, November 16, 1881, in Alfred P. James, "The First Convention of the American Federation of Labor," *Western Pennsylvania Historical Review*, January 1924, p. 29.

35. James, *op. cit.*, pp. 18-20.

36. One delegate for the first one thousand members, two delegates for four thousand members, three delegates for eight thousand members, four delegates for sixteen thousand members, and so forth.

37. The committee members were Richard Powers, president; Samuel Gompers, first vice-president; Charles F. Burgman, second vice-president; and Alexander C. Rankin, treasurer.

38. *Report of the First Convention of the Federation of Organized Trades and Labor Unions of the United States and Canada*, 1881, p. 24.

39. *Report of the Second Annual Session of the Federation of Organized Trades and Labor Unions of the United States and Canada*, 1882, p. 9.

40. Samuel Gompers, *Seventy Years of Life and Labor* (New York: E. P. Dutton and Co., 1943), I, 232.

41. "Report of Lyman Brant," *Thirty-First Annual Session of the International Typographical Union*, 1882, p. 53.

42. Letters of John J. Jarrett to W. H. Foster, August 21, 1883; Letter of Frank K. Foster to John Jarrett, Sept. 17, 1883. W. H. Foster would not run for a third term and was succeeded by his namesake. *Report of the Third Annual Session of the Federation of Trades and Labor Unions of the United States and Canada*, 1883, pp. 18-19, 20.

43. "Report of President George Clark," *Thirty-First Annual Session of the International Typographical Union*, 1883, p. 11.

44. *Report of the Annual Session of the Federation of Organized Trades and Labor Unions of the United States and Canada*, 1884, p. 17.

45. *Ibid.*, pp. 24-25.

46. Letter from Gabriel Edmonston to Adolph Strasser, November 22, 1884 in archives of the AFL-CIO.

47. Gabriel Edmonston to Secretary of the Interior, L. C. Lamar, March 10, 1885, in archives of the AFL-CIO.

II

The Knights of Labor and the Trade Unions

THE trade organizations had failed to establish an effective federation which could serve as the general representative of organized labor, and at the same time assume responsibility for organizing the unorganized. At best, the Federation of Organized Trades and Labor Unions of the United States and Canada, in its first five years, was an anemic and inactive organization, without substantial support from the major trade unions which it was unable to rally to its banner. Yet, despite its lack of achievement, the leaders of organized labor were conscious of the need for a closer alliance of trade unions.

[In the 1880's the hegemony of the trade unions over the economic interests of labor was seriously challenged by the Knights of Labor. The Knights pretended to represent labor in all its many fields of activity. Consequently it was not averse to establishing dual unions, invading the jurisdictions of already well-established labor organizations, and interfering with the trade activities of many trade bodies. It achieved its greatest growth in the mid-1880's; by the end of the decade, however, it had spent most of its force, and its advances in organization were already exhausted.]

The Noble Order of Knights of Labor was first organized by a small group of clothing cutters in Philadelphia, in 1869. For several years it was a small and modest organization. Uriah Stephens, its first head or Grand Master Workman, declared: "The Order is not a political one—it is more and higher. It is the parent of Principles, the house of reforms and educator of the masses." On another occasion Stephens stressed the elevation of man as the aim of the Order. He also believed that problems "in America are settled through the ballot box . . . to crystallize the principles into statute law to make them effective for the protection of the distressed and defrauded landless millions of toil."[1]

The Knights of Labor was first organized as a secret society. Almost from the outset non-garment workers were accepted as members. Called sojourners, they did not, at the beginning, have a voice in the management of the affairs of the Order. The locals, or assemblies as they were called, increased. A delegate body representing a number of assemblies, called the District Assembly, was first established in 1873. Soon the

Knights broke through their local boundaries, and local assemblies were formed in Western Pennsylvania. In response to the need for a national center, the first general assembly, or convention, was held in Reading, Pennsylvania, in 1875. Officers were elected and the Order began to welcome new members everywhere in the United States.[2]

The secrecy and ritual of the Order raised problems for the organization. Some Catholic prelates were convinced that the Knights of Labor was an oath-bound, secret, Masonic order; others that the Order was an advocate of Christian doctrine. Officially secrecy was eliminated in 1879, but was practiced in some localities until 1881. During the secrecy period a number of Catholic clergymen, believing that the Order was hostile to religion, sought to have Catholics withdraw their membership by having a ban placed against it by the Catholic Church. The intervention of Cardinal Gibbons and Archbishop Ireland was largely instrumental in preventing the ban from being issued.[3]

Beginning in the early 1880's, the Knights of Labor expanded rapidly, and in many places the Knights established local and even national labor unions. It is, however, difficult to discover any clear aims or principles which they espoused. Stephens, who led the movement in its initial phase, regarded the Order as the leader of all the downtrodden and oppressed, and he was suspicious of the Socialists, whom he regarded as "disturbers, who only gain entrance to labor societies that they may be in a better position to break them up."[4] In 1879, Stephens was succeeded as Grand Master Workman by Terrence V. Powderly. The latter had been a member of the Machinists' and Blacksmiths' Union and had been elected mayor of Scranton, Pennsylvania, on a labor ticket in 1878.

Powderly, like his predecessor, was not altogether clear on the purposes of the Order. Although the Knights of Labor conducted some of the more important strikes during the 1880's, Powderly never favored the use of this tactic. In his opinion, the strike "is a relic of barbarism, there are other means for righting wrongs."[5] Moreover, Powderly believed that strikes cause large fluctuations in the membership of the Order; men join during a walkout and are likely to leave once the dispute is settled.[6] In addition, he had more substantial reasons for opposing strikes. Such tactics, he felt, could not change many of the wrongs suffered by labor, such as inadequate apprenticeship laws and the unjust technicalities or delays in the administration of justice. Moreover, while the strike withdraws the supply of labor from the employer, "it also cuts off demand by throwing consumers out of employment, thereby purchasing power." Powderly believed that if the wages lost by strikers were set aside in a special fund and invested in cooperative enterprises, it would be possible to "soon amass a sum sufficient to erect shops and factories to give employment to . . . idle brethren. But I [Powderly] fail to see any lasting good in a strike."[7]

Powderly's views were shared by other leaders. Commenting on the failure of benefits to keep up with membership, the executive board concluded that the results "may be due in a great measure to the evil results which follow the inauguration and practice of the old system and relic of barbarism and trade unionism—strikes."[8]

In the course of its history, the Knights of Labor had evolved two structural types: the mixed assembly, made up of workers of various trades and, in some periods of the Order's history, professional men as well; and the trade assembly made up of workers in the same trade, and in fact a trade union. There was not much, therefore, that Powderly or the other leaders of the Order could do to suppress strikes as long as the Knights of Labor organized workers into trade assemblies. As long as the latter were chartered, the question of strikes would continue to bedevil the leadership.

The number of strikes became a problem, and Powderly did not know what policy to follow. He was opposed in principle and found strikes too expensive to support; yet he felt that "when you begin one you should make a success of it by every means." He was not always consistent in his view of this problem, for later he wanted to "stick to the original plan of the order, that of educating the members as to the folly of strikes."[9] At the same time, Powderly advised that a system for the support of members on strike should be devised, and the General Assembly decided that, even though strikes were "deplorable in their effect and contrary to the interests of the Order," they should be supported.[10]

[The purposes of the Knights of Labor were never given specific definition.]The chief interests of the Order seem to have been education, cooperation, the promotion of temperance, and discussions of the land question. Once Powderly described the order as "a connecting link between all branches of honorable toil," which "seeks to bind instead of loosen." It sought to take in all workers:

. . . the machinist, the blacksmith, molder, pattern maker, laborer, miner, and clerk; no lawyers, no bankers, no doctors, and no professional politicians. By combining all branches of trade in one common brotherhood, a complete system of communication and receiving intelligence is at once established . . . We teach the laborer, we discuss labor in all its interest at each meeting.[11]

[There is nothing in this statement, or for that matter in any other by the leaders, which would suggest an interest in collective bargaining or in establishing the union and union rules in the shop.]

Powderly and the other leaders believed that "isolated trade unions can accomplish nothing. One universal brotherhood of labor is needed." Yet, in the same letter in which he made this statement, Powderly advised the shoe workers to "establish their trade mark by which all other workingmen may know their mark."[12] The trade assemblies were in a real sense orphans of the Order. Moreover, the trade unions were beginning, in the early 1880's, to feel the competition of the Knights. When a leading trade union editor, J. P. McDonnell complained that the Knights of Labor were raiding trade union membership, Powderly replied that the Knights "make no attempts on trade unions at all, on the contrary they show the folly of separate action and endeavor to bring all workingmen into one organization."[13] Bringing all workingmen together could mean, in some circumstances, the formation of dual unions, and organizers of the Knights of Labor might not be too careful in their promises when establishing these organizations. It might be that the organizers of the Knights would form a dual union in a craft on strike, and such action would inevitably arouse the resentment of the leaders of the trade union involved. Some members of the Knights of Labor recognized this problem, and a resolution at the General Assembly, in 1883, proposed that organizers be instructed not to entice members of trade unions to establish trade assemblies by promises of support during a strike.[14] The suggestion was rejected.

A complaint of the interference of the Knights of Labor in the affairs of the International Typographical Union was made by President M. L. Crawford, who charged that:

. . . in some cities where assemblies of the Knights of Labor are organized, wholly composed of printers, a card authorized by our body is treated as secondary to one issued by these assemblies; that these assemblies pass upon all legislation before it is introduced in the local union; that they admit as members men who have not served their apprenticeship, as well as men who have "ratted" in our own organization; that men who hold working cards are compelled to work side by side with notorious "rats" in offices that are called union offices. This is all wrong.[15]

In an objective sense, the Knights of Labor had as much right to organize trade assemblies as the craft unions. Nevertheless, such organization made a conflict inevitable, especially when the leaders of the Knights acquiesced in the invasion of the jurisdictions of the trades. It was their view that "if these unions will parallel, it is proof conclusive that they should be brought into an order where the greatest good for the greatest number is afforded." Even mixed assemblies, those locals which recruited several grades and classes of workers, were encouraged to handle business affecting a group of workers in a particular trade. Nonmembers of the trade could be asked to retire, and then those remaining could transact trade business.[16]

The heads of the Knights of Labor were not oblivious of the differences between their organization and the trade unions. In their view:

The Order contemplates a radical change in the existing industrial system, and labors to bring about that change, while trade unions and other orders accept the industrial system as it is, and endeavor to adapt themselves to it. The attitude of our Order to the existing industrial system is antagonistic, and is necessarily one of war. It is, therefore, imperative that we adopt, in a large measure, the methods and machinery of successful warfare, in which the Knights of Labor must be looked upon as a great army, that it must be governed by certain discipline without which unity of purpose and harmony of action cannot be secured; that it must work from a center, and those intrusted with its government must be endowed with a large measure of discretion and authority. Emergencies arise in this Order such as cannot arise in trades' unions or others; emergencies which cannot be anticipated by law and which must be met promptly.[17]

It can be noted that, whatever claims one may make for the general advantage of the policies and program of the Knights of Labor, it is clear that the Order was not primarily a labor or trade union. It may have claimed to be something better or more desirable, but that it was neither concerned with nor interested in promoting the limited aspirations of trade unions is obvious from the pronouncements of its leaders.

However, despite the questionable interest of the Knights of Labor in the problems of trade unions, the Order insisted upon its right to establish dual unions wherever possible. Consequently, as the membership of the Knights of Labor expanded, the disputes over jurisdiction between the Order and the trade unions multiplied. Musicians, painters, tailors, molders, cigarmakers, steel workers complained about the invasion of their jurisdictions by assemblies of the Knights of Labor. The Iron Molders' International Union of North America demanded "the suspension of all iron molders from the Knights of Labor who have been suspended from our Union."[18] The Bricklayers' and Masons' International Union complained during the same time of the invasion of their jurisdiction, and listed a number of communities in which the union had to meet the competition of Knights of Labor assemblies.[19] Another warning came from the head of the International Typographical Union, who charged that there had "risen to influence in the councils of that great order an element, which, should it at any time attain supremacy, threatens the destruction of all distinct trade unions." He challenged the pretensions of the Knights to speak for all labor, and declared that "to abolish all lines and merge all trades into one organization would, in the present state of development of the labor movement, greatly increase the danger; and . . . would add nothing to the effective results of cooperation."[20]

The heads of the Knights of Labor were not altogether insensible to the developing conflict. Some of them recognized that in many branches of industry the membership of the Knights of Labor was in a minority.

Under these circumstances, the leaders of the Order nevertheless complained that "in large numbers of instances the Knights of Labor membership is unwillingly forced to submit to the dictation of the trades unions."[21] [It is obvious that the conflict could not be easily resolved as long as the trade unions and the Knights of Labor insisted upon occupying the same jurisdictions.] Even if dual unions had been acceptable to the trade organizations, the conflict over whose standards were to govern would inevitably arise. But the trade unions were not ready to surrender their insistence upon their exclusive right to govern the crafts and industries in which they functioned.

In the 1880's, a conflict between the Knights of Labor and the Cigar Makers' International Union arose. In most respects it was no different from the many others that had flared up over the years, except that this conflict could be described as a struggle over union labels. Over such an issue many organizations in addition to those directly involved could be drawn into the dispute.

Another important difference was the caliber of the leadership of the Cigar Makers' International Union. In its president, Adolph Strasser, this organization had an experienced and articulate spokesman who, with Samuel Gompers, another officer, had perhaps as keen an appreciation of the position of trade unions in modern society as any trade union leader of the period. Moreover, both of these men were in favor of a federation of trades, which they regarded as a necessary instrument for the advancement of labor. Gompers, who had been a member of the Legislative Committee of the Federation of Organized Trades and Labor Union for most of the latter's existence, already could boast of a detailed knowledge of, and extensive experience in, the trade union movement.

Conflict with the Knights began first as an intramural dispute in the New York cigar industry. New York was the focal point of the conflict— although other cigarmaking centers were also involved. The difference arose in an ideological controversy over political methods and philosophy to which certain unions were subject at the time. The initial causes of the split were the methods to be used legally to eliminate the manufacture of cigars in tenement houses. The Socialists favored independent political action, and their opponents favored backing candidates of the old parties who would promise to support the necessary legislation. In 1882 this issue arose in Local 144 of the Cigar Makers' International Union in New York. One of the old-party candidates, already a member of the state legislature, had sponsored a bill to outlaw the manufacture of cigars in tenement houses. The measure had been defeated at the preceding session by the narrow vote of forty-nine to forty, and the leaders of the Cigarmakers' Union, believing that every vote would be necessary if success were to be achieved at the next legislative session, supported the sponsor for reelection. They held it was more important to support proponents of this restrictive measure than to support a party with the "correct" ideology.

Within the union the ill feeling generated by these differences did not subside with the close of the campaign. In the subsequent election for officers of Local Union No. 144, the opposition to the head of the International Union elected its candidate, Samuel Schimkowitz, as head of the local. Challenging this action on the ground that the successful candidate was a manufacturer and therefore ineligible for union office, President Strasser declared the post vacant, believing that under the constitution he was authorized to decide such questions. The validity of Strasser's action was in turn challenged by an appeal to the Executive Board, which was asked to override his decision. The Executive Board ordered a new election; this was not held. The next convention, discussing the issues at length, concluded that the original suspension "was beyond the letter of the Constitution, but . . . [held] that said act was justified by the extraordinary necessities of the case."[22]

The dispute was not settled, despite the action of the convention, for the groups opposed to Strasser's policies seceded and organized the Cigarmakers' Progressive Union. After a short-lived separation, the two cigarmakers' unions reunited.[23] However, some of the more aggressive opponents of the Cigarmakers' International Union refused to return to the latter organization. Instead, they organized Local Assembly 2,814 of the Knights of Labor, and affiliated with District Assembly 49, New York, of the Knights of Labor, known as a center of anti-trade union sentiments in the Knights of Labor.

The dispute in New York intensified existing differences with the Knights. To protect their craft, the Cigarmakers' International Union had issued a blue label. The Knights of Labor in turn provided their employers with white labels to signify that members of the Order had been employed in the manufacture of cigars. Naturally the issuance of competing labels was a constant source of friction, and the Executive Board of the Knights of Labor reported that a dispute had arisen

. . . on account of the label on cigar boxes containing cigars manufactured by our members. It is claimed that the label, so used, comes in competition with one or more of the Union Labels in the cigarmaking trade, and works injury to the same. The Board can see no just grounds for such an assumption, and recommends that the Knights of Labor label be furnished to any Assembly ordering under their seal, to be used only by members of the Order upon goods manufactured by themselves. We believe, however, that no discrimination should be made in purchasing goods contained in packages bearing the label or seal of any recognized organization.[24]

Whatever merit such an attitude may have, it is not one that would be accepted by an American trade union with its concept of the inviolability of its jurisdiction.

Relations between the Knights of Labor and the Cigarmakers' International Union continued to deteriorate. In 1886, the Knights of Labor accepted a settlement in a general strike and lockout of the cigarmakers of New York, which was unacceptable to the Cigarmakers' International Union. Despite the opposition of the union claiming jurisdiction in the trade, the employers who settled were given the white label and supplied with help by the Knights. Of course, a trade union could only interpret such action as strikebreaking. Strasser and John S. Kirchner, a vice president of the International, complained to the General Executive Board of the Knights of Labor. "After listening to a statement from the gentlemen named, it was decided that three members of the Board should go to New York to investigate the matter at the earliest possible moment."[25] The committee spent much time in taking testimony which, because of bad feeling had to be taken independently by each group. In the end nothing was done to allay the bitterness between the two unions.

The Knights of Labor, then at the height of its power, was not ready to surrender on the question of the exclusive right of the unions to determine trade matters. Powderly blamed the trouble in New York on "socialistic fanatics. . . . Our label was the first in the field," he wrote, "and it was only [through] the organization of the Knights of Labor which made it possible for the International label to find a market that it became known at all."[26]

As a matter of fact, the General Executive Board of the Knights of Labor granted to all trade districts the right "to distribute such labels according to such laws and regulations as may be adopted by trade districts to protect the same," on condition, of course, that the regulations of the trade districts in this matter not be in conflict with the "general laws in regard to design and price to be charged for the label."[27]

Powderly asked whether "we are not justified in having a label to protect the wares of the thousands of members of our craft who are in this order?" He could not understand why the trade unions would refer to every unorganized man as a "scab," and he resented the efforts of the unions to so classify such workers. However, the differences between the unions and the Knights of Labor were deeper than the dispute over labels in the cigarmaking industry. While it may even be true that the ill feeling between Strasser, Gompers, and Powderly exacerbated an already bad relationship—Powderly disliked the other two and charged "Gompers had never come to see him only when he was drunk"—it would be an error to overstress these elements in the situation.[28]

The trade unions thought in terms of control of the exclusive jurisdiction of their trades; the Knights of Labor believed that, as the representative of all labor, the Order could set up any kind of organization. It was a basic conflict in outlook which could not be easily resolved.

While differences over socialism and politics accentuated the dispute between the Knights and the Cigarmakers' Union, such considerations played no role in the complaints of the International Typographical Union, an organization almost entirely divorced from the ideological currents that swept over some of the unions at the time. Nevertheless, this organization found the Knights of Labor continually encroaching upon its jurisdiction. In 1885, the ITU appointed a committee to discuss this problem with Powderly. The results were not at all encouraging. Powderly promised to comply with the wishes of the delegation and to eliminate the cause of the complaints. Yet a year later it was reported that "the cause of the complaint . . . exists to a greater degree at the present time late events have clearly shown; and also shown that Mr. Powderly either did not keep the promise made to your representatives, or that he is unable to control the organization of which he is the head in its attempted raids upon trade unions."[29]

The convention of the ITU nevertheless concluded that no conflict between the Knights and the Printers' Union was necessary. The Knights were again requested not "to dictate the course of action of distinct trades," and not initiate men expelled by the trade unions into its ranks. The Bricklayers' and Masons' International Union was another organization which was completely free from ideological disputes and was, at that time as it is today, a "pure and simple" trade organization. Yet, the secretary of the latter organization described the activities of the Knights of Labor as an attempt "to seduce subordinate unions of trades, crafts and their members individually to renounce their allegiance to their parent order," and charged that it "created disturbance and dissension to such a degree that decided and united action was necessary to prevent such encroachments."[30]

REFERENCES

1. Letters of Uriah Stephens to W. Olin, March 13, 1879; to John M. Cooper, January 5, 1879, in archives of Catholic University.

2. Norman J. Ware, *The Labor Movement in the United States, 1860-1895* (New York: E. P. Dutton and Co.)

3. Henry J. Browne, *The Catholic Church and the Knights of Labor* (Washington, D. C.: Catholic University Press, 1946), discusses the relations of the Catholic Church to the Knights of Labor in great detail.

4. Stephens to James S. Sullivan, August 19, 1879.

5. Powderly to Robert Lucas, December 6, 1879, letter in archives of Catholic University.

6. Letter from Powderly to L. J. Mooney, March 30, 1880, letter in archives of Catholic University.

7. *Sixth Regular Session of the General Assembly of the Knights of Labor,* 1882, p. 279.

8. *Ibid.,* p. 332.

9. Powderly to Joseph Buttond, June 20, 1880; and to W. A. Varner, February 8, 1883, letters in archives of Catholic University.

10. *Report of the Proceedings of the Seventh Regular Session of the General Assembly Knights of Labor,* 1883, pp. 405, 509-510.

11. Powderly to Brother Lawler, October 11, 1881.

12. Powderly to O. C. Hodgdoth, April 30, 1880, letter in the archives of Catholic University.

13. Powderly to J. P. McDonnell, September 24, 1882, letter in archives of Catholic University.

14. *Record of Proceedings of the Sixth General Session of the General Assembly, Knights of Labor,* 1883, p. 312.

15. *Thirty-Second Annual Session of the International Typographical Union,* 1884, p. 12.

16. Powderly to Fred Turner, September 18, 1884; to Daniel Shea, September 20, 1884.

17. *Report of Proceedings of Eighth Regular Session of the Knights of Labor,* 1884, p. 717.

18. *Seventh Session of the Iron Molders' International Union of North America,* 1886, p. 31.

19. *Proceedings of the Bricklayers' and Masons' International Union,* 1887, p. 80-87.

20. *Thirty-Fourth Annual Session of the International Typographical Union,* 1886, pp. 24-25.

21. *Report of Proceedings of the Eighth Regular Session of the General Assembly, Knights of Labor,* 1884, p. 716.

22. *Fifteenth Annual Session of the Cigarmakers' International Union,* 1883, pp. 2-8.

23. *Proceedings of the Sixteenth Session of the Cigarmakers' International Union,* 1885, p. 7; *Cigarmakers' Official Journal,* October 1885, pp. 6-8.

24. *Report of Proceedings of the Eighth Regular Session of the General Assembly, Knights of Labor,* 1884, p. 716.

25. *Report of the Proceedings of the Special Session of the General Assembly of the Knights of Labor,* 1886, p. 28.

26. Powderly to Henry Dettman, August 11, 1886, letter in archives of Catholic University.

27. *Minutes of the General Executive Board of the Knights of Labor,* December 20, 1887, in archives of Catholic University.

28. Powderly to Henry Dettman, August 11, 1886, in archives of Catholic University.

29. *Thirty-Third Annual Session of the International Typographical Union,* 1885, p. 125; *Thirty-Fourth Annual Session of the International Typographical Union,* 1886, p. 90.

30. *Twenty-First Annual Convention of the Bricklayers' and Masons' International Union,* 1887, pp. 62-63.

III

The American Federation of Labor: Its Formation and Early Struggle for Survival

MEETINGS OF TRADE UNIONS

The complaints by trade unions against the Knights were numerous and widespread, but they did not have their origin in the opposition of Gompers and Strasser, although these two men strongly favored resisting encroachments by the Knights upon trade organizations. Failure to find an amicable solution for the conflict finally led to action. On April 26, 1886, a confidential circular was issued[1] suggesting that an informal conference be held at Philadelphia to devise ways

. . . to protect our respective organizations from the malicious work of an element who openly boast "that trade unions must be destroyed." This element urges our local unions to disband, and it is doing incalculable mischief by arousing antagonisms and dissensions in the labor movement. Under cover of the Knights of Labor, and as far as we can learn, without authority from that body, this element pursues its evil work. "Rats," "scabs," and unfair employers are backed up by this element. Suspended and expelled members of trades unions are welcomed into their ranks. And these elements use the Knights of Labor as an instrument through which to vent their spite against trade unions. That this has been the case can be amply demonstrated by the Cigar Makers' and Typographical International Unions. Other trades have been more or less affected.

A conference was called for May 17th in Philadephia, at which it was planned to work out a program through which the antagonism between the Knights and the trade unions could be allayed.

Of the forty-three national and international unions which had received invitations, twenty accepted and sent twenty-two delegates.[2] The conference, held at the Donaldson Hotel in Philadelphia, opened on May 17th. William Weihe of the Amalgamated Association of Iron and Steel Workers was chosen to preside; P. J. McGuire was elected secretary, and W. H. Foster, assistant secretary.

In addition, letters approving the purposes of the meeting were received from a number of organizations, and individuals.[3]

The first session confined itself largely to electing officers and defining

31

the rules of the conference. Each delegate also "pledged himself to stand by the work of the conference in preventing any further encroachments or inroads on the trade unions by the Knights of Labor." Strasser, McGuire, Weihe, Fitzpatrick, and Chris Evans were named a committee to draw up a "treaty with the Knights of Labor, and to present an address to the conference for endorsement, setting forth the views of the trade unions, for presentation to the General Assembly of the Knights of Labor, at the special session to be held in Cleveland, on May 25th, 1886."[4]

CHARGES AGAINST THE KNIGHTS OF LABOR AND TREATY

The subsequent meeting declared that

. . . inasmuch as the trade unions have a historical basis, and in view of the success that has attended their efforts in the past, we hold that they should strictly preserve their distinct and individual autonomy and that we do not deem it advisable for any trade union to be controlled or to join the Knights of Labor in a body, believing that trades unions are the best qualified to regulate their internal trade affairs, nevertheless we recognize the solidarity of all labor interests. . . . certain elements in the Knights of Labor [are attempting] to destroy trades unions, and this element continually urges trades unions to disband, and join the Knights of Labor, and makes it a point to encroach upon the legitimate mission and prerogatives of trades unions, arousing antagonism and provoking dissensions in the labor movement to the delight of the capitalists of the whole country.

The officers of the national and international unions believed that a joint defense against the activities of the Knights of Labor was necessary. A treaty was drawn up as a consequence, and was submitted to the special convention of the Knights of Labor at Cleveland in May 1886. The treaty demanded:

1. That in any branch of labor having a national or international organization, the Knights of Labor shall not initiate any person or form any assembly of persons following said organized craft or calling without the consent of the nearest national or international union affected.

2. That no person shall be admitted to the Knights of Labor who works for less than the regular scale of wages fixed by the union of his craft; and that none shall be admitted in the Knights of Labor who has ever been convicted of scabbing, ratting, embezzlement, or any other offenses against the union of his trade or calling, until exonerated by the same.

3. The charter of any Knights of Labor assembly having a national or international union shall be revoked, and the members of the same be requested to join a mixed assembly or form a local union under the jurisdiction of their respective national or international trades union.

4. That any organizer of the Knights of Labor who endeavors to induce trades unions to disband, or tampers with their growth or privileges, shall have his commission forthwith revoked.

5. That whenever a strike or lockout of any trades union is in progress, no assembly or district assembly of the Knights of Labor, shall interfere until settled to the satisfaction of the trades union affected.

6. That the Knights of Labor shall not establish nor issue any trademark or label in competition with any trademark or label now issued, or may hereafter be issued, by any national or international trades union.[5]

[The proposals of the trade unions were drastic, and would have required the Knights of Labor to limit itself to educational work. While the answer submitted to the trade unions by the committee from the Knights was conciliatory in tone, there appears to be no recognition of the demand for exclusive control of jurisdictions by the trade unions.] Powderly never understood the trade unions' concern with autonomy. "We must have Strasser at Cleveland", he wrote; "let us elect him G[rand] W[orkman] and make the president of the Typographical Union G[rand] S[tatistician] then we will have all other unions fighting Strasser and Witter so they won't lose their autonomy."[6] Yet, he did not see the reasons for the disputes with the trade unions, and hoped to "put an end to the warfare." While admitting that errors had been made and wrongs done, Powderly was hopeful that the differences could be settled. He therefore suggested to P. J. McGuire that "it would be better to have the leading men of the labor societies meet at Cleveland . . . and make a statement on the wrongs perpetrated on them by the Knights of Labor to the General Assembly." While he believed the charges against the Order had been exaggerated, he hoped that conferences may make possible the avoidance of "the errors of the past . . . and [insure] the success of the future."[7] In Powderly's views the conference of trade unions at Philadelphia had been unduly influenced by the cigarmakers' controversy. But this analysis falls in the light of the presence of so many representatives of trade unions, and their acquiescence in the statements issued. The trade unions were not then, any more than now, inclined to become embroiled in conflicts not their own. In fact, the secretary of the Bricklayers' and Masons' International Union, an organization which was not inclined to become involved in the controversies of other unions, agreed "with the spirit of the resolutions and demands presented by the special committee of trade union officers."[8]

THE TREATY AND THE KNIGHTS

The treaty of the trade unions was placed before a special committee of the Knights, of which Frank K. Foster was chairman and Robert Schilling and George McNeill members. The three were active trade unionists and sympathetic to the trade union point of view. The other six members were obviously not hostile to unions, for the committee was convinced that:

. . . the basis upon which an agreement can be reached would necessarily include the adoption of some plan by which all labor organizations could be protected from unfair men, men expelled, suspended, under fine, or guilty of taking the places of union men or Knights of Labor while on strike or while locked out from work, and that as far as possible a uniform standard of hours and wages should be adopted, so that men of any trade enrolled in our order and members of trades unions may not come in conflict because of differences in wages and hours of labor. We also believe that a system of exchanging working cards should be adopted, so that a member of any craft belonging to different organizations could work in harmony together, the card of any member of this order admitting to work in any union shop, and the card of any union men admitting him to work in any Knights of Labor shop.[9]

On the floor the treaty aroused prolonged discussion. Some delegates favored a conciliatory approach; others wanted to ignore the trade union demands and even conduct more aggressive campaigns against them. The special assembly voted to appoint a committee to confer with the trade union group, and then report back to the regular convention scheduled for later in the year.[10] No committee was appointed at the close of the special session, and P. J. McGuire, one of the leaders at the Philadelphia meeting of the trade unions, sought to prod Powderly to appoint such a group. "It is the desire of the trades unions to meet with said committee," McGuire wrote, "and arrange for such reciprocal and fraternal relations as the cause in which we are all employed demands for the future." Powderly found it difficult to discover five men to act in this matter and he suggested that the "executive board will act in that capacity for the reason that they can be found together when wanted at a moment's notice." Moreover, the executive board was more fit to work out an agreement, in his opinion, than five who were "new and inexperienced."[11]

[On September 28, 1886, the trade union committee elected at Philadelphia, accompanied by Josiah Dyer, David Pascoe, secretary-treasurer of the International Typographical Union, and John S. Kirchner of the Federation of Trades, met the executive board of the Knights of Labor. The Executive Board suggested that the treaty proposed by the trade unions be considered by the forthcoming meeting of the General Assembly scheduled at Richmond, Virginia. It was suggested that, in cases of future encroachments or difficulties between trade unions and the Order, the facts be made known to the chief officer of the trade union involved whose jurisdiction was being impinged upon so that the dispute might be immediately settled by the executive board of the Knights of Labor if it involved an assembly of the Order. It was also suggested that a special committee be appointed by the Knights of Labor to investigate complaints of trade unions.]These suggestions were accepted by Powderly, who promised to recommend them to the coming session of the General Assembly.[12] [At least it was the view of the trade unions that they had received the "most positive assurances from General Master Workman T. V. Powderly and some members of the General Executive Board of the Knights of Labor that they will use every endeavor at Richmond to establish proper and satisfactory relations with the trade unions."]

[Nothing was done. Indeed, the Richmond meeting actually made more tense the already strained relations when it ruled that members of the Knights of Labor would have a choice of retaining their membership in the Order or in the Cigar Makers' International Union. This was an emphatic answer to the demands of the trade unions that the Knights of Labor confine itself to educational work and allow the trade unions to govern their own jurisdictions. It meant, of course, that the label of the Cigar Makers' International Union would be boycotted. Powderly, himself, was far from enthusiastic about this action, which could only be interpreted as a challenge to the pretensions of the trade unions. "I did not like to see it pass," he said, "but it became the will of the General Assembly and I have no alternative but to comply with it as far as I can."[13]]

✳ CONVENTION AT COLUMBUS, OHIO

Following the failure of the Richmond General Assembly to agree on a formula satisfactory to the trade unions, William Weihe, P. J. McGuire, Christopher Evans, P. F. Fitzpatrick and Adolph Strasser, on November 10, 1886, issued a call for a trade union convention to be held at Columbus, Ohio, on December 8th, for the purpose of establishing a federation of trades. The committee declared:

The time has now arrived to draw the bonds of unity much closer together between all trades unions of America. We need an annual Trades Congress that shall have for its object:

1. The formation of Trades Unions and the encouragement of the Trades Union movement in America.

2. The organization of Trades Assemblies, Trades Councils, or Central Labor Unions, in every city in America, and the further encouragement of such bodies.

3. The founding of State Trades Assemblies, or State Labor Congresses, to influence State Legislation in the interest of the working masses.

4. The establishment of National and International Trades Unions, based upon the strict recognition of the autonomy of each trade, and the promotion and advancement of such bodies.

5. An American Federation of Labor or Alliance of all National and International Trades Unions, to aid and assist each other, and, furthermore, to secure national legislation in the interest of the working people, and influence public opinion by peaceful and legal methods in favor of organized labor.

6. To aid and encourage the labor press of America and to disseminate tracts and literature on the labor movement.[14]

The sponsors of the Columbus meeting of trade unions placed control in the hands of the national and international unions. National and international unions were allowed delegates on the basis of size of membership.[15] On the other hand, local trade unions, unaffiliated with a national or international union were allowed one delegate.

While negotiations with the Knights of Labor were still going on, a number of trade unions at their respective conventions approved of the plan for a federation of trade and labor unions. Among those approving a federation was the International Typographical Union, whose president warned:

It is important that in the present state of public opinion upon the purposes of labor organization, the workingmen should not be compromised by affiliation in any degree with that class of irreconcilable agitators who, failing to appreciate the opportunities afforded by free institutions, advocate the principles and methods foreign to trade unionism. It is earnestly recognized that the representatives of this body to the next Federated Congress be instructed to oppose the admission of representatives from any but recognized bodies of organized labor.[16]

Even though the Printers' Union was never caught in ideological controversies, the leaders of the organization insisted that the new group be limited to a federation of trade unions.

The Molders' Union, which also approved the prospective federation at its convention in August 1886, emphasized another limitation that would have to be imposed upon such an organization. A committee, of which Frank Rooney, the California leader, was a member, suggested that

The time has arrived for the great national and international unions of North America to come together and by a common compact engage to sustain each other in all their efforts for material advancement of the least of its members. This combination able enough to guarantee to each organization the unqualified support of all the others, should also, and to make it successful, must leave to each the management of its own affairs.[17]

The desire of a number of unions for a federation of trades antedated the serious difficulties a number of them had with the Knights of Labor. Nevertheless, the differences with the Knights helped to canalize their interest and gave them a cause around which they could rally. However, [the unions that objected to the encroachments of the Knights were not ready to surrender their rights to a new federation, even if they themselves were its architects] The emphasis of the Molders' Union upon the autonomy of the independent union expressed the thinking of the trade union leaders.

The Federation of Organized Trades and Labor Unions would unquestionably have been glad to receive the new recruits from the trade unions, but its lack of success made it a questionable vehicle for a new movement. Even though a number of trade union leaders were active in this Federation, they wanted to make a new start with an organization which had not already been marked by defeat, one which in fact had never even begun to fulfill its mission. In the last report made by that organization, it summarized what was perhaps its most important and, in a sense, only significant activity, the campaign for the eight-hour work day.

The Legislative Committee of the Federation of Organized Trades and Labor Unions had changed their meeting place because it believed that:

The best opportunity that ever offered itself to make the Federation a strong and powerful body in the near future, is the conference of national and international unions. In order to come to an understanding with the unions which will be restored in that conference . . . we considered [it] advisable . . . to change the meeting place from St. Louis, Missouri to Columbus, Ohio, and the time from December 14th to December 7th, so as to give delegates an opportunity to participate in the meeting of both, and bring about, if possible, an amalgamation of both bodies.[18]

The twenty delegates present at this, the last convention of the Federation of Organized Trades and Labor Unions, were there, in fact, to wind up their organization. Twenty-eight delegates came initially to the meeting of the trade unions, and a number of delegates were accredited to both conventions. The trade union conferences thus opened with the twenty-eight delegates plus an additional twelve delegates from the Federation. Later, at the sessions, two other delegates appeared at the meetings. Twenty-five organizations with a membership of slightly below 317,000 were represented. The conference also received letters of sympathy from other organizations.[19]

McGuire opened the meeting, and John McBride of the Coal Miners and Mine Laborers was elected temporary chairman. He was escorted to the rostrum by Gompers. Committees on credentials, rules, and order of business, permanent organization, resolutions, and constitution were appointed. The trade union committee, which had conferred with the Knights on the treaty worked out at the Philadelphia meeting, was continued.

The preamble adopted by the American Federation of Labor was couched in the radical phrases of the time.[20]

[While the chief purpose of the meeting was to set up a federation and elect officers, it also expressed its views on several issues of the day. On politics, it urged "a most generous support to the independent political movement of the workingmen"—the only time such a view was to be advocated by the A. F. of L. In sympathy with the workers of the Pacific Coast, a demand for more rigid enforcement of the laws restricting the immigration of Chinese was demanded. The eight-hour work day was endorsed, but it was "deemed advisable for the present to establish the system of nine hours as a day's work in all branches of labor now working ten hours a day, where men are now working more than ten hours a day, we shall use every effort to aid and encourage them to still further reduce the hours of labor."

Strikes were approved, but the practice of "indiscriminate" support of walkouts by local central bodies was not held desirable. Instead of "appropriating moneys to every appeal in strikes," local bodies were urged to "reserve all their resources to contribute more liberally to official appeals made by this Federation, in behalf of bodies connected therewith, and [which] are also the only ones entitled to their support."

Four delegates, including John McBride and Gompers, were nominated for president. All withdrew, and Gompers was elected unanimously. George Harris and J. W. Smith were respectively elected first and second vice presidents, P. J. McGuire was chosen secretary, and Gabriel Edmonston, treasurer. The newly-elected officers were ordered to take over the organization immediately upon the adjournment of the convention. All funds of the Federation of Organized Trades and Labor Unions were turned over to the American Federation of Labor, and a per capita tax of one-half of one cent per member per month was imposed upon all national and international unions to finance the Federation.

The officers elected at the convention constituted the Executive Council, and it was their task to unify the labor movement. Formation of central labor councils and federations, promotion of the organization of unions, and the support of legislation favorable to labor were some of the duties imposed on them. In contrast to the previous federation, the American Federation of Labor created a full-time office, the presidency, with a salary of one thousand dollars a year, plus expenses incurred in the service of the organization. Other members of the Executive Council were paid at the rate of three dollars a day for time lost while serving the Federation.

GOMPERS AND MCGUIRE

While the American Federation of Labor had been formally organized, it could only be made a living reality by its permanent officers. The major task fell upon Gompers, who was the only full-time officer, and he was fortunate in that he could always call upon P. J. McGuire for advice and assistance. Gompers was born in London in 1850; he came to the United States at the age of thirteen. The next year he joined the Cigar Makers' Union of New York City. Subsequently he was active in the reorganization of the Cigar Makers' International Union, and was a member of the group supporting the efforts of President Adolph Strasser to modernize it. He was acquainted with the various intellectual and ideological currents within the labor movement of his time, and early in life he developed a strong belief in the desirability of labor pursuing a policy of economic action and eschewing independent politics. He was a delegate to five of the conventions of the Federation of Organized Trades and Labor Unions, and served on its Legislative Committee. Perhaps the chief reason he was chosen to head the American Federation of Labor was that full-time officers in the labor movement would not accept a post as unpromising as the chief office of a labor federation without funds and with a tenuous membership.

[Gompers was an ideal candidate for the post. Knowledgeable, with a bias in favor of trade unionism as against labor politics, he was a vigorous proponent of the trade union point of view, yet conciliatory with opponents within the organization. He understood as well as anyone the limits of the power of the Federation, and while he frequently tried to persuade he seldom used threats to force a point of view upon the affiliates.]

Peter J. McGuire, elected secretary, was born in New York City in 1852. He was apprenticed to a wood joiner, and became a member of his union in 1872. He was successively a Greenbacker, Socialist, and finally trade unionist. He organized the Brotherhood of Carpenters and Joiners in 1881, and served as its secretary for twenty years. He became popularly known as the father of Labor Day. He was Gompers' co-worker in the most difficult time in the A. F. of L.'s history. Not only was he shrewd and knowledgeable in the affairs of the labor movement, but he was a vigorous and astute organizer who gave his services freely to many organizations besides his own. McGuire was ready, during the time he was an executive of the A. F. of L., to help both in organizing workers in other crafts and callings, and in their negotiations with employers. Many labor organizations owe their beginnings to him, and many others profited from his tireless efforts on behalf of the cause. Shrewd, eloquent, and well-educated, he possessed a wide knowledge of foreign trade union movements as well as reform philosophies.[More than any others, Gompers and McGuire can be regarded as the architects of the labor movement.]

Upon the adjournment of the convention, a headquarters was obtained in New York City at a rent of sixteen dollars per month. The Federation began its existence with the balance of $160.52, which was turned over to the treasurer at the end of the Columbus convention. Money was scarce, and a large part of the work was to fall upon Gompers, aided by Secretary McGuire, Edmonston, and other members of the Executive Council.

AUTONOMY AS A BASIC PRINCIPLE

[The American Federation of Labor functioned from the beginning upon the principle of the autonomy of the national and international union. This meant that the sovereignty of the national organizations within their jurisdictions was recognized, and also their right to regulate their own affairs without interference from the Federation.]It is clear that, while it is doubtful whether the national unions would have agreed to join a central federation upon any other conditions, the consequent absence of authority placed the leaders of the A. F. of L. in occasional dilemmas. Not only would the Federation be taken to task for the derelictions of affiliates over which it had little or no control, but the A. F. of L.'s failure to mobilize needed financial resources for necessary political and economic activity would sometimes arouse resentment, even among those affiliates which knew the limits of the Federation's power in this area. Even though denied power to adjudicate issues, national unions insisted upon bringing their inter-unions conflicts, such as differences over jurisdiction, to the American Federation of Labor for settlement. The Federation was able to exercise influence only through suggestion and appeals to solidarity and the common interest of all labor. Occasionally—usually against the weaker unions—it could use more forceful means.

The American Federation of Labor took the position that it was necessary for the workers to organize

. . . so as to assist each other against the evils now afflicting our class. This possible, desirous, and necessary, working class unity has not yet been effected owing to the non-recognition on the part of all who have hitherto attempted it of the principle of autonomy, or the right of the several bodies composing the organization to self-government. [The American Federation of Labor avoids the fatal rock upon which all previous attempts to effect the unity of the working class have split, by leaving to each body or affiliated organization the complete management of its own affairs, especially its own particular trade affairs. Thus, the American Federation of Labor presents to the toilers of this broad land a form of organization under which each trade enjoys the most perfect liberty, while securing the advantages resulting from united action.[21]]

Conferences with Knights of Labor

During the first convention, on December 10th, a committee from the trade unions conferred with a committee from the Knights of Labor headed by John Howes, who acted as spokesman for the group.[22] [A. G. Denny, Louis Arrington, James McFeely, and G. P. Hall made up the Knight's committee. Paul F. Fitzpatrick headed the trade union committee; Strasser, Evans, McGuire, and Edward L. Daley of the New England Lasters' Union, also served.] The trade unions again presented the treaty, but the Knights' committee declared "we cannot consider that treaty. It has been rejected by our General Assembly." Nor would Howes consider any substitute. It was the position of his delegation that, as the Order had no grievances against the trade unions, the Knights of Labor could make no offer. Moreover, the committee from the Knights declared it could not even make recommendations. When the question of evidence arose, Fitz-patrick argued that "we have an abundance of testimony to show many grievances of where suspended and expelled members of trades Unions 'rats and scabs,' embezzlers of union funds, and unfair men generally, have been admitted to membership in the K. of L." There was consider-able discussion over this issue, and Howes admitted: "We cannot always regulate such matters, and there is likely to be conflict while there is a double jurisdiction of the Knights of Labor and the trades union in any occupation.[23]

In an interview with the *Ohio State Journal*, Howes declared that there need never be any difficulties with the trades unions. "Certain it was that the Knights did not invite it. They preferred peace always, and would concede points to obtain it when necessary, but revoking the charters of the Knights of Labor assemblies where there were trades unions engaged in the same line of work could not be considered."[24] Howes believed that the cigarmakers were the chief source of difficulty.

The committee from the Knights also believed that the trade unions leaders were not altogether sincere in their arguments, and that the grievances were used by some of them "to accomplish selfish purposes." Moreover, the committee pointed to the number of trade unions that found a hospitable home within the Order. In fact, they argued the Order "has given an opportunity to any trade to organize within the Order and perform its functions as a trade organization when the conditions involved would justify."[25] In fact, the statement expresses the basis for the objec-tions of the trade unions to the pretensions of the Knights. Leaders of the trade unions did not regard their organizations as inferior. On the con-trary, they looked upon them as the most obvious and natural type of labor combination. They did not believe that the tutelage of the Knights was desirable, nor did they look upon the leaders of the Order as fit to deter-mine when and what trade unions should be allowed an independent existence. In a sense the conflict was irreconcilable, as long as the Knights of Labor insisted upon chartering trade unions.

Unable to reach a satisfactory agreement, the meeting of the trade unions declared that the Knights of Labor

. . . have persistently attempted to undermine and disrupt the well-established trades' unions, organized and encouraged men who have proven themselves untrue to their trade, false to the obligations of their union, embezzlers of moneys, and expelled by many of the unions, and conspiring to pull down the trades' unions, which it has cost years of work and sacrifice to build; therefore, be it Resolved, That we condemn the acts above recited, and call upon all workingmen to join the unions of their respective trades, and urge the forma-tion of national and international unions and the centralization of all under one head, the American Federation of Labor.[26]

The differences with the Knights of Labor and the unions' inability to find a satisfactory settlement was the chief reason for bringing them together, but the sentiment for a federation of trades had been increasing among labor men, irrespective and independent of their experience with the Knights. In fact, the resolution setting up the American Federation of Labor made no allusion to the jurisdictional wars then going on, and merely argued that:

Many questions affecting the interests of the working classes . . . cannot be dealt with in special and separate trade and labor unions, and that end can be best attained by a federation of all trade and labor unions, through which all branches of labor may prove allies to any particular one that may be oppressed, and all may form one brotherhood for the defense and protection of the laboring masses.[27]

STRUGGLE FOR SURVIVAL

The American Federation of Labor was a new type of labor organization. No pure trade union federation with a full-time officer had ever before existed in the United States. Upon the shoulders of Gompers, who occupied the full-time office, fell the major, but by no means sole, responsibility for defining the policies and practices of the new body.

Problems other than financial also existed. Some of the unions which participated in the Columbus convention had doubts that the Federation would advantageously serve their interests. Such a fear was expressed by the Chief Organizer of the International Typographical Union on the ground that ["the constitution adopted at Columbus" would infringe "upon the individual rights of the unions."]

Julian Wright, one of the delegates from the International Typographical Union to the Columbus convention, was even more outspoken in his criticism. He insisted that the Federation constitution threatened the independence of the individual affiliates, for inasmuch as national and international unions would receive charters from the A. F. of L., they would, in fact, "derive their authority from the Federation." The objection to giving the Federation authority to issue charters to national and international unions could easily be met. In fact, the convention of the A. F. of L. met this objection at its meeting in 1887 by abolishing the requirement that national and international unions be given charters, and substituting instead the issuance of certificates of affiliation.

The above objection was a purely technical one, and could easily be met. However, one more serious, against the payment of per-capita taxes, was also raised. The convention of the International Typographical Union in 1887, voted not to "pay a per capita tax to any organization to which it may send delegates, believing that the calling together of representatives of trade organizations is for the purpose of consultation as to the best methods of strengthening their respective unions, and that actual expenses of such meetings shall be paid in equal part by the unions represented."[28] This was the policy the Typographical Union had followed with regard to the Federation of Trades and Labor Unions, to which it had made financial contributions. The objection was to the formal requirement that a given payment had to be made.

Acceptance of this view would have reduced the A. F. of L. to an annual meeting of delegates, with the organization performing virtually no activities. The opposition to the payment of per-capita taxes to the A. F. of L. was part of a movement within the Typographical Union to prevent it from affiliating with the American Federation of Labor, led among others by the editor of *The Craftsman*, the union's journal.[29]

FINANCIAL PROBLEMS

At the convention of the I. T. U. in 1888, the question of the payment of per-capita taxes was again considered. One of the leading opponents within the union of affiliation with the American Federation of Labor— David Pasco—had in the meantime been retired as secretary, and the convention voted to pay its obligations. Outstanding indebtedness was canceled, and the union paid only on its current membership. The efforts of the leaders of the Typographical Union to bring about affiliation were praised by Gompers who appreciated "sincerely their expressions of kindness to the A. F. of L. and earnestly hoped arrangements may be made so that your delegates may stand upon an equality with all others at the St. Louis session and assist at the helm of the Federation ship of state."[30]

While the I. T. U. was the only organization which formally refused to pay its per-capita tax, a number of other organizations were dilatory in meeting their financial obligations. Among the latter was Gompers' own organization, which led him to remind his old friend and colleague, Adolph Strasser: "You will imagine that if organizations such as the CMIU, which decidedly recognizes the necessity of the federation of Trades Union, fail to pay *per capita*, then others which look with greater indifference upon the movement become more lax in their duties." The letter failed to bring forth a payment or even a reply. One month later, Gompers again pleaded with Strasser to pay his obligations to the Federation. "Do you think it the wisest policy," he asked, "to assist in starving the Federation out of existence?"

Strasser excused his failure to make a remittance by the argument that the Cigar Makers' Union was being asked to pay more than its fair share of the Federation expenses. When assured that his union was only being asked to pay its proper per-capita taxes, Strasser remitted his contribution.[31]

The International Molders' Union of North America was another organization which showed some reluctance to pay its per capita. As this organization was one of the chief promoters of a federation of trades, its refusal was difficult to explain. Gompers appealed to the head of the Molders' Union to make its payment because it was "primarily through your efforts [that] the A. F. of L. was formed. . . . What would be said by those who would gloat over the downfall of the trades unions and through them the A. F. of L. if your organization would not be represented at the second session of the organization it helped to call into existence?"[32]

The failure of the unions to meet their financial commitments not only placed severe restrictions upon the functioning of the Federation, but imposed very great personal burdens upon Gompers. In April 1887, he complained to Gabriel Edmonston, the treasurer:

Money is coming in very slow, in fact so slow that it is discouraging. . . . If I only had the means I wouldn't care a straw but as it is I will have shortly to decide upon giving up the position, take a post at my trade or starve. If the unions of the country don't want a federation, then they don't and that settles it. If they do they ought to pay a little for the protection its very existence affords and should not insist upon doing what we protest against employers doing, i.e., exacting work without pay. There can be no question that I did a great deal of that in my long connection with the labor movement and am willing to do so again if I get a chance to get back at my trade. But with a large family depending upon me for support I cannot give my entire time without recompense.[33]

The seriousness of the financial situation was not exaggerated, for when McGuire asked reimbursement for expenses spent on Federation business, Gompers was forced to tell him: "There are no funds at my disposal or I would send the amount of the bill."[34] Conditions did not improve during the year, and in November 1887 the balance in the treasury was only $25.95.

SPEAKING CAMPAIGNS BY GOMPERS

Yet the work went on, and despite his personal need for funds Gompers always followed a policy of refusing compensation from labor groups for particular services. To an officer of a local union who asked Gompers to address a public meeting in his community, Gompers replied: "About the probable expense of the trip let me say that you know what the fare is, and with a slight additional necessary expense is all the outlay that is required for me. For my services I ask nothing."[35] Gompers believed that his trips were of great value to the movement. Usually taken as a lecture tour, they enabled him to meet the leading trade unionists in various communities and establish relations with them. He used these trips to bring active members in various places in touch with one another, and to organize local unions and enlist voluntary organizers. The extent of his activity is illustrated by a report in February 1888, in which the Executive Council was informed:

Thanks to your sanction I have had the opportunity of advocating the unity of labor in Syracuse, Rochester, Buffalo, Boston, Albany, Troy, Cleveland, Columbus, Cincinnati, Indianapolis, Louisville, Evansville, Nashville, Connellsville, Peoria, St. Louis, Springfield, Kansas City, Fort Scott, Denver, Lincoln, Omaha, Sioux City, Minneapolis, South Bend, St. Paul, Milwaukee, Chicago, Grand Rapids, Saginaw, Lansing, East Saginaw, and Detroit. [He planned to cover about a half dozen other cities then] to return to my home in New York from which I have been so long separated, about the tenth of next month. Throughout this trip I have found the unions in a healthy and active condition, and full of enthusiasm for the success of our common cause. The name of the American Federation of Labor is becoming . . . a household word and I believe that I have succeeded in arousing a general interest in its methods, and making its objects known in a most effective manner.[36]

Gompers enjoyed these trips and believed they were of great benefit to the labor movement. The Federation could not finance these campaigns out of its income, but no objections were raised against the trips as long as the Federation bore none of the expenses. Gompers usually tried to arrange these trips so that each locality would have to pay only a proportion of the cost, but if some locality failed to meet its share Gompers would pay out of his own pocket. Scarcely able to maintain his family, the failure of some local unions to meet their obligations, led Gompers to complain to the Executive Council: "I had traveled in midwinter nearly ten thousand miles, made about fifty speeches with the greatest success and came home about ninety dollars out of pocket."[37]

ORGANIZING

Travel and defense of the new Federation were merely part of the duties of the head of the movement, and in a sense only minor ones. The A. F. of L. could make itself felt on the labor scene only by gaining new recruits for its directly affiliated trade and federal unions, and for the locals of the affiliated internationals. Its principal function in this early period was the bringing together of the isolated and scattered local unions in a trade into an international organization. The Federation was in a strategic position to act as a clearing house for this purpose, since it could take the lead in calling a conference to which local unions in a particular trade would be invited. Thus, a number of local unions of barbers which had not yet established a national organization were urged by Gompers to try to organize the men of the trade in their home city. They were told they could then "become attached to the American Federation of Labor by applying for a charter (to this office) . . . I shall at an early date call for a conference of the barbers union to form a national trades union of them."[38]

The bringing of scattered locals of a trade together was one of the more important functions performed for the labor movement by the A. F. of L. However, the decision to exercise this function depended upon the existence of an interest by the Federation. Such an interest was said to exist if the A. F. of L. had at least a local union in the trade. While the Federation had the duty, wherever possible, of mobilizing workers into unions of their trades, the principle of autonomy which the internationals jealously guarded allowed for no interference in the affairs of a union or even a group of unions unless the principle of a prior interest had first been fulfilled.

A suggestion was made by the Secretary of a local of longshoremen in Saginaw, Michigan, that the A. F. of L. help establish a national union of longshoremen. There were at the time a number of local unions of that calling in existence which might be brought together. Gompers took the view that the A. F. of L., however, had "no right to interfere until it is empowered by one or more local unions." He recognized that it was of course important that a national union of longshoremen be organized, and recommended that "as aid in that direction you should urge the union in East Saginaw to become affiliated to the A. F. of L. thus making the next step comparatively easy." The Secretary was advised that, as soon as possible, members of the longshoremen's unions "should form a national organization" and Gompers supplied the names and locations of other unions in the trade and the officers of these independent locals. He suggested that informal relations be established as a preliminary to the unity in the trade. It took several years before such unity was achieved, but the encouragement of the Federation was of considerable value in bringing a national organization into being.[39]

Mobilizing Trade Unions Personnel

Another important service the Federation performed was the mobilizing of experienced trade unionists to organize workers in other trades. When the hair spinning workers of Philadelphia expressed a desire for a union, Gompers asked an officer of the Cigar Makers' International Union, John Kirchner, "if he could attend to this business."[40] Kirchner handled the "business" and a local union was established.

The Federation also became a center to which inquiries about organizing were directed by individual workers. Some, who did not know the name or location of the labor organization in their trade, if such existed, might know of the existence and address of the American Federation of Labor. Thus a worker who inquired about getting in touch with the long-defunct Machinists and Blacksmiths National Union was advised,

"The Machinists and Blacksmiths National Union succumbed during the disastrous panic of 1873 and has never reestablished itself," and given the name of the Amalgamated Society of Engineers, "of which John Hewitt is the secretary and the official to whom you should apply for information concerning local societies of this trade."[41] A copy of the letter was sent to Hewitt so that he might recruit a potential member into the union.

In giving advice on affiliation, care was always exercised to direct an applicant to the union of his trade, if such were in existence. A plasterer who sought to join a federal local was told "to join the national union of your trade,"[42] even though the particular national organization was not at the time affiliated with the American Federation of Labor. The policy followed in such instances was based upon both principle and expediency. It was not a wise policy to recruit workers into separate unions, in view of the Federation's desire to win the affiliation of national and international unions outside its ranks. Organization of their craftsmen would be regarded by the internationals as an invasion of their jurisdiction, and would inevitably arouse opposition. In addition, the Federation was opposed even at the outset to dual unions, and sought to prevent their development. On this principle, the application of an operators' and tailors' local union for affiliating directly with the A. F. of L. was temporarily rejected. The secretary of that organization was told that "all *bona fide* trades unions can obtain a charter from and affiliate with the Federation, but if a national organization of that trade exists they are requested to belong to that first."[43] However, the Journeymen's Tailors' Union, which had the jurisdiction in the men's tailoring trade, expressed no opposition to the affiliation of this local to the A. F. of L., and consequently the charter was granted. Gompers was a bit apologetic for the delay, and informed the local that "the object of our Federation is the formation or assisting in the formation of local, state, and national trade unions." He felt, however, that it was necessary to avoid chartering dual unions, as that "would be working in the power of error and wrong," and, with an obvious allusion to the Knights of Labor, "to follow the paths of the organization that has done so much injury in this direction."

The A. F. of L., in its desire to protect existing unions, had to consider their objections to the application of other trades unions to affiliate. Of course, if a *bona fide* organization requested affiliation, objections of a substantial nature were required to justify a denial. When the New York Pattern Makers' League protested the chartering of a metal trades local in New York, and presented only vague and general objections, the A. F. of L. refused to accede to the request on the ground that the complaints were not specific: "Merely to say that there are weighty objections is certainly no evidence," the local was told. However, the local was assured, "the American Federation of Labor is an organization opposed to unfair men in every form . . . it favors the formation of trades, and secures and maintains their autonomy and independence. The prospect of obtaining an application or any number of applications will not tempt the Federation to swerve the slightest from these principles."[44] The principle of autonomy of the national union was so firmly held to be the cornerstone of an effective national labor movement that locals in a trade were urged to join their national unions "even when such national unions do not belong to the A. F. of L."[45]

In carrying out this principle, which also meant following a policy of one union in a jurisdiction, the A. F. of L. faced the necessity of reconciling or merging two or more unions that had developed independently in the same trade. The Federation defined its position on these issues in order to appeal to the National League of Musicians to join the American Federation of Labor. Gompers argued that it is

. . . the duty of all workingmen to organize in unions of their respective trades and nationalize these unions, all to be devoted and cemented to each other upon matters affecting the general interests of wage-earners, while in *trade matters the autonomy of each union must be maintained.* We believe when the members of one union are threatened in their interests [it is our duty] to render such assistance as can be given and necessary. Yet never attempt to usurp the rights and independence of the union.[46]

[Following the principles enunciated in the above letter, the American Federation of Labor refused, for several years, to charter a national union of musicians until the heads of several of the organizations would agree to unite.]

AIDING LOCAL AND NATIONAL UNIONS

There were also occasions in which the heads of the A. F. of L. would be called upon to aid local and even national unions in negotiations with employers. In the summer of 1887 the National Union of United Brewery Workmen appealed for assistance in Boston. A strike had been called, and Gompers believed that, after ten days' negotiations, he had gained a satisfactory settlement from the employers. Instead, he found that the local leadership advised against compromising the initial demands. Gompers spoke out against "far reaching demands that the organization is totally not sufficiently equipped and disciplined to accomplish. It is one of the modes of shallow men to urge those with less experience to make more radical demands than the men feel themselves able to achieve and by that means have the men felt certain that the 'advisors' are true men."[47] In this instance, the terms secured by Gompers, and rejected by the strikers at the advice of their local leaders, were the best that could be obtained at the time. In fact, the strike was subsequently lost.

To prevent hasty and ill-advised action by the newly-organized was one of the tasks the Federation sought to accomplish. While there were a number of men with considerable trade union experience, they were by no means a numerous class. Consequently, advice on tactics was both necessary and valuable; but giving advice was a delicate matter and had to be done without any appearance that the autonomy or independence of the recipient was being violated. The more experienced leaders of the Federation were aware that newly-organized groups have a greater tendency to strike than long established organizations. They also knew that the new union is more subject to instability, and consequently it is necessary to curb the almost natural predilection for hasty action. To an inquiry by the secretary of a recently organized local union as to whether he should call a strike, Gompers advised:

If you see fit I answer yes. But there is something I dare not omit to call your attention to, namely, *Do not strike in haste and repent at your leisure.* New organizations are apt to strike when the time is inopportune or when they are unprepared for a stoppage. They are also liable to underestimate the power they have to contend against. I urge you therefore to be careful before the union takes a hasty or ill advised step. It is better in my opinion to keep on building the organization up. Strengthen your position so that you may have a good chance of victory before you strike. This may be a slow process but it is surest, in the end, and the quickest and by far the safest. It may be galling to wait for victory but defeat is worse. It is demoralizing and then you might be compelled to do the work of organization all over again a few years hence.[48]

In another instance, the secretary of a car builders' local union, after describing the low wages and undesirable working conditions existing in his plant, informed Gompers he was planning a strike soon. It was a recently-organized local, and conditions certainly justified the contemplation, if not the calling, of a strike.

My province [Gompers told him], is to advise and not to dictate. Therefore I will give you the benefit of my best judgment based upon extensive observations, and consider it my duty to acquaint you with the conclusions at which I arrive. . . . Unless present appearances are very misleading strikes of any kind will not be successful for some time to come, if the strikes are for an advance of wages. As a matter of fact, the tendencies of the present situation are in an opposite direction owing to a powerful combination of the employers. . . My advice is bide your time until you can take practical action; then plan your organization by all means at your command in the full belief that your time will come if you have the courage to wait. Lost strikes break up your organization faster than any other cause.[49]

Gompers was not averse to speaking out against violation by officers of the rights of the members when the occasion presented itself. A secretary of a local union notified Gompers he had called a strike without consulting the membership, and requested advice on how to proceed with the walkout.

It was very late in the day [he was told], to ask my advice after you went out on strike. . . . You should have given your union the first chance of endeavoring to investigate and thereafter decide upon the advisability of striking. As it is you placed the union in a position of making it an "affirmative nodding machine" without the power to say "no". . . . I do not denounce strikes but the ground should be well prepared and the chance of winning well calculated, the opposing forces not underestimated by momentary enthusiasm before entering into one.[50]

When advice was solicited, Gompers could respond promptly and without hesitation. A problem of a different kind was presented when events required the head of the Federation to intervene in the affairs of a subordinate union on his own initiative. Gompers did not believe he should remain silent when dangerous or harmful policies were pursued. Concern was shown when the Brewery Workers' Union sought to impose a boycott upon groups of breweries without first seeking a settlement of the dispute. Although it was an issue which fell within purview of the international and not of the A. F. of L., Gompers felt he was justified in intervening. He wrote to the head of the Brewery Workers' Union that he was obligated "to volunteer such advice as my experience teaches me should be given. You need not heed it. It is given for what it is worth, you can do as you please nevertheless." Instead of the calling of a strike, Gompers advised the issuing of a circular ("and I am willing to assist you in every way in its preparation") calling the attention of the employing brewers to the practices of some of their associates and asking their discontinuance. If the circular failed to bring the results, Gompers argued, other methods could be used to gain relief. "But your circular if issued first would place your organization in a position in which the bosses could not claim that without being requested to discontinue a practice they are threatened with a boycott."[51]

The request for the assistance of the American Federation of Labor in negotiating with employers was not unusual at the time. Whenever Gompers could not attend to the matter himself, he usually requested McGuire or some other trade unionist with experience in collective bargaining negotiations to assist. During difficulties between the Philadelphia *Tageblatt* and the German-American Typographia, both Gompers and McGuire participated in the discussion with the employer.

The officers of the Federation were under great pressure to help in organization and with other union problems. Both Strasser and P. F. Fitzpatrick, leading initiators of the Federation, were, nevertheless, critical of the progress made, and Frank Rooney, a leader in the California labor movement, described the A. F. of L. as impotent. The only answer that Gompers could make to these charges was that he had done everything humanly possible to keep the movement alive. He argued that "because it has not attained the degree of perfection we desire, is no reason to describe it as 'impotent'." Despite the disparagement of Rooney, Gompers was convinced "that the foundation of a great movement has been laid by the Federation."[52] Obviously, a number of trade union leaders were expecting considerably more from the new movement than its small staff and meager resources warranted. In addition to the direct aid the movement had given to trade unions, Gompers was convinced that the trade unions had gained many indirect advantages. These were "already noticeable in the way the Knights of Labor have partially kept their hands off the trades unions and the formation of national trades organizations and a more general recognition of the necessity and rights of each organization." Gompers was not concerned about the prestige of the A. F. of L. as long as it could "render successful aid in the formation and recognition of trades unions."[53]

There was also some disagreement between Gompers and the Executive Council on the desirability of publishing an official newspaper. A publication had been authorized, but it proved to be a drain on both the time of the officers, especially Gompers', and on the limited finances of the Federation. Yet Gompers believed the publication of a journal was necessary if the Federation's point of view was to be presented. He felt that the extra effort and expense would be amply repaid by having a means of answering charges against the trade unions, and of presenting their views on major questions. Despite Gompers' views in this matter, the convention of 1887 supported the Executive Council and abolished the *Union Advocate*, the first official organ of the American Federation of Labor.[54]

The heads of the movement were called upon to carry very heavy burdens. In fact Gompers had, earlier in 1887, complained to the Executive Council that a large part of his "time is taken up with running errands which time could be put to much better advantage. If I could be authorized to hire a boy to do this, he could also write the addresses on the wrappers for mailing our journals which would in itself be a great service. The wages of the boy would not exceed three and a half dollars per week and I believe would be a wise expenditure."[55] The hiring of the errand boy was authorized, and of course the abolition of the journal removed both editorial and business duties from Gompers' shoulders.

FIRST MILESTONE

Although the first year of the Federation's activity could scarcely be regarded as an overwhelming success, it was by no means a failure. [Perhaps its most important single achievement in this first year was the enlistment of ten internationals, several of which were among the leading trade unions of the time. The affiliation of the Amalgamated Association of Iron and Steel Workers of America, the Brewers' National, and American Flint Glass Workers Union was an indication of confidence of the large trade unions in the reorganized federated body.] Including the central bodies and single unions, the organizations represented at the convention in 1887 had a membership of over six hundred thousand. The annual income of the Federation can perhaps be regarded as some measure of the support the organization was able to gain. The old Federation throughout its entire existence of six years received $2666.70, which included the contributions made to finance the first meeting at Terre Haute. In its first year, the income of the new Federation was $2100.34. Yet, while the income might be regarded on a comparative basis as a satisfactory index of sentiment in favor of the A. F. of L., it was scarcely adequate to carry on the program of organizing the unorganized. Nevertheless, there still were, as was noted above, complaints against the high level of contributions required from international unions. Responding to the pressure from the affiliates, Gompers reluctantly advised the convention of 1887 to consider a reduction in the scale of charges to be paid by affiliates. The convention decided then that the per-capita tax should be cut in half, from one-half to one-fourth of a cent per member per month. It was the opinion of many delegates that the lower contributions would encourage several internationl unions, which had stood aloof because of the expense involved, to join the Federation.

The convention of 1887, by excluding two delegates from the Washington, D. C., Federation of Labor, reaffirmed the desire of the leaders that the Federation be exclusively a trade union body. These delegates were denied a seat because the group they represented "was not fully in sympathy with the trades union movement, as it was overwhelmingly composed of Knights of Labor Assemblies."[56] Another resolution of importance laid down the policy that only one organization was to be recognized in a single jurisdiction, and pointed up the basic opposition to the formation of dual unions.[57]

All incumbent officers were reelected. In fact, several officers accepted only after the convention insisted that they continue at their posts. P. J. McGuire, the secretary, was among those who wanted to retire because of the pressure of the duties in his own organization. At the unanimous request of the delegates, McGuire reconsidered his refusal.

The passing of the first milestone did not ease the burdens of the officers, but within the limits of its resources the organization carried on considerable activity. [Considering that the relations between separate international unions prior to the formation of the A. F. of L. had been sporadic, and at times even nonexistent, the new Federation gave them an agency through which they could appeal for financial, moral, and political aid during "time of trouble." In the lockout of the members of the Molders' Union by the Defense Association, the A. F. of L. issued a circular to all the unions connected with the Federation, pointing to the need of honoring the Molders' picketlines and providing other necessary aid. President Fitzpatrick of the Iron Molders' Union recognized that, while financial aid had not been needed by his members during the lockout, the ability of the labor movement to mobilize greater resources than could a single union would, in the future, be of great assistance to the Molders' Union as well as to other international unions.[58]

ORGANIZING THE UNORGANIZED

The Federation was also entrusted with the responsibility of organizing the unorganized. Since the Federation lacked the finances to employ full-time organizers, Gompers suggested to the Executive Council that active trade unionists be recruited to represent the Federation in unorganized areas and industries, as long as such "organizers . . . work according to the principles and within the lines maintained by the American Federation of Labor." The Council endorsed the proposal, and eighty voluntary organizers were appointed the first year. Gompers sought to gain the assistance of the officers of various unions in this campaign of enlisting trade unionists for this purpose. Officers of unions were importuned to help him organize workers in other trades. Thus the mere existence of the Federation, despite its lack of funds, not only enabled organizations to assist each other, but to organize the unorganized trades as well.

When Gompers heard that the head of the Molders' Union was planning a trip to the South, he expressed the hope the trip would be "productive of great good." At the same time, Gompers asked if he would take a few documents with him so that he might, if possible, "organize a few federal locals." During the same period, he urged McGuire: "Should you come across a good unionist during your trip, please let me know and I will appoint them 'organizers.'"[59]

In the program of organizing, differences were likely to arise on whether a national union should be established. Even in the first period of the A. F. of L.'s history, federal and local trade unions often sought to organize national labor unions. Sometimes such a step might appear inadvisable to the more experienced leaders of the Executive Council because of the insufficiency of the number of locals organized, or because the narrow geographical spread of subordinate units might not warrant the issuance of a national charter. However, the Federation had to assure its local unions that direct affiliation was not permanent, and that a national charter would be granted as soon as conditions were propitious. When several locals of hair spinners applied for a national charter, they were told it was not "practicable at present and will not be until more local unions of that trade are organized." The union was asked to "forward to this office the names and the addresses of good men employed in their trade in the various cities"[60] so that the Federation might render what help it could. While there were several locals in the trade affiliated with the A. F. of L., it believed that the time for a national union had not yet arrived.

The Federation played an important role in making available to isolated unions a center where they could obtain advice in the absence of a national organization in the trade. Without the influence and advice of the Federation, some of these local unions might not have been able to survive. Moreover, the Federation, while giving advice and encouragement, and sometimes financial support, could also help a local union to establish correspondence or even more direct relations with other unions in its trade or calling.

Organization was not the only problem facing the embryonic labor movement. Violators of trust, absconders, and incompetent administration were other difficulties confronting a number of unions. Suggestions on how to handle these problems were usually given, and, in these matters as in organizing, the A. F. of L. had the advantage of the experience of trained labor men which was available to the newly-organized unions.[61]

FINANCIAL AID

In 1888 the Federation began to make more direct financial contributions to its affiliates. The Executive Council considered the need of its more impoverished unions, such as the Coal Miners' Amalgamated Association. Many projects for aiding this Ohio coal miners' organization were discussed, and it was decided that the American Federation of Labor would bear the expense of an organizer in the coal regions. "His traveling and organizing tour to be in such places and subject to such purposes" as the officers of the Coal Miners' Union would direct. "The person to be appointed organizer is entirely left with you and I kindly ask you to give me the name of the gentleman so that together with the direction you may give him, I may issue to him a commission on behalf of the A. F. of L."[62]

At first the A. F. of L. agreed to pay the Coal Miners' Union organizer's salary and expenses for up to two months. "You are aware," the head of the Miners' union was told, "that the Federation has no bursting treasury. . . . The Executive Council of the A. F. of L. is anxious to be of some assistance to your new organization." In the spring of 1890, the Federation again engaged an organizer for the Coal Miners' Union.

While the Federation sought to be of aid to its affiliates, the amount of money at its disposal was not great. Some organizations, while jealous of their autonomous rights, believed that the Federation should force its affiliates to contribute to unions in distress or engaged in a serious dispute with their employers. At no time did the Federation expect, nor would it have been allowed, to mobilize the financial resources of affiliates in behalf of a particular cause or purpose. The leaders of the Federation recognized that the progress of labor is frequently accompanied by temporary reverses, and that every strike could not be regarded by the entire labor movement as an event upon which the future of the movement rests.

The heads of the A. F. of L. were also aware of the reluctance of many of their affiliates to donate large sums to other organizations, and no method of forcing them to do so existed. To a union fighting for survival, such arguments appeared insubstantial and evasive. When the head of a national union attacked the Federation for its failure to render adequate financial aid during a strike, the union was asked "a fair question. How much financial aid do you think, by the payment of a quarter of a cent, can be rendered to organizations whose aggregate payments (as was the case with yours) amount to from ninety-nine cents to one dollar and twenty cents?"[63]

On the other hand, the Federation made every effort to organize aid for its affiliates on strike or in serious difficulties with employers. On the motion of McGuire, an appeal for the striking anthracite miners was sent out and almost four hundred dollars collected on their behalf.[64] Financial aid, especially during strikes, was frequently sought by local unions directly affiliated with the A. F. of L. The Federation, with its small surplus, was not usually in a position to render much assistance, although it attempted to give such financial assistance as its finances allowed. The suggestion of Gompers that the American Federation of Labor be allowed to levy assessments to aid its affiliates was rejected by the unions. Sometimes local unions whose demands could not be met would threaten to withdraw from the Federation. It was clear that a number of organizations expected "too much from the Federation but in the course of time they begin to learn the objects of the A. F. of L. and are . . . proud of their connection and feel that all is being done for them that can be done and we do not make great promises and do nothing."[65]

Unions expected the new Federation to give more service than its financial and human resources made possible. There was constant pressure on the Executive Council to aid organizations with advice and finances. Although the Federation had little money, it was willing, as it did in the case of the Coal Miners' Union, to aid its organizations as much as its skimpy finances would allow. In addition, the members of the Executive Council were constantly requested to aid unions with negotiations and organizing. As all members of the Council except Gompers were officers of international unions, it meant that they would frequently have to neglect their own organizations to aid another.

As the pressure upon them mounted, several members of the Council tried to rid themselves of the added burden of serving the American Federation of Labor. William Martin, an officer of the Amalgamated Association of Iron and Steel Workers, sought to resign, and Gompers pleaded "in the name of our holy cause" for him to withdraw the resignation. McGuire was another who felt that his duties to his own union could not be effectively performed while he remained an officer of the American Federation of Labor. McGuire was continually called upon for advice and aid to other unions. Gompers feared that McGuire's resignation would indicate "a split in the Federation." Both McGuire and Martin withdrew their resignations, but Gompers himself became disaffected and informed the first vice-president of the A. F. of L., Daniel McLaughlin:

There are a number of circumstances which have arisen within a short time which compel me to ask the Executive Council of the A. F. of L. to accept my resignation of the office of President. I am desirous of accomplishing this with as little friction in the work of the Federation as possible. I ask you to please name the date when you will be ready to assume the office so that my resignation can take effect simultaneously with it.[66]

There is no record of the issue or differences, but he and the other members of the Executive Council who had threatened to resign continued their services to the American Federation of Labor.

CONVENTIONS OF 1888, 1889, 1890 AND 1891

An effort was made to get a high representation of unions at the convention of 1888. Fifty-one delegates were present, representing thirty-four organizations, nineteen of them national or international unions, with a membership of slightly below six hundred thousand. The Federation was in much sounder financial condition than at the preceding convention, despite the lowered per-capita tax. Its income of $4513.50 was more than twice as high as in the preceding year. What was even more significant was that $3585.48 of the total income represented payments for per-capita tax. There had taken place during the year "a growth of a regularity in the payment by the several organizations composing this body. This regularity is, of itself, a sufficient indication of the determination of our fellow-workingmen to stand together."[67] As compared with the preceding year's balance of only twenty-five dollars, the Federation could report more than six thousand dollars in its treasury.

Following the rule promulgated at the convention of 1888, the Executive Council refused to charter a local of cornice makers which refused to join the union in its trade. The American Federation of Labor would not accept this group on such terms. The organizer for the A. F. of L. was told that no men would be given a charter, "Who are recreant to the interests of their fellow workmen and who are in open rebellion to their national organization." The latter observation had reference to the hostility manifested by the local union towards the international in the trade, which was an affiliate of the American Federation of Labor. "The Tin, Sheet and Iron Cornice National Union is an affiliate . . . of the A. F. of L. and must be protected in its autonomy, independence and trade rights." To the argument that unless the A. F. of L. allowed this local to affiliate it would join the Knights of Labor, the answer given was, "As long as they remain unfaithful to their trade, the Knights of Labor can have them."[68]

Perhaps the most important action of the convention of 1888 was the launching, at the recommendation of Gompers, of a campaign for the eight-hour work day. This campaign had lapsed after 1886, and the A. F. of L. promoted its revival. Another important decision involved the affiliation of a second, or dual, union. The Amalgamated Society of Carpenters and Joiners asked to affiliate, but upon the objection of the United Brotherhood of Carpenters and Joiners, the request was refused. All the officers were reelected without opposition except Treasurer Gabriel Edmonston, who refused renomination.

The experience of the Federation during 1889 demonstrated that the organization was firmly established. The convention of that year was attended by seventy-four delegates, who represented fifty-three separate organizations. Even more significant was the increase in the representation of national and international unions, from nineteen in the preceding year to twenty-seven. Although none of the new national affiliates was destined to become a large organization, their attachment to the American Federation of Labor indicated that, increasingly, the latter was being regarded as the trade union central federation of the United States. Total membership of the Federation did not show any appreciable increase over the preceding year, but the finances were much improved. The Federation's income for the fiscal year 1889 was $6838.40, an appreciable increase over the preceding year.

The convention opposed the establishment of a political labor party "whereby workingmen may have representation of their own class." In the elections for membership on the Executive Council, all officers excepting the two vice-presidents were unanimously elected. It is of some interest that there existed opposition to the election of McGuire, who retained his office of second vice-president by a vote of 36 to 23. The coming of age of the A. F. of L. is attested by the declaration at the convention of 1889 "that the continuity of the American Federation of Labor be recognized and dated from the year 1881, in all future documents issued."[69] The Federation, while it demonstrated its ability to grow and prosper, still had to contend with the opposition of the Knights of Labor. Moreover, its policies on many issues remained to be defined, and strategy and tactics devised on the protean problems that faced the workers of the United States.

The Federation during the early years had to define its policies on collectivism, affiliation of political parties with central bodies, and the calling of general strikes. These issues inevitably aroused sharp differences of opinion and vigorous debate, but the organization was nevertheless building a firm foundation during this period.

[Much progress could be shown by the convention of 1890. One hundred and three delegates represented eighty-three organizations, twenty-seven of which were international unions. Total income for the fiscal year of 1890 was almost twenty-four thousand dollars. More than half of the income was, however, nonrecurring, raised to support the eight-hour strike of the Carpenters' Union. But the over nine thousand dollars of income for per-capita tax and supplies was the best index of the advances made by the A. F. of L.] This amount was considerably more than the total income of slightly more than sixty-eight hundred dollars in the preceding fiscal year. Aside from enactment of the usual resolutions, the highlight of the convention was the fact that Gompers was, for the first time, challenged for election. It was a demonstration run made by Thomas Morgan, who was angered by Gompers' leadership in the denying of a seat to the delegate from the Central Labor Federation. Morgan polled only 194 votes to Gompers' 1716.

During 1891, the heads of the Federation spent considerable time in healing a division in the ranks of the Brewery Workers' Union. A group of locals on the Pacific Coast refused to pay the assessments levied by the International, and as a consequence were suspended from membership. The suspended locals thereupon organized the Brewery Workmen's Union of the Pacific Coast, which sought representation in the various central bodies in that area. Gompers pleaded with the national officers to avoid "personalities or abuse of the men on the Coast," for "it is not the best way to bring about the desired results."[70] Gompers threw himself into this problem, and with the aid of several of the leaders of labor on the Pacific Coast, he was able to work out an arrangement satisfactory to both sides. Keeping unions together and easing factional quarrels could be performed by the heads of the American Federation of Labor who, on their own initiative, could intervene in a dispute within an autonomous union and prevent it from hardening into a permanent rupture. Such activity was usually carried on without much public knowledge, and little reward.

As compared to the convention of the preceding year, the one in 1891 was a tame affair. Although Gompers' role in the barring of the delegate from the Central Labor Federation had not been forgotten, few issues were presented over which much heat could be generated. Child labor was denounced, as was the use of convict labor to compete with free labor, school laws, and the eight-hour day on government work were endorsed. [For the first time the convention took note of the issuance of injunctions in labor disputes.]

[The Federation was, during this time, providing modest but important help for its affiliates. Even unions as well established as the United Brotherhood of Carpenters and Joiners frequently asked for loans or assistance. In 1891, a strike of carpenters at Pittsburgh led that union to appeal to the Federation for a loan, and three thousand dollars was temporarily given. In addition, a total of $2390 was loaned or donated to other organizations. Of the latter sum, two thousand dollars was sent to the United Mine Workers of America to aid its strike in Iowa, which the convention later voted to donate. In dozens of different ways—by advice, gifts, loans, and other aid—the American Federation of Labor was active in promoting the interests of the labor movement.]

REFERENCES

1. This was signed by Strasser, Peter J. McGuire, Secretary of the United Brotherhood of Carpenters and Joiners of America; Josiah Dyer of the Granite Cutters' International Union; Paul F. Fitzpatrick of the Iron Molders' Union; and W. H. Foster, Secretary of the Federation of Organized Trades and Labor Unions of the United States and Canada.

2. The delegates were George Harris, Coal Miners' Amalgamated Union; E. S. McIntosh, International Typographical Union; Chris Evans, Coal Miners' National Union; P. F. Fitzpatrick, Iron Molders' National Union; A. Strasser, Cigar Makers' International Union; P. J. McGuire, United Brotherhood of Carpenters and Joiners of America; Thomas O'Dea, Bricklayers' and Masons' International Union; Edward L. Daley, Lasters Protective Union of New England; T. J. Curran, Boilermakers' National Union; C. T. Sharp and Joseph Wilkinson, Custom Tailors' National Union; L. Stutzenberg, Metal Workers' National Union; H. A. Miller, German Typographical Union; J. K. Weir, Nailers', Rollers' and Heaters' National Union; E. S. Eaton, McKay Stitchers of New England; J.

Sheehan and James J. Black, Stereotypers Union of New York; and W. H. Foster, Federation of Trades and Labor Unions.

3. Letters were received from the Glass Blowers' Western League; Druggists' Glass Blowers' Association; Wool Hat Finishers' Union; Ohio Valley Trades Association; Telegraphers' National Association; National Silk and Fur Hat Finishers' Association; American Flint Glass Workers' Union; Amalgamated Carpenters; Amalgamated Engineers and Machinists' Union; Piano Makers' National Union; Hat Finishers' National Association; and the Mule Spinners' Association. Subsequently, letters were also received from the International Union of Plumbers, Gas Fitters and Steam Fitters; United Order of American Carpenters; Federation of Bookkeepers and Clerks; the United House Framers of New York and Vicinity; Lyman A. Brant, who was instrumental in the founding of the Federation of Organized Trades and Labor Unions; M. R. Witter, former president of the International Typographical Union; and the Workingmen's Assembly of Troy, New York.

4. All quotations in this section are taken from the report of Secretary O'Dea, who was a delegate to the Philadelphia conference, and endorsed the views although his union did not immediately affiliate with the American Federation of Labor.

5. *Ibid.*, p. 67.

6. Powderly to Fred Turner, May 1, 1886; to G. W. Andrews, May 3, 1886, letter in archives of Catholic University.

7. Powderly to L. Steenbach, May 1, 1886; to P. J. McGuire, May 11, 1886, letters in archives of Catholic University.

8. *Twenty-First Annual Session of the Bricklayers' and Masons' International Union*, 1887, p. 76.

9. *Report of Proceedings of Special Assembly, Knights of Labor*, 1886, p. 53.

10. *Ibid.*, p. 53.

11. P. J. McGuire to Powderly, June 10, 1886; Powderly to McGuire, June 17, 1886, letters in archives of Catholic University.

12. *Twenty-First Annual Convention of the Bricklayers' and Masons' International Union*, p. 78-79.

13. Powderly to J. F. Crainin, February 10, 1887, letter in archives of Catholic University.

14. *Twenty-First Annual Convention of the Bricklayers' and Masons' International Union*, 1886, p. 79.

15. One delegate for membership of less than four thousand; two delegates for four thousand or more; three from eight thousand or more; four delegates for sixteen thousand or more; five delegates for thirty-two thousand or more, and so on.

16. *Thirty-Fourth Annual Session of the International Typographical Union*, p. 24.

17. *Seventh Session of Iron Molders' International Union of North America*, 1886, p. 36.

18. *Ibid.*, p. 10.

19. These came from William Weihe, William J. Smith of the American

Flint Workers; J. P. Donnelly, Journeymen Plumbers' National Union; Thomas O'Dea, Bricklayers' and Masons' International Union; the Tailors' Progressive National Union; and several smaller organizations.

20. It declared: "Whereas, a struggle is going on in all of the civilized world, between the oppressors and the oppressed of all countries, a struggle between the Capitalist and the Laborer, which grows in intensity from year to year, and will work disastrous results to the toiling millions, if they are not combined for mutual protection and benefit. It therefore behooves the Representatives of the Trades and Labor Unions of America assembled, to adopt such measures and disseminate such principles among the mechanics and laborers of our country as will permanently unite them, to secure the recognition of the rights to which they are justly entitled. We therefore declare ourselves in favor of the formation of a thorough Federation embracing every Trade and Labor Organization in America."

21. Gompers to Web Weavers Amalgamated Association, March 5, 1888.

22. A. G. Denny, Louis Arrington, James McFeely, and G. P. Hall made up the Knight's committee. Paul F. Fitzpatrick headed the trade union committee; Strasser, Evans, McGuire, and Edward L. Daley of the New England Lasters' Union, also served.

23. *First Annual Convention of the American Federation of Labor,* 1886, p. 22.

24. *Ohio State Journal,* December 11, 1886.

25. *Report of the Proceedings of the Eleventh Annual Session, Knights of Labor,* 1887, p. 1447.

26. *First Annual Convention of the American Federation of Labor,* 1886, p. 23.

27. *Ibid.,* p. 18.

28. *Thirty-Fourth Annual Session of the International Typographical Union,* 1887, p. 112.

29. *The Craftsman,* November 2, 1887; December 24, 1887.

30. Gompers to W. S. McCreery, September 21, 1888.

31. Gompers to Strasser, March 10, 1888; April 7, 1888.

32. Gompers to P. F. Fitzpatrick, November 2, 1887.

33. Gompers to Gabriel Edmonston, April 22, 1887.

34. Gompers to P. J. McGuire, April 22, 1887.

35. Gompers to W. W. Christine, March 2, 1888.

36. Report of Gompers to the Executive Council, February 28, 1888.

37. Gompers to Frank K. Foster, May 23, 1888; Report to Executive Council, November 17, 1888.

38. Gompers to A. W. Parson, February 12, 1887.

39. Gompers to James A. McEachie, April 28, 1888; to George Fargo, May 19, 1888; to G. W. Reskin, April 8, 1887.

40. Gompers to John S. Kirchner, June 21, 1888.

41. Gompers to Joseph Gergenfeldt, June 21, 1888.

42. Gompers to A. M. Barber, March 5, 1888.

43. Gompers to Louis Thomas, February 24, 1887; March 2, 1887.

44. Gompers to John R. Nugent, February 18, 1887.

45. Gompers to Thomas Purdy, March 9, 1888; to E. W. Hilliker, March 10, 1888.

46. Gompers to Owen Miller, March 4, 1887.

47. Gompers to Louis Hebrand, July 1, 1887.

48. Gompers to George B. Wade, August 10, 1887.

49. Gompers to J. McWilliams, February 16, 1888.

50. Gompers to George Wade, April 7, 1888.

51. Gompers to Louis Hebrand, October 15, 1887.

52. Gompers to McGuire, March 2, 1887; to Strasser, March 3, 1887; to Frank Rooney, February 6, 1887.

53. Gompers to Josiah B. Dyer, May 2, 1887.

54. Gompers to Herman J. Traube, December 23, 1887.

55. Gompers to Executive Council, March 14, 1887.

56. *Second Annual Convention of the American Federation of Labor*, 1887, p. 9.

57. The resolution declared: "That the American Federation of Labor deems it unwise for two local or international organizations of any trade to exist in the same jurisdiction, and advise the amalgamation of trades in such instances. The Executive Council is instructed to use all means in its power to accomplish this end."

58. *Eighteenth Session of the Iron Molders' Union of North America*, 1888, p. 15.

59. Gompers to P. F. Fitzpatrick, April 8, 1888.

60. Gompers to M. G. Farnham, May 14, 1888.

61. Gompers to Henry Emrich, September 9, 1888.

62. Gompers to John McBride, December 31, 1888; April 14, 1890.

63. Letter to National Horse Collar Union, August 10, 1889.

64. Hugh McGregor to Gompers, February 17, 1888; *Third Annual Convention of the American Federation of Labor*, 1888, p. 4.

65. Gompers to John S. Kirchner, January 26, 1889.

66. Gompers to McGuire, February 25, 1887; to William Martin, April 22, 1889; to Daniel McLaughlin, May 23, 1889.

67. *Report of Proceedings of the Third Annual Convention of the American Federation of Labor*, 1888, p. 20.

68. Gompers to George Beckler, March 30, 1889; May 20, 1889.

69. *Report of Proceedings of the Ninth Annual Convention of the American Federation of Labor*, 1889, p. 27.

70. Gompers to August Delabar, May 18, 1891; to Ernest Kurzenknabe, June 25, 1891. Agreement between the United Brewery Workmen and Federation of Trades of Pacific Coast, signed by A. Furuseth, Charles F. Bechtold, James F. Valentine, Henry Kretlow, and August Delabar.

IV

Anarchism, Socialism, and the General Strike

THREE major issues involving anarchism or anarchists, socialism, and the general strike came before the A. F. of L. for decision during the 1890's. Socialism was the only question which the A. F. of L. was called upon to endorse directly. The other two—clemency for the Chicago anarchists convicted of the Haymarket Square murder, and the calling of a general walkout on behalf of the Pullman strikers—were not directly related to the unions affiliated with the A. F. of L. They were nevertheless of great enough importance to so affect the labor movement and the American Federation of Labor as to involve the A. F. of L. in these events.

THE SHORTER-HOUR MOVEMENT

The Haymarket case was an indirect result of the shorter-hour movement of the 1880's. Shorter hours of labor is one of the oldest demands of organized workers, and agitation for an eight-hour day had been carried on sporadically by many labor organizations since the Civil War. The demand issued by the Federation of Organized Trades and Labor Unions in 1884 for the establishment of the eight-hour work day on May 1, 1886, stimulated widespread activity on behalf of shorter working hours in many parts of the country.

The declaration in behalf of this objective can be regarded only as a propaganda "gesture," for the Federation had neither the means, the following, nor the authority to initiate, let alone direct, such a movement of workers. The Knights of Labor, which was invited to cooperate in this campaign, refused support. In fact, Terrence V. Powderly, like many other leaders of the Knights, looked toward political rather than economic action as the method for introducing shorter hours of labor. Yet the proposal of the Federation seemed to catch fire, and aroused widespread interest and enthusiasm within the ranks of organized labor, including sections of the Knights of Labor. Fearing that some groups within the Order might join in the shorter-hour movement, Powderly issued a secret circular in which he ordered assemblies of the Knights of Labor not to cooperate in the eight-hour movement.

In retrospect, the action of the Knights of Labor cannot be severely criticized. Its leaders mistrusted the use of the strike to achieve economic concessions, and regarded with suspicion, if not hostility, a proposal by the rival Federation of Organized Trades and Labor Unions. The Federation was weak financially and without widespread support of the large unions in the country. The ability of this declaration to arouse enthusiasm reflected the depth of the desire for the eight-hour work day among masses of workers. The eight-hour movement was to lead indirectly to a series of events which had serious repercussions upon the radical labor movements.

THE ANARCHISTS

In the inchoate radical movement of the 1870's an anarchist wing had arisen. At the Pittsburgh meeting in 1876 the anarchists established the International Working People's Association and issued a program of action. It was a vague and flamboyant platform which advocated "destruction of the existing class rule by all means, i.e., by energetic, relentless, revolutionary and international action." Of course, after the destruction of oppression, freedom based "upon cooperative organization of production"[1] would be organized. Chicago was a leading center of this largely verbal radicalism, and the movement made considerable progress in that city during the early 1880's, where it published an English official journal, the *Alarm,* and German and Bohemian newspapers. When the eight-hour campaign was first discussed, it was approved by the leaders of the Chicago anarchists. Albert R. Parsons, the editor of the *Alarm,* argued that more basic remedies were needed, and that as long as productive resources were privately held, the hours of work could not be controlled by labor. Consequently, movements for the eight-hour work day were a waste of time and a misuse of the workers' efforts. On the other hand, considerable enthusiasm for this program was manifested by local trade unions in Chicago, as elsewhere. In instances where the eight-hour work day was regarded as an unachievable goal, the objective was changed into a reduced work day. On May 1, 1886, widespread strikes were called in a number of industries to enforce the demand for shorter hours. Not centrally coordinated they were largely movements on a local basis. Of the 190,000 workers who had gone on strike for the shorter work day throughout the country, Chicago, with 90,000 strikers, had by far the largest number of any industrial center. New York City, which was second on the list in number of workers on strike, had 45,000.[2]

HAYMARKET SQUARE MEETINGS

The size and extent of the Chicago strike can be attributed largely to the activities of the local labor and radical movements. Unfortunately, "it was also the scene of an entirely unforseen development which did not grow out of that struggle and which had unfortunate consequences for the movement and for labor in general."³ A long strike against the McCormick Harvester Works that, initially had, no direct connection with the shorter-hour movement, imperceptibly merged into that movement. The Harvester Company had, during February 1886, locked out its workers who had been active in an earlier dispute. Among those who had gone on strike on May 1, 1886, were 10,000 lumber-shovers. As a group of these strikers were being addressed by August Spies, a leading anarchist and editor of the *Arbeiter Zeitung,* an anarchist German paper, at a point near the McCormick reaper works, a number of strike breakers left the plant for their homes. Immediately they were attacked by some of those present at the meeting. The police arrived, and in the clash that followed, "one striker was killed outright, five or six were seriously wounded, and an undisclosed number were otherwise injured. The police suffered less severely. Two or three were badly manhandled before the larger body of police appeared, six in all were injured."⁴ Indignant at the brutality of the police, Spies wrote a bitter denunciation of the episode in the columns of his paper, and issued a circular in which the following phrase, "Workingmen, arm yourself and appear in full force," had been inserted without his knowledge by the printer. Spies took exception to these words and they were stricken from most of the circulars.

A mass meeting was called for the following day, May 4th, to protest against the brutality of the police. It was addressed by Spies and Parsons, and while Samuel Fielden was speaking, the crowd began to leave because of a threatening rainstorm. Mayor Carter Harrison, who had been present at the meeting, had already left, as he was convinced that no violence would take place. Almost as the meeting was to end, a squad of 180 policemen, commanded by two police captains, formed in line and advanced upon the crowd. The speaker was ordered to halt his speech, and the crowd to disperse. Fielden cried that the meeting was peaceable. "At the same time, he, Spies and others on the wagon" from which the speakers addressed the meeting, "began to descend."⁵ Without any other warning, a bomb was thrown at the police, killing one and wounding many others.

Arrest and Conviction of Anarchists

Fear and anger swept the city. August Spies, Michael Schwab, Samuel Fielden, George Engel, Oscar Neebe, Adolph Fischer, and Louis Ling were immediately arrested. Albert R. Parsons evaded arrest, but surrendered during the trial. In an atmosphere of hysteria and panic, the defendants were brought to trial and convicted of the murder of Patrolman M. J. Degan. All defendants, except Neebe, were sentenced to death; Neebe to fifteen years in prison.

In labor and radical circles, the conviction was regarded as a gross miscarriage of justice. This view was later shared by John P. Altgeld, who, after his election as governor of Illinois, was to review the case. The American Federation of Labor, at the time struggling against the inertia and sickness which affects all infant organizations, asked for a pardon for the defendants. Gompers and Henry Emrich, a future treasurer of the American Federation of Labor and a leading trade unionist, were among fourteen labor leaders who charged, in a statement, that the men had been wrongly convicted. In their view:

Under the misguiding and corrupting influence of prejudice and class-hatred, those men have been condemned without any conclusive evidence, as acessories to a crime, the principals of which as well as the motive which may have actuated the same, are unknown. The execution of this sentence would be a disgrace to the honor of our nation, and would strengthen the very doctrines it is ostensibly directed against.[6]

Both Gompers and McGuire addressed meetings protesting the sentence. Gompers subsequently came with a delegation to plead with Governor Ogelsby for clemency. Dr. David seems to be a bit grudging in his recognition of Gompers' courage in this episode. Because Gompers argued that the execution of these men would "give an impetus to the so-called revolutionary movement," Dr. David describes "his plea for executive clemency upon a strange ground."

Gompers also declared to the Governor: "I believe that in some measure, however remote, the police of Chicago have been somewhat responsible for this trouble. I ask myself what good can come to the people of the State of Illinois; what good can come to the people of our country; what good can come to the good name of our country and our people if these men are executed?" Gompers was anxious that a terrible wrong be avoided, and the lives of innocent men not be snuffed out. Gompers' conduct in this situation contrasts sharply with the action of Powderly who, while convinced of the innocence of the convicted anarchists, would do nothing in their behalf.[7]

It was far more risky for the American Federation of Labor and its head, Gompers, to speak out against injustice and public hysteria than its larger and well-established rival, the Knights of Labor. While avoiding radical doctrines, the Federation, from then until the present, has never eschewed speaking out against oppression and injustice. Nor did Gompers escape criticism for his conduct. When a member of the Executive Council informed Gompers that he was being subjected to severe criticism for his espousal of the cause of the Chicago anarchists, Gompers regretted

the feeling in Chicago. . . . I abhor anarchy but I also abhor injustice when meted out even to the most despicable being on earth. I am opposed to the hanging of the seven Chicago anarchists for several reasons, among them the following are most important. They are not charged with committing murder. No person seems to know who threw the fatal bomb. Consequently, no connection was or could be proven between the party who threw it and the seven condemned men who are charged with inciting some "person unknown" to throw it. So long as capital punishment is part of the laws of our State and Country, if it could be enforced, no discrimination should be indulged in favor of one nor the law strained to shield another class. Then again apart from any other reason, if these men should be executed it would place a halo of martyrdom around them which would lead many to the violent agitation we so much deplore. In the interest of the cause of labor and peaceful methods of improving the conditions and achieving the final emancipation of labor I am opposed to this execution.[8]

After the execution, Smith again told Gompers that many labor men did not endorse his efforts on behalf of the Chicago anarchists. Gompers explained that he was "trying to keep a cool head and to view matters as they exist, to maintain the dignity and honor of our organization, and withal, to be manly and not cringing."

CENTRAL LABOR UNIONS IN NEW YORK CITY

Support of the campaign to prevent a miscarriage of justice did not mean that Gompers or the American Federation of Labor was any more kindly disposed to radical theories of reform or social reorganization. In fact, the American Federation of Labor soon took two steps which aroused strong feelings among Socialists against the A. F. of L., and especially against Gompers, who had inspired the moves.

The first conflict arose over the rechartering of the Central Labor Union in New York City, which had been organized in New York City in 1880. In the later part of the decade, it came under the influence of the Knights of Labor and Socialists. In August 1889, the Central Labor Union had defeated a resolution to establish a committee for the promotion of an eight-hour work day. Gompers criticised the action of "some men . . . so narrow in their views as to oppose a movement for the reduction in the hours of labor simply because it did not emanate from them." He hoped "the mistake may be rectified . . . the committee elected and all work for success."[9]

In February 1889, a number of unions withdrew from the Central Labor Union and organized a rival, the Central Labor Federation. The Central Labor Union had never sought to affiliate with the A. F. of L., or with its predecessor Federation. Nevertheless, when the Central Labor Federation applied for affiliation with the A. F. of L., and its rival protested, Gompers "endeavored to secure a reconciliation between the two contending organizations without avail, the feeling against each other being too severe." In fact there was "more feeling than evidence adduced." In commenting upon the differences between the two central bodies in New York City, Gompers showed partiality toward the Central Labor Federation, with which he was soon to become involved in a serious and far-reaching dispute. He pointed to failure of all affiliates of the Central Labor Union, except one local of the Granite Cutters, to join the American Federation of Labor. On the other hand, a large number of locals in the Central Labor Federation affiliated with the A. F. of L. Gompers' attitude towards these rivals is perhaps clearly indicated by his observation: "It is necessary to add that the Knights of Labor assemblies control the Central Labor Union."[10]

The efforts of Gompers and others to unite the two central labor unions finally led to a temporary merger of the two organizations. The Central Labor Federation surrendered its A. F. of L. charter, but after a short interval the rival factions again found that they could not live together in the same central body. Several unions thereupon withdrew and sought to reestablish the Central Labor Federation. Gompers was asked by the leaders of this movement, to return the charter of the Central Labor Federation, on the theory that the charter had been placed in his custody for safekeeping and had not been surrendered. Gompers disagreed, and informed Ernest Bohm, the secretary of the Central Labor Federation: "You say that the charter of the Central Labor Federation was delivered . . . for 'safe keeping.' Such is not the fact. When the charter was delivered to me it was surrendered with the statement that the Central Labor Federation had ceased to exist." However, Gompers assured the leaders of the movement to reestablish the Central Labor Federation "that I am in no wise in sympathy with the Central Labor Union in its conduct in matters connected with the labor movement, but this cannot sway my judgment in returning a charter to an organization which surrendered it when the books of this office already show that fact."[11] Gompers was stung by the charge that he was acting unfairly, and he told Bohm that "my record in the movement of labor entitles me at least to the distinction of being fair and if my sense of duty and loyalty to an organization, the interest of which is committed to my care, prevents me from complying with your request, I think it does not necessarily follow that I have ever been other than fair in my connection with the labor movement."

Gompers' decision was upheld by the Executive Council. The Central Labor Federation then applied for a new charter. However, a new obstacle was raised, because among the affiliated organizations supporting the request was the American Section of the Socialist Labor Party. Gompers could not "understand how a political party as such can be represented in a central trade union organization." But he added: "Of the merits or demerits of the 'Socialist Labor Party' it is not within my province to discuss but the representation of that party or any other political party in a purely trade union central organization is to my mind not permissible."[12] The Central Labor Federation, nevertheless, elected Lucien Sanial, a well-known Socialist, a delegate to the Detroit convention of the American Federation of Labor, and the dispute over his seating was regarded of sufficient importance to warrant the appointment of a special committee to consider the matter.

The committee, while recognizing the inevitability of differences in views and tactics among labor groups, held that:

The trade unions of America, comprising the A. F. of L. are committed against the introduction of matters pertaining to partisan politics, to the religion of men or to their birthplace. We cannot logically admit the Socialist Labor Party to representation, and shut the door in the face of other political organizations formed to achieve social progress. We are of the opinion that a political party of whatsoever nature is not entitled to representation in the American Federation of Labor.[13]

Sanial made two arguments in favor of admitting the Socialist Labor Party. First, he claimed that a precedent was set when the Socialist Labor Party in Baltimore had affiliated with the German Central Labor Union, which in turn was a member of the Baltimore Federation of Labor, an A. F. of L. affiliate. Such an argument was not conclusive, as the affiliation might have been allowed inadvertently. Moreover, this statement was challenged by the delegate from the Baltimore Federation of Labor. On the other hand, he tried to distinguish the Socialist Labor Party from other political parties because of the fundamental difference between that Party and the "old plutocratic parties," because the latter "are notoriously the political machines of the employing class, and as essential a part of the whole machinery through which they control, rob and oppress their wage-workers as is their industrial and commercial machinery." In Sanial's view, the Socialist Labor Party was "owned and controlled by wage-workers . . . who are in full sympathy with you upon all the economic principles thus far made by the American Federation of Labor, and who use this so-called 'political party' exclusively for the advancement of those economic principles and demands."

Gompers' position was that, regardless of one's political or social opinions, representation at conventions of a trade union body must be based upon "a card of membership in your trade union. The condition precedent . . . to representation, in a trade union movement is good standing membership of a trade union."[14]

During the debate Thomas Morgan, a leading Socialist trade unionist, suggested that a vote on the question be postponed and the issue submitted to a vote of the affiliated unions, which would then instruct their delegates to the next convention. It was feared that this proposal would only prolong the debate and thereby increase the dissension within the movement. Gompers called attention "to the venom that had been interjected by the advocates of the claimants for admission in their utterances through their own papers and public press." While lamenting the bitterness the dispute aroused among labor men, Gompers firmly believed that only by excluding political parties, regardless of their claims or principles, from affiliation with the American Federation of Labor, could "the purity of the Trade Union movement" be maintained. Even if "to maintain that stand drove him from the presidency of the American Federation of Labor (the greatest honor and gift in command of organized labor) he would not prove false to it."[15] As a matter of fact, Gompers was ready to grant a charter to the Central Labor Federation if the Socialists Labor Party would withdraw its affiliation. In his opinion, the Socialist Labor Party "could do a great deal for the trade union movement in the City of New York by withdrawing, for then quite a number of unions which were ready to join the Central Labor Federation but could not do so so long as the Socialist Labor was represented therein"[16] would affiliate.

Sanial was excluded by a vote of 1574 to 496, with the coal miners' delegation voting to seat him. Gompers was bitterly assailed in the Socialist press for his leadership in the fight. He believed that the criticisms were unjustified, and the bitterness which they engendered harmful to the movement. He, therefore, transmitted his views in a letter to Frederick Engels. He respected Engels' judgment, and told Engels that, as a student of "your writings and those of Marx and others in the same line I [Gompers] would not have your judgment formed upon the basis of erroneous information."[17] In detail, Gompers explained the reasons for the position taken by the convention of the A. F. of L., and assured Engels that it was not based upon opposition to a Socialist party.

In another letter, a specific denial that the action of the convention was motivated by opposition to socialism was made.

There has been a slander circulated [Gompers wrote] by the enemies of the trade union movement of America that the American Federation of Labor has placed its seal of disapproval upon socialism as a science, or a theory, or even as a system of society for the future. Such I beg to assure you is not at all the case. What we have decided is that a socialist political party, as a political party, cannot be represented in a trade union congress, but socialists or working people entertaining any other theory are entirely upon an equality with all other working men, providing they are members of the union of the trade, calling or profession they follow. In other words, we maintain that a man can hardly be esteemed to be a trade unionist unless he is a member of his trade union.[18]

Engels refused to become involved in American quarrels, and he failed to answer Gompers' letter. Subsequently, Gompers informed Friedrich Sorge, a friend and correspondent of both Marx and Engels, of his "absolute willingness to abide by his [Engels] judgment. I regret to say I never received a reply." Sorge sought to discover Engels' views on the issue, but he refused to commit himself. For years, Gompers had

honored the man [Engels] and knew his devotion to the cause of labor. An opinion from him would have had large weight with me and expression of it would no doubt have had some influence in determining the action of the Socialist Party, particularly in New York. They are in such desperate straits that they organized opposition unions to those in existence and declared boycotts on the products of bona fide unions.[19]

The Political Program

In opposing the affiliation of a political organization with a trade union federation, Gompers was espousing a principle which fundamentally did not conflict with any particular political philosophy. The conflict over the political program, introduced at the convention of 1893, was, however, of more fundamental character, in that it involved the endorsement or rejection of a basic Socialist doctrine, the "collective ownership by the people of all means of production and distribution"—one of the points in a larger program. The political program was introduced by Thomas Morgan, a leading Chicago Socialist and member of the Machinists' Union. It contained eleven planks, most of which would be or had been endorsed by conventions of the American Federation of Labor. The program called for: (1) Compulsory education; (2) Direct legislation; (3) A legal eight-hour day; (4) Sanitary inspection of workshop, mine, and home; (5) Liability of employers for injury to health, body, or life; (6) The abolition of the contract system in all public work; (7) The abolition of the sweating system; (8) The municipal ownership of street cars, and gas and electric plants for public distribution of light, heat, and power; (9) The nationalization of telegraphs, telephones, railroad, and mines; (10) The collective ownership by the people of all means of production and distribution; (11) The principle of referendum in all legislation.[20] The program was to be submitted for the consideration of the affiliated organizations, with the request that their delegates to the next convention be instructed on these issues. The proposal included the suggestion that the program be given "favorable recommendations." A foretaste of the future debate came with the adoption of a motion to strike the word "favorable" from the resolution. The motion passed by the narrow vote of 1253 to 1182.

At the next convention, in 1894, the political platform was the chief subject of discussion. Anticipating the arguments to be made, Gompers had emphasized in his report that most of the demands in the platform had already been endorsed by most labor organizations. He pointed out however, that:

Deftly dovetailed and almost hidden there is one declaration which is not only controversial, but decidedly theoretical, and even if founded upon economic truth, is not demonstrable, and so remote as to place ourselves and our movement in an unenviable light before our fellow workers, and which, if our organization is committed to it, will unquestionably prevent many sterling national trade unions from joining our ranks.[21]

The differences among the delegates to the convention hinged around two issues: independent political action, endorsed in the preamble, and collective ownership of the means of production and distribution.

The convention decided to consider each plank separately, and the debate started on a statement in the preamble that "the trade unionists of Great Britain have by the light of experience and the logic of progress adopted the principle of independent political action." This declaration, Strasser argued, was untrue, but even if it had been a correct statement of the policy of Britain labor, its endorsement would have committed the American Federation of Labor to independent political action. The preamble, after much debate, was defeated by a vote of 1345 to 861. The other points were adopted, in some instances with minor changes, until the tenth and controversial plank was reached. Strasser, who was bitterly opposed to collectivism, proposed to amend the collectivist clause by adding, "by confiscation and without compensation." A whole series of amendments were then presented, and the debate was long, and at times acrimonious.

McGuire, in opposing the collectivist resolution, claimed that he had read books on socialism in French and German, as well as English, but he was not concerned with the theoretical merits of the issue. Instead, he pointed to the "protests from 41 locals of the Brotherhood of Carpenters against introducing this question; 7156 members who promised to withdraw from our organization . . . if we act on these questions of a speculative character." In his view trade unions had "trouble and many difficulties to contend with to convert men to union principles, and why should we load ourselves with more than we can carry."[22]

During the discussion on the political platform, Patrick McBryde, secretary of the United Mine Workers of America, raised the question whether the American Federation of Labor could bind its autonomous unions to a particular political view. Gompers was of the opinion that the A. F. of L.

is a voluntary organization. The resolutions or platform adopted by it at conventions are expressive of the sentiments and demands of the majority of the organized workers affiliated with it. The resolutions and platforms can not be *imposed* upon any affiliated organization against its wishes, but the resolutions and platforms adopted are presumed to be observed by all organizations.[23]

[After a long debate, the motion to endorse the platform as a whole was defeated by a vote of 1173 to 735. The status of the program was again taken up and the delegates did not agree whether the political platform had been defeated by the rejection of it as a whole, or whether the adoption of the individual planks placed the Federation on record as favoring the particular planks.] John McBride, who had been elected to the presidency of the A. F. of L., was of the opinion that the convention had adopted the program. However, the convention of 1895 by a vote of 1531 to 359 declared "that the failure to adopt the planks as a whole was equivalent to rejection and therefore we declare that the American Federation of Labor has no political platform."[24]

Rejection of the political platform was attributed by the Socialists to the machinations of Gompers. From then on he became the chief target for their abuse. Gompers' attitude towards Socialists was to some extent determined by whether the latter were supporters of the trade union movement or its opponents. While they were political opponents, Gompers maintained friendly relations with many trade union Socialists. When the head of the Brewery Workers' Union asked Gompers to lead a class movement by endorsing independent politics, Gompers told him:

It is not necessary for them [the unions] to start a class movement. The trade union is the only class movement in the country or in the world. The movement often called a class movement is often nothing more than a party movement, and in the same degree as this party movement increases, in the same ratio does it lose its working class character. . . . You ask me to be a "leader of the American Federation of Labor and not only an officer." Where would you have me lead them? Where they have demonstrated their unwillingness to go?[25]

Gompers told him that he would rather surrender his post than advocate policies he opposed, or he believed were harmful to the labor movement.

Gompers not only helped the Brewery Workers' officers in their negotiations with employers, but defended their officers, who were Socialists, against what he regarded as unfair criticism. When the head of Coopers' Union attacked Charles F. Bechtold of the Brewery Workers' Union, Gompers expressed

. . . astonishment at your frequent use of language, regarding any brother official in the labor movement, which I think should not be employed. Of course, it may be your privilege but I am certainly of the opinion that it is not contributing to either good fellowship, and understanding of either your own union, any other union or the general labor movement. If you continue to call an officer of another trade union "czar and henchman" and repeat this often, if you use an appellation of the members of another union as "unskilled men who wear a pair of Dutch boots" the chances are that the other officer is likely to learn of it, and then may retort in kind, and then we shall have the spectacle of a squabble not only unbecoming and destructive of the best interests of the men of both trades, but it will also be an exhibition of hurling vile names and epithets at each other.[26]

Cable of the Coopers' Union had demanded that Gompers immediately answer whether he approved the conduct of the Brewery Workers' Union, and Gompers informed him he made no decisions until he had heard both sides in a controversy. It happened that Bechtold was a Socialist, and he and his union were opponents of Gompers, while Cable was a supporter. Nevertheless, on issues affecting the trade union movement, no distinction was ever made.

Gompers did not permit his opposition to socialism as a philosophy to color his attitude toward individual Socialists. When he learned of the suicide of Marx's daughter, he wrote to McGuire of his sorrow and described her as "a splendid woman, and one giving her talents to further the cause of labor, I felt badly when I learned of her death, shocked to find that it was suicide."[27] He did not show the same tolerance of Daniel DeLeon, especially when the latter inspired a dual trade union movement. Gompers also objected to the bitter recriminations and personal abuse which DeLeon poured on the heads of trade union leaders who failed to accept his policies.

SOCIALISM

Gompers welcomed the discussions of socialism on the floor of A. F. of L. conventions "because it armed our fellow trade unionists with the arguments to best defend the trade union position against the aggressiveness, onslaughts and attacks of the so-called socialists."[28] To Gompers, these debates were not only interesting but also welcome, since they gave him a chance to exhibit his forensic powers against his opponents. Other delegates did not look as tolerantly upon these annual fencing bouts. At the convention of 1895 a delegate, on the ground that convention costs of $576 a day were being wasted in political discussions, proposed: "That the convention declares that party politics whether they be democratic, republican, socialistic, populistic, prohibition or any other, should have no place in the convention of the A. F. of L."[29] It was adopted by a vote of 1496 to 158.

While the resolution inhibited the debate on political parties, it could not prevent discussions of socialism. Seven years later, at the convention of 1902, Max Hayes, a leading Socialist trade unionist delegate from the Typographical Union, asked that the convention "advise the working people to organize their economic and political power to secure for labor the full equivalent of its toil and the overthrowal of the wage system and the establishment of an industrial cooperative democracy."[30] The proposal was defeated by 4897 to 4171 votes, with 309 votes not cast. Despite the opposition of Gompers and his associates, an explicitly Socialist resolution nevertheless polled almost half of the total votes. The following year, the issue was again discussed. The debate was longer and more acrimonious.

The leaders of the American Federation of Labor were of the opinion that some Socialists, Debs among them, were responsible for the division of the labor movement on sectional lines. While they were never severe in their criticism of the Western Federation of Miners for promoting a dual labor federation, they had much less tolerance for the ideological dualism sponsored by certain Socialists. At the convention of 1903 ten resolutions favoring either independent political action or government ownership of the means of production and distribution were submitted. Many delegates participated in the debate.

John Mitchell, aside from Gompers the leading trade unionist of the period, paid a tribute to the activities of the Socialists and the aid they rendered during the anthracite coal strike. He singled out J. Mahlon Barnes, a leading Socialist and a member of the Cigar Makers' Union, for praise. Nevertheless, Mitchell regarded the efforts of the Socialists to commit the trade union movement to independent political action or to a particular social or political philosophy as unwise. Gompers showed more vehemence than was usual with him in discussions of public issues. He alluded several times to the role of the Socialists in the forming of the American Labor Union, which aimed to be a dual labor center to the Federation, and he ended his speech with the peroration that in his close study of socialism he had found Socialists economically "unsound; socially . . . wrong industrially . . . an impossibility."[31] The convention, by a vote of 11,282 to 2147, supported the committee's disapproval of these proposals. It was a decisive defeat of the Socialist resolutions. In the elections for office, a Socialist candidate, Ernest Kreft, from Philadelphia, polled only 1236 votes to Gompers 12,449 votes.

American Railway Union

The American Federation of Labor also faced another crisis in this period. It arose in 1894 as a result of a strike in the railway industry led by the newly-formed American Railway Union. Among the earliest organizations of labor were the railway operating unions or brotherhoods. Four had been established, beginning with the Brotherhood of Locomotive Engineers in 1863. The unions on the railroads were largely organized in one trade or calling. Several efforts were made to develop cooperation among these unions in the 1880's and 1890's, but they failed. Following the unsuccessful switchmen's strike in Buffalo, a number of leaders of railroad labor organizations established, on June 20, 1893, an industrial union of railroad labor, the American Railway Union. Eugene Victor Debs, the secretary-treasurer of the Brotherhood of Locomotive Firemen, was elected president, Sylvester Kelliher, the secretary of the Railway Carmen, secretary, and George W. Howard, vice president.

Relations between the American Federation of Labor and the leaders of the new movement had been friendly. Debs had been invited to address the convention of the A. F. of L. in 1892, and George Howard had congratulated Gompers in December 1893 "on your success at your last convention."[32] Whatever views Gompers may have held on the new venture, he did not offer any public statement on the new organization. It is true that Gompers inevitably opposed dual unions, and might consequently have regarded such a move as unwise. Yet he was not too close to the heads of the railroad unions. P. M. Arthur, the head of the Brotherhood of Locomotive Engineers, did not cooperate with other labor organizations, and the Brotherhood of Locomotive Firemen would not agree to eliminate the word "white" from its constitution and was therefore denied admission to the American Federation of Labor.[33]

The American Railway Union was an immediate success. In the space of one year, 465 locals with a membership of about 150,000 had been enrolled.[34] In its first brush with a giant railroad, the American Railway Union scored a decisive victory, growing evidence that the new industrial organization might become the dominant labor union on the railroads. The promising beginning was not to be realized. Against the wishes of its leaders the organization was drawn into the Pullman strike.

The Pullman Company had been created by an imaginative, industrial enterpriser, George Morton Pullman, who had helped to revolutionize railroad travel. Resourceful, combative, and dictatorial, he was able to win complete control of the service of supplying sleeping and parlor cars to the traveling public. Most of the manufacturing facilities of the Pullman Company were concentrated in Pullman, Illinois, a model community built by the head of the company. The firm, as well as the town, were completely dominated by this paternalistic employer. Charges for city services and rent were determined by the company, and were excessive as compared with those prevailing in independent communities. Shop discipline was strict, and policies were unilaterally determined by the company.

The depression of the 1890's presented the firm with the usual problems facing a business enterprise in a period of deflation. As business declined, the Pullman Company adopted the classical method of meeting such events, wage cutting. Charges for rent and other services were not, however, simultaneously reduced. The workers' answer to these pressures was organization of a union. By May 1894, the union felt strong enough

to request an adjustment of wages and rent and a review of shop grievances. The company agreed to reviewing grievances, but was unwilling
to make other concessions. Moreover, to show its attitude towards
organized action, the company discharged three members of the grievance
committee, despite the promises of the vice president that the spokesmen
for the men would suffer no reprisals.

On May 10, 1894, the meeting showed strong sentiment for a strike,
but upon the advice of the American Railway Union, the step was not
immediately taken. On the following day, a rumor spread that the company was planning a lockout, and in anticipation of this move a strike
was called.

A month later, the convention of the American Railway Union opened
in Chicago. In answer to the appeal of the Pullman workers for assistance,
a committee to seek a settlement of the walkout was appointed by the
convention. The company was adamant; it would not deal with the union
nor arbitrate the dispute. Rebuffed in its efforts to find a peaceful solution, the convention resolved that unless the Pullman Company agreed to
negotiate by June 26th, the members of the American Railway Union
would refuse to handle the company's rolling stock.

In retrospect, it appears not to have been the wisest decision. The
leaders, including Debs, were aware of the dangers inherent in this decision. Yet the pitiful stories of the strikers and the obduracy of the company moved the delegates to take this drastic step. It is likely that, had
the delegates been members of a labor organization with a longer history,
one in which defeat and victory are inevitably commingled, the decision
might have been different. Immediately the General Managers' Association, made up of twenty-four railroads in the Chicago area, announced it
would resist the boycott. Nevertheless, as planned, the boycott began on
July 26th, and it was immediately effective. In fact, thousands of members of the railway brotherhoods joined in the struggle, against the advice
and orders of their own officers. Violence accompanied the movement,
and it would appear that much of it was traceable to the lawless element
which utilizes such occasions, rather than to the actions of striking
workers.

The General Managers' Association did not remain inactive; it secured
injunctions against the strikers. The court orders were violated, and strike
leaders were prosecuted for contempt. The Federal government, on the
ground that the movement of the United States mails was being impeded,
entered the struggle and appointed several thousand marshals. When
they were unable to suppress the strike, President Grover Cleveland,
over the protests of Governor Altgeld, ordered troops to Chicago. Gompers
protested the sending of troops.

The strike, the intervention of federal troops, and the hostility of the

Pullman Company aroused the Chicago labor movement.[35] Events in Chicago inevitably had an effect upon the labor movement of the rest of the country. Requests were made that Gompers proceed to Chicago, and he at first rejected them. However, he protested against the use of troops in the strike.

On July 9th, a number of Chicago unions requested Gompers' presence in that city and he decided some action was necessary. Gompers reached the conclusion that the "extraordinary industrial situation compels some action by the Executive Council."[36] He thereupon called a meeting of the Executive Council for Chicago on July 12th. As was noted above, Gompers was on friendly terms with the leaders of the American Railway Union, and while he might have disapproved of their organization, it must again be emphasized that Gompers did not express any views. The heads of the international unions were invited; twelve representatives from national and international unions, the members of the Executive Council, and the representatives from two of the railway brotherhoods attended. E. E. Clark, Grand Chief of the Order of Railway Conductors, protested the holding of the meeting, and P. M. Arthur, head of the Brotherhood of Locomotive Engineers, would not reply to Gompers' invitation.

A committee from the Chicago Cigar Makers' Union appeared before the conference. This committee of eight was accompanied by Charles Dold, a leader of the Chicago labor movement and subsequently head of the International Piano Makers' Association. The committee, through Dold, requested the calling of a general strike on the ground that the strike of the "American Railway Union was not a question of organization but one of capital and labor. He thought the American Federation of Labor could settle it, but if they decided against it [the general strike] the A. F. of L. would be responsible for its defeat." Gompers asked Dold: "Could the contest be won if we had not come?" Dold answered that if the "Council had not come defeat would have been certain." At this point Dold was asked how a general strike could compel the Pullman Company to deal with its workers or to arbitrate. His answer was that "united action would accomplish it. United action would bring victory."[37] Dold and the committee from the Cigar Makers' local were undoubtedly reflecting the sentiment held by many groups and individuals in the Chicago labor movement.

A motion was then made to invite President Cleveland to attend the conference. The suggestion was opposed by John B. Lennon of the Tailors' Union, George W. Perkins, the head of Gompers' union, and P. H. Morrissey of the Brotherhood of Railway Trainmen. Gompers, Patrick McBryde of the Coal Miners' Union, and M. Garland of the Steel Workers' Union were among those who favored the proposal. It was adopted by a vote of 11 to 8. The following telegram was then sent to the President of the United States:

The gravity of the industrial situation of the country demands extraordinary and exceptional action of a conciliatory character at the hands of all men. Recognizing this fact the Executive Council of the American Federation of Labor and the undersigned Executive Officers of National and International Trades Unions and Brotherhoods of railroad organizations of America are in conference in the city. We ask you in the name of the working people and the entire citizenship of our country to lend your influence and give us your aid so that the present industrial crisis may be brought to an end, alike to the advantage of the people of our country and the institutions under which we live. We therefore ask you to come to Chicago and meet this conference, or if the state of public business does not warrant such a course that you will deputize some as your representative.

No answer was received from President Cleveland.

Debs appeared at the evening meeting, and presented the following conciliatory statement, which he asked Gompers to present to the Railway Managers' Association. Debs did not request the calling of a general strike:

The existing trouble growing out of the Pullman strike having assumed continental proportions and there being no indication of relief from the widespread business demoralization and distress incident thereto, the railway employees through the Board of Directors of the ARU respectfully make the following proposition as a basis of settlement. They agree to return to work at once in a body, provided they shall be restored to their former positions, without prejudice except in cases, if any there be, where they have been convicted of crime.

The proposition looking to an immediate settlement of the existing strike on all lines of railway, is inspired solely by a purpose to subserve the public good. The strike, small and comparatively unimportant in its inception, has extended in every direction until now it involves or threatens not only every public interest, but the peace, security and prosperity of our common country. The contest has waged fiercely. It has extented far beyond the limits of interests originally involved and has laid hold of a vast variety of industries in no wise responsible for the differences and disagreements that led to the trouble.

Factory, mill, mine and shop have been silenced. Widespread demoralization holds sway. The interests of multiplied thousands of innocent people are suffering.

The common welfare is seriously menaced. The public peace and tranquility are in peril. Grave apprehension for the future prevails. This being true, and the statement will not be controverted, we conceive it to be our duty as citizens and as men to make extraordinary efforts to end the existing strike and avert approaching calamities whose shadows are ever now upon us.

If ended now, the contest however serious in some of its consequences will not be in vain. Sacrifices have been made but they will have their compensation. Indeed if lessons shall be taught by experience the troubles now so widely spread will prove a blessing of inestimable value in the months and years to come.

The difference that led up to the present complications need not now be discussed. At this supreme juncture every consideration of duty and patriotism demands that remedy for existing troubles be found and applied. The employees propose to do their part by meeting their employers half way. Let it be stated that they do not impose any condition of settlement except that they be returned to their former positions. They do not ask the recognition of their organization or any organization.

Believing this proposition to be fair, reasonable and just it is respectfully submitted in the belief that its acceptance will result in the prompt resumption of traffic, the revival of industry and the restoration of peace and order.[38]

In addition to Debs, the statement was signed by George W. Howard, Vice President, and Sylvester Keliher, Secretary.

Gompers assured Debs that "we were all trade unionists and would do all we could to help our fellow workers in their present troubles." The conference would not approve of Gompers carrying the statement to the Railway Managers' Association by himself. Instead, it voted that Debs be allowed to select one or two persons from the conference who would then accompany Debs or some other representative of the American Railway Union for presentation to the Chicago Railway Managers' Association.

On the motion of George Perkins of the Cigar Makers' International Union, a committee of five—Gompers, McGuire, M. Carrol of the International Typographical Union, Martin Fox of the Iron Molders' Union, and M. M. Garland of the Amalgamated Association of Iron and Steel Workers—were appointed to draw up a statement on the railway conflict. Unanimously endorsed, the statement urged workers to refrain from participating in a general strike

Industrial contests cannot be entered into at the behest of any individual officer of this conference, regardless of the position he may occupy in our organizations. Strikes in our affiliated organizations are entered only as a last resort and after all peaceful adjustment of grievances have failed, and then only after the members have by their own votes (usually requiring a two-thirds and often a three-fourths vote) so decided.

The statement pointed out that the "public press, ever alive to the interests of corporate wealth have, with few exceptions, so maliciously misrepresented matters that to the public the working classes are now arrayed in open hostility to federal authority. This is a position we do not wish to be placed in, nor will we occupy it without a protest." The strike was recognized as an "impulsive vigorous protest against the gathering, growing forces of plutocratic power and corporation rule." While the conference expressed its sympathy for the action of the strikers, it "disclaimed the power to order a strike of the working people of the country."

Yet those present nevertheless recognized that a call for a strike from the labor conference might be answered by many trade unionists:

Appreciating the responsibility resting upon us and the duty we owe to all, we declare it to be the sense of this conference that a general strike at this time is inexpedient, unwise and contrary to the best interests of the working people. We further recommend that all connected with the American Federation of Labor now out on sympathetic strike should return to work, and those who contemplate going out on sympathetic strike are advised to remain at their usual vocations.

The two representatives from the railway brotherhoods objected to the favorable reference to the American Railway Union.[39]

Gompers was attacked for his refusal to place himself at the head of a general strike in behalf of the striking railway men. It is interesting to observe that not a single delegate criticized his conduct at the convention in that year. Almost sixty years later, a series of inferences intended to place the blame for the loss of the strike upon the American Federation of Labor are presented. "If," says Mr. Ray Ginger, "from June 26, the AFL had sought to keep the courts and Federal government from entering the dispute, if it had sought to counteract the misleading newspaper stories, if it had tried to restrain the strikebreaking actions of the Brotherhoods, it would have rendered great service to the strikers."[40]

Clearly Mr. Ginger implies that, had the Federation done its duty, the results would have been different. However, further questions arise out of his criticism. For instance, how, in reality, might the A. F. of L. have kept the Federal courts from entering the dispute? Ten years later, when the Federation had more than a million members, it was unable to keep the Federal courts out of the Hatters' dispute. And is there in fact any legal way for any labor organization, even today, to keep the Federal courts out of a dispute that the courts regard as coming in their province?

As to the Federation's failure to counteract newspaper stories—if this criticism is valid—labor can be so criticized today with equal validity. Even with the increasing resources of organized labor, and the growth of a labor press, the public press is still able to sway public opinion against labor's cause in a dispute, sometimes in decisive measure.

Superficially the third criticism seems more justified. Yet the record shows that the A. F. of L. had little influence on the railway brotherhoods; as a matter of fact, the latter were not inclined to cooperate even on matters that did not affect them as vitally as the rise of the American Railway Union. The Brotherhoods, which were unwilling to affiliate with the

Federation, were not likely to take the advice of Gompers on this matter. Two of them even refused to send representatives to the conference at the Briggs House, and the representatives from the other brotherhoods protested against any friendly observations concerning the American Railway Union. To believe that Gompers could have convinced them to commit "organizational" suicide would seem to require great faith in one's judgment.

When the convention of the A. F. of L. met in December 1894, Gompers discussed the part played by the Executive Council in the American Railway strike, and asked for a vote of confidence. The committee considering the report was of the "unanimous opinion that the course pursued by him [Gompers] and our Executive Council, in the strike of the American Railway Union, was the right and proper course for them to follow, notwithstanding that their sympathies must have run counter to their judgment." Not a single voice was raised against this statement, and Gompers bitterly assailed Thomas Morgan, who remained silent, although he had off the floor attacked Gompers' refusal to call a general strike. This statement by the committee was unanimously adopted. Yet the convention was literally full of Gompers' opponents, as Gompers was defeated for reelection by the delegates. Moreover, a number of Socialist delegates who had been angered by Gompers' opposition to their political program, including Thomas Morgan, the author of that document, were present at this convention as delegates. The convention was as unanimous as the labor conference at Chicago had been against the calling of a general strike. Several of those present at Chicago were in fact, opponents of Gompers, and they were by no means awed by his presence. They too had been unanimous against involving the movement in this risky type of venture.

All recognized that the decision was a difficult one, but the leaders of labor had tasted too many defeats to harbor any belief in their invincibility by the use of the strike weapon, irrespective of the numbers who had laid down, or might lay down, their tools. They were not concerned with demonstrations. Moreover, they recognized that a defeat is not necessarily fatal nor irretrievable. To call out on a general strike a labor movement that had been seriously weakened by unemployment in the depression of the 1890's would have been a quixotic gesture, one that might have seriously damaged the movement. The members of the Executive Council were not the ones who would order a demonstration strike. A hard and unsentimental decision was taken, and the future has justified its wisdom many times. To have antagonized public opinion, to have risked the welfare of loyal workers in a cause admittedly lost, would have been the action of sentimentalists or revolutionists, and not of responsible leaders of a trade union movement.

The Federation donated five hundred dollars, and issued an appeal for further financial aid, to help defend Debs and the other leaders who were being prosecuted for violating the injunction issued by the Federal courts against the strikers and the leaders. The total amount contributed to the "Debs' Fund" was $1386.41.[41]

REFERENCES

1. Henry David, *The History of the Haymarket Affair*, (New York: Farrar and Rinehart, 1936), p. 100; John R. Commons and Associates, *History of Labor in the United States*, (New York: The Macmillan Company, 1936), II, p. 295.

2. Commons, *op. cit.*, II, pp. 384-385.

3. David, *op. cit.*, p. 177.

4. David, *Ibid.*, pp. 190-191.

5. David, *Ibid.*, p. 204.

6. Quoted in David, *op. cit.*, p. 410-411.

7. See David, *op. cit.*, pp. 413-416.

8. Gompers to James W. Smith, October 13, 1887; November 15, 1887.

9. Gompers to August Delabar, January 25, 1889.

10. Gompers to Executive Council, May 21, 1889.

11. Gompers to Ernest Bohm, August 6, 18, and 28, 1890.

12. Gompers to Bohm, September 11, 1890.

13. *Report of Proceedings of the Tenth Annual Convention of the American Federation of Labor*, 1890, p. 20.

14. *An Interesting Discussion at the Tenth Annual Convention of the American Federation of Labor* (New York: The Freytag Printing Co., 1891), pp. 20, 21.

15. *Ibid.*, p. 21.

16. Gompers to August Delabar, May 19, 1891.

17. Gompers to Engels, January 9, 1891.

18. Gompers to Victor Delahaye, August 21, 1891.

19. Gompers to Sorge, November 21, 1891; November 27, 1891.

20. *Report of Proceedings of the Thirteenth Annual Convention of the American Federation of Labor*, 1893, p. 36.

21. *Report of Proceedings of the Fourteenth Annual Convention of the American Federation of Labor*, 1894, p. 14.

22. *A Verbatim Report of the Discussion on the Political Program Held at the Denver Convention of the American Federation of Labor, December 14 and 15, 1894* (New York: The Freytag Co., 1895), is the stenographic report of the debate.

23. *Report of Proceedings of the Fourteenth Annual Convention of the American Federation of Labor*, 1894, p. 41.

24. *Report of the Proceedings of the Fifteenth Annual Convention of the American Federation of Labor*, 1895, pp. 81-82.

25. Gompers to Ernest Kurzenknabe, December 5, 1896.

26. Gompers to James A. Cable, April 21, 1900.

27. Gompers to McGuire, May 20, 1895.

28. Gompers to John B. Lennon, December 28, 1901.

29. *Report of Proceedings of the Fifteenth Annual Convention of the American Federation of Labor,* 1895, p. 100.

30. *Report of the Proceedings of the Twenty-Second Annual Convention of the American Federation of Labor,* 1902, pp. 178, 179-183.

31. *Report of the Proceedings of the Twenty-Third Annual Convention of the American Federation of Labor,* 1903, pp. 188-199.

32. Gompers to Eugene V. Debs, October 3, 1892; to George W. Howard, December 28, 1893.

33. Ray Ginger, *The Bending Cross* (New Bruswick, New Jersey: Rutgers University Press, 1949), describes the opposition of Gompers, but there is nothing in the current record to indicate any concern by the heads of the American Federation of Labor.

34. *Report on the Pullman Strike of June and July 1894: Senate Executive Document No. 7, 53rd Congress, 3d Session* (Washington: Government Printing Office, 1895), pp. 130-131.

35. For a detailed description of the Pullman strike see Almont Lindsey, *The Pullman Strike* (Chicago: The University of Chicago Press, 1942).

36. Gompers to Debs, July 5, 1894; Gompers to McGuire, July 9, 1894.

37. Minutes of Executive Council, July 12, 1894.

38. Statement in Minutes of Executive Council, July 12, 1894.

39. Minutes of Executive Council, July 13, 1894.

40. Ginger, *op. cit.,* p. 149.

41. *Report of Proceedings of the Fifteenth Annual Convention of the American Federation of Labor,* 1895, p. 23.

V

The Resolution of the Conflict with the Knights of Labor

CHANGE IN VIEWS OF THE KNIGHTS

When the American Federation of Labor was reorganized, in 1886, the Knights of Labor was at the height of its power. The A. F. of L. principle of trade autonomy inevitably meant a limitation upon the claims of the Order as the all inclusive movement of labor in the United States. As long as the Knights of Labor retained the loyalty of thousands of workers, its attitude toward dual organization, politics, and trade autonomy would remain of great importance. Having initially taken a position that would almost automatically incite the suspicion and hostility of the trade unions, in 1887 the Knights of Labor made a conciliatory gesture by revoking its decision to expel from its ranks members who belonged to the Cigar Makers' International Union. In addition, those who had been expelled for belonging to that trade union were allowed reinstatement without payment of back dues.[1]

While this action represented a withdrawal from the extreme position of the Order in 1886, it by no means met the demands of the trade unions. To the latter, the groundwork of the case against the Knights was the readiness of the latter to invade their jurisdictions, and the Order was not willing to surrender this right as the price of appeasing the trade organizations. The Knights were willing to share their jurisdiction, but the unions would not accept such compromise. During a strike of steel workers at Mingo Junction, West Virginia, the Knights of Labor suggested to the Amalgamated Association of Iron and Steel Workers the setting up of a joint committee to direct the walkout. Inevitably, the proposal was rejected by the union, which led one of the national officers of the Knights of Labor to suggest formation of a national trades district "which will solidify and unite all workers engaged in the iron industry to the Knights of Labor, and bring them under one government."[2] Gompers was quick to seize the opportunity to attack the Knights, and in a letter to William Weihe, the head of the Amalgamated Association, explained the "methods of these people to first try and initiate a few simpletons and then claim jurisdiction to the detriment of the trade and then endeavor to 'wipe out of existence' a 'mere trade union.' "[3]

Dual organizations in a trade was a source of constant misunderstanding. When Paul F. Fitzpatrick of the Molders' Union asked the Knights of Labor to aid his union in a strike against the Defense Association, the answer was that the Knights were not involved in the controversy, and had "no right to drag into the contest thousands of members of the Knights of Labor."[4] Gompers was convinced that peace with the Knights was not possible.

Talk of harmony with the K. of L. [he wrote to McGuire], I tell you they will give us no quarter and I would give them their own medicine in return. It is no use trying to placate them or even to be friendly. They will not cooperate with a "mere" trades union as they call our organizations. The time will come, however, when the workingmen of the country will yet see and distinguish between a natural and artificial organization of labor.[5]

Gompers believed Powderly would do nothing to curb those in the Order who were warring on the trade unions, and he warned McGuire, who was inclined to be more trustful of Powderly's intentions, "not to place much reliance in his promises. His vacillation heretofore when confronted with any opposition has been too much for me to place confidence in what he says. It seems that the man who has the last word or argument with him has his support."[6]

CONTINUING CONFLICT

Whatever may have been Powderly's views on peace with the trade unions, the Executive Board of the Knights of Labor, on the motion of T. B. McGuire, decided that where

there is a National Trade District or Assembly whose product is protected by a label, this Board shall grant such national trade districts, within our Order, full power to distribute such labels according to such laws and regulations as may be adopted by the trade district to protect the same. Provided, such laws shall not conflict with general laws in regard to design and price to be charged for the label.[7]

Neither was the American Federation of Labor in a conciliatory mood. In its report to the convention of 1887, the Executive Council pointed to the difference between the words and actions of the leaders of the Knights. While the Knights sometimes expressed friendly sentiments toward the trade unions, the Council was convinced that the action of the Knights of Labor belied those words. Moreover, the Council was of the opinion that the Knights were determined to destroy the trade unions, and it therefore advocated unrelenting opposition to any interference with the independence and autonomy of the latter.[8] Even if the Federation were less eager to repel encroachments upon trade union jurisdictions, competition of dual unions in a trade would inevitably generate conflict. For example, when Typographical Union No. 2 requested the Knights of Labor to boycott an unfair employer, the latter replied that, before such action could be taken, Local Assembly of Printers No. 3,879 would have to make the request.[9] It is true that eventually the boycott was approved by the Executive Board, but only because a local assembly of the Order asked for such action. Certainly, the attitude of the Executive Board of the Knights is understandable, but the recognition of dual authorities in a trade tended to stimulate conflict, as the trade unions were not ready to concede parity to another group in the determining of conditions in the trade.

A somewhat similar problem arose in the Pennsylvania coal fields. The Mine Laborers Amalgamated Association of Pennsylvania complained of the invasion of its territory by the Knights of Labor.[10] Yet the principle of trade autonomy was so strongly imbedded in the consciousness of Gompers that he urged workers on surface cars to affiliate with a trade assembly of the Knights of Labor. Workers in that calling could not affiliate to the A. F. of L. except through the central labor union of some localities; consequently, Gompers advised them to "organize and form part of the national organization of their calling, District Assembly 226 of the Knights of Labor."[11]

This was, however, an unusual display of tolerance, one in which Gompers' belief in the importance of national trade organizations overcame his suspicion of the Knights. Nor did the Knights of Labor sympathize with or even understand the strong desire of the trade unions for a single autonomous organization in a trade. The resolution against dual unions, adopted by the A. F. of L. convention in 1888, was described by the official organ of the Order as designed

to practically force all members of the same craft into one organization. . . . [The resolution is] puerile, narrow and will prove abortive. It is useless to discuss such a proposition among men of experience in the labor movement for they understand well that it won't work.[12]

In fact, when some question over the chartering of a trade assembly of shoemakers arose, Powderly submitted a resolution "that nothing in this resolution shall be construed as to mean that there exists the slightest hostility to the formation of a National Trade Assembly of Shoemakers, nor shall it in any way apply to any other trade or calling."[13] While this resolution was adopted earlier than the one passed by the American Federation of Labor convention inveighing against the setting up of more than one union in a trade, the two resolutions can be regarded as expressing opposite views on the most crucial issue that confronted the labor movement of the time, the formation of dual unions. Yet, despite the differences, there was considerable opinion that an attempt should be made to find a basis for accommodation between the major labor organizations. At the suggestion of the Knights, a conference of the leading labor organizations was called. Gompers was unenthusiastic about the possibilities of peaceful coexistence, and informed McGuire that protests "have come to me from all over the country against any agreement with Mr. Powderly unless he shall give some tangible evidence of stopping the attempts to undermine the trade unions."[14]

Another objection raised by Gompers was to scheduling the meeting at Scranton, the home town of Powderly, "unless the Executive Council, whose servant I am and whose instructions I shall obey—orders me."[15] A conference was finally held between the two men, and Gompers "authorized . . . McGuire to affix my [his] signature to the manifesto agreed upon by our conference." At the same time, Gompers was happy that Powderly had "expressed a desire to rectify any wrongs that may have been done by the Knights of Labor and endeavor to prevent them in the future and that I take your word as an earnest of your desire."[16]

GENERAL LABOR CONFERENCE

Gompers and McGuire met with Powderly, John W. Hayes, and A. W. Wright of the Executive Board of the Knights of Labor and agreed to a broader conference on October 14, 1889, to which the leaders of the railway brotherhoods would be invited. The American Federation of Labor was interested mainly in two issues as they affected other organizations of labor. The most important consideration was to eliminate the issuances of charters for trade assemblies by the Knights, and to gain the latter's cooperation in the campaign for an eight-hour work day.[17] The discussions of October 14th failed, as the parties' views on labor organizations were basically too different to make agreement possible. For the purely trade-union demand for the eight-hour work day, the Knights of Labor showed no enthusiasm. Nor would the Order accept the A. F. of L.'s views on dual unions. Instead, the mutual recognition of cards and labels was proposed and the Knights also promised not to admit expelled members of trade unions. To the latter proposal the A. F. of L. replied that "where there exists a dual organization and authority in any trade, a conflict is inevitable and can only end disastrously to all interests."[18] The convention of 1889, which considered the relations between the trade unions and the Knights, was of the following opinion:

That the wage earner is the natural and proper guardian of the wage-earners' rights; that the most effective defense against encroachments upon those rights can be achieved through the medium of organization upon craft lines. It becomes imperative that the integrity of the trade union form of organization be zealously guarded; that this well-tested bulwark of labor be defended from overt attacks of jealous rivals as well as from the open antagonism of declared opponents. It does not seek to establish an autocracy of labor. It does, however, pledge itself to maintain the prestige and authority of its affiliated organizations, and to enter its most emphatic protests against the policy of any labor society which permits itself to be used as an ambuscade for the destruction of the trade union movement.[19]

AUTONOMY OF TRADE UNIONS AND THE KNIGHTS

The convention argued that much of the trouble in the labor movement was occasioned by the Knights of Labor chartering trade districts in crafts where national and international unions already existed, and the acceptance into membership by the Order of men who had proved unfair to their trade union. The convention found that despite repeated conferences between the representatives of the A. F. of L. and the Order, no satisfactory arrangement had been devised. Failure was attributed to the unwillingness of the Knights to recognize the "rightful authority of the trade unions in trade affairs." Consequently, the convention endorsed the position of the Executive Council at the conference of labor organizations.[20]

As the controversy remained unresolved, bitterness increased. In 1890, the Knights of Labor planned a meeting to review its differences with the A. F. of L. Powderly wanted to use the occasion to "reply to the numerous charges and accusations which have been made and circulated by the American Federation of Labor." In order that Gompers might not be forced to depend upon hearsay, he was invited to be present and occupy a seat on the platform. Powderly was hopeful that he would have the pleasure of sharing the platform with his guest should the latter "desire to reply to anything to which you take exception during the deliberations." Gompers scented a trap, and offered to debate with Powderly in accordance with the rules of such contests. He regarded a debate with several speakers before an audience of partisans not only a disadvantage to the presentation of his point of view, but a somewhat unfair arrangement. Powderly denied that he had intended to "challenge." Gompers to a discussion, and insisted that the latter had been invited to a meeting customarily held when the Executive Board of the Knights of Labor was in session.[21] The explanation was not accepted, and it evoked a tart comment from Gompers, who was convinced the invitation had been intended as a trap, and meant to be declined so that the declination could then be announced to the disadvantage of the A. F. of L. Whatever may have been the original purpose of the invitation, the exchange that followed indicates the reciprocal distrust with which each group of leaders viewed the other. Undoubtedly the ill feeling among the leaders widened the gulf between the organizations.

In 1891, the Knights of Labor took the lead in suing for peace. The terms were, however, such as the A. F. of L. was not likely to accept, and had in fact been rejected on several occasions. They again called for a mutual recognition of cards and labels, and the Knights offered to instruct its assemblies not to admit workers who had been suspended or expelled by a trade union, or who were in arrears in dues or assessments. On the other hand, the American Federation of Labor was to follow the same policy with regard to suspended or expelled members of the Knights of Labor. The committee from the Federation of Labor took the position that the A. F. of L.

is organized to maintain and strengthen the prestige, authority and autonomy of its affiliated bodies. Any proposition from an organization conducted upon an entirely different plan must be carefully considered as to its bearings upon the components of the American Federation of Labor. Each organization attached to the American Federation of Labor is guaranteed freedom from dictation or interference in managing its own affairs. Hence any agreement with another organization, even if satisfactory to the American Federation of Labor, can only come as a recommendation to its affiliated bodies. They are entirely free to accept or reject it.[22]

As proof of the independence and freedom of its affiliates, the American Federation of Labor pointed to the right of any of its affiliates to accept or reject the mutual recognition of working cards and labels with the Knights of Labor assemblies. The A. F. of L. again reiterated terms which would have relegated the Order to a minor role as an educational organization, and given complete control over trade affairs to the unions.

Once the A. F. of L. declared its inability to bind its affiliates, the Knights of Labor temporarily refused to negotiate further. In Powderly's view:

The counter propositions which have been placed before us by the A. F. of L. cannot be regarded by our Order in any other light than the views of individuals who represent no constituencies over whom they can exercise control. If the A. F. of L. could not act on the propositions of the Knights of Labor further attempt to make agreements with that body cannot but prove abortive for an organization not vested with sufficient authority to act on a proposition from a sister association has no legal authority to make a counter proposition.

Conferences and Decline of Knights

Not much change in the relations of the two organizations took place, and at the A. F. of L. convention of 1893 a committee of three was appointed, in response to a request by the Knights for a meeting of representatives of labor organizations to discuss means by which they might cooperate more closely. Gompers, McGuire, and Frank K. Foster were chosen as the A. F. of L. committee. As soon as the A. F. of L. had agreed to the meeting, the Knights of Labor lost its enthusiasm for the gathering.[24] The delay was presumably caused by the dilatory tactics of the leaders of the railroad unions, who were uncertain whether they wanted to attend. McGuire was angered at the delay, and told Gompers "if we have to wait for all these three organizations of railroad men . . . then we will wait until the walls of Jericho fall before another trumpet blast. I am in favor of proceeding with the conference, and favor Joseph R. Buchanan as a neutral party should call it without delay and place the present Knights of Labor on record."[25]

Buchanan was a leading labor editor, a member of the Knights and also a trade unionist.

Buchanan called a conference to promote "a closer union of the labor forces . . . the bringing together in one grand column the labor forces of America."[26] The leaders of the American Federation of Labor were optimistic about the results that would follow the meetings. In Gompers' view "the only purpose of the conference is to have existing organizations work harmoniously together upon all lines of action in the interests of the toiling masses of our country."[27]

The conference opened in St. Louis, on June 11, 1894. In addition to the Knights of Labor and the Federation, the Brotherhood of Locomotive Engineers, the Brotherhood of Locomotive Firemen, the Brotherhood of Railway Trainmen, Brotherhood of Railway Conductors, Farmers Alliance and Industrial Union, United Green Glass Workers' Association, and the Brotherhood of Electrical Workers were represented at the meeting. J. M. Bishop of the Knights of Labor proposed that a congress of labor organizations be held once a year, on Washington's Birthday. This meeting would devise a program of united action. Disputes between organizations of labor as to form of organization, jurisdiction, management of strikes, or any other differences would be settled by committees of arbitration chosen at this annual congress. Mutual recognition of working cards was to be established after July 1, 1894, so that a member of every "bona fide organization herein represented in any trade or calling" would be assured "recognition, assistance and support by all members of organized labor herein represented."

The Knights of Labor also suggested that where more than one local of the same craft existed in a community, joint executive committees be appointed to arrange wage scales and mutually satisfactory hours of work. In addition, the Order suggested that

In the coming campaigns and elections all members of organized labor cast their ballots against the two old political parties, and endeavor wherever possible to elect the third party candidates, unless said third party candidates shall avow themselves inimical to the interests of the masses; and believing, further, that the People's Party presents the most available means to an end, we suggest that they, at least for the present, receive the encouragement and support of united labor.[28]

[Whatever merit the proposals had as general propositions, the American Federation of Labor refused to relent in its insistence that the autonomy of the union in the trade or calling must be guaranteed, and that dual unionism be eliminated. The leaders of the Federation were convinced that no viable trade union movement could be built unless these principles were recognized. The major views of the Federation were upheld by a vote of thirteen to five, with the Knights of Labor, the Farmers Alliance, and the Railway Trainmen's delegations voting in opposition. Most important was the declaration upholding the position of the American Federation of Labor "that there should not be dual organization or authority in any one trade or calling; and that in all matters of trade conflicts, boycotts and trade labels the union particularly interested should have absolute authority and autonomy."[29]]

The committee representing the Federation also refused to endorse the People's Party, on the ground that, aside from the intrinsic merit of the proposal, such endorsement was beyond its powers. "The trade union movement has always urgently advocated an independent use of the ballot, but the Federation cannot with judiciousness imperil the economic integrity of its affiliated bodies by espousing partisanship, even in a third party form."[30] Consequently the delegates from the Federation refused to make any political commitments. Another consideration for withholding endorsement for any large scale political proposals was the pending discussion of the political platform submitted to the membership of the affiliates by the convention of 1893.

[This was the last serious attempt to find a working arrangement with the Knights of Labor, as the latter organization steadily declined in influence and in membership. Yet problems directly traceable to the existence of the Knights of Labor tended to arise for some time. In 1892, the convention of the Brewery Workers' Union voted to affiliate with both the Knights of Labor and the American Federation of Labor. In 1895, the Brewery Workers' Union was engaged in several disputes with its own locals and with the Executive Council of the A. F. of L.[31] The latter dispute arose as a result of the Council's refusal to endorse a boycott against a number of Alleghany County breweries. In considering the request for a boycott, the Executive Council found that the attempt of the National Union of the United Brewery Workmen to force its locals into the Knights of Labor "places that National Union in the attitude of hostility towards the interests of the American Federation of Labor, and we further find that much of the trouble has been caused by the dual position of the National Union of the United Brewery Workmen in being affiliated with the American Federation of Labor and the Knights of Labor."[32]

Another dispute involving the same organization concerned the refusal of Chicago Local No. 18 to pay an assessment. The local's refusal was based upon an objection to the affiliation of the National Union with the Knights of Labor. As the assessment was legal, Local No. 18 was suspended. Thereupon the Chicago Trades and Labor Assembly, an affiliate of the American Federation of Labor, was called upon by the National Union of the United Brewery Workmen to suspend the recalcitrant local. It refused to comply with the request and this policy was supported by the Executive Council of the A. F. of L., which did not look with favor upon the dual affiliation of the Brewery Workers' Union. When the matter was taken to the convention of the A. F. of L., it was found that the assessment was legal and that Local No. 18 would have to pay it, make arrangements satisfactory to the National Union, or stand suspended from the Chicago Trades and Labor Assembly. However, the convention blamed the difficulty on the

dual affiliation of the National Union with both the A. F. of L. and the K. of L. . . . and therefore recommended that the Brewery Workmen's National Union in their coming convention in September, 1896, take steps to dissolve National Trade District No. 35 of the Knights of Labor, lest suspension from the American Federation of Labor should follow and further representation at this convention be denied them.[33]

It was the last serious problem with the Knights of Labor, although differences between specific unions and trade assemblies continued for some time. In 1896 the American Federation of Labor decided that no central body affiliated with it was to admit delegates from any organization held to be hostile to the unions of the American Federation of Labor. This resolution was interpreted to bar assemblies of the Knights of Labor.[34] The Knights had, by the middle of the decade of the 1890's, ceased to be a serious rival to the A. F. of L., and Gompers was of the opinion that the Order had ceased to be a significant factor on the labor scene.[35]

REFERENCES

1. *Eleventh Session of the Knights of Labor*, 1887, pp. 1, 822.
2. William H. Bailey to General Executive Board, March 3, 1887, in *Ibid.*, p. 1379.
3. Gompers to William Weihe, February 25, 1887.
4. J. W. Hayes to Fitzpatrick, April 29, 1887.
5. Gompers to McGuire, April 22, 1887.
6. Gompers to McGuire, August 10, 1887.
7. Minutes of the Executive Board, of Knights of Labor, June 12, 1888, in archives of Catholic University.

8. *Report of Proceedings of the Seventh Annual Convention of the American Federation of Labor*, 1887, p. 26.

9. Minutes of Executive Board of the Knights of Labor, February 15, 1888, in archives of Catholic University.

10. Hugh McGregor to Hugh Mullen, Secretary of the Miners and Mine Laborers Association of Pennsylvania, March 2, 1888.

11. Gompers to E. J. Lake, October 22, 1888.

12. *The Knights of Labor*, December 15, 1888.

13. Minutes of Executive Board of the Knights of Labor, April 14, 1888.

14. Gompers to McGuire, April 21, 1889.

15. Gompers to McGuire, May 28, 1889.

16. Gompers to McGuire, June 27, 1889; to Powderly, June 27, 1889.

17. Gompers to Executive Council, September 7, 1889.

18. *Report of Proceedings of the Third Annual Convention of the American Federation of Labor*, 1889, p. 14.

19. *Ibid.*, p. 36.

20. *Ibid.*, p. 37.

21. Powderly to Gompers, June 19, 1890; Gompers to Powderly, June 20, 1890.

22. *Report of the Proceedings of the Eleventh Annual Convention of the American Federation of Labor*, 1891, p. 47.

23. Powderly to Chris Evans, February 3, 1892.

24. *Report of Proceedings of the Thirteenth Annual Convention of the American Federation of Labor*, 1893, pp. 52, 58.

25. McGuire to Gompers, March 27, 1894.

26. Circular issued under Buchanan's signature, in archives of A. F. of L.

27. Gompers to George W. Perkins, April 9, 1894.

28. *Report of Proceedings of the Fourteenth Annual Convention of the American Federation of Labor*, 1894, pp. 63-64.

29. *Ibid.*, p. 64.

30. *Ibid.*, p. 65.

31. Letter from K. Kurzenknabe, National Secretary, and Charles F. Bechtold, Assistant Secretary, of the National Union of the United Brewery Workmen, to the Executive Council of the American Federation of Labor, October 1, 1892.

32. Minutes of Executive Council, April 22, 1895.

33. *Report of the Proceedings of the Fifteenth Convention of the American Federation of Labor*, 1895, pp. 104-105.

34. *Report of Proceedings of the Sixteenth Annual Convention of the American Federation of Labor*, 1896, p. 85.

35. Gompers to T. C. Flynn, March 10, 1897.

VI

Organizing and Building National Unions

The American Federation of Labor sought to gain the affiliation of existing national and international unions and to establish such organizations in trades and callings where they were absent. While at the beginning some unions showed some reluctance to join the Federation, by the middle 1890's their suspicion and opposition were largely dissipated, and by the turn of the century the railroad operating crafts were the most important unions outside of the A. F. of L.

The American Federation of Labor was active in organizing on several levels. As soon as a sufficient number of local unions of any trade were organized, the heads of the Federation would endeavor to bring them "into correspondence with each other, and either to hold a conference or convention to form a national union." This was an important task, for as the A. F. of L. gained in prestige it could more efficiently perform this service for the labor movement. Moreover, the heads of the Federation could smooth over rivalries and soften differences between leaders and among locals and thereby facilitate their merging into one national union.

Gompers, reporting the formation of twelve new international unions in 1890, expressed the view that it was more desirable to start the national union "on its way to progress, though weak at first, than to have a fragmentary number of local unions of the same trade or calling without any central head or common concert among them."[1] Local unions already directly affiliated with the American Federation of Labor were required to affiliate with the national union as soon as the latter was established. Whenever a local union refused to comply with this rule its affiliation with the A. F. of L. would be canceled.

During 1891 Gompers reported that, as a result of the efforts of the American Federation of Labor, the Coopers' International Union had been revived, and the Electrical Workers "were organized into a national union from the various local unions affiliated to the Federation."[2]

In addition to organizing national unions in trades or callings where none existed, the A. F. of L. also established new local unions, whenever possible, for already affiliated internationals. This kind of support was

95

not exclusively given to affiliates of the American Federation of Labor, but applications for charters would be referred by the organizers of the A. F. of L. to unaffiliated international unions as well.[3]

Its major activity was establishing directly-affiliated trade and labor unions, groups of which subsequently became international unions.

While the trade unions could report some organizing activity in 1893, the depression which had fastened itself upon the economy was having a harmful effect upon labor organizations. Many unions lost large numbers of members, and the income of the Federation, if one excluded the contribution to the defense of the Homestead men, suffered somewhat. Per-capita taxes and supplies yielded over $15,000 for the fiscal year 1892, and only $12,820.96 in the following fiscal year. While the declines in income and membership were by no means catastrophic, and their size an indication of the viability of the new movement, the leaders had to recognize that their progress had been temporarily halted.

In 1894, income exclusive of the nonrecurring contributions for the defense of Homestead was above $15,000, $12,787.99 of which represented receipts for per capita and supplies. The following year, 1895, income from per capita and supplies was over $10,504, $8,392.95 of which was payment for per-capita taxes. The following year, 1896, both total income and per-capita began to rise, and per-capita tax payments were $10,057.86.

NUMBER OF CHARTERS FOR FEDERAL, TRADE, AND INTERNATIONAL LABOR UNIONS ISSUED BY THE AMERICAN FEDERATION OF LABOR, 1890-1905[a]

Year	Federal and Trade	Internationals
1890	274	8
1891	246	10
1892	277	8
1893	202	6
1894	167	5
1895	141	8
1896	267	11
1897	189	8
1898	182	9
1899	404	9
1900	834	14
1901	782	7
1902	877	14
1903	1,139	20
1904	228	11
1905	360	3

[a] Figures compiled from official proceedings.

In organizing, the Federation was as anxious to recruit the unskilled as the skilled. In fact, in 1897 Gompers warned:

With the invention of new machines and the applications of new forces, the division and subdivision of labor, many workers who have been employed at skilled trades find themselves with their occupation gone, and to which they have devoted long terms of years to acquire. Thus we see the artisan of yesterday the unskilled laborer of today.

The American Federation of Labor set up the federal labor unions, which broadly resembled in structure the mixed assemblies of the Knights of Labor, for the organization of unskilled, although the skilled were also taken into these groups.

Whenever federal labor unions are organized they are the recruiting grounds for the trade unions, both of the skilled and unskilled workers, and as soon as a sufficient number of one trade or calling, whether belonging to skilled or unskilled labor, they are required to form a union of those who follow the same trade or occupation. Thus our federal labor unions are the recruiting ground for the trade union movement.[4]

Originally federal labor unions were limited to workers in one trade, but a change was made in 1893, permitting workers of several trades to combine.

Lack of finances made it difficult for individual unions to support organizers in many areas, and such failure meant that the area might be completely neglected. It appeared to the A. F. of L. that organizing opportunities were present in New England in the late 1890's, and Gompers was aware that it might "be inconvenient and expensive" for each union to have its own organizer. He therefore sought to encourage joint organizing campaigns by several unions. On behalf of the A. F. of L., Gompers suggested to the Machinists, Molders, Painters, Printers, and Granite Cutters' unions that each of them contribute "a small amount to have an organizer in the field with each union carrying a small share of the expenses."[5] The unions involved did not follow through on the suggestion.

In 1897, in addition to chartering 189 federal and trade unions, organizers of the A. F. of L. organized over five hundred local unions which were then attached to the respective affiliates in their trades.[6]

In accordance with its policy of establishing national unions as soon as such a step was practicable, the American Federation of Labor called upon the core makers, in 1893, to set a time and place for establishing a national union. Several unions appealed for aid in organizing their jurisdictions in 1894.[7] Among those were the Retail Clerks, Carriage and Wagon Workers, Electrical, and Wagon Workers' unions. The convention recommended that "the incoming Executive . . . appoint such local organizers as are required, and adopt ways and means for their remuneration. This also applies to the Pattern Makers' National League of North America."[8]

In 1897, the A. F. of L. succeeded in forming from isolated locals of several trades four national unions, among them the Core Makers' International Union, which the Federation had sought to establish four years earlier. The organizing efforts of the A. F. of L. cannot, at this time, be minimized, for in the five-year period between 1896 and 1901, the A. F. of L. formed thirty-five international unions out of directly chartered federal and trade unions. Among the important organizations which are still functioning and which were thus organized are the Boiler Makers, Building Laborers, Lathers, Stationary Firemen's, Upholsterers, and Teamsters' unions.

Demands for organizing both industries and areas were made to the conventions of the A. F. of L. The convention of 1895 considered organizing the South, and Robert Howard of the Cotton Spinners Union of Fall River, and Frederick Estes, a printer from Ohio, were the first organizers to be sent there to establish unions. Gompers, who was down in the area on other business, looked the situation over and was convinced that Southern workers could be recruited into labor organizations. However, the officers of the A. F. of L. were keenly aware that organizing could only be supported if adequately financed, and they were often irritated at the tendency of conventions to vote in favor of campaigns without furnishing the financial means to carry them out.

ORGANIZERS OF THE SOUTH AND WEST

In 1896, the convention instructed the Executive Council to send organizers into the Western areas, especially the Inter-Mountain states. At the next meeting, Secretary Morrison pointed to the scant eighteen hundred dollars in the treasury and argued it was difficult to do much large-scale organizing with that amount.[9]

Yet the members of the Executive Council favored using whatever funds were available for organizing, even if only for short periods. They were "heartily in favor of any expense incurred in organizing."[10]

There were constant demands for assistance from various unions in different sections of the country. When a resolution instructing the Federation to organize the South was considered in 1898, Gompers suggested that "provision should be made to enable the officers to carry it out. If such provisions were not made, then the officers would have to report back to the next convention that they had complied with their instructions." The president of the International Typographical Union objected on the ground that organizing was the job of the internationals, which, he suggested, might cooperate together in joint organizing campaigns.[11] This discussion reflects the dilemma of the A. F. of L.; it was instructed to organize without always being provided with the "sinews of war." Moreover, as the internationals grew in size and power they became increasingly reluctant to make contributions needed for large-scale organizing.

When the convention of 1898 decided to send organizers into the Southern and Inter-Mountain states, Treasurer Lennon demanded that finances be provided. On his motion, the convention endorsed the levying of an assessment of two cents per member on all national, international, and trade and labor unions.

The convention of 1898 voted to send organizers into the Inter-Mountain states, largely in response to the dual movement sponsored by the Western Federation of Miners. The formation of a competitive federation was largely justified by the claim that the Federation had neglected the workers in the Inter-Mountain area. The directive was not carried out, as the expenditure was deemed inexpedient for the time because of the threatened Spanish-American War, and the large amounts spent on lobbying before Congress.

FULL-TIME ORGANIZERS

For the first time, in 1899, the Federation employed a number of full-time paid organizers. Prior to this time organizers had been engaged only on special projects and for limited periods. During the year the Federation had employed 17 organizers, whose time and expenses were paid in whole or in part by the A. F. of L. In addition, there were functioning more than 550 volunteer organizers, whose commissions had been renewed during the year. The A. F. of L. had gained 9 international unions, and had organized 405 federal and trade locals. In the next year, 1900, the results were even better, with 14 new internationals and 734 federal and trade locals affiliating. The greater result was due in part to the increased expenditure of the A. F. of L. in organizing. Almost up to the turn of the century, organizing was largely conducted by the Executive Council and volunteers. In 1894, the Federation reported an expenditure of $448.49 for this purpose. Not until 1898 was the cost of organizing separately listed. In that year only $1257 was spent for that purpose, but the following year the sum rose to $6373.66. Nevertheless, the officers of the Federation urged greater effort at recruiting new members, and Secretary Morrison called the labor movement's attention to the fact that "the spirit of organization is abroad." He urged the national and international unions to take advantage of the opportunities to organize their jurisdictions. He lamented the tendency of some unions to keep the heads of their organizations working at their trade, so that they could only devote evenings and Sundays to union business. He recommended that national and international unions should be urged to have at least one full-time paid officer devoted to the business of the organization.[12]

In 1900, for the first time in its history, the Federation had sufficient funds to keep general organizers in the field continuously. Up to June 20th, 20 organizers were in the field, active in different localities. The expense thus incurred gradually exhausted the treasury, and by the middle of July but $2000 remained, forcing, for a short period, the discontinuance of all but three organizers. These organizers worked either independently or were placed at the disposal of the affiliated unions. Over $16,000 were spent on this account. In addition, the Federation had 680 volunteers who occasionally aided the Federation in organizing.[13]

In the following year, expenditures for organizing almost doubled, from over $16,000 to over $32,000. The convention of 1899 had instructed an expansion of organizing activity, and having been provided with the means, the Federation utilized its funds. More than half of the total sum spent on organizing was for activity in the Western and Southern states.

The ratio of expenditures to total income of the American Federation of Labor spent for organizing is much higher than is indicated by the Table, for income includes assessments, which were substantial amounts in 1899, 1900, 1901, and 1905.

The amount spent on organizing actually constituted an even larger percentage of available income, for the Federation was required to set aside one-half of the per-capita paid by federal and trade unions into a defense fund to be used for the payment of authorized strike benefits.

INCOME, EXPENSES, AND EXPENSES OF ORGANIZING, 1898-1905[a]

Year	Income	Expenses	Organizing Expenses	Percentage of Organizing Expenses of Income (*Including Assessments*)
1897	$ 18,639.92	$ 19,113.83	$ 3,593.37	19.3
1898	18,894.15	19,197.17	1,257.00	6.7
1899	36,757.13	30,599.22	6,373.66	17.3
1900	71,125.82	68,373.39	16,399.74	23.1
1901	115,270.89	118,708.39	32,328.74	28.1
1902	144,498.21	119,086.74	28,186.11	19.5
1903	247,802.96	196,015.57	60,798.29	24.5
1904	220,995.97	203,991.15	83,242.23	37.7
1905	207,417.62	196,170.10	61,694.29	29.7

[a] Compiled from Annual Reports.

LOANS AND GRANTS

Income of the Federation influenced not only the scale of organizing the Federation could carry on, but the assistance it could render to affiliates. As a matter of fact, the persistent requests for aid from the national unions induced the A. F. of L. convention of 1893 to create a special fund from the monthly receipts from which the Executive Council could make those donations to affiliated unions it regarded as necessary. In 1892, the Executive Council lent to various unions a total of $3500 which was not returned, but the $2500 lent to the Carpenters' Union to help that organization in several disputes was returned within sixty days.[14]

In some instances the loans were repaid, but frequently the internationals or the locals which had received these grants were unable to repay them. In 1893, both the Electrical Workers' Union and the German American Typographia repaid their loans of five hundred dollars each, but the Federation still had five thousand dollars of loans outstanding. Most of the unions claimed that the large number of their members out of work prevented them from repaying their obligations.

In the following year, because of the severe unemployment, a large number of unions applied to the Federation for help. Over thirty-five hundred dollars was donated, including the contribution of five hundred dollars to the defense of Debs and thirteen hundred dollars to the United Mine Workers of America.[15] The donations to international unions came from the general fund and were not obtained from assessments, which was perhaps the best indication of the stability achieved by the A. F. of L. The Federation was thereafter prohibited from loaning money, but it could make donations.

Most of the $3467.01 donated in 1895 was for defense of individuals or for lecture tours. It led Secretary August McCraith to question some of the appropriations. He advised "it would be well for us to bear in mind when disposing of our resources in the present and future the pertinence and truth of the old maxim that charity begins at home." Nevertheless, the Federation continued to support its affiliates financially, whenever they needed help, in amounts which could be given. Donations of several thousand dollars were annually made.[16]

Financial support, even on the modest scale the Federation could provide, was undoubtedly of great assistance to the unions. The Federation supplied a needed margin, which sometimes made possible the survival of these organizations.

STREET CAR MEN

Of perhaps greater importance was the Federation's activity in bringing unions into existence, and preventing the divisive forces which exist in every newly-organized union from destroying it. As was noted earlier, the Federation was instrumental in the first years of its existence in reviving the Coopers' International Union, and in forming what is now the International Brotherhood of Electrical Workers. These were not sporadic acts, but were an integral part of the Federation's routine functions.

In 1891 the convention instructed the Executive Council "to issue a call for a conference of the organized street railway employees of the United States for the purpose of forming the whole into one organization." The Council was instructed "to provide a place for such conference, and delegate a duly authorized representative to open such conference in the name and by the authority of the American Federation of Labor."[17] The convention believed that convening of a conference by the American Federation of Labor for the establishment of a national union would carry more weight than such a call would if it were issued by one or several unions. Despite its slender resources, the American Federation was able to finance such conferences, and thereby remove a possible objection against the expense of these meetings which some local unions in a trade might raise. Perhaps as important was the fact that, being an outsider as far as the trade was concerned, the Federation could mediate between factions or even strong locals, each of which might insist upon controlling the new international union.

Under the authority of the Executive Council, the locals of street car men were called into conference in Indianapolis, Indiana, on September 21, 1892. In calling the conference, the A. F. of L. argued:

Experience has demonstrated . . . that singly and alone unions have too often been defeated in the contests with concentrated capital and the toilers must not only organize into unions of their respective localities but to have their unions formed into a national organization, thus enabling all to concentrate their efforts upon a given point to obtain success where otherwise by isolated action defeat would necessarily ensue.[18]

Two groups, the Brotherhood of Surface Car Employees and the Amalgamated Association of Street Railway Employees, were vying for control of the trade. At the convention, opened and temporarily directed by Gompers, the Brotherhood refused to merge with the new organization. Later the Detroit local of that organization was to appeal to the Federation for aid. However, since the members had their national union, the Federation could not "act unless it would be at the request of their national officers."[19]

The leaders of the Brotherhood had virtually promised to accept unity, and Gompers was keenly disappointed at the failure to establish one union among the surface car employees. The efforts to merge the several factions were continued, and at the convention of 1894 unity was achieved.

The Federation was able to take the leadership in this campaign because a number of locals of street car men were affiliated directly with it. In the tugging and hauling for position in the national union, differences between the leaders of the separate factions had been exacerbated. It was only through the efforts of the A. F. of L. that the breach in the organization was overcome and one union in the trade established.

MUSICIANS

In the case of the musicians, the problem of uniting several groups, each of which sought to assert its hegemony over the trade, was complicated by differences over the definition of a professional musician which determined eligibility for membership in a musicians' union. The first job of the American Federation of Labor was to convince labor men that the playing of musical instruments represented a distinct craft, and that the union in the trade had the right to set standards for those engaged in it. The issue arose because members of other unions—carpenters, plumbers, tailers, for example—who played in orchestras, insisted that they were not required to join a union of musicians, claiming that membership of other crafts gave them status as union musicians. Could a band made up of members of nonmusical unions be regarded as a union band? The existence of the American Federation of Labor provided a tribunal where such issues could be decided. While the Federation had no authority to impose its will upon any group, its decision carried some moral weight.

The question arose in several cities, but became acute in Milwaukee. In response to a request, Gompers raised the question with Frank J. Weber, the leader of the Wisconsin labor movement. Weber was at the time organizing longshoremen. Would he regard a man who was a member of the cigar makers' or carpenters' or any other union in good standing as a union member if he sought work as a longshoreman? Moreover, would Weber regard it "as a perfectly proper act of unionsim if in order to avoid becoming members of your union such cigar makers, carpenters, or printers or in fact any other trade or calling, would organize a separate and rival union of longshoremen or vessel unloaders?"[20]

The principle Gompers enunciated had to be followed if a union of musicians was to survive. Unless musicians were given hegemony over their trade, union men from other trades would have the power to set standards for musicians. The American Federation of Labor was fearful that a division between unionists over the definition of a union musician would not only be demoralizing to the members of the musicians' unions, but would lead to general strife and demoralization in other industries because such disputes tended to generate further differences. Gompers therefore took the position that each trade must be allowed to run its own affairs. While some of the policies of the musicians' unions may be regrettable, "yet so long as they do not change them, it seems to me that as a trade unionist and as members of the A. F. of L. we are in a measure bound by their decisions in their own trade, calling, profession or whatever you may please to call it."[21]

The musicians' unions were divided into several groups, some of which were directly attached to the A. F. of L. as local unions. The American Musicians of North America and the National League of Musicians of the United States were both trying to preempt the jurisdiction on a nationwide basis. In addition, there were a few locals attached to the Knights of Labor. The American Federation of Labor believed that it was necessary to combine all the groups in one organization, but felt that its chartering of a particular union might arouse the suspicion of its intentions and thereby nullify its objectives. Consequently, the A. F. of L. refused the plea of one of the organizations "to please grant us a charter, and order all musical unions holding a Federation charter to attend our convention and elect officers.[22]

A complicating factor was the attitude of the National League of Musicians of the United States. At its convention in Cleveland, in May 1895, the League decided "the musical profession . . . differs entirely from all others, and cannot be controlled or managed by strict trades-union methods or doctrines, as existing in your respective labor-organizations."[23]

The League objected to untrained musicians entering the field, and in order to protect itself and the public "against this invasion of incompetent imposters," it set up the examining board, "so as to distinguish between a musician and an amateur." Of course, musicians denied membership in the League would remain in the trade and sometimes join or establish unions which were in some cities affiliated with a central body of the American Federation of Labor.

The League recognized that

If charters to musicians' unions, not affiliated with the National League, are continued to be recognized and issued, then it is merely a question of time when our locals, who at present hold charters from your organization, will be called upon to decide between your organization and the National League as a National Protectorate, in order to escape the conflict of authority which naturally must arise by recognizing musical unions directly opposed to one another. Even if located in different sections of the country, the result must be the same, and trouble cannot be avoided, as the musical profession, is to a great extent, engaged in travelling, and under the laws of the National League, are prohibited from performing or employing musicians not belonging to the National League, when visiting other localities.[24]

The split among the musicians, in addition to the conflict it generated in the trade, produced differences in the labor movements of several cities. The objections to affiliation were overcome with the change in the officers of the League. They now asked that their position in the American Federation of Labor be clarified in the event that affiliation were acceptable. The officers were particularly concerned over the disposition that would be made of the twenty locals directly affiliated with the American Federation of Labor, and the power the union would have over its members. The League was informed that a national charter would be granted only if all local unions of musicians were to be accepted in the national organization. In turn, the League was assured that affiliation to the A. F. of L. would not interfere with the League's authority to act as the supreme power over its members. Moreover, its affiliation with the A. F. of L. "would be guaranteed absolute trade autonomy, and the central organization would not possess the right to interfere with the trade affairs of the League."[25]

The convention of the American Federation of Labor in 1895 ordered the Executive Council to call a conference to end the "interminable struggle which is going on all through the country between various factions of musicians and particularly in its attitude towards organized labor."[26]

Gompers had earlier pleaded with the leaders that

In the interests of the entire musical trade, as well as the whole labor movement, a new spirit should permeate the delegates assembled in the formation of the national union, and that spirit should have as its guiding purpose of organizing all musicians of the country into one intelligent, comprehensive organization, with its full rights, autonomy, independence and jurisdiction ceded to it. In the attainment of this purpose the American Federation of Labor will pledge its cooperation and support.[27]

Nevertheless, the National League of Musicians refused at its convention in the spring of 1896 to affiliate with the American Federation of Labor. Thereupon the Executive Council, with McGuire dissenting, decided to call the unions of musicians into convention for the purpose of setting up a national organization. It was agreed, at a meeting between the officers of the A. F. of L. and the conference of musicians' unions, that the A. F. of L. call and sponsor the convention, that all locals affiliated with the A. F. of L. were to be allowed to join the new Federation, and whereever more than one local union of musicians exist in a community they be amalgamated.[28]

On October 19, 1896, the American Federation of Labor invited all the musicians' unions in the United States to a convention. Representatives of twenty-seven locals appeared, and the American Federation of Musicians was organized. Peace was not immediately established in the musical trade, and the American Federation of Labor had to intervene in a number of local situations to prevent discrimination and to promote the unification of conflicting locals. At the urging of the American Federation of Labor, a local of musicians in Duluth, Minnesota, disbanded; yet the members were denied admission to the affiliate of the American Federation of Musicians. Gompers wrote the secretary: "We have a right to organize our unions but we have no right to deny men against whom there is no charge of unfair dealing, membership in our union, thus depriving them of an opportunity to earn an honest livelihood."[29]

While in this instance the local union which was attached to the new international refused to accept applicants, more frequently locals refused to affiliate with the American Federation of Musicians and sought direct affiliation with the American Federation of Labor. These locals were informed that such affiliation could not be accepted. Moreover, when the Chicago musicians' local refused to affiliate with the American Federation of Musicians but wanted to retain its affiliation with the Chicago Federation of Labor, Gompers assured the officers of the national musicians' union that "unless the Chicago union joins the American Federation of Musicians soon, I am sure it will become my duty to call upon the Chicago Federation of Labor to refuse the local organization recognition. This is in compliance with the constitution of the American Federation of Labor."[30]

There were difficulties in uniting the musicians into one national union in cities other than Chicago. The A. F. of L. urged the American Federation of Musicians to make concessions so that unity in the trade would be achieved in several localities, particularly Cleveland and Toledo, where an especially virulent conflict had developed.

Gompers called the attention of the national officers to another serious problem, the kind and number of local unions the American Federation of Musicians would allow to organize under its jurisdiction.

Many of our organizations [Gompers informed Secretary Jacob Schmalz] prescribe that a man may belong to the union where he resides or where he works, requiring the unions in the locality to form a kind of advisory board. You can readily see how such a matter may be necessary in cities . . . when perhaps the city in which a man lives may have absolutely no use for the class or kind of work in which he is a specialist. For that reason if he joins the union in the place where he resides, he would have no work and would have to move to a place where it is undesirable or inconvenient and sometimes next to impossible for him. These are matters which a national union must necessarily provide and I hope they will be given thorough consideration.[31]

It may appear strange that officers who had pretensions to national leadership would need the kind of advice and service the American Federation of Labor, at the time, offered. Yet the officers of many national unions, including the musicians, had little experience with the broader problems of administering more than one local union. The heads of the American Federation of Labor were aware of solutions to similar problems by other unions, and by their greater knowledge and experience could be of inestimable help to organizations struggling to win a place for themselves.

The American Federation of Musicians was not unappreciative of the efforts the leaders of the Federation exerted on its behalf. At its convention in 1897, the union instructed its delegates to the convention of the A. F. of L. to support Gompers for reelection. Gompers was unenthusiastic about this action, and declared:

I did not think I deserved a vote of censure, or one of confidence, at the hands of the musicians. I should dislike, however, any convention to adopt resolutions binding their delegates to vote for me for any office. In the convention of my own organization, I opposed such a proposition and secured its withdrawal. You can readily see my feelings in the matter. Organizations may vote as they will in reference to myself. I will not change my course toward them in the performance of my full duty to their interests.[32]

PAINTERS

Differences within the painters' organization, which had been established in 1887, arose out of a convention ruling in 1894 that the elected secretary was ineligible for office because his local was not in good standing in the national organization. As a result of this dispute, two factions, one with headquarters in Baltimore and the other in Lafayette, Indiana, claimed to be the legitimate union in the trade. Both factions sent delegates to the convention of the A. F. of L. of that year, and for the first time, the A. F. of L. was called upon to determine the legitimacy of a union in a trade. The credentials committee, which considered the conflicting claims, faced a dilemma, and it recommended that the convention seat the delegates of both factions, "and that the whole matter of dispute be referred to the incoming Executive Council, to, if possible, effect a harmonious solution."[33]

The American Federation of Labor began a long and patient effort to unify the two factions. President John McBride of the A. F. of L. drew up an agreement, but the Lafayette group rejected it on the ground that it could not surrender its autonomy or its right to self-rule, even to the American Federation of Labor. Thereupon the Executive Council decided to recognize the other group, the Baltimore faction.[34] The factional dispute was having an adverse effect upon union membership in the trade, and members were being discouraged from retaining their affiliation. Moreover, the dispute in the Painters' trade was involving other crafts. The head of one of the factions pleaded with the American Federation of Labor for action, for "while the matter [the split in the trade] is in abeyance our organization is disintegrating and many local unions are notifying us that unless matters are settled immediately the lapsing of their locals will be the result."[35] A proposal that the heads of the two unions in the trade resign, and that a joint convention select new leaders, was rejected. The American Federation of Labor insisted upon recognizing the group which was willing to accept its decisions on unity; but it continued to seek a united painters' organization.[36]

In 1897, the Executive Council appointed Gompers and McGuire to draw up a plan under which the two groups could be united. McGuire submitted the following proposal:

That the Executive Council advise and urgently recommend that each of the two representative national organizations of Painters, both known as the Brotherhood of Painters and Decorators of America, shall choose or elect five representatives to meet in a general conference March 16, 1898, at Buffalo, New York, with full power to agree upon such terms of consolidation or amalgamation that will unite both bodies in one organization, and thus put an end to the present factional quarrels which are so hurtful to the welfare of the painters and so damaging to the entire trade union movement.[37]

After joint terms of agreement were adopted, plans were to be arranged for the election of general officers, after which the heads of both unions were to retire from office.

Representatives from the American Federation of Labor appeared at the conventions of the two factions. Gompers, accompanied by the president and secretary of the International Typographical Union, met the head of the Lafayette faction, but the latter rejected the terms that had been offered. The Executive Council then recognized the Baltimore group as the regular faction of the Brotherhood of Painters and Decorators of America, and declared the Lafayette faction to be a dual or seceding body. Central bodies of the A. F. of L. were asked not to give encouragement or assistance to the locals of the seceding body. This action was taken

only as a last alternative after making every honorable endeavor to bring about amalgamation or unity of the two Painters organizations, and is firmly convinced that it is not at present the disposition of the seceding Painters organization, with headquarters at Lafayette, Indiana, to agree to any arrangement that does not involve the stultification of the parent body of the Painters now affiliated with the A. F. of L.[38]

Immediately the head of the Lafayette faction inquired whether the ousting of the locals of his organization by the A. F. of L. central bodies meant the beginning of an attack upon his union? Gompers assured him that "the A. F. of L. and its officers have no intention of fighting or starting a fight on any labor organization." However, Gompers informed him "when one side to a controversy . . . is willing to adopt propositions by which unity can be accomplished, it is not fraternal, it is not to the best interests of the trade, it is not to the best interests of labor that the other side should spurn the proposal for a meeting and conference to accomplish unity."[39] The recalcitrant faction had become the larger of the two, and the head of the group came to the convention of the American Federation of Labor in 1898 and asked for the floor. McGuire objected to this request, but Gompers asked that he be heard so that he might convince the delegates that "he was in the wrong."[40] Gompers did not want to close the door to unity, and he was not ready to repulse any friendly overtures, even by one who had refused to meet with a committee from the Executive Council.

Soon thereafter, Gompers again appealed for a settlement of differences, for it was "needless . . . to call attention to the sad sight witnessed by all lovers of unionism, now presenting itself by reason of the division in the trade. Intelligent men have long ago held that no two bodies could claim jurisdiction over one trade without antagonism and conflict."[41] Gompers was distressed by the conflict, and he received complaints that the Painters' Union affiliated with the A. F. of L. had allowed unfair men to join one of its locals. Yet he did not see how he could ask that the charter be revoked as long as the conflict between the factions continued.[42]

Peace and unity could only be restored by mutual concessions. When the head of the Baltimore group inquired whether he should send written proposals to the other group, Gompers advised "written propositions are of themselves rigid. They are seldom, if ever, calculated to bring about unity of action."[43] Hence, he advised the dispatching of a committee which would negotiate. The American Federation of Labor convention again instructed the Executive Council to unify the painting trade. Gompers informed both organizations that the American Federation of Labor would pay the expenses of any meetings held for this purpose. With the aid of Gompers and other members of the Executive Council, a unity program was agreed upon by committees from both organizations. Under the auspices of the American Federation of Labor, elections were held, officers chosen, and the results accepted by both factions.[44]

The unification of the warring painters' factions took almost six years. Such efforts were of great importance in the early years, when the organizations were not as well established and deviation from the international by a group could be more easily accomplished.

THE TEAMSTERS

The Teamsters' Union was another union which owes its birth to the A. F. of L. Initially, it was built out of locals that had been largely established by the American Federation of Labor, and the A. F. of L.

"nursed" the organization along for several years, when division and factional warfare threatened to destroy the youthful organization.

In November 1898, the A. F. of L. called a convention of team drivers for the establishing of a national union. A Team Drivers' International Union was formed, officers elected and a constitution, largely written by Secretary Frank Morrison, devised. The American Federation of Labor asked all the teamster locals directly affiliated with it to join the new International.[45]

Owner drivers presented the new union with its first serious problem. George Innis, the head of the new national union, informed the American Federation of Labor that some locals had owners and hack drivers in their ranks, who themselves were unwilling to employ union men. He felt that as long as the owners dominated the locals the ordinary driver would not join the union.[46]

For a time the issue remained in abeyance, but the Teamsters' Union was soon wracked by a serious dispute over the amount of dues to be charged. Upon the recommendation of John B. Lennon, Treasurer of the A. F. of L., the Team Drivers' International Union raised its dues at its convention in 1901. Immediately, the major local in Boston, Local No. 25, seceded and initiated plans for forming a rival international. The American Federation of Labor was called upon for advice and assistance, and Gompers immediately recruited a group of Massachusetts labor leaders to use their influence to prevent the split in the ranks of the teamsters.[47] It was largely the American Federation of Labor which prevented a permanent split in the organization over this issue. The plan worked out at the headquarters of the A. F. of L. "for stamping out the dissension in Boston proved to be a complete success. The local put up a splendid fight with about 2,000 of their members at the meeting but it is needless to say that when we turned the big guns on them, it only took a few hours to win the battle."[48] The "big guns" were the representatives of the American Federation of Labor who were able to convince the Boston membership of the need for accepting the decision of their convention.

Soon thereafter, the Executive Council was called upon to intervene in a more serious controversy—whether the union should allow membership to owner-drivers. Gompers, Treasurer Lennon, and Vice President Kidd were appointed to seek a settlement that would eliminate the division in the ranks of the teamsters. A new organization had been formed— the Team Drivers' National Union—which claimed to have forty-seven locals with almost 28,000 members. It applied for affiliation with the A. F. of L. All the locals of the new teamster organization—which had been formed partly because of its members' opposition to allowing owner drivers union membership—were in Chicago, and the new union presented a serious problem for the American Federation of Labor. Gompers was anxious to seal up the division and asked the Team Drivers' International Union

to have a representative of your organization meet with a representative of the applicants [the other teamsters' union] at headquarters in this city during the time the Executive Council of the American Federation of Labor will hold its session here. . . . You can readily understand that if there is to be some kind of amalgamation, it will have to be done by conference, and this can be better accomplished when some members of the Executive Council are present.[49]

At the same time, the Executive Council of the A. F. of L. voted, by five to three, to ask the Team Drivers to eliminate the clause allowing owner drivers membership in the union.

Innis was informed that

The constitution of the American Federation of Labor prescribes that the organization shall be composed of wage earners. Team drivers have complained bitterly that in unions made up of drivers of teams, owners and employers, the men who work for wages have their courage crushed out of them with no power to correct grievances because of their fear of discharge or discrimination which can be easily though indirectly, exercised should they have the temerity to bring forward a matter before the meetings of their unions.

Moreover, the Executive Council of the A. F. of L. informed Innis:

There is a deep seated conviction among a large number of team drivers that employers of labor have no right to become members of any local union and that conviction is fully shared by members of the Executive Council of the American Federation of Labor. . . . It is perhaps entirely superfluous to call attention to the Chicago situation, you and a few members of your Executive Board were present and know of the awful contest which we waged and the efforts made by my colleagues of the Executive Council of the American Federation and myself to endeavor to bring about the affiliation of the team drivers of Chicago with your international union. The main contention being that the men in Chicago objected to being associated with your organization for the single fact that it contained employers.[50]

As a result of the pressure, the Team Drivers' International Union removed the objectionable clause from its constitution, so that employers who controlled more than one team were no longer eligible for membership.

More active steps to bring the two teamsters' unions together were taken at the A. F. of L. convention in 1902. A committee was selected to meet with representatives of the two unions and devise a program for merging the two organizations. When they proved unable to agree, the Executive Council was again called upon to intervene. It broke the deadlock by devising a formula which gave each union one vote for each one hundred members. The formula was accepted by both unions, and a convention was prepared by the American Federation of Labor, with its representative acting as temporary chairman.[51]

The type of service given by the A. F. of L. in the teamster dispute was of inestimable value in building the labor movement, and a number of unions profited from the intervention of the heads of the A. F. of L. in times of factional splits.

Not only did the leaders fear the effect of a division in a trade or calling on the organizing possibilities in that trade or calling, but they also sought to avoid the repercussions upon the general labor movement. Dual organization created difficulties in central bodies because local unions were likely to find support from other labor bodies in their home communities. Immediate attempts were always made to reunite divergent factions, and even when rebuffed, the leaders of the Federation could, without loss of face, try again when tempers had cooled and persuasion was more possible. The efforts sometimes continued over a number of years, and the steps taken to restore unity were usually not publicized, even at conventions of the American Federation of Labor.

Unions as well established as the International Typographical Union sometimes found the American Federation of Labor could perform useful services in a difficult situation. When this union was confronted by a secession of printing pressmen, who wanted an organization of their own, the head of the Typographical Union appealed to the American Federation of Labor. At the suggestion of the Executive Council Gompers helped to bring about a workable solution of the problem.[52]

The unification of the teamsters' organization did not immediately end the dissension within the trade. Cornelius P. Shea, who had become the head of the united organization, was not the kind of a leader who could eliminate factionalism. He involved his union in a bitter strike at the Montgomery Ward plant in Chicago, during which Shea and several other leaders of the Chicago teamsters were indicted for extortion. Shea's conduct aroused the membership, and the head of the San Francisco Joint Council appealed to the Executive Council of the American Federation of Labor to remove Shea from his office. The Joint Council of Teamsters in San Francisco held Shea "to be utterly unfit to hold the high office by which he has been honored. He is a disgrace to himself, a dishonor to the teamsters of the country and a stain to the labor movement."[53] As the International Brotherhood was chartered as an autonomous union, the Executive Council had no power to intervene. The members of the organization provided their own remedy in 1906 by ousting Shea and electing Daniel J. Tobin in his place.

Tobin was to serve as president of this union for more than forty years. He, however, took hold of a badly divided organization. In addition to his own union, a dual group, the United Teamsters of America, was seeking to organize the trade. Again the American Federation of Labor intervened, and sought to heal the rift. This time, however, an acceptable peace formula was not devised. Yet Tobin recognized "that all that was possible for any person to do towards bringing both organizations together was done by you, Gompers." The latter would not relax his efforts toward healing the breach, despite the lack of enthusiasm on both sides. Tobin assured Gompers that his "untiring efforts on behalf of unity in the Teamster ranks was fully appreciated."[54] Unable to bring unity into the ranks, the American Federation of Labor denounced the deception practiced by the seceders, proclaimed the International Brotherhood of Teamsters as the only bona fide union in the industry, and ordered its central bodies not to accept the affiliation of teamsters' unions not chartered by the International Brotherhood.

Assessments and Defense Funds

The leaders of the Federation recognized its responsibility to aid affiliates in time of need. Thus the convention of 1887 submitted a proposal authorizing an assessment of five cents per member per week upon affiliates for the support of a strike. It was submitted to the affiliated unions and defeated. The defeat of this proposal, by the international unions, showed, in Gompers' view, that

Either the identity of interests of the toiling masses of our country have not been sufficiently recognized, or the unions are acting upon the belief that each should help itself before attempting to aid the other. In truth, however, the establishment of the former would successfully accomplish the latter. While there may be no present prospect of success in the adoption of this proposition, I recommend that the subject be continually kept before the attention of our organization, so that they, in the course of time, may see the necessity and benefit of adopting this measure.[55]

On the other hand, in 1889 establishment of an assistance fund was approved, the monies provided by an assessment of two cents upon every member of the unions of the Federation. The fund was to be used for support of workers during a strike or lockout. Disbursement of the fund was placed in the hands of the Executive Council, which had the authority to impose the assessment of two cents per member for five consecutive weeks. The essential difference between this fund and the one rejected in 1887 was that the first would have created a fund under the control of the Executive Council of the A. F. of L.; the latter was to be raised only for specific purposes, with the A. F. of L. acting as a conduit and disburser. Unions failing to meet the assessment were to be suspended. It was recognized by the leaders that this requirement ran counter to the principle of voluntarism, which the international unions and the leaders of the Federation regarded as the cornerstone of the American Federation of Labor. Yet the great need for funds and support, especially when unions were engaged in a labor dispute, overcame the fear of centralized power.

Voluntary and Compulsory Assessments

The Federation was almost always willing to issue appeals for voluntary contributions, but usually the response to such appeals was only fair. In his report to the convention of 1889, Gompers declared:

We insist upon the autonomy and independence of trade unions. In the contest to maintain this principle, I take second position to no man. Yet in its advocacy and to further the high mission with which the trade union movement is charged, we, each of our organizations, should stand ready and prepared to render every assistance to protect and advance the interest of any of our fellows with the same fervor and enthusiasm as if we were the ones the blow was directed against.[56]

The authorization for the imposition of an assessment came at a propitious time—when the American Federation of Labor had urged its affiliates to embark upon campaigns for the shorter work day. It was first used in 1890 to raise funds in aid of the members of the Carpenters' Union, who were seeking to establish the eight-hour day. The Federation collected $12,486.94 for this purpose, and an additional $1,220.94 in response to appeals for voluntary contributions. Gompers urged that the right of the Federation to levy assessments be continued, and the system be extended so that directly affiliated federal and trade unions would also be required to contribute. He also recognized that a special defense fund had to be established for the federal and trade unions so that they could be assisted in their ordinary disputes with employers.

Whatever views the unions might have held on the need for mutual support, many were opposed to being taxed for the defense of another group of workers. This attitude was not altogether motivated by selfishness. In some instances the assessment would be levied at a time when some unions were themselves involved in disputes with employers, and finding the burden of supporting their own members out on strike difficult to bear. Such unions were not ready to assume added financial responsibilities. Members of others objected to being taxed for workers in other trades. Thus the Granite Cutters' National Union decided to withdraw from the A. F. of L. because its members refused to pay the assessment levied in support of the eight-hour strike of the Carpenters' Union. Rather than permit this union to withdraw its affiliation, Gompers urged the Executive Council to cancel the union's obligations, which the Council approved.[57]

While the Granite Cutters' Union was the only one that wanted to cancel its affiliation rather than pay the assessment, other national organizations actively opposed the levy. As a result of the experience of the Federation, Treasurer John B. Lennon recommended that the Executive Council's authority to impose assessments be relinquished. He felt that such authority conflicted with the principle of autonomy of the international union. He argued that assessments should be collected only from the strongest organizations; that the amounts that could be collected were small and thereby "a delusion to organizations that depend upon it for assistance in case of any great strike or lockout."[58]

The assessment was nevertheless retained, but the total requests for funds could seldom be met from the income of these assessments. Gompers then suggested that the Federation be allowed to make small assessments to raise a fund for making loans to affiliates. The suggestion was rejected by the convention of 1891. The convention of that year also considered a proposal to set up a "sinking fund" of five hundred thousand dollars to be raised by a levy, the size of which was to be determined by the Executive Council. The amounts contributed by each union were to be under the joint control of the union and officers of the Federation, and could be drawn upon to aid strikes and lockouts approved by the heads of the Federation. The convention asked the Executive Council to formulate a program based upon this proposal. The Council found that the depressed state of business and employment during 1893 made the time unpropitious for the submission of the plan.[59] In 1898 the power of the Executive Council to levy an assessment was temporarily abolished. In 1898 the Treasurer, John B. Lennon, suggested a broader program. Instead of authority in the Executive Council to levy an assessment to support a specific union on strike, his proposal required all unions to pay the A. F. of L. assessments along with their per-capita taxes. The plan, submitted with the approval of Gompers, would have established a defense fund of some magnitude, since it required all affiliated unions to pay an annual per-capita tax of five cents. Organizations which had contributed for at least one year would, in the case of strikes or lockouts, be eligible to draw upon this fund for an amount of three dollars per week for each striking member. The Executive Council was given the authority to investigate the strike or lockout with the purpose of settling the dispute and had the right to deny the request for assistance. In fact, for unions asking this support, the American Federation of Labor would have been able to exercise considerable authority. As finally adopted, the creation of the defense fund was left to the discretion of the Executive Council, the mandatory requirement having been deleted by the Committee on laws.

A year after its enactment, the resolution was characterized "as not even ornamental."[60] The consequence was that the old power to levy an assessment was restored to the Executive Council, except that the assessment was to be one cent per member per week for a maximum of ten weeks. The conditions under which the levy could be imposed were the same as formerly. The power was used sparingly, and a number of unions found the assistance of great aid in times when their unions were facing difficulties with employers. Gompers, among others, was not satisfied with the A. F. of L.'s limited power in this area, for the Federation was faced with constant pleas for financial help. Yet the unions, especially the large and stable ones, were not ready to tax themselves for the benefit of the weaker organizations or the unorganized. Nor were they ready to endow the A. F. of L. with sufficient resources so as to enable it to strike out on an independent course.

Gompers, who frequently had to reject pleas for financial aid during a strike, felt it superfluous

to say . . . how keen I [Gompers] feel the absence of a fund which could be of such valuable assistance to our fellow workers in cases of the kind as one in question, but in spite of all recommendations and advice which are recommended to our organizations and to the working people generally, they only see the necessity for such a fund when they themselves are engaged in conflict, and either vote down such a proposition when they are at peace, or else when such a proposition is by chance adopted, as it was last year, they make it discretionary, and do not avail themselves of it. It occurs ofttimes that such requests are made to this office, and it causes me no little pang when I am compelled to answer as I do in this instance.[61]

The same issue came before the convention in 1901. John B. Lennon, a member of the Executive Council, was aware of the continual appeal of unions for aid, and he therefore proposed an annual levy by the Federation of ten cents per member, with the right to increase the levy up to fifty cents per member per year. The funds collected by these taxes were to be used exclusively in support of strikes and lockouts. No appropriation was to be made unless the union involved had strictly complied with the laws of its own organization. Moreover, funds were not to be used for the first 4 weeks of any strike or lockout unless 10 per cent or more of a union's membership were involved. The proposal would have given the Executive Council of the A. F. of L. the power to investigate before an appropriation was made, and, moreover, the Council would have been given the power to discontinue payments whenever it held such a step advisable.[62] The proposal was rejected without a recorded vote. By allowing the Executive Council of the A. F. of L. to administer the fund and to decide on the desirability of paying strike benefits, the adoption of this proposal would have given the Council power over purely trade matters of autonomous national and international unions. Moreover, it would have favored the weaker unions, as those organizations with large memberships could build up their own defense funds; in addition, the larger organizations would make the larger contributions which could then be used for supporting smaller and weaker unions.

Gompers also recommended the enlargement of the power of the A. F. of L. to levy assessments. He asked also that the Executive Council be directed to levy an assessment early in the year, the fund so created to be at the disposal of the Council to be used in behalf of the affiliated organizations "engaged in a protracted struggle, one which their means will not permit them to singly support." Gompers was convinced that a system of "mutual financial assistance is essential to the success of the trade union movement of every industrial country."[63] The committee viewed "with decided disfavor the idea of the establishment of a defense fund by the American Federation of Labor." Gompers' recommendation was unanimously rejected on the ground "that it is an unsafe policy to offer any incentive for members of an affiliated body to undertake a strike upon the money contributed by other trade unionists." The committee instead urged that the international unions, by a system of adequate dues and assessments, build up their own finances for protective purposes.

The issue reappeared at the convention of 1909, and provoked considerable debate. The proposal at this time called on the Executive Council to devise a program for assessing the members of national and international unions in aid of workers out on strike. The rules under which the funds were to be distributed were also to be devised by the Council. James Duncan argued that the financing of the labor movement was the responsibility of the international unions. Moreover, if a large union were to become involved in a labor dispute, it could easily exhaust the fund, and little would be left for other organizations. Mitchell criticized the proposal as "impracticable" and pointed to the large sum that would have been needed had every striker in the anthracite coal region in 1902 received as little as two dollars a week in benefits. He also objected to the vesting of power in the Executive Council to determine when its affiliates could strike, as such power would have to be granted if such a proposal were adopted. "If," he argued, "we want to go back to the Knights of Labor and submit the affairs of each organization to the judgment of men who are not familiar with them, then . . . refer this to the Executive Council, with the recommendation that they must report some plan next year for the centralization of funds."[64] The plan was defeated.

DEMAND FOR MORE GENEROUS SUPPORT

A serious controversy arose over assessments as a result of the request of the Western Federation of Miners, after the latter union had joined the

A. F. of L. Engaged in a bitter dispute within the Northern Michigan copper mines, the head of Western Federation of Miners, Charles Moyer, requested the Executive Council in August 1913 to "come to our assistance financially and that all organizations of the A. F. of L. be authorized to hold meetings for the purpose of soliciting funds. A victory in the State of Michigan means the organizing of approximately one hundred thousand metal miners in the northern mineral mines."[65] The Executive Council endorsed the appeal.

The appeal for voluntary aid was answered by contributions of $217,357.36, of which the A. F. of L. collected directly $55,173.82. The United Mine Workers of America sent to the Western Federation of Miners, either directly or through the A. F. of L., $102,091.43. The contributions were not, however, adequate to sustain the strikers, and President Moyer requested the Executive Council to levy an assessment in behalf of the strikers. The request was refused, by a vote of eight to one, with Gompers not voting. The argument against the levying of an assessment was that many international unions were in financial difficulties and unable to pay it. Failure would automatically have to lead to suspension from the Federation, as an assessment, under the constitution, occupied the same position as per-capita.

The United Mine Workers of America took up the fight on behalf of the metalliferous miners. A virtual demand that Gompers appear and explain the refusal was made by the Coal Miners' convention. Daniel Tobin, the head of the Teamsters' Union, had wired to the Executive Council that it had been called a collection of "worm-eaten, fossilized booze fighters" by one of the delegates. Tobin demanded that someone be sent to the convention to answer the charges, and as usual that someone was Gompers. It was an unfriendly audience that was waiting to hear him. He repeated the argument that many international unions were not in a position to levy assessments, as they were engaged in strikes of their own. He also argued that an assessment would not be adequate to support the strike, since President Moyer estimated that thirty thousand dollars was needed weekly. He then pointed to the aid given by the Federation to the strikers: the sending of Vice President Mitchell and Treasurer Lennon to the strike area, in addition to organizers; and the successful efforts of the A. F. of L. to have a Congressional investigation of the strike made. Finally, he pointed to the refusal of the last convention to approve an assessment in behalf of the strikers. The delegates listened, but were not convinced.[66]

The internationals were again polled, in 1913, on a proposal that the American Federation of Labor set up a defense fund. The international unions were asked whether they would be willing to vest power in the hands of the Executive Council of the American Federation of Labor to "levy, collect and distribute, in accordance with the rules to be provided, a tax upon each member directly under the jurisdiction of the A. F. of L., through its affiliated national and international unions for the purpose of meeting the expense of any strike or lockout of a national character."[67] Twenty-six internationals expressed their opposition to this plan; nineteen favored it; twenty-two were undecided. A number of unions which opposed the program expressed the view that such a plan would lead to too much concentration of power in the hands of the Federation. The International Association of Machinists, then dominated by Socialists, "could not conceive the possibility of such power being reposed in the A. F. of L. by any national or international organization affiliated therewith." Even more emphatic was the reply of the United Brotherhood of Carpenters and Joiners of America, which was convinced that once the A. F. of L. became involved in the strikes of its affiliates, it would "mean the beginning of the end of the usefulness of the A. F. of L." The other objecting unions found the administration of such a program to be too difficult; others believed it would lead to a proliferation in the levying of assessments which many unions would not be able to pay; and almost all opposed the vesting of plenary power over the affiliates in the American Federation of Labor.

Gompers for many years favored the levying of assessments. He also sought to establish a defense fund that could be used to aid affiliates. These recommendations were always rejected. In some instances, unions were not financially able to pay an assessment. Thus, the United Mine Workers of America asked to be exempted from paying the assessment in the nine-hour strike of the Machinists' Union, and later only paid on part of the membership. In 1910 the United Mine Workers of America asked to be excused from meeting the assessment for the legal defense of the Hatters. Throughout its history this union most readily responded to the needs of other unions or causes. At that time the Miners' Union was engaged in strikes, however, and was straining its resources to support its own members.

The problem of assessments also arose in the McNamara case. On the basis of the then-membership of the A. F. of L., the twenty-five cents assessment requested of every member should have raised approximately $435,000. Only $237,000, or about 55 per cent, was raised. The sum included the large contribution of the Bridge and Structural Iron Workers, the union directly involved. The inadequacy of the response becomes clearer when it is recalled that the McNamara case was one where the need for funds was great and compelling, and where the full resources of the labor movement were utilized to raise the funds needed to form an adequate defense. The heads of the Federation were aware of the unwillingness of affiliates to contribute and of their own inability to compel independent unions to donate monies, no matter how grave the need or righteous the cause.

Between 1889 and 1924, the A. F. of L. levied sixteen assessments: one each for ten, five, and four cents, two for three cents, three for two cents, and eight for one cent. A total of $216,131.88 was collected, which does not include the numerous voluntary contributions made in behalf of various causes and organizations by the affiliates. In every instance where an assessment was levied, there were unions which could not pay the tax.

Gompers changed his views of the desirability of a central defense fund administered by the Federation. He feared that a central defense fund might lead to

the creation of a dictatorship of the few over the lives of the workers, and I am as much opposed to such a dictatorship in the organized labor movement of our country as I am opposed to the dictatorial powers which the legislative and executive bodies of our government undertake to enact into laws, and the judiciary interpreting and stretching and usurping powers over constitutional rights guaranteed to the people, and particularly when they are working people.[68]

REFERENCES

1. *Report of Proceedings of the Tenth Annual Convention of the American Federation of Labor*, 1890, p. 14.

2. *Report of Proceedings of the Eleventh Annual Convention of the American Federation of Labor*, 1891, p. 12.

3. *Report of Proceedings of the Twelfth Annual Convention of the American Federation of Labor*, 1892, p. 17.

4. *Report of Proceedings of the Seventeenth Annual Convention of the American Federation of Labor*, 1897, p. 15.

5. Gompers to the Mechanists, Molders, Painters, Printers, and Granite Cutters' unions, May 28, 1897.

6. *Report of Proceedings of Seventeenth Annual Convention of the American Federation of Labor*, 1897, p. 32.

7. Gompers to William Anderson, secretary of Brotherhood of Brass Workers' Union, August 15, 1893.

8. *Report of Proceedings of Fourteenth Annual Convention of the American Federation of Labor*, 1894, p. 35.

9. *Report of Proceedings of the Seventeenth Annual Convention of the American Federation of Labor*, 1897, p. 88.

10. James O'Connell to Gompers, June 16, 1897.

11. *Report of Proceedings of the Eighteenth Annual Convention of the American Federation of Labor*, 1898, p. 100.

12. *Report of Proceedings of the Nineteenth Annual Convention of the American Federation of Labor*, 1899, p. 29.

13. *Report of Proceedings of the Twentieth Annual Convention of the American Federation of Labor*, 1900, p. 35.

14. *Report of Proceedings of the Twelfth Annual Convention of the American Federation of Labor*, 1892, p. 18.

15. *Report of Proceedings of the Fourteenth Annual Convention of the American Federation of Labor*, 1894, pp. 18-19.

16. *Report of Proceedings of the Fifteenth Annual Convention of the American Federation of Labor*, 1895, p. 19.

17. *Report of Proceedings of the Eleventh Annual Convention of the American Federation of Labor*, 1891, p. 42.

18. Circular in the archives of the American Federation of Labor.

19. Gompers to Samuel Goldwater, October 3, 1893; W. J. Law to Gompers, October 21, 1893.

20. Gompers to F. J. Weber, August 24, 1893.

21. Gompers to F. J. Weber, August 24, 1893.

22. Albert Harmon to Gompers, June 15, 1894.

23. Alexander Bremer to John McBride, July 25, 1895.

24. Bremer to McBride, July 25, 1895.

25. James Duncan to Owen Miller, April 29, 1895.

26. Gompers to Frank H. Wade, September 1, 1896.

27. Vote Book of Executive Council, March 2, 1896.

28. Vote Book of Executive Council, May 6, 1896.

29. Gompers to Frank Wade, September 3, 1896.

30. Gompers to Owen Miller, November 20, 1896.

31. Gompers to Jacob J. Schmalz, April 5, 1897.

32. Gompers to Owen Miller, June 16, 1897.

33. *Report of Proceedings of the Fourteenth Annual Convention of the American Federation of Labor*, 1894, p. 27.

34. August McCraith to the Brotherhood of Painters and Decorators, March 4, 1895.

35. W. S. de Veaux to John McBride, January 10, 1895.

36. John McBride to Frank Mooney, May 17, 1895.

37. Minutes of Executive Council of the A. F. of L., February 22, 1898.

38. Minutes of the Executive Council of the A. F. of L., February 23, 1898.

39. John Barrett to Gompers, July 24, 1898; Gompers to Barrett, July 27, 1898.

40. *Report of Proceedings of the Eighteenth Annual Convention of the American Federation of Labor*, 1898, pp. 50-51.

41. Gompers to John Barrett, March 9, 1899.

42. Gompers to Executive Council, March 27, 1899.

43. Gompers to Francis Kneeland, July 10, 1899.

44. "Official Proceedings of the Conference to Unite the Brotherhood of Painters and Decorators of America," Vote Book of the Executive Council of the A. F. of L., June 21, 1900.

45. Circular issued by the A. F. of L., February 6, 1899.

46. George Innis to Frank Morrison, March 16, 1899.

47. Gompers to James Duncan, R. W. Carrity, John F. Tobin, and John F. O'Sullivan, October 24, 1901. Tobin was a leading socialist.

48. Innis to Frank Morrison, September 30, 1901.

49. Gompers to George Innis, September 27, 1902.

50. Gompers to George Innis, August 28, 1902.

51. Minutes of the Executive Council, January 16, April 21, 1903; *Proceedings of the Joint Convention of the Team Drivers' International Union, the Teamsters' National Union and Proceedings of the Convention of the International Brotherhood of Teamsters*, 1903, p. 5.

52. William Prescott to Gompers, April 14, 1893; Gompers to Prescott, April 18, 1893; Gompers to Executive Council, April 18, 1893.

53. E. T. O'Day to Executive Council of the American Federation of Labor, undated, but written in the winter of 1905.

54. Daniel Tobin to Gompers, October 1, 1907; November 7, 1907.

55. *Official Report of Proceedings of the Second Annual Convention of the American Federation of Labor*, 1887, p. 22; *Report of Proceedings of the Third Annual Convention of the American Federation of Labor*, 1888, pp. 11-12.

56. *Report of Proceedings of the Ninth Annual Convention of the American Federation of Labor*, 1889, p. 17.

57. Gompers to Executive Council, January 28, 1891.

58. *Report of Proceedings of the Eighth Annual Convention of the American Federation of Labor*, 1891, p. 20.

59. *Report of the Twelfth Annual Convention of the American Federation of Labor*, 1892, pp. 31-32; *Report of Proceedings of the Thirteenth Annual Convention of the American Federation of Labor*, 1893, p. 41.

60. *Report of the Proceedings of the Nineteenth Annual Convention of the American Federation of Labor*, 1899, p. 146.

61. Gompers to Daniel Harris, who had asked the A. F. of L. for aid in a strike, April 6, 1900.

62. *Report of the Proceedings of the Twenty-First Annual Convention of the American Federation of Labor*, 1901, p. 197.

63. *Report of Proceedings of the Twenty-Second Annual Convention of the American Federation of Labor*, 1901, pp. 15, 185-186.

64. *Report of Proceedings of the Twenty-Ninth Annual Convention of the American Federation of Labor*, 1909, p. 216.

65. Moyer to Gompers, August 22, 1913.

66. Gompers to Executive Council, January 15, 1914; February 4, 1914.

67. *Report of the Proceedings of the Thirty-Fourth Annual Convention of the American Federation of Labor*, 1914, pp. 62-66.

68. Gompers to W. E. Bryan, December 31, 1921.

VII

Depression and Recovery

UNEMPLOYMENT

The decline of business and employment had, up to the emergence of the American Federation of Labor, almost always proved fatal to the existing labor movement. The great depression which spread over the economy in the early 1890's was to test the mettle of the A. F. of L. According to the Executive Council more than three million workers were out of work. Gompers, in his report to the convention of 1893, attributed the growth of unemployment to the increases in production which were unaccompanied by parallel increases in consuming power.

In a society where such abnormal conditions prevail there must of necessity be something wrong at the basic foundations, and it requires but little study to come to the conclusion that the ownership and control of the wealth, of the means of production, by private corporations which have no human sympathy or apparent responsibility, is the cause of the ills and wrongs borne by the human family.[1]

Gompers' remedy was not socialization, but "a guarantee that employment, remunerative and healthful is accorded to all." He again emphasized the importance for providing immediate relief, and reducing the hours of labor. He believed that "a practical, just and safe equilibrium can be maintained in the industrial world for the fast and ever increasing introduction of machinery, by a commensurate reduction of the hours of labor."[2]

The American labor movement was able to survive, and Gompers was "elated by the manner [in] which we have withstood its fearful effects." He was convinced that lessons had been learned during the depression which "upon the first revival of industry give an impetus to our movement unparalleled in the history of America."[3]

The difficulties facing the unions as a result of lessened employment continued into 1895, and Secretary McCraith reported to the Executive Council that

Secretaries generally complain of dullness, a reduction of membership and a few have suspended. The continued depression has compelled members to change both location and employment, thus weakening the union. . . . A large

123

number of unions, national, state and local are in arrears; they have been notified by letter and indirectly in the Federationist, and will no doubt settle later on. For the present we have no money for special appropriations or anything of a cost nature.[4]

EFFECT OF DEPRESSION ON A. F. OF L. ACTIVITY

The slump in income affected the Federation, and forced it to neglect many essential activities because of lack of funds. President McBride apologized for not being able to support the Utah eight-hour case then coming before the courts.

We are not in a condition, financially, to aid you. The hard time . . . has made every labor union feel its blighting effect, and today there are few organizations in a position to help themselves, while nearly all are compelled to neglect, for the want of funds, things that should be attended to. This condition of things has multiplied the demands upon us for financial aid and so lessened the ability of our affiliated bodies to pay per capita tax that we have been almost swamped financially and are, temporarily at least, under the necessity of refusing to grant meritorious requests.[5]

Some issues or events of more than normal significance were considered. For example, the Thirteenth convention considered a resolution "making it obligatory on the part of corporations and the representatives of capital to treat and negotiate with the representatives of labor in conference or otherwise." It was defeated by a vote of 1052 to 1243. On the other hand, the convention asked for a law which would prohibit employers from interfering with the organizations of their employees. The convention also approved a resolution sponsored by the International Typographical Union endorsing government ownership of the telegraph system. Publication of a monthly magazine was authorized, and the first issue of the *American Federationist* appeared in the following year. Gompers had always been anxious to publish a regular journal.

The convention declared that the

pardoning of the so-called Chicago anarchists by Governor Altgeld, of the State of Illinois, is but a simple act of justice. *Whereas*, the conviction and incarceration of Fielden, Schwab and Neebe was the result of class prejudice and persecution at a time when the public mind was influenced with passion; and *Whereas*, the Governor of Illinois, in the face of a set resolve of the capitalist class to the contrary, had had the courage to defy power and opposition, in defense of innocence and justice, thus proving his honesty and sincerity of heart; therefore be it *Resolved*, by the American Federation of Labor in convention assembled, that we indorse the Governor's action and accept the reasons he assigns as in line with the true facts of the case.

The resolution was unanimously adopted without a single voice of protest from the floor.[6]

OPPOSITION TO GOMPERS

Considerable criticism was directed against Gompers at the convention of 1893 for the issuance of a souvenir book. This type of publication had been issued at convention time for several years. Questions of the use of money and the general financing of the enterprise had been raised. A special committee of five had been appointed to look into the matter. It reported that the "Executive Council are blameless in the matter. We find that a souvenir had been contracted for by the President Gompers, and the amount received for the same, has, we believe, been expended by him in the interest of the Federation."[7] At the same convention, the Executive Council was enlarged to include four instead of two vice presidents.

Contests for offices at conventions were becoming more frequent. It would indicate that they were now regarded of some importance, since at the early conventions delegates had to be urged to accept election.

At the convention of 1891 for example, H. J. Burt of the Flint Glass Workers, and August Delabar of the Bakery Workers had opposed Gompers. Together they had received 655 votes to 1378 for Gompers. The second vice presidency and the office of treasurer were also contested in that year. William A. Carney of the Iron and Steel Workers was chosen over Edward Coogan of the Lasters' Protective Union for the vice presidency and John B. Lennon, a tailor, was chosen treasurer over the opposition of August Delabar. Only the latter two officers were challenged at the convention of 1892, and both were reelected.

Up to 1893, opposition to Gompers for the office of the presidency was nominal. This was certainly true in 1890, when T. J. Morgan, a leading Socialist, opposed him. His opposition was more formidable at the convention of 1893. His opponent that year was John McBride, a leading trade unionist and officer of the United Mine Workers of America. P. J. McGuire declined the nomination in favor of McBride. Gompers was reelected by the narrow margin of 1314 to 1222.[8]

DEFEAT OF GOMPERS

At the convention of 1894, the situation was to be different. Gompers had noted that because of depressed business and employment the Denver convention was likely to be dominated by local people from the Denver area. In his opinion, this would mean that a local rather than a national view was likely to predominate. The convention was destined to be a hectic one, as the political program, presented by the Socialists, was to be the chief topic of discussion. There were seventy-seven, or eighteen fewer, delegates present at the convention of 1894 than there had been in the preceding year. Moreover, there were sixteen fewer organizations represented in 1894. More than four hundred fewer votes were cast for the office of the presidency in 1894 than in 1893. The main reasons for the lower representation were the large unemployment and the financial difficulties suffered by many unions.[9]

In the contest for the presidency, Gompers was again opposed by Mc-Bride, and the latter was elected by 1170 to 976 votes. It is true that Gompers had lost some Socialist votes, but he gained the votes of two delegates from the Carpenters' Union, the Molders' Union delegation, the votes of the delegates from the Iron and Steel Workers' Union. It should, however, be noted that the voting in 1893 was reasonably close and that almost any shift in sentiment or differences over any issue might have been adequate to defeat the incumbent. Gompers' defeat in 1894 seems attributable to the smaller number of delegates in the later year.

JOHN MCBRIDE

McBride had been a pioneer leader of the Coal Miners' Union, and he had helped to establish the organization in his native state, Ohio. In 1888, he had sought the endorsement of the A. F. of L. for the United States Commissioner of Labor. Gompers placed the matter before the Executive Council which refused to get involved. The same policy was in the next few years followed with other requests for political endorsement by others, and the refusal to support McBride in no way reflected hostility toward him.[10]

John McBride was born in Wayne County, Ohio, in 1854, and went to work in the coal mines at the age of nine. He joined the Ohio Miners' Union in 1870, and in 1883 he became its president. He served in the Ohio legislature in 1883 and 1885, and was the Democratic candidate for Secretary of State in 1886.

In many respects, the man who temporarily succeeded Gompers was quite unlike him in both temperament and experience. Gompers was acquainted with the various brands of radicalism then struggling to win influence over the labor movement. He was also sensitive to the limitations of his position. Moreover, Gompers had never developed the imperious attitude one sometimes finds among heads of all types of organizations, including labor. He had been an officer of his union, but never headed the organization. His espousal of autonomy of international unions, as well as his knowledge of the Federation, made him recognize that while he might persuade he had no power to coerce. He might, it is true, ask for the expulsion of a recalcitrant union, but this was a dangerous and self-defeating process, and could in time lead to the disintegration of the A. F. of L.

McBride had other ideas of the functions and duties of the head of the movement. As head of the United Mine Workers of America, he had participated in many battles to establish the union in the coal fields. He was elected to office at a time when economic conditions made the expansion of the unions difficult. Many unions found it difficult merely to maintain their positions. As a result, McBride could, at the end of his term, report little progress and few innovations. McBride also suffered from illness and for some time he was unable to conduct the business of the Federation. As McGuire, the first vice president, was the secretary treasurer of the United Brotherhood of Carpenters and Joiners of America and a full-time officer, McBride asked James Duncan, the second vice president, to serve in his place. In making this decision, he failed to consult the Executive Council, and one of the members found this decision "hard to believe."[11]

McBride tried to follow a forceful policy in relation to the national and international unions, over which he had no control. He was outspoken and quick to take offense. Instead of trying to placate and persuade those who differed with him, he sought to bully and threaten. He denied the head of the Brewery Workers' Union a chance to reply to a criticism published in the *American Federationist,* and when the latter insisted upon criticizing the Executive Council, he was told that he had maligned the Executive Council's personal characters "by assigning as reasons for the action taken causes having no existence in fact, but which had their source in your imagination and distorted brain."[12]

An officer of the International Machinists' Union who protested against the chartering of a rival, the International Association of Machinists, was informed: "You assume a knowledge which you do not possess, and writing me as you do you simply exposed your ignorance as an official and gave evidence of your boorishness as a man."[13] In a dispute with the head of another union over organizing a group of cornice workers alleged to be "unfair men," McBride charged the information that had been given to him was not true.

The members . . . have been charged with being expelled or suspended members of other unions, with having scabbed. . . . Your International Association cannot afford, neither can we, to stand idly by while being charged with having, fostering, scabs in our ranks, and your organization, by its indifference and negligence, assumes such a position and forces us to either proceed summarily against your association or stand equally guilty.[14]

McBride also became involved in a controversy with the International Furniture Workers' Union, and the latter preferred charges against him. An investigation by a special committee absolved him of all guilt.[15] On top of all of his controversies, McBride published an article in the *New York World* endorsing compulsory arbitration,[16] in spite of the Thirteenth convention's rejection of this stand.

In his report to the convention of 1895, McBride expressed the view that the preceeding convention had adopted the political platform. He argued "that wage workers cannot hope to be free in the shops, mines and factories while trudging in a party slavery to the polls." He, however, warned of allowing distant ideals to stand in the way of practical action. He recognized that the mission

of the trade unions has always been that of regulating the conditions of employment, and the securing of proper remuneration therefore, in the interests of those who work for wages, it must not be forgotten that the trades union movement has a general mission, and a world-wide work to perform in its efforts to establish the brotherhood of man regardless of creed, color or nationality.[17]

In the elections for office, Gompers was returned to the presidency. He defeated McBride by a vote of 1041 to 1023, or a majority of 18. McBride was supported by many old line trade unionists, and was nominated by James Duncan, who was to serve with Gompers on the Executive Council for many years. The two delegates from the Brewery Workers' Union, an organization that had supported McBride in 1894, voted for Gompers in 1895. The bitter controversy between the head of the Federation and this union undoubtedly influenced their votes. There were contests for three of the vice presidencies, McGuire alone being unanimously elected.

James Duncan, the incumbent second vice president, was comfortably reelected, but Duncan, who was to become a leading collaborator of Gompers, was opposed by Charles Reichers of the United Garment Workers. In this contest McGuire and Gompers were on opposite sides; Gompers supporting Reichers, a Socialist, and McGuire, Duncan. The reasons for Gompers' opposition were not disclosed, but it may have been because Duncan had nominated McBride for reelection. James O'Connell, whose union, the International Association of Machinists, had just been allowed to affiliate with the Federation, was chosen third vice president over Rhody Kenehan of the Horseshoers' Union. For fourth vice president, the failure of any candidate to gain a majority on the first ballot necessitated a runoff, and on the second ballot M. M. Garland of the Iron and Steel Workers defeated William D. Mahon of the Street Car Men's Union. The latter was a Socialist at the time, but he was to become subsequently a pure and simple trade unionist and a close collaborator of Gompers.

Recovery in Business and Organizing

The secretary was able to report to the convention of 1896 that the A. F. of L. had made a satisfactory recovery, due in large part to the efforts of the 267 voluntary organizers. Despite the higher income which followed the rise in activity and membership, the Federation could report a balance of only about seven hundred dollars. Its lack of resources did not prevent local unions and even internationals from appealing for aid, and often the requests could only partly be met, if at all. Much of the activity of the Federation, at the time, was not even reported to the conventions. Gompers, Duncan, Lennon, and O'Connell were continually on the move helping other unions with their problems. Even organizations as well established as the International Typographical Union occasionally appealed to the A. F. of L. For example, James Duncan was directed by the Executive Council to help the Typographical Union negotiate a contract with the Arena Publishing Company in 1898.

In one month Gompers helped the Bicycle Workers' Union negotiate an agreement with the National Cash Register Company, and he helped the Journeymen Horseshoers' Union settle differences with Annheuser Busch Brewing Company in St. Louis. He aided, too, the Tobacco Workers' National Union in negotiations with the Brown Tobacco Company and Liggett and Myers. James O'Connell assisted the Wood Workers in Chicago in negotiating an agreement, the Shoe Workers in the same city, and the Brewery Workers in Rochester, New York. When the members of the Executive Council could not furnish the aid, the heads of the Federation would enlist some other labor men.[18] In behalf of a group of railroad men who were unable to negotiate a satisfactory agreement, the A. F. of L. enlisted the service of Henry C. Barter, the Secretary of the International Longshoremen's Union. The head of the same union was enlisted to aid the shoemakers in Rochester, New York, in a dispute between them and their employers. These are only a few of the cases of direct aid given by members of the A. F. of L. to the labor movement.[19]

Convention of 1896

In his report to the convention, in 1896, Gompers noted that trade unions were as a rule without a platform of principles.

declaratory of purpose to which the flights of imagination often soar, but which so frequently, but simply, appeal to the passions. . . . The trade unions are the business organizations of the wage earners . . . to secure for the toilers relief from the long hours of burdensome toil, and find work for those who cannot find work at all, to fight for full enfranchisement of labor, not only at the polls, in the halls of legislation, but far more important than all these, in the factory work shop and mine.[20]

He advised that the Federation continue on its practical path. More-over, he advised the trade unions to "exercise care in the expressions of our declarations, so that our motives and purposes may not be misunder-stood by friends or foes. Dealing with the real, rather than the ideal, we easily discern the differences between the consciousness of our rights and hatred of others. . . ."[21]

One practical step was to increase dues so as to strengthen the power of the union. The A. F. of L. could not affect the dues of internationals, but it could prescribe the charges for its federal and trade unions. Mc-Guire's proposal that the latter be required to charge at least fifty cents a month dues evoked a long debate, and it was approved by a vote of 40 to 28.

On political questions, the convention of 1896 reaffirmed its approval of the free coinage of silver at a sixteen to one ratio. Such resolutions had been approved by the conventions of 1893, 1894, and 1895. Because of the political overtones of this issue, as the demand for free coinage of silver had been a plank in the Democratic platform in the campaign of 1896, the convention denied that "in the adoption of the principles of free coinage we in any degree endorse any political party that may have made free coinage a partisan political question." Although the resolution was opposed by delegates who were Socialists, and several who were sup-porters of the Republican Party, it was adopted by a vote of 1915 to 362.

PRESIDENTIAL CAMPAIGN

The role of the A. F. of L. officers in the presidential campaign of 1896 came under scrutiny. Organizers had been instructed by the Executive Council that they were not to become engaged in active campaigning for any political party. William C. Pomeroy, a delegate from the Hotel and Restaurant Employees, and an organizer of the American Federation of Labor, was charged with signing a political circular endorsing the Re-publican Party. His commission had been canceled by the Executive Council, and there was now a demand that he be denied a seat at the convention of 1896. The circular had also been signed by a James A. O'Connell, who was confused with the head of the International Associa-tion of Machinists, James O'Connell. The latter charged "a lie had been attempted in the name of the Federation. He [O'Connell] was not there to question a member's political rights, but . . . no man had right politically to represent himself to be an officer of the Federation according to our constitution, to sign his name to any political document."[22] After a long debate, Pomeroy was denied a seat.

A charge was also made by Secretary McCraith that Gompers had violated the nonpartisan policy of the American Federation of Labor by supporting the Democratic candidates in the presidential election of 1896. The convention considered the charges in executive session and voted its "fullest confidence" in Gompers.[23] McCraith was not a candidate for reelection, and he was replaced by Frank Morrison, another printer who was to serve for more than forty years. In discussing McCraith, five years after he retired, Gompers described him as

difficult personally [but] so far as financial honesty is concerned, cannot be questioned. He was also a competent official. He did seek to impose his theories upon the movement, regardless of the attitude of the organization. It was this which caused any friction between him and me. He seemed to suspect everyone of wrongdoing who did not agree entirely with him in his theories of philosophical anarchy. This, with an additional failing of overweening conceit which prompted him to imagine that he "knew it all and that there was no depth" to any one whose studies and convictions of the social problem did not coincide absolutely with his, was his gravest fault. This fault made it exceedingly difficult for any one to get along with him, and which brought upon his retirement.[24]

CONVENTIONS OF 1897, 1898, AND 1899

The convention of 1897 was in a sense uneventful. Perhaps its most important decision was to raise the per-capita tax on national and international unions from one-fourth to one-third of a cent per member per month, and of federal and trade unions from one to two cents per member per month.

The convention considered the request for aid by striking textile workers at Atlanta, Georgia, and a special committee reviewed the problem of these workers. The convention suggested that the Executive Council give such aid as was possible, and send one of its members to help the strikers. This direction was subsequently carried out.

During 1898, the American Federation of Labor faced another challenge. Ideological and regional dual unions were being organized, neither of which was to become a serious threat. Closely related to the revival of dual unionism was a movement for the withdrawal of single unions from the American Federation of Labor. Such proposals were submitted to the convention of the Carpenters' Union, and received only five votes; a similar one was defeated on a referendum within the International Typographical Union. Gompers attributed the movement for the withdrawal of international unions from the A. F. of L. to Socialist influences, and denounced such efforts as "treachery" which if successful, would inflict serious damage upon the labor movement and the rank and file within the unions.[25]

The convention of 1898 renewed its endorsement of the free coinage of silver. James Duncan, a member of the Executive Council, urged a more cautious approach, but he was overruled, and the convention reiterated its views on the subject.

The Executive Council was also divided on increasing the per-capita payments to be made by members of federal unions. On this question, Gompers drew a distinction between his belief in high dues for members of internationl unions and those who are members of organizations directly affiliated with the A. F. of L. He favored high dues as a general principle, because it was necessary for the success of the organizations. However, he did not believe it was wise to place too great burdens upon the unskilled workers, over one hundred thousand of whom belonged to federal labor unions. Nevertheless, the convention, by a vote of 47 to 17, voted to increase the per-capita tax of federal locals.

The convention of 1899 met when the labor movement was in the midst of the first great revival after a serious business depression. The predictions of the leaders, that once having withstood the decline in employment they would be in an excellent position to win new adherents with the first improvement in business, were amply borne out. The Federation still lacked the finances to engage in extensive campaigns on its own, but it had already demonstrated its usefulness to furnish aid— financial, organizational, and moral—to the labor movement. During that year the Order of Railroad Telegraphers affiliated, the first union of railroad employees to join. The convention also endorsed a recommendation of Gompers that central labor unions authorize the formation of building trades' councils. Such councils had been formed by building trades' unions beginning with the 1880's, and were at times a source of division within the local labor movements. Under the rule adopted, city centrals would allow building trades' councils to function, on the theory that the workers in these organizations had special problems to handle.

A resolution asking the release of Alexander Berkman, an anarchist who had been imprisoned in 1892 for his assault upon H. C. Frick during the Homestead strike, was adopted. Berkman, a youth of nineteen, had been deeply moved by the violent struggle at Homestead. He decided to avenge the attacks upon the strikers, and attacked Frick in his office; for this assault he was subsequently sentenced to twenty-two years in prison. In the opinion of the convention, the sentence was

excessive and far beyond the limit of the law, brought about by the excitement and prejudice prevailing at the time the offense was committed, and that the ends of justice had been fully satisfied with the four years of imprisonment of Alexander Berkman, considering the act as one committed by a misguided youth, and that clemency could be extended in this case, as in many similar ones in times gone by.[26]

Gompers, on his own, subsequently appealed to Senator Boies Penrose, the leader of the Republican Party in Pennsylvania, to use his influence to have Berkman released. Despite these efforts the pardon was not granted, and Berkman was not released until 1906.

Whether the Federation should express its sympathy for the Cuban people in their fight for freedom from Spain also aroused some debate. Samuel Donnelly, the head of the International Typographical Union, believed in concentrating upon wages and hours at home. On the other hand, Andrew Furuseth favored freedom, but he feared the resolution would help to encourage incendiary action in Cuba, which would result in an increase in the government debt and the creation of a permanent army. Gompers spoke at length in favor of the resolution. For him

Liberty, truth and freedom was the basis of the make-up of the world. He was a trade unionist in America and England, but he would be a socialist in Germany, and in Russia a nihilist. . . . It was necessary for the different classes interested in Cuba to unite to achieve their purpose as it was for wage workers to unite with the capitalists in baronial times.[27]

References

1. *Report of Proceedings of Thirteenth Annual Convention of the American Federation of Labor*, 1893, p. 11.

2. *Ibid.*, pp. 11-12.

3. Gompers to Tom Mann, May 10, 1894.

4. August McCraith to Executive Council, April 22, 1895.

5. John McBride to Edward Gaby, July 1, 1895.

6. *Report of Proceedings of the Thirteenth Annual Convention of the American Federation of Labor*, 1893, p. 31.

7. *Ibid.*, p. 56.

8. Among leading trade unionists who supported McBride were P. J. McGuire and the rest of the delegation from the Carpenters' Union; Martin Fox and Joseph Valentine of the Molders' Union; the entire delegation from the Mine Workers' Union; the Iron and Steel Workers' delegation, and a number of others. The delegates from the Shoe Workers, Bakers, Brewery Workers, Tailors, Longshoremen's, and Sailors' unions were among those who supported Gompers.

9. Gompers to McGuire, November 1, 1894.

10. Gompers to Executive Council, June 29, 1888; to William Martin, January 5, 1889; to John McBride, July 7, 1888.

11. John B. Lennon to August McCraith, February 17, 1895.

12. McBride to Charles F. Bechtold, July 15, 1895.

13. McBride to Daniel J. Sullivan, August 2, 1895.

14. McBride to James F. Hughes, June 15, 1895.

15. Minutes of Executive Council, December 7, 1895.

16. P. J. McGuire to August McCraith, February 18, 1895.

17. *Report of the Proceedings of the Fifteenth Annual Convention of the American Federation of Labor*, 1895, p. 17.

18. Gompers to Executive Council, April 26, 1898.

19. Gompers to D. J. Keefe, August 31, 1898; Gompers to Henry C. Barter, January 28, 1899; *Report of Proceedings of the Seventeenth Annual Convention of the American Federation of Labor*, 1897, p. 43.

20. *Report of the Sixteenth Annual Convention of the American Federation of Labor*, 1896, p. 12.

21. *Ibid.*, p. 2.

22. *Ibid.*, p. 37.

23. Samuel Gompers, *Seventy Years of Life and Labor* (New York: E. P. Dutton and Co., 1925) I. p. 378; Samuel Gompers, *American Federationist*, August 1896, pp. 129-130.

24. Gompers to James E. Bell, January 31, 1901.

25. Gompers to McGuire, October 4, 1898; *Report of Proceedings of the Eighteenth Annual Convention of the American Federation of Labor*, 1898, p. 17.

26. Gompers to Boies Penrose, April 19, 1899; *Report of Proceedings of the Sixteenth Annual Convention of the American Federation of Labor*, 1896, p. 55.

27. *Report of Proceedings of Sixteenth Annual Convention of the American Federation of Labor*, 1896, p. 53.

VIII

Homestead, the Bituminous Coal Strike, and the American Federation of Labor

HOMESTEAD

The battle of Homestead, Pennsylvania, between strikers of the Carnegie Steel Company and a boatload of Pinkerton guards seeking to approach the plant of the company by barges on the Monongahela River, shook the labor movement. Homestead was a leading steel-producing community, and relations between the Carnegie Steel Company and the Amalgamated Association of Iron and Steel Workers of America had for years been friendly. In 1889, Henry C. Frick, who had already established a reputation as an anti-union employer, was appointed manager of the Company's properties. When negotiations for a renewal of the contract started in the spring of 1892, the company demanded a reduction of wages for some of the departments and a change in the date of the expiration of its contract. Obviously believing the demand would be rejected, the company contracted with the Pinkerton Detective Agency, which was to supply it with armed guards in the event of a walkout.

Andrew Carnegie was not in the country, having taken his usual vacation in his native Scotland. He later claimed the strike was allowed to take place without his approval. "No grief of my life," he wrote Gompers twenty years later, "approaches that of Homestead. My rule was never to have a strike, never think of employing new men. Never:—Confer with the old men, and assure them we never would try to do without them . . . You know from experience what it is to suffer unjustly."[1]

No agreement was reached and, as anticipated by Frick, a suspension of work followed on June 29, 1892. At the beginning of the strike, a picket line was thrown around the plant, and it was not possible to enter the premises without encountering the resistance of the pickets. Thereupon the Company decided to move the armed guards up the Monongahela River in barges and to land them undetected on the Company's property, where they presumably would be able to reopen the plant. The plan failed, for at the prearranged signal, armed men, women, and children assembled to prevent the guards from landing. When the gang plank was shoved out from one of the barges, and a landing attempted, warnings were shouted and, in the excitement, a shot was fired—by whom was never ascertained. It was the opening of a general battle.

In the meantime, the tug which had towed the barges with their human cargo withdrew, closing any avenue of escape. The battle lasted for twelve hours, ending at five in the afternoon. Three guards and seven workers were killed and many wounded. On the promise of Hugh O'Donnell, the leader of the strikers, that they would be given safe passage, the guards surrendered. The crowd, maddened by the violence and bloodshed, was in no mood for magnanimity or compassion. The hapless guards were assaulted and unmercifully beaten by their captors, despite the efforts of the leaders to prevent reprisals. Peace was restored, and on July 10th, after cessation of the violence, the militia arrived and took charge of law enforcement.[2]

As soon as Gompers learned of events in Homestead, he sought to be of assistance to the workers involved. As a first step he established a committee to seek to prevent the recruitment of strikebreakers. Union men were placed on guard "at all labor agencies in and around New York to persuade unfair workmen from taking the places of their striking brothers at Homestead."[3] Another step was to propose the calling of a session of the Executive Council at Pittsburgh, close to the center of the battle. He, of course, first sought the approval of William Weihe, head of the Amalgamated Association of Iron and Steel Workers. Weihe was assured that Gompers was "anxious to do whatever lies in my power and will be to the advantage of the Association in this contest. For this reason, I have submitted a proposition to the Executive Council for the purpose of holding a meeting in Pittsburgh."[4] Weihe did not think the meeting of the Council would be helpful at the time, and in response to his wishes the meeting was not scheduled. It was held later in the strike.

In the middle of July, Hugh O'Donnell, Hugh Ross, and five others were charged with the murder of one of the Pinkerton guards. In September, almost two hundred more indictments for murder, riot, and conspiracy were returned by the Grand Jury.

In the defense of the indicted, and in mobilizing aid for the strikers, the American Federation of Labor played an important role. On August 19, 1892, the Executive Council issued its appeal for the Homestead strikers. It urged workers to remain away from the plant, and union men to support the strikers financially. Subsequently, December 13th was designated as "Homestead Day," and union men and sympathizers were requested to donate a portion of a day's pay to aid the strikers. The Executive Council actively participated in the planning of the defense, and at Gompers' suggestion W. W. Ervin was retained as one of the attorneys. The American Federation of Labor raised over seven thousand dollars in behalf of the strikers and the men on trial. Three defendants were brought to trial and quickly acquitted by the jury. The strike was, however, broken by the Company.[5]

In the Homestead episode, the American Federation of Labor clearly demonstrated its value to a constituent union. As a first step it immediately associated itself with the cause of the workers. The Federation, through its officers, actively participated in the planning of the case and raised considerable funds for the support of the men involved and their families. Considering the age and resources of the Federation at the time, its efforts in Homestead dramatically demonstrated the value of the organization to the constituent unions.

THE COAL MINERS

The coal miners were among the workers who in the 1890's received considerable aid from the American Federation of Labor. In a sense, the ability of the Federation to provide aid, even though necessarily on a small scale, demonstrated the utility of the A. F. of L. to the unorganized. In contrast with many workers of the time, conditions in the mining camps made recruiting and maintenance of unions extremely difficult. Moreover, the coal miners had not yet achieved the cohesion and unity which have since become characteristic of the workers in that industry.

Almost from the beginning the A. F. of L. had helped the Miners' Union with funds and organizers. One of its first acts on behalf of a constituent union was the appointment, at the suggestion of Gompers, of an organizer for the Ohio coal fields in 1888. When the United Mine Workers of America was established, the Federation again financed organizers for the union in the coal industry.[6] In 1892, the American Federation of Labor donated five hundred dollars to the strike of coal miners in Tennessee. This was in addition to a donation of five hundred dollars to the metal miners on strike and in the stockades in Coeur d'Alene, Idaho. The donations represented almost one-third of the balance in the A. F. of L. treasury.

After the unsuccessful strike of 1894, the United Mine Workers of America faced difficult times. Unable to pay its per-capita tax, Secretary W. C. Pearce wrote that, as the union had no funds, it would be forced to accept suspension from the A. F. of L. for failure to meet its contributions. Gompers refused to accept this proposal. He believed it was the duty of the A. F. of L. to relieve the "organization from a burden it cannot at the moment bear, and thus not necessarily lose its valued membership." Funds were donated to the union so it would be able to meet its commitments. Because the convention of the American Federation of Labor had decided against the making of loans to affiliates, Gompers asked the Executive Council "to make a donation [of one thousand dollars] recognizing the necessity which must prevail in the United Mine Workers' Union."[7]

Despite the empty treasury and low state of their membership, the United Mine Workers of America believed in 1897 that conditions were favorable for the establishment of the union in the bituminous coal fields of the middle west, and in Pennsylvania and West Virginia. The leaders held that the demoralization that had spread over the coal fields, with the constant wage-cutting, would encourage the miners to seek relief through united action. The convention of the United Mine Workers of America demanded an increase in tonnage rates and authorized the Executive Board to negotiate the increases or call a strike at a propitious time. Failing to gain any concessions, the district presidents and the General Executive Board called a strike for July 4, 1897. As soon as the strike was called, Michael Ratchford, the head of the union, appealed to Gompers for aid. It was Ratchford's view that the success of the strike might be determined by the ability of the union to force a suspension of operations in West Virginia, a largely unorganized state. He, therefore, appealed to the American Federation of Labor to help with three or four organizers who would seek to enlist the support of the West Virginia miners. W. D. Mahon, Robert Askew, and Frank J. Weber were immediately dispatched to West Virginia, after William Weihe, a member of the Executive Council, had approved this action. Other members of the Council were then asked to approve the steps taken.[8] Gompers also requested the Council to make suggestions "relative to the miners' struggle and as to what can be done in reference to it. At the request of Ratchford, a circular appealing for aid for the strikers was issued by the Federation."[9] Gompers believed that not enough funds could be raised to take care of all needs of the strikers, but it was hoped that sufficient sums would be gathered to take care of emergency cases. Gompers would have liked to send large "sums if the funds of the A. F. of L. permitted. . . . What do you think if we appropriate a few hundred dollars?"[10] Gompers inquired of McGuire.

As the strike continued, the American Federation of Labor appealed to its affiliates to aid the miners with organizers. Among those who entered the coal fields were several members of the Executive Council, including Gompers, Treasurer John B. Lennon, and Vice Presidents Weihe and O'Connell. The repression and the injunctions faced by the union in West Virginia placed the strikers at a serious disadvantage. Ratchford appealed to Gompers for a conference of trade union leaders to decide on methods for meeting the problem. When the request was received, immediate action was necessary if the meeting was to be effective. Unable to summon the Executive Council into session on so short notice, Gompers nevertheless called the conference on his own responsibility. In defense of his action, he argued that a conference would aid the strike, and the attendance of a large contingent from the trade unions and the Executive Council would direct the meeting into practical rather than propaganda channels. At the meeting at Wheeling, West Virginia, on July 27, 1897, officers of "seventeen national unions and three railway brotherhoods assembled." James R. Sovereign of the Knights of Labor and Eugene V. Debs were also at the conference. In addition, offers of support came from a number of other unions. Several of those present made statements. Gompers, Sovereign, and Ratchford were appointed a committee to visit the Governor and demand the right of free speech and assemblage in West Virginia. An appeal for financial aid was also issued.[11]

When the committee protested against the action of the courts, the Governor indicated that he did not favor the injunctions that had been issued against the strikers by some of the judges. When, because of the opposition of the Governor, some of the state courts failed to enforce the injunctions, the mine operators appealed to the federal tribunals, where they procured a sweeping order from Judge Jackson against the strikers and their leader. However, Gompers, O'Connell, Ratchford, Frank J. Weber, and other labor men violated the stringent order without prosecution.[12]

The strike continued and Ratchford, on his own volition, called a meeting for St. Louis, Missouri, for August 30, 1897. To the distress of Gompers, McGuire, and other members of the Executive Council, Gompers' name was appended to the call without his permission. The latter found himself in a dilemma, as the call asked the reform organizations, scientific societies, trade unions, and all others to send delegates to St. Louis for the conference. Gompers did not like to be compelled to meet with groups that had no direct responsibility for labor. However, he feared repudiation of the meeting "might have a disastrous effect upon the miners' cause, and hence I am forced into silence against the unwarranted use of my name." The program of the St. Louis meeting was an innocuous document and another meeting was called for Chicago on September 30th.[13]

The Chicago meeting was also opposed by the Executive Council. However, after hearing Ratchford, the Council decided to continue the financing of organizers in West Virginia. In a statement, signed also by Ratchford, the Council declared:

The American Federation of Labor, believing only in practical methods, has today decided to continue to support [the coal miners of West Virginia] with organizers and money until a complete victory is won. To this it calls on its unions and on the public to not halt in their full and unmeasured aid to this worthy movement. . . . We can see no need for the labor convention in Chicago. . . . We advise our unions not to be represented there. The money it would cost to send delegates had better go to help the suffering miners and their families. It is not by conventions, with irresponsible talk, inflammatory declamations, and revolutionary buncombe, that the cause of labor can be advanced. Violent appeals to the passions of the multitude can serve no good purpose. It is only by systematic organization of the working people in trade unions, with united hearts and united funds, and a fraternity of purpose which knows no bounds of creed, color, nationality, or politics, that will uplift the masses.

The statement closed with appeal to citizens to rise unitedly at the polls to root out evil influences in American life.[14]

The American Federation of Labor continued its support of the strikers, and when the Central Competitive field agreement was signed Gompers expressed his gratification at the victory, and pointed to the wide support which the A. F. of L. had given directly and which it had helped to mobilize on behalf of the coal miners. In the opinion of Gompers, without the aid of the A. F. of L. and the trade unions the miners could not have remained out on strike for more than two weeks.[15]

Despite a substantial victory, the United Mine Workers was without funds and, for the time, unable to meet its obligations to the A. F. of L. Over the opposition of John B. Lennon, the Executive Council donated the sum necessary so that the Miners' Union could make its per-capita payment.[16]

Another donation was subsequently made so that the Miners' Union could meet an assessment levied by the A. F. of L. In addition, the A. F. of L. retained two organizers in West Virginia, as requested by the head of the United Mine Workers of America. One of them, Chris Evans, had been an officer of the union, and was well known throughout the coal fields. It was only when work was completely resumed and the Miners' organization withdrew its support of the strikers in West Virginia that the A. F. of L. discontinued financing the organizers in that state. The bituminous strike, which was of tremendous importance not only for the establishment of the United Mine Workers of America as an effective organization but as a demonstration of the new collective bargaining by unions, was greatly aided by the direct support the American Federation of Labor gave, and even more, mobilized. As a central federation, the A. F. of L. took the lead in making appeals and in inducing other organizations of labor to supply money and men needed in the conflict. It is not possible to judge whether Gompers' statement that the miners could not have won was correct, but there can be no doubt that the contribution of the A. F. of L. made victory easier and more certain.

REFERENCES

1. Andrew Carnegie to Samuel Gompers, November 1, 1912, in Easley Collection at the New York Public Library.
2. The facts are found in *Senate Report No. 1280, 52D Congress, 2D Session, 1892.*
3. Gompers to Executive Council, July 7, 1892; to M. Dampf, July 8, 1892.
4. Gompers to William Weihe, July 7, 1892.
5. *Report of Proceedings of the Thirteenth Annual Convention of the American Federation of Labor,* 1893, pp. 18-20.
6. John McBride to Chris Evans, April 11, 1892.
7. Gompers to Executive Council, February 16, 1894, *Vote Book,* October 13, 1894.
8. *Vote Book* of Executive Council, July 12, 1897.
9. Gompers to Executive Council, July 19, 1897.
10. Gompers to McGuire, July 31, 1897.
11. *American Federationist,* August 1897, pp. 119-121.
12. *Ibid.,* October 1897, pp. 159-160.
13. *Proceedings of the United Labor and Reform Convention, held in Chicago, Illinois* on September 27, 28, 29, 1897.
14. Statement adopted by Executive Council of the American Federation of Labor, and endorsed by M. D. Ratchford, President of the United Mine Workers of America, Minutes of Executive Council, September 27, 1897.
15. Gompers to McGuire, September 14, 1897; McGuire to Gompers, September 8, 1897.
16. *Vote Book* of Executive Council, October 13, 1897.

IX

Shorter Hours

PREPARING CAMPAIGN

Soon after its reorganization, the American Federation of Labor, at the suggestion of Gompers, picked up the campaign for a shorter-hour work day which had been launched by the old Federation. At the convention of 1887, Gompers declared that "as long as there is one man who seeks employment and cannot obtain it, the hours of labor are too long."[1]

At the next convention, in 1888, Gompers again emphasized the importance of achieving shorter hours of labor. He recognized that the eight-hour movement in 1886 might not have been altogether successful. He argued that it was always difficult to gain improvements, but that the benefits which had accrued to labor by reason of the eight-hour campaign were sufficiently impressive to warrant another effort in the same direction. He advised that some action to promote the shorter work day should be taken, and "we should not content ourselves with the passage of a resolution meaning nothing. If this convention should decide to engage the attention of the working people to the adoption of the eight-hour work day it should take such steps as would lead to practical action and results."[2]

A special committee considered the entire question, and the convention adopted its plan for establishing the eight-hour work day, and it recommended that plans be made to win the shorter work day by May 1, 1890. However, a general movement or strike in all industries, as in 1886, was to be avoided. Instead, the question was to be submitted for a vote to the affiliated unions seeking the reduction in hours for their members. Unions which cast the largest majority in favor of the eight-hour work day were to receive the support of all the organizations affiliated with the American Federation of Labor. The union which cast the next highest majority was to be next in line for similar support.[3]

The campaign was undertaken with the belief that the fixing of a target would concentrate the efforts and interests of the workers upon a given objective. To a member who complained that there was too much concentration upon a limited aim, Gompers explained:

We want eight hours, we are determined to have eight hours, we shall try to aid those who are in a condition by May 1, 1890, to obtain eight hours and

142

hope to obtain their assistance in return at some future time. The end of the labor movement, the end of the agitation for the reduction of the hours of labor, will not end in 1890; so long as there is one person seeking employment and cannot obtain it, so long will there be work for our organization.[4]

The campaign for the eight-hour day was well organized and, considering the resources of the movement, much time and effort were spent on promoting the objective. A proclamation was issued by the Executive Council urging workers to direct their energies toward achieving this goal. Simultaneous mass meetings were held in 240 cities and towns on February 22, 1889; 311 meetings were held on July 4th, and 420 on Labor Day of that year. Special organizers were retained to spread the gospel, pamphlets and circulars were issued urging and defending the shorter work day, and an effort was made to create a favorable public opinion to this demand.

At the convention of 1889, Gompers suggested that one or two trades affiliated with the A. F. of L. be selected to seek to establish the eight-hour work day in their crafts or callings and that other affiliates contribute a specified sum per member to aid the union or unions undertaking the campaign; and, in the event it proved necessary, such unions would strike to enforce this demand. He suggested that the convention authorize the Executive Council, acting in conjunction with the officers of the union selected, to initiate the campaign. The convention of 1889 accepted Gompers' proposal.[5] The recommendations were adopted, except the section on assessments. Instead, the convention authorized the Executive Council to levy an assessment of two cents per week per member upon all national, international, and federal and trade unions for the purpose of aiding the union engaged in a strike, throughout its jurisdiction, for the eight-hour day.

The A. F. of L. next appealed to the Knights of Labor for cooperation in this campaign. The Knights were asked to throw in their "lot with us, without restraint or reservation. If our efforts are crowned with victory, the working people will be proud of those who have stood by and for them."[6] The Knights refused the invitation, as they had done in 1886.

Carpenters and Miners

On March 17, 1890, the Executive Council nominated the United Brotherhood of Carpenters and Joiners of America to make the first attempt. The American Federation of Labor sought to have unions not involved in the strike make loans to the Carpenters' organization, as it believed the assessment would be too slow in raising the funds needed in a strike of these dimensions.[7] The loan proposal fell through, and consequently the assessment was imposed, resulting in the raising of over twelve thousand dollars. The American Federation of Labor was criticized for not doing more. However, Gompers denied he was "at fault nor were the officers of the American Federation of Labor. More than $12,000 . . . was sent to headquarters and placed at the disposal of the United Brotherhood of Carpenters and Joiners of America to aid in their struggle. I do not pretend to say that this is a vast sum but that it materially aided is well known to those who knew of the circumstances."[8] The eight-hour campaign was highly successful. According to Secretary McGuire, the movement established shorter hours for carpenters in 137 cities, and favorably affected 46,197 members of the trade and countless others in various branches of the building trades.

The Executive Council had selected the Coal Miners' Union as the organization to follow the Carpenters' campaign. On March 10, 1891, an appeal was issued by the A. F. of L. pointing to the brilliant success of the shorter-hour campaign of the Carpenters' Union, "so that it requires but a reminder to bring all of the toilers of the country to a full realization of the importance of the eight-hour work day in the trade selected to lead in our present movement—the coal miners."[9]

Complications developed when the Miners' Union was unable to call a general strike in the industry, since the economic conditions in the industry were too unfavorable for such a contest. The union canceled the strike in every district except Iowa. Thereupon the Executive Council sought to find another trade willing to seek the eight-hour work day. Secretary Patrick McBryde of the United Mine Workers of America denied the eight-hour movement had been canceled by the Miners' Union, saying that it had only been deferred. Moreover, McBryde asked that funds intended to finance the eight-hour campaign be diverted to the support of the striking miners in Iowa. The Executive Council refused because the Iowa strike, by reason of its limited nature, could not be regarded as a movement to establish the eight-hour day in a trade within the meaning of the resolutions enacted by the convention of the A. F. of L.

McBryde, who had bitterly protested and denounced the Executive Council for its narrow interpretation, was informed by the Executive Council:

We cannot ignore the official notice received from Secretary McBryde that the United Mine Workers of America had declared the Eight Hour Movement of the Miners "off," nor could we justify our position before the organized wage workers of the country were we to approve the application for financial assistance in support of an Eight Hour strike of the Iowa miners, when no such reservation was made in the official notification of the May 1st movement. Hence we believe that the money intrusted to our care was not intended to be expended in the manner of your application.[10]

30 0.0 0

However, the Council offered to loan the Miners' Union two thousand dollars, with a promise that the cancellation of the loan would be placed before the next convention. The convention canceled the loan.

The depression of the 1890's temporarily suspended the campaign for the eight-hour work day. At the convention of 1895, the convention voted "that the whole force and power of the American Federation of Labor shall be concentrated upon the issue of a shorter work day, and the Executive Council be requested to secure the fullest discussion by the press, the pulpit and the platform."[11]

The year passed without the Federation taking any important steps in the eight-hour campaign, although a number of unions sought to establish an eight-hour work day in their jurisdictions by negotiations or strikes. The convention of 1896 decided to set up an advisory board, made up of the representatives of those unions with headquarters in Indianapolis, Indiana, the headquarters city of the American Federation of Labor. Officers of the Federation were to meet with this committee once a month for discussing and planning the campaign for the shorter work day. A series of mass meetings were to be held to promote the campaign for shorter hours, and the retaining of special organizers and the publication of special leaflets and pamphlets were ordered. In order to carry out the campaign and aid financially the striking union, John B. Lennon, the Treasurer of the A. F. of L. and a member of the Executive Council, suggested that an assessment of five cents per member be levied upon every member, the levy to be paid prior to April 1, 1897. The proposal was overwhelmingly rejected, by a vote of 1871 to 300, and a substitute for an assessment of one cent approved.[12]

PRINTERS

The American Federation of Labor continued to urge the establishment of the shorter work day upon its affiliates. In 1900, the campaign of the Granite Cutters' International Association was aided by the A. F. of L. Many unions made shorter hours one of their chief objectives, and the Executive Council always stressed the advantages of gaining such a concession. The International Typographical Union decided to enforce this demand upon the book and job trade on September 1, 1905. According to J. W. Bramwood, the secretary of the Union, more than "two hundred . . . local unions had trouble on this account." The American Federation of Labor levied an assessment upon its members and contributed $52,619.52 to the International Typographical Union.[13] While this was a small sum as compared with the amounts raised by a 10 per cent assessment imposed upon the wages of its members by the International Typographical Union, "it was an earnest of . . . [a] desire to be helpful to our brothers engaged in one of the greatest contests ever conducted by a trade union."

CHANGE IN TACTICS

Increasingly the effort to establish the shorter work day was conducted by the unions on a limited basis, rather than throughout an entire jurisdiction. The convention of 1906 instructed the Executive Council to discover the desires of the affiliates in this matter. On the basis of the replies, the next convention urged "persistent agitation to shorten the hours of labor in each trade, by such process as may be most practicable in their respective interests." A change in sentiment over the tactics to pursue toward achieving the eight-hour work day is evident. The convention no longer believed it was advisable to seek universally the eight-hour day, as some trades and callings were still working ten hours a day and in some even longer. Hence, workers and their unions were advised to strive continually for a reduction in the hours of labor, and to place this demand at the top of the agenda for the improvement of the conditions of labor.[14]

LEGISLATION

Reduction of the hours of labor continued to be a major interest of the American Federation of Labor. Differences arose, however, over the methods to be followed. The convention of 1913 endorsed the establishment of the eight-hour work day for women and children by legislation, but was not explicit on the methods other than those employed by trade unions for achieving this end in industries employing men. Because of the charge, made in several states, that the American Federation of Labor opposed the enactment of shorter-hour legislation for men, a charge which handicapped the campaigns for these objectives in several states, resolutions were introduced at the convention in 1914 favoring legislation for the general shortening of the work day. The resolutions committee, however, recommended that "the regulation of wages and the hours of labor should be undertaken through trade union activity, and not to be made subjects of laws through legislative enactment, excepting insofar as such regulations affect or govern the employment of women and minors, health and morals; and employment by federal, state or municipal government."[15]

The views of the resolutions committee provoked a long and at times bitter debate. On the side of the opposition to the enactment of legislation on wages and hours were Gompers, Duncan, and John P. Frey. Mitchell was on the other side, and pointed to the demand of workers, especially in the Western states, for legal regulation of the work day. He argued that the Federation with all its energy and strength and effort over the years had not been able to reduce the hours of labor. "Have you a right, then," he asked, "to deny to all the men and women in these various states the right to legislate themselves into a legal eight-hour day?"[16] Gompers vehemently argued against legislative intervention, and insinuated that the proposal stemmed from Socialist sources. He wanted the convention to keep to the "charted road" of trade unionism, and avoid being entrapped by politics and legislative action. The committee's views were upheld by a vote of 11,237 to 8107 with 607 not voting.

The issue was again before the convention of 1915, brought in by a resolution from the Illinois Federation of Labor, sponsored by John Fitzpatrick, one of the leaders of the Chicago labor movement. The resolution asked that "we . . . hold solid for the eight-hour work day by legislation, both industrially and politically."

Again the resolutions committee declared "the regulation of wages and the hours of labor should be undertaken through trade-union activity, and not to be made subjects of laws through legislative enactment, excepting insofar as such regulations affect or govern employment of women and minors, health and morals; and employment by federal, state or municipal government." The same arguments were repeated, with Gompers expressing an extreme suspicion of government—something he seldom did at conventions. He was

unwilling to place within the power of a political agent, call him what you please, the right to govern my industrial liberty, or the industrial liberty of my fellow workers. There never was a government in the history of the world and there is not one today that when a critical moment came, did not exercise tyranny over the people. The second premise of the advocates of the eight-hour law is this: They imagine, or back in their brain is this thought, that these working people are unorganizable, and therefore the strong arm of the law should come in and "protect" them. Now there is nothing more unstable and untrue that any working people are unorganizable.

Gompers denied that there were workers who would permanently not organize, for through the "exercise of some special injustice by a great corporation or employer . . . they organize and struggle and bear burdens and make sacrifices to secure the best of conditions." Gompers then explained that the only demand that he would make upon Congress is to do for the workers "what we cannot do for ourselves."

Primarily, Gompers wanted "the government to secure us by law the right to exert and exercise the normal human activities of self-development and associated effort, to bear the burdens of the struggle for industrial improvement and freedom . . . freedom to fight and freedom to achieve."[17]

Neither Gompers nor any one else explained why it was dangerous or harmful to obtain the shorter work day through legislation; or why a government which could protect the weaker members of society—women, children, seamen—by wage and hour legislation would inflict serious damage to other groups if the latter were included in such legislation.

In fact, the argument used by Gompers and his supporters was largely doctrinaire. It may be true that there are dangers to the liberties of the people in large and powerful governments—especially to the working people—but there was no proof that the enactment of general wage and hour laws would either injure the morale of the worker or endanger the movement.

Many leading trade unionists recognized the fallacy of Gompers' position, and the vote on the question would indicate that an increasing number of delegates found the arguments against regulation unconvincing. Gompers was able to win the victory, as the resolutions committee recommendations were adopted by a vote of 8500 to 6396 with 4061 votes not cast. It is obvious that the report was adopted by a minority, and that many delegates refrained from voting so as not to inflict a severe defeat upon Gompers. The large negative vote in part indicated the growing opposition to the established views of the Executive Council, including Gompers.[18]

REFERENCES

1. *Proceedings of the Second Annual Convention of the American Federation of Labor*, 1887, p. 11.

2. *Report of Proceedings of the Third Annual Convention of the American Federation of Labor*, 1888, p. 11.

3. *Ibid.*, p. 29.

4. Gompers to Edward Plant, December 21, 1889.

5. *Report of Proceedings of the Ninth Annual Convention of the American Federation of Labor*, 1889, p. 30.

6. Gompers to Powderly, October 17, 1889.

7. Gompers to William Weihe, April 30, 1890.

8. Letter to a correspondent, November 6, 1890.

9. Circular issued on March 10, 1891, by the A. F. of L. over the signatures of Gompers and Chris Evans.

10. Gompers, on behalf of Executive Council, to John B. Rae, May 26, 1891.

11. *Report of Proceedings of the Fifteenth Annual Convention of the American Federation of Labor*, 1895, p. 76.

12. *Report of Proceedings of the Sixteenth Annual Convention of the American Federation of Labor*, 1896, pp. 72, 78.

13. *Report of Proceedings of the Twenty-Sixth Annual Convention of the American Federation of Labor*, 1906, p. 17.

14. *Report of Proceedings of the Twenty-Seventh Annual Convention of the American Federation of Labor*, 1907, pp. 286-287.

15. *Report of Proceedings of the Twenty-Fourth Annual Convention of the American Federation of Labor*, 1914, p. 421.

16. *Ibid.*, p. 434.

17. *Report of Proceedings of the Thirty-Fifth Annual Convention of the American Federation of Labor*, 1915, pp. 502-503.

18. *Ibid.*, pp. 503-504.

X

Dual Unionism

By the middle 1890's it appeared that victory in the conflict with the Knights of Labor would go to the American Federation of Labor. This would mean the elimination of dual and competing unions. But the hoped-for surcease from this evil was not to follow, for the American Federation of Labor was soon confronted by ideological and regional dual union movements.

The Socialist Labor Party, representing orthodox Marxist socialism, in the 1890's came under the influence of Daniel DeLeon, a lecturer on international law at Columbia University. At first a single taxer, he soon left that group and joined the Socialists. In 1891 he became the editor of *The People*, the official organ of the Socialist Labor Party, succeeding Lucien Sanial, the delegate whose credentials had been questioned at the Detroit convention in 1890. Next, as has been noted, the Socialists tried to win endorsement of their program of socialization and independent political action at the A. F. of L. convention of 1894 and failed. DeLeon then sought to capture the fading Knights of Labor but in this venture he was also unsuccessful.

He later decided to organize a trade union movement of his own, one which would endorse his views and respond passively to his orders. A conference of followers, attended by delegates from the New York Central Labor Federation, the United Hebrew Trades, the Newark, New Jersey, Central Labor Federation, and District Assembly 49 of the Knights of Labor, on December 10, 1895, formed the Socialist Trade and Labor Alliance. The organization of the new federation of labor was announced at a mass meeting to which several well-known Socialist trade unionists, among them J. Mahlon Barnes, a member of Gompers' Union, and John F. Tobin, the head of the Shoemakers' Union, had been invited. The latter two, delegates to the convention of the American Federation of Labor then meeting in New York, were unaware initially of the special purpose of the meeting and delivered speeches.[1] The Socialist Trade and Labor Alliance was to serve as an "ally and supplement of the Socialist Labor Party in bringing those masses who cannot directly be reached by . . . [the] party organization—and we want to emphasize that point."[2]

149

DeLeon's concept of the function of trade unions was similar to Lenin's in that he believed they should be an adjunct of a "revolutionary" political party. The American Federation of Labor, just emerging from a serious depression and seeking to establish unity on the economic front, regarded the new federation as a serious threat. Moreover, attacks upon the trade unions by DeLeon, whose talent for denunciation and vituperative phrases was far above the average, convinced the heads of the A. F. of L. that he and the other leaders of the Socialist Labor Party, supported by a few unthinking workers, were plotting to destroy the trade unions.[3]

The threat of the Socialist Trade and Labor Alliance to the A. F. of L. did not materialize. Though it managed to organize a few local unions temporarily, it served primarily to exacerbate the already deteriorating relations between the Socialist movement and the leaders of the American Federation of Labor. The autocratic leader of the Socialist Labor Party was reasonably well versed in political and social theory, but he had little understanding of American labor. DeLeon was, moreover, largely a verbal revolutionary; he believed in carrying on the class struggle on a "civilized plane." His bitterness and intolerance helped to broaden the gap between the leaders of the trade unions, whom he described as "labor fakirs," and the Socialists. The animus generated by DeLeon's tactics were sometimes unfortunately directed at Socialists who were not in sympathy with his polemical methods or with his views on trade union movements.

WESTERN FEDERATION OF MINERS

More serious was the defection from the A. F. of L. of the Western Federation of Miners, a union of metalliferous miners, organized in Butte, Montana, in May 1893. For a time the union in the industry reflected the violent spirit of the Western mining camps. The American Federation of Labor, anxious to become the spokesman for all organized workmen, looked toward the affiliation of the Western Federation of Miners as it did of other unions. During the metal miners strike in Coeur d'Alene, Idaho, in 1892, the American Federation of Labor protested the conduct of the authorities and donated five hundred dollars for the defense and relief of the miners imprisoned in the "bull pen." The Idaho miners became part of the Western Federation of Miners.[4] The A. F. of L. had little money, and while the amount does not seem large, it was equal to the sum donated for the defense of the Tennessee coal miners, also victims of prosecution during a strike in that year. In July 1896, the Western Federation of Miners joined the A. F. of L., and Edward Boyce and Patrick Clifford attended its convention that year as delegates. It was during a bitter strike in Leadville, Colorado, that the metal miners' delegates sought assistance. The Executive Council and the convention both endorsed the strike, but the A. F. of L. unions contributed little money,

"scarcely enough to cover the costs of canvassing."[5] The resolution of
support for the Western Federation of Miners had been drawn by
Gompers "with the full knowledge of Mr. Boyce. . . . It was distinctly
expressed by Mr. Boyce that he did not expect any financial assistance as
the result. It was also understood that Mr. Boyce was to write me advising
me from time to time as to in which manner I could be of some service
to the miners in their struggle."[6]

Gompers was aware even before the miners' delegation had left the
convention that they were dissatisfied with the attitude and the leadership
of the A. F. of L., and favored withdrawing from it. He was, therefore,
anxious that a representative of the American Federation of Labor attend
the metal miners' convention in March 1897 and explain the A. F. of L.'s
position—its lack of finances and control over affiliates. Gompers was
aware that "these men are engaged in an awful conflict . . . and the
antagonism they have to contend with is something that has brought
their strength and courage in relief."[7]

Gompers, who was always willing to speak directly and courteously on
issues he believed of importance to organized labor, wrote a long letter
to Boyce telling him of the rumors that the Western Federation of Miners
planned to sever its affiliation with the A. F. of L., and urging him to avoid
this step. He hit out at the argument that the Federation had been derelict
in its support of the Leadville miners in their strike.

All know [Boyce was told] that our organizations pay but one-quarter of a
cent for each member per month into the funds of the American Federation
of Labor. No one can conceive of the idea that a great fund can be created from
such a small contribution, and it is equally known to all that we have no
mysterious power by which, touching a rock, great riches can be had and
given to our fellow workers. Even the fact that our fellow-unionists may be
engaged in a most just and righteous struggle, does not give us the means
by which to create large funds to help them, unless the members in our organization in the first instance are willing to pay their share and bear the burden
by which such a fund can be created.[8]

Gompers went on to argue that advocating the creation of a fund is not
enough, for every member of the Federation shared to some extent the responsibility for the absence of a sufficient reserve to support workers engaged in strikes.

Gompers both pleaded and warned against the separation of workers
along sectional lines, and told Boyce he was aware

of the defects of the American Federation of Labor as any one can point
them out to me. With some others we have endeavored to remedy these defects; we have tried by all honorable means to organize workers in their unions,
to make these organizations in their national unions in our Federation as effective as possible. That we have not accomplished more is not due to the men

who recognize its shortcomings, it is because the great mass of labor have thus far failed to realize their full duty to themselves and to each other. Our unions and our Federation is and can be only that which we make it. If it does not fill the expectations of some of us, it becomes our duty to struggle on and on, in order to make it a most thorough, compact, and perfect organization to fight the battles of labor today, and to secure the rights of the toilers for all time.[9]

Boyce answered that there were easier ways to win battles for labor than "sitting down in idleness until the capitalists starve us to death in idleness and hunger." He also informed Gompers that he did not regard himself as a trade unionist, but he disclaimed all knowledge of plans to withdraw the Western Federation of Miners from the A. F. of L.[10] Gompers again reiterated his views that labor could not afford to divide on sectional lines. To Boyce's claim that he had written Gompers, on February 16th, requesting financial aid for the Leadville miners on strike, Gompers answered that the letter had not been received, and if it had, either an assessment or an appeal to unions for help would have been issued by the Executive Council.

Boyce had also informed Gompers that the "men of the West are one hundred years ahead of their brothers in the East," and that there were easier ways to gain concessions than strikes. Gompers doubted that this was the language of "the hero of the Leadville strike; this is not the language of the man I know you are; it is not the language of men who fought great battles and have stamped the progress of their struggles on the pages of human history and human progress." Boyce wanted "to get out and fight with the sword or use the ballot with intelligence." Gompers ridiculed the notion that there was an easier way of winning battles than the strike, nor would he admit the inferiority of the workers of the East, in establishing their rights, to those of the West. As for Boyce's

suggestion that the resort must be the sword, I prefer not to discuss. I only want to call your attention to the fact, however, that force may have changed forms of government but never attained liberty. . . . The conception which is a matter of growth, a matter of education, and is a matter of progress, proceeds in the same ratio that the people conceive their rights and will manfully, heroically, and with self-sacrifice, stand for it and which no power in the form of government can withstand.[11]

Boyce sent a perfunctory reply, in which he informed Gompers he favored a Western movement.

WESTERN LABOR UNION

According to reports reaching Gompers, the convention of the Western Federation of Miners favored continuing affiliation with the A. F. of L., but Boyce ignored that view. In December 1897, the Executive Board of the Western Federation of Miners polled its locals on a proposal to call

a conference of all labor[12] organizations of the West for the "purpose of
bringing them into closer touch upon all matters pertaining to the interest
of labor. As the laboring people of the West have never met together to
discuss matters of interest to them or advance their interests, the Executive Board favors such action."[13] When the majority of locals responded
affirmatively, a conference was called at Salt Lake City for May 10, 1898.
Of the 119 delegates who attended, 77 were metal miners.[14] In his opening remarks, Boyce attacked the existing labor organizations and charged
that those which had their headquarters in the East had ignored the problems of Western labor. He therefore advised a new organization, comprising unions east of the Pacific Ocean and west of the Mississippi River.
Others located in different areas were to be allowed affiliation as long as
they accepted the principles of the new organization. The delegates established the Western Labor Union, and Walter MacArthur, a leading
trade unionist of the Pacific Coast, believed it was "only the Western
Federation of Miners under another name. Of course Boyce dominated
everything, sometimes openly, but for the most part in the committee
room. Boyce's influence with the miners is unquestionably strong. The
majority believe him sincerely, and all of them fear to oppose him."[15]
MacArthur did not believe the new movement would amount to much.

The schism introduced by Boyce lasted a number of years, and the
Western Federation of Miners was perhaps the chief driving force in the
subsequent formation of the Industrial Workers of the World. Boyce himself did not long remain an active trade unionist. He struck it rich pros-
pecting, and retired from the labor scene to a more comfortable existence.

However, the dual union tendencies sponsored by Boyce undoubtedly
reflected the views of the metal miners, who looked upon the workers of
the eastern part of the country as effete and overcautious. The metal
miners, faced by ruthless and tough employers, found it necessary to
adopt the same aggressive militant attitude to survive. In the spring of
1899, the Western Federation of Miners was again involved in a strike
at Coeur d'Alene, Idaho. During the strike, the concentrator of the Bunker
Hill and Sullivan Company at Wardner, Idaho, was dynamited, and
federal troops were requested by Governor Steunenberg on the ground
that an insurrection existed beyond the power of the state to control.
Federal troops could be called as the Idaho National Guard was absent
in the Philippines.[16] General H. C. Merriam was put in charge, and he
arrested several hundred men who were quartered in unsanitary box cars
and warehouses, called the "bull pen." Only those who had permits from
the Governor's representative could work in the mines. General Merriam
in a statement accused the Western Federation of Miners of being a
criminal conspiracy. Gompers assailed the statement, and forced a re-
traction. He asked the Executive Council to give him "authority to take

whatever action within the law and within reason to remedy the wrong committed against the union of miners, and to make such further efforts as shall prevent a recurrence of such a wrong being perpetrated upon any organized body of wage workers."[17] Gompers had informed the Executive Council, on May 16th, that the conflict between the Western Federation of Miners and the mine owners "makes it necessary for us to do all that we can to give them whatever moral support we can."[18]

At its meeting the Executive Council endorsed the fight of the metal miners, appropriated five hundred dollars for their defense, and issued an appeal for financial aid in their behalf. Boyce wanted the A. F. of L. to call a special convention, but Gompers was opposed on the ground that experiences in the American Railway walkout and bituminous coal strikes of 1897 with similar meetings would not justify such a step.[19] At the instructions of the convention of 1899, the Executive Council "undertook to secure an investigation regarding the labor troubles of last year in Idaho, and the treatment accorded to the miners who were imprisoned in the stockade known as the 'bull pen.'" The convention also demanded that federal troops be withdrawn.

While Gompers emphasized the undesirability of the split in the labor movement, he as well as the other members of the Executive Council sought to be of help to the Western miners. Gompers recognized that Boyce exerted much influence toward the division of the labor movement on sectional lines, but he held the view that "as the representative of the organization of the men involved [Boyce] must have some influence with us and our action."[20] Moreover, the A. F. of L. always hoped that, in time, the Western Federation of Miners would find its way back to the main stream of the labor movement. Consequently, criticism of the leaders was avoided; there was only regret at their unwisdom. This attitude towards the leaders of the Western Federation of Miners contrasted with the bitterness against DeLeon. The latter was not a worker, nor a leader of workmen. He was an interloper, an intruder into the labor movement, whose vituperative phrases had stung Gompers. Even character assassination, which DeLeon had developed to a fine art, would have been forgiven if DeLeon had not sought to undermine the unions by denouncing their leaders in the midst of strikes or on other occasions. When DeLeon attacked the leaders of the bituminous coal strike, Gompers angrily replied that "there is not a charge or insinuation which the skinflint employer, or corporation thug or apologist or villainous newspaper penny-a-liner has launched against labor organizations which this *Agent Provocateur* has not rehashed, embellished and served up just at the time when it will serve the interests of the capitalist class best."[21]

On the other hand, when Gompers was told that he was being attacked by Boyce and Debs, he merely replied:

That is their business. I shall simply go on in my work as I see the light and duty. . . . I may be wrong, but somehow I cannot escape the conclusion that success in the labor movement, that advantages to the workers, improvements in their conditions, and the establishment of justice among men, in other words, the time for which we are all hoping and praying, lie through the road of hard work, through organization, close application and, if necessary, bear burdens and temporary sacrifices, and even bear the ill will of Mr. Debs and others who have never yet succeeded in any effort they have undertaken.[22]

Gompers was sharp in his criticism of Debs' role in the launching of the American Labor Union and the I. W. W., but he never evinced any personal bitterness towards him.

The American Labor Union

The A. F. of L. avoided all criticism of the Western Federation of Miners. And when Gompers was informed of a suspicion that the Western Labor Union was being supported by corporation donations, he replied that "in the interests of the men themselves, as well as our movement, I hope this is not true."[23] Committees from the Executive Council were sent to confer with the Western Federation of Miners and the Western Labor Union in hope that the breach could be healed. In several communities, notably Denver, the existence of the Western Labor Union had led to serious dissension, and Gompers sought to mobilize a number of international unions in the struggle. During the convention of the Western Labor Union in June 1902, an afternoon was set aside to discuss the division in the labor movement. After listening to Frank Morrison, Debs, who was present as a guest, took the platform and leveled a sharp attack against the American Federation of Labor, charged that trade unions "had outlived their usefulness," and called for the extension of the Western Labor Union to the remainder of the country. Acting upon this suggestion, which also came from other sources, the organization shifted its headquarters to Chicago, and changed its name to the American Labor Union.[24] Despite the belief that a class organization was the only means of rallying the workers into organizations, the American Labor Union, like its predecessor the Western Labor Union, was a complete failure.

Cripple Creek Strike

Yet the Western Federation of Miners was not regarded with hostility. When a local of metal miners was organized, the A. F. of L. representative was instructed that "there is no reason why a local union of any trade should not become affiliated with its respective national organization."[25] Nor did the American Federation of Labor ignore the brutal attacks upon the Western Federation of Miners in Colorado. A strike had started at the mills of the Colorado Reduction and Refining Company in Cripple Creek over the discharge of a number of union men. The strike was supported by all the miners, and it appeared that the company would have to withdraw the dismissals. Instead, company sympathizers were deputized, militia sent into the area, and the pickets dispersed. As the contest continued, a citizens' alliance was organized, strikers imprisoned and deported without trial by deputies, and soldiers sent by Governor Peabody.[26]

A circular drawn up by Duncan and Gompers denounced the "rule of gun and bayonet" and charged the Colorado government with carrying out the "bidding of the most unscrupulous organization of men who are prompted by no other thought or purpose than avarice, greed and power —the mine owners organized as the Citizens Alliance." The circular charged Governor Peabody with doing their bidding and being completely dominated by these unscrupulous and ruthless men.[27] Unions were asked to aid the metal miners financially, and the A. F. of L. itself donated one thousand dollars. There was a feeling among A. F. of L. affiliates, especially in the West, that a conference of trade unions should be called at Denver to consider the situation. The proposal was, however, rejected by the Executive Council by a vote of 8 to 3.

LAUNCHING OF THE INDUSTRIAL WORKERS OF THE WORLD

Any hopes that the support of the A. F. of L. would soften the support of the Western Federation of Miners for a dual labor movement were, however, not realized immediately. Instead, the Metal Miners' Union decided to participate in the launching of a new dual body. In the fall of 1904, a group of six persons active in the radical and Socialist movements, among them William Trautman, editor of the *Brauer Zeitung*, and Isaac Cowen of the Amalgamated Society of Engineers, whose union had been expelled from the A. F. of L., met and decided to convene a larger conference in the hope of preparing plans for the launching of a new labor federation. The outcome of this first conference was the issuance of a letter, signed by Debs, among others, inviting about sixty unionists and active Socialists to a secret meeting. All except Max Hayes and Victor Berger, leading members of the Typographical Union and Socialist Party, accepted. Twenty-nine persons appeared at the second meeting in January 1905, among them the three top officers of the Western Federation of Miners. Debs was also present, as was a representative from DeLeon's Socialist Trade and Labor Alliance. A manifesto was issued, and a convention called for June 1905.[28]

When the Executive Council of the A. F. of L. learned that the Western Federation of Miners had joined the new attempt to set up a dual labor federation, it voted to cease supporting the metal miners. In addition, the Council demanded an accounting be made to determine whether the funds donated by the A. F. of L. and its affiliates had been used for the purpose for which they were intended.

Instead of answering the request, the leaders of the Western Federation of Miners responded with an attack upon the heads of the A. F. of L. But Gompers refused to reply in kind. Instead, he pointed to the donation of $10,000 made by his union, the Cigar Makers' International Union; the $1000 donated by the Glass Bottle Blowers; the $1000 by the Theatrical Stage Employees; and by the United Mine Workers of America, $27,000. Gompers was aware of the remarks of President Charles Moyer and Secretary William D. Haywood of the Western Federation of Miners.

They said some very mean things, not simply in their latest utterances, but all through. President Moyer, in his official report to the last convention of the Western Federation of Miners, devotes the major portion of his report to an attack upon the labor movement, upon the American Federation of Labor, and particularly me. I don't intend to retaliate in kind, either here or anywhere else, but I repeat that if we are going to have any kind of confidence in our fellow union men we must be in a position to assure them that the money they contribute for any purpose is devoted to that purpose. There is nothing further from my mind than to place a stigma upon the organization or its officers. They and I differ very materially as to our relative understanding of the trade union movement. They have a right to differ from me, and they have a right to sturdily defend their position, just as I have a right to defend the position I take; but that does not form the right for them or for myself, for their organization or for our organization, to divert money contributed for the legal defense of the men involved in Colorado, especially when it is alleged they have largely expended that money to put on foot an organization that was launched to be the antagonist movement of the American Federation of Labor.[29]

No one rose to defend the Western Federation of Miners and its use of funds donated by other organizations of labor affiliated with the A. F. of L. The convention unanimously approved the views of President Gompers.

MOYER, HAYWOOD, AND PETTIBONE CASE

The affiliation of the Western Federation of Miners with the Industrial Workers of the World was not destined to be of long duration. However, before the separation the Western Federation of Miners was to undergo another severe trial, in which the A. F. of L. was to play a role. On December 30, 1905, former Governor Frank Steunenberg of Idaho was killed by a bomb as he was opening the gate of his home. He had been governor during the troubles at Wardner, when many members of the Western Federation of Miners were arrested and held in the bull pen. The Idaho officials believed that the murder had been perpetrated by agents of the union, but instead of requesting the authorities of Colorado to arrest and extradite the suspects, two officers, Charles H. Moyer and William D. Haywood, and a former member, George A. Pettibone, were seized late in the evening of February 17, 1906, taken in separate carriages to the railroad station, and hurried in a special train to Boise, Idaho, to face charges of murder. Gompers said that the manner "of their unwarrantable and brutal abduction from their homes, the State of Colorado, to Idaho, justifies the suspicion and belief that there is a scheme afoot to fasten guilt upon them for the Steunenberg murder."[30]

Even though the kidnapped men were not officers of unions affiliated with the American Federation of Labor, the incident aroused widespread anger and protest among labor men. A movement to call a special convention of the A. F. of L. was instituted, although it failed to gain the approval of a majority of the Executive Council. William Mailey, a member of the Executive Board of the Socialist Party, was sent on a confidential mission to the American Federation of Labor by the secretary of the Socialist Party, J. Mahon Barnes. On his way to Washington, Mailey called conferences of union officers in Chicago, Indianapolis, and Cincinnati, and received the approval for a special convention from the officers of twenty national unions.[31] While the heads of these unions approved of a conference, the issuance of the call was in the hands of the American Federation of Labor. Gompers, Morrison, and O'Connell, who were in Washington, were

resentful of the outrage committed upon Moyer, Haywood and Pettibone in their illegal and immoral abduction from their own state in a brutal manner, but as to whether a national conference of all labor organizations should be called under the auspices of the American Federation of Labor, for this specific purpose, and this alone, is a subject upon which Messrs. Morrison, O'Connell and I have some grave doubt; nor are we satisfied that it would even accomplish any good results for the men. It may indeed react to their detriment. If anything, it should take the form that will have at least some assurance that it will be of a practical and tangible character. Agitation is one thing; tangible and practical results are another. [The] matter is submitted to the Executive Council without prejudice.

Two members of the Executive Council, Mitchell and Valentine, voted for a conference; one, Morris, asked for a special meeting of the Executive Council of the A. F. of L., which would speak for the entire labor movement, and the majority opposed any conference.[32] It was Gompers' view that "everything within our power that can be done will be done for these men, and this too, whether a convention is called or not."[33]

FIRST CONVENTION OF THE INDUSTRIAL WORKERS OF THE WORLD

Haywood and Pettibone were acquitted and Moyer released from jail, but the Western Federation of Miners had in the meantime severed its connections with the Industrial Workers of the World. The latter organization had been established in June 1905, and its proceedings were closely followed by Gompers, who immediately reported them to the members of

the Executive Council. Daily, Gompers received a synopsis and an evaluation of the activities of the preceding day from an agent, who not only
showed a wide knowledge of the personalities at the convention, but
whose appraisal showed him to have had a keen understanding of trade
unionism and labor tactics. Gompers' informant reported that

many of the delegates who seem to be taking a prominent part in the gathering
represent no one but themselves and are not even members of trade unions. . . .
In the hall I met a goodly number of acquaintances who are members of
unions affiliated with the A. F. of L. and who are socialists but not one of them
was there representing his union, and indeed a number to whom I spoke
were rather bitter against the new venture and expressed loyalty to the A. F. of L.
although criticising some of its policies.[34]

There was a clear indication to the observer who reported the convention proceedings that there was a struggle between the theorists and the
practical trade unionists. The most adroit of the latter group, in his
opinion, was D. C. Coates, the head of the American Labor Union, who
had succeeded to that post when Daniel J. McDonald resigned the presidency. Coates favored industrial organization as understood by many
members and officers of the A. F. of L. In contrast were the theoretical
minded, led by "Father" Thomas J. Haggerty, whose organization chart,
displayed at the convention, was described by Coates as "Haggerty's
wheel of fortune," a description Gompers was subsequently fond of using.
As the convention went on, Coates was described as "easily the most
dangerous man in the convention" from the viewpoint of the A. F. of L.
The others were held to be too impractical and lacking in organization
sense, and therefore of no consequence. In his opinion, the makeup and
organizational structure were such as to make failure inevitable—"the
entire affair has been satisfactory from the standpoint of the A. F. of L."[35]

From the standpoint of the American Federation of Labor, the leaders
were convinced that no trade union movement could, at the time, develop
significant strength on the basis laid down in the program of the Industrial
Workers of the World. The latter organization contained within itself
too many discordant elements. After the internal splits of 1906 and 1907,
the organization became one that concerned itself largely with the
migratory workers of the West and the exploited immigrants of the East.
It attracted considerable attention by engaging in free speech fights, and
it led some dramatic industrial battles, but it was never a serious rival to
the A. F. of L. As a matter of fact, it sought to organize in few places
where a going labor union functioned, although the United Textile
Workers of America exercised jurisdiction in the textile industry, where
some of the more dramatic struggles of the I. W. W. were conducted.
Gompers did not believe the program of comprehensive industrial union-

ism was the answer to the structural problems facing the trade union movement. He was especially opposed to any program that would imperil existing organizations. He was of the opinion that any "attempt prematurely to force . . . amalgamation brings reaction and failure in its wake." He argued that the trade unions were alert to changes in their industrial environments and the numerous jurisdictional disputes were themselves evidence of efforts by unions to expand their membership into new channels.

While the Industrial Workers of the World were never a serious challenge to the hegemony of the A. F. of L. over the labor movement, the former organization subsequently stimulated a wider interest in industrial unionism, a demand for which began to express itself in resolutions at the conventions of the American Federation of Labor. In view of the relations between organizations of labor, and the role and power of the A. F. of L., a proposal for redrawing of jurisdictions which was implied in such resolutions would inevitably arouse serious opposition at the conventions of the American Federation of Labor. Yet, three decades later, the issue was to arise as a practical problem of adjustment within the trade union movement, and the absence of statesmanship was to lead to the great breach within the labor movement. But for the moment, the demand for industrial unionism was not significant within the A. F. of L., nor a serious threat from without.

The Western Federation of Miners, once it had separated from the Industrial Workers of the World, gravitated towards the main branch of the labor movement. Formal application for affiliation with the A. F. of L. was made in June 1910. Its claim for exclusive jurisdiction of workers in and around the metal mines encountered opposition from some craft unions. Early in 1911, the American Federation of Labor agreed to issue a charter to the Western Federation of Miners "on the basis of the jurisdiction of the United Mine Workers of America" with the reservation that a few local unions of machinists be allowed to retain their affiliation with the International Association of Machinists. "The reservation can in no way affect the control of the mining industry by the Western Federation of Miners" which was assured of the cooperation of the machinists.[36] The Western Federation of Miners would, however, not surrender it rights to the craft unions in areas where the latter had no workers organized in the metal mines.

Gompers sought to work out a compromise so that the Western Federation of Miners would be admitted to affiliation, but without the craft unions forfeiting their claims. Instead the metal trades unions raised more formidable objections to the invasion of what they regarded as their jurisdictional rights. Nevertheless, the American Federation of Labor, which had sought to find some compromise acceptable to all the unions involved, and failed, issued a charter to the Western Federation of Miners on May 9, 1911. The United Mine Workers of America had been a vigorous supporter of the metalliferous union, and the Executive Council was anxious to eliminate what had, in the past, been the chief source for dual movements.

REFERENCES

1. N. I. Stone, *The Attitude of the Socialists Toward Trade Unions* (New York: Volkszeitung Library, 1900), p. 6; *The People,* December 15, 1895.

2. *Proceedings of the Ninth Annual Convention of the Socialist Labor Party,* April 1896, p. 33.

3. *American Federationist,* April 1896, p. 33.

4. *Report of Proceedings of the Thirteenth Annual Convention of the American Federation of Labor,* 1893, p. 22.

5. Vernon H. Jensen, *Heritage of Conflict* (Ithaca, New York: Cornell University Press, 1950), pp. 59-60.

6. Gompers to William Blackman, March 21, 1898.

7. Gompers to George A. Whitaker, March 6, 1897.

8. Gompers to Boyce, March 9, 1897. This letter started an exchange between Gompers and Boyce, subsequently published in a leaflet.

9. *Ibid.*

10. Boyce to Gompers, March 16, 1897.

11. Gompers to Boyce, March 16, 1897.

12. Gompers to Executive Council, June 30, 1897.

13. Circular in American Federation of Labor archives. It was signed by Boyce and James Maher, secretary-treasurer.

14. Gompers to Executive Council, May 20, 1898.

15. Walter MacArthur to Gompers, May 20, 1898.

16. *Coeur d'Alene Mining Troubles: Senate Document 142, 56th Congress, 1st Session* gives a detailed report on this episode. Jensen, *op. cit.,* pp. 72-95 deals with it and its causes.

17. Gompers to Executive Council, June 30, 1899.

18. Gompers to Frank Morrison, May 16, 1899.

19. Gompers to Boyce, June 20, 1899.

20. Gompers to James Duncan, September 26, 1900.

21. *American Federationist,* August, 1897, p. 117.

22. Gompers to Carl Browne, September 29, 1902.

23. Gompers to Julian Pierce, January 25, 1902.

24. Morrison to Executive Council, February 12, 1902.

25. Gompers to M. L. Owen, January 2, 1903.

26. Jensen, *op. cit.*

27. Circular issued by the American Federation of Labor, June 20, 1904, in archives of the A. F. of L.

28. Paul Brissenden, *The I. W. W.: A study of American Syndicalism* (New York: Columbia University Press, 1920) covers the origin and early activity of the I. W. W.

29. *Report of the Proceedings of the Twenty-Fifth Annual Convention of the American Federation of Labor,* 1905, pp. 253-254.

30. Report to Executive Council, June 16, 1906.

31. Among them the United Mine Workers of America; the United Brotherhood of Carpenters and Joiners of America; the Bricklayers' and Masons' International Union; the American Federation of Musicians; the Hotel and Restaurant Employees International Union; and the International Molders' Union.

32. Report of Frank Morrison to Executive Council, January 30, 1907.

33. Gompers to Ernest Bohm, January 30, 1907.

34. *Vote Book,* June 27, 1905.

35. *Ibid.*

36. Moyer to Gompers, February 20, 1911, September 2, 1911.

XI

Intervention in the Affairs of Affiliates

The Principle of Autonomy of Affiliates

In conformity with the principle of autonomy and independence, the Executive Council of the American Federation of Labor was never granted authority to interfere in the internal affairs of affiliates. Moreover, the international unions, which dominated the Federation from the beginning, would have repelled any attempt by the officers of the A. F. of L. to meddle in their affairs. In fact, several international unions only joined the A. F. of L. when they were assured that their independence would not be in the least impaired. The leaders of the Federation, some of whom were also heads of international unions, were convinced that only on the basis of the complete independence of the international union could a viable federation of labor be built.

However, the principle of autonomy posed a serious problem for the A. F. of L. At times the policies or practices of affiliates might violate trade union standards, or they might affect unfavorably a particular union, and even more, the entire labor movement. Certainly the central organization could not follow a policy of extreme restraint and refuse to advise the less experienced leaders on important issues, ones that might have a serious effect upon the membership. Even more difficult for the Federation were the intra-union disputes, which were likely to arouse strong feelings.

In practice, all intervention in the affairs of affiliates was not of the same order. Usually the issue upon which the Federation intervened would influence the reaction of the affiliated organization. The size of the union might also determine the reaction of an affiliate to advice or intervention by the Executive Council. The stronger and the more stable the union, the less ready it usually was to accept advice or interference by the A. F. of L.

Disputes Within a Union

Disputes within an organization were, at times, submitted to the head of the A. F. of L. Such questions were properly within the province of the international union, and Gompers was "loath to give decisions in matters that arise between organizations, it seems to partake too much

163

of dictatorship."[1] Yet there was a feeling, even among the internationals, that the A. F. of L. as the representative of the labor movement at large was obligated, at least, to urge officers of affiliates to carry out their duties effectively. Taking cognizance of several complaints against the head of the Barbers' Union, Gompers wrote him that "it behooves you to do all in your power to see the movement does not retrograde."[2] The criticism was ignored, and Gompers called attention to the belief that "with proper efforts unions could easily be started in nearly all large cities. I trust you will attend to this matter and come up to the expectations of your fellow craftsmen who honored you by making you their standard bearer."[3] As the complaints continued, Gompers had to inform their authors: "Of course I am powerless to more than advise as to what action should be taken. For that reason I will call on him [Finkelstein] today and endeavor to persuade him to perform his duty or if he is unable to resign and allow some other officer to undertake and perform his functions."[4] Eventually conditions in the Barbers' Union improved, and Gompers' efforts in behalf of better administration may have contributed to this result.

Whenever information on incompetent management or inefficiencies of locals reached the American Federation of Labor, it would be transmitted to officers of the international union involved. A union of molders in Chicago was losing membership—the local A. F. of L. organizer attributed this to a failure of leadership. The head of the Molders' Union was urged to do something "at once to prevent still further disintegration in the ranks of said union."[5] Gompers was not averse to offering friendly advice to union officers, but he made certain that such advice would not be regarded as an interference in the internal affairs of affiliates. When the head of the Boot and Shoe Workers planned a long trip to Europe, Gompers warned him that "frequently have young organizations been ruined forever by inattention in a shorter period than two months."[6] Gompers' advice was heeded and the trip, which would have taken the head of the union from his office for some time, was canceled.

DISPUTES BETWEEN UNIONS

A more difficult problem confronted the American Federation of Labor when a dispute over trade union practices arose between two independent unions. When Josiah B. Dyer of the Granite Cutters' National Union complained to Gompers that carpenters were taking the jobs of the members of his union engaged in a labor dispute, Peter J. McGuire retaliated with a claim against the granite cutters.[7] Gompers could only regret the absence of provisions in the laws of the organizations "by which a better standard of ethics and mutual assistance" could be evolved. He hoped that both officers would make recommendations to their respective unions so as to arrive "at a clear understanding and cooperation upon such matters."

The necessity of cooperation between unions during labor disputes was recognized. When a federal labor union over which the A. F. of L. had power sought to take the job of union carpenters on strike in Saginaw, it was warned that if it continued the practice its charter would be revoked.[8] In the latter case the American Federation of Labor had the authority to act and to insist upon a given standard of conduct. However, unions "affiliated with the A. F. of L. maintain their autonomy and independence in the questions of their profession, trade or calling uninterfered with by any officer of the Federation either in a national or local character."[9]

As international unions held first authority to regulate trade questions in their jurisdictions, the right of central bodies to interfere in the carrying out of agreements became an issue when the St. Louis Trades and Labor Union of St. Louis, Missouri, ordered the musicians' union of that city out on a sympathy strike. When the latter refused, it was suspended and denied a seat in the St. Louis central body. An appeal was taken to the Executive Council, which held that unions when making contracts should consider the interests of all labor organizations affected. However, "the constitutional autonomy accorded affiliated bodies prohibits them [the St. Louis Trades and Labor Assembly] from interfering with bona fide contracts of local unions."[10] A similar issue involving the same two unions came before the convention of the American Federation of Labor in 1899. The musicians, according to the charges, made themselves "thoroughly obnoxious to the affiliated bodies by their attitude to the striking stage employees." Expelled from the Detroit Council of Trades and Labor Unions, the musicians appealed to the A. F. of L. to override this decision. The committee, which considered the issue at the convention, believed that the musicians "acted in complete violation of every principle of trade unionism," and recommended that the expulsion be upheld. However, the convention accepted the view of Andrew Furuseth, who argued: "It was clear that the Detroit musicans employed in theatres had not acted as union men"; but he did not think all the musicians should be condemned for the action of the Detroit men. In the end the dispute was submitted to the American Federation of Musicians, whose Detroit local was involved in the controversy.[11]

The right of affiliates to manage their own affairs was given greater emphasis when a central labor union, the Cincinnati Labor Council, sought to reject a delegate from one of the local unions on grounds that he was not fit to belong to the central body. President McBride intervened and stated that

each organization is the judge of and has the right to select its own representatives, and the rule has applied not only to national conventions of the A. F. of L., but to its central bodies. If any man or set of men are elected to your central body who has been guilty of anything that could disqualify him or them from serving in that capacity, charges should be preferred against them in the union to which they belong, and the case settled on its merits.[12]

The rule against intervention was, however, not always strictly followed, and the A. F. of L. insisted that the Tin, Sheet, Iron and Cornice Workers expel one of its locals because it had allowed unfair men to join. "Your international association," McBride insisted, "cannot afford, neither can we, to stand idly by while being charged with having, and fostering, scabs in our ranks, and yet your organization by its indifference and negligence assumes such a position and forces us to either proceed summarily against your association or to stand equally guilty."[13] The American Federation of Labor revoked the charter of this international union, and only when the local against which charges had been made ceased to exist was the international again welcomed by the A. F. of L.[14] Had the principle of autonomy been strictly observed in this instance, the American Federation of Labor would not have had any grounds for intervention. However, the sheltering of "unfair" men by a national union was considered a question concerning the interests of the entire movement, which afforded a basis for the action.

In 1897, Gompers called attention to the danger of allowing employers, supervisors, and merchants to join the organizations of labor, insisting that there was an "absolute necessity to maintaining the clear-cut character of our movement as a wage-earners' movement." He believed that if employers or supervisors were allowed to join unions they tended to restrain free expression of opinion and the criticism necessary for an effective organization. Gompers' view was endorsed by the convention. Soon the A. F. of L. had to apply this principle.[15] When questions such as employment during strikes or support of unfair men arose, the unions might recognize this as a problem that transcended the rights of a particular group. The honest management and integrity of unions raised another type of issue.

COMPLAINTS BY MEMBERS

The absence of a tribunal to which members might appeal after they had exhausted their remedies within their own unions led some to assume that the American Federation of Labor could provide such a forum. It appears that the heads of the A. F. of L. did not look with disfavor upon such a possibility. When a member of the Retail Clerks' National Protective Union charged the convention of his union with improper action at its convention, the Executive Council would not consider the charges, because "the complaints or grievances submitted have not been officially placed before the Executive Board of the Clerks National Association as required by their laws. All rights of complaining unions should first be exercised and exhausted within their own national unions before coming to the A. F. of L. with their complaints and grievances."[16] The causes that gave rise to the dispute could not be ascertained.

Subsequently, the Executive Council suggested that the legislation which aroused opposition be repealed. In this decision the Federation sought to lay down the conditions under which complaints against officers of affiliates would be considered. Implicitly, at least, the right or authority of the A. F. of L. to consider disputes or complaints arising within its affiliates was not disavowed, as the refusal to intervene was based upon the principle that a complainant had first to exhaust his remedies within his own union.

In fact, the A. F. of L. during the same year intervened in a dispute between the members and locals and the international officers of another international union, the Hotel and Restaurant Employees International Alliance. Charges of fraud had been made against several of the international officers, and the Executive Council investigated the charges. At first, an effort to devise an amicable settlement was made, and a special convention of the union called for this purpose. A committee from the A. F. of L. was present in an effort to work out an agreement. The settlement was not effective in allaying the differences within the union.[17] The A. F. of L. was determined to "have the organization . . . rid . . . of the element which has tended to bring it into disrepute for personal and mercenary reasons."[18] After the old officers had been removed by the American Federation of Labor, it furnished the union with financial aid and advice. Gompers drew up several circulars for the officers, and he insisted that those who had been removed cease claiming membership in the American Federation of Labor.[19] Intervention in this instance was based upon the belief that the officers of the particular union were not fulfilling their duties towards the workers in their jurisdiction, and that the Federation in such cases had a duty—transcending the principle of trade union autonomy—to take action.

In the case of the American Agents' Association a similar issue was involved. An investigating committee had reported to the Cincinnati Labor Council that "certain individuals with very shady reputations . . . have taken up the matter of trades unionism in this vicinity as a means of furthering their own selfish purposes financially and politically, and who have for years been causing strife in the labor ranks."[20] The Council of Cincinnati therefore protested against the recognition of the American Agents' Association because the latter was not a bona fide labor organization. It was further charged that its president, Charles H. Sidener, "is not a wage worker and consequently not entitled to recognition in the Trades Union Movement."[21]

Sidener's right to act as a delegate to the convention of 1899 was challenged. When he failed to answer the charges against him, the convention decided to revoke the charter of the American Agents' Association, and gave the Executive Council thirty days in which to carry out this mandate.[22] However, before taking final action, the Executive Council decided to allow the accused a hearing.

A special committee of Gompers, Morrison, and Andrew Furuseth heard the charges, and concluded that the membership of the American Agents' Association was grossly exaggerated, that a number of locals claimed by the officers did not in fact exist, and that the head of the union used a nonunion print shop in which to publish his official newspaper and the union labels used by his organization.[23]

While the bookkeeping system used left something to be desired, the Executive Council believed that adequate grounds for the revocation of the charter existed without raising the question of the personal integrity of the officers. In conveying the decision of the Executive Council, Gompers sought to soften the blow by declaring simply that the American Agents' Association had an insufficient number of bona fide local unions for the organization to "retain its charter as a national trade union." He called upon the legitimate locals of the quondam international union to reaffiliate directly with the American Federation of Labor. The heads of the Agents' Association pointed to their independence and autonomous rights to carry on the business of their organization, but the Council rejected these arguments, on the narrow ground that the American Agents' Association was not a legitimate trade union.[24] Gompers did not care to engage in recriminations, and, in compliance with his suggestions, the charter was revoked on narrow grounds, the failure of the American Agents' Association to show a sufficient number of members and locals to justify its retention of a charter as an international union. The question of the right of the A. F. of L. to intervene was avoided, although practically the Federation did impinge upon the autonomy of an independent organization.

In the above instances, the A. F. of L. was convinced that the organizations involved were administered in conflict with the principles of trade unionism. Instances arose, however, where the issues involved were not as clear cut. A particular act or policy might be out of harmony with the practices of the labor movement, resulting in complaints by one or more members or locals to the A. F. of L. As a rule, the Federation appealed to the officers of the union directly, offering suggestions but emphasizing the right of the international union to reject the advice given. When the International Union of Steam Engineers refused to charter a local of its craft in New York City, Gompers sought the reversal of the decision. To him, "it was obvious that with the better and thorough organization of the engineers of New York, it will add considerable prestige and power to the International Union, the organization in whose success I feel so much interest."[25]

Disputes between locals and their internationals were even greater difficulties. Usually such disputes are charged with emotion and are likely to arouse strong feelings among the participants. When a local of the Amalgamated Meat Cutters and Butcher Workmen appealed to the A. F. of L. against its international, Gompers informed the secretary of the international union that "the local desires to have the matter reviewed and decided within the lines of trade union authority, and if this be so, it occurs to me that such a desire should not be discouraged. If you consent thereto, I shall review the matter . . . and render a decision . . . binding on both sides."[26] In this instance Gompers sought to develop appellate authority, which this and other unions rejected as undesirable.

ATTACKS UPON INDIVIDUALS

Yet Gompers always stood ready to help affiliates settle disputes among individuals or factions. He regarded himself as the servant and guardian of the welfare of all affiliates, irrespective of the views of the leaders on politics or social questions. Discussing assistance which he and McGuire had given to the Brewery Workers' Union in its negotiations with employers, Gompers warned against the harsh penalty imposed upon a former leader of the organization, August Priesterbach, who had been expelled. Gompers urged that

It is hardly the wisest thing to expel a man from membership in his union when any other mode of punishment is possible. If Mr. Priesterbach has been guilty of wrong doing (and if he has been punished, it is fair to assume he has), there is another form of punishment other than expulsion. Expulsion is the highest penalty any organization of labor can mete out to any man, no matter how grave his crime be to any organization, to society, to mankind, it condemns him to starvation. I do not submit this to you as an isolated expression of my judgment upon a matter of this kind; but I have opposed expulsion as a matter of principle in the union of my own trade, in the national conventions of the Cigar Makers' International Union, as well as upon the public platform. Recently . . . I was asked this same question, and my answer was that there are other ways to punish a member, guilty of unfair conduct toward his organization, than expulsion. . . . You know of course, that Mr. Priesterbach has been an active factor in your national union; he has had the confidence of the members for a very long time, and had the respect of a good many men outside of your organization as well as those of it; and while he may have, and no doubt has, been guilty of a mistaken and wrongful course, yet I believe that he could be dealt with in much more effective as well as rational and humane manner.

Gompers recognized that technically he had no right to enter this issue. He offered his services toward "bringing about an understanding by which the dignity and the interests of your national union can be maintained and yet bring about a peaceful solution of the pending controversy, I shall only be too glad to serve you and the organization."[27] Gompers' intervention in the dispute within an autonomous union was on his own initiative, but he regarded it his duty to seek to prevent open schisms or injustice against individuals.

TECHNICAL CHANGE

The interests of the labor movement might require intervention or advice even when no question of the rights of individuals was involved. Some unions with a long and strong craft tradition might regard the introduction of machinery with fear and suspicion, and instead of seeking to control the new jobs would seek to bar the production workers from their ranks. The heads of the A. F. of L. always avoided public controversy with their affiliated unions. Yet their public silence does not mean that they were unconcerned or that they did not urge a more realistic policy. When the Coopers' Union refused membership to machine workers, Gompers spoke out against the policy.

If [he informed James A. Cable] you refuse to organize them under the jurisdiction of your international union, you cannot deny them the right to organize; and the question then arises whether they are to be encouraged to have an organization independent of your International union or the general labor movement under the banner of the American Federation of Labor, and thus arouse their rivalry and possible antagonism to your organization and the movement, or, on the other hand, adopting the wiser policy of organizing them, recognizing them, having them attached to your International union, and thus help to root out the many evils of child labor, long hours, low wages, now prevailing among the machine coopers.[28]

Gompers pointed to the success with which the International Typographical Union had handled the analogous problem of the introduction of the typesetting machine. Instead of opposing the new devices, the Typographical union insisted that its members be given the first opportunity to operate the new machines under union conditions and wages. Gompers recognized the difference in the positions of the Coopers' and Typographical Unions. In the case of the former, a large number of the workers in its jurisdiction were in the union; the Coopers' controlled a relatively small part of its jurisdiction. Yet Gompers insisted that the prudent policy for the Coopers' Union would be recognition of the machine, then work "for an improvement in the conditions of the men in the trade, whether they work with the ordinary tools or with a machine."[29]

The question took on an even more serious aspect when a local of the Coopers' Union in Milwaukee refused to allow its members to operate machinery, but permitted its operation by nonunion workers. A dispute over the issue caused a strike, which also affected other trades; these appealed to the Executive Council of the A. F. of L. The Council avowed "that if the Coopers' International Union was to grow, was to become a factor for the protection and advancement of the interests of your trade, it was necessary that the policy should be changed and coopers allowed to operate machinery, providing fair union conditions could be obtained."[30] There was, however, a serious obstacle to an adjustment in that the delegates to the convention of the Coopers' Union had adopted provisions which forbade members to operate machinery.

The Council thereupon advised a liberal interpretation of the union rules, for it was "decidedly averse to the violations of the laws of our organization; but, there is a time in the life of an organization when if a strict interpretation of the laws would threaten the very existence of our movement, a liberal interpretation of the laws must be made, in order to protect the interests of those who have entrusted them to our keeping."

In order to protect the interests of the Coopers' Union, the Council insisted that the strike be settled and the use of machinery recognized. It pointed to the gains in wages and hours that had been made under the contract, and "these in themselves are great achievements, but over and above all is the question that employing coopers throughout the country may understand that the Coopers' International Union is prepared to do business with them, and upon a basis which will recognize the machines, accord the right of the coopers to operate them under fair and honorable conditions."[31]

It was largely due to the prodding of the Executive Council that the Coopers' International Union reversed its position and decided to accept the machine.

In the case of the machinery issue involving the Coopers' Union, the dispute affected other organizations. The A. F. of L. was willing to give advice, but even in this situation the Federation had no means by which it could force its views upon affiliates.

It was even more difficult for the A. F. of L. to interject itself into disputes that involved a single organization and its subordinate locals. Yet, Gompers' sense of duty to the labor movement frequently overcame his views on non-interference. Finding that a local union of electrical workers in New York City was encouraging "unfair men," Gompers wrote to the head of the Brotherhood of Electrical Workers:

While in no way desirous of interfering with your jurisdiction or the autonomy of your Brotherhood, yet it seems to me that the best interests of your organization would warrant you in taking every action to rid it of any odium which attaches to the conduct of Local Union No. 12. I am sure that if any local union would [so] conduct itself in the International Union of which I am a member, I would at once request the International President to revoke its charter.[32]

The local was subsequently requested to follow better trade union practices.

It was relatively easy for the heads of the A. F. of L. to speak out against the encouragement of "unfair men," for this involved a question of trade union principle. Much more difficult was intervention in a dispute between two local unions which involved jurisdictional rights. Appealing for an end to discrimination by one local union of painters and decorators against another, Gompers pleaded, after apologizing:

Of course I am not desirous of interfering with the business of your union, but suggest the advisability of mutual recognition of your and their cards and that a fraternal spirit may be manifested by the members of your craft and unions. Regardless of all differences of opinion upon other matters, it seems that the working people of any particular craft should cooperate in their efforts rather than antagonize each other, and I ask you to give this matter your early consideration in order that a mutual understanding may be arrived at.[33]

At the same time, Gompers wrote to the secretary of the Carpenters' Council of New York, asking his cooperation in eliminating the conflict among the painters of that area, for, "[if the policy is] continued, it will only call forth retaliation and that is something we certainly ought to try to avoid in the labor movement."[34]

SECESSION

Differences between a local union and its international not only endangered the stability of the organizations involved, but sometimes created difficulties for the A. F. of L. because of the support the recalcitrant local might receive from the labor movement. The A. F. of L. was likely to be drawn into these differences by the protests of the International against central bodies chartered by the Federation. Even when such possibilities were absent, the A. F. of L. sought to advise and "direct" the affiliates so that they would follow practices that were in harmony with the principles of trade unionism. When two locals of the American Federation of Musicians threatened to secede unless the international changed its rules on traveling musicians, the Executive Council of the A. F. of L. ordered Gompers "to tender the good offices of the A. F. of L. to the end than an adjustment of the controversy between the Musicians of Denver and Chicago may be had."[35] Largely as a result of Gompers' efforts a formula for settling the differences between the locals and the parent organization was devised.

BREWERY WORKERS

An even more serious problem arose when a group of locals seceded from the parent organization. As early as 1891, the heads of the American Federation of Labor were instrumental in healing a serious rift within the Brewery Workers' Union. The Pacific Coast locals of that organization objected to an assessment levied by the international, and withdrew from the national organization when their protests were unheeded. Immediately the A. F. of L. stepped in to heal the breach. It proposed waiving the assessment, but the international refused. Efforts to find a formula were continued. The A. F. of L. agreed that the men on the Pacific Coast misinterpreted their duty to the international, but was "of the opinion that indulging in personalities or abuse of men on the Coast is not the best way to bring about the desired results." It urged the head of the Brewery Workers' Union to offer "some counter propositions" which would lead to "harmony between your fellow craftsmen of the two coasts."[36] It was largely because of the insistence and the efforts of the committee of the A. F. of L. that a settlement was devised under which the Brewers Union of the Pacific Coast agreed to rejoin the national organization by paying the current per-capita and assessment.[37]

BOILER MAKERS

The Executive Council tried to serve the interests of the labor movement and prevent the splits which occasionally took place in single organizations from hardening into permanent division. When several lodges of the Brotherhood of Boiler Makers and Iron Ship Builders of America in the Pittsburgh area seceded, the Executive Council tendered "its good offices as intermediary to conciliate and help to bring about adjustment and unity so much desired." However, the Executive Council found it necessary

to disavow any intention on our part to meddle or interfere with the internal affairs of your organization, for such is farthest from our purpose, but we find a schism in an international trade union, no matter if it be small, but which may possibly grow and widen the breach and bring about rivalry and antagonism from which the workers necessarily suffer. We believe that it is our imperative duty to tender the very best services of which we are capable to avoid the possible consequences and dangers involved.[38]

Feeling ran high, and for a time it was not possible for the Council to get the two groups to meet. Eventually, with the help of Gompers, a formula was worked out which enabled unity to be reestablished.

ELECTRICAL WORKERS

The Executive Council usually offered its services when an internal conflict within an affiliate became serious and tried to find a compromise by which the dispute could be resolved. In the case of the International Brotherhood of Electrical Workers, delegates from two factions, each claiming the right to the name and the prerogatives of the organization, appeared at the convention of the A. F. of L. in 1908. A special committee recommended that President Gompers request locals of both factions to send delegates to a joint convention, that law suits begun by each faction against the other be withdrawn, and that the funds be placed in a special bank in the headquarters' city, Springfield, Illinois, the bank to be designated by President Gompers. A special representative of the A. F. of L. would decide all differences that might arise in the carrying out of the agreement.

The recommendations of the committee were accepted by both factions at the convention, but only one—the group led by Frank J. McNulty—would carry out its commitments. The Reid-Murphy group would neither withdraw its law suits nor agree upon a bank for desposit of the union funds. Consequently, the Executive Council recognized the faction willing to comply with the mandates of the convention.[39]

However, formal recognition did not prevent the seceding union from carrying on its activities, and the Council could not by mere fiat prevent division in the ranks. Efforts to mend the rift in this union were continued. Eventually central bodies of the A. F. of L. complied with the mandate that the seceders were not to be sheltered, but the leaders of the Federation could not avoid concern for the large number of electrical workers outside the regular organization. The Federation hoped to bring the factions together, but it insisted that only the locals affiliated with the faction recognized by the A. F. of L. were to be allowed membership in A. F. of L. central bodies, for under the A. F. of L. constitution no local union suspended, expelled, or seceded from its national union could retain its affiliation with a central body of the A. F. of L. Gompers argued that "to allow a central body or a state branch to recognize a seceding or dual union, carries with it an implied understanding that they may sit in judgment upon the merits of disputes that may arise within the ranks of trades, a right which is primarily that of the international organization of the trade."[40]

The Federation continued its efforts to heal the breach for several years. Committees were elected annually to arbitrate the dispute. When the regular faction refused to proceed with an arbitration because its opponents would not withdraw the pending law suits, Gompers informed the officers that "neither side to a controversy has the right to withdraw from the arbitration." At the same time, he sharply criticised Frank Duffy, a member of the Executive Council who had been chosen as one of the arbitrators, who because of the dilatory tactics of one of the factions sought to resign his post. Gompers wrote Duffy:

To say that I am astonished at the course you have pursued is putting it mildly, for though you were selected as a member of the special committee by one of the parties to the dispute among the Electrical Workers, you, like the other members of the committee, were a special committee of the A. F. of L. In so far as I am either personally or officially concerned, I must decline to consider it, much less to accept it. . . . Addressing myself to what I regard to be a most important and extraordinary procedure, I must prevail upon your conscience and your sense of duty to yourself as an executive officer of one of the greatest organizations of labor of the country; your duty to the men you represent, your duty to the Electrical Workers, as well as to the cause of labor generally, demands that you withdraw your resignation and continue your effort to secure and bring an amalgamation of the Electrical Workers of America.[41]

The division in the ranks of the electrical workers led to scabbing and dissatisfaction that threatened the unity of the labor movement in California. A Light and Power Council had been formed in San Francisco by the Machinists, Boilermakers, Stationary Firemen's, and the Reid-Murphy, or seceding faction, of the Electrical Workers' Unions. This Council became engaged in a strike against the Pacific Coast Gas and Power Corporation, and the strike was subsequently endorsed by the California Federation of Labor, the San Francisco Trades Council, and a number of the building trades.

The regular faction of the International Brotherhood of Electrical Workers injected itself into the strike and signed a contract for a lower wage than the one demanded by the striking electricians. This aroused a storm in the California labor movement, and its delegate to the 1913 convention of the American Federation of Labor called for a condemnation of such methods. A substitute, offered by Wharton of the Machinists' Union, would have required the withdrawal of all men by the International Brotherhood of Electrical Workers who had replaced those on strike. This proposal was defeated by a vote of 12,772 to 5504, and the Executive Council was directed to proceed to San Francisco and work out a solution to the differences.[42]

Gompers, Mitchell, Hayes, Valentine, and Lennon proceeded in San Francisco to seek peace, and they spent ten days in continual session with the contending groups. In the end they were able to work out an agreement. Gompers believed the ten days "spent in conference to settle this matter have achieved results not only for San Francisco, but for the country as a whole." Asked whether there had been any compromise, Gompers replied that compromise was inevitable: "Our ranks are made up of very different people and sometimes their opinions must clash."[43] Under the terms of agreement, the seceding locals were restored to full rights to the International Brotherhood of Electrical Workers, which had already won a victory in the courts of Ohio.

PRESSMEN

The limitation of the authority of the Federation was clearly shown when it sought to mend a break in the ranks of the International Printing Pressmen and Assistants' Union. Several locals in the New York area charged President George L. Berry with using the property of the International union for his own purposes. Supported by the Central Federated Union of New York, the charges were brought to the attention of the Executive Council. Upon learning of the charges against him, Berry suspended the protesting locals. As it appeared that the Pressmen's Union might be faced with a full scale secession movement, the Executive Council decided to intervene on the ground that the jurisdictional conflict that might follow a secession might adversely affect all of the unions in the printing industry.

With some diffidence the Executive suggested that

In view of the desirability and necessity of restoring harmony among the ranks of pressmen, and if the International Printing Pressmen's Union represented by its President or Executive Board is agreeable to the following course, the Executive Council of the American Federation of Labor tenders its good offices for the purpose above assigned, namely, that a committee be created as follows: Two representatives of the International Printing Pressmen's Union, two from the four printing pressmen's locals of New York City and two representatives selected by the Executive Council. The duty of the Committee shall be to bring about unity and cooperation among organized pressmen of America under the jurisdiction of the International Printing Pressmen and Assistants' Union.[44]

This friendly attempt to mediate a dispute within the Pressmen's Union was described by Berry as

Indefensible . . . an unfair and unwarranted usurpation of power by the Executive Council that deserves a severe rebuke. . . . It may be said by the Council that they have taken no position inasmuch as they have left it to the President of the International Printing Pressmen and Assistants' Union to determine whether they shall proceed or not. A position of this kind is vitiated by the fact that the Executive Council did resolve and it has presumed that there existed chaos or lack of harmony in the ranks of the International Printing Pressmen and Assistants' Union.

Berry went on to declare that his union was under no obligation to the Executive Council, and told it in fact to mind its own business.[45] The members of the Executive Council thereupon decided not to pursue the matter any further. Several declared that Berry was mistaken in his charges against the Council, but they saw no possibility of intervention without his consent. In fact the Federation had to insist upon the seceders being denied seats in the Central Federated Union of New York.

Although Berry regarded the intervention of the Executive Council as presumptuous, he did appeal for aid in negotiations with the Chicago Publishers Association. The publishers expressed no desire to deal with the Pressmen's Union, but consented to a conference with Duncan, Mitchell, and Lennon, a committee from the Executive Council "because it had been called by the American Federation of Labor and out of courtesy to the request and efforts of the Executive Council."[46] The Executive Council spent considerable effort and in the end was successful in bringing about an agreement.

SEAMEN

During the same period, a split also developed within a division of the International Seamen's Union, the Atlantic Coast Seamen's Union. The seceders charged that incompetency and mismanagement had led to large-scale losses in membership on the Atlantic Coast and the Great Lakes, and requested the intervention of the Executive Council of the A. F. of L. The charges were supported by the Central Federated Union of New York, which declared that the continuance of the evils within the Seamen's Union threatened to injure the entire labor movement around New York City. Vice President Duncan, who was presiding over the Executive Council, informed the committee protesting conditions in the Seamen's Union that the A. F. of L. "has no jurisdiction over the internal affairs of international organizations," and with that statement requested the representatives "to proceed with whatever they had to say in regard to their contentions."[47] The Executive Council proposed to both parties the appointment of a joint committee, with members of the Executive Council to join the discussion in an attempt to work out the differences, but the objections of the officers of the international organization involved, the International Seamen's Union, ended the efforts of the Executive Council as a peacemaker.

SUSPENSION

Any effort by the American Federation of Labor to impose standards of behavior upon its attached unions would have been resisted and have led to eventual secession by the internationals involved. The Federation could always revoke the charter of a union refusing to obey its mandates, but such a policy held serious dangers to the A. F. of L., and Gompers continually fought against such a step. He believed that affiliation with the A. F. of L. compelled a union to remain "within the bounds," to some degree, "for the wishes of the affiliated unions, as expressed by the judgment of the A. F. of L."[48]

When the Executive Council, despite Gompers' opposition, decided to suspend the charter of the Brewery Workers' Union, Gompers was

more oppressed and depressed . . . than I have ever felt in all my life. . . . No doubt you can imagine the position in which I am placed in being required as President of the A. F. of L. to carry out a policy with which I am in essential variance and against the enforcement of which my judgment revolts. . . . I believe that no opponent in our movement could under any circumstances deliver it so effective and harmful a blow. I have repeatedly heard men resent the statement that the American Federation of Labor is the "parent body" to the trade union movement, a statement with which you and I not only agree but affirm; and yet we see some of these men who stoutly resent the expression or the thought that the American Federation of Labor is the "parent body" of trade unions, vote to revoke a charter of an international trade union. I am not only heart sore; I am astounded.[49]

Gompers regarded this issue of such great importance that he seriously considered resigning the presidency. His public opposition to the decision of the Executive Council drew a rebuke from James Duncan, the first vice president, who pointedly told Gompers he was not the entire Council. Gompers admitted he had violated a fixed rule of not discussing Council business or revealing votes of members, but said he would prefer to disobey the instructions of the convention rather "than to deal a heavy blow to the trade union movement and to the American Federation of Labor."[50]

In these matters, as many others which were controversial, the members of the Executive Council did not explain their action, or attempt to shift the blame for certain decisions to some members. Nor was there any effort to inform the labor movement or the public that the Executive Council had intervened in a given situation. If the Council tried to mediate and failed, and the international insisted upon its rights, the Executive Council believed it was obligated to act in conformity with the provisions of the A. F. of L. constitution. Of course, when the name of the Federation or a basic moral issue was involved, as in the case of the Agents Union and the Hotel and Restaurant Workers, the Federation did intervene. However, it was not regarded as prudent to try to settle every internal dispute that faced every international union.

STEREOTYPERS

A dispute within the International Stereotypers and Electrotypers Union which led to the revocation of the charter of the Chicago local and the expulsion of one of the leaders of the local, L. P. Straube, placed the A.

F. of L. in this kind of a dilemma. The Chicago Federation of Labor sided with the local, and recognized its delegates. The International then demanded that the local be expelled from the Chicago central body.

Straube, who became the center of the controversy, was a well-known Chicago trade unionist, and was actively supported by the leaders of the labor movement in the city. He was also a member of the Commercial Portrait Artists' Union, which now sent him to represent it in the Chicago Federation of Labor. Thereupon, the head of the International Stereotypers and Electrotypers protested to the Executive Council, which asked the Chicago Federation of Labor to deny a seat to Straube.

Aware of the injustice to an active trade unionist, the Executive Council of the American Federation of Labor requested the international to rescind the expulsion and "give Brother Straube an opportunity to earn a living at his trade." It also instructed Gompers to appear before the Stereotypers' convention and plead for his reinstatement. Instead of yielding to Gompers' pleas for justice and forgiveness, the convention voted that

In view of the fact that Samuel Gompers, President of the American Federation of Labor, in a public address delivered before this body in convention assembled, requested that the reaffiliation of an expelled member of this union be taken out of the hands of the Convention [and] be placed in the hands of the Executive Board, the convention respectfully declares that the request is not a proper one to make . . .[51]

Having failed to bring about a settlement, the Federation could do nothing but insist that the constitution be obeyed by its central organization. While the Chicago Federation complied with the order to unseat Straube, every delegate present at the meeting when the order of the Executive Council was read protested the decision. The issue was carried to the convention of 1915. The defense made by the international union, which forced the exclusion of Straube, was that its action was warranted by its own laws. The action of the Executive Council was upheld by the convention by the narrow vote of 97 to 89, after which Gompers declared that this question involved "the law, practice and safety of the movement."[52] Subsequently Straube was reinstated, largely as a result of the efforts of the Executive Council. However, the council would not publicly rebuke an affiliate on an issue which involved the latter's internal affairs.

MEN'S GARMENT WORKERS

In the dispute in the men's garment industry, the A. F. of L. faced a similar issue. The officers of the United Garment Workers of America were out of touch and out of sympathy with the thousands of immigrant workers in their organization in New York and Chicago. Strikes in Chicago in 1910, and in New York in 1913, conducted without the full support of the international officers, widened the rift between the local and international leaderships.

The union, in both the Chicago and New York markets, was dominated by leaders of immigrant origin, many of whom were Socialists. The national leaders, on the other hand, were traditional unionists, who were convinced that the immigrant garment workers were incapable of building a stable organization. Suspicion between the local and national leaders increased when the national leaders sought to settle both the Chicago and New York strikes on terms deemed unfavorable by strikers.

The successful strikes in the leading clothing markets increased the influence of the insurgent locals. It appeared that they had gained a sufficient accretion in their strength to challenge successfully the international officers at the forthcoming convention of 1914. To forestall such a possibility, the international union officers disenfranchised many locals controlled by their opponents. On the theory that they were being denied their rights and that the convention was controlled by usurpers, the delegates from the insurgent locals, with the cooperation of other delegates sympathetic to their viewpoint, withdrew from the convention of 1914, and organized themselves in what they at first called the legitimate United Garment Workers of America. The A. F. of L., however, continued, in line with its historic policy, to recognize the old officers. The delegation from a sister union, the International Ladies' Garment Workers' Union, to the A. F. of L. convention of 1914 sought to have a committee appointed to investigate and bring about unity of the two groups.

"In view of the fact that the subject matter . . . deals with the internal affairs of an organization other than the one which asks for the appointment of the committee, and that to proceed with the proposed inquiry might be construed as recognizing a seceding faction," the resolution was rejected by the A. F. of L. convention. Two members of the committee which recommended rejection of these proposals, the heads of the Electrical Workers' and the Seamen's Unions, had themselves faced secession movements in their own organizations and were clearly out of sympathy with rebellious factions. The president of the Brotherhood of Electrical Workers believed that if a firm stand had been taken on the secession in his union, the seceding group would not have acquired as much support as it had.

Failing to win the intervention of the A. F. of L., the seceders established the Amalgamated Clothing Workers of America, which became a great union despite its nonaffiliation with the A. F. of L. The Executive Council made an effort, despite the vote of the convention, to initiate negotiations between the leaders of the United Garment Workers of

America and the leaders of the seceding group. In this instance the regular leaders also objected, and the matter was not pursued any further.

The Executive Council then ordered one of its affiliates, the United Hebrew Trades, a central body of unions of Jewish workers, to expel its locals aligned with the seceders, in conformance with the constitution, which denied affiliation with A. F. of L. central bodies to locals seceding from national unions belonging to the A. F. of L. Instead of yielding immediately to the instructions of the Executive Council, the United Hebrew Trades asked that efforts to bring the two groups together again be made. The request was rejected.

The United Hebrew Trades was again ordered to disaffiliate the seceding locals of garment workers. The United Hebrew Trades informed the Council that to abide by "your decision we would make a precedent of sacrificing the very moral foundation upon which our organization stands. We ask you no more than would be expected of any body civic that sits in judgment, namely, to give the accused a chance to plead his case." Duncan, Valentine, and Hayes favored reconsidering the case, but all insisted that the United Hebrew Trades must comply with the decision, and expel the garment workers' locals.[53] The recognized officers of the United Garment Workers insisted that the seceders were being led by New York Socialists, manipulated by the *Forward*. Following refusal to oust the seceding garment workers, unions affiliated with the A. F. of L. were required to withdraw from the United Hebrew Trades.

The issue was again debated at the convention of 1915, and an attempt was made to question whether the Executive Council had allowed the seceding clothing workers their day in court. Gompers defended the Council, and insisted that its members could only devote a limited amount of time to the business of the Federation.

CONCLUSION

Irrespective of any other consideration, the A. F. of L. could not have acted differently from its course in this instance. Moreover, no special rule was applied in this situation but the usual custom of not recognizing seceders. This rule was followed in the other cases mentioned earlier. In the dispute within the Printing Pressmen's Union, Frank Morrison, the secretary of the A. F. of L. and himself a printer and conversant with conditions in the Printing Pressmen's Union, sounded a note of despair in his letter circulating Berry's righteous answer to the offer of the Executive Council to arbitrate. The powerlessness of the A. F. of L. in the men's garment workers' dispute perhaps illustrates the rule against nonintervention at its worst. There can be no doubt that the Amalgamated Clothing Workers of America, made up at the time of the dissident group within the United Garment Workers of America, was correct in its revolt against a crass attempt by a group of officers to stay in office, irrespective of the will of the majority. Certainly, the Amalgamated Clothing Workers of America demonstrated over time that it, rather than its opponent, was the union capable of organizing the men's clothing industry.

Nevertheless, the principle that was followed in this instance was the only one which would have made the Federation a living reality. An attempt to make every difference within an organization, every division within the ranks of a union, its own would have destroyed the Federation. The Unions would not have allowed a tutelary authority to rise above them, and determine the management of their internal affairs.

In 1919 the American Federation of Labor was again brought into a controversy between locals of the International Printing Pressmen and Assistants' Union and the top officers. This time, two other international unions in the printing industry appealed to the Executive Council and requested that the city central body of New York be ordered not to support the seceding group among the pressmen. The Council called upon the locals to return to their "allegiance of the International Printing Pressmen and Assistants' Union at once," and Gompers was sent to New York to confer with the seceders. It took some time before the issues were resolved.[54] A similar problem arose in the secession of several locals of the Teamsters' Union in New York in 1921. The head of the international immediately demanded that the locals be ousted from the Central Trades and Labor Council of Greater New York. As in the pressmen's case, Gompers called a conference of the contending parties, and was successful in working out an agreement which restored unity.[55]

However, the A. F. of L. would even avoid using its limited influence in controversies within unions which did not lead to an open schism. Thus when the International Longshoremen's Association complained of the refusal of the New York locals to accept the award of the National Adjustment, the Executive Council replied it could not "inject itself into a strictly trade struggle between factions in a national or international union. . . . The dispute should be solved by those who have the power to enforce its rules and decisions. . . . The Executive Council, as you know, has no control over the actions of members of national or international unions."[56]

REFERENCES

1. Gompers to Charles E. Miller, May 11, 1888.
2. Gompers to Edward Finkelstein, March 3, 1888.
3. Gompers to Finkelstein, April 10, 1888.
4. Gompers to Fred L. Berger, October 18, 1888.
5. Gompers to Paul Fitzpatrick, February 14, 1889.

6. Gompers to H. J. Skeffington, July 17, 23, 1889.

7. Gompers to Josiah Dyer, June 19, 1890.

8. Gompers to P. J. McGuire, June 6, 1890.

9. Gompers to Owen Miller, May 8, 1891.

10. Minutes of the Executive Council of the American Federation of Labor, April 2, 1893.

11. *Report of Proceedings of the Nineteenth Annual Convention of the American Federation of Labor*, 1899, pp. 133, 146.

12. John McBride to Frank L. Rist, June 12, 1895.

13. McBride to James F. Hughes, June 15, 1895.

14. *Report of Proceedings of the Seventeenth Annual Convention of the American Federation of Labor*, 1897, p. 18.

15. *Ibid.*, pp. 88-89.

16. Minutes of Executive Council, October 24, 1898; Gompers to Fulton Williams, October 23, 1898.

17. Quote in Executive Council Minutes, October 16, 1899; Executive Council Minutes, October 25, 1898; *Report of Proceedings of the Eighteenth Convention of the American Federation of Labor*, 1898, pp. 114-115.

18. Gompers to Owen Miller, October 10, 1899.

19. Gompers to Fred C. Dressler, October 21, 1899; to Thomas Tract, December 12, 1899.

20. Report to Central Labor Council of Cincinnati, Ohio, by the Special Investigating Committee appointed to look up the matter of granting a charter to the Kenton and Campbell Counties Trades and Labor Assembly, April 4, 1899.

21. To the Executive Council of the American Federation of Labor from the Cincinnati Labor Council Committee, January 15, 1900.

22. Gompers to Charles H. Sidener, January 20, 1900.

23. *Hearing of the Defense of the American Agents' Association*, held at the headquarters of the American Federation of Labor, January 29, 1900.

24. Gompers to Charles Sidener, April 20, 1900; Sidener to Gompers, April 6, 1900.

25. Letter to P. F. Doyle, March 4, 1899.

26. Gompers to Homer D. Call, November 22, 1899.

27. Gompers to Charles F. Bechtold, October 7, 1899.

28. Gompers to James A. Cable, president of the Coopers' International Union, in *American Federationist*, September, 1899, p. 160.

29. *Ibid.*

30. Gompers to James A. Cable, November 18, 1899.

31. *Ibid.*

32. Gompers to H. W. Sherman, January 29, 1900.

33. Gompers to Officers and Members of the Operative Painters Protective and Benevolent Union, June 27, 1890.

34. Gompers to James Doyle, June 27, 1890.

35. Gompers to Owen Miller, October 8, 1901.

36. Gompers to August Delabar, May 18, 1891; to Ernest Kurzenknabe, June 25, 1891.

37. Agreement between the Brewers Union of the Pacific Coast and the National Union of United Brewery Workmen, January 14, 1892.

38. Executive Council of the A. F. of L. to John McNeill, December 13, 1903, December 15, 1903, December 16, 1903.

39. Vote Book of Executive Council, December 14, 1908.

40. Vote Book of Executive Council, October 18, 1909.

41. Gompers to Frank Duffy, March 14, 1910; to F. J. McNulty and James F. Noonan, March 14, 1910, in vote book, March 14, 1910.

42. *Report of the Proceedings of the Thirty-Third Annual Convention of the American Federation of Labor*, 1913, pp. 377-381.

43. *San Francisco Call*, December 6, 1913.

44. Resolution in Vote Book of the Executive Council, August 11, 1913; Report of Frank Morrison to Executive Council, August 23, 1913.

45. George L. Berry to Morrison, August 11, 1913.

46. Minutes of the Executive Council, November 2, 1913.

47. Minutes of the Executive Council, August 6, 1913.

48. Minutes of the Executive Council of the American Federation of Labor, May 19, 1906.

49. Gompers to Lennon, May 8, 1907.

50. Gompers to Duncan, May 1, 1907; Duncan to Morrison, April 13, 1907.

51. Vote Book, October 25, 1915.

52. *Report of the Proceedings of the Thirty-Fifth Annual Convention of the American Federation of Labor*, 1915, p. 392.

53. A. I. Shiplacoff to Executive Council, July 25, 1915; August 26, 1915, Vote Book.

54. Minutes of the Executive Council, December 18, 1919.

55. Minutes of Executive Council, October 24, 1921; Agreement on the Settlement of dispute between International Brotherhood of Teamsters, Chauffeurs, Stablemen and Helpers and New York locals, in A. F. of L. archives.

56. Minutes of Executive Council, October 7, 1921.

XII

Jurisdictional Problems

EXCLUSIVE JURISDICTION

At its organization, the A. F. of L. had no power to decide the jurisdiction of its affiliates. In fact, any attempt to make such decisions was always implicitly, and at times even explicitly, challenged by some unions, even some which on other occasions insisted that their rights to their jurisdictions be enforced by the Federation. The declaration by the convention of 1888 that the A. F. of L. deemed "it unwise for two local, national or international organizations of any one trade to exist in the same jurisdiction, and advise the amalgamation of trades in such instances" was the first statement on this question.[1] The Executive Council was instructed to use its influence toward eliminating competing unions. The convention in the following year was again instructed to "make a persistent effort to bring about an amalgamation of all dual organizations existing in any one trade, and especially so of any that may exist in the case of unions affiliated with the American Federation of Labor."[2] The principle embodied in these resolutions—one organization in a trade— was tested almost immediately when the Amalgamated Society of Carpenters and Joiners applied for affiliation with the American Federation of Labor. At the protest of the United Brotherhood of Carpenters and Joiners, its rival was refused a charter. The convention approved this action by the Executive Council, but in 1890 the Amalgamated Society was allowed to join the A. F. of L.[3]

While the principle of one union in a jurisdiction had general acceptance within the labor movement, conflicts were unavoidable as long as more than one union claimed the right to organize a particular group of workers. Union jurisdictions were not always sharp and clear enough to eliminate such disputes. Moreover, changes in materials and techniques would stimulate rival claims to jobs and frequently became a source of conflict. Another factor in promoting differences was the granting of jurisdiction over a particular group of workers to more than one union, as was likely to happen when those unions had been established prior to the formation of the American Federation of Labor. It was therefore natural that disputes of this character would be carried to the American

Federation of Labor, largely because no other tribunal existed for considering such issues—nor would one have been considered by the unions. The A. F. of L. accepted these duties without enthusiasm, and sought to effect voluntary solutions. Thus the convention of 1892 recommended that the Furniture Workers' Union and the United Brotherhood of Carpenters and Joiners, the two unions involved in the first jurisdictional dispute, find some method of getting together. The committee did not believe "it lies within their province to take any other action, as the constitution gives to each body the right to control its own affairs."[4]

The early conventions of the A. F. of L. would have preferred to avoid intervening in jurisdictional disputes. Nevertheless, at the convention of 1893 the Tin, Sheet-Iron, Cornice and Sky Light Workers' Union filed a complaint against the United Brotherhood of Carpenters and Joiners of America because the latter was "usurping the right of other union men carrying the card of our International Union." The convention approved a resolution that members of the Brotherhood of Carpenters and Joiners refrain from putting in tin gutters, putting up corrugated sheet iron or any other work not part of the carpenters' craft.[5] Of course there were no means by which the Federation could compel the Carpenters' Union or, for that matter, any other organization, to accept its dicta. The convention took a "determined stand against the many internal fights among affiliated organizations," and the Executive Council was instructed to discourage such disputes by enforcing the clauses in the A. F. of L. constitution which gives to each trade the right to manage its own affairs, and imposes on the Executive Council the duty to bring about the unity of organizations in the same trade. The difficulty with that advice was that every trade involved in a dispute took the position that certain jobs were in its trade jurisdiction. Consequently these disputes were brought before the Executive Council and the conventions of the A. F. of L. for adjudication. Despite their insistence on the right to determine their own jurisdictions, many unions alternately voted on such questions at conventions and at other times were parties to a complaint. The leaders of the Federation, who favored settlement of jurisdictional disputes by negotiation and tolerance, were sometimes forced to use pressure in enforcing the decisions. As pressure could more be easily applied to weak than to strong unions, the Federation was more likely to use "force" upon the weaker ones, but only after successive efforts at a settlement had been made.

As unions were established and expanded their activities, jurisdictional questions tended to increase. At the convention of 1896, several unions presented jurisdictional complaints. The lathe operators' union protested against a worker, employed in its jurisdiction, who refused to join that union on the ground he already belonged to the International Association of Machinists. The grievance committee of the convention held that he would have to pay the regular dues to the lathe operators' union as long as the latter held a charter in that trade. A dispute between the Electrical Workers' Union and National Alliance of Theatrical Stage Employees was decided in favor of the former, and, for the first time, a dispute between the Coopers' and Brewery Workers' Unions came before the convention. It was believed that a settlement had been reached, but the division among the workers employed in breweries was to be long and recalcitrant, with the dispute becoming more serious with time. While the dispute over the brewery workers was longer and more tenacious than most jurisdictional controversies, it was typical in that the unions involved refused to accept adverse rulings, and thus the dispute would reappear at the following convention.[6]

THE BREWERY INDUSTRY CONFLICT

In 1896, the National Union of Steam Engineers was chartered by the A. F. of L., and in the following year the stationary firemen were organized on a national basis. The establishment of these unions brought a serious jurisdictional problem. These unions demanded the right to organize the members of their crafts around breweries; on the other hand, the Brewery Workers' Union contended that when the Brewery Workers' Union was organized in 1888 it had been given the right to recruit coopers, firemen, engineers, and teamsters into its organization.[7] The Federation had taken the position, at its convention in 1898, that "all union men should belong to a union of their craft," and the issue between the several craft unions and the United Brewery Workers' Union became increasingly serious. During 1899, the Brewery Workers were asked by the Executive Council of the A. F. of L. to comply with the resolution that "unions having workers of another craft or calling, as members of their union, should insist that they belong to the union of their craft or calling where such exist."[8] This controversy was not a typical clash over jurisdiction, as the form of organization was also involved: the Brewery Workers' Union insisted upon being recognized as an industrial union.

At the convention of 1899, it was decided that a union seeking a charter from the A. F. of L. would be required to

State and define in its laws all the branches or trade over which it claims jurisdiction, and should such laws cover branches of trades already chartered by the American Federation of Labor, then such charter shall be denied until passed upon by the American Federation of Labor in convention assembled, when the claims of all parties shall receive a hearing. Should a charter be granted by the American Federation of Labor to a distinct branch or trade formerly a part of another body, the parent body from that time forward shall be estopped from receiving into its ranks members of unions of the branch or trade chartered.[9]

The rule adopted was obviously designed to serve for cases such as the Brewery Workers' Union, in which the claim of prior organization was the basis upon which a union argued for its right to retain craftsmen whose respective craft organizations were subsequently established.

While the convention and the Executive Council could legislate on this question, the Brewery Workers' Union refused to accept the decisions. The issue was again submitted to the convention of 1899. There was considerable discussion on the floor, with one delegate objecting to the transfer of workers between organizations "like a flock of sheep." In the end, the Executive Council was instructed to appoint a committee to settle the differences between the engineers, firemen, and brewery workers' unions. The failure of the Executive Council to compel obedience to its decisions was criticized by James A. Cable, the head of the Coopers' Union. The latter objected to the calling of a strike by the Brewery Workers' Union against the employment of a member of the coopers' organization. He charged Gompers with showing lack of vigor in carrying out the decisions of the conventions and committees of the A. F. of L. It was Cable's opinion that there should be "a power somewhere in the labor movement strong enough to adjust these questions of jurisdiction." Gompers pointed to the inability of different trades "to determine where the line of one trade ends and the other begins, and each asks for arbitrary and final decisions from the executive head of the American Federation of Labor."[10]

The gravamen of the Coopers' Union complaint was that the A. F. of L. was not compelling the United Brewery Workers' Union, an industrial organization, to release craftsmen to the craft organizations whose members were employed in the breweries. Gompers recognized he could do little to compel obedience, and he therefore argued that

[One of the] greatest factors which had contributed to the growth, the influence and the power of the American Federation of Labor, and with it the national and local trade union movement, has been the fact that its officers have not been clothed with power to order, decide and enforce questions of trade disputes between unions. . . . By always acting as an advisor and mediator only exercising its functions and duties voluntarily granted by the trades unions to the American Federation of Labor, it has been potent in adjusting innumerable disputes of all kinds to the advantage of all labor and all organizations.[11]

This moral authority Gompers always sought to exercise, but not always to any avail. The Brewery Workers' Union had forced the replacement of a cooper with a worker from its own organization, the latter being paid a lower wage. Again a complaint was made by the Coopers' Union, and Gompers sought to use his influence towards a settlement. He wrote to the Brewery Workers' Union that he made

no pretense of being able to decide the fine lines of demarcation of trade jurisdiction, but it appears to me, and I think it will appear to most every other person, that a hoop driving machine should be operated by a cooper. I am not asking you to give up your work to the coopers or to others, but the fact remains that when a union man is doing certain work, that work coming under the jurisdiction of his trade, he should be permitted to continue, more especially when the wages paid him are higher than the wages which are offered to the workman of another trade. After all, the question is that the man is a union man associated with his fellow workers.[12]

The Executive Council tried a compromise, and decided that engineers and firemen who were members of the National Union of United Brewery Workmen could remain in that organization, and the cards of these workers were to be recognized by the Engineers' and Firemen's Unions. On the other hand, the Brewery Workers' Union was to refrain from issuing charters to engineers and firemen and all applications for such charters were to referred to the respective craft unions.[13]

The question came up again at the convention of 1900, and the grievance committee which considered the complaints of several craft unions against the United Brewery Workers recognized that enforcing a decision under which the Brewery Workers' Union would be compelled to divest itself of all craftsmen employed in breweries might work serious injury upon the Brewery Workers' Union. It was recommended that the Brewery Workers' Union be given jurisdiction over employees in breweries. However, coopers and other craftsmen engaged on new or repair work were to join the unions of their crafts, and firemen, engineers, or other crafts, now under the jurisdiction of the United Brewery Workers, were to be allowed to remain members of their craft organizations without interference from the United Brewery Workers. The proposal left craftsmen who were members of the Brewery Workers' Union in the latter organization. An amendment from the floor that all engineers and firemen be instructed to join the union of their craft was defeated by a vote of 2999 to 1902. Gompers, Duncan, and Lennon voted for the more severe restrictions, while Vice Presidents Kidd and Mitchell and Secretary Morrison voted for the more liberal proposal. The Grievance Committee pointed to the inability of the convention "to legislate for any affiliated body" and the committee therefore recommended that the unions involved in disputes seek to come to an understanding on the basis of an interchange of cards.[14] Despite the efforts of the Federation, the issues in dispute remained unsettled, as the Brewery Workers' Union refused to obey the decision.

The majority of the members of the Executive Council were members of craft unions. However, their opposition to the Brewery Workers' Union did not arise from the fact that the latter sought to operate on an industrial basis. In fact, Gompers severely reprimanded a local of the Teamsters' Union which had entered into a contract with a group of breweries in Cincinnati, Ohio. Gompers found that they did not represent a single beer driver and that

This wholly unwarranted contract was entered into to continue for a term of three years, and this too without a word of consent or assent from the men involved or interested. It is plainly evident . . . that the contract entered into between Team Drivers' Union No. 13 and the Cincinnati Brewery Employers' Exchange was irregular, improper, and ought to be annulled. In regard to the question as to under whose jurisdiction beer drivers properly come, it is but necessary to say that beer drivers have been part of the United Brewery Workers' International Union since its formation and affiliation with the American Federation of Labor, more than twelve years prior to the organization of the Team Drivers' International Union.[15]

Whatever may have been the personal views of particular members of the Council, the problem facing the A. F. of L. in this area was to find workable compromises.

With the help of the Executive Council of the A. F. of L., an agreement setting up joint conference boards of the Firemen's, Engineers', and Brewery Workers' unions was worked out for the cooperation of the three unions, but a special convention of the Brewery Workers' Union rejected this arrangement. Thus the controversy continued. In the meantime, strikes of one union against the other plagued the industry. At the convention of 1904, it was decided that the Brewery Workers' Union would not be allowed to organize engineers, firemen, and teamsters. The latter union, organized by the A. F. of L. in 1899, had become of some importance. It was decided that engineers, firemen, and teamsters employed in breweries could withdraw from the United Brewery Workmen's Union and join their respective unions without prejudice or discrimination. Whenever a majority of men employed as engineers, firemen, or teamsters in any brewery were members of the respective unions of these crafts, the organization or organizations representing such majority was to appoint a committee to act jointly with the United Brewery Workmen's Union in negotiations with the employer. Failure to comply with the provisions of the recommendations within six months after the adjournment of the convention was to lead to a revocation of the charter of the organizations failing to carry out the instructions.

These proposals failed to solve the controversy. The Executive Council then appointed Adolph Strasser to act as arbitrator. Strasser found that all the three unions—engineers, firemen, and brewery workers—were guilty of violating the decisions of the Executive Council and the conventions of the A. F. of L.

Strasser ruled again that in breweries where the majority of engineers and firemen are members of their respective crafts, they were to appoint committees to act jointly with the Brewery Workers' Union, the latter organization to have representation equal to all the other unions. However, he ruled that hereafter the Brewery Workers' Union was not to admit to membership any engineers, firemen, or teamsters, but to refer all members of these trades to their respective organizations. While holding each of the unions guilty of unfairness, Strasser suggested that all disputes and charges except scabbing be kept off the floor of the convention of the A. F. of L. for at least three years, and that those unions which violated the ruling of the convention should have their charters revoked. The Executive Council pleaded with the unions "for moral compliance" with the decision.

When the Brewery Workers' Union refused to obey the rulings of the Executive Council and various conventions, its charter was revoked—over the strong protests of Gompers. The charter of this union was canceled on May 30, 1907, but a demand for its reinstatement was made at the following convention. Gompers, who believed that the Brewery Workers' Union was in error, yet spoke out against suspending charters:

[I do] not believe in the revocation of charters as a remedy for the grievances that come up in the labor movement. I am not asking the favor of the Brewery Workers when I make that statement, because I want to couple it with the further statement that I believe the Brewery Workers are wrong; and this conclusion does not come because they believe or do not believe in a philosophy of the trade union movement I do, or because they and I are at variance on that question. My judgment on trade union affairs is not formed on whether a man differs or agrees on any economic or philosophical proposition. The concrete position of the Brewery Workers is wrong. They have never been able to demonstrate either in the conventions of the American Federation of Labor, or before the committees of the American Federation of Labor or before any person specially appointed to investigate this question, they have never been able to demonstrate to any impartial body brought together, large or small, that they were right. Every body of men that has considered the question in controversy between the Brewery Workers and the Engineers and Firemen has absolutely decided that the Brewery Workers were in the wrong. You will readily observe, then, that when I say I believe and know they are in the wrong, and yet I vote, and will, so long as I have the power of voting, against the revocation of their charter; but they ought to be made to feel the decision and judgment of the labor movement that they are in the wrong.

In the end, the charter was restored, on the motion of Gompers from the floor of the convention.[16]

The jurisdictional difficulties of the brewery industry are unique only for their duration. The number of these disputes increased annually, totaling over four hundred between 1890 and 1924. The Federation found these differences a source of difficulty and frustration. The convention of 1900 observed that each

party has apparently been accorded jurisdiction over the field immediately in dispute by American Federation of Labor charter. Particularly is this the case when the dispute involves one of what we might term the composite charters granted by the American Federation of Labor. And often, as a result, we find ourselves confronted with the undesirable task of limiting on the one hand what is popularly regarded as trade autonomy, or, on the other, of disintegrating a composite organization which, while in existence, has demonstrated its ability both to protect and advance the interests of its members to a remarkable degree. In such cases we are strongly of the opinion that narrow conceptions of strict trade autonomy should give way to the policy which, in our judgment, will best serve the interests of the workers immediately involved, and best promote the power of the general movement. We desire further to say that this body can not, in our opinion, presume, by resolution or otherwise, to transfer bodies of men from one organization to another, unless with their consent.[17]

MACHINISTS AND PRINTERS

The Federation did not favor splitting existing unions, nor did it as a matter of principle oppose industrial organizations, but it could not refuse to hear the complaints of affiliates against one another.

At the end of the century, a dispute arose between the International Association of Machinists and the International Typographical Union over which was to have jurisdiction of machinists employed in printing plants. James O'Connell, the head of the International Association of Machinists, complained to the Executive Council, of which he was a member, that

our affiliation with the A. F. of L. guarantees to us the autonomy of our trade and full jurisdiction over the machinists' craft. I, therefore, in the name of the International Association of Machinists, request you, as the executive of the A. F. of L. take this matter up at once with the International officers of the I.T.U. in accordance with the laws governing the A. F. of L.[18]

Gompers pleaded for calmness, reason, and compromise. When Chicago Local No. 16 of the International Typographical Union refused to work with members of the Machinists' Union, O'Connell became more insistent upon the rights of his union. In a letter to Gompers, he charged that the lockout of machinists constituted "a flagrant violation of trade autonomy, and we demand of the American Federation of Labor protection under our affiliation."[19] As a member of the Executive Council and as one of the leading trade unionists of his time, O'Connell was well aware of the limits of the Federation's power.

Under the constitution of the International Typographical Union, union law is not subject to compromise or arbitration. At its convention in 1898, the I.T.U. declared that machinists operating linotype machines would generally be required to belong to the International Typographical Union. Gompers was anxious to find a solution, and he was distressed by the intransigence of both parties, an intransigence which he believed was injuring the general labor movement. In letters to the heads of both the Machinists' and Printers' unions, he pointed to their responsibilities, lamented appeals to pride, and pleaded for an amicable settlement.

If your organizations [they were told], persist in the course outlined [engaging in jurisdictional disputes] it simply means that in all organizations a union man will take sides in every city and town throughout the country; and that which has taken a lifetime of effort; that has caused years of uninterrupted work, sacrifice, and untold money expenditures, that is, the unity and solidarity of the labor forces of the United States, is in danger of being destroyed and the workers rendered helpless to defend and protest, much less advance, their interests . . . it is one of the saddest moments of my life to be compelled to record the fact that in cool, calm deliberation two such powerful organizations as yours are arraying themselves in preparation for a conflict, the trying consequences of which no one can now fully foretell. Is it not likely that the best interests of both your organizations are being jeopardized by your attitudes; and is it not likely that the interests opposed to your organizations and their members are intensely interested in this strife and antagonism, to thereby not only weaken and destroy the efficiency to protect your respective crafts, but that this internecine strife may lead to the disruption of the labor movement and the demoralization of our forces.[20]

Gompers regarded all jurisdictional disputes as harmful, and one between two such powerful organizations as the "most serious and dangerous incident that came under my notice in the American labor movement." Nevertheless his advice and pleas were unheeded, and the relations between the two organizations were exacerbated when O'Connell, in a confidential letter, accused members of the International Typographical Union of "ratting or scabbing our men out of their positions." The secretary of the Typographical Union, John W. Bramwood, sent a copy of the letter, which had been shown to him, to Frank Morrison, the secretary of the A. F. of L., with a request that it be shown to Gompers. The latter immediately wrote to O'Connell that he "was astounded that you should ever harbor thoughts on the line you have written, much less to pen them and publish them." The Executive Council considered a part of the letter as applying disrespectfully to all members composing the I.T.U. O'Connell submitted an apology and withdrew the statement as it applied to the membership of the I.T.U.[21]

This dispute went on from year to year, with the machinists, who were the weaker craft in this situation, continually complaining to the A. F. of L. The president of the International Typographical Union did

not think the membership will ever consent to allow the A. F. of L. to handle the machine tender question, for our membership who have had experience in machine offices, know very well that harmony in our ranks depends upon our controlling machine tenders. I think I stated in one of my previous letters to you that frequent cases had come to the notice of this office where machine tenders, previous to their admission to the I.T.U., were the cause of continual friction between the foreman of the composing room and the men under him, and the proprietors. Since we have assumed control of machine tenders, this friction has been done away with, for the machine tenders understand thoroughly that they are governed by the I.T.U. law, and that a violation of them means expulsion and loss of their situation.[22]

As a matter of fact the members of the Executive Council were plainly told that the printers would not obey any decision not in their favor, and a member of an arbitration committee appointed to settle the dispute was convinced that if a decision was made that would not be "satisfactory to the printers, the printers would ignore it." He saw no purpose in spending his time in such fruitless endeavors.

Another member of the Executive Council was convinced that the linotype operator machinists should be under the control of the Printers' Union, and he believed that "the strict autonomy of trades in a narrow sense is because of the different methods of production disappearing . . . and every trade may as well appreciate this fact and act in accordance, as to butt [its] heads against a stone wall in opposition." The proposal offered for the handling of this problem, made by John B. Lennon, long-time treasurer of the Federation, was similar to one adopted in the 1930's in the organization on a large scale of the manufacturing industries. Lennon believed "the principal craft in the manufacture of any product should control the establishment even if it does to some extent infringe upon what many trade unionists insist upon as being trade autonomy."[23] As a principle Lennon's suggestion was rejected, although it was virtually the position the A. F. of L. had to take in the case of the coal mining industry. A similar view has been adopted in practice in manufacturing industry, but only after the great organizing drives of the 1930's and 1940's, sparked to a large extent by the rise of the Congress of Industrial Organizations.

COAL MINING AND THE SCRANTON DECLARATION

Whatever theory may prevail, the hard fact of the practicability of a solution always faced the leaders of the Federation. Unions were not always consistent on this issue. The International Association of Machinists, while engaged in bitter long-time controversy over several hundred linotype machinists, could yet support industrial unionism at the conventions of the Federation. Whatever rule or decision the Federation might have adopted on this issue, it is likely that the strong affiliated unions would have ignored it whenever such a rule treaded upon their jurisdictional rights. In the case of the coal mining industry the jurisdictional problem took a novel form. When the United Mine Workers of America was chartered, no conflict of jurisdiction existed between its claims and those of other unions. This changed when in 1900 the Brotherhood of Blacksmiths demanded the right to organize members of its craft employed in and around coal mines so "that our members everywhere shall not be disturbed or intimidated by any other trade labor organization." Gompers was not sympathetic to these demands, and argued "the miners have great responsibility by reason of the contracts they have entered into with the mine owners; and is not quite so easy when once organizing men under the jurisdiction of their national organization to turn them over, more especially if these men have secured some property right in the organization in the shape of benefits."[24]

Soon thereafter, the Engineers', Firemen's, Machinists', and Pattern Makers' unions also complained against the invasion of their jurisdictions by the United Mine Workers of America. Under the decree of the convention of the A. F. of L. in 1899, the unions challenging the Mine Workers' organization had a valid case, for the convention of that year declared the "principle of trade autonomy guarantees to the weaker crafts the same measure of protection that the stronger bodies can maintain for themselves." Moreover, each affiliated craft was presumed to have complete jurisdiction "over its members irrespective where they may be employed."[25] Yet, the principle could not, as was already noted, be enforced against a strong union. The claims of the craft unions for the right to organize members of their respective trades employed around the coal mines were creating serious friction and danger of an open clash in some of the Illinois coal mining communities.[26]

President Mitchell of the United Mine Workers of America took cognizance of the attacks upon the jurisdiction of his union and advised the convention of 1901 that it was necessary for one organization to have complete jurisdiction in and around the mines. He argued that there had been instances where craftsmen, members of the unions of their trades, had caused strikes and idleness of many members of the United Mine Workers of America, even though these craftsmen represented a small percentage of the total employees. Following his lead, the convention of the United Mine Workers of America in 1901 declared that it had "jurisdiction of all men employed in and about coal mines, excepting foremen, etc., and we would recommend that the incoming officers be directed to organize into the United Mine Workers of America all engineers, firemen, blacksmiths, carpenters, and others who may now be members of other trade organizations."[27]

Gompers, who had discussed the question with Mitchell, echoed the sentiments of the coal miners. He explained that craftsmen working in and around the coal mines were not likely to comprise a large part of the labor force. Yet under some circumstances, it would be possible for approximately 3 per cent of all workers, the number of craftsmen, to force a shutdown of the mines, and thereby compel the remaining 97 per cent to follow suit. According to Gompers, the United Mine Workers of America found such conditions intolerable, and insisted that the craftsmen become members of its organization.[28]

As mining communities were not typical industrial towns, a basis for differentiating between mining and other industries existed. On the motion of James Duncan, the first vice president and a close collaborator of Gompers, a special committee on autonomy was appointed at the convention of the A. F. of L. in 1901. On the committee were Gompers, Mitchell, and Duncan, the most influential members of the Executive Council. They brought in what has become known as the "Scranton Declaration" which defined the rights of affiliated unions within their jurisdictions. The "Declaration" recognized the need for applying "the principle of autonomy consistent with the varying phases and transactions in industry." The committee found it "impossible to define the lines of demarcation where one trade or form of labor ends and another begins, and that no hard and fast rule can be devised by which all our trade unions can be governed or can govern themselves." The committee urged tolerance and forbearance in the handling of this issue. The committee's report attributed the growth of the American Federation of Labor to its organization "on trade lines" and found it unnecessary and inexpedient to depart from this fundamental principle. It urged adherence to organization on trade lines as closely as possible in view of the great changes "in methods of production and employment." The report found, however, that

Owing to the isolation of some few industries from thickly populated centers where the overwhelming number follow one branch thereof, and owing to the fact that in some industries comparatively few workers are engaged over whom separate organizations claim jurisdiction, we believe that jurisdiction in such industries by the paramount organization would yield the best results to the workers therein, at least until the development of organization of each branch has reached a stage wherein these may be placed, without material injury to all parties in interest, in affiliation with their national trade unions.

This statement was not intended to vitiate any earlier decision of the Executive Council or conventions on jurisdictional disputes between affiliates.[29]

The report further declared that the interests of the trade union movement would be promoted "by closely allying the sub-divided crafts, giving consideration to amalgamation and to the organization of district and national trade councils to which should be referred questions in dispute, and which should be adjusted within allied crafts' lines." The report concluded with the statement that the A. F. of L. is a voluntary association and therefore could not adopt "methods antagonistic to or in conflict with established trade union laws."[30]

The "Declaration" was an attempt to meet a practical problem rather than to lay down a principle to govern the structure. The same convention which unanimously approved the "Declaration," refused to approve a requirement that all unions present to the A. F. of L. a statement in writing defining the jurisdiction covered by them for use as a guide to the settling of subsequent jurisdictional disputes. It was not regarded as a practical method because of the rapid changes going on in industry.

The "Scranton Declaration" was a necessary compromise and, in fact, exposed the lack of power of the A. F. of L. to enforce any rule with respect to jurisdiction upon a powerful affiliate. In a sense, the "Declaration" confirmed what was already obvious in other jurisdictional disputes, notably those involving the Brewery Workers' Union and Printers' Union.

The claims of the coal miners could be handled more easily, for an argument for the exceptional character of coal mining communities could be made. However, among the several reasons for making the distinction, perhaps the most important was the inability of the Federation to enforce an adverse decision upon the United Mine Workers of America. By limiting the principle to "isolated areas" the Federation satisfied the craft unions that industrial organization would not be permitted to operate under the aegis of the Federation in non-mining communities, where such forms of organization might seriously endanger the latters' positions. There was in fact nothing the craft organizations which were affected by the decision could do, as the coal miners would not have obeyed any decision that separated the craftsmen employed in and around the mines from their organization. Had the view of John B. Lennon been followed, the Federation might have tried to work out some arrangement whereby the union with the principle interest in a plant would hold control even if such control violated the principle of trade autonomy. In such case, the "Scranton Declaration" would have been broadened. But the affiliated unions were not yet ready to accept such a radical departure from trade autonomy. It was forty years later, when confronted by the rise of the C.I.O., that the Federation adopted a variation of Lennon's principle. The contrast of the unwillingness of craft unions to concede a principle, but their readiness to accept a practical policy, is noticeable in the difference in the attitude between the several crafts toward the organization of their craftsmen by the Coal Miners on the one hand, and the Brewery Workers' Union on the other. The Firemen's, Engineers, and Teamsters' unions were involved in both situations. In the case of the Miners' they made their protests, but as neither they nor the A. F. of L. could do much to compel the Miners' Union to "disgorge" the craftsmen it organized, the craft unions were willing to accept a "rule of exception." In the brewery industry, the craft unions had the support of their members employed in other industries. The craftsmen were not isolated and could find support elsewhere.

METALLIFEROUS MINERS

An analogous problem faced the A. F. of L. when the Western Federation of Miners applied for a charter covering all workers in and around the metalliferous mines. To a large extent both logic and history appeared to support the claim. The Western Federation of Miners was, however, numerically weaker than the union in the coal industry; moreover, some of the craft unions in the metal trades held a few contracts in the metalliferous mining industry. As relations between the miners' unions were close at the time, the United Mine Workers of America strongly supported the claim for an inclusive industrial charter for metal miners. It was a knotty problem, and as usual in such circumstances, Gompers was deputized by the Executive Council to devise an acceptable formula. He urged the Western Federation of Miners to accept a charter, and then allow time and negotiation to settle its jurisdiction. The metal trades unions, which were largely involved, refused to accept this compromise, and instead asked "that all national and international organizations affiliated with the A. F. of L. shall have absolute jurisdiction over their craft and membership thereof in territory claimed by the Western Federation of Miners."[31]

The two miners' unions, aroused by the attempted raid of the craft organizations, demanded:

That a charter be issued to the Western Federation of Miners on the basis of the jurisdiction of the United Mine Workers of America. It was found that there was some difference between the coal mining and mineral mining organizations in respect to the organization and employment of machinists which did not relatively apply to other trades, and, therefore, it is made a provision of the issuance of this charter that members of the machinists' locals now existing in mining camps are not to be required to join the Western Federation of Miners in order to follow their trade in the mining camp.[32]

The United Mine Workers of America, the most powerful union in the A. F. of L., actively resented the proposals of the Executive Council. At its convention the U. M. W. A. characterized the Council's efforts at compromise as an effort to harass the Western Federation of Miners, and the convention resolved that "every objection raised against the issuance of a charter on jurisdictional lines applies with equal force to the U. M. W. A. and is a covert menace to that complete control of the industry, which we believe essential to our organization and the protection of workers in general."[33] But the Executive Council had to take the craft unions into account; and the Western Federation of Miners could, if it had the power, function as an industrial union with or without the approval of the A. F. of L. Since the Federation could not ignore the protests of its own affiliates, a compromise settlement was finally made recognizing the rights of the craft unions in the metal mines. The compromise did not have the enthusiastic approval of the Western Federation of Miners. Here it was not actually principle, but expediency or practicality that determined policy. Practicality in this case meant not interfering with any jurisdictional rights the craft unions had already obtained.

The Federation was conscious of the structural and jurisdictional problem and Gompers, in his report to the convention of 1903, criticized the "attempts to force the trade unions into what has been termed industrial organization."[34] He may have been anticipating the resolution introduced by the delegate from the Wisconsin Federation of Labor, which requested that a committee be appointed to study the possibilities of grouping the trade unions on industrial lines.[35] This was the first resolution for reorganizing the Federation on industrial lines, and it came from a central body dominated by Socialists. At the next convention Victor Berger, the first Socialist member of Congress, in a resolution described "trade autonomy in unionism" as "the application to the labor movement of the outworn principle of individualism," and demanded a "modern alignment of the united working class against the growing rapacity of manufacturers' and citizens' alliance organization, instead of the disgraceful, petty and destructive quarrels between union officers."[36] This resolution was, as were the others which followed, defeated, but at the convention of 1912 the debate on this question took a more significant turn.

INDUSTRIAL UNIONISM

Inspired perhaps by the dramatic struggles of the Industrial Workers of the World, the industrial union resolution sponsored by the United Mine Workers of America in 1912 found widespread support at the convention. After a long, and at times acrimonious, debate, the industrial resolution was defeated by a vote of 10,934 to 5929. Not for two decades would the proponents of structural reform find as many supporters for their program on the floor of A. F. of L. conventions.

In part the failure of the I.W.W. to establish industrial unions and to become a significant force in industry lessened the appeal of industrial unionism. The resolutions submitted to conventions of the American Federation of Labor had at best propaganda value. The inability of the

Federation to impose its view of jurisdiction upon affiliates, or perhaps to have its view accepted, precluded any possibility that an endorsement of industrial unionism would have any effect upon changing the claims or the jurisdiction of affiliates. Yet the willingness to endorse industrial unionism of unions representing more than one-third of the membership at the convention of 1912 showed that sentiment on this issue had undergone a drastic change. Such endorsement did not necessarily mean that the particular organization was ready to surrender any of its jurisdiction to an industrial union claimant. For example, the top officers of the International Association of Machinists supported industrial unionism at the A. F. of L. convention in 1912, yet they joined with several other unions in the metal trades in protesting against the invasion of their jurisdiction by the Carriage, Wagon and Automobile Workers' Union— a protest which incidentally led to the latters' expulsion from the A. F. of L.[37] It is also signicant that members of the Executive Council privately regretted this expulsion, although they did not openly oppose the action of the convention. Obviously an expression in favor of the industrial form of organization would not have forced any craft union to surrender its jurisdiction, nor compelled unions to amalgamate with each other.

The discussion of this entire question was in fact surrounded by an air of unreality, because approval or disapproval of industrial unionism by a convention of the A. F. of L. would not have changed the power relations between unions, and it might have multiplied disputes and even encouraged secessions. There was no way for the A. F. of L. to compel its affiliates to change their structure except by persuasion, which historically had not been effective against the stronger organizations. And at the time there was no practical problem of structural adjustment in any industry except the brewing industry, where the union was harassed by the claims of the craft organizations but nevertheless managed to remain within the A. F. of L.

In the 1920's the issue reappeared in a new form. Resolutions endorsing industrial unionism were presented to the conventions of 1921 and 1922. In 1921 a resolution was introduced by a delegate from the Casper, Wyoming, Trades and Labor Assembly, who had been an editor of an Industrial Workers of the World newspaper. He spoke at length, but his resolution, and the one submitted in the following year, were defeated without a recorded vote.

The amalgamation movement, which was dedicated to the reorganization of the American trade union movement on an industrial basis, went into high gear in 1923. The movement was inspired by William Z. Foster, who even then had had a varied career in the labor and radical movements. Foster had been a member of the Industrial Workers of the World, and attended the Budapest international trade union conference in 1911 as a representative from that body, where he had engaged in a heated argument with James Duncan, the representative of the A. F. of L. While abroad, Foster became disenchanted with the I.W.W. and embraced instead the French variety of syndicalism, which called for "boring within" the trade unions so as to convert them to a more radical program. Foster tried to establish a movement devoted to this purpose prior to World War I, and failed. He then joined the Brotherhood of Railway Carmen, and was a leader in the organization of the Chicago stockyards and packinghouses and the steel industry during and immediately after World War I. Having established himself as an able organizer by the success achieved in the steel industry, even though recognition was never forced from the unwilling managements, Foster revived his prewar schemes for reorganizing the labor movement of the United States. This time, however, his endeavor was conducted under Communist auspices.

The amalgamation movement called for a breaking down of jurisdictional boundaries between unions and their reconstruction on an industrial basis. Foster, whose Communist connections had not yet been revealed, managed for a short time to gain a substantial following, which caused the Executive Council to take notice of the campaign. A program, declared the Executive Council, of amalgamating unions against the wishes "of the organizations involved, against their interests, and in accordance with a plan evolved for the satisfaction of personal or revolutionary ends, can be regarded only with the most unrelenting hostility."[38] The same report pointed to the large number of voluntary amalgamations of unions that had taken place without the pressure or even the aid of the Federation. The three resolutions endorsing amalgamation, one of which was submitted by William F. Dunne from the Butte Trades and Labor Council and later editor of the *Daily Worker*, were defeated. The resolutions committee argued that unions within the A. F. of L. were always free to federate or amalgamate, and that the Federation had no power to compel such action. Moreover, the resolutions were held to be a potential source of division, and the good faith of the sponsors was questioned.[39]

One of the factors which kept the discussion of industrial unionism on what might be described as an academic plane was the absence of unionism in those industries in which questions of union structure might have become a source of difficulty. In the building, railroad, and printing industries, where the major fraction of organized workers were then employed, differences over jurisdiction did exist, but there were few attempts, except in the case of competing unions in the same trade, to eliminate entirely a regularly established union. The unions in these industries might become involved in serious jurisdictional difficulties but they were not ready to merge with one another into one big industrial union.

The question of structure would only become a real problem when the possibilities of organizing large segments of manufacturing industry, especially those engaged in mass production, existed in fact. Neither the leadership of most of the major unions nor of the A. F. of L. were then ready to meet this challenge. The formula suggested by Lennon—control of the jurisdiction by the union with the principle interest—would have worked, and a suggestion as direct and simple and yet far-reaching would have aroused neither the bitter hostility nor the feverish enthusiasm generated by the program of industrial organization.

Events in the 1930's, when the efforts to force unions to adopt certain practices led to the great split in the labor movement, demonstrated the wisdom of the early A. F. of L. policy of solving structural problems on a practical basis, and preventing the question of the structure of one or more unions from becoming an ideological issue. Had Gompers policy of procrastination and tolerance been followed, it is likely that the unions which formed the C. I. O. would not have been expelled from the American Federation of Labor. Instead time, the great solvent, would have been allowed to do its work.

AMALGAMATION OF RELATED TRADES

The American Federation of Labor tried to prevent the development of unions which covered only a narrow jurisdiction. In the case of the custom tailors, the paper hangers, and a number of others, the Federation refused to issue a charter, on the ground that the jurisdiction was too limited to allow for growth of a viable union. In instances where two or more unions existed in one or closely-related jurisdictions, the Federation would seek to bring the two groups together and encourage merger. Thus the steamshovelers and dredgemen's unions, the steam and operating engineers, the sawmill and wood workers, the hod carriers and cement workers, the art and glass workers and painters, the metal workers and machinists, the electrotypers and stereotypers, the coppersmiths and sheet metal workers, and the brass and iron molders were some of the groups of workers whose unions merged under the persuasion and influence of the A. F. of L. However, at times the A. F. of L. was compelled to use its ultimate power—the revocation of charters—to induce this result. There were several such instances.

The first was in 1901, when the American Federation of Labor revoked the charter of an affiliate because its jurisdiction conflicted with other A. F. of L. unions. The Amalgamated Society of Engineers, an English union of mechanics, was chartered by the A. F. of L. early in its history. As unions were established in the various crafts in the metal trades, they came into conflict with the Amalgamated. The Boilermakers', Machinists', and Pattern Makers' unions complained of the invasion of jurisdiction by the English organization. The American Federation of Labor sought to solve the problem by an agreement with George Barnes, the secretary of the English organization, under which the members of his union in the United States would retain their rights to benefits but would transfer their membership to other unions. At the same time the Amalgamated Society was asked to surrender its jurisdiction in the metal and machinery industry in the United States. When the agreement failed to receive compliance, the charter was revoked.[40]

The same problem existed among the carpenters. In 1888 the Amalgamated Society of Carpenters and Joiners applied for affiliation to the A. F. of L. McGuire, who was then secretary of the United Brotherhood of Carpenters and Joiners of America, at first protested, but subsequently agreed to it.

In 1901, each of the Carpenters' unions complained of the encroachment of the other. Gompers suggested a meeting between representatives of the two organizations to work out an arrangement whereby conflict would be avoided. However, in the following year, the Brotherhood demanded at its convention that the Amalgamated be ousted because of its violation of trade union principles. Gompers replied that "the Amalgamated Society of Carpenters has held its charter from the American Federation of Labor for many years. That the same was issued with the consent of the U. B. and the A. S. C., the representatives of the A. F. of L. having been called in to assist in the adjustment of differences thereto existing."[41]

The Executive Council found that the difficulties which followed from competing unions could not be entirely avoided and it recommended that the Amalgamated Society might observe the working rules of the other Carpenters' Union, and its members continue as beneficiary members of their own organization. Beginning with modest cooperation, the Council believed that in time the two unions might amalgamate if such a course were found to be in the best interests of members of the craft. Had the suggestions of the Executive Council been followed, the dispute might have been immediately settled. Instead strikes and boycotts were started by the members of one union against the other. In New York, the United Brotherhood of Carpenters and Joiners called a strike and forced a suspension of all building operations on the ground that its rival was recruiting delinquent members of the United Brotherhood. Through the intervention of the Executive Council of the A. F. of L., peace was temporarily restored.[42]

To find a remedy for the difficulties, which inevitably affected other building trades, the Executive Council appointed Adolph Strasser as arbitrator. He suggested unification, but the two unions could not agree on a formula.[43] Thereupon, the Executive Council suggested that committees from both organizations meet with a committee from the Executive Council. "Of course the attendance of any representative from the

Executive Council is to be dependent entirely upon the wishes of either or both organizations, and if the representative of the Executive Council would be acceptable, that they act in a conciliatory or advisory and helpful capacity, rather than in any other." Both organizations were assured that the Executive Council only sought to restore harmony in the trade. The unions were warned against unnecessary bitterness, and urged to show a fraternal spirit.

While the Amalgamated was ready to discuss the differences, its rival, the United Brotherhood, would agree to a meeting only if the creation of one organization of "Carpenters and Joiners, comprising all the branches of wood working industries, as enumerated in Section 61 of the Constitution of the United Brotherhood was considered."[44]

The dispute dragged on for more than ten years, with each organization refusing to make concessions. Finally the A. F. of L. convention of 1911 decided that, unless a program of amalgamation were devised by the two unions, the Federation would intervene and set the terms. Gompers was instructed by the Executive Council to meet with the Carpenters' Unions and seek an agreement within ninety days after the adjournment of the convention. The Amalgamated refused to send delegates to the conference. But the A. F. of L. was reluctant to revoke the charter, and the date fixed for revocation was pushed back several times in the hope that an agreement would be voluntarily consummated.

The aggressive attitude of the United Brotherhood toward its trades justified the Federation's insistence that an amalgamation take place. Of course the aggressive attitude of the United Brotherhood towards its rival, the Amalgamated, the Brotherhood's unwillingness to accept compromise, such as the exchange of cards or even recognition of the United Brotherhood's working rules by the other union, gave the Federation no choice, especially when the United Brotherhood could point to the violation of its charter rights. It may have been true that the officers of the United Brotherhood acquiesced in the granting of the charter. Yet the present officers could insist that there was no evidence that a surrender of jurisdiction was ever contemplated. The United Brotherhood was fearful that its position might be threatened by an alliance between the Amalgamated Carpenters and Joiners and some of the other building trades unions. That this fear was not groundless was demonstrated in a number of areas where the Amalgamated had been able to win control and force the members of the United Brotherhood from their jobs. Another problem competing unions raised was discipline in the ranks. Each of the carpenter unions complained that the other had been recruiting unfair men, or those who had been suspended or expelled from the other organization. As the much larger union, the United Brotherhood set out to eliminate its rival and create one union in the trade. In the end the Council was forced to act, and it revoked the charter of the Amalgamated in 1913.

The locals of the Amalgamated immediately became ineligible for membership in any central organization directly or indirectly chartered by the A. F. of L., which meant that they could not affiliate with any of the building trades councils chartered by the Building Trades Department.

Soon thereafter an arrangement was made on beneficiary benefits to be provided and per-capita to be paid to the United Brotherhood of Carpenters and Joiners and all other questions at issue. The Executive Council of the American Federation of Labor was informed that "the big fight between the United Brotherhood of Carpenters and Joiners of America and the Amalgamated Society of Carpenters and Joiners became a thing of the past. They were amalgamated in January, 1914."[45]

THE WOOD WORKERS

In planning to dominate all wood working, the United Brotherhood of Carpenters and Joiners operated on two fronts. The first was the carpentering trade; the other was wood working, where the Amalgamated Wood Workers' International Union occupied the jurisdiction. The Amalgamated was a merger of the Machine Wood Workers' Union and the Furniture Workers' International. In 1894 the Machine Wood Workers had come to an agreement with the United Brotherhood under which the latter surrendered some branches of the wood working industry. The rights that had been conceded under the agreement were acquired by the Amalgamated Wood Workers. Without their knowledge, the United Brotherhood abrogated its agreement, and the A. F. of L. convention of 1901 found the United Brotherhood guilty of an improper extension of its jurisdiction. If the convention decision had been carried out, the Brotherhood would have been forced to restrict itself to its original jurisdiction. This meant that members of the Carpenters' Union would be replaced in shops and planning mills, a point which that union refused to concede. Consequently the issue was carried to the convention of 1902, which decided that each union name five members to a committee and, if the committee were unable to reach agreement, that an outside arbitrator be chosen by the committee. The committee deadlocked, and P. J. Downey, who was chosen as the arbitrator, ruled that the work in planning mills and factories belonged to the Wood Workers.

Despite this adverse ruling, the Carpenters' Union came into the convention of 1903 and demanded that the charter of the Wood Workers be revoked. The latter reciprocated and made the same demand with respect to its rival. The convention ruled that the arbitrator's award would have to be accepted, but nothing was done.

The following year the convention decided that, unless the award of the arbitrator was accepted, the United Brotherhood would be suspended. However, the Executive Council would not accept this drastic solution, and instead tried to work out an arrangement satisfactory to both groups.

In the spring of 1905 Gompers met with committees of the two unions, but was unable to get them to agree to any proposals. The United Brotherhood wanted an amalgamation of the two organizations; the Wood Workers were seeking an agreement whereby the jurisdiction of each would be delimited and recognized by the other. Finally, in 1906 a merger agreement was devised, but the Wood Workers' membership would not approve the terms.

In 1909 the convention of the A. F. of L. endorsed a merger, and instructed the Executive Council to carry it out. However, the heads of the Wood Workers refused to confer with the officers of the Carpenters' Union. Thereupon the issue was again submitted to a convention of the A. F. of L. The Wood Workers now insisted upon becoming a semi-independent department within the Carpenters' Union. In 1911 the A. F. of L. convention decided that if amalgamation were not achieved by July 1 of the following year, the charter of the Wood Workers would be revoked. As in the case of the Amalgamated Carpenters, this step finally forced a merger.

It was ten years between the first demand of the United Carpenters and the forcible merger of the two unions. In the interim the A. F. of L. sought by persuasion to find some compromise that would enable the two unions to live peacefully together, or to have them merge voluntarily. It was only at the insistent demand of the Carpenters' Union that the final step of compelling another organization to merge or depart from the family of the Federation was taken.

RAILWAY CARMEN

The situation with the railway carmen presented a somewhat different problem to the American Federation of Labor. The International Association of Railway Car Workers was affiliated with the American Federation of Labor. Outside of the A. F. of L., the Brotherhood of Railway Carmen also operated in this jurisdiction, and was in fact the more successful union of the two in terms of organizing the workers in the craft. In 1909 the Brotherhood sought to affiliate with the A. F. of L. This step was opposed by the International Association. As the 21,000 membership of the Brotherhood was almost five times as great as that of the A. F. of L. affiliate, the Federation faced a dilemma. It could refuse to charter the Brotherhood of Carmen and thereby keep a large group of workers outside of the ranks of the central organization. On the other hand, it could ignore the rights of its own affiliates. As a first step the Federation issued a charter of affiliation to the Brotherhood of Railway Carmen. This placed two unions in the same jurisdiction, which not only violated a principle of the Federation but the Federation's constitution, which, under Article 11, Section 9, forbids the chartering of a union, when such action would be "a trespass on the jurisdiction of existing affiliated unions without the written consent of such unions."[46]

It was not the aim of the A. F. of L. to leave the two car worker unions free to compete with the inevitable jurisdictional disputes. Instead the Federation sought to bring the two unions together, and when the International Association of Railway Car Workers refused to accept what were regarded as reasonable terms, the convention of 1911 ordered its charter revoked. Subsequently, this organization sought to spread itself so as to cover all of the shop crafts. It was not successful in organizing many workers, but it had sufficient nuisance value to draw a sharp rebuke from the Railway Employees Department, two years after it was ousted.[47]

PLUMBERS AND STEAM FITTERS

The dispute between the National Association of Steam and Hot Water Fitters and Helpers of America and the United Association of Plumbers, Gas Fitters, Steam Fitters and Steam Helpers lasted for almost two decades. The Steam Fitters were the first to organize, in 1888. The Plumbers formed a national union the following year and affiliated with the A. F. of L. When the Steam Fitters sought an A. F. of L. charter, they urged that as a distinct trade, they should be allowed to maintain a separate union. The Plumbers, already affiliated with the A. F. of L., protested on the ground that the two trades, while distinct in one sense, overlapped sufficiently so that the granting of a charter to the Steam Fitters would violate their jurisdictional rights, and the existence of two unions in the pipe-fitting trade would inevitably lead to friction. Instead of a separate union of Steam Fitters, the Plumbers' Union suggested that steamfitters be required to join the Plumbers' Union. They offered that representation on the union executive board be equally divided between the two crafts; that all issues affecting steamfitters be referred for decision to the steam fitter members of the board; and that at conventions, only delegates from steam fitter locals be allowed to vote on issues affecting that segment of the pipe fitting trade. These proposals were rejected by the Steam Fitters' Union, which claimed the right to operate their own organization and the right to affiliate with the American Federation of Labor. Since the interested organizations could not agree, a committee from the A. F. of L., to which the matter was referred, decided that steam fitting was a separate and distinct trade from plumbing, entitling the Steam Fitters to a charter. However, the A. F. of L. held that steam fitters who were members of the Plumbers' Union could remain in that organization, and that steam fitters in areas with an insufficient number of steam fitters to form a local of their own be allowed to join the plumbers' organization, as the latter had a larger potential membership.[48] The Executive Council hesitated to issue a charter on these terms, and Gompers was deputized to work out another solution. He failed, and the Steam Fitters' Union was issued a conditional charter with the conditions undefined in 1898.[49]

The forecast of the officers of the Plumbers' Union that the chartering of its rival would only be a source of dissension and difficulty was quickly realized. Both organizations violated the dicta laid down by the committee of 1898 and the Executive Council of the A. F. of L. The Plumbers' Union continued to enroll steam fitters, and the latter organization sought to broaden its jurisdiction by adding "General Pipe Fitters" to its name. Both unions complained to the Executive Council, and an exchange of cards between the two unions was suggested. Gompers, Mitchell, and Kidd, members of the Executive Council, patiently corresponded and met with committees to devise a formula whereby each union would recognize the membership of the other. Such exchanges, it was hoped, would help to develop friendly feelings and eventually lead to amalgamation of the two unions.

Failing to bring about an agreement or even a truce, the issue was placed before the convention of 1901. It ruled that the Plumbers' Union must give up the steam fitters it had enrolled in violation of the decision of the earlier convention, and further that the Steam Fitters' Union would have to revert to its original name. Moreover, the convention ordered that committees from the two unions meet within ninety days after adjournment and arrange for the mutual exchange of cards, or, better still, work out an amalgamation recognizing the autonomy of the two crafts interested. If the committees were unable to work out an agreement, the Executive Council was ordered to appoint a committee to consider the question. The Executive Council, while suggesting that the amalgamation of the two unions would be the best solution, recommended that the terms upon which the Steam Fitters' Union was admitted to the A. F. of L. be carried out, and that the demand of its rival, that its charter be annulled, be rejected. However, the issues were by no means settled, for the Plumbers' Union believed that the Steam Fitters ought to be in a separate division in their organization, while the latter argued that the solution to the problem was an alliance between the two independent unions.[50]

The failure of the Steam Fitters' Union to agree to the proposals set forth by the Executive Council led to the revocation of its charter by the convention of 1903, but two years later the A. F. of L. convention recommended that the case of the Steam Fitters' Union be reopened by the Executive Council, with a view toward restoring its charter. Many supporters of the Steam Fitters were unions employed in the building trades. When the issue again came before the Executive Council, James Duncan, the first vice president, favored returning the problem to the convention. His proposal was defeated by a vote of three to four, and

Gompers' motion to restore the same charter rights as the union had formerly enjoyed was adopted by the same vote, four to three.[51]

The readmission of the Steam Fitters to the A. F. of L. strengthened the position of this group, who now demanded that the United Association of Plumbers eliminate from its title all reference to steam fitters, who were asked to transfer to the Steam Fitters' Union. The Plumbers Union was also requested by the Council to cease forming new locals of steam fitters, and both organizations were to be allowed to organize men of either craft who would then govern themselves in accordance with the constitution of the union involved. Steam fitters' locals were to be allowed to operate wherever a contractor could secure a steam fitting contract. These proposals were not accepted by the Plumbers' Union, which demanded consolidation of the two pipe fitting organizations.

It was the opinion of John R. Alpine, the head of the United Association of Plumbers, Steam Fitters and Steam Fitters' Helpers, that

Our steam fitters have their condition improved by being with us. We place no restriction upon our steam fitters. If they bring a good card with them, we accept them from all portions of the country. Such is not the case with the International Association of Steam Fitters. They give difficult examinations. The course of business indicates that the steam fitters and the plumbers are so closely identified that it is suicidal to try to disassociate them. Steam fitters do plumbing and are engaged on iron pipe work and have been paid the prevailing rate of wages.

On the other hand, the steam fitters' organization insisted that the mere existence of an independent steam fitters' union compelled the Plumbers' Union to treat members of the craft more fairly.[52] The dispute went on, with the Federation continually seeking a formula that would bring the groups together or at least into a peaceful alliance. Building trades unions not involved in the dispute directly, generally believed that the existence of two unions in the pipe fitting trade tended to create jurisdictional disputes which led to loss of work and unnecessary suspension of work. The A. F. of L. convention of 1911 decided that another effort to unify the two pipe fitting unions be made. In the event of failure, the Executive Council of the A. F of L. was authorized to lay down the conditions under which a merger would take place. After May 1, 1912, per-capita taxes were to be received from only one organization in the pipe fitting trade, at which time one charter was to be revoked.

The program for amalgamation was approved by the convention of 1912. However, it was rejected by the Steam Fitters' Union. The heads of the Plumbers' Union then turned to the steam fitters' locals directly. Denied affiliation with the A. F. of L., the Building Trades Department, and local building trades councils, many of the locals decided to affiliate with the Plumbers' Union. After several years, the steam fitters became a division of the United Association of Plumbers, Steam Fitters and Steam Fitters' Helpers, now called the United Association of the Pipe Fitting Trades.[53]

The American Federation of Labor had sought to find a formula which would enable the two unions to work out a mutually satisfactory solution. The insistence of the officers of the Steam Fitters' Union upon retaining the identity of their union gave the Federation, in the end, no alternative but to cancel the charter of this organization. The crafts were so closely intertwined that the existence of two unions made jurisdictional disputes inevitable, disputes which involved other unions of the A. F. of L. Consequently, the Federation felt that its revocation of a charter was justified despite the principle of autonomy of each independent union.

The Federation, in all the cases involving a "forced" merger—the carpenters, woodworkers, carmen, and plumbers disputes—in the end favored the stronger organization. In the dispute between the plumbers and steam fitters, the A. F. of L. had the excuse that the charter of the steam Fitters' Union was a conditional one, even though the conditions were never defined. In the other instances, the Federation yielded to the pressure of the more powerful union, although it tried for a time to find a solution which would enable the weaker union to exist. In yielding to pressure, the A. F. of L. was influenced by the attitude of the unions whose jurisdictions were in the same industry with the contending organizations. The existence of more than one union in a craft would have, at the time, stimulated jurisdictional disputes, which the A. F. of L. was anxious to prevent. The A. F. of L. sided with the more powerful unions; it could find no alternative to such decisions.

REFERENCES

1. *Report of Proceedings of the Third Annual Convention of the American Federation of Labor*, 1888, p. 21.

2. *Report of Proceedings of the Ninth Annual Convention of the American Federation of Labor*, 1889, p. 21.

3. Gompers to Executive Council, November 20, 1888; Gompers to McGuire, November 20, 1888; October 24, 1890.

4. *Report of Proceedings of the Twelfth Annual Convention of the American Federation of Labor*, 1892, p. 33.

5. *Report of Proceedings of the Twenty-Third Annual Convention of the American Federation of Labor*, 1893, p. 43.

6. *Report of the Proceedings of the Sixteenth Annual Convention of the American Federation of Labor*, 1896, pp. 42, 101.

7. Minutes of Executive Council Meeting, April 14, 1899.

8. Minutes of Executive Council, October 18, 1899.

9. *Report of Proceedings of the Nineteenth Annual Convention of the American Federation of Labor*, 1899, p. 156.

10. James A. Gable to Gompers, August 24, 1900, and Gompers to Gable, August 31, 1900.

11. Gompers to Gable, August 31, 1900.

12. Gompers to Charles Bechtold, August 25, 1900.

13. Minutes of Executive Council, July 19, 1900.

14. *Report of the Proceedings of the Twentieth Annual Convention of the American Federation of Labor*, 1900, p. 184-185.

15. Circular Letter by Gompers, January 25, 1901.

16. *Report of Proceedings of the Twenty-Seventh Annual Convention of the American Federation of Labor*, 1907, pp. 276-277.

17. *Report of the Proceedings of the Twentieth Annual Convention of the American Federation of Labor*, 1900, p. 184.

18. Letter of Gompers to Samuel B. Donnelly, April 20, 1899, in which the letter of O'Connell is quoted.

19. O'Connell to Gompers, July 13, 1899.

20. Letters to O'Connell and Donnelly, June 24, 1899.

21. O'Connell to his members, July 17, 1899, Bramwood to Frank Morrison, August 7, 1899; Gompers to Bramwood and O'Connell, August 17, 1899; O'Connell's statement, October 18, 1899.

22. Samuel Donnelly to Frank Morrison, January 13, 1899.

23. Thomas I. Kidd to Gompers, May 15, 1900; Lennon to Gompers, July 17, 1899.

24. Slocum to Gompers, July 12, 1900; Gompers to Slocum, July 18, 1900.

25. *Report of the Proceedings of the Nineteenth Annual Convention of the American Federation of Labor*, 1899, p. 136.

26. T. K. Heath to Gompers, August 17, 1900.

27. *Minutes of the Twelfth Annual Convention of the United Mine Workers of America*, 1901, p. 90.

28. *American Federationist*, March, 1901.

29. *Report of Proceedings of the Twenty-First Annual Convention of the American Federation of Labor*, 1901, p. 240.

30. *Ibid.*, p. 240.

31. Moyer to Gompers, September 2, 1910; Minutes of the Executive Council, February 20, 1911.

32. *Ibid.*

33. *Minutes of Executive Council*, January 20, 1911.

34. *Report of the Proceedings of the Twenty-Third Annual Convention of the American Federation of Labor*, 1903, p. 19.

35. *Ibid.*, p. 161.

36. *Report of Proceedings of the Twenty-Fourth Annual Convention of the American Federation of Labor*, 1904, p. 113, 132.

37. *Report of the Proceedings of the Thirty-Fourth Annual Convention of the American Federation of Labor*, 1914, p. 182.

38. *Report of the Proceedings of the Forty-Third Annual Convention of the American Federation of Labor*, 1923, pp. 38-39.

39. *Ibid.*, pp. 265-268.

40. *Report of Proceedings of the Twenty-Second Convention of the American Federation of Labor,* 1902, p. 141; Letter of Gompers to George N. Barnes, October 17, 1901.

41. Quote in Gompers to Duffy, October 16, 1902; also Gompers to Duffy, September 10, 1901, and October 7, 1901.

42. Statement of Executive Council, November 17, 1902; Minutes of Executive Council, June 20, 1903, January 23, 1903.

43. *Minutes of Executive Council,* September 17, 1904.

44. Vote Book, September 17, 1904; Gompers to W. D. Huber, September 17, 1904.

45. Duffy to Gompers, February 21, 1914.

46. Letter of Frank Morrison to Executive Council, September 20, 1909; Circular issued by International Association of Railway Car Workers, August 10, 1910.

47. Circular Letter issued by the Railway Employees Department, signed by A. O. Wharton, December 10, 1913.

48. Report of Committee on Dispute Between National Association of Steam and Hot Water Fitters and Helpers of American and United Association of Plumbers, Gas Fitters, Steam Fitters and Steam Fitters Helpers, 1899, to Executive Council, in A. F. of L. archives.

49. Letter of W. J. Spencer to Gompers, July 19, 1899; Gompers to Spencer, October 17, 1899; Gompers to W. L. Onstott, October 17, 1899.

50. Minutes of Executive Council, April 14, 1902.

51. Executive Council Vote Book, June 20, 1906.

52. Vote Book, March 9, 1908.

53. *Report of Proceedings of the Thirty-Second Annual Convention of the American Federation of Labor,* 1912, p. 106; *Ibid.*, p. 101.

XIII

The Departments

The American Federation of Labor was based upon the right of each international union to manage its own affairs. Yet in many industries craftsmen of different unions worked alongside each other, and their mutual, and at times conflicting interests could not be entirely ignored. Occasionally circumstances pitted one group of workers against the other in contract negotiations and strikes; and the problems arising out of the existence and crossing of picket lines by workers not involved in a dispute were matters that bedeviled the unions from the beginning of their history.

Gompers had foreseen these problems, and in his report to the convention of 1888 mentioned the possibility of eventual reorganization of the A. F. of L. on the basis of industrial divisions. Under the plan he suggested, industries such as iron and steel, railroad, metal and machinery, and building construction would each hold conventions of the several unions in their industries which would legislate upon their respective problems. The industrial divisions, in turn, would be accorded representation at the conventions of the American Federation of Labor.

NATIONAL BUILDING TRADES COUNCIL

These suggestions were not recommendations for action or for changes in the structure of the Federation, but were merely speculations on the future of the A. F. of L. But the American Federation of Labor's suspicion of any effort to unite the separate crafts on a national basis led it to deny approval to the National Building Trades Council of America which had been established two years before. Made up of building trades councils, national building trades unions, and local unions of the building trades which had no national organization, the National Building Trades Councils sought to combine the building trades unions for mutual support.[1] The A. F. of L. convention in 1899 refused to endorse this movement because it found that it "sometimes assumed an attitude of rivalry and hostility, not only to the American Federation of Labor, but often to unions connected with the regular organizations of the craft, going so

213

far as to charter and recognize independent unions frequently organized for the purpose of antagonizing existing organizations."[2]

In contrast to its objections to a national council, the Federation endorsed local building trades councils as part or sections of central labor unions. These sections were to handle business connected with their industry.

[They] should have absolute authority to determine questions affecting building trades unions, and this applies also to other trade union councils or sections a part of the central labor union so far as their respective trades are concerned. The metal trades unions have part of the title of "council," and so have others. . . . What is wanted is the building trades councils shall be known as such or building trades sections, making their own choice as to name, and that they should be a part of central labor unions.[3]

The convention reiterated the views of President Gompers that building trades sections and similar sections in other industries should be organized on a local basis under the control of central bodies. This view that the building trades councils should be subordinate to the central bodies was based upon the argument that issues may arise in which nonbuilding trades unions also had an interest, and that the building trades alone were not to have the power to decide such issues.

Despite the rebuke at the hands of the A. F. of L. the National Building Trades Council justified its existence on the ground that

It has been found necessary, owing to the necessity of special mode of procedure in adjusting their grievances, to form a national federation separate and distinct from any other jurisdiction, to enact legislation for building trades councils and unions by building trades councils. This in no wise interferes with the loyalty and allegiance to the American Federation of Labor of our unions, all of whose nationals with few exceptions are a part thereof.[4]

W. H. Steinbiss, who headed the Council, wanted the right to settle jurisdictional disputes among building trades unions. Such authority would mean that the decisions of the Federation in this area would be circumvented. The A. F. of L. convention of 1901 reiterated its opposition and deprecated

the idea of National Building Trades Council. The thought that this movement is secretly approved by the National Unions at interest is entertained by some. If this be so, these unions are not, in our opinion, alive to the dangers which the future may have in store for them, for we can well conceive that should this movement proceed unrestrained the National Unions may yet find themselves confronted with a well-developed secession movement in their own midst. That seems to us the logical sequence of this regrettable severance.

Implicit in the A. F. of L.'s position was the fear that a national building trades council might usurp the functions of the Federation itself. The convention of 1903, therefore, also reiterated its opposition to the establishment of a separate building trades authority on a national scale.

STRUCTURAL BUILDING TRADES ALLIANCE

During the same year a number of building trades' unions met at Indianapolis and declared that the problems of the industry were not receiving adequate attention at the conventions of the American Federation of Labor. Consequently they decided to organize the Structural Building Trades Alliance. Jurisdictional disputes and dual-union problems, it was believed, could be more effectively handled by a central organization of unions in the industry. The constitution gave to each international union equal representation at conventions. The national organization was also to establish local alliances, which were to support striking member-unions by sympathetic walkouts after approval by a two-thirds majority and by the international unions involved. Formation of the Alliance was justified by the claim that the building trades were peculiarly dependent upon each other, as they were in reality subdivisions of one general industry, and yet distinct from each other, "since their handicraft is of a distinctly different character."[5] The Structural Building Trades Alliance did not arouse much enthusiasm in Federation quarters. Local alliances often clashed with central labor unions in their communities over the respective authority of these bodies.

The concern shown by leaders of the A. F. of L. over the formation of a "Building Trades Department" was not due to failure to understand the need for this form of organization, but to the fear that the unions in the building trades might decide to go their own way. Many of the unions in the building trades had already shown a readiness to affiliate with department-like organizations, which were not even chartered by the American Federation of Labor. Neither the National Building Trades Council nor the Structural Building Trades Alliance was part of the American Federation of Labor, and both organizations encouraged the affiliation of local non-A. F. of L. unions and even national unions. The leaders of the A. F. of L. were sensitive to the possible threat of a cohesive group within a single industry to the hegemony of the A. F. of L. over the general labor movement. It was this fear, rather than opposition to the structural change, which accounts for the hesitancy of the leaders of the Federation.

A bitter dispute between the Pittsburgh building trades and their employers led to the calling of a conference of building trades unions, at the instructions of the 1906 A. F. of L. convention. The first meeting in December 1906 was followed by several conferences between heads of the national unions involved and members of the Executive Council of the A. F. of L. The sentiment for some kind of departmental alliance among the unions in the building trades was too strong to be resisted by the A. F. of L. In August 1907 committees from the Structural Building Trades Alliance and the Executive Council agreed upon a program for mobilizing the unions in the building trades into a department. The A. F. of L. convention of 1907 agreed that it should charter a building trades department, to be made up of national and international unions, and that the department be clothed with authority to issue charters to local building trades sections.[6]

BUILDING TRADES DEPARTMENT

In pursuance of this declaration, a conference of forty-one delegates from twenty building trades unions decided in February 1908 to establish a building trades department to be composed of national building trades unions chartered by the American Federation of Labor, and generally employed in "erection, repair and alteration" in the building trades industry. The department was authorized to set up local building trades councils and settle jurisdictional disputes. Instead of equal representation for all international unions, as in the Structural Building Trades Alliance, unions were allowed a compromise form of proportional representation.[7]

James Duncan, the first vice president of the A. F. of L., who was present at the organizing meeting as one of the representatives of the American Federation of Labor, had serious reservations. He was concerned about the assumption of authority by the Building Trades Department to adjust jurisdictional disputes. He regarded this authority as a serious threat to the Federation, and a possible source of rivalry. He was convinced that

A jurisdiction decision by this Department, to be final would subordinate, in as far as transaction of their own business is concerned, the laws of every national and international union to the Department. . . . Again, can a department or sub-division of a main body assume more power or authority over affiliated organizations than the main body assumed?

He derided the confidence of the founders of the Building Trades Department that all jurisdictional disputes would be settled within ninety days of their submission. Such a feat would be, he said, "the eighth wonder of the world." In contrast, William Huber, the head of the United Brotherhood of Carpenters and Joiners of America, saw no threat of dualism in the Department, and he was convinced that its rules were in strict conformity with the policies of the American Federation of Labor.[8] Soon after the formation of the Building Trades Department, the Structural Building Trades Alliance held a special convention, and instructed its officers to close out its affairs as soon as the Department received a charter from the A. F. of L.[9]

In greeting both the initial conference and the subsequent convention, Gompers warned of the danger of dividing the movement. He told the first convention that

[He hoped] that the men of the Department would see to it that, though they understood to have the interests of the men in the building trades primarily advanced, they would never do anything that would weaken the bonds of union of the building trades unionist with the trade unionists of other branches of labor. . . . Nothing would be more disastrous to the interests of the men of labor of all trades and callings—the building trades included—than any weakening or severance of the bonds of unity.[10]

The Building Trades Department soon demonstrated that the fears of the A. F. of L. leadership that the Department might try to arrogate to itself some of the powers of the Federation were not altogether unfounded. Jurisdictional disputes had existed in this industry almost from the beginning of the formation of the American Federation of Labor. These disputes, while they caused losses to workers and industry and even aroused public opinion against organized labor, were always settled by the use of Fabian tactics. The leaders of the A. F. of L. relied on tolerance, reason, and negotiation to settle these disputes, rather than the force they did not possess. On the other hand, the heads of the Building Trades Department favored stronger action.

When the International Association of Steam and Hot Water Fitters and Helpers of America and the United Brotherhood of Carpenters and Joiners of America refused to obey the decisions of the Department in jurisdictional disputes, they were suspended. The Building Trades Department then asked, in January 1911, that the charters of the two unions be revoked. Unaccustomed to hasty solutions of jurisdictional disputes, and opposed to the use of compulsion, the Federation postponed its decision. Soon thereafter, the officers of the Building Trades Department wanted the Executive Council of the A. F. of L. to decide whether the course pursued by the Department was right or wrong, and if the latter, the Council was "to point out a way in which the Department could proceed that would enable the Department to maintain discipline among the building trades."[11]

The Council would not argue the manner of achieving discipline; but, it pointed out that

Enforced compulsory obedience to edicts and decisions have never proven successful, . . . suspension of International Unions and revocation of charters, are not calculated to harmonize existing differences, nor bring the members of an international union so suspended into a better frame of mind in order that an award may be accepted by them.

The Council was convinced that suspensions and revocations of charters would only breed antagonism. It argued

[The] most enlightened and advantageous discipline comes with time and experience and is suggested and later self-imposed. It is something not yet generally understood how perfectly safe freedom is, and this truism applies to the administration of the organized labor movement as much as it does to any government on the face of the earth.[12]

The convention of 1911 supported the Executive Council, and declared that suspension of charters was primarily the responsibility of the American Federation of Labor. It added that revocation of charters had never been regarded as an effective method for solving jurisdictional disputes. The Department was asked to reinstate the suspended unions. This particular experience reduced the pretensions of the Building Trades Department. Clearly, the Federation was not prepared automatically to endorse a policy which, in a large sense, was antipathetic to the spirit of the A. F. of L.—a policy in this case fraught with peril for the entire labor movement.

METAL TRADES DEPARTMENT

While the A. F. of L. feared that a department in the building trades might lead to the creation of a dual authority within the labor movement, it showed no such suspicion of a closer alliance in the metal trades. Such an alliance had been suggested originally by President James O'Connell of the Machinists' Union in 1896. In 1900, in a letter to eight unions in the metal trades, Gompers urged them "to form some council or trade alliance for the purpose of mutual support. There is no reason why this council should not be formed."[13]

A temporary alliance was formed by the unions in the metal trades. In the following year they set up the Federated Metal Trades. Seven unions were represented and officers were elected.[14] It was greeted with approval by Gompers who declared, "there are no unions affiliated more faithful in adherence to the principles and policies of the American Federation of Labor than are these metal trade unions." Gompers wrote to the head of the Federated Metal Trades: "I shall personally and officially do what I can to aid it."[15] It failed even to get started.

The first failure at federation in the metal trades did not discourage the heads of the unions. In March 1906 another attempt at unity was made, but this effort also failed, although the leaders of the metal trades' unions did approve of federation "with the object of effecting a more complete organization of these districts which influence the conditions prevailing in the industrial centers."[16]

Finally, following the A. F. of L. approval of the Building Trades Department, thirty-one delegates from nine unions in the metal trades held a convention and set up the Metal Trades Department. Its chief objective was to establish metal trades councils and promote closer relations by the unions in the industry, and widen the cooperation with unions outside the Department.

A proposal to allow the local metal trades unions to direct sympathetic strikes in support of organizations in employer-disputes was rejected.[17] In 1910 the Metal Trades Department sought to gain the cooperation of the Building Trades Department to refuse to "handle the products of firms against which the metal trades have strikes."[18] The proposal was rejected.

In the following year a measure aimed at wider cooperation by the unions in metal trades was enacted. It required that, whenever 75 per cent of the national and international unions inaugurate a general movement for the purpose of advancing the interests of the affiliated organizations or in defense against wage reductions, all affiliated local organizations would be obliged to take a strike vote in accordance with their own rules. The returns on the strike vote were to be deposited with the head of the Metal Trades Department, and if it were found that the strike had been approved by two-thirds of the total votes cast, a strike call would be issued by the President of the Department. Failure by an affiliate was to be a cause for suspension of the offending affiliate from the department.

This measure, in effect, transferred the authority over strikes from the international union to the department, and the International Molders Union of North America protested that

No department of the American Federation of Labor, through its conventions or otherwise, has any power or authority to in any way infringe upon, interfere with or set aside the laws, rules and regulations provided for in the constitution of any of the national or international organizations affiliated with the American Federation of Labor. Unquestioned autonomy over its internal affairs is guaranteed to each affiliated organization in Section 2, Article II, of the constitution of the American Federation of Labor.[19]

The A. F. of L. was, therefore, compelled to reexamine the powers of the departments, for in addition to the difficulties encountered by some of the organizations of the Metal Trades Department, serious controversies had arisen in both the Railway Employees, and Building Trades Departments.

RAILWAY EMPLOYEES DEPARTMENT

In the railroads, as in the building and metal trades, local federation of unions preceded the formation of national alliances. As early as 1892, a system federation composed of railroad unions was established on several Western railroads. The strike of the American Railway Union in 1894 put an end to these organizations, but by the end of the first decade of the century cooperation and joint action by several of the craft unions on single railroad systems was revived. Craft agreements with the railroads were simultaneously abrogated on the Wabash Railroad in 1908, and a formal system federation organized.

These developments, coming at the time when unions in other industries were devising methods for closer cooperation, encouraged the railroad unions in 1908 to establish the Railroad Employees Department.[20] The Department was organized for promoting the interests of railroad employees by legislation, and also for protecting their interests on the job. H. B. Perham of the Order of Railroad Telegraphers was chosen president of the department, which was chartered by the American Federation of Labor in February 1909.

The federation movement soon encountered the opposition of the railroads, obviously fearful that joint negotiations would place them at serious bargaining disadvantage. At the time the federations of crafts on single systems sought to establish the principle of joint negotiations with the carriers, the Railroad Employees Department was inert and ineffective. The Department concentrated its energies largely on lobbying for legislation before Congress, and played virtually no role in the negotiations of agreements or the development of economic policies by the unions.

In the meantime, developments outside of the Railroad Employees Department were bringing certain of the unions in the railroad industry into closer alliance. Both the Harriman lines and the Illinois Central refused to recognize or to negotiate with the system federations established on their roads. The refusal led to a strike, which began on September 1, 1911, of six internationals and the federal labor unions. It continued for several years and was marked by violence and bitterness. The unions were willing to engage in a long-drawn struggle because they believed the railroad companies were not dealing equitably with the workers organized in single crafts, and that there was a tendency by the carriers to make concessions to the stragically-placed unions, while holding out against the weaker ones.

The strike also called attention to the weakness and lack of activity of the Railroad Employees Department. The convention of the International Association of Machinists in 1911 instructed its president to seek a conference of unions to organize a federation of the system federations. In the meantime, sentiment for extending the strike to other Western railroads spread among the railroad crafts. The Association of Western Railways denied that the roads had any jurisdiction in the matter in dispute between the unions and the Harriman and Illinois Central lines. After several meetings, the Federation of Federations of Railway Employees was established in April 1912. Subsequently, it merged with the Railroad Employees Department, and the organization has since been known as the Railway Employees Department.[21]

With the subsequent formation of the Label Trades Department, for promoting the purchase of union-made products, and of the Mining Department, the new structural form was complete—except for the establishment of the Maritime Trades Department in the 1940's.

The latter three departments were not very effective; the Mining Department ceased to exist in 1926, and the Maritime Trades Department until recently has not been more than a paper organization. As the Label Trades Department was created to promote sentiment for the purchase of union made goods and services, it could not by its very character develop differences concerning the authority of the department over affiliates, or over the division of power between it and the American Federation of Labor.

DIFFERENCES WITHIN DEPARTMENTS

As has been observed, the International Molders' Union complained of the attempt of the Metal Trades Department to usurp powers which resided in the International Union; there was also a complaint that the Railroad Employees Department refused affiliation with a regularly-chartered international of the American Federation of Labor; and that the Building Trades Department was seeking to determine jurisdictional questions that were within the province of the American Federation of Labor.

The convention of 1914 was called to consider the rights and prerogatives of the departments as a unit, and to clarify the relationship existing between the various types of affiliated organizations.

A jurisdictional dispute had arisen between the International Association of Marble Workers, an A. F. of L. affiliate, and the Bricklayers' and Masons' International Union. Almost from the beginning of its history, the American Federation of Labor had sought unsuccessfully to win the latter's adherence. Under the leadership of its secretary, Patrick O'Dea, the Bricklayers' and Masons' International Union had consistently refused to join the A. F. of L., even though at times affiliation was at least nominally urged by some of the officers.

It was inevitable that in a jurisdictional dispute between an affiliated and non-affiliated union, the Federation would side with one of its internationals. However, it was charged that three unions of the American Federation of Labor—the Journeymen Stone Cutters, the International Union of Steam Engineers, and the United Brotherhood of Carpenters and Joiners—had entered into an agreement with the Bricklayers' and Masons' International Union to destroy the Marble Workers and other unions affiliated with the A. F. of L.

When the Executive Council criticized the conduct of the United Brotherhood of Carpenters and Joiners, it was told that the "Carpenters are going to protect themselves in their claims which justly and properly belong to them," and the Brotherhood questioned the authority of the A. F. of L. to prohibit an affiliate from entering into an agreement with other organizations, whether affiliated or not affiliated with the American Federation of Labor. One of the sore points with the Carpenters was the large number of strikes caused by unions with relatively few members. This they held to be wrong and harmful to the best interests of the Carpenters' Union; they were also dissatisfied with the methods of representation which gave the smaller unions relatively greater power within the Department. They insisted that the agreement entered into with the Bricklayers' and Masons' International Union would not be broken, as such conduct was against the policy and spirit of the Brotherhood.[22]

The powers of departments were discussed in detail at the convention of 1914, and the laws of the A. F. of L. were amended so that

The fundamental laws [of departments were] to conform to, and be administered in the same manner as the laws and procedures governing the American Federation of Labor. No department, local council or railways system federation of same shall enact laws, rules, or regulations in conflict with the laws and procedure of the American Federation of Labor, and in the event of change of laws and procedure of the latter, department, local councils, and railway system federations are to change their laws and procedure to conform thereto.

There was some objection to this clause by Arthur Wharton, the head of the Railway Employees Department, who feared that it might be interpreted to mean that joint negotiations with an employer by several unions were prohibited; he called attention to the method of joint negotiations by the unions in the mechanical sections of his department. Duncan, the first vice president of the A. F. of L. and spokesman for the resolutions' committee, admitted that the organizations in the Railway Employees Department had ceded to the Department authority which they had refused to give to the A. F. of L., but he argued that an organization aggrieved by a decision of the Railway Employees Department could appeal to the Executive Council of the A. F. of L., and ultimately to the convention.

Another change was the adoption of a section which described each department as

the official method of the American Federation of Labor for transacting the portion of its business indicated by the name of the department, in consequence of which affiliated and eligible organizations should be part of their respective departments and should comply with their actions and decisions, subject to appeal therefrom to the Executive Council of the American Federation of Labor.[23]

Under the amended rules the pretensions of the departments were curbed and their decisions made subject to appeal to the A. F. of L. Moreover, the departments were themselves explicitly recognized as instruments and agencies created by the A. F. of L. for performing independent services for their affiliates. They could not establish regulations or assume authority over affiliates which the Federation did not exercise unless the unions were themselves willing to surrender such power.

As it was now explicitly stated that the departments were agencies of the A. F. of L., subject to the latter's appellate procedures, the Bricklayers' and Masons' International Union, which had rejected affiliation with the A. F. of L. for many years despite the advice of its chief officers, finally joined the A. F. of L. in October 1916. The Building Trades Department had supported the Marble Workers in the controversy with the Bricklayers' and Masons' International Union. The affiliation of the Bricklayers' Union to the A. F. of L. was undoubtedly aided by the inability of this union to join the Department of its industry unless it also joined the A. F. of L.

REFERENCES

1. *Constitution and Laws of the National Building Trades Council of America,* 1901.
2. *Report of Proceedings of the Nineteenth Annual Convention of the American Federation of Labor,* 1899, p. 156.
3. Gompers to M. P. Carrick, April 30, 1902.
4. W. H. Steinbiss to Frank Morrison, January 23, 1001.
5. William J. Spencer, "The Structural Building Trades Alliance," *The Carpenter,* December 1905, p. 4. Vote Book of the Executive Council of A. F. of L., September 14, 1904.
6. *Report of Proceedings of the Twenty-Seventh Annual Convention of the American Federation of Labor,* 1907, p. 303.
7. One delegate for the first four thousand or less members; two delegates for four thousand members or more; three delegates for eight thousand members or more; four delegates for sixteen thousand members or more; five delegates for thirty-two thousand members or more, with each delegate given the right to cast one vote. This was a compromise of conflicting demands for equal representation for all unions regardless of size, and higher representation based on membership.
8. Report to Executive Council by James Duncan and William Huber, February 19, 1908.
9. *Official Report of the General Conference of the Building Trades Affiliated with the American Federation of Labor,* 1908; *Proceedings of the First Annual Convention of the Building Trades Department, American Federation of Labor,* 1908.
10. *Report of Proceedings of the First Annual Convention of the Building Trades Department,* 1908, p. 2.

11. William Spencer to Executive Council, June 13, 1911.

12. Executive Council to William Spencer, June 17, 1911.

13. Gompers to John Mulholland, November 12.

14. *Machinists' Monthly Journal,* June 1901, p. 469.

15. Gompers to E. J. Lynch, February 20, 1903.

16. *Iron Molders' Journal,* April, 1906, p. 260.

17. *Report of Proceedings of the First Annual Convention of the Metal Trades Department,* 1908.

18. Report from Metal Trades Department to American Federation of Labor, January 19, 1911, in Vote Book of Executive Council.

19. Joseph F. Valentine to Executive Council of the A. F. of L., February 29, 1914.

20. Testimony of A. H. Wharton, *Report of the Commission on Industrial Relations* (Washington, Government Printing Office, 1916), X, 9760-9763.

21. *Meeting of Railroad Employees Department in Rochester on November 9, 1912: Official Proceedings of Convention of Federation of Federations of Railway Employees,* 1912.

22. Duffy to Gompers, June 8, 1914; Duffy to James Kirby to Gompers, August 6, 1911.

23. *Report of Proceedings of the Thirty-Fourth Annual Convention of the American Federation of Labor,* 1914, pp. 447-454.

XIV

The National Civic Federation

CHICAGO CIVIC FEDERATION

The National Civic Federation, which became a serious source of contention between the heads of the A. F. of L. and its more radical trade union opponents, was an outgrowth of the Civic Federation of Chicago. The latter group, founded in 1894 soon after the Pullman strike, aimed to develop a better understanding of social and economic problems in the community. At its first meeting it considered the utility of conciliation and arbitration as a means of eliminating active labor strife. In 1898 its leaders manifested interest in expanding the organization, and a number of public men, including Gompers, were approached on the advisability of launching such a national group.[1]

NATIONAL CIVIC FEDERATION

In September 1899 representative men were asked to serve as advisers on the projected national organization. John Mitchell was among them, and he immediately sought Gompers' reaction. The latter believed that even "if no positive affirmative advantage may come the advantage may be in preventing hostile or inimical action being taken." Gompers did not believe "there can be any harm at all in accepting a position as a member of the advisory council."[2] It is obvious that the leaders of the A. F. of L. approached the new movement with skepticism, but they saw no harm to the labor movement in associating with others to promote the study of public questions.

Initially the National Civic Federation, established in 1900,[3] sought to study general issues of contemporary concern; but under the leadership of Senator Mark Hanna, especially after the steel strike of 1901, its energies were largely directed toward devising methods for maintaining industrial peace, and promoting collective bargaining.[4] The Socialists, and even some non-Socialist trade unionists, did not regard these steps with favor. To them the program of the National Civic Federation to lower the heat of industrial controversy was a threat to the militancy of labor. Nor were the open shop anti-union employers more kindly disposed to the new venture. The advocacy of peace and understanding between capital and labor was to them a dangerous doctrine which would serve to strengthen unionized labor and in the end undermine the employers' position.

John Kirby, the head of the National Association of Manufacturers, bitterly assailed the National Civic Federation, particularly because of the membership of leading labor unionists. He could not, in

conscience wink at the great danger to the best interests of our common country that lies hidden in the endorsement, by your organization [the National Civic Federation] of these men and doctrines they preach and which in so far as they can they execute in the name of the Civic Federation, and for which that organization will, some day, have to recognize its responsibility.[5]

Among the departments set up by the National Civic Federation, those on trade agreements and welfare work were the most important agencies for promoting industrial peace. Senator Hanna, who became active from the outset, was elected chairman and then president of the organization. Gompers was chosen vice president. In addition to these two, Ralph Easley, the secretary, and John Mitchell of the United Mine Workers of America, who became head of the Trade Department in 1908, were the most active in promoting the labor relations activities of the organization. Hanna served until his death in 1904, and was succeeded by August Belmont, who resigned in 1907. Seth Low, the former mayor of New York City, was then elected, and he held office until 1916.

The period from 1900 to 1916 was the most important in the labor activities of the group. It offered its services to labor and management, and intervened in both the steel strike and in the machinists' strike of 1901. The Civic Federation also tried unsuccessfully to "head off" the anthracite strike of 1902, and failed. Still, according to Easley, in the first years of its existence the National Civic Federation helped to settle more than one hundred strikes, and wholly or partially failed in eighteen other instances. In 1903 the work of conciliation was placed on a departmental basis and John Mitchell was made co-chairman of the division.[6]

The leaders of the Civic Federation were convinced that modern industry needed organized labor if serious social tensions were to be averted. On the other hand, Gompers was of the opinion that the National Civic Federation offered a forum for presenting labor's point of view, a forum in which labor men and the men of business could meet and perhaps, by better acquaintance, overcome mutual suspicions. Gompers, while cooperating with the National Civic Federation from the beginning, had no illusions about the benefits which labor would derive. He did not believe that the heads of labor were deluding themselves "into the belief that the millennium has been established by the formation of the executive committee of the Industrial Conference of the National Civic Federation. 'Peace on earth, good will towards men' is the hope not yet attained, and as far as we can observe, is a long way from achievement." He nevertheless welcomed the desire for peaceful labor relations by employers, which he attributed to the growing power of the labor movement.[7]

From the beginning, leaders of the American Federation of Labor found their connections with the National Civic Federation helpful, even though the Civic Federation was not always successful in converting leaders of industry to a sympathetic view of the labor movement. Yet they could not gainsay the efforts of the Civic Federation in behalf of more peaceful collaboration between management and labor through recognition of unionism. In 1901 the heads of the Civic Federation recognized the "tremendous importance to the industrial welfare of this country that every influence be brought to induce Mr. [J. P.] Morgan and his friends to 'start right.'"[8] They did not completely succeed in having Morgan "start right," but the heads of the American Federation of Labor could see no reason why they should seek to discourage these efforts on behalf of union recognition and collective bargaining. Labor leaders friendly to the Civic Federation denied that their militancy was in the least affected by the relations to it.

Aside from direct conciliation of labor disputes, the National Civic Federation issued studies on industrial, political, and social questions. Annual dinners were also held, and usually attended by representative men from labor, businesses, education, and the clergy. As a leading officer, Gompers used these occasions to espouse the philosophy of trade unionism.

ATTACKS FROM THE RIGHT AND LEFT

The Civic Federation was increasingly attacked from the left and right. The National Association of Manufacturers regarded the Federation as "an annex to the A. F. of L." On the other hand, a Socialist resolution by Victor Berger, at the A. F. of L. convention of 1905, stigmatized the "hypocritical attempt of the Civic Federation plutocrats to convince organized laboring men that the 'interests of capital and labor are identical.'" Certain labor leaders were charged with cooperating in the attempt to blind the workers, and Berger pointed "with sorrow to the close intimacy and harmonious relations established between Samuel Gompers and other labor leaders with the great capitalists and plutocratic politicians." The resolution then called upon the convention to declare that such cooperation was not in the interests of labor. The resolution was unanimously rejected, and at Gompers' request another endorsing his membership in the Civic Federation withdrawn.[9]

Despite the opposition encountered from the two extreme groups, the National Civic Federation had the support of the majority of labor leaders.

Mitchell retired from the presidency of the United Mine Workers of America, and became a full-time head of the Trade Agreements Department of the National Civic Federation. He had held his post only a short time when his union, at its convention in 1910, declared that a member of the United Mine Workers of America could not hold office in the Civic Federation. Forced to choose between his union and the Civic Federation, Mitchell resigned his post with the latter. The resolution opposing dual membership had been enacted by an alliance between the Socialists and President Tom L. Lewis. The latter had served as vice president under Mitchell, and had opposed many of the latter's policies. He now had his revenge for years of frustration. Similar resolutions were introduced and enacted in other unions. Mitchell regretted the action of his union "not so much because it requires me to choose between the two organizations, as because of the unjust attack upon the National Civic Federation which . . . has stood consistently as an advocate of industrial peace."[10]

The offensive against the National Civic Federation was led by the Socialists, and Morris Hillquit, a lawyer and occasional Socialist theoretician, regarded the "game played by the Civic Federation" as "the shrewdest yet devised by the employers of the country. It takes nothing from capital, it gives nothing to labor and does it all with such an appearance of generosity, that some of the guileless diplomats of the labor movement are actually overwhelmed by it."[11]

Hillquit, in the same letter, summed up the basis for the Socialist opposition to cooperation between the A. F. of L. and the National Civic Federation. In his view, shared by all Socialists, the Civic Federation introduced into the labor movement a "subtle and insidious poison . . . robs it of its independence, virility and militant enthusiasm; it hypnotises or corrupts its leaders, weakens its ranks and demoralizes its fights. The Socialist Party is employing all efforts at its command to save American labor from the malign influence of the National Civic Federation."

The views of Hillquit were also held by many non-Socialist trade unionists, and steps to bar membership of officers of the A. F. of L. in the National Civic Federation were started. The issue came before the convention of the A. F. of L. in 1911. Three resolutions, one of them introduced by the heads of the United Mine Workers of America, attacked the activities of the National Civic Federation, and demanded that officers of the A. F. of L. sever their relations to it.

The resolutions committee examined in some detail the expressed purposes of Civic Federation, heard the testimony of a number of officers of trade unions that the Civic Federation had aided them in securing

conferences with employers, leading to subsequent adjustment of grievances, and that no evidence had been presented to show that the Civic
Federation had ever shown hostility by word or act to trade unionism,
although some of its members were unfriendly to organized labor.

In reporting on the resolutions, the committee found that

[The] Civic Federation was organized in part for the furthering of the adjustment of disputes between employees and their employers through the methods
of friendly conference, conciliation or arbitration, when mutually acceptable,
and the consummation of joint contracts and agreements covering the terms
of employment. In addition, to bringing together representative men from all
groups for the public discussion of the questions affecting the relations of
employers and organized workmen. The organization, we find, at the time of
its inception, set the official seal of its approval upon the recognition of trade
unions by employers, and as endorsing the consummation of formal agreements covering the terms of employment and organized workmen.[12]

The attack upon the National Civic Federation was led by several
delegates from the United Mine Workers of America, including its president and Mitchell's successor, Tom L. Lewis, who were acting under
instructions from their organization. One of the more serious complaints
charged that leaders of labor fraternized with anti-union employers at
the banquets of the Civic Federation. Moreover, it was charged that
many anti-union employers supported the Civic Federation financially,
and yet these same employers would not recognize the unions of their
workers.[13] The real aim of the Civic Federation, its opponents insisted,
was to blunt the edge of the workers' militancy, to chloroform the trade
union movement and thereby expose the worker to greater exploitation.

Mitchell, who represented a union leading the opposition to the
National Civic Federation, spoke out against outright condemnation.
He told that he had helped to organize the National Civic Federation,
and that for eight years he had been simultaneously an officer of the
United Mine Workers of America and the National Civic Federation;
during this period the union had grown at a greater rate than it had
before or since. He pointed to the activity of the Civic Federation in settling strikes, its influence in behalf of enlightened labor legislation, and
while he could no longer be a member of the National Civic Federation
because of the action of the convention of his union, he pleaded for
rejection of the condemnatory resolution. Other officers of labor unions
described the aid they had received from the Civic Federation in their
negotiations with employers.

On the other hand, several Socialist delegates found membership in
the National Civic Federation incompatible with leadership in the labor
movement. Gompers, however, was convinced that the Civic Federation
performed useful service, and that cooperating labor people did not sur-

render their views nor their militancy. He had no delusions that the formation of the National Civic Federation ushered in a new era in the relations
of labor and management. Nor did he believe that it was a substitute for
organization. However, he stated:

With the increasing power and influence of our great labor movement, which
must of necessity continue to gather further numbers and strength . . . that
time has come when the power is being reckoned with by the representative
employers of labor, who have concluded that antagonism to organized labor
is vain and unprofitable, and who see the wisdom of a policy of conciliation.
They realize it is better, more intelligent and progressive.[14]

In the end, the right of leaders of the A. F. of L. to continue membership in the Civic Federation was sustained by a vote of 11,851 to 4924,
with 465 votes not cast. The opposition made an impressive showing
despite defeat, and it showed the rising influence of the Socialists in the
American Federation of Labor.[15]

At this stage the National Civic Federation concentrated largely on
attempting to convince aggressive anti-union industrialists of the desirability of collective bargaining. The organization was far ahead of its
time. Although the Civic Federation accepted donations from any employer, even those bitterly opposed to unionism, it never, in the years
up to the end of the first World War, compromised in its belief that the
future of American industry must be in the direction of dealing with
organized labor.

There can be no doubt that the propaganda and authority of the Civic
Federation helped to dilute the influence of the militant anti-union employers. The attacks of David Parry, John T. Kirby, C. W. Post, and other
aggressive anti-unionists are the best testimony of the attitude of the Civic
Federation in the matter of unionism. The Civic Federation was not only
helpful in bringing labor officers and employers together, but Easley,
Mark Hanna, Seth Low, and others utilized their knowledge of and their
relations to men of business to help prevent and settle labor disputes, and
thereby were often instrumental in minimizing opposition to dealing with
unions by employers.

Even the meetings and dinners, which were the sharpest point of scorn
of the Socialists, brought union leaders and heads of business together,
and there is no indication that Gompers or Mitchell, to mention the two
most active labor leaders in the Civic Federation, were ever restrained
from presenting their views because of the presence of the august personalities from the business world. Moreover, Easley, with his extensive
connections, was not averse to warning labor men of the plans of business
if these plans were of interest to labor. Thus, in October 1920 Easley
warned Gompers of an impending drive on the unions financed by United

States Steel Corporation, Standard Oil, and Julius Rosenwald.[16]

During World War I, the chief interest of Easley was diverted toward uncovering spies and anti-American activities. After the Bolshevist Revolution of October 1917, Easley became steadily more concerned in fighting radicalism, and his attitudes did not always have the approval or support of Gompers. In 1921 he asked Gompers to support legislation for limiting freedom of speech, and for the denaturalization of non-native born citizens who "refused to bear arms." Gompers considered it "untimely and unwise to put the questions regarding the annulment of citizenship and the curtailment of freedom of speech and of the press. There is altogether too much interference by the government now with the constitutionally guaranteed rights." Gompers recalled that no one had been more pronounced in his opposition

to the theories espoused, so called radicals and radical groups, and I have been and am doing my share to attack and counteract them. I am quite convinced that any attempt on the part of the government to "stamp out" by law free expression of opinion particularly in time of peace will not only be ineffective but will bring about the very opposite result to the desired.[17]

Easley and the National Civic Federation increasingly concentrated their efforts on fighting radicalism and Soviet Russia. Within the ranks of organized labor its influence, especially after the death of Gompers, steadily declined. In 1935 the convention of the A. F. of L. instructed its officers to resign their posts with the National Civic Federation. For a number of years the latter had ceased to perform those tasks which had originally attracted the leaders of labor. From the point of view of the labor movement at the time, the National Civic Federation had little to offer, and the delegation of the United Mine Workers of America sponsored the resolution that severed all official relations between the A. F. of L. and the National Civic Federation.

REFERENCES

1. Gompers to Ralph Easley, November 22, 1898, in archives of the A. F. of L.

2. Mitchell to Gompers, April 7, 1900; Gompers to Mitchel, April 9, 1900.

3. Among the labor leaders on the advisory committee which called the meeting in December 1900 were Gompers, Mitchell, McGuire, E. E. Clark of the Order of Railway Conductors, Frank P. Sargent of the Brotherhood of Railway Trainmen, T. J. Shaffer, James Lynch of the International Typographical Union, H. C. Barter of the International Longshoremen's Association, and many others.

4. The conference in 1900 set up several departments, among them the National Committee on Conciliation and Arbitration, whose purpose was to

formulate policies and measures and to enter into active service in the cause of peace and harmony in the industrial world, and declared "its purpose to be the prevention of those most threatening of all industrial disturbances, the strike and the lockout." The National Committee, in a Mimeographed Statement (in archives of A. F. of L.) urged "full and frank conference between employers and workmen, with the avowed purpose of reaching an agreement as to the terms of employment." The statement emphasized the value of trade agreements as aids to industrial peace and urged "that they should be generally adopted." The statement advocated the expansion of trade agreements so that they would cover as many workers as possible, and education and cooperation as the means by which employers and workers can be best restrained from committing unwise acts. Finally, the National Committe was "to establish and maintain a Board of Commission composed of the most competent persons available, selected from employers and employees of judgment, experience and reliability," who were to aid in the promotion of the above objectives and who were "to make known to workmen and employers that their counsel and aid will be available if desired in securing that cooperation, mutual understanding and agreement already indicated as the general purpose of this National Council on Conciliation and Arbitration."

5. John Kirby to Seth Low, December 27, 1909.

6. Figures are taken from a confidential report in the Easley papers in the New York Public Library.

7. *American Federationist*, February 1902, p. 71.

8. Easley to Gompers, April 1, 1901.

9. *Report of the Proceedings of the Twenty-Fifth Annual Convention of the American Federation of Labor*, 1905, p. 182.

10. Mitchell to Seth Low, February 16, 1911, in archives of Catholic University.

11. Letter of Morris Hillquit to Ralph Easley, June 6, 1911, in Easley Papers, New York Public Library.

12. *Report of the Proceedings of the Thirty-First Annual Convention of the American Federation of Labor*, 1911, p. 218.

13. Frick donated one thousand dollars, August 17, 1911. Easley papers of New York Public Library.

14. *American Federationist*, February 1902, p. 71.

15. Mother M. Green, *The National Civic Federation and the American Labor Movement*, 1900-1925 (Catholic University unpublished doctoral dissertation examines the Civic Federation in considerable detail. Mother Green allowed me to read her study, and I am grateful to her for aid and insights.

16. Memorandum to Gompers from Easley in Easley papers at the New York Public Library, no date.

17. Easley to Gompers, December 29, 1921; Gompers to Easley, December 30, 1921.

XV

Changes Within

MEMBERSHIP CHANGES

From many points of view the membership increases of the A. F. of L. might be regarded by the leaders with considerable satisfaction. From 1897 to 1904 the enrollment climbed steadily. It dropped in the next year and then leveled out, with minor fluctuations, in the period between 1905 and 1910. It began to climb again in 1911, and by 1915 stood at almost two million.

MEMBERSHIP OF THE AMERICAN FEDERATION OF LABOR 1897-1915
(*in thousands*)

Year	Membership	Year	Membership
1897	264	1907	1,538
1898	278	1908	1,586
1899	349	1909	1,482
1900	548	1910	1,562
1901	787	1911	1,761
1902	1,024	1912	1,770
1903	1,465	1913	1,996
1904	1,676	1914	2,020
1905	1,494	1915	1,946
1906	1,454		

Despite the real gains in this decade and a half, the Federation suffered what in retrospect appear to have been serious reverses. The defeat of the union in the steel industry, the loss of positions by the affiliated organizations in the metal and machinery industries, and the growing aggressiveness of anti-labor employers on both the economic and political fronts raised serious questions as to the efficacy of the Federation's policies to meet the tasks which faced the labor movement. In addition, the extreme anti-governmentalism espoused by the Executive Council, whose chief spokesmen were Gompers and Duncan, inspired opposition not only by Socialists but by many trade unionists who believed that government had a role in protecting standards and improving the conditions of labor.

233

McGuire

The oppoistion directed its attacks against the leading proponents of the Federation policies, with Gompers always the chief target. After 1900, he had to face his opponents without the advice or support of his comrade-in-arms, P. J. McGuire. For the first time since the reorganization of the American Federation of Labor in 1886, McGuire was unable to participate and help guide the deliberations of a convention. When it came to the election of officers, Gompers made a moving speech in which he "expressed regret that P. J. McGuire could not have been at the convention, but shattered health caused by the severe and untiring labor in the movement prevented his presence at this time." There was a contest for the vacancy on the council, and Denis A. Hayes of the Glass Bottle Blowers' Association was chosen.

McGuire's departure from the organized labor scene carried with it an element of great personal tragedy. He had been active in the radical and Socialist movements as a youth, and was one of those who turned from the broader panaceas to trade unionism as the means for raising the standard of life of the workers. He launched a four-page journal, *The Carpenter,* in 1881 and sent out the call for the first convention of the United Brotherhood of Carpenters and Joiners. He gave himself unsparingly to his own organization and to the general labor movement. In the first two decades of its existence, McGuire was a tower of strength to the American Federation of Labor. He directed his own union, and he also contributed innumerable hours to organizing workers in other trades and negotiating with employers on their behalf. Few important decisions were made without his advice.

McGuire seemed to lack Gompers strength and ability to shake off the cares of office. He sometimes ran into financial difficulties, and in 1896 his friends collected several hundred dollars to help him meet his debts.[1] In the next two years there was a visible slackening of his activity, and by 1899 and 1900 his participation in the sessions of the Executive Council of the A. F. of L. became sporadic. Gompers, while pleading with him to renew his activity, knew well of the stress and physical illness from which McGuire suffered. In the last days of December 1900, McGuire told Gompers that he was feeling better, and Gompers was

delighted to receive and read the contents of your letter of December 29th, and took occasion to show it to some of your dear friends here, who I know feel gratified as I do that your health is improving, and with it your courage re-- turned, for they know the splendid service you can still perform in the great cause for which you have unceasingly worked for many years. It is an honor as well as a pleasure for me to know that jointly we have struggled so hard, a sincere gratification that we have lived to see some of the fruition of our labors.[2]

When McGuire told Gompers he was scheduled to address a meeting at Reading, Pennsylvania, the latter hoped it would lead to good results for the Carpenters' Union and for the general labor movement, "and last but not least, for yourself. If you were to go away from the office at Philadelphia for a couple of weeks," Gompers told him, "I feel confident that your meeting old friends and making new ones in the labor movement, . . . would have the effect suggested."[3] McGuire failed to attend the Reading meeting. His health was poor, but McGuire's sickness was not completely physical. Gompers learned of his reluctance to leave his office and pleaded with him to make the trip so as to get away from the stress and pressure of work. It was a painful plea, and Gompers begged his old comrade not to "consider my importunities . . . impertinent. You know the strong regard and friendship I have always held for you, and the recognition of your splendid powers. My extreme anxiety for the good of the movement and for your welfare, I trust, will be accepted as my excuse."[4]

McGuire was physically ill and mentally exhausted, a burned-out leader who had turned to drink. Gompers' letters to him show a deep concern for the welfare of a man who, second only to him, might well be regarded as the architect of the American Federation of Labor.[5] At the convention of the United Brotherhood of Carpenters and Joiners of America in 1900 there was dissatisfaction expressed with the management of the secretary's office, on such matters as the handling of claims for a death benefit, and failure to submit a regular report to the convention. McGuire's prestige was sufficiently high so that, despite the criticism, he was reelected to the post he had held since he had founded the union in 1881.[6] An opponent to McGuire, William D. Huber, was elected to the presidency, at the time an unpaid job. Frank Duffy, who was to succeed McGuire in the Secretary's post, was elected to the General Executive Board.

McGuire's books had been audited at the convention of 1901, but suspicion persisted that all was not in order. A later audit in April 1901 revealed shortages and erasures in the books of account. McGuire claimed he could explain the condition of his books, and he advised the members of the General Executive Board, in session in Philadelphia, not to delay their departure. At the next meeting, his books were in even worse shape, and he again failed to explain discrepancies in the accounts. The Secretary failed to carry out his promise to the Executive Board. Finally, President Huber found him in a saloon. Huber claimed the "general officers were lenient with Brother McGuire . . . We regarded what he had been in the past, we respected old age, and respected the fact that he was an able man, and had done a great deal for the organization." McGuire claimed that all would be in order, and an outside firm of accountants was brought in to make the audit. Their report showed the accounts were not in balance, but that there was no evidence of deliberate dishonesty.[7] McGuire defended the irregularities with the claim of ill health which forced his absence from the office.

The discovery of the shortages was followed by McGuire's suspension from the office of secretary, and his replacement by Frank Duffy. President Huber had been advised by his attorney that, to recover the funds, criminal charges would have to be brought. The advice was followed and McGuire was arrested on Huber's warrant.[8] McGuire was not without friends in the Brotherhood; cries against prosecuting McGuire were raised in many locals. Huber and Secretary Duffy found themselves bound to defend their action, and denied that they had been motivated by spite or venom against a political rival. An investigation by John Morrison, who was in charge of advertising in the *American Federationist*, convinced him that McGuire "was not morally guilty" although he conceded that no one could make sense out of McGuire's books. The controversy wracked the Brotherhood, but in the end a settlement was arranged under which McGuire agreed to pay to the Brotherhood one thousand dollars immediately and another in two installments. He also agreed to forfeit all salary due him from the union. McGuire's parting words were advice against disharmony and splits in the union. His departure under a cloud was sad and painful.

Gompers was not convinced that McGuire was dishonest, and the suppression by the Executive Board of an entire issue of *The Carpenter* in which McGuire explained the neglect of his duties as due to illness, convinced him that "it is a case of persecution rather than in defense of the organization." Gompers attributed the shortages in McGuire's accounts to a dishonest clerk who had been forced upon him by the General Executive Board. Gompers knew that McGuire had handled "hundreds of thousands of dollars for the Brotherhood and for the general labor movement, and has had opportunities to 'make money' and I know that he has not a dollar in the world. It is truly pitiable, and he is in awful condition."[9]

McGuire did not resume his labor activity. On February 18, 1906, he died. His death was announced in *The Carpenter*, and an editorial commemorating his achievements printed. A memorial fund was started by a number of locals, and an appeal issued for the relief of Mrs. McGuire, who had been left penniless. Almost six thousand dollars were collected by the Carpenters' Union, and a number of locals contributed directly to the widow. The Executive Council, meeting on March 19th, paid tribute to his contribution to the labor movement.[10]

At its convention of 1906, the A. F. of L. declared that "the late P. J. McGuire . . . contributed in no small degree to the successful launching of the eight-hour movement, the establishing of Labor Day, and the founding of this great American Federation of Labor" and expressed its "sincere and heartfelt regret at the irreparable loss which the labor movement of America has suffered."[11]

THE STEEL STRIKE

In 1901, the Federation gained almost a quarter of a million members, the largest annual increment to that date. The resulting increases in income enabled it to engage more organizers, who also aided the international unions in recruiting. The convention of 1901 was also called upon to settle a dispute between Gompers and John Mitchell, head of the United Mine Workers of America, second vice president of the A. F. of L., and the president of the Amalgamated Association of Iron and Steel Workers, which had arisen as a result of the steel strike of 1901.

The Amalgamated Association was one of the oldest unions in the United States, having been organized in 1876 as a result of a merger of previously existing unions. Its representatives attended the first convention of the Federation of Organized Trades and Labor Unions in Pittsburgh in 1881, where the head of this union presided at several sessions. The union prospered and was recognized as one of the more powerful and better-managed organizations of labor in its time. With the growth of the large multiplant corporation in the industry, the union found that some companies would shut down the organized plants while allowing their non-union properties to operate. Such a policy constituted a threat to the union, for by a process of induced erosion the power of the union could gradually be diminished and eventually extinguished. To meet this danger, the Amalgamated Association of Iron and Steel Workers of America at its convention of 1901 decided: "Should one mill in a combine or trust have a difficulty, all mills in such combine or trust shall cease work until such grievance is settled."

This principle was written into the union's constitution almost at the same time that the United States Steel Corporation was organized, just a few months before negotiations of a new contract were to begin between the union and the corporation's operating subsidiaries. There were some misgivings among the promoters of the United States Steel Corporation as to whether the flotation of securities would encounter public criticism or resistance, especially in the event of a strike.[12] Negotiations, in the hands of T. J. Shaffer, a former Methodist minister, and John Williams, the secretary of the union, were begun with the American Steel Hoop Company, one of the subsidiaries of the United States Steel Corporation. The opinion in A. F. of L. quarters was that Williams was the strong man in the Amalgamated.

Although there was accord on a scale of prices, the company refused to sign for the mills which had not been under contract in the preceding year. Consequently no agreement was reached. Both the American Sheet

Steel Company and the American Tin Plate Company similarly were ready to accept the scale demanded by the union, but refused to accept the unionization of their unorganized mills. Finally, the union was offered what in retrospect was a great concession. The American Steel Hoop Company offered to sign for all mills except one; the American Sheet Steel Company offered to add five mills operated as non-union in the preceding year; and the American Hoop Company offered to sign for all mills that had been under contract with the union the last year. These offers were refused, and strikes were called.

On July 27 George Harvey, editor of *Harpers' Weekly*, entered the controversy and arranged for a meeting in New York between J. P. Morgan, Shaffer, and John Williams. Charles Schwab, the head of the United States Steel Corporation, was present at the interview. It was proposed that work would be resumed at the plants of the three companies on strike, and that the heads of the union should urge acceptance of this plan. Williams seemed opposed, and quarreled with Schwab. Neither Shaffer nor Williams would agree to recommend the acceptance of the agreement by the General Executive Board. Consequently, when the agreement was submitted to the Board it was rejected.

Schwab believed the leaders of the union were obligated to fight for the agreement, which he, Gary, and Morgan had accepted. He thereupon wrote to Shaffer that he "read with astonishment" the refusal of the General Executive Board to "adopt your advice."[13] During the interview the union officers were assured by Morgan that he was not hostile to organized labor, that on the contrary he wanted to maintain friendly relations with the unions. He insisted that normally he would not be opposed to recognizing in all the mills, but at the time such an arrangement was impracticable. This does not coincide with the subsequent revelations of the investigations of the United States Steel Corporation by the Stanley Committee of the United States House of Representatives, which showed that the board of directors of the United States Steel Corporation was opposed to any extension of unionism in its plants. However Ralph Easley, secretary of the National Civic Federation, who played a role in arranging some of the conferences between Morgan and the union representatives, claims that some of the constituent companies would never have consented to become a part of the United States Steel Corporation had they not been assured that their mills would be conducted on an open shop basis. This was, according to Easley, "the reason for the resolution adopted by the United States Steel Corporation . . . declaring it was opposed to any extension" of unionism "in mills where it did not exist."[14] In any event, no settlement was reached, and the union subsequently called out all of its members employed in the mills of all subsidiaries of the United States Steel Corporation. After the strike had been thus extended, the United Mine Workers of America Executive Board suggested that President Mitchell use his efforts, whenever possible, to help settle the strike.

Shaffer asked Gompers to come to Pittsburgh, and that a conference of all national unions or at least of a meeting of the Executive Council of the A. F. of L. be called. Gompers refused on the ground that such conferences would be a sign of weakness, and argued that the situation in the steel industry was not analogous to the one that existed during the bituminous coal strike of 1897 when the A. F. of L. had called such a conference.

In the meantime, the National Civic Federation intervened and sought to bring about a termination of the dispute. Ralph Easley, its secretary, with the cooperation of Mitchell, Frank P. Sargent of the Brotherhood of Locomotive Firemen, Henry White of the United Garment Workers' Union, and Professor J. W. Jenks, conferred with Shaffer, Williams, and Michael Tighe. The Civic Federation was authorized to submit a proposal to the United States Steel Corporation that the strike would be terminated if all the union mills in the preceding year would again be recognized under the new contract. This offer was submitted to the company officers in New York by the above-named group from the National Civic Federation, with the addition of Gompers. The union offer, in effect a request for the reestablishment of the status existing before the strike, was far inferior to what the companies had originally offered.[15]

However, conditions had undergone some change, for the companies had succeeded in reopening a number of mills with strikebreakers and they were no longer ready to surrender those mills to the union. Instead they suggested a much less favorable settlement, offering to sign for all union mills of the preceding year except those which the companies had already reopened with strikebreakers. The Advisory Committee of the Steel Union was informed by the group negotiating on its behalf "that these were the best conditions which can be secured as a result of this strike; that it is the last offer for an arrangement which the company will entertain, and that we must be in the position to accept these conditions today or all negotiations will be off." The committee was convinced that it was to the interest of the union to accept the new terms.

The offer was read to Shaffer and Williams over the telephone, and acceptance urged upon them. The companies had managed to start nine mills that had operated under union agreements the preceding year. Gompers, Mitchell, and other members of the committee pleaded with the steel companies to postpone opening another mill so that the General Executive Board of the Amalgamated Association might have time to consider the settlement without further prejudice. But the strike dragged on, with the union steadily losing control of the situation. Finally, on

September 14th, Shaffer signed an agreement under which the non-union mills were to remain as such, and "no attempts to organize" were "to be made" and "no charters" were "to be granted." Under this agreement no question of a worker's connection with the strike or membership in the union was to be raised in determining his reemployment. The outcome of the strike was disastrous to the Amalgamated Association of Iron, Steel and Tin Workers, and to the labor movement generally.

ATTACK ON GOMPERS AND MITCHELL

A week after the strike ended, Shaffer issued a confidential circular to his members, accusing Gompers of not giving him adequate support in the strike, and charging that Mitchell had failed to carry out an agreement with Shaffer to call out the coal miners if the United States Steel Corporation did not accept the terms Mitchell had outlined. Another charge was that Mitchell had promised to have Frank P. Sargent, the head of the Brotherhood of Trainmen, call out the members of his union if the demands were not met. Other charges were made relating to the conduct and the kind of cooperation Gompers gave the steel strikers. Gompers and Mitchell denied Shaffer's allegations, and offered to submit his charges to a committee of leading union men for examination.[16]

The pertinent question is whether the requests from Shaffer to Mitchell and Gompers were reasonable ones. The International Executive Board of the United Mine Workers of America had met during the strike, and had suggested that Mitchell intervene and seek a settlement, but they did not mention a sympathetic strike. The notion that Mitchell could order the trainmen, members of one of the more conservative unions, out on strike does not seem a very likely one. Mitchell was as knowledgeable as most labor men of his time, and he must have known the reluctance of the Brotherhood of Railroad Trainmen and their officers to engage in any strikes, much less those called in sympathy with workers in another industry. Shaffer did not claim that Sargent, the head of the Railroad Trainmen, had made any such promise. He must have known the unlikelihood that a union leader from one organization could successfully order the workers from another industry and union out on strike.

There is another kind of question also involved in this dispute. Should Mitchell in any case have ordered his miners out of the pits in behalf of the Steel Workers' Union? The conflict between short-run and long-run interests is always difficult to decide, but in retrospect it does not appear that the strike should have been called. A union, like a business and for that matter any other institution, cannot assume too many immediate risks on the theory that its long-run interests will thereby be served. The Amalgamated Association was originally offered substantial concessions from the companies on the control over non-union plants. It is true that they would not sign for all plants, but the reduction in the number of non-union plans would have automatically reduced the flexibility of the companies and strengthened the position of the union.

In the light of Easley's testimony, the view that Morgan was not opposed to organized labor cannot be entirely dismissed. However, a union in control of the major plants of a company is able to bargain and strengthen its position. It might have demonstrated its responsibility and thereby broken down the resistance and opposition of some members of the United States Steel Corporation. Later experience has shown that unions do not and cannot always impose their demands if they insist that multiplant firms accept unionization for all units as a condition for making an agreement.

On the other hand, unions gaining a foothold by organizing some plants can generally extend their positions to the remaining ones of the same company. It is true that it had been a common practice among some firms in the industry to shut down unionized plants if possible, and allow the unorganized ones to operate. But as the Amalgamated had previously organized non-union plants, acceptance of the original offer might have simplified its future task of extending the organization of the industry.

In precipitating an extensive and risky strike the union engaged in a gamble a prudent organization would have avoided. The entire strike demonstrated a reckless incapacity on the part of Shaffer and other leaders of the Amalgamated Association, an incapacity which was to be costly to the union. There is also a question whether the attitude of the leaders of the Amalgamated and the ease with which the union was defeated did not influence the policies of the Corporation. Moreover, if there was actually a split among the officers of the United States Steel Corporation on the question of union recognition, Shaffer's conduct undoubtedly strengthened the group that was opposed to union organization.

Gompers had no power to call a strike, and it is doubtful if he would have gained the approval of the members of the Executive Council had he suggested such a call. In the case of the United Mine Workers of America, Mitchell had just gained grudging recognition from the anthracite coal operators after the intervention of Mark Hanna. With the coal operators in the anthracite districts dissatisfied with their arrangements, and anxious to rid themselves of the restrictions of the union, a violation of contracts would have seriously weakened the anthracite miners' position. Moreover, sympathetic support of the steel strikers by the coal miners and the workers in other organized industries would have seriously weakened the position of organized labor, which was seeking to establish in the public mind a reputation for reliability in the observance of its contracts. It would have lent weight to the charges by anti-unionists that the unions were a potential danger to social stability. And it is doubtful if an extension of the walkout to other industries would have affected the outcome of the strike. At best, it would have been a quixotic gesture which would have aroused widespread fear in the public. It would have undermined the claims of organized labor that it was a responsible institution, and jeopardized many of its gains. It is true that the steel strike was perhaps the opening gun in a long campaign to disestablish unionism in some of the more important sections of American industry. Yet it is possible that the attitude and policies of Shaffer contributed to the strengthening of the very anti-union forces he sought to control.

As one considers the struggle and the ensuing controversy from the vantage point of the present, one must conclude that the policy of the Amalgamated Association at the time was deficient in realism, based on an overestimate of its own strength in disregard of prudence and the gradualism characteristic of the wiser union leadership of the time. In seeking to involve a large number of workers in other industries in a dispute in which they had no direct interest, the leaders of the Amalgamated were only compounding their initial error. There is no record that the Amalgamated ever made an analogous sacrifice. In charging Gompers and Mitchell with violation of their trust, Shaffer was showing a disregard for the truth motivated by a desire to shift the blame for the abysmal failure in policy. Leaders of labor in the 1940's and 1950's have faced this problem of the division of plants controlled by a single company between union and non-union, and as a rule have not been willing to run the risk of losing the organized plants in order to gain the non-union units. There is of course a difference, because of the existence of the federal labor relations laws and the greater acceptance of unionism. Yet the sacrifice of the present to meet possible and perhaps never existing dangers in the future, especially when the policies of the company in question are not clearly defined, is not a mark of an adroit or even competent labor leadership. The facts, as they have been developed, show that Shaffer was not only deficient as a leader, but his demands upon Mitchell and Gompers could never have been carried out by responsible labor leaders.[17]

The Strike of the Machinists

The International Association of Machinists had only become affiliated with the A. F. of L. in 1895, and dated its beginnings to 1888, but the union early became an important affiliate. Its head, James O'Connell, became a member of the Executive Council of the American Federation of Labor. Moreover, O'Connell was an active member of the Council, aiding many organizations other than his own to enroll members and negotiate contracts with employers. Under his leadership, an agreement had been signed on May 10, 1900, with the National Metal Trades, the so-called Murray Hill agreement. Under it differences between members of the National Metal Trades and the International Association of Machinists which could not be settled directly were to be submitted to a committee made up of the heads of the two associations or others appointed by them. The findings in such disputes were to be final and binding and were to serve as precedents for the adjudication of similar cases.[18] Present at the conference at which the agreement was signed were the officers of a number of unions in the metal trades; Gompers was present as a representative of the unions in the metal trades directly affiliated with the A. F. of L.

Speaking for the unions present, Gompers expressed the hope that cooperation between the unions and industry would be achieved and that similar agreements would be established in all the metal and machinery trades.[19] Gompers believed that a great deal of good had been accomplished at the first conference and suggested, in a letter to all the unions in the metal trades, that they come together to establish "some council or trade alliance of a national character for the purpose of mutual support. There is no reason why this council should not be formed, and why the affiliation of every national union composing it should not be secured."[20]

It should be noted that the A. F. of L. was the organization which sought to bring about wider unity and cooperation among the unions in the metal and machinery industry. This was incidental to the main problem, for the unions soon found themselves faced with employer opposition to concessions the labor organizations believed were necessary and reasonable. Moreover, a dispute soon arose over whether certain demands, mainly the nine-hour work day, fell within the province of the local and individual employer or were within the jurisdiction of the National Metal Trades. A complicating difficulty was that in a number of cities unsatisfactory relations had arisen between the unions and the local metal trades employers. In St. Louis, for example, "the unions of the different branches of the trade have made requests for reasonable concessions upon the employers, who refused to consider the matter, stating that the question should be considered and adjusted by the National Metal Trades Association and the national unions interested, and declined to take the matter up locally."[21]

However, the National Metal Trade refused to consider the wage question on a national basis. As a result, a strike was called by the International Association of Machinists on May 20, 1901. Following the calling of the strike, the administrative committee of the National Metal Trades Association charged the union with breaking its contract. Soon thereafter the National Civic Federation, acting through its secretary, Ralph Easley, intervened. The latter hoped to send some men who were sympathetic to the labor movement into the meeting of the National Metal Trades Association so as to prevent "a general war on the union, as some of its hot headed members are advocating".[22]

FINANCIAL ASSISTANCE

The National Civic Federation sought to bring about a settlement through a compromise. The union was willing to submit the wage question to arbitration, providing the employers would institute a fifty-four hour work week and reinstate all strikers without prejudice. The Metal Trades Association rejected these conditions, and renewed its charge that the union had been guilty of an irresponsible violation of contract.[23] As the strike continued the International Association of Machinists found itself in need of financial support, lacking the means to provide even for the basic needs of the strikers for any protracted period. It appealed to the American Federation of Labor for aid, and the latter levied an assessment upon the members of the constituent unions, with one member of the Council opposed. Another, John Mitchell, favored the assessment, but he pointed to the strikes in several coal districts as proof of the inability of his union to pay the charges imposed. It was finally agreed that the United Mine Workers of America would contribute on the basis of a membership of one hundred thousand rather than for all of those on its rolls. Under this arrangement, the Miners' Union was able to meet its obligation, and yet was not required to pay more than its finances allowed.

Over thirty-three thousand dollars was raised by the American Federation of Labor. Gompers was of the opinion that some of the money should be used for the support of the metal and machinery workers, on strike in San Francisco, who were not affiliated with the Machinists' Union. This proposal was opposed by O'Connell, who argued that the funds had been raised for his organization. Nevertheless, the Executive Council by a vote of five to three decided to accept Gompers' recommendation, with the aim of demonstrating to employers in the Pacific Coast area that the strikers there were not forgotten by their fellow unionists in other parts of the United States. It was also intended to impress the workers of the Pacific Coast with the realization that the American labor movement had an interest in their problems. Consequently, three thousand dollars was sent to San Francisco, and twenty-eight thousand given to the International Association of Machinists.

The strike itself did not achieve its objectives, and the National Metal Trades Association, which had signed an agreement with the union in the preceding year, became a bitter opponent of all organized labor. Aggressive and irreconcilable employers had gained dominance over the National Metal Trades Association, a dominance feared by, among others, Ralph Easley. The policies followed by the International Association of Machinists at the time did not help to allay this hostility. James O'Connell, one of the abler men in the labor movement, had favored a conciliatory policy, and had even warned his members that "fighting the piecework question is absolutely suicidal," but his views were not accepted. It was not a time for the moderates on either side. Among the metal trades employers, the anti-unionist and open shopper became predominant. The union survived, but its strongholds became the railroad shops and roundhouses and the navy yards, where the attitude toward unionism was less hostile. Of course, some shops in the metal trades dealt with the union and made concessions, but on the whole the nine-hour strike was lost. In this conflict, the A. F. of L. played a helpful if a subordinate role. Not only did it raise needed funds, but it financed a number of organizers who were active in the field attending to the duties so essential in a great strike.

THE ANTHRACITE STRIKE OF 1902

In contrast to the defeats in the steel and metal machinery industries, organized labor, aided by the Fabian statesmanship of John Mitchell, one of the great leaders of the United Mine Workers of America, by 1900 was able to establish the union in the anthracite coal fields where it had been virtually nonexistent for a quarter of a century. The foothold was gained largely as a result of the shrewd and conciliatory policies of Mitchell. Another contributing factor to the union's success was the presidential contest of that year.

Believing that a prolonged strike in the anthracite fields might have unfavorable repercussions upon the fortunes of the Republican candidate, Senator Mark Hanna and a powerful financial group intervened in the walkout, leading to its termination and the limited recognition of the union and some improvements in wage scales. The coal companies, however, would not participate in the establishment of a joint conference which would have enabled the union and management to handle grievances and other questions, as requested by the union in 1901. But for a time the union did not press for further concessions.

The anthracite coal fields had been, prior to 1900, completely unorganized since the 1870's. During that period a number of evils had developed in the industry. Proper weighing of coal was absent, and charges at the company stores were often excessive. In addition, a drastic change had taken place in the ethnic composition of the labor force. The Irish, Scotch, Welsh, and American miners had become a minority and were replaced by Eastern Europeans—the Slav, Croat, Pole, and Italian. Hard working and many with peasant backgrounds, this group had failed to establish a viable union, although there were occasional stirrings which indicated that all was not serene in the anthracite coal fields. The policies of the companies did not encourage organization, and the United Mine Workers of America which had established its dominance over the Central Competitive Field in the bituminous industry was not looked upon with favor by leading operators.

The union, nevertheless, decided to compel recognition of its right to bargain for its members. On February 14, 1902, the representatives of the three anthracite districts and the president of the United Mine Workers of America, in a joint request, asked the leading operators to meet them in a conference of representatives of miners and operators. Hitherto, the agreement with the operators had been a verbal one. The proposal was promptly rejected by the heads of various coal companies. Some of the company officers objected to a uniform scale, sought by the union; others argued that periodic negotiations of the terms of the labor contract tended to create unrest and agitation; and some contended that the differences in the conditions of mining bituminous and anthractie coal were such as to militate against the common practices sought by the union. Failing to get a favorable response, the three anthracite districts of the union met in convention and drew up demands for wage increases, changes in working conditions, and recognition of the union.

The leaders of the miners then appealed to the National Civic Federation. Its chairman, Senator Mark Hanna, invited the parties to a conference in New York City. The issues were explored but no agreement was reached. Thereupon the conference was adjourned for thirty days, at the expiration of which representatives of the union and the operators met again. At the suggestion of the National Civic Federation, Mitchell and the district presidents met with the leading officers of the principal coal-carrying roads in the anthracite area. Mitchell reconvened his executive board, and again appealed for a settlement. In the meantime, the National Civic Federation suggested arbitration and, in the event of inability to agree upon the arbitrators, offered the names of Archbishop Ireland and Bishop Potter. George F. Baer, the head of the Philadelphia and Reading Coal and Iron Company, was quick to answer that

Anthracite mining is a business, and not a religious, sentimental, or academic proposition. The laws organizing the companies I represent in express terms impose the business management on the president and directors. I could not if I would delegate this business management to even so highly respectable body as the Civic Federation, nor can I call to my aid as experts in the mixed problem of business and philanthropy the eminent prelates you have named.[24]

Failing to win any concessions, the leaders of the anthracite miners ordered a temporary work suspension pending the determination of the steps to be taken by a convention. The convention met on May 15th and by a vote of 461 to 349 determined to continue the strike. Six days later the union proposed that concessions alone be given to the engineers, firemen, and pumpmen employed in and around the mines; when these were rejected, this group was also called out. Virtually all of the approximately 150,000 anthracite mine workers were out on strike. It was a long and grueling contest, but the ranks of the miners held firm.[25]

As the strike continued, a demand for a national strike of all coal miners arose in the ranks. Bowing to the insistent appeals, a convention was called. Mitchell was of the opinion that the future of the labor movement depended upon obedience to contractual commitments, and that nothing could be gained by a wholesale violation of contracts. The convention of 2253 delegates, which met on July 17th, rejected a general strike in the mines. Instead it voted to donate fifty thousand dollars from the national treasury and request the districts to contribute whatever sums they could. In addition, assessments in support of the strike were imposed upon all unionized miners employed in the bituminous coal fields.

An appeal to the people was also issued which declared that

The arbitrary assumption by the employers that neither the miners nor the public have any rights that are entitled to consideration by them, have forced us to organize, not for the purpose of taking from the operators that which belongs to them, but for the purpose of securing, by business methods, better treatment than we have received in the past and fair recompense for our labor. We have sought to accomplish this end by conciliatory methods. As proof of our sincerity we point to the joint convention system of adjusting wages and conditions of employment from year to year which we have by our persistent efforts introduced and firmly established in a great majority of the bituminous fields of the United States. We have faithfully lived up to the letter and spirit of every contract we have made, nor shall we violate them now.

As the strike continued from week to week, a point was reached at which the lowered coal supplies were less than were necessary for normal needs. Continuance of the strike meant serious economic harm and even severe suffering by householders dependent upon anthracite fuel. The anthracite coal strike became a national problem, and a plea from communities and officials of government was issued which induced President Theodore Roosevelt to intervene. In a telegram, on October 1, 1902, he invited John Mitchell and the heads of the leading coal-hauling anthracite railroads to a conference at the White House on October 3rd. At the meeting, President Roosevelt pointed to the public's vital concern in the controversy, and the "urgency, and the terrible nature of the catastrophe impending for a large portion of our people in the shape of a winter-fuel famine" which justified his intervention.

The President suggested immediate resumption of coal mining. Upon the completion of the President's statement, Mitchell immediately proposed that the representatives of the miners and operators seek a settlement directly and, failing to arrive at a satisfactory agreement, submit the issues to an impartial board of arbitration.

The conference then recessed; upon reassembling, the operators denounced the lawlessness of the strikes and rejected Mitchell's offer. They declared that if given adequate protection they would solve the fuel crisis by restoring production, blaming the lack of output on the lawlessness of the miners and the failure of government to furnish safeguards. Miners in each colliery, under the operators' proposal, could settle grievances directly with their employers, and failing to do so, the issue could be determined by the judges of the local Court of Common Pleas of the district. The operators pointed to the fact that Mitchell was not a resident of Pennsylvania, and that he had gained his mining experience in the bituminous coal fields. They insisted that the miners had been guilty of lawlessness, and troops would restore order and the digging of coal. Consequently, they refused to arbitrate.

Roosevelt then asked Mitchell if he would agree to the miners returning to work, after which the President would appoint a commission to investigate the issues in dispute, promising to use his influence to obtain operator acceptance of the commission's recommendations. Since the operators had not committed themselves to accept such recommendations, it was a difficult position for the union. But it was adroitly handled by the officers led by Mitchell.

He called upon the strikers to meet in mass meetings, irrespective of their membership or nonmembership in the union, on October 8th, and to declare whether they wanted to return to work. Meetings were held and resolutions were overwhelmingly adopted that the miners would not return to work until their demands had been granted. From the beginning, Mitchell had been averse to accepting the President's terms for ending the walkout, since they contained no guarantees that the union would be unmolested in carrying out its activities. From the point of view of the United Mine Workers of America, the crucial issue was the recognition of the union. Consequently, Mitchell informed the President that

Having in mind our experience with the coal operators in the past, we have no reason to feel any degree of confidence in their willingness to do us justice in the future; and, inasmuch as they have refused to accept the the decision of a tribunal selected by you, and inasmuch as there is no law through which you could enforce the findings of the commission you suggest, we respectfully decline to advise our people to return to work simply upon the hope that the coal operators might be induced or forced to comply with the recommendations of your commission.[26]

In the meantime, the entire National Guard of Pennsylvania was sent into the anthracite counties to maintain order, but little coal was mined. The impasse was broken on October 13th, when the operators proposed that the President of the United States appoint a commission to consider the issues, and the companies promised to accept the recommendations. In the request to the President, the kinds of individuals to be appointed and their qualifications were specified. President Roosevelt subsequently

found that the desire of the operators to have as a member of the commission "a man of prominence, eminent as a sociologist" allowed him to
appoint as one of the seven-man tribunal, E. E. Clark, Grand Chief of the
Order of Railway Conductors, for the term "sociologist means a man who
has thought and studied deeply on social questions and has practically
applied his knowledge."

Mitchell notified the President that the presidents of the anthracite
districts had agreed immediately to call a delegate convention to which
they would recommend acceptance of the arbitration proposal. The convention unanimously voted to accept the recommendation of its officers.
Mitchell informed the President of the decision, and took the occasion to
inform the President and the public that, had the union's offer of arbitration or impartial investigation been accepted before the strike, no walkout, with all of its inconvenience to the public and the losses that followed,
would have taken place. He admitted and lamented the violent acts by
the strikers, but charged that the coal and iron police had been guilty of
greater violence. He informed the President, "We do not, however,
exult over our opponents; we appeal to them now, as we have from the
first, to turn their eyes to the future, and to cooperate with us in an effort
to establish better relations between employer and employee for the advantage of both."[27]

A long hearing upon the issues was held, and the conduct and abilities
of John Mitchell made a deep impression upon the public. The report
granted the union increases in wages, and recommended that a board of
conciliation be set up, to be made up of a representative from the operators from each of the three districts and a representative of the organization representing a majority of the mine workers of the districts. Persons
having grievances before the board were to have the right to elect a
person to represent them before it. Miners were also given the right to
elect check weighmen, an important demand at the time. No discrimination in employment was to be practiced because of membership or nonmembership in a union. The award ran to March 31, 1906.

The strike was a great victory for the union. It enabled it to crash
through barriers that had existed for over a quarter of a century. Its importance for the American Federation of Labor was that it reinforced the
views of the Federation leadership that the future lay in the direction of
collaboration with employers through the trade agreement, and that while
the labor movement must be prepared at all times to lay down its tools
and strike, the unions could gain much more by moderation and by appealing to reason and fairness than by espousing a verbally militant doctrine
that might arouse strong feelings against labor organizations. The views of
Mitchell were reflected in his adroit appeal to public sentiment, in his
reasonableness, in his readiness to compromise as long as he did not

surrender completely the union's position.

John Mitchell became, next to Gompers, the most eminent labor leader of the time. Mitchell was born at Braidwood, Illinois, in 1870. At the age of twenty, he became an officer of the Illinois district, and later a member of the legislative committee of his union. Elected vice president of the United Mine Workers of America in 1898, he assumed the presidency the same year upon the resignation of Michael Ratchford. Mitchell was re-elected the following year, and served until 1910, when he refused to stand for reelection. In general, Mitchell shared Gompers' views on social and political questions, believing that the greatest gains could be achieved by labor through trade union action. He was less doctrinaire than Gompers on the role of government in economic affairs, and saw no danger in pro-tective legislation for men. Soon after his great successes in the anthracite coal industry, a movement was started to have him oppose Gompers for the presidency of the A. F. of L., but he refused. In the National Civic Federation, and in public activity, Mitchell advocated peaceful collabora-tion of labor and management through collective bargaining. After his voluntary withdrawal from the presidency of his union, he headed the Trade Agreement Department of the National Civic Federation. He died in 1919.

CONVENTIONS OF 1902-1905

At the convention of 1902, the Executive Council criticized the effort of the Milwaukee Trades Council to call a conference of city central bodies with a view of unifying them around a common center, seeing in the move the dangers of dual organizations.

In the election for office, all incumbents were unopposed except Thomas I. Kidd. The latter, president of the Amalgamated Wood Workers' In-ternational Union, was challenged by Frank Duffy, the secretary of the United Brotherhood of Carpenters and Joiners of America, whose union was then engaged in a bitter jurisdictional struggle with the Carpenters' Union, insisting that the Wood Workers' International amalgamate with it. The convention also raised the salaries of the permanent officers of the Federation by increasing the president's salary to $3000 a year, and the Seretary's salary to $2500 a year.

Steps were taken at the same convention to prevent unions from exercis-ing pressure upon the Executive Council by withholding per-capita taxes. Two unions had threatened to withdraw unless favorable decisions were made by the Executive Council. Upon Gompers' recommendation, the rule was adopted that whenever any effort was made by a union to in-fluence a decision by threats, the Executive Council was to refuse to deal with the issue until the threat was withdrawn.

The convention endorsed disability insurance. Introduced by Victor L.

Berger, the Socialist leader from Milwaukee, the resolution instructed the Executive Council and all friends of labor "to procure the enactment of national laws to protect disabled workmen, and to provide a system of national insurance for their assistance during enforced idleness." Another resolution introduced by Berger calling for a government pension of twelve dollars a month to every worker over sixty who had earned less than one thousand dollars a year, was defeated by a vote of 90 to 85.

During 1905, the A. F. of L. levied an assessment on behalf of United Textile Workers of America, and collected over $33,000. A number of unions were given grants, the largest, $5500, going to the United Garment Workers of America. The Federation also took steps to prevent the proliferation of international unions in a given trade. Several local unions in the silk industry were refused affiliation and were asked to join the United Textile Workers. In addition, the stone masons' application for a charter was rejected because the union sought to occupy the jurisdiction of the Bricklayers' and Masons' International Union, which notably was not a member of the Federation. Carpet mechanics were advised to affiliate with the Upholsterers' Union and several others were given similar advice.

The Executive Council also noted the inadvisability of issuing charters too hastily. In the case of the International Union of Building Employees, made up of a number of locals formerly directly affiliated with the A. F. of L., the Council observed that

[The international] was instituted prematurely and officered poorly, and constituent locals so diverse that they were unable to successfuly carry on the work of an International Union. We believe, however, that it might be possible to prosper, and we rendered it every assistance within our power, including financial aid. Notwithstanding this, however, the effort proved abortive. It caused diffusion of effort, by which the interests of the members were being neglected and frittered away. We therefore found it necessary to revoke the charter of the International and issue charters to the local unions without cost.[28]

Despite the growing opposition, the Federation's leadership remained intact. Vehement arguments took place on the floor of conventions, but the leaders were able to ride out any storms blown up by their opponents. Sometimes the opposition tried to embarrass the heads of the Federation, as when Victor Berger sought in 1905 to oppose the recommendation that the salary of the President be increased to five thousand dollars a year. He was, however, able to get only 20 out of the 356 delegates to support the move.

Only when a post on the Executive Council was newly created, or became vacant because of death or retirement, was there likely to be a contest for the position. As a rule a delegate or two, one usually a Socialist from Wisconsin, would register a negative vote against the unanimous election of Gompers. The right to dissent was generally unchallenged, although at one convention, in 1906, the right of J. Mahlon Barnes, a delegate from the Cigar Makers' Union, to vote against Gompers was questioned on the ground that it violated the instructions of the convention of his union. Barnes insisted upon his right and his vote was allowed.[29]

THE RICE AND BRANDENBURG INCIDENTS

In 1907 there was an attack upon the character of Gompers which was noted by the convention of that year. Henry Rice, the advertising solicitor of the *American Federationist,* had been dismissed for dishonesty by Gompers. He then declared that he had given money to Gompers and that he had received funds from Gompers. After his dismissal he charged Gompers with dishonesty, and his statements were circulated by the Manufacturers' Association. Gompers was able to show that Rice had been dishonest in his dealings with the Federation, and that after his discharge he had fraudulently issued publications ostensibly of the Federation and that he had sold advertising space in those publications and retained the proceeds.

The Brandenburg incident was an attempt by an agent of the National Manufacturers' Association to compromise Gompers. Broughton Brandenburg claimed to be the head of a bureau of the National Manufacturers' Association which had for its task the exposure of the immorality of labor leaders. He charged that Gompers had, in 1895 at Little Rock, Arkansas, confessed his immoral conduct under the impression he was dying during a serious illness. Brandenburg offered to withhold this information and to "take care" of Gompers financially, if Gompers would resign from the presidency two months after his reelection. Gompers, in New York on business in connection with plans for the establishment of a Building Trades Department, informed other members of the Executive Council of Brandenburg's plans.

As Gompers had never signed such a statement in 1895, Brandenburg then sought to have Gompers sign a statement repudiating his entire activity in the labor movement. Gompers would not accommodate him, and soon thereafter the charges against Gompers were published in the journals of the National Manufacturers' Association. Brandenburg was subsequently arrested for passing forged checks. He jumped bail, and was later caught and sentenced to a term in prison.[30]

At the convention of 1907, after hearing a statement under a special order of business, Victor Berger rose and made an unusual declaration: "For some years past it has been my lot to come here and vote against the unanimous election of President Gompers. This year I promised to move to make his election unanimous." He then asked for a standing vote of confidence, "accompanied by three cheers for President Gompers."[31]

OPPOSITION

While the Federation would close ranks against an attack from outside critics, within the organization critics were not inclined to soften their attacks upon the policies of the Federation. In a large measure this came from the Socialists, who were gaining increasing influence within the trade unions between 1900 and 1915. These Socialists, leaders of a number of trade unions, opposed dual unionism and did not look with favor upon doctrinaire Marxism which influenced Socialist views in all countries. However, they wanted the Federation to espouse independent political action and industrial unionism, and to engage in more aggressive organizing.

The dissatisfaction with the policies of the Federation was especially great in the ranks of the United Mine Workers of America, the largest affiliate. Many of its younger leaders were Socialists, and they objected to the Federation's views on government intervention, industrial unionism, and independent politics. In addition, there was a widespread feeling among the coal miners that the Western Federation of Miners was suffering discrimination because its charter rights were being restricted.

The feeling against the A. F. of L. was largely directed against Gompers. His appearance at the convention of the United Mine Workers of America in 1914 led to a personal attack upon him by Duncan McDonald, a leader in the Illinois district and a Socialist. He accused Gompers of being drunk at the convention of the A. F. of L. which McDonald had attended as a delegate from his union. This was not the first time McDonald had a brush with Gompers. During the convention of 1912, McDonald was reported to have publicly impugned the unionism of Gompers by charging the latter smoked non-union made cigars. Gompers addressed the convention on a "question of high personal privilege," and asked McDonald whether the statement that he was "not a good unionist" was made by him to the press. McDonald answered: "I did not make that statement." Gompers accepted that disavowal in good faith, and declared he was satisfied.[32]

Then, from the sanctuary of his own convention, McDonald now hurled charges of drunkenness at Gompers, who did not sit idly by. He charged his accuser with being a liar and slanderer. The pecksniffian charges were hurled at the elected leader of the greatest labor organization in the history of the United States, one who had devoted, at the time, forty-five years of his life to labor organization. It was no secret that Gompers took a drink, and more than one or two. But it had never been charged that drinking ever interfered with the manifold duties he tirelessly performed. In some months, he dictated more than a thousand letters, appeared before government boards, legislatures, and public bodies, and was called upon to help settle strikes. He traveled widely and spoke endlessly at public meetings. It has been testified by people who knew him that whatever he did after working hours, he was always prompt and attentive to business during the working part of the day. All attest that he was always businesslike and courteous. McDonald himself did not charge that Gompers drank during the convention or that he was incompetent to conduct the business of the convention; he whined that he and his wife could not sleep because Gompers was in the next room having a gay party.[33]

The dissatisfaction of the coal miners with the policies of the Federation also showed itself in the refusal of John P. White, the head of the United Mine Workers of America, to serve as a vice president and member of the Executive Council of the A. F. of L. after he had been elected in 1913 to succeed John Mitchell. White's objection to serving was that he was offered the seventh vice presidency, while Mitchell had been second vice president. White's position was based on the erroneous view that a vice president's rank on the Council was determined by his numerical position. While there is no indication of harsh feeling in White's letter of rejection, his attitude was undoubtedly influenced by the eagerness of some groups within his union to express dissatisfaction with the policies of the A. F. of L.

In answering White Gompers reviewed the history of the Executive Council, and showed that newly elected members were usually placed at the bottom of the list, and that they moved up in regular order as vacancies occurred. In only one instance, in 1900, had this procedure been violated. The first vice president, P. J. McGuire, did not seek reelection that year and James Duncan moved up to the first vice presidency. O'Connell, who was third vice president, was prevailed upon by Gompers to allow John Mitchell to take the second vice presidency, and he, O'Connell, continued at his old post the third vice presidency. Not again, until William Hutcheson was elected to replace Duffy as first vice president in the 1940's, was the rule of succession violated. Gompers pointed out that all vice presidents were equal in power and authority irrespective of their numerical position. White was convinced that there had been no intent to slight either him or his union, but he nevertheless refused to accept "the honor."[34] Evidently White believed that he had blundered and acceptance of the office would be a public admission of an error. Later that year, in response to the urging of the Executive Council that the United Mine Workers of America ought to be represented on the Council, William Green, the Mine Workers' Secretary-Treasurer, accepted the eighth vice presidency.

At the same time in 1914, Duffy, who was secretary of the United Brotherhood of Carpenters and Joiners, replaced Huber who had been the president. The transfer of the post on the Executive Council from the president to the secretary-treasurer had little effect, except that Gompers might have found William Hutcheson, who later became head of the Carpenters' Union, a more exacting member of the Executive Council than Duffy.

The shift of the office from the president to the secretary of the United Mine Workers of America had important repercussions upon the future leadership of the A. F. of L. Had the post on the Executive Council of the Federation been accepted by White, the tradition that the president of the United Mine Workers of America serves on the Executive Council of the A. F. of L. would have continued and, would in fact, have been "firmed up." It would have meant that John L. Lewis instead of William Green would have been on the Executive Council at the time of Gompers' death. It is of course not certain whether the post would have gone to Lewis since the other members of the Council who made the temporary selection of a successor might not have selected a man with the imperious temper and autocratic inclinations of Lewis. One conclusion, however, seems reasonably certain: if Green had not been a member of the Executive Council, he probably would not have been elected to the presidency, for his prior record reveals no activity or reputation of a character that would have brought him to the fore for consideration for the office.

At the convention of 1912, the Socialist delegates decided to present a candidate against Gompers. Max Hayes, a member of the Typographical Union and a leading Socialist trade unionist, was chosen to make the "demonstration run." He made a very creditable showing, polling 5073 votes to Gompers' 11,974, with 296 not voting. His support came from the Bakery, Brewery Workers, Machinists, Coal Miners except Mitchell, Western Federation of Miners, the Painters, Tailors, and Typographical unions.[35]

The rising influence of the Socialists resulted not only from the increasing attractiveness of their program, but also from the intensified opposition to the labor movement from industry and government. Faced by the resolute opposition of industry, the government, and the courts, workers increasingly responded to the gospel of socialism, especially in its milder versions. The decision in the Hatters' case had led, according to Gompers, to "a state of apprehension and misgiving . . . among some of our most active trade unionists." Joseph Valentine, the head of the International Molders' Union and a member of the Executive Council, was fearful that the labor movement was confronted with a serious crisis, a view shared by other members of the Council who were disturbed by the rise in sentiment for independent political action.[36]

The extreme violence that the workers met in their efforts to organize strengthened the opposition to the moderate views of the Federation leadership. The tragedies in the Michigan copper areas, with the death and deportation of strikers, were followed by an even more shocking one at Ludlow, Colorado. The events there stirred the hearts and minds of all labor, and greatly contributed to the bitterness increasingly shared by organized and unorganized workers. The United Mine Workers of America had established a district organization in Colorado at the turn of the century, but the violence and opposition of the Colorado Fuel and Iron Company, a Rockefeller concern, doomed the organization after a long strike in 1903-1904. In 1910 an effort to reestablish the union again ended in failure, despite a long strike.

After a respite of a couple of years, the United Mine Workers of America, under the direction of Vice President Frank J. Hayes, made another attempt to establish the union and collective bargaining with the employers. While workers joined the union in large numbers, the companies were still adamant in their refusal to deal with the miners' organization. This led to a strike in the fall of 1913. Recognition of the union was the principal issue, but an increase in wages, observance of the Colorado mining laws, discharge of armed guards, and the right to choose one's own boarding house and doctor were also demanded by the miners. The start of the strike was accompanied by evictions of miners from company-owned houses. Tent colonies were established by the union on land adjacent to the mining properties. Armed guards deputized by the sheriff were imported, and their presence increased the tension.

After the killing of a union organizer by a Baldwin-Felts guard at Trinidad, violence became frequent. When an armored automobile raked the tent colony, and the miners offered resistance, the sheriff of Los Animas County asked Governor Ammons to send troops. At first refused, they were dispatched to the strike area on October 16th. The militia men were regarded with friendly feelings at the outset, but when they began to intimidate strikers sentiment changed. The officers of the troops did not try to discourage the hostile conduct of the militia. An investigation made at the request of the Governor, by a committee appointed by the President of the Colorado Federation of Labor, found Adjutant General Chase, the commanding officer, unfit, and also found that some of the militia had formerly been employed as mine guards. Arrests, deportations, and violence became common experiences for many of the strikers.

The earlier violence reached its climax in the terrible tragedy of Ludlow. In a battle between a detachment of militia, under the command of Major Pat Hamrock, and the miners, one of the former was killed. Subsequently the Greek strike leader, Louis Tikas, and another miner were captured by the militia; a Lieutenant Linderfeldt broke a rifle over the head of Tikas, who with his comrade was later killed on the pretext that they had tried to escape. This was only a prelude to more ghastly conduct by the militia. The militia raked the tent colony at Ludlow and set it on fire. Eleven children and two women were smothered in the flames. A coroner's jury held the Guardsmen responsible for the deaths.

The strikers reacted with the same kind of violence. In pitched battles, a number of mines were captured, guards killed, and the mines burnt. Finally Governor Ammons appealed to President Wilson for troops. On April 29, 1914, they were ordered to Colorado, with Secretary of War Garrison asking miners and mine guards to surrender their arms. Federal troops restored peace, but they could not settle the strike. Thereupon President Wilson as well as a committee from the House of Representatives proposed a settlement. John D. Rockefeller was asked to intervene since he controlled the coal company which dominated the Colorado mining district. He refused to make any concession on the question of recognition and, despite the urging of President Wilson and a Congressional committee, he persisted in his refusal. Undoubtedly the intransigence of Rockefeller and other leading industrialists did much to weaken the position of the more moderate wing of the labor movement, which was already under attack because of the Ludlow tragedy and the violence in Michigan.[37]

At the convention of 1912 the Executive Council was instructed to provide information on laws restricting the hours of labor. In its report to the convention of the following year, the Council observed that economic organization of labor was the most potent method of restricting hours of work. An exception was made in the case of women, as they do not organize as readily as men. Consequently they deserved the protection of society.

At the convention of 1914, several resolutions advocating the reduction of hours of labor by law came before the delegates. Instead of endorsing laws for this purpose, the resolutions committee advised trade union action to achieve the goal. The report aroused one of the bitterest debates in the conventions of recent years, and found John Mitchell arrayed against Gompers. Mitchell argued that refusal to endorse regulation of working hours by law would in fact repudiate the efforts of workers in a number of Western states to gain shorter hours of labor through legislation. Gompers defined his position exactly when, in answering a question of a delegate on the difference between a law limiting the hours of labor and limiting the issuance of injunctions by the courts, he replied:

In the law to limit and regulate injunctions we propose to clip the power of the court insofar as labor is concerned, and in an eight-hour law for men it is to give the courts still greater power than they now have. Is there no difference? It is a fact, admitted not only by all lawyers, but by every thinking, earnest labor man, that once you give a court jurisdiction over any matter the court will find a way to exercise that jurisdiction. Place it in the power of the courts to take jurisdiction, to assume jurisdiction, to acquire jurisdiction, or to have jurisdiction accredited to them, and they will leave no stone unturned to exercise it to the detriment of the men and women of labor, who, after all, in all times have been compelled to suffer the tyranny and oppression of oligarchy, under whatever name it might be known.[38]

The following year, the desirability of shorter hours for men by government rule was again debated. The same vehemence was shown, and Gompers again noted that he asked only for freedom to organize:

The only demand which I will make of Congress is to do for the workers what we cannot do for ourselves—where the Government is the employer to secure the shorter work day by law, because it can be secured no other way. But primarily I want the Government to secure to us by law the right to exert and exercise the normal human activities of self-development and associated effort, and to bear the burdens of the struggle for industrial improvement and freedom, and so that we may fight the battles, not by a piece of paper dropped in an urn or a beautifully carved ballot box, but by the scars of battle, by the hunger of the stomach, of the weeping and the wailing of life, and still stand true to the battle line of labor. That is the fight I am making. I want freedom to fight and freedom to achieve and I will never consent to anything else.[39]

On the basis of Gompers' argument, he and the others espousing his views would have favored laws such as the National Labor Relations Act and the anti-injunction acts, but not laws determining minimum wages and maximum hours except for those marginal groups. The sources of Gompers' opposition to reliance on government were both philosophic and practical. The leaders of the Federation, who made its policies over time, believed that ten workers in a shop might be able to seek concessions in a particular plant, but several thousand might be powerless if they had to convince a legislative body to grant them relief. In addition to fearing the dispersion of energy and the diversion of interest and division in the ranks that political action might engender, many had a philosophical objection to strengthening government; they were in a sense philosophical anarchists. Their theoretical convictions were buttressed by experience, as they witnessed the use of government power in behalf of the employer. For the same reasons, fear of government power, they opposed collectivist ideas. Tyranny in the name of labor was as onerous and objectionable as in the name of any other group.

Nevertheless, changes were taking place which were loosening the dominance of the older views. Had these shifts within the Federation continued, the more extreme anti-governmentalism of the dominant group would have been set aside. World War I actually hastened the process of change. However, severe losses in membership and prestige suffered by the labor movement in the period immediately following the war, and the hostile social climate which surrounded the labor movement in the 1920's, aborted the shift before it had been completed. In consequence the American Federation of Labor showed itself, in the period between 1924 and 1933, in one of its least vigorous cycles. It seemed as if a reaction to the great organizing campaigns during and immediately after the war, and to the losses which the unions suffered as a result of the employer offensive, debilitated its energies. Beginning in 1916, the A. F. of L. faced a range of new problems, as the war expansion opened new opportunities for organizing as well as for service by the labor movement.

References

1. Gompers to John S. Kirchner, February 5, 1896.
2. Gompers to McGuire, January 2, 1901.
3. Gompers to McGuire, March 11, 1901.
4. Gompers to McGuire, March 19, 1901.
5. Gompers to McGuire, May 1, 1901.
6. *Proceedings of the Eleventh General Convention of the United Brotherhood of Carpenters and Joiners of America,* 1900, pp. 81-82.
7. "Report of Finance Committee," *Proceedings of Twelfth Regular Convention of the United Brotherhood of Carpenters and Joiners of America,* 1902, pp. 12, 27, 38-40.
8. "Report of General President W. D. Huber" in *The Carpenter,* February 1902, pp. 2-3.
9. Gompers to James Duncan, November 26, 1901; to Jerome Jones, September 29, 1902.
10. "His career in the trade union began at a time when it was almost considered a disgrace to be a participant in the labor movement. He was one of the pioneers who blazed the way on this North American Continent for the great army of organized labor that is now marching towards the accomplishment of the objects for which the trade union was founded. No body of men in the trade union were closer to P. J. McGuire or knew him better than the members of this Council, and we did desire to give expression to the fact that we found at all times an earnest, efficient and valiant co-worker in the cause of labor. His ability was very great; certainly none in the movement were more able, and but few were his equals. The particular monuments that he has left behind him are the Brotherhood of Carpenters and Joiners, and the American Federation of Labor; for it can justly be said that his great force of mind and character were particularly devoted to the upbuilding of these two organizations, and that he was a very great factor in promoting their success, and when, in the future, the history of the trade union in America is written, we are sure that name of P. J. McGuire will be found very close to the head of the list of

those who made the movement a success." Minutes of the Executive Council, March 19, 1906.

11. *Report of Proceedings of the Twenty-Sixth Annual Convention of the American Federation of Labor,* 1906, p. 226.

12. Ralph Easley to Louis D. Brandeis, November 4, 1912, in the manuscript division of the New York Public Library.

13. *Journal of Proceedings of the Amalgamated Association of Iron, Steel and Tin Workers of America,* 1901, pp. 6203-6304.

14. Letter of Easley to Brandeis, November 4, 1912, in New York Public Library.

15. Statement of Steel Strike in Mitchell Papers at Catholic University.

16. *Journal of Proceedings of the Amalgamated Association of Iron, Steel and Tin Workers,* 1902, p. 6320; Samuel Gompers, "The Steel Strike" *American Federationist,* October 1901, pp. 415-426.

17. The view presented here differs from the one on the same question in Selig Perlman and Philip Taft, *History of Labor in the United States,* 1896-1932, (New York: The Macmillan Co., 1935). The one presented here seems the accurate view. In writing the material in the *History of Labor,* I did not have access to the letters of Easley and Mitchell. Moreover, my observations in the last 25 years have convinced me that my earlier view was an error, and the more complete evidence would tend to indicate that Shaffer and the other leaders of the Amalgamated Association completely misjudged the situation. Their defeat encouraged antiunionism, strengthened the anti-union forces immeasurably, and could have been avoided, at least for the time being. No one can say with certainty that the United States Steel Corporation was not merely making concessions for tactical reasons, but it is always possible to strike, and the greater control the union exercises, the greater its power of resistance. The strike should not have been called in the first place; but to expect the labor movement to stake what might well be its entire existence to prevent the loss of the steel strike, would seem at this juncture to have been an act of folly.

18. *Machinists Monthly Journal,* June, 1900, pp. 311-313.

19. Conference between unions in the metal trades and National Metal Trades Association, in archives of A. F. of L.

20. Gompers to John Mulholland, November 12, 1900. Similar letters were sent to the heads of the Molders' Metal Polishers' Machinists' Metal Mechanical and Electrical Workers Unions.

21. James O'Connell to Henry F. Devins, November 9, 1900.

22. Easley to Gompers, June 3, 1901.

23. O'Connell to Easley, July 1, 1901; Henry F. Devins to Easley, July 7, 1901.

24. *Report to the President of the Anthracite Coal Commission of May-October, 1902.* (Washington: Government Printing Office, 1903), p. 35. Telegram from Ralph Easley to Mitchell, May 14, 1902, in archives of Catholic University.

25. *Proceedings of Special Convention of the United Mine Workers of America,* 1902.

26. *Documents Relating to the Anthracite Strike of 1902* (No place or date, or publisher), p. 123.

27. *Ibid.*, p. 131.

28. *Report of Proceedings of the Twenty-Fifth Annual Convention of the American Federation of Labor,* 1905, p. 62.

29. *Report of Proceedings of the Twenty-Sixth Annual Convention of the American Federation of Labor,* 1906, pp. 249-254.

30. *New York Times,* January 5, 1911.

31. *Report of Proceedings of the Twenty-Seventh Annual Convention of the American Federation of Labor,* 1907, p. 266.

32. *Report of Proceedings of the Thirty-Second Annual Convention of the American Federation of Labor,* 1912, pp. 356-358.

33. Daniel Tobin told how, after his first election for president of his union, he had met Gompers and they had gone out together for a "social evening." The next day "I met him in his office and he hardly recognized me except that I was the newly-elected President of the International Brotherhood of Teamsters, and he would be glad to listen to what I had to say. One of his principal qualities was that while he could spend a social hour with his friends, that he could relax and fraternize, the next day you could not expect that he would deviate one iota from the straightforward business." Daniel Tobin to John Frey, in Frey Papers, folder 193, Library of Congress collection. It was also said that Gompers frequently attended burlesque shows. It was the same one regularly attended by Justice Oliver Wendell Holmes. There is, however, no record that they ever met at this theater.

34. Gompers to White, December 12, 1913, January 8, 1914; White to Gompers, December 18, 1913; Executive Council to White, January 20, 1914.

35. For Hayes' views see: Max Hayes, "The Rochester Convention of the A. F. of L.," *The New Review,* January 4, 1913.

36. Report to Executive Council, February 28, 1910, April 27, 1910.

37. *Report of United States Commission on Industrial Relations,* Vii, p. 6866-6902; IX, p. 8190-8198; John Fitch, "Law and Order in Colorado," *Survey,* December 5, 1914, pp. 242-247.

38. *Report of Proceedings of the Thirty-Fourth Annual Convention of the American Federation of Labor,* 1914, p. 440.

39. *Ibid., Thirty-Fifth Annual Convention,* 1915, pp. 485-503.

XVI

An Organized Attack upon the Labor Movement

CITIZENS' ALLIANCES

THE GAINS achieved by organized labor beginning with the late 1890's soon brought forth a reaction in the camp of business. Employer organizations which had heretofore been neutral or favorable to the claims of unionism became hostile and bitter opponents. Large corporations supported, on the whole, the anti-union campaigns which were given impetus by several cases under the Sherman Anti-Trust law and the decisions of the Supreme Court. Beginning in 1903, unions found their activities increasingly restricted, and their growth impeded by the militant opposition of employer associations as well as by the unfavorable decisions of the courts.

The National Association of Manufacturers, initially under the leadership of David M. Parry, was one of the more militant leaders in the drive to reduce the influence of unions in industry. David M. Parry sounded the keynote of the campaign in 1903, when he denounced organized labor as "socialistic," saying that it "knows but one law . . . the law of physical force—the law of the Huns and Vandals, the law of the savage."[1] The principles drawn up by the NAM ran directly counter to the demands of organized labor. Boycotts, blacklists, strikes, lockouts, and the closed shop were unalterably opposed. The NAM did not limit itself to a mere pronouncement of principles but, under the leadership of Parry, J. W. Van Cleave, and John Kirby, Jr., it carried on a widespread and unremitting campaign to curb the major activities and to reduce the power of labor organizations. Tireless and energetic as propagandists, these leaders of business rallied large numbers of employers to their views, and were undoubtedly a factor in the changed climate of opinion confronting the unions in the first decades of the century.

The citizens' alliances which proliferated throughout the country at the turn of the century were another cause of concern to the unions. "During the spring and summer of 1903 the general movement of organization against trades-union tyranny reached the joint where it became desirable that there be some central organization or union of

262

the various associations."[2] With this end in view, thirteen leaders in the anti-union movement, among whom were Kirby, Parry, and Marshall Cushing of the National Association of Manufacturers; Frederic W. Job of the Chicago Employers' Association; E. F. Brul of the National Metal Trades; and J. C. Craig, president of the Citizens' Alliance of Denver, called a congress. More than two hundred and fifty delegates assembled in Chicago on October 29, 1903, to launch the Citizens' Industrial Association as a clearinghouse with a permanent headquarters in Indianapolis, Indiana.

The Association declared:

The present industrial conditions have become so deplorable by reason of the indefensible methods and claims of organized labor that the time has come when the employing interests and good citizenship of the country must take immediate and effective measures to reaffirm and enforce those fundamental principles of American government guaranteeing free, competitive conditions. In its demand for the closed shop organized labor is seeking to overthrow individual liberty and property rights, the principal props of our government. Its methods for securing this revolutionary and socialistic change in our institutions are also those of physical warfare.[3]

Branches were established on a craft or industry basis; these in turn were amalgamated into local groups so that the members could oppose organized labor effectively. J. Van Cleave, one of the leaders, wanted employers to cease advertising in the *American Federationist* and to avoid purchasing union-made goods.[4] The Citizens' Industrial Association lasted only a few years, but during its existence generated some public support which undoubtedly inflicted grave wounds upon the organizations of labor.

BELLIGERENT GROUPS

While the above associations were largely engaged in the molding of public opinion, the National Founders Association and the National Metal Trades Association were engaged in active opposition to union organization on the plant level. The former, established in New York in 1898, started as an association for dealing with the unions employed by its members. In 1899 an agreement with the Iron Molders' Union of North America was signed which set up methods for settling differences between workers in the foundries and their employers. The agreement failed. Friction between the Molders' Union and the industry steadily increased, and by 1904 relations between the Association and the Molders' Union completely collapsed. From this time on the Founders' Association increasingly opposed unionism. It promoted the open shop and members engaged in strikes or lockouts were furnished strikebreakers, had their work made up by other employers, and were given monetary aid.

Equally active against organized labor was the National Metal Trades Association, made up of metal products producers who employed machinists, pattern makers, brass workers, coppersmiths, platers, polishers, buffers, iron ship builders, blacksmiths and boilermakers, carpenters and helpers employed about the machine shops. Founded during a strike of pattern makers in New York City in 1899, the Association became national in scope two years later. It reached an agreement with the International Association of Machinists, but its abrogation by the union led the Metal Trades Association to adopt a militant anti-union policy, a policy which was in effect until the 1930's. The Association combated strikes and "provided a secret service system, by which members can place in their shops *special contract operatives* who will report on the loyalty of the workmen and even the foremen. Through these, the employer can learn of any agitator in the shop almost as soon as the agitation begins."[5]

These organizations and the National Erectors Association, organized among firms engaged in steel erecting, were among the leading national opponents of organized labor on the economic level. In 1902 the Anti-Boycott Association was established by employers who declared themselves "aware of the far-reaching consequences and dangerous extent of the boycott, threatening capital by arbitrary proscription and labor by tyrannical persecution."[6] The Association aimed to blunt one of organized labor's favorite and widely-used weapons, the boycott.

THE BOYCOTT

From the beginning of its history, the American Federation of Labor had not only utilized the boycott, but found that it was at times used in trivial and even frivolous disputes. As far back as 1885, serious misgivings were expressed by the convention of the old Federation about the tendency of some unions to utilize the boycott too freely. As a result the convention decided that, before a boycott would be endorsed, the reasons for its imposition would have to be made known to the Legislative Committee.[7] As the requests for endorsement of boycotts increased, the Federation found it necessary to set up more stringent standards for their approval.

In 1897 the convention enacted a regulation requiring the Executive Council to determine the terms under which the "unfair" firm was operating; whether the union making the request was trying to enforce the boycott; and the position of any other unions having members in the plant of the employer in question on this issue. The following year, the convention of the A.F. of L. disapproved of local, national, or international unions "sending out any circular calling for a boycott unless the same is first endorsed by the A. F. of L., and in case the boycott circular is sent out without such endorsement, the Executive Council will feel justified in refusing to sustain the boycott." In order to prevent hasty and ill-advised action, the convention of 1899 decided that the Federation was not to endorse a boycott unless the request was made by a directly-affiliated national or international union, and then only after a full investigation had been made.[8]

As a rule, when an application for the imposition of a boycott was submitted to the Executive Council of the American Federation of Labor, Gompers would communicate with the employer, apprising him of the request to place the firms' products on the "unfair list." If the firm's answer was not satisfactory, its name would be placed on the "unfair list," which was circulated among labor organizations and carried by the *American Federationist*, the official organ of the A. F. of L.

Placing of boycotts in many instances became a purely formal procedure, and sometimes even led to embarrassments of other unions, which protested against boycotts that had been imposed at the request of sister organizations. For example, when the American Federation of Labor placed a Rock Island, Illinois, farm machinery company on its "unfair list" at the request of the United Brotherhood of Carpenters and Joiners of America, the International Brotherhood of Blacksmiths protested that "it is not business policy to publish the names of firms as being unfair until a thorough and careful investigation of the merits of the case has been made."[9] Sometimes a question arose of the justification of a boycott under given circumstances. In one case, the international officers first disapproved of a strike of one of their locals, but having tried and failed to gain a satisfactory settlement they then appealed to the Executive Council of the A. F. of L. to endorse a boycott. This request was rejected by the Executive Council who held that the strike could and should have been avoided.[10]

It is obvious that the position of the Executive Council became increasingly more difficult in this area, as it had been given some discretion in the approval or rejection of a boycott. Though the Executive Council could approve or disapprove the imposition of a boycott, as far as it affected the Federation, it had no control over the action of national or international unions. The large increase in requests for boycotts finally led to the adoption of a rule that national and international unions were to be limited to three requests, and directly affiliated unions to one, a year.

It is difficult to estimate the effectiveness of this technique upon sales or other activities of firms coming under the ban, but the constant request upon the American Federation of Labor for approval of boycotts would indicate that the boycott was not without influence upon sales. Therefore, as anti-union employers broadened their attack, their attention was inevitably focused upon this weapon of labor.

DANBURY HATTERS

The courts were called upon to intervene, and decisions soon revealed the danger the use of the boycott held for organized labor. The right of labor to use the boycott was raised in *Lawlor v. Loewe,* or the Danbury Hatters' case, which directly involved the United Hatters of North America, and indirectly the American Federation of Labor as well. On or about March 1, 1901, this union demanded that Dietrich Loewe and Company unionize its making and finishing departments and use the union label on its products. The Loewe Company refused and notified the United Hatters of North America that "if attacked, shall use all lawful means to protect our business interests."

In July 1902, the Hatters' Union, despite the warning, called a strike and proclaimed a boycott against the products of the Company. In an advertisement in the local press, the Company announced it would hold all the "members of all Labor Unions, individually and collectively responsible for all damages which . . . [it] may sustain in . . . [its] property or business by reason of the unlawful acts of such Labor Unions or any of the officers or agents."[11] Nevertheless, the boycott continued and (despite the replacement of union workers in the plant), it effectively reduced sales. Thereupon the Company, in September 1903, started a suit aginst 240 members of the Hatters' Union in the federal court of Connecticut, claiming treble damages amounting to $240,000, under the Sherman Anti-Trust Law. It "was the first attempt of its kind ever made in this country to hold union members responsible as members for the acts of their union officials."[12] The homes of the workers in Danbury, Bethel, and Norwalk, Connecticut, were attached pending the outcome of the suit. Manufacturers in the industry and other anti-union employers financed the Company's action through the American Anti-Boycott Association. It took almost fourteen years for the issues to be decided.

The first question determined by the United States Supreme Court, in February 1908, was whether the Sherman Anti-Trust Law could be applied to unions seeking to prevent the distribution of products in interstate commerce. The Court [*Dietrich Loewe et al. v. Martin Lawlor et al.* U.S. 389 (1908)] held the union could be sued. In the first trial the Company recovered a large verdict. This was reversed on technical grounds. The American Federation of Labor then intervened, and at its suggestion Alton B. Parker and Frank Mulholland were added to the list of attorneys. In the second trial, the jury awarded the full amount of the damages claimed, $252,130.90; the award was upheld by the United States Supreme Court. In holding individual members of the local liable for the actions of their organization, Justice Holmes, speaking for the Court, declared that

[If members of the union] paid their dues and continued to delegate authority to their officers unlawfully to interfere with the plaintiffs interstate commerce in such circumstances that they knew or ought to have known, and such officers were warranted in the belief that they were acting in the matters within their delegated authority then such members were jointly liable.[13]

The American Federation of Labor had spent $98,756.02 in the trials and appeals of the Hatters' Case, and sought to have Congress appropriate $290,000 for meeting the verdict, on the theory that the law had been mistakenly applied. Congress refused, and the burden had to be borne by the members of the union, upon whose homes and slender bank accounts the Company had placed liens. The seizure could not be allowed by the labor movement, and upon the unions and their members fell the responsibility of saving the homes and bank accounts of the Danbury hat workers. The convention of 1915 voted to call upon the workers of the United States to donate one hour's pay on January 27, 1916, for meeting the verdict. The money collected, added to the amounts donated by the United Hatters of America, was sufficient to pay the damages. According to Walter Gordon Merritt, the Danbury Hatters' case cost the labor movement a little more than $420,000.[14]

In addition to the expense and money losses which the suit inflicted upon the organizations of labor, the A. F. of L. was forced to revise its boycott strategy. Perhaps abolition of the boycott might better describe the action of the A. F. of L. Following the first decision in the Hatters' case, the attorneys of the A. F. of L., in conference with several members of the Executive Council, suggested that the "We Don't Patronize" list regularly carried in the American Federationist be discontinued. In the opinion of counsel

The A. F. of L., its affiliated organizations, their officers and members, as well as the Executive Council of the A. F. of L. could not only be proceeded against under the penalty of a possible one year's imprisonment, five thousand dollar fine, or both, at the discretion of the court but that those firms carried upon the 'We Don't Patronize' list could sue for threefold damages of their claim they lost by reason of the boycott.[15]

Following the decision of the Supreme Court in the Hatters' case, a meeting of farmer and labor organizations was called by the Executive Council. A protest against the decision was made to Congress, with a plea for relief. In addition, a statement to the workers of the United

States called attention to the inequity of the ruling and the threat the decision held to the rights of labor.

BUCK'S STOVE AND RANGE COMPANY

A more direct blow was also aimed, in 1907, at the American Federation of Labor by James Van Cleave, the president of the National Association of Manufacturers. Van Cleave was the head of the Buck's Stove and Range Company of St. Louis. He had threatened to raise a million and a half dollars to fight labor organizations, and he advocated a boycott of of union-made goods by business men. It was inevitable that he would refuse to deal with organized labor. Placed on the "We Don't Patronize" list, the company sued, in the Supreme Court of the District of Columbia in the fall of 1907, to prevent the American Federation of Labor from carrying its name. Soon thereafter, Gompers was warned by the company's attorneys of the penalties for violating the injunction. Immediately, Gompers reported to the Executive Council:

[If] we are enjoined from doing the things we have a lawful right to do, and we perform them, the injunction to the contrary notwithstanding, it will have the effect of riveting attention to the outrageous procedure on the part of the courts to the issuance of these unwarranted injunctions, and do more than anything else to secure either a favorable decision from the courts, or relief at the hands of Congress.[16]

A defense on the legal front had to be prepared, and counsel retained. Gompers sought the services of Richard Olney, who had been Cleveland's attorney general, and who had played a role, then not known, in the dispatching of troops to Chicago during the strike of the American Railway Union. Olney refused to serve, and Alton B. Parker, who had been on the Court of Appeals of New York State and the Democratic candidate for President of the United States in 1904, was the next choice. Parker advised the Federation to base its argument in the case "exclusively upon liberty of the press." He advised that

the name of Cleave's Buck's Stove and Range Company be taken out of the column of the "We Don't Patronize" list of the *American Federationist,* and that I [Gompers] write an editorial dealing with the subject, making such criticism as my judgment warrants in the editorial, and maintaining the contention we are right, if necessary, to the higher courts. He said, that such an editorial should unquestionably be in violation of the terms of the injunction, but that it would disassociate the question from every so-called "unfair list" or "We Don't Patronize" list, and that if Judge Gould should summon me to show cause why I should not be punished for contempt of court, a clean-cut issue of the liberty of the press would be presented.[17]

Gompers followed the advice of counsel and criticized the decision of the court in an editorial in the *American Federationist.* Consequently, he, Morrison, and Mitchell were summoned before the Supreme Court of the District of Columbia, upon the petition of the Buck's Stove and Range Company, to show cause why they should not be adjudged in contempt of court. Mitchell was charged that, as a vice president of the American Federation of Labor, he had entertained a resolution at the convention of the United Mine Workers of America, over which he presided, endorsing a boycott against the Buck's Stove and Range Company. Morrison, as an officer of the A. F. of L., had allowed to be circulated magazines and resolutions endorsing the boycott against the same company; Gompers was charged with writing editorials endorsing the boycott. All three were found guilty by Judge Gould, who imposed sentences of six months, nine months, and one year's imprisonment respectively upon Morrison, Mitchell, and Gompers. The decision was upheld in the Circuit Court of Appeals. However, on the ground that the petition originally filed by the Buck's Stove and Range Company was civil in character, and the punishment of Gompers, Mitchell, and Morrison, meted out by Judge Gould, was criminal in nature, the Supreme Court in 1911 reversed the findings of the lower courts. However, the right of the Supreme Court of the District of Columbia to punish in a proper proceeding for contempt, if any had been committed against it, was recognized.

In the meantime, J. W. Van Cleave had died, and the management of the Buck's Stove and Range Company was taken over by Frederick W. Gardner, who had no desire to carry on the contest with the unions which had initially inspired the court action. In a conference with Gompers, a satisfactory agreement was worked out between the Company and the unions in its plant which provided that the company withdraw its attorneys from the case, and the litigation between the Buck's Stove and Range Company and the American Federation of Labor be terminated. Gompers insisted that the "contempt cases be prosecuted to a final decision upon the questions involved before the Supreme Court of the United States." The lawyers for the Federation, however, were of the opinion that the whole case was moot and that if the court were informed of the satisfactory relations now existing between the parties and, moreover, that the company had declined to prosecute the contempt cases further, the case would inevitably be thrown out of court or come "to a happy end." This solution was not regarded with favor by the defendants, and Gompers informed the Executive Council: "It was a course against which my whole nature revolted and against which I emphatically protest."[18] Gompers was authorized by the other two defendants to draw up a letter, which was signed by the three.

It was the view of the defendants that the course suggested by the attorneys in the case was inadequate.

[For] several years labor has sought the opportunity to make a test of the principles involved before the courts wherein the constitutional and inherent rights would be raised and met. Such a case presented itself when the Buck's Stove and Range Company under its old management obtained the injunction against the American Federation of Labor, its officers and affiliated organizations and their members. With great earnestness and unanimity it was decided that a case, not of our own making, but nevertheless a case, had been found wherein these principles could be tested, and with a clear understanding of what the possible consequences might be, it was determined that the test should be made.[19]

The lawyers were directed not to emphasize the changed relations between the company and the unions in its plant, and to seek a decision on the issues.

C. W. Post, a leading open-shopper and anti-unionist, was also dissatisfied by the turn of events. He was a stockholder in the Buck's Stove and Range Company and he tried to prevent an agreement with the union. When he failed, he started a suit for $750,000, and also failed in this effort. When the case reached the United States Supreme Court on appeal, the court, upon learning that the dispute between the unions and the Buck's Stove and Range Company had been settled, dismissed the case as moot. It, however, upheld the right of the Supreme Court of the District of Columbia to punish by a proper proceeding for contempt if any had been committed against it.

Judge Wright then appointed a committee of attorneys, the same lawyers who represented the Buck's Stove and Range Company, to inquire whether there existed good cause to believe that Gompers, Mitchell, and Morrison had been guilty of contempt of court. Refusing to grant a change of venue, the case was heard by Judge Wright. An apology was requested, which the defendants refused to make. Moreover, Gompers was perturbed by the turn of events, not because of the danger of imprisonment, but because the issues raised in the first instance could not be adjudged in the second contempt proceedings. He informed his attorneys: "I would chafe under the restraint of my liberty were I incarcerated in jail, but I have preferred to go to jail for a year upon the Supreme Court confirming the decision and sentence of Justice Wright, rather that to have obtained my freedom from jail upon a technicality."[20] Gompers, Mitchell, and Morrison were again sentenced respectively to a year, nine months, and six months in jail for contempt of court in their failure to obey the original injunction. Upon appeal, the District Court of Appeals in May, 1913, upheld the verdict but reduced the sentences to thirty days of imprisonment for Gompers and fines of five hundred dollars each for the other two defendants. On appeal to the United States Supreme Court, the judgment of the courts below were reversed on

technical grounds. The original issues were therefore never decided.
The effect of this case as well as the one against the Hatters' was to
strengthen the more radical elements in the Federation. They were living
proof, to many, that the government and the courts were solidly aligned
against the workers; that the gospel of socialism with its emphasis upon
class war and class differences was given living exegesis by these
decisions.

References

1. Quoted in Albion G. Tayler, *Labor Policies of the National Association of Manufacturers* (Urbana, Illinois: University of Illinois, 1927), p. 35.

2. *The Preliminary Convention of the Citizens' Industrial Association of America,* 1903, p. 3.

3. *Ibid.,* p. 17.

4. *Proceedings of the Second Annual Convention of the Citizens' Industrial Association of America,* 1904, pp. 27-29.

5. Clarence E. Bonnett, *Employers Association in the United States* (New York: The Macmillan Co., 1922), p. 112.

6. Walter Gordon Merritt, *History of the League of Industrial Rights* (New York: League for Industrial Rights, 1925), p. 11.

7. *Report of the Proceedings of the Federation of Organized Trades and Labor Unions of the United States and Canada,* 1885, p. 27.

8. *Report of the Proceedings of the Twenty-Seventh Annual Convention of the American Federation of Labor,* 1897, p. 91; *Ibid., Twenty-Eighth Annual Convention,* 1898, p. 133; *Ibid., Twenty-Ninth Annual Convention,* 1899, p. 161.

9. Letter of Robert B. Kerr, General Secretary-Treasurer and Organizer of the International Brotherhood of Blacksmiths, to Gompers, June 24, 1901.

10. Letters of James A. Cable, Secretary-Treasurer of the Coopers' International Union, to Gompers, December 22, 1900, January 14, 1901; Cable to Frank Morrison, December 12, 1900.

11. Quoted in Walter Gordon Merritt, *Destination Unknown* (New York; Prentice Hall, Inc., 1951), p. 15.

12. *Ibid.,* p. 17.

13. Lawlor v. Loewe, 235 U. S. 522, (1915).

14. Merrit, *op. cit.,* p. 24.

15. Report to Executive Council, Vote Book, May 17, 1908.

16. Report to the Executive Council, September 20, 1907.

17. Gompers to Executive Council, January 10, 1908.

18. Gompers to Executive Council, December 29, 1910.

19. Gompers, Mitchell, and Morrison to Alton B. Parker, Jackson Ralston, and Frank L. Mulholland, December 28, 1910.

20. Gompers to Ralston, May 11, 1911.

XVII

Steel and the McNamaras

THE STEEL STRIKE OF 1909

There was obviously a coordinated plan to reduce the strength and influence of the trade union movement. In a number of industries organized labor was finding itself continually harassed by organized employer opposition. The steel industry not only opposed unionism, but led in encouraging similar policies in other industries. The union in this industry, the Amalgamated Association of Iron and Steel Workers, had been seriously weakened by the unsuccessful strike of 1901. The union was given a reprieve of several years in that it was not formally expelled from the properties of the United States Steel Corporation until the summer of 1909. However, the union refused to be ousted without a struggle.

In July 1909, the U. S. Steel Corporation announced it would no longer recognize the union. The Amalgamated Association then called upon the A. F. of L. for aid in the "war of extermination against the Amalgamated Association of Iron Steel and Tin Workers." The Tin Plate Workers, who had a union of their own, suffered the same fate. The head of the Amalgamated Association believed organized labor had no choice but to close down non-union as well as union plants. He called on the A. F. of L. "to see to it that every possible assistance is given to the Amalgamated Association if a strike is necessary."[1] After several fruitless attempts to gain a reprieve which would allow the union to exist, the Amalgamated and the Tin Workers' Unions called a strike on July 1, 1909.

Some sentiment existed for calling a general conference of trade union officers, but the heads of the two organizations involved could not agree on a policy in this matter. The Executive Council of the A. F. of L. was also divided. Hayes, O'Connell, and Lennon opposed the calling of a general trade union conference, although the latter was willing to agree if the two unions involved were willing to sponsor such a meeting. The issue was then transferred to the convention of the A. F. of L. for decision. The latter declared the United States Steel Corporation

the most formidable and aggressive enemy the movement has to contend with; that we believe the thorough organization of all branches of its business

272

is the most necessary work that can engage the attention, time and effort of the American Federation of Labor and its affiliated National and International organizations, and that we recommend that a meeting be held during the sessions of the convention of the executive officers of all organizations represented, together with the President and Secretary of the A. F. of L. to consider and outline a campaign of organization among the employees of the United States Steel Corporation, and to consider and devise ways and means of making the strike of the affiliated organizations, now pending, more effective, to the end that they may be brought to a successful conclusion.[2]

Gompers invited the international unions to send representatives to the Pittsburgh meeting, and thirty-six unions responded. The meeting, held in Pittsburgh, on December 13, 1909, issued calls for financial help and for the sending of organizers. On January 1, 1910, a "Plan of Action and Appeal" was published. Each national and international union was asked to assign at least one organizer, who would work under the direction of P. J. McArdle, the head of the Amalgamated Association, the principal union in the controversy. The Amalgamated Association was advised to merge with the Tin Plate Workers' Association. Labor was asked to send contributions, for workers of both striking organizations, to be sent to John Williams, the secretary-treasurer of the Amalgamated Association.

The conference appointed special committees to wait upon the President of the United States, the Speaker of the House, and the President of the Senate for the purpose of laying before them the grievances from which labor suffered from the corporation. In addition, special committees were appointed to wait upon the governors of states and representatives of counties and municipalities where the United States Steel Corporation had plants, to present to those officials a catalogue of wrongs committed by the Corporation against labor.

In addition, a committee of nine was appointed to draw up a statement to be presented to President Taft during a conference. In the statement the A. F. of L. declared

[The federal government] is not impotent to enquire, when a great national trust, doing interstate business, engaged in government contracts for ordnance and armor plate, and recipient of governmental protection in the form of a favorable tariff schedule has undertaken to directly lower the standard of living of more than one hundred thousand of its workmen, and indirectly all workmen, by the exercise of a power independent of any government and destructive of personal rights under our government.

The corporation was charged with being an illegal combination in restraint of trade, with excluding American labor from employment, charging excessive prices, degrading labor by long hours and low wages, tyrannically preventing the organization of labor, denying free speech and assemblage, exercising powers beyond and in defiance of law in local communities. The continued existence and methods of the corporation were held to be "a menace not only to labor, but to the business men yet outside of its baneful power and influence, and particularly to the perpetuation of our republic based upon the independence, character and sovereignty of the masses of our people."[3]

The committee called for an impartial investigation of the charges. Frank S. Monnett, a former attorney general of Ohio, and A. G. Ballard prepared the legal evidence which, together with economic and sociological facts, was also presented to President Taft. Specific charges were made against the United States Steel Corporation. Attorney General George Wickersham, to whom the charges had been sent by the President, found that the facts presented "to show that the United States Steel Corporation and its subsidiary companies, and their officers and directors, are engaged in a combination to restrain interstate and foreign trade and commerce in steel and iron and their products, and in endeavoring to monopolize the same" could not be acted upon "until the Supreme Court of the United States shall have decided the appeals now under consideration by it from the judgments of the circuit courts in the proceedings against the American Tobacco Company and the Standard Oil Company of New Jersey." As for the "number of assaults and batteries, and acts of oppression . . . committed by officials of the various subsidiary companies in different parts of the country,"[4] these were not regarded as questions for the courts of the United States, but had to be dealt with, according to the Attorney General, by the states.

In the midst of the strike in the plants of the United States Steel Corporation, a sudden revolt started in the unorganized plant of the Bethlehem Steel Company at Bethlehem, Pennsylvania. This demonstration aroused widespread attention, and resulted in an investigation by the United States Senate, an investigation sponsored by the A. F. of L. During the investigation the United States Steel Corporation ended Sunday work, and it was widely believed that this step was the outcome of the agitation initiated by the A. F. of L.

The American Federation of Labor was also instrumental in bringing about an elaborate investigation of industrial conditions in the steel industry by the Stanley Committee of the House of Representatives. Many unions furnished organizers and financial aid, but the struggle was too uneven for the organizations of labor. On August 10, 1911, the unions ended their strikes in all plants except Waynesburg, Pennsylvania. A constant flow of funds was needed, and the $39,649.41 donated by the other labor organizations was insufficient to sustain the workers on strike.

The defeat of the union in the steel industry meant that the major producers would now operate on an open shop basis and would no longer recognize even the few outside labor organizations they had acknowledged since 1901. Not until 1937 were the large steel producers formally to recognize unions not under their direct control. It was a defeat for the organizations of labor, and for the A. F. of L., but the unions not involved in the struggle with the steel industry were unwilling, and very likely unable, to mobilize the men and financial resources to challenge successfully the giants in steel. Moreover, public sentiment was then too lethargic with respect to the rights of labor to compel, even if the courts had permitted, the industry to yield to the majority of their workers and grant their unions recognition.

The McNamara Case

Closely related to the difficulties of labor organizations in the steel industry were the problems faced by the Bridge and Structural Iron Workers. The Iron Workers' Union, founded in 1896, had held contracts with some of the large employers in its industry in the first years of the century. Difficulties between the union and the larger companies were, however, on the increase. The American Bridge Company, a subsidiary of the United States Steel Corporation, dealt with the union up to 1905. When the union demanded that the erection of a steel mill at McKeesport, Pennsylvania, be done with members of the union, the Company refused. Refusal led to a break in relations.

It has been maintained that the United States Steel Corporation feared that the granting of this demand would have been the entering wedge for the extension of the union's power over the erection of steel. From this vantage point, it was feared the union could initiate a campaign for organizing of the fabricating mills, which the United States Steel Corporation was unwilling to allow. What is perhaps more likely is that the Company was not willing to strengthen the position of any labor organization, having in view their eventual exclusion from the company.

The Bridge and Structural Iron Workers accepted the challenge of the American Bridge Company. Moving to the attack, it declared a strike against Post and McCord Company in New York in 1905 on the assumption that this firm was a subsidiary of the American Bridge Company. Almost at the same time an open shop campaign was initiated in the steel construction industry under the leadership of the National Erectors' Association. Formed in 1903 as the National Association of Manufacturers and Erectors of Structural Steel and Iron Work, the organization adopted the shorter title when it inaugurated the open shop campaign in the industry in 1906. "The object of this Association shall be the institution and maintenance of the open shop principle in the employment and erection of steel and iron bridges and buildings and other structural steel and iron works."[5] Under the leadership of Walter Drew, the National Erectors' Association became a powerful and not always scrupulous leader of the anti-union forces in the industry.

Engaged in a nationwide struggle, beginning in 1905, the International Bridge and Structural Iron Workers sought the aid of the American Federation of Labor. The latter appealed for financial aid for the iron workers in 1905, and in 1906 the A. F. of L. sought to settle differences between the iron workers and the Building Employers' Association of New York, differences in part due to the difficulties in steel.

The Central Federated Union of New York called upon the Executive Council to enlist the aid of the other building trades' unions in behalf of the iron workers. Gompers favored calling a special meeting of the Council in New York, so as to mobilize the other unions behind the iron workers, but only Huber and Mitchell would support his plea. Hayes, Duncan, Lennon, and Keefe voted against the meeting and it was never held.[6] The iron workers were hard pressed by their anti-union opponents, a factor that probably contributed to the emergence of more militant leadership within the union. In 1905 Frank M. Ryan and John J. McNamara were elected respectively president and secretary-treasurer, and they turned to the use of dynamite.

In the five years between 1906 and 1911, eighty-seven structures erected by non-union labor were dynamited. The campaign of violence was directed by McNamara, and union funds were used to finance the campaign. Ortie McManigal, a member of the union, and James B. McNamara, a brother of the secretary-treasurer, were the leaders in this publicly unknown branch of the union's activity. Anti-union elements were not entirely without knowledge, as H. S. Hockin, a member of the Executive Board of Iron Workers' Union, was on the payroll of employers.

Los Angeles, California, was at the time a center of anti-union activity. Under the leadership of the Merchants' and Manufacturers' Association, and the inspiration of Harrison Gray Otis, the publisher of the *Los Angeles Times,* a constant and aggressive campaign against unionism was carried on. The American Federation of Labor had levied an assessment, which raised over fifteen thousand dollars, to help the California labor movement resist the onslaught and to finance the campaign of unionization in Los Angeles. The *Los Angeles Times* was of course completely unorganized. On October 1, 1910, its building was dynamited, with a loss of twenty lives and property damage of over a half a million dollars.

At the time of the explosion Gompers was in St. Louis arranging for the forthcoming convention. Interviewed about the tragic event, he denounced the perpetrators and declared, "It was inconceivable that a union man should do such a thing," but he went on to say that if such

STEEL AND THE McNAMARAS

a crime had been committeed by a member of organized labor, the entire labor movement could not be held responsible for the deed of a single unhinged individual.[7] Almost immediately the *Los Angeles Times* charged the deed was the work of an agent of the labor unions.

Employer organizations in and outside of Los Angeles followed the lead of the *Times*. The Merchants' and Manufacturers' Association promptly appropriated fifty thousand dollars for discovering the guilty. Responsibility for the explosion was immediately placed upon the labor movement, although an investigation by the California State Federation of Labor claimed that the evidence showed the explosion had been caused by gas and that anti-union forces led by Otis were using the event to arouse feeling against organized labor.[8]

Convinced, not without justification, that powerful forces were at work in California to destroy the trade unions, the leaders of labor were shocked and aroused when John J. McNamara was seized at Indianapolis, on April 22, at 5:30 P.M., during a session of the executive board of his union. The other members of the board were not allowed to leave the room. In the meantime, McNamara had been taken before a police judge, who in spite of his lack of authority in such cases, granted extradition. He was transported to Los Angeles, where he, his brother J. B. McNamara, and Ortie E. McManigal had been secretly indicted for murder.

The first reaction of the kidnapping, as it was properly characterized, was to call a meeting of the heads of unions in Indianapolis. The conference was attended by Gompers and the heads of the Carpenters', Barbers', Teamsters', Bricklayers', Bookbinders', Printers', and Locomotive Firemen's unions. The conference

raised the question whether union officers are to be denied rights enjoyed by other persons, and whether it was proper to ignore the legal rights of labor organizations. The conference also declared its belief that every individual accused of crime is entitled to a fair and speedy trial before an unprejudiced judge and jury. To this end money is a necessity, and we propose to see that John J. McNamara is supplied with money to make an adequate defense and to be able to avail himself in every way of the facilities that are open to every man accused of crime to establish his innocence.[9]

The statement was signed by the heads of the unions present at the conference.

The participation in McNamara's kidnapping of William J. Burns, the head of a private detective agency, who had been assisted by Walter Drew of the National Erectors' Association, assured the officers of labor unions that a plot to railroad leading officials of organized labor to death or to long terms in prison was being perpetrated in order to lay the groundwork for a general attack upon all organized labor.

The issue was too important for the heads of the American Federation of Labor to ignore, even had they been inclined to do so. In fact, the organizations of labor looked to Gompers and the Executive Council to take the lead and provide finances, publicity, and an adequate defense. The first problem was to secure funds for defense and for other aid for the imprisoned. In a letter to the California Federation of Labor, which had already taken steps to aid the defendants, Gompers expressed his gratification "that our fellow workers of the Coast proposed to take their stand and financially as well as morally aid in the protection of the legal rights of Secretary McNamara and our other accused men."[10] The International Association of Bridge and Iron Workers, through its president Frank Ryan, expressed a desire to engage Clarence Darrow as chief counsel, with the Federation to have the responsibility of paying for his service. On May 21, 1911, Gompers informed Darrow that he, Morrison, Ryan and Leo Rappoport, the Chief counsel for the union, had decided to engage him to conduct the case, and authorized Darrow to hire assistants.[11]

In the meantime Victor Berger, a Socialist Representative in Congress, introduced a resolution for an investigation of the arrest and extradition of John J. McNamara. Gompers was unable to attend the hearing, so he submitted a statement in support of the adoption of the resolution in which he denounced the kidnapping and argued:

It is not appropriate here even to refer to the guilt or innocence of Mr. Mc-Namara. That many of our fellow citizens and I believe in his innocence is not a question for your committee to consider, but that a great outrage and violation of fundamental guarantees has been committed; that the subject is one deserving of the investigation of a special committee of the House of Representatives; that at least in the future the same travesty on law and outrage of justice may be prevented should appeal to every right thinking and patriotic American citizen.[12]

The main problem facing the defense was that of raising sufficient funds to assure an adequate defense. This was no easy task. When Andrew J. Gallagher of the San Francisco Labor Council asked the A. F. of L. for fifteen thousand dollars, he was told that only thirteen thousand dollars had been raised at the time.

The one bit of progress made in the first weeks was the retention of Darrow, who stood very high in the opinion of the leaders of labor. When Darrow withdrew from the mayoralty race in Chicago in 1903, Gompers expressed his enthusiastic approval of this step, as an elected officer could only inforce the law on the statue books. He considered the withdrawal as a "great advantage to the cause which is so near to you," telling Darrow "that the great gifts of heart and brain and your splendid attainments can be utilized by you as one of the great tribunes to whom all the people can always appeal, with all the earnestness and force of your nature."[13] Darrow's stature as a labor lawyer and as a tribune for the oppressed was greatly increased by his successful defense of Haywood and Pettibone.

The Executive Council of the A. F. of L., and officers of the Building Trades, Metal Trades, and Label Trades Departments discussed, on June 12, 1911, the financing of the defense. Gompers, Morrison, Frank Ryan, and O. A. Tveitmore, who was the secretary-treasurer of the California Building Trades Council, were appointed as a committee to handle all matters with Darrow. It was then decided that all "bills and attorneys' fees and expenses incidental to the defendants at Los Angeles should be O.K.'d by Attorney Clarence Darrow before any should be paid." Lennon, James Short, president of the Building Trades Department, Tveitmore, and John Mitchell were the committee to devise methods for raising funds. All national and international unions were to be asked to donate at least twenty-five cents per member; the same request was to be made directly to chartered unions.

Frank Morrison, the secretary of the A. F. of L., was chosen secretary of the McNamara Legal Defense Committee, without compensation. A conference of officers of national and international unions was called for June 29, 1911, at Indianapolis, and a Ways and Means Committee on the McNamara Defense, made up of Gompers, Morrison, Short, William J. Spencer, James O'Connell, A. J. Barres, and Thomas Tracy of the Union Label League, appointed.

Darrow appeared before the meeting at Indianapolis, and declared that

Inasmuch as he and other counsel would be required to remain in Los Angeles for an indefinite period, close up their business offices in their home cities; that because of the number of witnesses from all parts of the country, whose constant attendance at Los Angeles would be necessary during the entire period of the examination, preliminaries, and during the trial; that because of these it would be necessary to raise a fund of not less than three hundred and fifty thousand dollars.

James Duncan, first vice president of the A. F. of L., favored aid to the Bridge and Structural Iron Workers in the collection of funds, but he advised against the Federation assuming direct responsibility for the case. The other members of the Executive Council were of a contrary opinion. They were all convinced that the charges against the McNamaras were part of the campaign initiated by anti-union employers and the steel industry to destroy the labor movement, and secure in their faith in the innocence of the men on trial in Los Angeles, they threw themselves into the herculean effort to raise sufficient funds for the defense.[14] The size of the sum needed astonished the members of the conference, and there was considerable expression of concern. The members of the conference were "fully persuaded, however, of the innocence of the accused men" and "directed that every effort be made to create as large a fund as possible, declaring at the same time that we were not under any circumstances obligated to raise any stipulated sum."[15] The conference at Indianapolis endorsed the proposals of the Executive Council. Gompers was somewhat disappointed at the attendance, but he hoped it would lead to good results. Edward Nockles, the secretary-treasurer of the Chicago Federation of Labor and an active participant in the defense, advised Morrison early in August that there was great need for funds. Morrison pleaded with the unions to advance money on account and reimburse themselves by collecting the twenty-five cents per member. The defense was expensive.[16]

In addition to Darrow, Cyrus F. McNutt, Joseph Scott, and Le Compte Davis, Job Harriman, and E. M. Hilton were retained by the defense. Investigations and preparation were expensive, and most of the burden fell upon the officers of the American Federation of Labor. Gompers toured the Pacific Coast and discussed the McNamara case at his meetings. He visited the McNamaras in prison, and they fortified his "conviction of their innocence."[17] Subsequently, he took the unprecedented step of endorsing Job Harriman, a lawyer for the defense and the Socialist candidate for mayor of Los Angeles. While he disagreed with many of Harriman's political beliefs, Gompers was convinced that "he places human lives before dollars, and if elected will give the toilers in Los Angeles a square deal."[18]

The selection of a jury began on October 11, 1911, but as the trial proceeded Darrow became convinced that the prisoners could not be successfully defended. According to Anton Johansen, a union leader closely connected with the defense, the burdens were too much for Darrow, and he became increasingly pessimistic about the outcome. Moreover, he was harassed by shortages of finance and fear as an undated letter to Tveitmore reveals.

I am going to have assurance of the money that I need or finish up Jim's case without putting any more money in it and then quit the farce. I am simply not going to kill myself with this case and then worry over money and not know what to do. [Darrow then criticized the methods used to raise funds, which he believed could not be done] by sitting in the office and sending out letters or going to conventions and passing resolutions. I only wish some of the fellows had my job and had to raise money. Up to February 1st, 350,000 will be needed; we have but 170,000. The case may run two years longer. Jim's probably until April 1st. I could hurry except that the longer it takes the sooner the other side will get tired. After February 1st it will need at least 20,000 a month—if it can't be done for God's sake let me know, so I can fix my plans if it can be done do it. But if it isn't made definite and quick, I am going to assume that it won't come in any considerable amount and will curtail in every direction.[19]

Darrow knew the limitations of the A. F. of L. in raising funds, and that it could only appeal to its affiliates, but he saw only his own problem. At the convention of the A. F. of L. in 1911 Gompers appealed for greater financial aid, pointing to the great cost of preparing an adequate defense.[20] Even before the jury had been completed, a sensational development had taken place on November 28th. The chief investigator for the defense had been arrested and charged with bribing a juror. According to Darrow, he faced the possibility of endless trials, as there were twenty separate indictments against each of the two defendants—McManigal had turned state's evidence.

Darrow became convinced that the only way he could save the lives of his clients was to have them, if acceptable to the prosecution, plead guilty and receive a prison sentence. Darrow consulted Le Compte Davis, another attorney for the defense; Lincoln Steffens, the publicist; E. W. Scripps, the newspaper publisher; and Fremont Older, a leading San Francisco editor. All agreed with his view that there was a duty to save the defendants' lives. Darrow believed that the state had a strong case, that the defense had little counter evidence to offer, and that J. B. McNamara could not be put on the witness stand as he could not "sustain himself on cross examination."[21] Despite their initial reluctance, the defendants agreed to the proposal, but the district attorney

could not act without consulting with some of the others interested, and that would require word from the Erectors Association of Indianapolis. The negotiations dragged on for a number of days. Then, Mr. Fredericks [the district attorney] reported that Mr. Drew, of the Erectors Association was willing to accept the proposition.[22]

James McNamara pleaded guilty to murder and John McNamara to dynamiting of the Llewellyn Iron Works, which had been dynamited on Christmas Day, 1910. Resentment and disillusionment spread among the organized workers and their friends, and the feeling was instrumental in completely destroying the chances for the election of Job Harriman, one of the lawyers for the defense. Harriman had led all other candidates in the primary. Darrow recognized that

to a certain extent, the mayoralty campaign which ended on December 5th, five days after the guilty plea, [and] the case went together, and while I had never been a Socialist I was more or less in accord with that view, and thoroughly sympathetic with the aims of the party. On account of Mr. Harriman, I was sorry to have the plea of guilty entered, but, on the other hand, the lives of my clients were at stake, and I had no right or inclination to consider anything but them.[23]

The closeness of the outcome of the mayoralty campaign very likely influenced the industrial interests of Los Angeles, not known for their magnanimity or kindness, to accept the guilty plea.

Darrow realized the consternation and disappointment the plea of guilty would cause in the ranks of labor, and on November 23rd he wired Gompers asking that Tveitmore, Nockles, John Fitzpatrick, or Johansen be sent out to Los Angeles immediately. Obviously he wanted someone, close to and in the confidence of the Ways and Means Committee, near during his negotiations with the prosecution. When Darrow had changed the plea, he wired Gompers: "There was no avoiding step taken today. When I see you I know you will be satisfied that all of us have done everything we had to accomplish the best. Hope you will believe we realize our responsibility and did the best that could be done."[24] As soon as the guilty plea had been announced, the conference of international officers reconvened and condemned

crime and violence, whether developing in trade unions, in commercial enterprises, or in the conduct of daily newspapers. There can be no distinction as the quality of participants in crime, no palliation of crime, no excuse for crime; and the present enlargement of a particular crime committed by a member of a trade union, one among the millions of wage earners, or by an officer of a trade union, one among thousands of such officers, smacks of an attempt to cover up crimes in other quarters and to enlarge the opportunity for criminals in high places, and this effort is by the interests that are suspected of controlling the utterances of supposedly public mouthpieces and molders of public opinion.[25]

The statement pointed to the belief of the union officers that McNamara had been the victim of a "foul conspiracy" and that the unions had only done their duty under the conditions "that then existed." Unions, the statement declared, had been as free of crime as any institution "in the history of any other organized human effort," and it thereby severely criticized the "inflammatory, vicious and mischievous denunciation of trade unions, their officers and their members." The statement argued that the manner in which the arrest was made, the holding of the executive board of the union incommunicado, and the hurrying of J. J. McNamara "by circuitous routes" to California, all convinced the labor movement of the innocence of the men on trial. The statement was signed by the officers of all the unions that originally signed the appeal for the McNamaras, plus a general officer of the International Association of Machinists, whose headquarters was not in Indianapolis.

The McNamara Ways and Means Committee also had to consider the effect of the admission of guilt upon the labor movement and upon public opinion. Darrow was requested to meet with the committee in Washington, but he was unable to do so. He wired that he was unable to tell how soon he could leave, and that "Nockles goes east tomorrow night will have him see you and I will go as soon as possible."[26] Nockles, who was in Los Angeles, wired the Ways and Means Committee that he hoped "you will stand by Darrow. Full report will show that everything possible was done." The Ways and Means Committee decided to stop all payments, after the pleas of guilty had been announced.

Organized labor was shaken by the outcome, and the leaders sought to explain their position. The Ways and Means Committee issued a statement deploring violence and exculpated the labor movement from responsibility for the crimes of the McNamaras. It cited the manner in which the head of an international union had been seized, and the violent antagonism of the National Erectors Association, among others, to organize labor as proof that its belief in the innocence of the McNamaras was due to the illegal manner in which the representatives of the employers had acted. There were no recriminations against the guilty men, although satisfaction was expressed that the majesty of the law and justice had been maintained and the culprits commensurably punished for their crimes.

The case aroused, at least temporarily, intense feelings against the organized labor movement. The Socialists, who were not above stepping into the maelstrom, saw in the violence of the McNamaras the logical outcome of the A. F. of L.'s denial of independent political action. Beset from all sides, and forced to bear more than his share of the burden of vituperation, Gompers did not take kindly to the criticism of the Socialists, which he interpreted as the result of their failure to control the economic movement of labor.[27]

Following the McNamara trial, fifty-four officers of the International Association of Bridge and Structural Iron Workers were indicted in Indianapolis in January 1912 for conspiracy to transport dynamite in interstate commerce. The indictment claimed the conspiracy had been formed in 1907. Indictments against three were dropped. A member of the executive board, H. S. Hockin, testified against his colleagues. He had directed the dynamiting of bridges and buildings, and at the same time was keeping some employers and later Detective William J. Burns informed of the movement of the dynamiters.[28]

In the end thirty-eight were convicted. President Frank Ryan was sentenced to seven years in prison, other defendants to sentences from one year and a day to six years. Five who pleaded guilty received suspended sentences. The convictions of two were subsequently reversed by the higher courts. An attempt was made to implicate the A. F. of L. and especially Gompers, whom William J. Burns, the private detective, was anxious to convict. The A. F. of L. and its officers were innocent and the Indianapolis grand jury brought no charge against them.

In the meantime, Darrow was indicted in Los Angeles on charges of trying to corrupt two jurors. His chief investigator, who had been caught trying to bribe jurors, had turned state's evidence and implicated Darrow. Darrow was in a difficult financial situation, and a report was circulated that he had charged Gompers with knowing beforehand of the guilt of the McNamaras. Gompers was deeply aroused at the report. This Darrow denied, and asked the Federation to help finance his defense.[29] Gompers accepted Darrow's denial, but explained the difficulties in raising money for the defense. In a letter to Darrow, he wrote

Believing, aye, almost firmly convinced of the innocence of the McNamaras, we strained every nerve to raise as near as possible the amount of money you suggested would be necessary for their defense. Upon learning that they were guilty, the first intimation of which was conveyed to the rank and file as well as to the officers of the labor movement through their confession, I am free to say to you that in my judgment any general appeal for funds to defend you or the men under indictment would fall upon indifferent ears and elicit little, if any, response at this time. If I had the means, or the control of means, I should be glad to place it at the disposal of you and the other men, but I have none.[30]

When the heads of the United Mine Workers of America and the Western Federation of Miners issued an appeal for funds, and requested the A. F. of L. to do the same, Mitchell and Hayes voted for the appeal; John Alpine was opposed; and Lennon, Perham, Valentine, Morrison and Huber voted to postpone consideration of the issue until the meeting of the Executive Council.[31]

Darrow was acquitted in the first trial, and then tried on a second indictment for bribing a second juror. The jury failed to agree, and the charge was dismissed. With the heads of the union convicted, the Iron Workers' Union faced many problems. Members of the Executive Council suggested that Gompers attend the convention of the union, and stress the support of the Federation, but not commit the A. F. of L. to any financial burdens.[32] A number of leaders of organizations of labor addressed the convention. All urged the maintenance of the union, and none tried to lecture the delegates on the conduct to be pursued, except the absolute necessity for standing firm and protecting the organization. James O'Connell, John P. White, Daniel Tobin, and William Bowen of the Bricklayers' Union, were among the speakers. Gompers, who was there on behalf of the Executive Council, urged the delegates to defend and retain their union, for otherwise it will mean "slavery and death and destruction to the Bridge and Structural Iron Workers, because your organization must live; it must live that you must meet the situation as you find it and deal with it as earnest, honest, intelligent men, who want to serve their fellow workers."[33] The delegates acted upon the advice, and reelected President Frank Ryan, who was out on bail.

The dynamite cases placed the labor movement on the defensive with the public. However, as one examines the statements made by the labor leaders of the time, one finds no note of apology or recrimination against the McNamaras. Instead, they argued that it was the bitter anti-union policy of the organized employers which caused men, made deseperate by the tyranny and injustice and denial of rights, to turn to violence. There has been considerable speculation as to whether the leaders of labor were aware of the guilt of the McNamaras.

The evidence in Gompers' letters suggests that he, certainly, was firmly convinced of the innocence of those charged with the dynamiting. He was deeply shaken by the pleas of guilty but he accused no one of bad faith. In a typical letter on this subject, he assured Albert H. Walker that he had

been absolutely convinced of the innocence of the McNamara brothers, from all the information I was able to gather at the time and from my knowledge of general events and circumstances, particularly as regards the unwarranted attacks of the Manufacturers' Association and of General Otis upon the general labor movement and upon myself, and as thoroughly satisfied in my own mind of their innocence, as I am now astounded and shocked by their confession of the terrible crime they have committed.[34]

Eleven years later, in 1922, Gompers, asked by a hostile newspaper whether he had pleaded in behalf of the McNamaras, declared:

The president of the American Federation of Labor did sign the call mentioned in the above question because at that time he was satisfied beyond any question of doubt that the defendants in the case were innocent and that assistance in their defense was imperative if they were to be saved from an unjust conviction. The action was legitimate, it was American and it neither requires nor occasions regret. When the dramatic plea of guilty was entered none was more astounded than the president of the American Federation of Labor, but until that time there was no honorable course to pursue except to act in accordance with a sincere belief.[35]

Aside from Gompers' statements, his whole career suggests that he would not have risked the name and prestige of the entire labor movement in behalf of a cause which might have inflicted serious damage to all the unions, no matter how remotely they were connected with the violent deed. While he was willing to speak out and defend the movement against its antagonists, he was not inclined to run risks in behalf of "dubious causes." Despite the adverse effect of the case on public opinion, the membership of the A. F. of L. did not decrease, and in fact, largely as a result of the gains in the women's clothing industries rose immediately after the McNamara case.

COMMISSION ON INDUSTRIAL RELATIONS

Soon after the McNamara episode had run its course, a committee influenced largely by this case urged appointment of a commission by Congress to investigate industrial relations. It was made up of leading liberals and social workers, among whom were Jane Adams, Louis D. Brandeis, Stephen Wise, and Father John A. Ryan. Among the topics suggested for investigation was the manner in which wage rates were determined, the handling of grievances, and industrial relations.[36] The American Federation of Labor favored these proposals, and Morrison and Mitchell participated, as representatives of the A. F. of L., in the discussions on the scope and personnel of the commission. On August 23, 1912, the law setting up a commission of nine to study the relations between capital and labor, with capital, labor, and the public each to be represented by three members, was enacted. The A. F. of L. proposed two members of the Executive Council, Lennon and O'Connell, and "fairness required that these [railway] brotherhoods should be represented by one of their choice."[37] The committee promoting a commission on industrial relations criticized the two members of the Executive Council as too conservative. Timothy Healy, the head of the Brotherhood of Stationary Firemen, denounced the views of the committee as "arrogant."

President Taft himself favored Duncan and Mitchell, but as neither would serve without the endorsement of the Executive Council, he had no alternative but to appoint the two recommended by the A. F. of L. Taft's appointees were not confirmed, and it was left to his successor, President Wilson, to fill the posts. An effort to have Wilson select someone from the left wing of the labor movement was started by the committee on industrial relations, and Ralph Easley charged that there was an attempt by some of those around the *Survey*, a reform weekly, to have William D. Haywood, the leader of the Industrial Workers of the World, appointed to the Commission. He warned Wilson's secretary, Joseph Tumulty, "that much pressure is being brought on President Wilson by a group of radical social reformers, Socialists and Anarchists to induce the President to appoint a representative of the Industrial Workers of the World upon the contemplated Industrial Relations Commission."[38]

In the end, Lennon, and O'Connell, both members of the Executive Council, and A. B. Garretson of the Order of Railway Conductors were the labor representatives. The hearings provided the country with much information on industrial conditions and the causes of industrial warfare. It also drew aside the curtain from many neglected economic areas, and revealed exploitation and oppression which helped to mitigate in the public mind the revulsion against the violence of the McNamaras and other members of the Iron Workers' Union. This was especially true in the revelations on the Ludlow, Colorado, coal strike, with its terrifying slaughter of women and children in the tent colonies by National Guardsmen. Even more important from the point of view of the organized labor movement, the Commission did help in the creation of a more hospitable climate for organized labor, and by attracting attention to serious evils helped the public to forget the dynamite cases.

REFERENCES

1. P. J. McArdle to Gompers, August 7, 1909; Gompers to Morrison, August 7, 1909.

2. Circular issued by the American Federation of Labor, November 27, 1909.

3. Gompers, O'Connell, G. W. Perkins, McArdle, E. S. McCullough, J. D. Pierce, J. W. Hayes, and Charles E. Lawlor to President W. H. Taft, January 6, 1910.

4. George W. Wickersham to Gompers, March 28, 1910.

5. Article III of the constitution, quoted in Luke Grant, *The National Erectors' Association and The International Association of Bridge and Structural Ironworkers* (Washington: United States Commission on Industrial Relations, 1915), p. 13.

6. Report to the Executive Council of the A. F. of L., February 27, 1906.

7. *St. Louis Star Globe,* October 2, 1910.

8. The most detailed description of events and public reaction after the explosion is found in Grace Heilman Stimson, *The Rise of the Labor Movement in Los Angeles* (Berkley and Los Angeles: University of California Press, 1955), pp. 366-406.

9. *The Bridgemen's Magazine,* June 1911, pp. 325-327.

10. Letter to California Federation of Labor, May 19, 1911.

11. Gompers to Olaf A. Tveitmore, May 19, 1911; Gompers to Darrow, May 21, 1911.

12. *Hearings Held Before the United States House Committee on Rules, House of Representatives,* May 27, 28, 1911, pp. 6-7.

13. Quotation is from Gompers to Darrow, March 5, 1903; Gompers to Andrew J. Gallagher, March 5, 1911.

14. Gompers to Duncan, March 19, 1912.

15. Minutes of Executive Council, January 12, 13, 1911; Report to Executive Council, January 6, 1911.

16. Gompers to Duncan, July 7, 1911; Nockles to Morrison, August 1, 1911.

17. *Los Angeles Record,* September 13, 1911.

18. *Wheeling* (West Virginia) *News,* September 18, 1911.

19. Darrow to O. A. Tveitmore, undated.

20. *Report of Proceedings of the Thirty-First Annual Convention of the American Federation of Labor,* 1911, pp. 313-315.

21. Clarence S. Darrow, *The Story of My Life* (New York: Charles Scribner's Sons, 1934), pp. 182-183; *The Bridgemen's Magazine,* November 1912, pp. 728-729.

22. *Ibid.,* p. 183.

23. Darrow, *op. cit.,* p. 184.

24. Darrow to Gompers, December 1, 1911; Darrow to Gompers, November 23, 1911.

25. *The Bridgemen's Magazine,* January 1912, pp. 6-7.

26. Telegram from Gompers to Darrow, December 6, 1911; night letter from Darrow to Gompers, December 7, 1911. Nockles to Gompers, telegram, December 6, 1917.

27. *American Federationist,* February 1912.

28. *Grant, op. cit.,* p. 105.

29. Letter of Darrow to Former Senator R. F. Pettigrew, March 4, 1912.

30. Letter from Gompers to Darrow, March 16, 1912.

31. Vote Book, March 13, 1913.

32. Vote Book, February 4, 1913.

33. *The Bridgemen's Magazine,* March 1913.

34. Letter from Gompers to Albert H. Walker, December 8, 1911.

35. Gompers to the editor of the *New York Commercial,* December 9, 1922. It would be impossible to find a more distorted and mean description of the McNamara case than that given by the late communist and Titoist Louis Adamic, *Dynamite* (New York: The Viking Press, 1931), p. 251. Adamic explains the quashing of the Buck's Stove and Range case as due to the McNamara confession.

36. Paul U. Kellogg, *Work-Relationships and the Democracy* (New York: Committee on Industrial Relations n. d.).

37. Letter of Gompers to President Taft, September 9, 1912.

38. Quote from Easley to Joseph Tumulty, June 17, 1913; Easley to William B. Wilson, June 18, 1913.

XVIII

Legislation and Political Action

EARLY POLITICAL OBJECTIVES

The American Federation of Labor had from 1881 shown a concern for political problems. Yet there was some resistance on the part of a number of delegates to the first convention, in 1881, even to the discussion of political questions. Though a resolution urging the restriction of child labor was enacted, John Jarrett, who presided, ruled that resolutions on the regulation of interstate commerce by Congress and the forfeiture of railroad land grants for nonfulfillment of contract were foreign to the purpose of the convention. Jarrett was not entirely consistent, for on his motion the conference approved a tariff on foreign-made goods.

While the convention did not develop an elaborate political platform, it called for the enactment of compulsory child education laws, uniform apprentice laws, a national eight-hour day law, the repeal of contract prison labor, the abolition of the truck system of wage payment and the substitution of payment in lawful money, a mechanic's lien law which would give a worker a prior lien upon property for the payment of wages, the repeal of the conspiracy laws, and the establishment of a bureau of labor statistics in the states.[1] In addition, the prohibition of Chinese immigration, enforcement of sanitary laws in mines and factories, and the establishment of licensing provisions for stationary engineers and firemen were requested.

At the second meeting, the endorsement of a protective tariff was rescinded, and demands for the abolition of contract laborers and for the enactment of an Employers' Liability Act which "will give employees the same right to damages for personal damages that all other persons have" were added to the legislative program.[2]

The Federation had few funds for lobbying, and it delegated to the Federation of the District of Columbia the authority to represent it on legislative matters before Congress. Gabriel Edmonston, a member of the Legislative Committee and a resident of Washington, helped to prepare bills before Congress and occasionally testified before Congressional committees on legislation affecting labor. The political platform of the first Federation changed little through its entire existence. It always recommended that labor organizations seek to secure representation in legislative bodies, but it did not as yet define its own position on the tactics to be used to achieve this end.

The first convention of the reorganized Federation, in 1886, endorsed independent political action, and the representative of the Journeymen Bakers' National Union "favored more radical action on the part of the Trades' Unions than had heretofore been the rule."[3] Presumably these observations referred to political action, as the Bakers' Union at the time was dominated by Socialist leaders and thinking. Aside from demanding the enforcement of the restrictions against Chinese immigration and the improvement of the apprentice laws, the first convention did not concern itself with many legislative matters. It seems that in view of the obstacles in unifying the trade unions, the leaders sought to avoid a discussion of controversial issues. This would explain why Gompers and McGuire, who had expressed opposition to independent political action at other times, did not object to the resolution endorsing this policy.

The convention of 1887 showed more concern with political action and advised the members of the Federation to pay more attention to legislation. It was charged that members of labor unions

suffer greatly, not only from the enactment of unjust laws and the inefficiency of unenforced laws, but also from the discriminating dispensation of the law. Laws have been passed in the interest of the workingman [which] are not enforced because he neglects himself to enforce them . . . We therefore recommend to all the membership the necessity of resorting to the use of the ballot and demanding of all candidates for public office a public pledge of support to the measures desired by them before voting for them.[4]

At the next convention, Gompers, in his report, advised against the forming of a third, independent, political party on the ground that recent experience (evidently in the New York City mayoralty campaign) had made such action unwise. Gompers' recommendation was phrased in tentative terms, in which he alluded to the need of concentrating labor's effort upon the attainment of the eight-hour work day.[5]

Gompers kept informed on labor legislation and intervened with legislative bodies or government executives when legislation affecting labor was pending. In a letter to Governor David Hill of New York Gompers in 1888 protested against a bill that would have made the law establishing Saturday as a half-holiday inoperative for nine months.

The tendency of the times [he told the Governor] is to give to Sunday its old puritanical character, to make it a day of rest and religious observance. Truly, then a half-holiday on Saturday devoted to amusement, exercise, and recreation should be afforded the workingman. It cannot be claimed that the productivity of labor is diminished by this half holiday. . . . It is asserted that the State of New York is at a disadvantage with other States by reason of this law. If we recognize the beneficient effect upon the health and comfort of our people then the so-called disadvantage is an argument not worth consideration. It is doubtful if any useful legislation over which the several states have absolute control can or will be adopted simultaneously, one must lead the many, and there is no reason why the Empire State should not be the first. To repeal the law now would only have the effect of deterring other states from adopting a similar law.[6]

DIFFERENT POLITICAL VIEWS

There were differences, and they existed from the beginning of the A. F. of L., over the political tactics to be pursued, but they did not for a time come to the surface. The convention of 1889 rejected an endorsement of independent political action, and in the following year the debate on the admission of a delegate from the New York Central Labor Federation indirectly involved this issue.[7] Had the A. F. of L. recognized the propriety of the affiliations of the Socialist Labor Party, it would have been committed to independent political action, for the special character of the Party and its peculiar relation to the labor movement would have been inferentially admitted. Gompers emphasized in his report to the convention of 1891 that the refusal to allow a political party to affiliate directly with the economic labor movement did not imply that political action by labor was repudiated.[8] Gompers always argued that the worker should be concerned with politics and legislation. He wanted, however, "to wean the workers from being political followers of any party by whatever name known."[9]

The leaders of the A. F. of L. believed that political action meant support of those candidates who were favorable to the policies and to the legislation sponsored by labor. In 1894, McGuire asked the Executive Council to send a man through New Hampshire in behalf of the candidacy of Senator H. W. Blair "in view of his past services and efforts in behalf of the eight-hour law and the labor movement generally."[10] Endorsement of a political party was regarded by the leaders of the trade unions as partisan politics. This label was applied to all political parties and included those espousing socialism as well as the so-called old parties. There was, in their opinion, a difference between lobbying for labor legislation and supporting candidates on the basis of their records, and endorsing a political party. It will be recalled that August McGraith, the Secretary of the A. F. of L., believed that Gompers had violated the rules of the Federation in supporting the presidential candidacy of Bryan in 1896. The convention found no grounds for the charges.

In the following presidential campaign the question of the propriety of an executive officer of the A. F. of L. supporting a presidential candidate, William Jennings Bryan, was again raised, when Treasurer John B. Lennon inquired if he could take the stump for Bryan. Gompers commented that

There are a number of earnest republicans in your national union, as well as the other organizations of the A. F. of L., who would not take kindly to the notion if we, who are elected as officers by their votes as well as the votes of others, were to publicly and practically officially, use the offices, or the influence which these offices given, to secure the defeat of their party, and the success of the party to which they are opposed. If you were to take the stump for Mr. Bryan, or I were to do so, don't you think that other unionists would be equally justified to take the stump for McKinley—yes, Mr. Debs, or Mr. Maloney? Some are positively honest in so doing; others are not, yet all are classified alike. In my judgment, we shall be doing our duty to our fellow-workers, hence to all the people of our country, in a far better way by confining our active work to the trade union movement.[11]

While Gompers was opposed to having the officers of the A. F. of L. active in political campaigns, he voted with the majority of the Executive Council, in 1896, against prohibiting A. F. of L. organizers from "mixing in politics." The objection to such a proposal was that the A. F. of L. might be charged with accepting money from Hanna, the Republican national chairman, and that it would represent an interference with individual rights. O'Connell, Duncan, and McCraith voted to prohibit, but McGuire, Gompers, Garland, and Lennon overruled them.[12] At the same time Gompers, on behalf of the Council, urged unions to remain out of politics.[13]

Despite the objections to direct political involvement, the heads of the Federation were continually active in promoting or opposing legislation of interest to all or to some group of workers. The convention of 1895 instructed the Executive Council to promote legislation favorable to labor. However, a resolution for the appointment of a legislative committee for that purpose was not accepted until the next convention. At the meeting in 1896 Gompers proposed that representatives of the Federation be stationed in Washington (the offices of the A. F. of L. were then in Indianapolis) during the sessions of Congress to guard and further the legislation sought by the A. F. of L. Following the convention's approval, Andrew Furuseth was appointed legislative agent, and one hundred dollars was appropriated for his salary and expenses.[14] Furuseth appeared before Congress, and he presented the views of the A. F. of L. on pending legislation. These did not always meet with the approval of organizations outside the A. F. of L., as for example, Furuseth's unsuccessful efforts to have seamen exempted from the Erdman Act, supported by the four railway brotherhoods.[15]

POLITICAL DEMANDS

Interest in legislation and politics increased, especially after 1891 when the question of the issuance of injunctions in labor disputes came before a convention of the A. F. of L. An injunction restraining striking printers from picketing had been issued by a Pennsylvania Common Pleas Court. There was considerable concern over this development, and minority and majority recommendations were made by the resolutions committee on how to handle this issue. The Executive Council was authorized to contribute funds for the appeal to the higher courts. Subsequently, the injunction was upheld in the Pennsylvania Supreme Court.

Gompers was convinced that the affirmance of the lower court's decision was due to an inadequate presentation of the issues in the briefs. "I would suggest," he told the Executive Council, "that a friendly case should be brought about before the court of Pennsylvania with an injunction issued argued upon the merits of its continuance and permanency, and if decided against us and it be carried to the various courts without a single right being waived I feel certain that the decision of the Supreme Court will be overturned by that same body."[16] Gompers' confidence was soon shaken by several other adverse court decisions in the space of a few months. He became convinced that the "orders issued by Judge Ricks, Taft, Billings and Lawrence . . . [are] certainly more than a mere coincidence." The similarity of these decisions, the closeness in time in which they were handed down, indicated to Gompers that these decrees were part of a studied campaign to injure organized labor.[17]

Throughout the early years the Federation's legislative program was relatively simple. After President McKinley's inauguration he was visited by the Executive Council and asked to sponsor legislation deemed necessary by the A. F. of L. Later, Gompers appealed to President McKinley for legislation that would make the "Government of the United States if not . . . a model employer at least a fairly generous employer of its workmen and so far as is possible to become the direct employer thereof, instead of the costly and ungainful of the contractor and sub-contractor with the loss of profit these imply."

On the limitation of the rights of the courts to issue injunctions in labor disputes, the A. F. of L. declared:

Within the past few years a new weapon has been brought into play in the disputes between employer and the employed theretofore unknown to the law as it has been applied . . . to either criminal, the political or the police powers of the state—the now well-known weapon of the judicial injunction restraining workmen from doing certain things recognized by the codes as perfectly within the lawful limit of their rights.[18]

During the year, the Executive Council drew up a short set of proposals which were submitted as a memorial to Congress. The first demand on the labor agenda was the amendment of the eight-hour law so that it would apply to public works whether done directly by government or by contractors or sub-contractors. Other demands called for a remodeling of the immigration laws so as to give greater protection to American workers and their families; reform in the currency laws to assure the American people against financial panics; and liberal appropriation for public works. In calling for

the prompt adoption of these relief measures at the hands of Congress, we firmly believe some degree of prosperity may be restored and the conditions of the people bettered. We assure you the millions are now in no disposition to be trifled with. They are fast becoming desperate, and deep are their mutterings of discontent. They desire to realize some of the prosperity so freely promised on the stump six months ago. Over three millions of willing workers are idle; shall they appeal to you in vain? Shall the interests of trusts, syndicates, monopolies, corporations and monied men remain of more importance than the welfare of the toilers? We trust no.[19]

By 1902, the question of the use of the injunction in labor disputes led the Executive Council to place this matter near the top of its legislative agenda, second only to the demand for legislation establishing an eight-hour work day for government employees. In 1902, the Council declared that "injunctions of a flagrant, unjustifiable, outrageous character are continually issued, and honest law-abiding, and faithful citizen-workmen are thrust into prison for periods from one to nine months." Such court orders, the Council charged, invaded "the legal and moral rights of the workers to perform perfectly legal and legitimate acts, to carry on their efforts to a successful determination." Affiliated unions were urged to call attention to this evil in their mass meetings and celebrations during Independence and Labor days.[20]

THE BILL OF GRIEVANCES

The efforts of the Federation did not lead to successes on the legislative front. In February 1906, Gompers informed the Executive Council "that as far as legislation and administration are concerned, as they apply to the interests of labor, [they] are of the most unsatisfactory and unpromising character. There seems to exist an utter disregard of either the interests, the requests or the protests of labor." Congress was not inclined to act favorably on labor-supported legislation, and Gompers was satisfied that some kind of "demonstration and protest to be made at the earliest possible moment to those responsible for legislation and administrative acts" was necessary.[21]

After consultation with several members of the Executive Council,

Gompers called on the international unions to appoint representatives to participate in preparing a memoranda to be presented to the President, the Speaker of the House, and the president pro-tempore of the United States Senate. Representatives from fifty-one international unions attended at the meeting and drew up a "Bill of Grievances." The statement set forth the complaints of labor organizations against the failure of Congress to enact an effective eight-hour law for government workers; the failure to regulate effectively convict labor and immigration, especially Chinese. Another matter protested was the refusal of Congress to grant equal rights to seamen and to impose "in the guise of a bill to subsidize the shipping industry, a provision . . . which would make compulsory naval service a condition precedent to employment on privately owned vessels." The statement charged that anti-trust legislation had been perverted so that it was applied to labor in violation of the personal liberty as guaranteed by the constitution. Another complaint was the misuse of the injunction, which the A. F. of L. contended had been used to subvert personal freedom and hamper the activities of labor unions. The Federation also protested the domination of the House Committee on Labor by those hostile to the demands of the organized workers; the denial to government employees of the right of petition to Congress for redress of grievances; and the threat that the exercise of the rights of petition would be followed by instant dismissal from the Federal service.[22]

Changing Tactics

The drafting of a statement to Congress and the President represented a concentration of energy and highlighting of political demands, and was in fact a new departure. Moreover, the A. F. of L. was not content with mere presentation of demands. At the initiative of the Executive Council, a Labor Representation Committee, with Gompers, O'Connell, and Morrison as members, was established. The Committee launched a campaign against labor's most persistent legislative enemies, and called upon union men to support for Congress candidates favorable to the demands of organized labor.

As a first objective, the Labor Representation Committee sought the defeat of Congressmen Charles E. Littlefield of Maine, a sworn enemy of organized labor and a powerful member of the judiciary committee. As the election in Maine came in September, the Federation was able to test its new policy on a limited scale. Gompers entered the campaign on August 18th, and spoke to the largest meeting in the history of the State. He addressed nine other meetings, and was followed by other leaders of organized labor. A number of unions sent organizers into the area, and the labor forces succeeded in stirring up interest and riveting attention upon the district and the issues in the campaign.

The Republican Party became sufficiently concerned to send in several of its elder statesmen, including Speaker Joseph Cannon, Secretary of War William Howard Taft, and Senator Albert Beveridge of Indiana, a noted spellbinder. President Theodore Roosevelt issued a statement that the defeat of Littlefield would be "a positive calamity to his district and to the country at large." Labor was unable to defeat Littlefield in a strong Republican district, but his majority was reduced from 5419 in 1904 to under 1000 in 1906.[23]

The campaign to defeat labor's enemies and elect its friends to Congress continued during the remainder of the campaign. An appeal for funds was issued, and $8,225.94 was contributed, $8,147.19 of which was spent. In several districts where candidates of the principal parties were hostile to organized labor, independent trade union candidates were nominated. The decision on whom to support was left in the hands of the local labor people, on the theory that they were the best judges of the merits of the candidates in their own districts. Information on the performance of Congressmen on bills of interest to labor was transmitted to their home districts to aid their constituents in making their decisions. While the Republican Party succeeded in maintaining its control over the House of Representatives, it was achieved by a much lower majority, and Gompers was convinced that organized labor's participation in the campaign was in part responsible for this outcome. Moreover, he believed that labor's campaign would have a salutary effect upon the members, and that more attention would be given to labor's demands.[24]

Not all unionists were satisfied with the steps taken on the political front. Socialists and others who favored independent political action by labor were critical of the limited commitments made by the Executive Council, and took occasion, during the discussion of the President's report to the convention of 1906, to criticize the policies pursued. Victor Berger was quoted by Gompers as having written: "Most undoubtedly the American Federation of Labor shows signs of decay in spite of the mighty numbers marched forth in the reports of Gompers and Mitchell. All its proceedings are senile. Sam Gompers, the President and leading spirit, has more and more developed into an empty, self-complacent old fool."[25] The views and actions of the Executive Council on the political plane were supported by the convention.

The campaign of 1906 actually marked an important departure for the A. F. of L. Prior to that time, the leaders always urged their members to show an interest in political activity and to support candidates sympathetic to the claims of labor. In this year the Federation essayed a more active, and for that reason a somewhat different, role. The continued refusal by the leaders to take a further step and embrace independent labor politics obscured this essential change in policy. Socialists could think of political action only in terms of an independent party, although some were willing to concede that the party could be instead a labor party. What most Socialists were after was an independent class party of labor, a demand which the leaders of the Federation would never accept. But while the leaders of the Federation would not accept a class party, they were increasingly bedeviled by problems which had their primary origin in political or government institutions. More aggressive political activity was inevitable once laws or administrative rulings adversely affected the position of labor. This became increasingly apparent as the labor injunction was used more and more to cripple essential activities of organized labor.

The issuance of injunctions continued as a major problem. A conference of labor and farmer representatives called by the A. F. of L. on March 1908 again asked Congress to curb the issuance of labor injunctions by the federal courts. Repeated again was the demand for an eight-hour law for all workers employed upon government work. The same year, representatives of the American Federation of Labor appeared and presented their position to the conventions of the Republican and Democratic Parties. In addition to the above demands, the A. F. of L. asked for recognition of labor's right to organize; for trial by jury in contempt cases not committed in the presence of the courts; and the enactment of an employer liability law. Endorsement of an amendment to the Federal constitution to grant suffrage to women, and the establishment by the Federal government of a Department of Labor and Bureau of Mines were also requested.

The labor representatives were not hospitably received by the Republican delegates, who reiterated the right of the courts to intervene in labor disputes. More favorable was the treatment accorded the delegation at the hands of the Democrats.

In 1910, organized labor fared better politically. The progressive tide that had been slowly rising swept fifteen trade unionists into Congress, eleven of whom were Democrats, three Republicans, and one Socialist. William B. Wilson, former secretary-treasurer of the United Mine Workers of America, one of those elected, was appointed chairman of the House Labor Committee.

The experience of the A. F. of L. delegations to the Republican and Democratic conventions in 1912 were largely a repetition of 1908. The delegation was rebuffed by the Republicans and welcomed by the Democrats. The split in the Republican ranks by the third-party candidacy of Theodore Roosevelt, and the increase in progressive sentiment, led to the defeat of the Republican candidate and the capture of the Congress by the Democrats. President Wilson was friendly to labor. Ten days after he took office, Gompers wrote to him and gave him the detailed reasons why labor should be exempted from the Sherman anti-trust law and why the issuance of injunctions in labor disputes by the federal courts should be regulated.

In Gompers' view, it was "impossible to legislate equitably for labor and capital under the same law. Certainly it is not class legislation to make different provisions for two things inherently different, aiming at different purposes and employing different methods. The provisions of no law will admit of universal indiscriminate application." Gompers insisted that labor was asking only for justice; that workers should not be "persecuted for entering into any combination or agreement having in view the increasing of wages, the shortening of hours, or the bettering of conditions of labor, or any act in furtherance thereof not in itself unlawful."

Gompers insisted that labor was not asking for the right to commit unlawful acts, but only to have rights destroyed by judicial usurpation restored. He took up the question of precedent and custom as forces that should be obeyed and supported, and declared:

The mere fact that a law or a legal precedent exists, does not necessarily imply that it works justice. Oppression and wrong may become established, and under the cloak of authority and regularity take on prestige and a sanctity usually ascribed to accepted rules of justice. These are the insidious forces that have fought labor under the guise of conspiracy laws, and now seek to accomplish their purpose by interpreting the Sherman Anti-Trust law as a modernized conspiracy act.

Gompers insisted that if the activities of labor unions were to be classified as conspiracies, it was time to examine the subject and inquire whether these "conspiracies" did not promote the interests of humanity. He asked the President to consider the needs and the position of labor and the ends of justice before he decided on the steps to be taken.

It was a long letter, almost thirteen double-spaced typewritten pages, addressed to a man just taking over a burdensome office. Nevertheless, Wilson graciously answered: "I am sincerely obliged to you for writing it, and you have no occasion to apologize for the length of the letter. I shall take it home with me and go over it very carefully indeed, for I am sure you know my disposition in matters of this kind."[26]

THE CLAYTON ACT

The relief sought by labor for twenty years appeared to have been granted by the enactment of the Clayton Act, signed by President Wilson, on October 15, 1914. Section 6 of the law declared "The labor of a human being is not a commodity or article of commerce." In its report to the convention of 1914 the Executive Council declared the enactment of the labor sections of the Clayton Act as "securing to the workers of America those fundamental principles of industrial liberty which were among the chief features of the Bill of Grievances and were the objectives of the political policy which the American Federation of Labor inaugurated in 1906." The Clayton Act was described as labor's Magna Charta,[27] but the United States Supreme Court in *Deering v. Duplex Printing Company* (254 U.S. 443, 1921), held that the Clayton Act did not prevent federal courts from restraining actions they deemed illegal. As matters turned out, the Clayton Act gave labor much less relief than its sponsors had hoped for.

SEAMEN'S ACT

However, the Federation was successful in 1915 in gaining one of its objectives—the enactment of a law granting rights and protection to seamen on vessels of United States registry. Sponsored by Senator LaFollette, the law regulated the hours of labor in port and at sea, allowed for inspection, at the demand of a majority of the crew, of the seaworthiness of any vessel engaged in foreign commerce; regulated more favorably the arrangement of sleeping quarters; and abrogated the penalty of imprisonment of American seamen as a penalty for quitting work on a vessel of the United States in a foreign port; prohibited the allotment of wages to creditors on American vessels; and set standards for improved food, safety and inspection.

SCIENTIFIC MANAGEMENT

Scientific Management was another issue which indirectly impinged upon politics and legislation. As developed by Frederick W. Taylor, it emphasized efficiency and production, and tended to neglect, at least at the beginning, the worker and the effect the new techniques might have upon his skill or welfare.

The 1911 convention of the A. F. of L. considered the question and pointed to the efficiency of the American worker and warned against speeding up and stop-watch methods which inevitably led to an increase in the accident rate. Gompers also pointed to the wide acceptance by non-union employers of Scientific Management as a reason for suspicion.[28]

Yet Gompers, despite his public pronouncements—evidently influenced by the hostility to Scientific Management shown by the metal trades unions in the Federation—was not too certain of his grounds. In fact, he found "very little data that could be used to controvert the claims of 'scientific management.' The working men have intuitively rebelled against these plans, but often they have been without available information that could be used in a public argument or before congressional or legislative committees in such a way as to substantiate their contentions properly."

Gompers wanted a factual report, one on conditions "as they are, rather than recommendations as to what the workers ought to do. The workers must solve their own problems in accordance with their own experience."[29] Despite their doubts, the Federation nevertheless maintained, at the request of its affiliates most concerned with the problems raised by Scientific Management, an opposition to the system. Resolutions attacking the methods of Taylor and his co-workers were passed by several A. F. of L. conventions, and investigations of its use in government arsenals and shipyards were sponsored. At the request of the Machinists' Union, the convention of 1914 voted to have the system of Scientific Management abolished and its introduction prohibited—"particularly the time study and premium or bonus features" in the workshops of the government.[30]

Subsequent conventions issued similar pronouncements, but they were, of course, ineffective in prohibiting the development of more efficient methods of operation and measurement of performance in government and industry. As Gompers himself was aware, the workers' reaction was an intuitive one, and he recognized that inevitably systems of scientific management and time and motion study would be opposed because of their novelty and because they tended to undermine the traditional methods of wage fixing. In this respect the Socialist leader of the International Association of Machinists, William H. Johnston, showed himself less progressive and perceptive than his predecessor, James O'Connell, who early in the century advocated the acceptance of piece work by the Machinists' Union, which he then headed. Had O'Connell's advice been followed, it is probable that it might have dulled the edge of some of the anti-union opposition of employers, especially powerful in the metal trades. Moreover, as the largest single group in the metal trades, the attitude of the Machinists' Union naturally influenced the views of other organizations of labor, and in other industries as well.[31]

The political activities of labor were enlarged during and after World War I. In fact, the political tactics to be pursued then again became a subject of debate and contention.

REFERENCES

1. *Report of the First Annual Session of the Federation of Organized Trades and Labor Unions of the United States and Canada*, 1881, pp. 3-4.

2. *Report of the Second Annual Session of the Federation of Organized Trades and Labor Unions of the United States and Canada*, 1882, p. 11.

3. *Report of Proceedings of the First Annual Convention of the American Federation of Labor*, 1886, pp. 16-17.

4. *Report of Proceedings of the Second Annual Convention of the American Federation of Labor*, 1887, p. 25.

5. *Report of Proceedings of the Third Annual Convention of the American Federation of Labor,* 1888, p. 19.

6. Gompers to Governor David B. Hill, May 30, 1888.

7. *Report of the Proceedings of the Ninth Annual Convention of the American Federation of Labor,* 1889, p. 24.

8. *Report of the Proceedings of the Eleventh Annual Convention of the American Federation of Labor,* 1891, pp. 15-16.

9. *Report of the Proceedings of the Twelfth Annual Convention of the American Federation of Labor,* 1892, p. 13.

10. McGuire to Gompers, October 1, 1894.

11. Gompers to John B. Lennon, October 15, 1900.

12. Minutes of the Executive Council, March 20, 1896.

13. Gompers to Henry Weisman, June 27, 1896.

14. Minutes of the Executive Council, December 16, 1895.

15. Gompers to W. S. Carter, August 20, 1896.

16. Gompers to Executive Council, January 8, 1893.

17. Gompers to Peter Breen, March 31, 1893.

18. Gompers to President William McKinley, November 18, 1897.

19. Vote Book of the Executive Council, April 21, 1897.

20. *Vote Book,* April 1, 1902.

21. Gompers to Executive Council, February 13, 1906.

22. *Textbook of Labor's Political Demands* (Washington: American Federation of Labor, 1906).

23. *Rumford Falls, Maine, Times,* September 8, 1906.

24. *American Federationist,* December 1906, pp. 970-973.

25. *Report of the Proceedings of the Twenty-Sixth Annual Convention of the American Convention of the American Federation of Labor,* 1906, pp. 183-204.

26. Gompers to President Woodrow Wilson, March 14, 1913; Wilson to Gompers, March 17, 1913.

27. *Report of the Executive Council of the American Federation of Labor to the 34th Annual Convention of the American Federation of Labor,* 1914, p. 1.

28. *Report of Proceedings of the Thirty-First Annual Convention of the American Federation of Labor,* 1911, pp. 76-77, 287.

29. Gompers to Frey, August 31, 1913, in folder 138 of the Frey papers in the manuscript division of the Library of Congress.

30. *Report of Proceedings of the Thirty-Third Annual Convention of the American Federation of Labor,* 1913, p. 299; *Ibid., Thirty-Fourth Annual Convention,* 1914, p. 466.

31. Milton J. Nadworny, *Scientific Management and the Unions* (Cambridge, Massachusetts Harvard University Press, 1955) examines in detail the response of organized labor to Scientific Management.

XIX

Immigration, Negro Labor, and the A. F. of L.

CHINESE IMMIGRATION

The immigration question first came before the A. F. of L. in 1881, with the demand for restricting the importation of contract laborers and stopping the inflow of Chinese settlers to the United States. Later the A. F. of L. also favored more severe restrictions upon non-Oriental immigration.

Agitation against the Chinese began in California prior to the Civil War, and was based upon a combination of economic and racial dogmas. The California legislature as early as 1855 tried to restrict the landing of Chinese immigrants in that state. This was, of course, prevented by the United States Supreme Court as an encroachment upon the exclusive right of the Federal government to regulate foreign commerce. The latent hostility toward the Chinese could readily be stirred into open violence by demagogues, especially in periods of unemployment. The sandlots agitation of San Francisco, led by Dennis Kearney in the late 1870's, is one of the more notable instances of the power of the agitators against Oriental labor.[1]

While there were undoubtedly racial aspects to the agitation against the Chinese, the basic objection of labor leaders was to the competition of Chinese workers in the labor market. That they undercut native and other immigrant workers, and that their living standards and demands were lower than white workers', there can be no doubt. Testifying before a Senate committee investigating labor conditions in 1883, Adolph Strasser, the head of the Cigar Makers' International Union, claimed that eight thousand Chinese workers were employed in cigar-making in California. "At one time," he testified, "there were only 25 cigar-makers left on the Pacific Coast or in San Francisco, all the rest having been driven out by the cheap labor of these imported coolies."[2]

The first convention of the reorganized Federation in 1886 protested against the evasion of the Chinese exclusion act through the intervention of the courts of the United States, and declared its "full accord with the workingmen of the Pacific Coast in the fierce struggle for existence to which they are subjected by reason of competition with Chinese." The convention also demanded "rigid enforcement of the laws . . . to prohibit Chinese immigration, and the passage of such further laws by Congress as may be necessary to effectually prevent the use of the Courts, as a back door to admit such immigration."[3] These policies had earlier been enunciated by the conventions of the preceding Federation of Organized Trades and Labor Unions.

Chinese immigration continued to be a source of concern and protest by officers and members of the unions affected by the competition of Chinese workers. In 1887 the San Francisco Cigar Makers' local union not only protested against the "immense number of Chinese landed on fraudulent certificates," but charged that "hundreds of Chinese girls are brought here for the purpose of prostitution." The convention reiterated the earlier views of the A. F. of L. for more severe restrictions upon the entry of Chinese into the United States.[4] The economic grounds for that attitude were stated clearly by Gompers earlier in 1894 when he declared:

The basic purpose of all legislation of the United States relating to exclusion of Chinese persons has been to save the working classes of this Republic from competition with Chinese laborers. Legislation has not been directed against persons because they are subjects of the Emperor of China, but because of Chinese blood and status of laborers. Therefore, if the policy of exclusion is to be continued for the purpose that gives it existence, the acquisition of the Philippine Islands, largely populated as they are by Chinese persons and persons of Chinese descent, should not militate against our policy of protecting our people against the evil effect of Chinese invasion. There is no antipathy on the part of American workmen to Chinese because of their nationality, but a people . . . who allow themselves to be barbarously tyrannized over in their own country, and who menace the progress, the economic and social standing of the workers of other countries, cannot be fraternized with.[5]

The same view is reiterated by the Executive Council. In a letter to President Theodore Roosevelt, the Council said:

Mr. President: we need not remind you of the evil of Chinese competition, but it may be well to suggest that there is nothing which the working people understand so well, there is nothing upon which we are so united, and there is no question upon which we will be so capable of distinguishing between the chaff and the wheat, as on this question. We realize it means bread, butter, reproduction, life and we have faith that you will take such steps as you consistently can to avert from us and our civilization this pending danger.[6]

Unemployment and depressions would inevitably heighten the opposition of organized labor to the inflow of new workers. While all new immigrants tended to compete with those already in the United States, the much sharper difference in the standards of living of Chinese workers, the differences in their cultural background, sharpened the opposition to them. Urging action to retain restrictions upon Chinese immigration, Gompers remarked that the "appalling sight is witnessed of millions of our fellow men and women actually idle and literally without the means of sustaining life. If at any time the flood gates of immigration should be opened, certainly in the presence of such an awful crisis, wisdom, patriotism, statesmanship and humanity forbid the step."[7]

In 1902, the A. F. of L. issued *Chinese Exclusion: Meat vs. Rice,* which contained statements on Chinese immigration from a number of sources, including newspaper articles, books, and pamphlets, writers, military men, and diplomats, the head of the California Bureau of Labor Statistics, and the Special Committee of the Board of Supervisors of the City and County of San Francisco appointed to investigate Chinatown in 1885. Some of the material dealt with living conditions of the Chinese, and attacked their moral standards. Testimony was cited that Chinese women had been enslaved and forced into prostitution. It undoubtedly contained statements that were unfair and overdrawn.[8]

In retrospect the pamphlet of the Federation favoring Chinese exclusion is certainly a biased portrayal of Chinese civilization and Chinese character, but it was not far from the general picture held by virtually all groups in the American community at the time. When one examines the argument of the American Federation of Labor, it does not appear unduly extreme. There is no doubt that it could have been said of the Chinese in 1900 that they "live more cheaply; they send their money out of the country to China; most of them have no intention of remaining in the United States, and they do not adopt American manners, but live in colonies, and not after the American fashion." The argument of the American Federation of Labor was that the Chinese worker was an aid toward reducing the standards of the American laborer. The Federation, by collecting news reports and underwriting their authenticity, and even more their typicality, was guilty of stimulating prejudice against the Chinese. Yet, while not exculpating the authors of their responsibility, one must consider the time and circumstances under which the pamphlet was issued.

The American Federation of Labor reiterated its opposition to Chinese immigration on a number of other occasions. It made

no pretense that the exclusion of Chinese can be defended upon a high ideal, ethical ground, but we insist that it is our essential duty to maintain and preserve our physical condition and standard of life and civilization, and thus to assure us the opportunity for the development of our intellectual and moral character. Self-preservation has always been regarded as the first law of nature. It is a principle and a necessity from which we ought not and must not depart. Surely, America's workmen have enough to contend with, have sufficient obstacles confronting them in their struggle to maintain themselves in their humanizing movement for a higher and a better life, without being required to meet the enervating, killing, underselling, and underliving competition of that nerveless, wantless people, the Chinese.[9]

EUROPEAN IMMIGRATION

In 1883 the Federation of Organized Trades and Labor Unions demanded the enactment of laws by Congress to "prevent the importation of all foreign laborers under contract."[10] For a time the leaders of the Federation believed that such legislation would adequately meet the needs of the workers of the country, but they frequently protested the lax enforcement of this law.[11]

At the convention of 1891 the issue was discussed on another level. There was not only a protest against the conduct of the shipping companies and the "wily speculator" who "stimulate unnecessary and unhealthy immigration," but it was argued that immigration "is an efficient means by which effete institutions of some of the European countries are perpetuated, and thus economical, political and social reforms postponed or avoided."[12] The convention took no action on the recommendation by Gompers that some "regulation and restriction" of immigration was necessary. The convention would not go beyond asking that legislation be enacted to restrain and restrict artificially stimulated immigration and that all contract and assisted immigrants be prevented from coming into the United States.[13]

As a matter of fact, the Executive Council had refused to endorse, by a vote of four to one with Gompers voting with the majority, McGuire's proposal for a suspension of immigration for one year. The Council did approve legislation authorizing the President of the United States to suspend all immigration into the United States whenever the needs and interests of the United States warranted such action.[14] It was also the position of Gompers that "organized labor of this country had no desire to keep out desirable immigrants who come here of their own volition, but emphatically protested against the importation of undesirable immigrants in the shape of contract laborers, and look to the next Congress to amend the law so that it will be more difficult to violate and easier to convict all the violators."[15] This letter, in fact, reflected the attitude of most of the delegates, and it was not until 1896, after the return of Gompers to the presidency, that the issue was again seriously considered.

Gompers alluded to several restrictive bills before Congress, and declared the convention could not be neutral. A special committee, of which McGuire and Lennon were members, recommended the endorsement of the Lodge-Corliss bill, providing for an educational test for immigrants. The recommendations opposed "extreme measures of restriction" as "contrary to the spirit of our time and the welfare of our country," and favored stricter enforcement of present measures to guard against entrance of criminal and pauper elements, punishment for violators of the alien contract law, and stricter qualifications for naturalization. The recommendations were opposed by leading trade unionists, and the matter was referred to the Executive Council with a requirement that it report back to the next convention on the issue.[16]

At the following convention in 1897, it was reported that the organizations which polled their members on immigration, in compliance with the instructions of the convention of 1896, reported a majority favoring restrictions. The committee of the convention considering the question favored mild restrictions on "the lines of the educational test," and opposed suspension of immigration for five years as proposed in one of the resolutions.[17]

In 1900 the Federation refused to endorse restrictions upon immigration, rejecting a resolution which would have required the Executive Council to devise a bill for this purpose.[18] The A. F. of L. made the first concession to restriction by its endorsement of an educational requirement. It was believed that such a requirement would

be beneficial to the more desirable classes of immigrants, as well as to ourselves. It is good for them, no less than for us, to diminish the number of that class which by reason of its lack of intelligence, is slowest to appreciate the value of organization, and furnishes the easiest victims of the padrones, and the unscrupulous employer. It is good for them as well as for us to raise the average intelligence of the Republic. . . . And even the countries from which the immigrants come may be spurred, by the standard which we set up, to provide better facilities for the education of their people, to the profit of those who remain at home, as well as for those who come to us.[19]

The American Federation of Labor's attitude toward immigration was influenced by the large number of immigrants coming to the United States.

[Advocacy of] exclusion was not prompted by any assumption of superior virtue over our foreign brothers. We disavow for American organized labor the holding of any vulgar or unworthy prejudice against the foreigner. We recognize the noble possibilities in the poorest of the children of the earth who come to us from European lands. . . . It is not on account of their assumed inferiority, or through any pusilanimous contempt for their abject poverty, that, most reluctantly, the lines have been drawn by America's workingmen against the indiscriminate admission of aliens to this country. It is simply a case of self-preservation of the American working classes.[20]

John Mitchell, another leader of the American Federation of Labor, argued:

The American wage earner, be he native or immigrant, entertains no prejudice against his fellow from other lands; but . . . our workmen believe and contend that their labor should be protected against the competition of an induced immigration comprised largely of men whose standards and ideals are lower than our own. The demand for the exclusion of Asiatics and Hindus, is based solely upon the fact that, as a race, their standard of living is extremely low and their assimilation by Americans impossible. The American wage-earner is not an advocate of the principle of indiscriminate exclusion which finds favor in some quarters, and he is not likely to become an advocate of such a policy unless he is driven to this extreme as a matter of self-preservation.[21]

Mitchell pointed to the tariff on manufacture and argued that American workers should similarly be protected against unreasonable competition. He pointed to the following advertisement in a Pittsburgh, Pennsylvania, newspaper: "Men Wanted, Tinners, catchers, and helpers, to work in open shops. Syrians, Poles and Roumanians preferred. Steady employment and good wages to men willing to work. Fare paid and no fees charged."[22]

While Gompers was ready to argue that the protection of American workers against Oriental immigration involves "the larger question of racial preservation," he always returned to the basic economic point that Oriental workers "have driven white workers out, have established conditions and wages that are incompatible with American standards of work and life."[23]

The attitude of the A. F. of L. toward the immigrant may also be derived from the Federation's efforts to protect him against discriminatory legislation. Gompers protested against a rider to the "Urgent Deficiency Bill," which would have withheld protection from alien laborers employed in construction of the Panama Canal and in the Canal Zone under the estatutory limitations of hours of service which applied to other laborers and mechanics. Gompers claimed that such action would sweep aside a principle enunciated as early as 1868, arguing that no one could assume that a work day longer than eight hours in the "torrid zone" could "be wise, economic or humane." He declared:

It is essential that a longer work day should not apply in a territory under a burning sun and in a miasmic atmosphere. [In answering the argument that the provision applied to alien laborers, and that therefore, American need not concern themselves, he said] . . . such distinction can have no place in our consideration, for in truth then, the present eight-hour law should not apply to alien laborers who are now employed by the government or on work performed for the government of the United States.[24]

As restrictive measures, the A. F. of L. supported the literacy tests, and after World War I the quota laws, so as to limit the importation of foreign labor. The Executive Council, in asking the continuance of this type of legislation, pointed to the opposition of reactionary employers, paying the lowest wages, to legislation that would curtail the flow of immigrants. Among such was James A. Emery, a leading lobbyist for the National Association of Manufacturers, "who thrives on the compensation he receives from labor-baiting employers." Spokesmen for the Bethlehem Steel Company also appeared in 1923 before the Congressional Committee considering the bill, and declared that their company had to pay too high wages because of the restriction of immigration. These arguments of industry, which historically favored free immigration, undoubtedly underline the reasons for the opposition such a policy encountered from the American Federation of Labor.[25]

NEGRO WORKERS

The American Federation of Labor has always welcomed the worker into its ranks irrespective of race or religion. Not as much can be said for the affiliates, many of whom discriminated against the Negro worker and would not accept him in their ranks. When an announcement was made, at the convention of 1891, that the National, subsequently International, Association of Machinists had been organized, John B. Lennon, who was to serve as treasurer for almost thirty years, and who was always active on the Executive Council, introduced the following resolution: "That it is the sense of this convention, and it looks with disfavor upon trade unions having provisions which exclude from membership persons on account of race or color, and that we most respectfully request that the National Machinists' Union remove from their constitution such conditions, so that all machinists shall be eligible for membership."[26] The resolution was adopted by a vote of fifty-one to three. Earlier the secretary of the Journeymen Barbers' Union had complained of racial and religious discrimination, and Gompers had assured him "that much injury is done our cause by the injection of questions of nationality, race or religion. Our employers care very little what we are so long as we work cheap."[27]

This was, of course, a general statement, but the attitude on Negro workers and their rights within unions was soon given more precise definitions. In a letter to R. T. Coles, Gompers explained:

The sentiment of organized labor of the country is decidedly in favor of maintaining and encouraging the recognition of the equality between colored and white laborers, so much so that at the last convention of a national union of machinists which is particularly located in the South and which prohibited colored machinists from becoming members, the Federation resolved to call for a convention of all machinists' unions for the purpose of forming a national union which shall recognize no color line.[28]

Gompers made several attempts to strike the word "white" out of the constitution of the Machinists' Union, but "instead of treating my [Gompers] communications with respectful consideration, they have attacked me, my motives, and used such flimsy pretexts as would convince one of the uselessness of continuing the argument."[29] Gompers urged the National Association of Machinists to strike out the racial clause, "which though in itself is so objectionable and unmanly practically accomplishes no good."

Gompers visited the Philadelphia convention of the International Association of Machinists in 1893, but before he was allowed to address the delegates, the racial issue had been decided "with unseemly haste."[30] The American Federation of Labor would therefore not allow the International Association of Machinists to join its ranks, nor would it agree that the International Machinists' Union, an affiliate, would have to merge with the other organization. In a letter to the head of the International Association of Machinists, Gompers stated that the A. F. of L. "was instituted upon the idea that to the union of the trade belongs absolute jurisdiction on all matters connected with that trade. That principle is just as applicable to your Association as to any other. The recognition of this cardinal principle, however, did not deny us the right of expressing the sentiments of trade unionism against any matter involving the general interests of the labor movement."[31] Gompers then traced the history of the discussions between himself and the heads of the International Association of Machinists on the race issue. The Federation would not grant a charter until the restriction upon Negro members was eliminated. Gompers alluded to the agreement to the elimination of the word "white" from the Machinists' constitution. "It was a solemn compact and clear understanding and must be lived up to without evasion or reservation."[32]

The convention of 1894 endorsed the views of the Executive Council in declaring that the "working people must unite to organize irrespective of creed, color, sex, nationality or politics." After Gompers' defeat for the presidency in 1894, the affiliation of the International Association of Machinists was still pending. James Duncan, who acted as president for several months because of the illness of McBride, informed the International Association of Machinists:

[As] long as you have the word "white" establishing the color line as a part of your constitution either your action must be changed or your lodges and your national body must stand debarred from all affiliation with us. . . . I believe yours is the only national union, that at present, has the color line as distinctly formed, while at the same time many crafts refused to admit a colored man without having any such provision in their constitutions, the matter being left absolutely with the local unions as whether or not they admit colored applicants.[33]

The International Association of Machinists for many years followed exactly the procedure suggested by Duncan. It is unfair to suggest that Duncan was the author of the evasion, for the national and international unions wishing to discriminate on the basis of race or color had themselves hit upon that method. Nevertheless, Duncan's acquiescence in the evasion of the principle of racial equality in organizing placed the sanction of the highest acting officer upon a reprehensible practice which subsequently was adopted by many other national and international unions. The A. F. of L. subsequently allowed unions to retain discrimination clauses, although the A. F. of L., as distinct from its affiliates, was never guilty of such practices.

At the orders of the Executive Council George L. Norton, a Negro organizer, was sent to New Orleans in the spring of 1892. Soon there were inquiries and complaints from white members of the A. F. of L. unions. Gompers instructed that he not try to organize any white laborers if they showed any objection to him on account of his color. In his letter Gompers cited the need

to address you upon a subject which is of an exceedingly delicate nature and one which probably will hurt me more to speak of then you even to read, for you must be aware of the fact that so far as I am concerned I never have made distinction between the white and black man in the matter of our identity of interests and the necessity of organizing and bringing them together in one fold. . . . If I believed for a moment that race prejudice could be overcome I would certainly extend your authority to all, but I am satisfied that any other course than the one suggested would only intensify the feeling and bring about results opposite to what we may desire and hope for.[34]

The following day Gompers again wrote:

It is because of this that I wrote you in the strain that I did yesterday, and it hurts me very much to be compelled to ask you to exercise greater discretion and not run counter to the men who have these prejudices, and possibly in that way obviate rather than intensify the feeling of bitterness. In any union which has sufficiently advanced in their conception of the identity of interests of labor regardless of color, you are fully authorized to proceed, but in those cases where it would hurt yourself, the colored workmen, the white workmen, as well as the general interests of the American Federation of Labor, I kindly suggest to you be very discreet and allow our agitation and time to work the desired changes.[35]

Obviously a white organizer in New Orleans had complained to Gompers about Norton, and Gompers informed him that Norton had been appointed at the suggestion of the Executive Council. Gompers nevertheless urged that the two men confer, and an effort be made to organize Negro workers. Acknowledging that there "is no necessity to run counter to the social distinctions made," Gompers pointed out that

The wage workers ought to bear in mind that unless they help to organize the colored man, they will of necessity compete with the workmen and be antagonistic to them and their interests. The employer will certainly take advantage of this condition and do all they can to even stimulate the race prejudice. In many cases where the race prejudice cannot be utilized, national or religious prejudices are harped upon and brought into play. As a man whom I have every reason to believe you are, serious, earnest and honest in the desire to see our fellow wage-workers improve their condition, I ask you to examine into this question more closely to see whether I am not right. View it in a common sense manner. Start out the investigation not with the old prejudices that you may have heard from infancy, but study it in the light of the historical struggles of the people of all nations, and you will find that I am right.[36]

Gompers took the position that the A. F. of L. did not compel its international affiliates to accept colored workmen, any more than it compelled its affiliates to accept those of any other race or nationality. The A. F. of L. opposed, however, the barring of colored workers because they were colored. "If a man or set of men array themselves for any cause against the interests of the workers, their organizations have the right to say their membership is barred. It should be at the wrongdoer against labor; it should not be a nationality or race against whom the doors are barred."[37] However, the American Federation later admitted internationals which barred Negroes by constitutional amendment.[38]

The position of the Federation was not an easy one. Fearful of allowing too many unions to exist outside its fold, it faced the dilemma of losing a number of internationals which would not affiliate if compelled to eliminate their racial clauses or to eliminate discrimination against the Negro in their ritual. In 1909, the Federation admitted both the Brotherhood of Railway and Steamship Clerks and the Brotherhood of Railway Carmen, both of which openly and specifically discriminated against Negro workers. "Presumably the belief had come to prevail that it was wiser to attempt to purge a union of racial antipathy after admitting it to fellowship, than to risk its loss by demanding repentance as a condition of affiliation."[39]

Prejudice against the Negro was widespread, and the question was whether organizations of labor could be set up in the South if the leaders insisted upon retaining white and Negro workers in the same union. In urging acceptance of the Negro into the union, Gompers informed one of his organizers that there was

no sentiment . . . about the matter connected with the Negro laborers whether they be molders or other workers. I do not [he argued] for a moment entertain the belief that by our simple declaration that we shall make friends of the Negro laborer. Their previous condition, their former absolute dependence upon their master (and now their employer) have deprived them of learning that it is necessary for them to rely upon themselves and upon each other, but I am confident that organized workingmen will take a more liberal view of the situation, or rather a more practical view, that the Negro workmen will to a very much greater extent make common cause with us in our struggles . . . I beg of you to believe that in this matter I strip myself absolutely from all sentimental considerations and base it upon what I am confident will best serve the interests of labor to help, though it may be slow and gradual, in the solution of this great problem.[40]

Despite the efforts of the A. F. of L., unions in Southern communities would not accept Negroes as members. The Federation was then faced with the question of whether it would devise some method to meet the situation, destroy its organizations in the South, or encourage the creation of a "purely" Southern labor movement. Some of the internationals faced the same problem during this period. When some of the Southern locals protested against the admission of Negroes, President Huber of the Carpenters' Union declared: "We are banded together in a grand Brotherhood for the purpose of elevating the conditions of our entire craft, regardless of color, nationality, race or creed. Prejudice on these lines, racial, has no standing in the labor movement, and we cannot consistently deny admittance in our organization to any man because he belongs to the African race." Huber denounced the discrimination against the Negro by some locals as "discreditable to our Brotherhood" and demanded that the practice be stopped.[41] The same problem was faced by the Brotherhood of Painters and Decorators, and Secretary M. P. Carrick lamented the feeling against the Negro worker who, he argued, was a good union man.[42] Yet the two organizations were forced by the insistence of their Southern membership to establish separate locals in some communities. In fact, *The Carpenter* was for months flooded with bitter denunciations of President Huber's views.

Gompers reported the difficulty the A. F. of L. faced in the refusal of locals to accept colored members, and the failure of city central bodies in the south to seat delegates from Negro locals. The solution devised by the Federation was to permit the organization of separate locals of Negro workers and separate city central bodies. At the same time Gompers declared: "I am free to say that I should prefer that there be unity of organization as well as unity of purpose."[43] Neither Gompers nor the other leaders considered this solution, forced upon them by circumstances, as felicitous, but unless they had been ready to surrender the organizations of the South, they had to accept the compromise. Gompers declared at the same convention:

Realizing the necessity for the unity of the wage-earners of our country, the American Federation of Labor has upon all occasions declared that trade unions should open their portals to all wage-workers, irrespective of creed, color, sex, or politics. Nothing has transpired in recent years which has called for a change of our declared policy upon this question; on the contrary, every evidence tends to confirm us in this conviction; for, even if it were not a matter of principle, self-preservation would prompt the workers to organize intelligently, and to make common cause.[44]

Whatever its own view, the Federation could not determine the admittance policies of the autonomous unions; as long as they met the other formal requirements of the A. F. of L.,[44] the latter could not inquire into the conduct of its affiliates. To the extent that the Federation could help to organize Negro workers, it sought to do so. In 1902 Gompers expressed his gratification that the colored workers of Richmond, Virginia, were becoming affiliated with the labor movement. During this time, he inquired of Secretary William Dobson of the Bricklayers' and Masons' International Union, then not affiliated with the A. F. of L., whether he would grant a charter to a local union of colored bricklayers "or whether charter should be granted by the American Federation of Labor."[45]

When the question of organizing colored firemen was raised, Gompers wrote to F. P. Sargent, the head of the Brotherhood of Locomotive Firemen, and expressed the hope that "some action may be taken for the interests of the colored firemen, as well as for the interests of the Brotherhood as regards the relation of the colored firemen to your organization."[46]

Gompers insisted that Negro workers must be organized "in order that they may be in a position to protect themselves and in some way feel an interest in our organized white workmen or we shall unquestionably have their undying enmity." He advised that, where the color line is sharply drawn, "it would perhaps be best to first form local unions of colored workers, and then have a central body composed of those organizations."[47] There was, of course, a question of Negro organizers. Much of the activity of the Federation in the first two decades was carried on by volunteers. When a Negro applied for a commission as organizer in St. Louis, the Executive Council, as was customary in such circumstances, ordered a check of the applicant's background and qualifications. When the St. Loius Trade and Labor Council refused an endorsement the A. F. of L. automatically denied the credentials.[48]

The method of getting approval of the locality was always followed where an individual requested that he be given credentials. Whenever a question arose about Negro workers being refused entry into an international union, the A. F. of L. usually offered a federal local union as a substitute.[49] Gompers believed that the Negro was a good and loyal union man, and he regarded the Article of the A. F. of L. constitution which provided for separate locals and central bodies of Negro workers as a necessity only because integrated locals and central bodies were not found possible. He denounced efforts to deprive Negroes of jobs and deny them a right to join a union.[50]

The Federation evolved the policy of itself organizing workers denied membership by affiliated internationals. Such a policy did not meet the problem, for it frequently meant that the Negro would be denied the expert guidance and leadership built up by the unions operating in given jurisdictions. However, without power to enforce its dicta, the Federation was faced with the choice of ignoring the problem publicly, and trying to win the unions over to a fairer and juster racial policy. Of course, the amount of interest the Federation would show in breaking down the barriers for Negro workers was always influenced by conditions. Yet, the record shows that the Federation, as distinct from it affiliates, was always anxious to organize the Negro, and did so whenever possible.[51]

Gompers' constant reiteration of his plea for organizing Negro workers into unions was later shown to have been not only morally correct, but wise even from the most narrow organizational point of view. The large northward migration of Negro workers during World War I made their recruitment into unions a vital necessity. The request for organizing of Negro workers came before the Buffalo convention in 1917, and the issue was referred to the Executive Council.[52] Leaders of Negro organizations became more vocally critical of the discrimination and neglect of the thousands of Negro workers. Early in 1918 a group of Negro leaders appealed to the A. F. of L. for greater efforts to bring the Negro workers into the organization of labor. John R. Shillady, secretary of the National Association for the Advancement of Colored People; Fred Moore, editor of the New York *Age;* Emmet J. Scott, special assistant to the Secretary of War; Thomas Jesse Jones, educational director of the Phelps Stokes Fund; and Eugene Kincle Jones, secretary of the National Urban League, appealed to the Executive Council for greater organizing efforts among Negro workers.

A meeting of the committee and the Executive Council was arranged. Speaking for the Council, Gompers tried to clarify the position of the A. F. of L. He pointed to the welcome always given to Negro workers by the A. F. of L. He explained the issuance of separate charters as a concession, and declared that he was opposed to the practice on principle. While he did not regard separate unions on racial grounds as desirable, he believed it was at the time, the only way in which unions could have been established in the South. He then pointed to the limits of the Federation's power.

Subsequently the committee presented several proposals which it believed would facilitate the organization of Negro workers by A. F. of L. unions. Most important, the committee wanted a statement that would clarify the position of the Federation on the race issue.[53] In addition, the committee recommended that a Negro organizer be employed by the A. F. of L., and that the Council meet with the committee for periodic consultation. The Council did not accept the suggestions, but it indicated that the cooperation of Negro leaders would be welcomed in the future.

In the meantime, the failure of the international unions to organize the Negro wage earner was to react unfavorably upon the activities of many of the organizations of labor. World War I had accelerated the migration of Negro workers to northern industrial plants, and the discriminatory attitudes of some unions were now more serious, both to the Negro workers and to their white members.

At the convention of 1919, two resolutions on the organization of Negro workers were submitted. One of them decried the failure of unions to admit Negro workers, which had made it "possible for the unscrupulous employer to exploit the one against the other to mutual disadvantage of both." The other resolution requested a charter be issued for colored workers. As Negro workers were widely distributed in industry and in skill, the issuance of such a charter would have been, according to the resolutions committee, a trespass upon the rights and jurisdictions of many unions. The convention therefore recommended that the organization of Negro workers be given special attention by the Executive Council.[54] The failure of some of the unions of the American Federation of Labor to accept Negroes for membership undoubtedly offered employers a prolific source of strikebreakers. The head of the National Committee for Organizing the Steel and Iron Workers estimated that there were 30,000 Negro strikebreakers employed during the great steel strike of 1919. John Fitzpatrick found that the "Northern Negro is alive to the situation and cannot be used to any great extent, but the Southern Negro is brutally exploited and has no real knowledge of the situation in which he is being used."[55]

At the convention of 1920, a resolution urging the elimination of racial lines in the constitutions of the Brotherhood of Railway Clerks was submitted. The convention voted to request the elimination of such clauses from the constitution.[56] However, the request was not granted, and in 1921 two resolutions protesting the discrimination against Negro workers were submitted to the convention. The law committee disapproved of these resolutions because "the American Federation of Labor cannot interfere with the trade autonomy of affiliated national or international unions." Considerable criticism followed the presentation of this report, and Gompers stated that the A. F. of L. had, itself, always urged the organization of Negro workers. "That is the policy and the principle of the American Federation of Labor, but it cannot enforce that declaration upon the affiliated international unions if those international unions decline or refuse to adopt them."[57]

The convention voted to instruct the Executive Council to call a meeting of the organizations affected, with a view toward finding a solution. Gompers attempted to have the unions in question act on the recommendations of the convention, and he was unable, for a time, to get a response to his communications.

On July 7, August 3, and November 3, 1921, Gompers wrote asking for a meeting, but his communications were not acknowledged until December 10th. Martin F. Ryan, the head of the Brotherhood of Railway Carmen, perhaps summarized the difficulties of the A. F. of L. in trying to protect the rights of Negroes.

Brother Gompers [Ryan wrote] I may say for your information that the question of admitting the Negro to membership in our Brotherhood has been a matter of consideration, discussion and controversy for a number of years. Personally I have been very much in favor of the adoption by our Brotherhood of some plan or scheme that would admit the Negro to membership, and with this thought in mind I submitted a very strong recommendation in my report to our Convention.

Ryan's recommendation was rejected, and instead the convention of the Brotherhood of Railway Carmen voted to organize Negro workers in separate locals which were to "be under the jurdisdiction of the nearest white local, and shall be represented in any meeting of Joint Protective Board, Federation meeting or convention where delegates may be seated, by white men." Under those conditions Negroes, Ryan declared, would be entitled to all "rights and privileges otherwise guaranteed by our organization, including out-of-work stamps, death and total disability benefits." In view of the action of his union, Ryan was disinclined to attend a conference for eliminating discrimination against the Negro.[58] Nor were other unions more amenable.

The settlement was of course unsatisfactory from many points of view, but Gompers was not able to arrange a conference of other unions which discriminated against Negroes. Yet he always hoped that the relaxation of barriers would be a first step to greater rights. This is obvious from an agreement he helped to devise between the Machinists, Blacksmiths, Boilermakers, Electricians, and the Firemen and Oilers' unions, under which the latter agreed to admit colored helpers of the above crafts to its organization whenever the above International unions did not themselves accept Negro workers to membership. The A. F. of L., which had always organized Negro helpers in federal labor unions, was asked to transfer such locals to the International Brotherhood of Firemen and Oilers. The various shop craft organizations agreed to negotiate agreements for helpers in their respective trades. Gompers' suggestion "that in view of the temporary character of the arrangement" the Firemen and Oilers' Union agree to transfer Negro helpers whenever the respective craft international would accept them, illustrates his views.[59]

REFERENCES

1. Ira B. Cross, *A History of the Labor Movement in California* (Berkley, California: University of California Press, 1935), p. 129.
2. *Report of Committee of the United States Senate Upon the Relations of Labor and Capital* (Washington: Government Printing Office, 1885), I, p. 452.
3. *Report of the Proceedings of the First Annual Convention of the American Federation of Labor,* 1886, p. 21.
4. *Report of the Proceedings of the Second Annual Convention of the American Federation of Labor,* 1887, pp. 23, 30.
5. *Report of Proceedings of the · Fourteenth Annual Convention of the American Federation of Labor,* 1894, p. 70.
6. *American Federationist,* June, 1902, p. 333.
7. Gompers to Adlai E. Stevenson, April 14, 1894.
8. *Some Reasons for Chinese Exclusion: Meat Vs. Rice* (Washington: American Federation of Labor, n. d.).
9. *Report of Proceedings of the Twenty-Fifth Annual Convention of the American Federation of Labor,* 1905, p. 31.
10. *Report of the Third Annual Session of the Federation of Organized Trades and Labor Unions of the United States and Canada,* 1883, p. 2.
11. *The Boston Daily Globe,* December 12, 1889; *Report of Proceedings of the Tenth Annual Convention of the American Federation of Labor,* 1890, pp. 24-25.
12. *Report of Proceedings of the Eleventh Annual Convention of the American Federation of Labor,* 1891, p. 14.
13. *Report of the Proceedings of the Twelfth Annual Convention of the American Federation of Labor,* 1892, pp. 14, 28.
14. *Minutes of Executive Council,* January 16, 1893.
15. Letter to Senator David B. Hill, chairman of the Senate Immigration Committee, June 23, 1893.
16. *Report of Proceedings of the Sixteenth Annual Convention of the American Federation of Labor,* 1896, pp. 99-100.
17. *Report of Proceedings of the Seventeenth Annual Convention of the American Federation of Labor,* 1897, pp. 96-97, 103.
18. *Report of Twentieth Annual Convention of the American Federation of Labor,* 1900, pp. 148-149.
19. *American Federationist,* December, 1902, p. 935.
20. Samuel Gompers "Immigration, Up to Congress," *American Federationist,* January, 1911, pp. 2-3.

21. John Mitchell, "Protect the Workman," *American Federationist,* January, 1911, p. 7.

22. *Ibid.,* p. 7.

23. Gompers to Senator Ellison D. Smith, May 1, 1914.

24. Gompers to President Theodore Roosevelt, February 10, 1906. In view of the attitude of the A. F. of L. on immigration, the article by Professor Arthur Mann, "Gompers and the Irony of Racism," *Antioch Review,* Summer of 1953, seems strange. Written with unacademic venom, the article attributes to Gompers and the A. F. of L., racism and anti-foreignism. Professor Mann exhibits little understanding of the problems and attitudes of trade unionism, nor did he base his article upon an adequate examination of the documentary material. Trade unions face certain types of problems in the labor market, and the English Miners' Union, whose secretary is a Communist and many of its leaders Socialists, opposed the use of Polish miners and the importation of Italians for work in the mines, even though serious shortages of manpower existed. These are manifestations of self-interest and not racism. On a number of occasions, the A. F. of L. made its position clear that its attitude was not based upon racism, but economic necessity. The pamphlet *Meat Vs. Rice,* attributed by Professor Mann to Gompers, was not written by him, but it was issued by the American Federation of Labor. Moreover, it is largely a compilation of material from public sources. Professor Mann attributes responsibility for an article written in the *American Federationist* in 1895 to "his journal." Professor Mann should have known that Gompers had been defeated in 1894, and the magazine was edited by John McBride. In fact, Gompers opposed exclusion of non-Oriental immigrants in 1894. Professor Mann fails to mention that the majority of the unions voting on immigration in 1896 voted for some kind of restriction. The entire article is of a caliber which one would not ordinarily notice, were it not that a reputable historian, Richard Hoffstadter, *The Age of Reform* (New York: Alfred A. Knopf, 1952), p. 178, uses this screed as a basis for his description of the A. F. of L.'s policy on immigration.

25. *Report of Proceedings of the Forty-Third Annual Convention of the American Federation of Labor,* 1923, p. 38.

26. *Report of the Proceedings of the Tenth Annual Convention of the American Federation of Labor,* 1890, p. 29.

27. Gompers to the Secretary of the Journeymen Barbers' Union, July 30, 1890.

28. Gompers to R. T. Coles, April 28, 1891.

29. Gompers to Harry E. Easton, April 30, 1891.

30. Gompers to the Executive Council, May 17, 1892.

31. Gompers to James O'Connell, November 3, 1893.

32. *Ibid.*

33. Duncan to W. S. Davis, April 1, 1895.

34. Gompers to George L. Norton, May 16, 1892.

35. Gompers to Norton, May 17, 1892.

36. Gompers to John M. Callahan, May 17, 1892.

37. Samuel Gompers, "Why Affiliate with the Federation," *American Federationist,* July, 1896, p. 103.

38. Herbert R. Northrup, *Organized Labor and the Negro* (New York: The MacMillan Company, 1944), pp. 10-11.

39. Sterling D. Spero and Abram L. Harris, *The Black Worker* (New York: Columbia University Press, 1931), p. 89.

40. Gompers to W. S. Grisson, April 16, 1897.

41. *The Carpenter,* January 1903, p. 3.

42. M. P. Carrick to Gompers, March 5, 1903.

43. Gompers to James E. Porter, May 23, 1900, June 18, 1900.

44. *American Federationist,* April 1901, pp. 118-120.

45. Gompers to James Brown, June 13, 1902; to William Dobson, July 16, 1902.

46. Gompers to C. W. Heinke, May 17, 1902; to P. F. Sargent, May 17, 1902.

47. Gompers to J. A. Summers, February 5, 1903; to David U. Williams, February 16, 1903.

48. Gompers to J. B. Powell, February 12, 1901; Gompers to David Kreyling, August 3, 1901; Kreyling to Gompers, August 12, 1901.

49. Minutes of Executive Council, October 16, 1912; Gompers to George Hull, June 1, 1911.

50. Gompers to W. H. Paul, May 31, 1911; Gompers to Booker T. Washington, February 16, 1912; Minutes of Executive Council, January 16, 1914.

51. Bernard Mandel, "Samuel Gompers and the Negro Workers 1886-1914," *Journal of Negro History,* January 1955, attempts to portray Gompers as a race baiter. Written from the Marxist-Leninist point of view, the author does not show much knowledge of the internal politics of the Federation, the limits to the power of the President or of the Executive Council. Of course, the A. F. of-L. could always issue ukases, but there was and is not today any means for compelling obedience to these orders. Gompers had too much experience to try to impose his views upon unwilling organizations, nor did he believe a frontal attack was the most effective method for gaining results. Yet he always tried, frequently without success, to win the unions over to a more enlightened and humane policy.

52. Minutes of Executive Council, February 10, 1918.

53. Spero and Harris, *op. cit.,* pp. 108-109.

54. *Report of Proceedings of the Nineteenth Annual Convention of the American Federation of Labor,* 1919, pp. 305-306.

55. John Fitzpatrick to Gompers, March 30, 1920.

56. *Report of Proceedings of the Fortieth Annual Convention of the American Federation of Labor,* 1920, pp. 351-352.

57. *Report of Proceedings of the Forty-First Annual Convention of the American Federation of Labor,* 1921, pp. 431-433.

58. Martin Ryan to Gompers, December 10, 1921 is the source of the quotations. Gompers to Executive Council, December 21, 1921.

59. Gompers to Executive Council, Dec. 21, 1921.

XX

Pan-American Labor and the Mexican Revolution

Porto Rico

Because of the direct relations between Porto Rico and the United States in this century, the problems of Porto Rican labor have occupied a special place in the American Federation of Labor. In 1899, the convention of the A. F. of L. declared that "Porto Rico has by armed force been conquered and annexed." In the following year, Santiago Iglesias of the *Federacion Libre of Porto Rico* appealed for aid in organizing the workers of the Island. The convention of that year demanded that the workers of Porto Rico be granted the right to free speech and assembly, urged international unions to translate their constitutions and literature into Spanish, and voted an assessment for organizing the Porto Rican workers.[1]

Soon after the adjournment of the convention of 1900, Santiago Iglesias was appointed an organizer for the A. F. of L. in Porto Rico. Iglesias came to Washington and Gompers took him to see President Theodore Roosevelt with whom his organizing commission was discussed. The President through his secretary asked that Iglesias not be molested as long as he confined himself to organizing. Despite the request, he was arrested because he had left the jurisdiction of the court while free on his own recognizance on a charge of murder which was an outgrowth of a strike directed by Iglesias. Gompers protested to President Roosevelt, who intervened with Governor William Hunt. Nevertheless, Iglesias was sentenced to a term in prison, but the verdict was subsequently set aside by the higher courts. To encourage organization, the A. F. of L. agreed to charter any unions which its affiliated internationals refused to accept. In 1903, Gompers visited Porto Rico and encouraged the workers to join unions. The A. F. of L. at the same time demanded that Porto Ricans be granted American citizenship. Over the years, the A. F. of L.'s interest in the workers of Porto Rico has continued.

In a real sense, this interest might be regarded as an extension of its concern for workers of the United States. The A. F. of L.'s desire to help the workers of other Latin American countries build their labor

320

organizations and improve their living conditions was a manifestation of a fraternal spirit which stretched beyond the nation's boundaries and encompassed workers from other lands.

MEXICAN REVOLUTION

Even though the two movements were not too close, the American Federation of Labor showed its sympathy for the fight against tyranny in Mexico.[2] A resolution of protest against the arrest in Los Angeles in 1907 of the libertarian Mexican anarchists, Ricardo Flores Magon, Antonio I. Villarreal, Librado Rivera, and other members of the Mexican Liberal Party was presented by J. Mahlon Barnes. At the instructions from the convention, the Executive Council sought a Congressional investigation of the persecution of political refugees, and President Gompers, in a letter to President Taft, called his attention to the perversion of the instrumentalities of the American government in behalf of Mexican tyranny.[3]

During the revolution against the government of Porifiro Diaz, fear was expressed that the United States might intervene. The convention of 1912 not only declared itself for a "hands off" policy, but expressed its "cordial greetings and best wishes to the men in Mexico now struggling to abolish age-long wrongs by striking the shackles from the limbs and minds of men and women, and to abolish the present land tenure."[4]

The government of Diaz was overthrown by Francesco Madero, who sought to institute some basic reforms. Before he could even put the beginning of his program into effect, he was overthrown by Victoriano de la Huerta, who murdered both President Maderos and his Vice President. The United States government refused to recognize Huerta. Soon thereafter a successful revolt was led by the Constitutionalists, under the leadership of Venustriano Carranza. Peace was not, however, immediately restored, as one of the generals of the victorious army, Pancho Villa, now began a campaign against his former chief, Carranza. After a trying period, the revolt was suppressed, and the liberal Carranza government was able for the time being to hold power.

The Executive Council expressed its satisfaction with the Constitutionalists and hoped for a speedy termination of its campaign against its adversaries. At the same time, the Council pleaded for

humanitarian consideration even to those who have been guilty. And that in our judgment such a policy would have a tranquilizing effect, promoting the successful inauguration of the new constitutional government of Mexico and would tend to unite the people of Mexico in support of an orderly government of the country. And it is also earnestly hoped and respectfully suggested that some definite declaration be made, not only upon the lines indicated above but should be coupled with an avowal of purpose that the Constitutionalists will carry into effect a rightful and justifiable division of the lands of Mexico for the working people.[5]

What pleased the leaders of the American Federation of Labor most was the readiness of the Carranza government to grant the Mexican workers the right to organize unions. Convinced that the revolutionary government was working in the interests of labor, the Executive Council instructed Gompers to inform President Wilson of its favorable attitude. In a letter to the President, on September 22, 1915, Gompers reviewed the struggle of the Mexican people for greater freedom and a better life.

There has been going on just across our southern boundary a battle which is part of the world-old struggle for freedom [Gompers informed the President]. Although that struggle may be associated with many things that are not in accord with our ideals, yet I am sure that these things are the first crude efforts of a people long accustomed to despotism and denial of the rights of free citizens to realize ideals of freedom.

Gompers then traced the history of the successful revolt, the efforts to establish freedom, and the failure of the first revolution. Huerta, who gained power by the sword, was soon displaced by Carranza, whom Gompers regarded as the

recognized friend of the working people and the real leader of the people generally in Mexico. He has granted to the wage earners the right of organization and has secured them opportunities for carrying out the legitimate purposes of organization. He has been thoroughly in sympathy with the ideals of greater opportunity and freedom of the masses of the people. The working people have been supporting him. They have adjourned as lodges and trade unions to enlist in the Carranza army with their union officials as the officers of their regiments. . . . It is with the desire that we Americans who have so much liberty and so much opportunity should use our influence to aid those who are less fortunate, that as representative of the labor movement of America we urge upon you recognition of General Carranza as the head of the Mexican government.[6]

The statement drew a sharp criticism from Frank Duffy, a member of the Federation's Executive Council and secretary of the United Brotherhood of Carpenters and Joiners of America. At this time the "International unions" of the A. F. of L. were under severe attack by the Archbishop of Quebec, who urged Canadian Catholics to avoid those organizations and instead, join the Catholic unions of Canada. Duffy now charged that the attitude of the Archbishop was due to the Federation's support of the Carranza government, which in his words, was guilty of "terrorizing Mexico, pursuing priests and martyrizing the Sisters and causing death everywhere." Duffy demanded that the "persecution of any man or set of men, or any people or race on account of their religious faith or political beliefs" be protested. At Duffy's insistence, the Executive Council ordered an investigation of the charges of religious persecution.[7]

Yet Duffy would not admit, at least to outsiders, that the Federation had been guilty of conscious wrong-doing. In a letter to Monsignor Kelley, Duffy explained that the Federation

has done much good for the protection, betterment and advancement of the wage workers generally. We are unalterably opposed to the persecution of any one on account of his religious faith or political beliefs. In fact, religion has no standing in our movement. . . . What I mean is that religion has no part in the labor movement, neither has nationality or politics. A man in our movement is at liberty to perform his religious duties as he sees fit without hindrance from any one. If religion, nationality and party politics were allowed to be discussed in our meetings, we would be divided and that would be the end of the labor movement.[8]

Despite formal recognition of the Carranza government, relations between the United States and Mexico deteriorated. Trouble along the border, which the A. F. of L. declared was fomented by interests in the United States hostile to international peace, led to the seizure of several American soldiers by the Mexican government. Gompers, in the name of the American Federation of Labor, sent fraternal greetings to the *Casa Del Obrero Mundial,* and invited it to send a delegation to El Paso, Texas, for a meeting with representatives from the A. F. of L. Louis Morones and Salvador Gonzales were sent to meet with the Executive Council in Washington. Frank Duffy disapproved the invitations, and protested to Gompers that members of the Executive Council had not been consulted nor their advice sought.[9] Vice President Duncan urged the delegates to organize the industrial workers into unions, and begin steps for distribution of land among the peons. At the close of the meeting, the Mexican delegates were questioned on the government's policy toward religion. They denied that there had been religious persecution or interference with the right to worship. This seemed to end all opposition, for the joint statement issued by the Federation and the Mexican labor delegates was signed by all members of the Executive Council including Duffy.[10]

The statement declared that closer relations between the workers of the two countries will be a "constructive force in bringing about understanding necessary for better relations between our countries and for maintaining peace founded upon a proper regard for the rights of all." Relations between the two countries were, at the time, strained, and a general conference for developing amicable relations between the two labor movements was held to be inadvisable. Instead, a joint commission of two members was chosen to remain in Washington until the crisis passed. John Murray was chosen as the Federation's representative.

While the conference was in progress, the danger of armed intervention in Mexico by the United States became acute. Throughout the crisis period, going back to the first day of the revolution, the A. F. of L. had watched developments in Mexico with friendly understanding, always trying to mitigate the possibilities of an armed clash between the two countries. Gompers and other members of the Executive Council were in close touch with Colonel Edmundo E. Martinez, whose report Gompers placed before President Wilson. The A. F. of L. had worked hard for recognition, with much of its activity not publicly known. The friendly relations between the A. F. of L. and the national administration and President Wilson were, in this instance, fully utilized. Now the Federation saw its efforts jeopardized by this rising demand that the government intervene and force the release of the American troops imprisoned in Mexico. Gompers appealed directly to Carranza to avert this tragedy. "In the name of common justice and humanity," he said, "in the interest of a better understanding between the peoples and the governments of the United States and Mexico, for the purpose of giving them opportunity to maintain peace and avoid the horrors of war, upon the grounds of higher patriotism and love, I appeal to you to release the American soldiers held by your officers in Chihuahua." President Carranza replied promptly: "In replying to your message dated yesterday, I would state that the government in charge has ordered the liberty of the American soldiers whom the Mexican forces took as prisoners at Carrizal."[11] Upon receipt of the message, the Executive Council, then in session, expressed its sincere appreciation for the actions of the Mexican government. Later the convention directed the Executive Council to set up a Pan-American Federation of Labor with the cooperation of the unions from other Latin-American countries.

The view of the convention was in harmony with the earlier conference held between the delegates from Mexican labor and representatives of the A. F. of L. The Pan-American conference was based upon the "manifesto" issued on February 10, 1917, drafted by John Murray, which declared "no relations between the Pan-American countries can be permanent that are not based upon the will of the masses of the people and in accord with the concepts of justice. We deem it an essential step toward democracy and justice that there shall be established for the masses who have hitherto been without regular agencies for expressing their views and desires, opportunities that will enable them to have a voice in helping and determining international affairs."

In December 1917, the Pan-American Conference committee was organized, and it sought to establish a meeting ground for all bona fide labor organizations in the Latin American countries. All organizations were to be autonomous within their own countries. It was the view of the conference that the working people of the several countries should seek to gain improvement in their conditions through their use of economic power, and should concentrate upon better wages, shorter hours and improved conditions of employment, and also seek legislative enactments guaranteeing the rights of free speech, press, and assembly.[12] Gompers was also able to convince President Wilson that friendly labor in Latin America would be valuable to the United States, especially during the war. A newspaper published in English and Spanish, edited by John Murray and Canuto A. Vargas, was issued, and plans for setting up a Pan-American Federation proceeded.

Gompers was particularly anxious that the Mexican workers create an effective economic movement, that they become aware of the "power of economic organization and direct attention to common interests and problems of the workers—interests and problems which extend past national boundary lines and intermingle wherever the industrial and commercial interests of our countries extend."[13] Not only did Gompers give general advice, but in several conferences with representatives of Mexican labor he discussed "practical problems of organization and methods that might be helpful in establishing the Mexican labor movement upon a basis that will give the workers the greatest freedom for development, protection and betterment."[14]

On November 13, 1918, seventy-two delegates, forty-six from the United States, twenty-one from Mexico, and the remainder from Guatemala, El Salvador, Costa Rica, and Columbia, met at Laredo, Texas, and established the Pan American Labor Federation. Mexican labor was represented by the *Federacion Regional Obrero Mexicana* (Crom), organized at Saltillo, in March, 1918. The objectives sought were modest —the improvement in the working conditions of the workers of the United States and Latin America, and the promotion of better understanding between the peoples of the Western hemisphere. Sharp criticism was expressed by several Mexican delegates of the discrimination practiced by some American unions against Latin American workers in the United States. A demand that the American Federation of Labor aid in obtaining the release of wartime political prisoners was also made. In the end an agreement was reached upon all points of controversy, with the A. F. of L. delegation promising to seek improvement in the treatment of Mexican immigrants and justice for political prisoners in the United States. Officers of the Pan-American Federation were established in Washington, and the A. F. of L. donated several thousand dollars to maintain the various activities. John Murray was chosen English-language secretary, and Canuto A. Vargas, Spanish-language secretary. James Lord was named treasurer, and Gompers, chairman.[15]

It had been decided at the first convention that the second meeting was to be held at Panama, but because transportation facilities were not adequate, the meeting by unanimous agreement was transferred to New York City. Delegates from Peru, El Salvador, Nicaraugua, the Dominican Republic, and Mexico were present. Soon after the convention opened, Delegate Borran asked Gompers whether the resolutions adopted at the first meeting had been carried out. He was informed that the A. F. of L. had sent a delegation of five to the Paris Peace Conference, where they had tried to have incorporated in the peace treaty guarantees of human rights. After discussion of problems relating to the South American countries, the convention considered the immigration issue. A number of the Central American delegates felt strongly that the United States discriminated against foreign workers. Gompers, after his election as chairman for the ensuing term, felt it necessary for him to explain the position of the United States and of the American Federation of Labor on this question. He reviewed the history of American immigration policy:

If the workers of all countries [he informed the conference] were well organized and had established standards of life and labor commensurate with the life and standards established here, there could be and would be no objection. The doors would be thrown open and the hand of welcome and fraternity extended to all who come of their own volition. If I had the right to determine the conditions upon which immigration to the United States might be legally afforded, I would say that any man or woman—workman or workwoman who came with a good clean union card of good standing membership in the union—I would be perfectly willing to say, "Come into America," because you are fighting for the right and for standards and for life! But you cannot do that, not under the law. You cannot establish that as a condition precedent to entrance to the United States. And so far as my feeling in the matter is concerned I say that the man who is selfish enough and is ignorant enough to fail or refuse to join the union of his trade wherever he may live, is not the man about which it is necessary to so much concern ourselves.

All officers were reelected.[16]

Mexico City witnessed the third congress of the Pan-American Federation in January 1921. Delegations from the United States, Porto Rico, Mexico, the Dominican Republic, Guatamela, and El Salvador were present. The Pan-American Federation of Labor furnished a ready forum to which South and Central American representatives of labor could bring their complaints against conditions in the United States as they affected their nationals, or against the conduct of the representatives of the United States government in their native countries. Through its delegate to the convention of 1921, the Dominican Republic presented a statement of conditions prevailing in that country, then under the control of American military authorities. These complaints, on instructions of the Executive Council, were placed before the President of the United

States. Gompers outlined the complaints of the Dominican people about the importation of cheap labor, the imposition of a censorship, and the existence of a severe military rule which annulled the ordinary civil guarantees.[17] Gompers was subsequently informed by Secretary of State Robert Lansing that the censorship had been abolished, and that the Department of State "will give careful study to the present conditions."[18]

In addition to appealing to the United States government, the Executive Council of the American Federation of Labor sent a committee to investigate conditions on the spot. The committee, Peter J. Brady and Anthony McAndrew, denounced the miserable wage and working conditions prevailing in the Dominican Republic, and urged the regulation or suppression of the importation of lower-paid workers. It was the opinion of the committee that "the sugar interests should be regulated and controlled and further efforts on their part to secure additional land should be prevented at least during the military occupation of the United States."[19]

The committee outlined an affirmative program of reform which it believed was necessary for the benefit of the Dominican people, as well as for the development of a friendlier attitude towards the United States. First, employers and employees were urged to work out amicable arrangements for cooperation through their organizations; other matters called for were the establishment of an eight-hour day for the civil service employees; a wage high enough so that civil service employees could support their families and themselves in decency and comfort; the establishment of decent wages and the eight-hour day in private employment, especially in the sugar industry where wages were depressed by the importation of cheap labor; the elimination of tariffs on foods, olothing and other necessaries of life; the appointment of "fair price" committees to regulate the prices of food and other necessities; and the adoption of a compulsory education law. In addition, laws for regulating child labor and factory conditions, the recognition of the right to organize and strike, and the improvement of sanitary facilities were advocated. Finally, it was urged that American military forces be removed from the properties of the sugar planters so that they might not serve to intimidate workers. The congress, after hearing the report, expressed its approval of the work of the committee, and recommended that a telegram be sent to the President of the United States protesting against the continued occupation of the Dominican Republic.

It was the consensus of the delegates that the efforts of the A. F. of L. to prevent armed intervention by the United States had alone justified the existence of the Pan-American Federation of Labor. At the suggestion of Gompers, a resolution pledging the Pan-American Federation "to aid in maintaining the independence and autonomy of all the Pan-American countries" was adopted. The same officers, except John Murray who had died before the convention, were reelected. In place of Murray, Chester M. Wright was elected English-language secretary.[20]

The closer relations between the Latin American labor movements, especially the Mexican, and the American Federation of Labor were reflected in the efforts of the A. F. of L. to secure American recognition of the Mexican government by the government of the United States. The convention of the A. F. of L. in 1921 went on record in favor of recognition of the government of Mexico of Alvaro Obregon. Shortly after the convention several American citizens were kidnapped in Mexico. Consequently, in transmitting the views of the convention to the Secretary of State, Gompers considered it

appropriate and timely to say that these incidents in no wise change the position of the American Federation of Labor on the question of recognition. Quite the contrary, our position is strengthened, for it is easy to see the hand in these incidents of the political enemies of the Obregon Government. As long as recognition is denied to the Mexican Government, its political enemies who happily are very few in number and of no nationwide importance, will feel encouraged and emboldened in their reprehensible attempts to create trouble and embarrassment for the Obregon Government.[21]

When the United States Government appointed two commissioners to confer with representatives of the Mexican government in May 1923, James Lord, the head of the Mining Department of the American Federation of Labor, was sent by the Executive Council of the A. F. of L. to act as an observer, although officially he represented the Pan-American Labor Federation. Recognition was arranged in the fall of 1923, following which a conference between representatives of the Mexican Federation of Labor and the A. F. of L. was held at El Paso, Texas.

For Gompers, the establishment of friendly relations between the two peoples was very gratifying:

In doing so, let us hope that the European labor movement will profit by our example and likewise bend their efforts towards the establishment of the closest and most cordial relations between the European peoples. The labor movements of our respective countries, the United States and Mexico, will be glad to render any assistance within their power, not only to the labor movements of the rest of the American republics, but also to the labor movements of Europe. But in any event, the entity of our respective labor movements in the Western Hemisphere must be maintained in that autonomy and independence so necessary to their safety and well-being and to their complete freedom of action.[22]

In December 1923, the officers of the American Federation were informed that arms and ammunition were being furnished to Mexican insurgents by Americans through American ports. The State Department was immediately apprised of these activities which, Gompers was convinced, were in violation of the desires of our government. To make his position clear, he informed the State Department:

I feel strongly in regard to events in Mexico at the present time because of my desire for the triumph of the principles of democracy and because I am so abundantly confident that the choice of the Mexican people as expressed in their present government, was wise and marked for that country a striking measure of progress and attainment. I am confident that this view is shared, not only by yourself, but by all of the officers of our government and I am equally confident if there are Americans who have found opportunity to encourage the rebellious movement and to equip it with munitions of war, the practice will be stopped upon discovery.[23]

Gompers did more than appeal to the State Department. He called upon trade unionists to aid the United States government to detect gun running and smuggling of military supplies to the rebel forces headed by General de la Huerta. An appeal by the Pan-American Federation to the International Federation of Trade Unions to ferret out any shipments of arms to the Mexican revolutionaries was also made. That the activity of American labor was effective is evidenced by the attempt of the leaders of the Mexican revolt to convince the A. F. of L. that their efforts were directed only against the red influences within the Obregon government and not the government itself. The A. F. of L. did not swallow the "red bait" and, instead, denounced the duplicity of the leaders of the revolt who were playing the dual role of pretending to be radicals and at the same time appealing to foreign investors as a conservative group. Gompers refused to communicate with any of the leaders of the revolt, and proclaimed his support of the established Obregon government.[24]

While most attention was given to Mexican affairs, the Pan-American Federation, acting through its executive, was also concerned with conditions in other South and Central American countries. In the dispute between the republics of Chile and Peru over the ownership of the provinces of Tacna and Arica, the Pan-American Federation of Labor submitted a memorandum in which the hope was expressed for a satisfactory solution to this vexing border dispute.[25]

At the instructions of the 1921 convention of the Pan-American Federation of Labor, the Executive Committee also inquired from our State Department what course it planned to follow in the evacuation of American troops from the Republic of Santo Domingo. Secretary Hughes assured Gompers "that the Government of the United States will withdraw its military forces from the Dominican Republic within a period of eight months."[26]

The Pan-American Federation also raised the question with the

American government over its relations with the Republic of Nicarauga. In a letter to President Calvin Coolidge, Gompers called his attention to the policy of the Pan-American Labor Federation of aiding "in the maintenance of the independence and autonomy of all the Pan-American countries." Gompers enclosed in his letter a statement from the Nicaraguan Federation of Labor in which the United States government was charged with having supported the revolution in 1910 against the constituted government. Moreover, the document charged the United States with encouraging a "despotic dynasty under which the people are oppressed politically and economically." An investigation of conditions in Nicaragua was subsequently made during the summer of 1924 under the auspices of the Pan-American Labor Federation. A series of recommendations was made for the improvement of economic and political conditions. In the same year, the convention of the A. F. of L. criticized the machinations of "powerful groups of American captains of finance who with the sanction of Latin-American groups of scheming politicians have acquired control over the financial and natural resources of these countries."[27]

The fourth convention of the Pan-American Federation of Labor met in Mexico City. It was destined to be the last convention that Gompers was to attend, and he led a delegation of six, five of whom were members of the Executive Council. Delegations from the labor movements of Mexico, Nicaragua, Panama, Santo Domingo, and Guatemala were present when the conference opened on December 4th. A large number of resolutions on economic and political problems were adopted. One resolution urged that "the principle of self-government by free people and the principle of self-government in industry are one and identical, the first functioning through political institutions and the second through those institutions which the trade union movements have established." A resolution calling for the release of several Mexican revolutionaries serving life imprisonment as the result of the death of a member of a Texas sheriff's posse was demanded, and support for the Mexican government declared. Several resolutions dealt with problems of organization of workers, and several requested the governments of the different countries to liberalize their rules governing labor unions. A number of resolutions dealing with the relations of the American government to those of the Central American states were adopted, and the executive board directed to investigate, and if necessary take steps, to remedy the evils reported to exist.

Gompers, who presided, was unable to continue his duties through the entire congress. He became ill on December 8, 1924, and, although one of the American delegates, Matthew Woll, believed his condition was not serious, he was to die soon thereafter. Gompers was reelected president, and a new office, vice president was created; it was filled by

Louis N. Morones. James Lord, who had been treasurer from the beginning of the organization, retired on account of ill health, and Matthew Woll was elected in his place. The other officers were chosen for another term. With the death of Gompers, the Pan-American Labor Federation lost its strongest and most active supporter. For Gompers, the Pan-American Federation was a dream of the workers of the Western hemisphere united through their national autonomous trade unions for the promotion of peace and the common welfare of all countries. He was aware of the backwardness of the labor movements of many of the Latin-American countries, their primitive outlooks and their tendency to substitute rhetoric for solid organization. Yet he hoped that, despite all shortcomings, the labor movements would build a Pan-American Federation of Labor uniting the free people of the two continents around a bastion of democracy and freedom.

Gompers was succeeded in his office as head of the Pan-American Federation of Labor by William Green, who continued the policies of his predecessor. When the American Secretary of State, Frank B. Kellogg, issued a statement in 1925 which seemed likely to jeopardize the amicable relations between Mexico and the United States, Green requested from the Secretary a record of the incidents in which the Mexican government had failed to make proper indemnification for property losses of American citizens. Green expressed his serious concern "that there should be even the implication that our government would lend aid and support to a movement against the constitutional government of Mexico. It is unthinkable that our government would lend aid and support to a movement against the constitutional government of Mexico."[28]

In 1925, when there were reports that the United States government planned to lift the embargo against shipments of arms across the border, Green wrote:

The officers and members of the American Federation of Labor would view such a development with feelings of deep apprehension. We are strongly opposed to any action on the part of our Government, which would tend to cause civil war in Mexico or a break in the diplomatic relationship between the two countries. There does not seem to be sufficient reason or justification for such action at this time. It is the firm opinion of the membership of the American Federation of Labor that if the differences between the United States and Mexico cannot be settled by direct negotiation they are proper subjects for arbitration. We favor [submitting] the differences that have arisen from the application of the Land and Mineral Laws in Mexico to an impartial court of arbitration for final settlement.[29]

In addition to taking action where there were threats of intervention by the United States in the affairs of Latin-American countries, the A. F. of L. and the Mexican Federation of Labor tried to work out a mutually acceptable immigration policy.

Despite the real contributions made by the Pan-American Federation of Labor towards international goodwill and closer relations with the organized workers of Latin America, it was not destined to survive, in spite of the fact that its fifth congress, in July 1927, found more countries represented by more delegates than any previous meeting. In addition to the American Federation of Labor and the Mexican Federation of Labor, nine South and Central American countries sent representatives to the gathering. In his opening speech to the convention, President Green inferentially summarized the problem facing the Pan-American Federation, when he declared "the Pan-American Federation of Labor is really the child of President Gompers."[30] Without Gompers' guidance, without his tolerance, his understanding, and his mediatory ability founded upon respect for the opinions of others, the organization could not easily survive. The American Federation of Labor overshadowed all the other organizations in size and power; it paid virtually all of its expenses, and while the fifth convention went through the motions of a deliberative body, it had lost its soul and inspiration with the departure of Gompers.

REFERENCES

1. *Report of Proceedings of the Nineteenth Annual Convention of the American Federation of Labor,* 1899, p. 16; *Report of Proceedings of the Twentieth Annual Convention of the American Federation of Labor,* 1900, p. 140.

2. Louis L. Lorwin, *Labor and Internationalism* (New York: The Macmillan Company, 1929), pp. 277-301, deals with the relations of Pan American labor to the A. F. of L.

3. *Report of the Proceedings of the Twenty-Eighth Annual Convention of the American Federation of Labor,* 1908, pp. 259-260.

4. *Report of the Proceedings of the Thirty-Second Annual Convention of the American Federation of Labor,* 1912, p. 256.

5. Letter from the Executive Council of the American Federation of Labor to R. Zubaran, United States Representative of Mexican Constitutionalists, July 25, 1914.

6. Gompers to President Woodrow Wilson, September 22, 1915.

7. Frank Duffy to Reverend Francis Kelley, April 5, 1916.

8. Duffy to Reverend Francis Kelley, April 14, 1916; Kelley to Duffy, April 10, 1916.

9. Duffy to Gompers, May 25, 1916.

10. Minutes of Executive Council, July 1, 1916.

11. Gompers to Carranza, July 29, 1916; Carranza to Gompers, July 30, 1916.

12. Lorwin, *op. cit.,* pp. 288-289.

13. Letter of Gompers to the members of the *Confederation de Sindicatos Obreros,* July 19, 1916.

14. Gompers to Chester M. Wright, July 21, 1916.

15. *Pan American Labor Press,* December 4, 1918.

16. *Report of the Proceedings of the Second Congress of the Pan-American Federation of Labor,* 1921, p. 55.

17. Gompers to President Woodrow Wilson, November 29, 1919.

18. Secretary of State Robert Lansing to Gompers, January 31, 1920.

19. *Report of the Proceedings of the Third Congress of the Pan-American Federation of Labor,* 1912, p. 39.

20. *Ibid.,* pp. 37-55, 93.

21. Gompers to Secretary of State Charles E. Hughes, July 1, 1922.

22. Gompers to Ricardo Trevino, General Secretary, *Confederacion Regional Obrera Mexicana,* November 7, 1923.

23. Gompers to Secretary of State Charles E. Hughes, December 18, 1923.

24. Gompers to President Alvaro Obregon, January 29, 1924.

25. Memorandum addressed to the Official Representatives of the Republics of Chile and Peru to the Washington Tacna-Arica Conference by the Pan-American Federation of Labor Executive Committee.

26. The Executive Committee to Secretary of State Hughes, May 28, 1921; Hughes to Gompers, June 18, 1921.

27. *Report of the Proceedings of the Fourth Congress of the Pan-American Federation of Labor,* 1923, p. 103.

28. William Green to Secretary of State Frank B. Kellogg, June 15, 1925.

29. Green to President Coolidge, March 28, 1927.

30. *Report of Proceedings of the Fifth Congress of the Pan-American Federation of Labor,* 1927, p. 7.

XXI

The Churches and Organized Labor

THE American Federation of Labor welcomed all organized wage earners, and always opposed the formation of confessional or denominational unions. Discussions of religious subjects were never encouraged, and the convention of 1896 placed them under the ban. Gompers' outlook might be described as positivistic and secularist. In the early years of the century he, Colonel Robert Ingersoll, and others signed an appeal for support of the lectures of Harry Frank, a well-known secularist lecturer.[1] Nevertheless, Gompers did not allow his own religious or lack of religious opinions to intrude into his activity as a union officer. He was not averse to defending the labor movement against critical clergymen, as when he politely informed the Washington Presbyterian Ministers Association that the worker should be helped to a better life now rather than wait for his reward in the hereafter.[2]

PROTESTANT CHURCHES

The Presbyterian Church was the first Christian denomination to show a formal interest in the labor problem. In October 1901, a commission of three bishops, three presbyters, and three laymen was appointed to study the labor question, and in 1906 the General Assembly of the Presbyterian Church not only urged another study be made of the labor problem, but also suggested the development of fraternal "relations with workingmen and their organizations."[3]

For the first time a representative of an organized church was a fraternal delegate to the convention of the American Federation of Labor. Gompers and other leaders of the A. F. of L. showed a keen awareness of the need for tolerance on religious matters. The establishment of the Department of Church and Labor by the Presbyterian Church was to lead to the first formal relations between a church and the A. F. of L.

Reverend Charles Stelzle, an ordained minister and a member of the International Association of Machinists, who had been placed in charge of the Department, was allowed to address the convention of 1905. He was able to declare that the Department of Church and Labor "is the only official organization of the kind in the world." He pleaded for

334

better understanding between the church and organized labor, and described the evils he knew at first hand, and his anxiety to promote cooperation between the two institutions for their abolition. Subsequently, a resolution was adopted recommending to all affiliated city and state branches that, whenever practicable, they exchange fraternal delegates with the various city and state ministerial associations.[4] The following year, the Executive Council voted to seat a fraternal delegate from the Department of Church and Labor of the Presbyterian Church in the United States of America, under the same conditions as delegates were seated from the Farmers' Educational and Cooperative Union, the Women's International Union Label League, and the Women's Trade Union League.[5]

CATHOLIC COOPERATION

In that year, Charles Stelzle was the delegate, as he was for the two following years. In 1909, however, Stelzle represented the Federated Council of Churches of Christ of America. At this convention, the address of Reverend Stelzle greatly impressed Father Peter E. Dietz, then visiting his first convention of the American Federation of Labor.

"Conversing later with some of the leading Catholic trade unionists at the convention, Dietz learned that they were not a little ashamed of the fact that Protestantism was officially on record in support of the American Federation of Labor, while their own church remained aloof." This experience influenced Father Dietz to organize an association which a year later became the Militia of Christ for Social Service.[6] The head of the organization was P. J. McArdle of the Amalgamated Association of Iron, Steel and Tin Workers. Thomas J. Duffy, the head of the Brotherhood of Operative Potters, was chosen secretary. Peter Collins, a leader of the McNulty faction of the International Brotherhood of Electrical Workers, John Mangan, a power in the Steam Fitters' Union, John Mitchell, James O'Connell, and Frank Duffy were among the officers. Mitchell and O'Connell were members of the Executive Council, and later Dennis Hayes and John Alpine, who were also on the Council, were elected to the directorate of the Militia of Christ.

For those Catholics who joined the Militia of Christ, it represented, as it did for John Mitchell, a movement

for constructive social reform, and whether there be any justification for the charge there is a widespread impression that our Church is just a little over-conservative in matters of this kind; therefore, it seems to me that our people should adopt and pursue a systematic program for social betterment; that we should identify ourselves with the movement to promote legislation, that is, constructive legislation, for the protection of that great part of the people in our country who are least able to protect themselves.[7]

Many leading trade unionists of the Catholic faith did not look with approval upon the Militia of Christ, and as a matter of fact, despite the affiliation of leading trade union officers, the Militia of Christ largely remained a paper organization carried in the "vest pocket" of its executive secretary, Father Dietz. There is little trace of its activity within the trade union movement, except that it gave the Socialists another purported reason for the failure of Socialist ideology to dominate the mind of American Labor.

The theory that Catholic influence prevented American Labor from endorsing socialism and independent political action never gained a following outside of radical and anti-Catholic circles. The opposition to socialism in the early years was led by men such as Gompers, and McGuire, who was not a practicing Catholic although he was of a Catholic family and died in the Church. Lennon, Duncan, Kidd, and McCraith, who carried the attack against the Socialists, were of Protestant origin, McCraith being a philosophical anarchist without much religion of any kind. Moreover, the A. F. of L.'s defense of revolutionaries and anarchists refutes the implication of domination by the Church.[8] When Professor Francisco Ferrer was executed by the Spanish monarchy in 1909, the Executive Council declared that "The cause of free speech, free press and free education have found in Ferrer another martyr, the more regrettable in an age when civilization boasts of having replaced the tortures and brutality of mediaevalism by toleration end enlightenment."[9]

THE PRINCIPLE OF SECULAR UNIONS

At the convention of 1913 two resolutions critical of the German Christian unions were introduced. One, from the International Longshoremen's Association, was signed by T. V. O'Connor, W. B. Jones, Thomas Harrison, and Simon P. O'Brien; the other was submitted by the Painters' Union, at the time strongly influenced by Socialists. One of the resolutions declared the Christian unions of Europe as "subversive of the essential unity of the International Labor Movement." The other resolution, after alluding to the conduct of the Christian unions of Europe, charged "clergymen of this country with taking sides with capital against labor, as was shown by the action of a Catholic bishop in West Virginia against striking coal miners, and by the actions of Protestant preachers joining the militia in Michigan against the miners, and other cases that are known to the trades unionists."

The later resolution called on the convention to condemn any movement, "Christian or Catholic," which was harmful to the labor movement and urged workers not to support them. The resolutions committee argued that the injection of religious issues would be harmful to the labor movement, and pointed to the exclusion of sectarian questions from the conventions of the American Federation of Labor as one of the sources of its strength. In keeping with established custom the convention refused to pass judgment upon the conduct of the labor movements of other countries. The conclusions of the resolutions committee were supported by all the delegates except one.[10]

In the same year, James Kirby, the president of the United Brotherhood of Carpenters and Joiners of America, complained to Gompers that he had found during his trip to Lower Canada "the Catholic clergy utterly arrayed against the International Trade Movement. . . . We are fighting this proposition and will continue to do so as we realize that if they are not beaten at home, they will spread and it is our intention to give them all the fight they want."[11] Kirby sought the cooperation of the A. F. of L. against the Canadian Catholic unions, and he was anxious to drive them from his jurisdiction. It should be noted that Frank Duffy, secretary of Kirby's union, was on the directorate of the Militia of Christ, and a devout Catholic always ready to defend his Church. However, he also dreaded the spread of sectarian unions.

In 1910, Father Peter E. Dietz addressed the convention as the fraternal delegate from the American Federation of Catholic Societies. His position was the same as that of the Reverend Stelzle, who had represented either the Presbyterian Church or the Federal Council of Churches of Christ since 1906. In 1915 Father Dietz sought closer and more formal relationships with the A. F. of L. for his organization. He called attention to the fraternal spirit existing between the American Federation of Catholic Societies and the American Federation of Labor, and the fair interpretation of the American labor movement which the Catholic Societies had made through its meetings, conventions, and publications. It was the opinion of Father Dietz that "this has contributed not a little to the growth of the American Federation of Labor in numbers and moral influence both within the labor movement, and outside of it."

Father Dietz noted that there had been "some criticism of the fraternal delegateship at the recent convention at Philadelphia. Whether just or unjust, we need not now consider, but it has raised the very proper question, how it might be possible to make the relation more vital, definite and progressive." Father Dietz pointed to the similarity of aims of the two organizations, declaring that "the American Federation of Labor aims to better the material, intellectual and moral interests of the American workingman, with special emphasis upon the material; the aim of the American Federation of Catholic Societies is the same with the emphasis primarily on religion."

An outline of the fields of possible cooperation was given. Father Dietz believed that

There would be unanimity of opinion resulting from the principle that the state shall not do for associations and unions, what they ought to do for themselves without state aid; e.g., hours of labor, minimum wage, social insurance, etc. (2) Industrial education without discrimination against the parochial school system would be to the point on the score of compromise. (3) There would be no compromise on policies that would adopt fundamental tenets of Marxism, prohibition by legislation, or any other socially unsound.

Father Dietz called for a "virile relationship" between the two organizations, one that would not only lead to an exchange of fraternal delegates between the organizations on all levels, but would call for cooperation by committees from the two organizations on issues such as industrial education, legislation and social service, strikes, etc.[12]

The letter was distributed to the members of the Executive Council for discussion at their meeting. Gompers and Duffy were appointed to draw up an answer. In a long letter the suggestion for closer cooperation with the A. F. of L. was firmly rejected. First, the letter pointed out that the American Federation of Labor "must unite and organize irrespective of creed, color, sex, nationality or politics." While the Executive Council accepted the view "that the American Federation of Labor aims to better the material, intellectual, and moral interests of the American working people," it declared it "an error to state that special emphasis is placed upon the material, for as sure as cause is related to effect, the intellectual and moral development of the working people is essentially dependent upon their material wellbeing. The very fact as you point out that the aim of the American Federation of Catholic Societies is primarily concerned with religion, is itself a bar to the American Federation of Labor to enter such agreement with a religious body as you propose."

In addition, the Executive Council, while acknowledging that cooperation on some of the proposals mentioned by Father Dietz might be generally acceptable, stated that "upon others there are wide and diverse opinions." As for inviting delegates from the Catholic Societies, the Executive Council declared that no organization, with the exception of the trade union movements of foreign countries, have ever been invited to send fraternal delegates to the conventions of the A. F. of L. "Those associations or commissions which have sent fraternal delegates, have found a cordial reception at our conventions, a kindly greeting, and an interesting and sympathetic audience." The Federation was anxious that such relations continue, and continue on that basis.

The Executive Council pointed to varied religious, national, and political backgrounds of the membership.

There may be here and there employers [the Council declared], who give preference to workers of their own nationality, politics, or religious faiths, but the rule, the general, aye, the nearly universal rule is, that the first consideration of employers is how can they get the most out of the workers for as little compensation as possible, and the questions of the religion, nationality, and politics are driven to the background. If there be one lesson to the toilers more trenchant than another, it is that they must stand united for the principles of fraternity, sympathetic cooperation, and solidarity in furtherance of their rights and protection of their rights and welfare. We trust, therefore, that the American labor movement as understood and carried on by the American Federation of Labor be left free from the influences, policies and tactics which have to their great detriment divided the workers in several other countries.[13]

CANADIAN CATHOLIC UNIONS

In 1915 the unions of the American Federation of Labor were sharply attacked by Archbishop Cloutier of Three Rivers, Quebec, who charged the "neutral societies, contrary to Catholic unions, advocate the hatred of classes and strikes." He urged Catholic workers to withdraw from international organizations, described as "evil and subversive," and align themselves with the Catholic Canadian unions. The attack aroused serious concern among the members of the Executive Council. In letters requesting information on this question, Gompers hoped that "the statement of the Archbishop may not be representative of the general church policy." This was interpreted by Frank Duffy as implying that the Catholic Church was anti-labor, and he angrily submitted a long list of statements by Catholic prelates favoring organization of labor. Duffy attributed the opposition of some of the clergy to the A. F. of L.'s endorsement of the revolutionary Mexican government of General Carranza.[14]

A number of unions, among them the United Brotherhood of Carpenters and Joiners of America, discussed the steps to be taken to counteract the propaganda of Archbishop Clouthier. The head of the Commission of Religious Prejudice of the Knights of Columbus charged that Gompers had been "scandalously misrepresented in the pastoral letter issued by the Bishop of Three Rivers judging by the translation."[15] In the period following World War I the problem continued to plague the Canadian unions affiliated with the A. F. of L.

The Council was convinced that unity was essential between the workers of Canada and the United States, but that division along religious lines might spread across the border. Considerable concern was shown about a report that a Protestant trade union movement would be launched in Ontario to counteract the one being promoted by the Catholics. It was the opinion of the members of the Council that a campaign against the secession movement in Canada had to be inaugurated, based on an explanation of the A. F. of L.'s position rather than on at attack on the Church.[16] A committee, made up of Woll, Daniel Tobin, and Duffy, was appointed to devise methods for meeting this problem. Suggestions were made that the committee call upon the Apostolic Delegate and acquaint him with the position of the Federation on many of the important social and economic problems, in the hope that the campaign against the American unions in Canada would be eased. The investigation conducted by the Federation showed that the Catholic unions in Canada were limited to Montreal, Sherbrooke, and Quebec, and that only a few unions were seriously affected, among them the Carpenters' Union.

Cooperation among the organizers of the A. F. of L. and the various unions was advocated as a means of combating the Catholic organizations. A mass of data was assembled, showing the less favorable wage scales and working conditions of the Catholic unions as compared to those of the Canadian organizations. In striking out against the Canadian Catholic unions, Gompers wanted it clearly understood that

there is no matter of religious faith involved in any manner whatsoever in considering this subject. It is not only the privilege, but the right of every man to follow the faith or religion that is his and no man must interfere with it. The sole purpose is that in the movement to protect and promote the rights and interests of the working people they should not fall into the error of dividing the organization upon religious grounds and thereby do not only themselves but all other injury.[17]

REFERENCES

1. I have not come across any derogatory reference, or favorable, for that matter, to religion in his letters or speeches.

2. Samuel Gompers, "Ministers Discuss Labor," *American Federationist*, August 1902, pp. 435-443.

3. Resolution in A. F. of L. archives.

4. *Report of the Proceedings of the Thirty-Fifth Annual Convention of the American Federation of Labor*, 1905, pp. 152-154, 178.

5. Minutes of the Executive Council, June 21, 1906.

6. Mary Harrita Fox, *Peter E. Dietz, Labor Priest* (Notre Dame, Indiana: University of Notre Dame Press, 1953), p. 45.

7. Quoted in *Ibid.*, pp. 51-52.

8. See the article by Mark Karson, "The Catholic Church and Unionism," *Industrial and Labor Relations Review*, July 1951, pp. 527-542.

9. Minutes of Executive Council, October 19, 1909.

10. *Report of Proceedings of the Thirty-Third Annual Convention of the American Federation of Labor*, 1913, pp. 313-314.

11. James Kirby to Gompers, October 13, 1913.

12. Peter E. Dietz to the Executive Council of the A. F. of L., January 12, 1915.

13. The Executive Council to Father Dietz, September 24.

14. Gompers to Duffy, August 3, 1916; Duffy to Gompers, August 16, 1916; Gompers to William Green, August 3, 1916.

15. P. H. Callahan to L. G. Jourdain, June 5, 1916.

16. Minutes of Executive Council, February 26, 1921.

17. Circular letter sent by A. F. of L. to all national and international unions, July 11, 1921.

XXII

Defense and War

Historically, the A. F. of L. had opposed imperialism and conquest and advocated peace and disarmament. In 1887 the Federation, after declaring that the "working class, the class that always has to bear the brunt of war, has the most profound interest in the establishment and maintenance of peace," endorsed an arbitration treaty with Great Britain and Ireland as the more effective method of settling international differences. Peace and disarmament as a method for its achievement were subsequently approved at a number of conventions. In 1895, the A. F. of L. endorsed the struggle for Cuban liberty, and in the following year the convention approved a statement of Gompers that "liberty, truth and freedom were the basis of the make-up of the world and must be obtained before the Cuban proletariat could be organized."[1]

After the war with Spain, the convention of 1898 expressed its apprehension of the disposition and government of Porto Rico and the Philippine Islands. It warned against the imperialism which threatened the United States, and against forcing

our system of government upon an unwilling people; against the maintenance of a huge standing army, that has no place in a republic such as ours . . . against the manifold dangers attendant upon European and Asiatic entanglements, and as workingmen emphatically protest against the unfair competition of the wretched peoples who would become, without voice or vote, our fellow citizens.[2]

To the convention of 1899, Gompers denounced the annexation of Hawaii, "in spite of protests of the people." The violation of the principle of self-rule in the Philippine Islands was sharply attacked, and the convention warned against the extension of the "territoried" domain or the increase of the standing army to more than 25,000 enlisted men and officers.[3]

WORLD WAR I

At the outbreak of World War I, the A. F. of L. lamented the reversal of sentiment which led to such low evaluation upon human life. "The

342

power to declare war," declared the Executive Council, "must be put in the people or their chosen representatives." The convention approved education for peace, and the establishment of international understanding and agencies that will prevent war.[4] The convention of 1914 also adopted a resolution for the holding of a labor conference at the same time and place as the general congress which would be held at the close of the European war to determine conditions of peace. The convention of 1915 emphasized the need for the establishment of friendly relations between nations and the avoidance of war.

In 1916 the A. F. of L. declared that "the way to prevent war is to organize for peace." The Executive Council came out for a "voluntary union of nations, a league for peace, to adjust disputes and difficulties and to take the initiative in constructive efforts to direct and facilitate world progress in accord with highest concepts." The convention the same year unreservedly attacked militarism, which it described as a "brutalizing institution," and "large standing armies as a threat to the existence of civil liberty. . . . Our experience has been that even this citizen soldiery, the militia of our several states, has given cause for gravest apprehension." The convention opposed any training which would inculcate militarism, and directed the president to investigate it.

COUNCIL OF NATIONAL DEFENSE

As the war in Europe went on, the government of the United States became increasingly concerned with its outcome. In August 1916, Congress established by law the Council of National Defense, made up of the secretaries of War, Navy, Interior, Commerce, and Labor. An advisory commission of seven members, one of whom was Samuel Gompers, was subsequently appointed by the Secretary of War. Gompers was made chairman of the committee on labor, including conservation of health and welfare of workers. After receiving the approval of the Executive Council Gompers informed Newton D. Baker of his acceptance, and stated that he saw his responsibility "to give a spirit and purpose to plans for national preparedness that shall make human welfare the paramount consideration."[5] The job carried no salary, but it is evident from the correspondence and memoranda that Gompers did not intend to be a mere figurehead. Under the terms of his appointment he was the "sole medium of communication between the Committee on Labor and those bodies or their officials [the Council of National Defense]." He had the "right of supervisory administration and final decision in all matters involving communication of any kind between any member or committee of the Committee on Labor and any Government official or any other person or persons wherein such matters relate to any phase of the functions of the Committee on Labor."[6]

As war approached, Gompers recommended the utilization of the skills of labor union officers in the supply departments of the armed services. He pointed, in a memorandum to President Wilson, to the difficulties of labor union officers attending officers' training camps, in which officers for the expanding American army were being trained. President Wilson was sufficiently impressed to send the memorandum to Secretary of War Baker with a notation asking whether it was "not possible to make use of them [labor union officials] in the commissary or other similar departments."[7]

From his vantage point in the advisory commission, and from his wide knowledge of events, Gompers saw the approach of war, and he became anxious that organized labor be prepared with a program. He advised Speaker Champ Clark that there need be no apprehension entertained that "the working people will fail in the performance of duty and to give service for the safety, integrity and the ideals of our country."[8]

More than passive loyalty was needed at this conjuncture, for the heads of the A. F. of L. were convinced that the labor movement had to cooperate actively in the handling of the problems of defense and, if necessary, war. In the opinion of the leaders, unless the labor movement was ready to make constructive suggestions, "it would have to accept directions decided by other groups and thereby forfeit any opportunity for helping to guide policy." Following consultations with the heads of unions stationed in Washington, the Executive Council called a meeting of heads of national and international unions and the Executive Council.[9]

If in this formative period [the unions were informed], the labor movement shall clearly enunciate what part it is willing to take in defense of the Republic, it will be in a position to have a voice in deciding the whole plan of national preparedness for defense, but if the labor movement should hold aloof and should refuse to proclaim a constructive program, all wage-earners will be forced to accept conditions and methods determined by those who do not understand or sympathize with the aims or purposes of the labor movement.

Gompers urged the officers of the unions to consider the necessities of the situation, and to meet in Washington on March 12, 1917, to discuss the issues confronting the country and the labor movement.[10]

POSITION OF A. F. OF L. IN WORLD WAR I

The Executive Council met on March 9, 1917, and, after a discussion of three days, drew up a statement defining the position of the American labor movement in peace and war; it was signed by 148 representatives of seventy-nine affiliated national and international unions, five unaffiliated organizations, and five departments of the A. F. of L. The declaration, *American Labor's Position in Peace or in War,* recognized that war was a possibility and that now was the time to take steps to avoid conflict when "constructive agencies for peace" can still be established. The statement pointed to the importance of industrial potential in modern warfare and of the workers who man the industries. Therefore, it was held "fitting that the masses of the people of the United States should take counsel and determine what course they shall pursue should a crisis arise necessitating the protection of our Republic and defense of the ideals for which it stands." While the conference reiterated labor's suspicion of militarism, it conceded that a nation is justified in defending its rights—"the labor movement distrusts and protests against militarism, because it knows that militarism represents privilege and is the tool of special interests, exploiters and despots . . . [but] it holds that it is the duty of a nation to defend itself against injustice and invasion." The declaration also called for the recognition of the equal importance of industrial service and military service, and demanded that, in the interest of safeguarding the rights of wage earners, organized labor should have representation on all agencies administering national defense policies.[11]

On April 7, 1917, a meeting of labor, management, and representatives of the public was called by Gompers to discuss the conservation of human resources and increasing productivity. As it was believed that employers, irrespective of their attitudes towards unions, had a responsibility for maintaining continuous output, increasing productivity, and the protection of the health standards of wage earners, the invited were not limited to those who were friendly to organized labor. More than 150 persons attended, including representatives of leading international unions, the railway brotherhoods, employers, and welfare experts in a number of industries and the general public. A permanent organization was formed, and an Executive Committee elected to deal with various phases of labor and production problems. Gompers was its chairman, Matthew Woll his assistant, and Secretary of Labor Wilson served as secretary.[12]

National committees were appointed to give attention to the war phases of such problems as wages and hours, mediation and conciliation, welfare work, women in industry, cost of living, domestic economy, and the general problems of employment.

The Executive Committee of the Committee on Labor adopted a Declaration which caused considerable dissatisfaction in the ranks of organized labor. The resolution called upon the Council of National Defense to

issue a statement to employers and to employees in our industrial plants and transportation systems advising that neither employers nor employees shall endeavor to take advantage of the country's necessities to change existing standards. When economic emergencies arise requiring changes of standards, the same should be made only after such proposed changes have been investigated and approved by the Council of National Defense.

The Council of National Defense was also requested to urge

the legislatures of the States, as well as all administrative agencies charged with the enforcement of labor and health laws, the great duty of rigorously maintaining the existing safeguards as to the health and welfare of workers, and no departure from such present standards in state laws or state rulings affecting labor, should be taken without a declaration of the Council of National Defense that such a departure is essential for the effective pursuit of the national defense.

Opposition to the part of the statement "advising that neither employers nor employees shall endeavor to take advantage of the country's necessities to change existing standards" appeared immediately. Daniel Tobin, the president of the Teamsters' Union, wrote that he had many complaints from his members, and that Gompers had no authority to make such commitments. In Tobin's opinion, before any such pledge could be made a special convention of the A. F. of L. should have been called, and

the International officers should have been asked to consult with their several unions and get instructions so that when they did attend the special convention of the A. F. of L. they would be in a position to know the feeling of their membership. I want to say to you the International I represent will continue to fight and struggle, even to the extent of striking for better conditions, war or no war.

Gompers denied that he had made any statement, or that he had agreed that there "shall be no strikes of any kind during the war." He went on to explain that he had only in mind the safeguarding of existing standards, and that moreover, he only had reference to

large industries and the transportation systems whose operations are essential to the prosecution of the war. They are not intended to cover every petty labor difference in the country, though it is hoped that patriotic regard will be held by all citizens to the need of a possible maximum of industrial peace everywhere. It is, of course, not expected by the committee that negotiations, or even strikes, now on in various occupations shall be wholly suspended irrespective of the merits of the questions under discussions.[13]

The Executive Committee amplified its statement by declaring that the phrase, "no departure from such present standards," was intended to mean "no lowering of present standards." The Committee also made known that no promises had been made that there should be "no strikes during the war." Gompers believed that the declaration in no wise precluded the effort to obtain necessary improved conditions.[14] In its second statement, the Executive Committee suggested that

No arbitrary change in wages should be sought at this time by either employers or employees through the process of strikes or lockouts without at least giving the established agencies, including those of the several states and of the Government, and of the Mediation Board in the transportation service and the Division of Conciliation of the Department of Labor in the other industries, an opportunity to adjust the difficulties without a stoppage of work occurring.[15]

Despite the attitude of the war agencies, certain employer groups were actively seeking the repeal of labor and welfare legislation in a number of states. Such appeals were usually based upon the argument that repeal was necessitated by the shortage of labor. Gompers was perturbed by these efforts. He charged that

[Employers] have never taken the pains to use carefully and for the purpose of conservation any factor in production which was not expensive. . . . It has been the settled policy of large corporations, such as the steel companies, to have always available a mass of unemployed. These can be called on whenever needed and dismissed as the temporary needs cease. As a result, these great corporation managers, when they find they cannot readily pick up a hundred men for one or two hour's extra work, feel they have been denied a condition that assured cheap labor, and have at once declared a scarcity of workmen.

Gompers also insisted that servants and retainers be drawn into war work, and only then, he argued, should a claim of the existence of a scarce labor supply be seriously considered.[16]

Gompers' views on the existing labor question were not unnoticed by the employer side. Daniel Willard, the chairman of the Advisory Committee, found himself "unable to accept fully what I understand to be your views concerning the labor question generally as it confronts us at the present time." In turn, Gompers called Willard's attention to the number of times the Advisory Commission and the Council of National Defense had been apprised of "unfair discrimination, injustice, invasion of lawful rights of workers." Gompers also protested the failure to appoint labor representatives on war agencies, and against efforts to prolong the work day beyond eight hours. He pointed to the experience of England in unduly prolonging the hours of work in the early period of the war, and the harmful effect it had on production. Gompers also defended the expectation of unions that they be recognized for collective bargaining with employers.[17]

WAR-TIME LABOR AGREEMENT

In the meantime, the importance of organized labor in the war effort was inferentially recognized by the appearance of President Wilson at the Buffalo convention in 1917. It was the first time the A. F. of L. had received such recognition, and the President made a plea for the avoidance of industrial conflict and for increased cooperation between labor and management as a means of promoting the war effort. While Wilson was in many respects the president whose views and actions were more favorable to organized labor than of any of his predecessors, his appearance was yet full recognition of the increased importance of labor. The new, even if temporary, status of labor was also observable in the effort to devise workable programs of cooperation between labor and the war agencies.

On June 19, 1917, an agreement was signed by the Secretary of War, Newton D. Baker, and Gompers. Under this agreement, an adjustment commission of three persons was appointed by the Secretary of War; the labor member was nominated by Gompers. The agreement stipulated that local union rate of wages would be paid for construction work on cantonments. The agreement was later extended to repair work. John R. Alpine, the head of the Plumbers' Union, was appointed to the adjustment commission.[18]

In the meantime, serious difficulties arose in the construction and ship-building industries. William Hutcheson, the head of the Carpenters' Union, insisted that workers had a right to quit work unless satisfactory arrangements could be made. Yet neither he nor any other leader of the trade union movement wanted to embarrass the government or interfere with the war effort. To obviate the difficulties, Louis B. Wehle drew up a plan whereby the Navy accepted the essentials of the agreement negotiated with the Secretary of War. Under the arrangements disputes over wages, hours of labor, or other conditions of employment were submitted to a board of three persons, one nominated by the United States Shipping Board, one representing the public, and the third, or labor representative, nominated by Gompers. As both the metal trades and the building trades were engaged in ship building, Gompers nominated two persons, one of whom sat on the committee when the matter under consideration concerned largely construction of steel ships; otherwise a representative of those workers engaged in the construction of ships of wooden hulls served.

[Wehle] discussed the matter with Assistant Secretary [Franklin D.] Roosevelt. He has agreed that a naval officer shall sit on the Emergency Construction Committee and that the Navy would hereafter accept from the Emergency Construction Committee the names of contractors to whom contracts are to be awarded. Since it has been arranged that a representative of organized labor is to sit in with the Emergency Construction Committee at the selection of contractors, the contractors who will hereafter be selected for naval land work will be fairly sure to have their relations with labor upon a sound basis.[19]

The program for settling disputes in the shipbuilding industry was accepted by the various government divisions involved, the Metal Trades

Department, the Building Trades Department, and the single unions whose members were affected. Under this arrangement A. J. Barres, the secretary of the Metal Trades Department, was nominated by Gompers for this Board. Subsequently, a more detailed agreement was reached, and the basis for wage setting more precisely defined.

The Baker-Gompers agreement gave the unions certain rights, in that prevailing union conditions with regard to wages and hours were accepted as standard. Both contractors and government agencies employing labor, however, were not always anxious to encourage union conditions and union organization. As a consequence a constant stream of complaints was transmitted to the labor office in Washington, and Gompers was kept busy trying to bring the government and its contractors into line so that the agreement would be obeyed and discontent among workers allayed. For example, the heads of the government arsenal in Rockford, Illinois, refused to confer with representatives of the unions representing the workers employed there. At the intervention of Gompers, the heads of the arsenals were ordered to admit business agents of the building construction unions on the premises.[20] In some instances, government contractors refused to pay overtime rates for work after eight hours a day. In these instances Gompers would intervene and take the matter up with the War Department, which usually ordered that the agreement be followed.[21] Many unions complained of the inability of union contractors to bid for war orders, and in these instances the labor division intervened with the War Department to request a correction of the situation.

Soon Gompers faced an attack from the labor side. After the signing of the original Baker-Gompers agreement, the A. F. of L. was informed that the "Government cannot commit itself in any way to the closed shop. . . . The word 'conditions' is, of course, clearly understood to refer only to the arrangement in the event of overtime, holiday work and matters of that kind." Gompers acknowledged that the understanding given above was correct, and "the question of the union shop was not included."[22]

Unaware of the limitations of the Gompers-Baker agreement, William Hutcheson, the head of the Carpenters' Union, charged that the government was aiding anti-union employers. As soon as such complaints arrived at the office of the committee of labor, they were immediately funneled to the government agency against which the complaint had been made, with a request for rectification of the grievance. While commending Gompers on the promptness with which he handled complaints, Hutcheson demanded that government contractors and government-employers adopt the union shop. He pointed out that

There was quite a feeling among our membership that [this] was the opportune time to advance their wage and it was no easy task on the part of the general officers to restrain them from doing so and we feel that when firms . . . are given contracts by our Government and permitted to employ non-union men therein even though they may be paying the wage and working the hours established by our organization, that it tends to jeopardize and retard, and even tear down the conditions and standards as established, and we feel that in all fairness and justice to our membership as citizens of this country that the Government should take steps to see that only contractors as comply with the standards and conditions as established be given governmental contracts.[23]

Hutcheson interpreted the phrase, "union conditions must be followed," in the Baker-Gompers agreement as requiring the establishment of a union shop on government work. As was noted above, no such arrangement was contemplated in the agreement, and was, in fact, explicitly rejected on behalf of the government.

Laboring under the belief that the union shop would be enforced, the officers of the Carpenters' Union had prevented their members

from ceasing work for the enforcement of conditions that they thought should be brought about because of the fact that they were of the opinion that the understanding arrived at between yourself pertaining to hours, wages and overtime rate and conditions as in effect on June 1st would be made applicable and would mean the recognition of the union or closed shop so long as that condition prevailed in that locality where the work was under course of construction. If this is not recognized by the Government officials we will have to assume the same attitude towards the Government work that we would in reference to the work of any contractor or builder, which I am frank to admit would mean the ceasing of work to enforce our conditions.[24]

Gompers replied that he could not get away from the fact that the Government was involved in a serious war, and that he had been trying to gain a promise for the recognition of union wages, hours, and conditions of employment as standards that were to govern the employment of labor by the Government or its contractors. He pointed to the attitude of other unions with large numbers of members engaged by the government, none of which demanded or was given the union shop. He then informed Hutcheson:

If you desire to continue to assume the position stated in your letter, you must do so with the realization that practically all other trades engaged in various capacities for the Government have assumed an entirely different position. It is not my purpose to dictate any mode of procedure, but only to lay before you the facts as they exist with the hope that mature judgment will be exercised in dealing with the problem which concern our organizations and our Government in this crisis.[25]

While Hutcheson agreed that it would be difficult for the Government to accept the union shop and thereby debar non-union workers from employment, he clearly indicated that the Baker-Gompers agreement was in fact a deception, for had he been aware of the interpretation given to "conditions" as not meaning the union shop, he would have not placed himself in a "ridiculous position before our membership on various occasions when they were anxious and desirous of ceasing work because of non-union workmen being employed, and through the efforts of the undersigned [Hutcheson] were prevented from doing so."

Gompers reiterated his belief in the union shop, and the hope that the Carpenters' Union would obtain it throughout its jurisdiction. Yet Gompers was puzzled that

anyone can fail to understand this fact that the Government of the United States, representing all the people of the United States, cannot enter into an agreement to employ exclusively members of any one organization. I firmly believe that there are very few men who for conscientious reasons would refuse to become members of a trade union, but even if there be but a few and they are American citizens, the Government of all the people of the United States, cannot be asked to deny these citizens the right to work for the Government, or for Government contractors, upon the ground that they are not members of a union.[26]

While Gompers was under attack from the labor side for not doing enough to assure the labor movement an opportunity for gains in membership, opposition to his policies also came from anti-union employers and their agents who feared his activities would encourage the spread of labor organization. The National Erectors Association complained against the restrictive practices of labor organizations, and pointed to the absence of unionism in "the great basic industries to which the government must look to in carrying out the war preparation program." The National Erectors Association warned against allowing the unions to expand under the cover of the war.[27]

GRIEVANCES OF LABOR

The refusal of employers to deal with their workers through a union and the insistence of some employers on paying less than the over-time rate after eight hours of work a day, were common complaints. Whenever complaints came in, they were immediately forwarded to the government division concerned, and prompt replies requested. Many difficulties were straightened out by this method. For example, an employer who refused to bargain with the union in his plant and thus faced a strike, was able to have federal troops placed outside of his establishment to intimidate the pickets. The matter was brought to the attention of the Committee on Labor, and the Seretary of War was informed that

Men doing their daily work in production that is necessary for military defense or maintaining the civil life of the nation are doing their part for the common cause. In order to insure uninterrupted output of necessary supplies there must be accorded to workers opportunity to settle differences with employers. This can be accomplished by inducing employers and employees to talk over their differences and reach an understanding. Anything that would enable the employer to take advantage of force against his employees would militate against cooperation which must be based upon mutual confidence and understanding.

The soldiers were ordered withdrawn immediately by the Secretary of War, who agreed that "federal troops must not embarrass the peaceful process of adjusting industrial differences that may arise. I am confident that the future will furnish no such embarrassments."[28]

Nevertheless, serious grievances arose over the refusal of employers to observe the wartime truce, or their interpretation of the meaning of the truce as allowing the employers to operate under the same non-union conditions they did before the war. Complaints of discrimination against workers for joining unions were quite common. Guilty of discriminatory practices were such concerns as the United States Steel Corporation and the Western Union Telegraph Company, but there were also complaints against similar practices by smaller enterprises. As a consequence a growing restiveness developed among workers, which their leaders could not easily allay.

Warnings against the possible consequences of these employer practices were not uncommon. Among many, Warren S. Stone, head of the Brotherhood of Locomotive Engineers, demanded from Gompers that either employers be ordered to cease their anti-labor activities, or the wartime restraint on strikes, self-imposed by labor, be abrogated.[29] Stone's protest followed discrimination by a number of railroads against workers who joined unions. Hutcheson was another leader who was quick to point to the failure of the A. F. of L.'s war-labor policies. When Gompers appealed to him to help end a strike of carpenters at the Norfolk navy yard, Hutcheson answered that if Gompers and the other building trades' unions had cooperated with his organization, the difficulties in question would never have arisen.[30]

The A. F. of L. was anxious to have labor represented in war agencies dealing with labor questions. In January 1918, Gompers called the attention of the railroad brotherhoods to their lack of representation upon government boards dealing with railroad problems, and requested the heads of these organizations to help him work out a policy on the railroads acceptable to the unions.[31] While in this issue the A. F. of L. took the lead in urging upon labor organizations the need for participating in the making of governmental decisions affecting the workers in their industry, the A. F. of L. also supported the protests of the United Mine

Workers of America against the union being excluded from the government policy-making bodies in the coal industry. Failure to give the United Mine Workers of America proper representation on such bodies meant that the legitimate voice of the organized mine worker would be stifled, which, it was argued, "would lead to sullen resentment in the mining communities of our country, and undesired during this crisis, in the mining industry."[32] Following this protest, the United Mine Workers of America was given representation.

TRAINING OF LABOR

The devising of a training program in industry was another issue that led to dissatisfaction and dispute. The Shipping Board found that it would require at once thousands of machinists, but that workers with such skills were not immediately available in such large numbers. When Gompers' advice was asked, he suggested a conference between representatives of government agencies requiring these skilled workers, and the unions involved. As a result, representatives of the Machinists, Molders, Blacksmiths, and Pattern Makers' unions met with Gompers and representatives of the Shipping Board. To objections raised by several of the union representatives, Gompers made the following argument:

If we take hold of this proposition, as well as every other proposition, upon a broad minded basis, we will not lose, we will win. The same as those trades which balked against the introduction of a new machine, fought it, and then the machine survived and the organization was destroyed. The organization which took a broad view to accept the machine, but asked for its control, secured it, and are in a better position today than before the introduction of the machine. That is the invariable rule.[33]

Based upon the analogy of the introduction of machinery, the metal trades unions were urged by Gompers to accept some dilutions of skills and some relaxation of apprenticeship requirements.

Gompers pleaded the existence of a great national need for skilled workers, a need which could not be supplied out of the ordinary sources of labor supply as the reasons for changing customary policies. If the unions cooperated they would, in Gompers' opinion, have a voice in determining the conditions which would be introduced. If, however, they took a purely negative position they ran the danger of having their views completely ignored. Some reluctance was expressed by the representative of the International Association of Machinists to dilution of standards in his trade, but after some discussion, he agreed to help devise new rules for the training program.

The existence of one individual and one organization with the primary responsibility for advising the government on basic labor questions made it possible not only for organized labor to speak with one voice and exercise maximum influence upon the war agencies employing labor, but it allowed for the funneling of complaints against employers, legislators, and other groups who sought to use the war emergency as a pretext for suppressing civil rights or for the revocation of established standards in industry. Whenever there was a move to revise standards of hours or conditions of employment, on the ground that such action was necessitated by the war emergency, the initiators of such projects would always be informed that revisions were not to be made until approved by the Council of National Defense. In the matter of suppression of civil rights, the situation was more serious, for such action was usually inspired by local interests and carried out without the approval of the federal authorities; in fact, against their wishes.

ILLEGAL ASSAULTS

Reports of illegal action by citizens' committees and local officials came to the A. F. of L. from many sections of the country, especially the Rocky Mountain areas and Western States. This mob spirit was most seriously manifested in the deportations of workers and their sympathizers in Arizona because they were on strike or protesting against industrial conditions.

When the documents and information had been carefully considered, President Gompers secured a conference with the President of the United States and asked him to take some action to protect the rights of the peaceful law abiding workers within that state. . . . In this same conference similar conditions in other states were also presented. President Wilson, fully appreciative of the seriousness of the conditions, asked the Council of National Defense to take the matter under advisement.

At the request of the Council, President Wilson appointed a commission, made up of Secretary of Labor William B. Wilson, J. L. Spangler, Verner Z. Reed, John H. Walker, and E. P. Marsh. Felix Frankfurter was appointed secretary. It was the duty of the commission to seek the causes of discontent, and develop a better understanding among workers and employers.[34]

The President's Mediation Commission, as it was called, severely condemned the deportations of strikers at Bisbee, Arizona. It charged that "the deportations were wholly illegal and without authority in law either State or Federal." The deportations were carried out under the direction of the sheriff of Cochise County, with the aid of the officers of the company against which the strike for improved labor conditions were directed. The excuse given was that members of the Industrial Workers of the World were involved. The commission recommended that such occurrences be made a criminal offense under federal law to the full extent permissible under the Constitution.[35]

WAR LABOR POLICIES BOARD

As the war continued it was felt that another agency should be established to deal with over-all labor questions. In the summer of 1917 Gompers recommended the establishment of a War Labor Board of five members, with a representative from each of the following: the Department of Labor, the A. F. of L., the special government boards dealing with labor, employers, and technical and professional labor. This board was to collect data and formulate plans for allocating labor supply and to deal with any other question affecting labor. The suggestion was not accepted.

Another proposal called for the appointment of a director of labor so as to eliminate strikes and competitive bidding for workers, on the ground that "officers of labor unions confess to finding it increasingly difficult, and frequently impossible to hold their men." This program was rejected as too drastic and unnecessary. President Wilson, in the meantime, had requested the Secretary of Labor to provide a broad and coherent program for meeting all labor needs, and transferred the labor functions to the Secretary of Labor who became, in fact, the War Labor Administrator.[36] Soon thereafter the War Labor Policies Board was appointed to devise a common policy. According to Gompers, Frankfurter's appointment by Secretary of Labor Wilson was at the advice of the President of the United States.[37]

Soon after his appointment, Frankfurter requested the heads of each of the government war agencies to appoint a representative to the Labor Policies Board. He also called on Gompers for advice. The latter wrote to each of the agencies suggesting that either a labor representative be appointed to the Board or that a labor advisor be selected for the representative of each department. Franklin Roosevelt, who represented the Navy, was among those appointed to this Board. Frankfurter also met with the Executive Council of the A. F. of L. and discussed with its members the policies that would in their opinion promote the war effort. Frankfurter was advised that it would be helpful to formulate wage policies on a national rather than on a local level. Negotiations with the heads of unions, it was believed, would lead to greater uniformity in wages and working conditions and thereby help to lower labor turnover.[38]

WAR LABOR CONFERENCE BOARD

One of the principal problems confronting the War Policy Board was the working out of an effective method for allaying the increasing and spreading discontent in industry, and the devising of an effective method for preventing strikes and lockouts. Gompers and other leaders of organized labor did not look kindly upon tripartite government boards for the settling of labor disputes. On several occasions Gompers had recommended boards with representatives of labor and industry and government agencies directly engaged in war production. The suggestions were unacceptable, and finally the question was submitted to a War Labor Conference Board, made up of five representatives nominated by the A. F. of L., and five representatives from the employer side recommended by the National Conference Board, with each group appointing a chairman who was to preside on alternate days. It was the duty of this board to devise a national labor program for the period of the war. The Conference Board recommended the establishment of a War Labor Board for conciliating and mediating every conflict in the field of production affecting the effective conduct of the war. Local boards were to be set up to hear controversies, and the National War Labor Board was to be given power to subpoena the parties and hold hearings on the issues. Failure of the Board to reach a unanimous decision was to be followed by the appointment of an umpire, who also was to be appointed by unanimous vote of the members; otherwise, he was to be drawn by lot from a list of ten nominated by the President of the United States.

The War Labor Conference Board enumerated a set of principles to govern the relations of employers and employees during the war. Workers were to be allowed the right to organize and bargain collectively through representatives of their own choosing, and employers were to refrain from interfering or abridging this right in any way. Employers were to be allowed to form associations, and no interference in these activities was to be attempted by organized workers. No coercion was to be used by workers to compel others to join unions, nor by employers to discouraged organization by their workers. Wherever the union shop existed, it was to be continued, and the same rule was to be applied to wages, hours, and other conditions of employment. Where non-union and union men and women worked together and the employer met only with employees or representatives at work in his establishment, the continuance of this condition was not to be brought before the Board as a grievance. However, this rule was not to be interpreted as denying the right of workers to organize into labor unions, a right recognized by the War Labor Board.

It was also stipulated that established safeguards for health and safety in industry were not to be relaxed. If necessary, women were to be allowed to perform the work formerly done by men. In all instances where the law required it, the basic eight-hour law was to be enforced. In all other cases, the hours of labor were to be arranged with due regard to the needs of the government and the welfare, health, and comfort of workers. Limitation on production was to be avoided. A plan for distributing labor was outlined, and the custom of the locality in fixing wages, hours, and other conditions of employment was to be recognized. Explicitly, "the right of all workers, including common laborers, to a living wage is hereby declared. In fixing wages, minimum rates of pay shall be established which will insure the subsistence of the worker and his family in health and reasonable comfort."[39]

WAR LABOR BOARD

The labor members of the War Labor Conference Committee, Frank J. Hayes, William L. Hutcheson, Thomas J. Savage, Victor A. Olander, T. A. Rickert, subsequently became members of the War Labor Board. Frank P. Walsh, who had been the chairman of the Commission on Industrial Relations, was their choice as chairman. The Board contained the heads of the two largest unions in the A. F. of L., the United Mine Workers of America and the United Brotherhood of Carpenters and Joiners of America, and a member of the Executive Council, Thomas A. Rickert.

On the whole, the Board's activities met with the approval of the A. F. of L. The influence of former President William Howard Taft, who represented the public and was appointed by the employer group, was helpful in averting serious stoppages. Perhaps the most important contribution from the view of organized labor was the Board's recognition of the right of labor to organize and to bargain collectively through representatives of its own choosing.

Many employers were less happy about the work of the War Labor Board. The inability of many employers to prevent the expansion of unionism was interpreted as a sign of partiality of the War Labor Board to organized labor. In fact, Basil Manley, who replaced Walsh as chairman of the War Labor Board, charged that:

Even during the period of hostilities there was no effective cooperation on the part of the five employer members appointed by the National Industrial Conference Board and their alternates. On the part of certain of them, at least, there was not only no cooperation, but active attempts to hinder the effective functioning of the Board and its usefulness.[40]

During the war, these members were restrained in their hostility by patriotic feeling. Another restraint was the major role played by government in the economic life of the country. Once the armistice had been signed, the inhibitions forced upon them by patriotism or necessity evaporated, and they reverted to their customary habits of fighting labor unions. Yet even during the hostilities, according to Manley, an employer member advised employers "not to submit to the jurisdiction of the Board" and since the armistice he had referred to the umpires' panel set up by President Wilson as a "stacked deck."

Neither did the Board arouse unanimous enthusiasm in the ranks of labor. The International Molders' Union, in urging the discontinuance of the War Labor Board, declared: "Our experience has been that the results obtained through the assistance of the National War Labor Board have not been in keeping with the spirit of the proclamation of the President of the United States as far as giving the workers justice and equity."[41]

While on the whole the Executive Council favored the War Labor Board, it was reluctant to have the United States Government control all wages—a suggestion advocated by some heads of war agencies. It objected to a proclamation stabilizing wages in the metal and other trades which, it was informed, was to be issued by President Wilson, and the Council was "apprehensive of the far-reaching effect and influence such a proclamation would have." The Council asked that the proclamation be postponed until it could more carefully marshall its views against such a proposal.[42]

Even though the A. F. of L. was opposed to giving the government control over wage policy, it urged that the Council of National Defense be permitted to deal with problems of the postwar adjustment.[43] While President Wilson was willing to think along the lines suggested, he, because of other duties and perhaps because of subsequent failure in health, did little to put these suggestions into practice.

AMERICAN ALLIANCE FOR LABOR AND DEMOCRACY

In addition to other war activities, American organized labor established the American Alliance for Labor and Democracy to oppose the influence of pacifist and anti-war elements within the labor movement. The American Alliance was the response of the A. F. of L. to the efforts of the People's Council, a "militant" pacifist organization, to gain influence within the labor movement by forming workingmen's councils on the Russian model. Especially influential in certain circles of the New York labor movement, the People's Council had the endorsement of several unions affiliated to the A. F. of L.

The Central Federated Union of Greater New York became concerned with the propaganda of the Council, in view of the large foreign population in its area. With the approval and support of Gompers, the Central Federated Union of New York began to combat this influence. It declared that

It is the duty of the people of the United States, without regard to class, nationality, politics or religion, faithfully and loyally to support the government of the United States in carrying the present war for justice, freedom and democracy to a triumphant conclusion, and we pledge ourselves to every honorable effort for the accomplishment of that purpose.[44]

The efforts of the People's Council were condemned.

Steps were now taken to enlist not only trade unionists, but Socialists who supported the government of the United States in the war. John Spargo and Charles Edward Russell, well-known Socialist publicists, and Joseph Barondess, a veteran of the Jewish labor movement, joined in the campaign. The main effort to combat the propaganda of the pacifists fell upon the Central Federated Union of Greater New York which, early in July 1917, appointed a committee of leading New York labor officials to plan a counter effort. On July 21, 1917, the first conference, attended by Gompers, Morrison, Organizer Hugh Frayne, Joseph Barondess, and several representatives of the National Labor Publicity Committee, was held. The conference was enlarged, its activities increased, and on August 6, 1917, the American Alliance for Labor and Democracy was launched.

It was hoped that the Alliance would initiate a campaign of education through the distribution of literature and the scheduling of speakers so that the war aims of the government of the United States might be better understood by workers, and the efforts of pacifist elements to gain a following prevented. On August 17th, a call for a national conference at Minneapolis, Minnesota, for September 5, 6, and 7, 1917, was issued. The call was signed by a number of pro-war Socialists and leaders of organized labor. The meetings were attended by 199 delegates who decided to place the Alliance on a permanent basis and elected Gompers as its chairman, and Robert Maisel as secretary and director. A number of others were selected to be members of the Executive Committee.

The American Alliance aimed to align wage earners in a patriotic organization opposing dual loyalties and the spread of "that brand of socialism known as the Bolsheviki in any part of these United States of America"; sought to eliminate profiteering in food stuffs, and aimed to devise a program of reconstruction. To spread the influence of the American Alliance, a weekly news service was established, and leaflets and pamphlets were published on topics affecting labor, such as "labor and the war, patriotism, socialism, bolshevism, government regulation, profiteering, reconstruction and general industrial readjustment."[45] The Alliance was active during the war, and was reasonably effective in presenting the views of patriotic American labor. Once the war was over, there was hope that the Alliance would continue through the reconstruction period. It, however, had no program upon which it could rally its followers. In fact, one of the members of the Executive Committee, Frank P. Walsh, resigned as soon as hostilities had ended. The secretary, Robert Maisel, had other plans. He wanted to transform the Alliance into an anti-radical intelligence service. In January 1919, Gompers was informed by Matthew Woll that the solicitation of funds by the director of the Alliance might prove embarrassing to the A. F. of L. Gompers, who was then in Europe, immediately wired: "Must insist discontinuation soliciting funds for any purpose." Soon thereafter the American Alliance was discontinued.[46]

REFERENCES

1. *Report of Proceedings of the Sixteenth Annual Convention of the American Federation of Labor,* 1896, p. 84.

2. *Report of Proceedings of the Eighteenth Annual Convention of the American Federation of Labor,* 1898, p. 84.

3. *Report of Proceedings of the Nineteenth Annual Convention of the American Federation of Labor,* 1899, pp. 148-149.

4. *Report of Proceedings of the Thirty-Fourth Annual Convention of the American Federation of Labor,* 1914, pp. 48-49.

5. Gompers to Newton D. Baker, October 31, 1916; Baker to Gompers, October 30, 1916.

6. Advisory Commission, Council of National Defense, *The Labor Committee, Plan of Administration* (mimeographed and undated).

7. Memorandum from President Wilson to Secretary Baker, March 31, 1917.

8. Gompers to Speaker Champ Clark, February 10, 1917.

9. Report to Executive Council, February 28, 1917.

10. Circular letter issued by the American Federation of Labor to all of its national and international unions, March 2, 1917.

11. *American Labor's Position in Peace or in War:* Statement issued by the American Federation of Labor, March 12, 1917.

12. The other members were V. Everitt Macy, President of the National Civic Federation; James Lord, President of the Mining Department of the A. F. of L.; Elisha Lee, General Manager, Pennsylvania Railroad Company; Warren S. Stone, Grand Chief of the Brotherhood of Locomotive Engineers; A. Parker Nevin, National Association of Manufacturers; Frank Morrison, Secretary of the A. F. of L; Lee K. Frankel, Metropolitan Life Insurance Company; James O'Connell, President of the Metal Trades Department of the A. F. of L.; and Louis B. Schram of the Accident Department of the National Civic Federation.

13. Daniel Tobin to Gompers, April 12, 1917; Gompers to Tobin, April 17, 1917. President J. W. Kline of the Brotherhood of Blacksmiths' Union also protested and many local officers also wrote protests.

14. Gompers to Edward Anderson, April 10, 1917.

15. Amplification of Declaration Adopted by the Executive Committee, April 16, 1917.

16. Statement of Gompers, May 25, 1917.

17. Daniel Willard to Gompers, June 16, 1917; June 22, 1917; Gompers to Willard, June 19, 1917.

18. Memorandum of Agreement for the adjustment and control of wages, signed by Newton D. Baker, Secretary of War and Gompers, June 19, 1917.

19. Memorandum submitted to Gompers, Baker, and Josephus Daniels by Louis B. Wehle, August 9, 1917.

20. Walter Lippman to Gompers, August 20, 1917; Ordway Tead to Charles McGowan, August 3, 1917.

21. Walter Lippman to William E. Bryan, August 3, 1917.

22. Louis B. Wehle to Frank Morrison, June 20, 1917; Gompers to Wehle, June 22, 1917.

23. Hutcheson to Gompers, July 12, 1917, and August 1, 1917.

24. Hutcheson to Gompers, September 19, 1917.

25. Gompers to Hutcheson, October 21, 1917.

26. Hutcheson to Gompers, October 5, 1917; Gompers to Hutcheson, October 15, 1917.

27. Daniel Drew to Advisory Commission of Council of National Defense, July 11, 1917.

28. Gompers to Newton Baker, June 1, 1917; Baker to Gompers, June 2, 1917.

29. Stone to Gompers, May 3, 1917; J. J. Konekamp to Gompers, July 28, 1917.

30. Hutcheson to Gompers, April 3, 1918; Gompers to Hutcheson, April 10, 1918.

31. Gompers to W. S. Carter, January 19, 1918.

32. Statement issued by the United Mine Workers of America, May 21, 1917.

33. Memorandum of the conference of international officers, chairman of Committee on Labor and representatives of the U. S. Shipping Board, in archives of A. F. of L.

34. *Report of Proceedings of the Thirty-Seventh Annual Convention of the American Federation of Labor,* 1917, pp. 88-89; *Senate Committee Print No. 7, 74th Congress,* 1936, 2nd Session, p. 164.

35. *Report of President Wilson's Mediation Commission on the Bisbee, Arizona, Deportations,* issued on November 5, 1917.

36. Secretary of Labor Wilson to President Wilson, April 29, 1918.

37. Gompers to Executive Council, May 23, 1918.

38. Memorandum from Felix Frankfurter to Gompers, May 23, 1918; Memorandum of the Executive Council of the A. F. of L., July 24, 1918.

39. *Senate Committee Print No. 7,* p. 236.

40. Memorandum to President Wilson from Basil Manley, February 25, 1919, in National Archives.

41. Joseph Valentine to Secretary of Labor William B. Wilson, May 13, 1918, in National Archives.

42. Executive Council to President Woodrow Wilson, November 11, 1918, in National Archives.

43. Gompers to President Woodrow Wilson, November 27, 1918.

44. Resolution adopted on June 29, 1917.

45. Outline of a Plan for the American Alliance for Labor and Democracy.

46. Frank P. Walsh to Gompers, December 31, 1918; Woll to Gompers, January 24, 1919; Robert Maisel to Gompers, February 26, 1919; Woll to Gompers, February 26, 1919.

XXIII

Changes During and After World War I

The beginning of World War I stimulated interest in organization among workers, and swelled the ranks of many unions. Problems of adjustment to changing circumstances as well as dissatisfaction with traditional policies spread through the ranks.

MEMBERSHIP IN THE AMERICAN FEDERATION OF LABOR 1916-1924
(*in thousands*)

Year	Membership	Year	Membership
1916	2,072	1921	3,906
1917	2,371	1922	3,195
1918	2,726	1923	2,926
1919	3,260	1924	2,865
1920	4,078		

The per-capita tax per month on all national and international unions was raised to seven-eights of one cent in 1917, and to one cent in 1921. On federal and local trade unions, the per-capita tax as raised to fifteen cents per month in 1915, to twenty cents in 1919, and twenty-five cents in 1920. In 1920, the amount of the latter per-capita placed by the Federation into the defense fund of directly affiliated federal and trade unions was raised from five to twelve and one-half cents. During the period, the trade unions not only gained in numbers, but in many instances organizations were established in new firms and even in industries formerly closed to organized labor.

Despite the large gains in membership, dissatisfaction with the policies of the leadership was on the increase. Some of the opposition came from old Socialist opponents of the entrenched officers, but there was also a growing feeling among non-Socialists in the A. F. of L. that the heads of the Federation were not sufficiently vigorous or had been too long in office. In 1917 the treasurer of the American Federation of Labor, John B. Lennon, who had served twenty-eight years, was defeated by Daniel Tobin by a vote of 13,478 to 9102. Tobin was nominated by Frank J.

Hayes, the vice president of the United Mine Workers of America and a Socialist. He was strongly supported by the Indianapolis group, by unions whose headquarters were located in that city, and by a number of unions dominated by Socialists.

The following year another veteran, James O'Connell, the second vice president of the A. F. of L., who had first been elected to the Executive Council in 1895, was forced to decline nomination because his union, the International Association of Machinists, had decided by referendum vote of the membership that if its president, William H. Johnston, wanted to run for any office in an organization to which the Machinists' Union was affiliated, the delegates to the convention would support his candidacy. As Johnston was a candidate for vice president of the A. F. of L., O'Connell felt he was obligated to refuse reelection to the Executive Council.

Another member of the Executive Council, H. B. Perham, was defeated by Thomas A. Rickert of the United Garment Workers of America. While the withdrawal of O'Connell was brought about by the influence of the Socialists in the Machinists' Union, the defeat of Perham had no significance, except to indicate that a desire for change existed.

The large increases in membership during the war, the widespread dissatisfaction that followed the armistice and military demobilization, the aggressive attacks upon organized labor by employers, and the necessity for working out solutions to many new and difficult problems, intensified opposition to the policies of the Executive Council and even to its members as individuals. Although the Federation leadership was able to maintain its positions on various issues and its power within the A. F. of L., the challenge was serious.

Attack upon Gompers

Tobin had clashed with Gompers over the conduct of a meeting called to define the policy of the trade unions toward World War I. He refused to serve on a committee headed by Gompers and wrote him that he had "no confidence in a committee that you are endeavoring to organize because of the fact that things will have to run as you want them to run or they can not run at all." Tobin's anger was aroused by the refusal of the meeting of the executives of national and international unions, in March 1917, to approve the postponement for three or four days of the issuance of the declaration in support of the government of the United States in the event of war. Tobin's proposal was "voted down by nearly every member of the Council."[1]

The convention at which Tobin was elected treasurer was held after the declaration of war by the government of the United States, and Tobin was somewhat embarrassed by his earlier position. Even sharper was the reply of the president of the International Typographical Union, Marsden Scott, to the same invitation: "Having no confidence whatever in your integrity," he wrote to Gompers, "I decline to serve on your committee."[2] Neither Tobin nor Scott differed from Gompers on trade union philosophy. Essentially, they looked at most trade union problems in similar fashion, though Tobin lacked the philosophic breadth and acute intelligence of Gompers. Scott was a member of the more conservative faction in his union, the Wahnetas, and his differences were obviously personal. But such differences cannot be entirely discounted in a large organization, and the trade union officers whose internationals were quartered in Indianapolis were able to establish close personal relations as well as to discuss their grievances against the A. F. of L. With the proliferation of jurisdictional disputes, every international union could present some complaint against the failure of the Federation to act in its behalf.

HEALTH INSURANCE

Differences were also appearing among the older trade union leaders. The increased importance of government in economic affairs, at least temporarily during World War I, and the greater friendliness of the Wilson administration towards organized labor, softened the anti-governmental attitude of many leaders of organized labor. When Gompers opposed health insurance, James Lynch, a former head of the International Typographical Union, strongly objected. He called Gompers' attention to the support of a health insurance program by the entire labor movement in New York State, where Lynch was then serving as Labor Commissioner. In Lynch's view the opposition to the program of health insurance consisted "mainly of the Merchants and Manufacturers Association, profit-taking insurance companies, organized doctors of the State, and Christian Scientists." Lynch, on most issues, was a supporter of the A. F. of L.'s official policies, but he rejected its views on health insurance.

Gompers would not accept the above argument. In his opinion, the worker should be provided with an adequate income, and then allowed to distribute his expenditures in accordance with his tastes. In Gompers' opinion, the view that

the state should provide sickness insurance for workers is fundamentally based upon the theory that these workers are not able to look after their own interests and the state must interpose its authority and wisdom to assume the relation of parent or guardian. There is something in the very suggestion of this relationship and this policy which is repugnant to a free born citizen. It seems to be at variance with our concept of voluntary institutions and of freedom for individuals.

In addition, Gompers expressed the fear that the administration of a system of government health insurance would require a large bureaucracy which might endanger the liberty of individuals, including workers. "When once a political agent is authorized to take care of the health of the citizens," he argued, "there is no limit to the scope of his activities or his right to interfere in all of the relations of life. Even home would not be sacred from his intrusions."[3]

The Executive Council was not in agreement on this question, and when a statement critical of health insurance was submitted for its approval, Vice President William Green proposed the following amendment:

We hold that the impairment of the earning power of a worker through sickness should be a fixed charge upon industry. Provision should be made by which medical care and hospitalization, sufficient to take care of the worker and his family should be supplied, during periods of illness. We favor a plan of State Health Insurance which will provide for the collection of a fund through the instrumentality of the state out of which weekly benefits and the expense of medical care would be paid.

The amendment, moreover, suggested that the plan be financed by employer contributions and that no interference with the rights of the worker be permitted.[4]

The amendment was not accepted, and instead, a committee of five was appointed to consider and report on the question. The committee was later authorized by the convention. After hearing witnesses, the committee concluded that

Compulsory health insurance means the surrender by the wage earner of rights and liberties of action that would be dangerous to his individual and collective welfare. Acceptance of paternalistic benevolence carries with it obligations that can do nothing but lead to the control of a great many of the activities of the organizations of labor that now are unhampered by state or other interference, and while it is true that in some instances compulsory insurance may bring some relief from poverty, it is a mere palliative, for economic justice, when established, will bring the relief sought for and in greater measure, if obtained by the workers through organization and this can only be done through freedom of action. Any surrender of a right on the part of an individual or organization to the state means certain control by the state and no one can tell how far reaching that may be.[5]

Failure to get unanimous endorsement for this view prevented the issue from being presented to a convention. Both William Green and Frank Morrison favored health insurance.

UNEMPLOYMENT INSURANCE

The attitude of the A. F. of L. on health insurance reflected its opposition to other forms of social insurance, except insurance against industrial accidents and annuities to aged workers. Unemployment insurance was opposed and the misgivings of the A. F. of L. were based upon the belief that "when the government undertakes the payment of money to those who are unemployed, it places in the power of the government the lives and the work and the freedom of the workers." Instead of unemployment insurance, the A. F. of L. at that time approved public works financed by government, financing of homes by government credit to workers at low interest rates, and the erection of housing for the unemployed.[6] The opposition to unemployment insurance was based largely upon fear of government, a fear supported by the long experience of the A. F. of L. with the executive and judicial branches of the government during labor disputes.

Gompers also expressed opposition to such a program on other grounds. In his opinion, the enactment of unemployment insurance would make unemployment a permanent evil. Why such a result would follow, he never made clear, but he was firmly convinced that government intervention for the relief of the unemployed would be a serious evil, not only for labor but for the entire country. In Gompers' view the worker should be paid enough for his labor so as to permit him to provide for periods of idleness. He also believed "it is paternalism that will destroy initiative and encourage dependency." Such laws, he concluded, "are not advocated for the good of the workers. They are advocated by persons who know nothing of the hopes and aspirations of labor which desires opportunities for work, not for compulsory unemployment insurance."[7] In his view, a system of unemployment insurance would place in the hands of the government the right to determine who would and would not be eligible for unemployment insurance, and under such a system "the labor movement would lose its voluntary character and its effectiveness, and there would be brought about a condition of affairs in our country whereby the toilers would be rendered ineffective in their work for the protection and promotion of their rights and interests."[8]

The fears of Gompers have not been realized, even though the administration of the unemployment compensation laws in some states may be subject, from the point of view of organized labor, to criticism. Yet there can be no question that unemployment compensation laws have been of inestimable benefit to all workers, including those who are members of unions. The dangers visualized by Gompers and others have not been realized, for the only sanction that a state can impose upon a worker for refusal to accept a given job is denial of benefits. Moreover, refusal of employment in a plant on strike is, in the United States, universally recognized as a valid reason for the rejection of a job by an unemployed worker, and is not considered a valid reason for denying benefits. Strikers are usually denied benefits for the duration of the strike or for stated periods during the strike.

CANDIDACY OF JOHN L. LEWIS

The growing opposition to the heads of the A. F. of L. reached its greatest strength in 1921, with the candidacy of John L. Lewis for the presidency of the Federation. Lewis had been elected head of the United Mine Workers of America in 1919, and was recognized as a brilliant and forceful leader. For the first time in almost thirty years, Gompers was to face a serious challenger at a convention. One of the unusual elements in the campaign was the intervention of the Hearst press, which conducted a sharp and irresponsible campaign against Gompers.

Gompers was nominated by George Perkins, the head of the Cigar Makers' International Union, and William Green performed the same office for Lewis. Gompers was elected by 25,022 votes to 12,324 for Lewis. While the delegation from the United Mine Workers of America was split, with three delegates—Frank Farrington, Robert Harlin, and Alexander Howatt—voting for Gompers, the United Brotherhood of Carpenters' delegation voted as a unit for Lewis. This action perhaps reflected the antagonism of the head of that union, William L. Hutcheson, towards Gompers. The entire delegation of the International Association of Machinists voted for Lewis, reflecting the hostility of this organization, which at that time was headed by a Socialist and LaFollette progressive, to the Gompers' regime. The other seven of the largest ten unions—Railway Carmen, Railway Clerks, Electrical Workers, Painters, Seamen, Teamsters, and Street and Electric Railway Carmen—voted (with the exception of the Railway Clerks, whose delegation voted six out of seven for Lewis) unanimously for Gompers. The majority of Socialists voted for Lewis. Max Hayes, who made a "demonstration" run against Gompers in 1912, cast his vote for Lewis, although the rest of the delegation from the International Typographical Union, including Charles Howard, the future secretary of the Committee for Industrial Organization, supported Gompers. Similarly, the delegation from the International Ladies Garment Workers Union split, with four delegates, including its president, Benjamin Schlessinger, voting for Gompers and two other delegates for Lewis.

After the voting, Gompers for the first time expressed his gratification at his election to a convention of the American Federation of Labor. He only did so, he claimed, because the results demonstrated that a chain of newspapers could exercise no control over the labor movement. Lewis, in thanking the delegates who had voted for him, observed that some who had promised him support had changed their minds, which he agreed was their right and privilege. He disclaimed any connection with the vituperative campaign of the Hearst chain.

There was also a contest for the office of sixth vice president between the incumbent, Thomas A. Rickert, and James P. Noonan, the head of the Brotherhood of Electrical Workers. An unusual feature of this contest was the nomination of Rickert by Gompers, the first time he had nominated a candidate for the Executive Council. Rickert was elected by 24,463½ to 12,278½ votes.

The convention of 1921 marked the high point of the formal opposition to the ruling group in the Federation. The postwar losses of membership and the conservative turn in the climate of opinion were to have repercussions upon the labor movement. Moreover, with the death of Gompers in 1924, a member of the United Mine Workers of America was to become the head of the A. F. of L.

REFERENCES

1. Tobin to Gompers, March 30, 1917.
2. Marsden Scott to Gompers, March 28, 1917.
3. James M. Lynch to Gompers, December 18, 1918; Gompers to Lynch, December 23, 1918.
4. Minutes of Executive Council, May 19, 1919.
5. Minutes of Executive Council, January 8, 1920.
6. Statement in archives of the A. F. of L.
7. Gompers to L. P. Ray, November 2, 1921.
8. Minutes of Executive Council, December 16, 1918.

XXIV

Reconstruction and Political Freedom

THE RECONSTRUCTION PROGRAM

In view of the dislocation and changes that followed the war, the American Federation of Labor felt it necessary to devise a reconstruction program. Acting on the instructions of the convention of 1918, the Executive Council appointed John Frey, B. M. Jewell, John Moore, G. W. Perkins, and Matthew Woll as a Committee on Reconstruction. The program, submitted by this committee and approved by the Executive Council and the convention of 1919, called for the establishment of industrial democracy. It pointed to the importance of "codes of rules and regulations" within industry, in which,

Except where effective trade unionism exists, [a code] is established by arbitrary or autocratic whim, desire or opinion of the employer and is based upon the principle that industry and commerce can not be successfully conducted unless the employer exercises the unquestioned right to establish such rules, regulations and provisions affecting the employees as self-interest prompts.

The Reconstruction Program challenged the existence of conditions which denied the workers a voice in the setting of the rules and regulations in the plant, and declared that it was essential for workers to have the right to organize into trade unions "and that effective legislation should be enacted which would make it a criminal offense for any employer to interfere with or hamper the exercise of this right or to interfere with the legitimate activities of trade unions."

The Program called for a policy of "better" wages, fewer working hours, and improved working conditions. It insisted that in countries where wages are highest, both material and spiritual progress are the greatest. "The American standard of life must be maintained and improved," the Program declared, and there must therefore be no decrease in real wages. On the contrary, in many instances wages should be raised. "The workers of the nation demand a living wage for all wage-earners, skilled or unskilled—a wage which will enable the worker and his family to live in health and comfort, provide a competence for illness and old age, and afford to all the opportunity of cultivating the best that is within mankind."[1]

Shorter hours were urged as a means of improving health and productivity, and a limitation of the work day to eight hours, with overtime permitted only under unusual circumstances. Women were to be paid the same pay as men for equal work performed, and it was urged that they not be permitted to perform work disproportionate to their strength. Abolition of child labor was proposed, by prohibition of the employment of minors under sixteen years of age and the restriction of the employment of children less than eighteen years of age to not more than twenty hours within any one week and with not less than twenty hours of school during the same period. The right of public employees to organize and to bargain collectively over their terms of employment was advocated. In discussing cooperation, the Report declared: "To attain the greatest possible development of civilization, it is essential, among other things, that the people should never delegate to others those activities and responsibilities which they are capable of assuming themselves. Democracy can function best with the least interference by the state compatible with due protection to the rights of all citizens."

Consequently, wherever producers could, through cooperative effort, eliminate the middleman, such a step was held to be a useful one. Cooperative dairies, canneries, packing houses, grain elevators, distributing houses were advocated for the farmers, and consumers cooperatives as a means of eliminating profiteering and excess charges for foods and other necessities. In addition, it was held that "participation in these cooperative agencies must of necessity prepare the mass of the people to participate more effectively in the solution of the industrial, commercial, social and political problems which continually arise."

The right of the United States Supreme Court to declare federal and state legislation unconstitutional was criticized, and steps were urged by which legislation declared unconstitutional could be reenacted by Congress or the legislature of the state involved without the subsequent action being subject to review by the Supreme Court.

On political action, the Report pointed to the disastrous experience of organized labor in America with political parties of its own, and therefore reiterated support of the traditional nonpartisan political policy. On government ownership, the Report declared that "public and semi-public utilities should be owned, operated or regulated by the government in the interest of the public." Subsequently, several members of the Executive Council were to base their support of government ownership of railroads upon this statement, while others were to argue that the statement was not intended to commit the Federation to a policy of government ownership. The right of the workers on the railroads to organize and bargain collectively, irrespective of the future disposition of the railroads, whether they be retained by the government or transferred back to private ownership, was demanded. Government ownership of all wharves and docks connected with public harbors used for commerce and transportation was advocated. Improvement of inland transportation, and development of water power by state and federal governments were also urged. A graduated tax upon all usable lands above the acreage cultivated by the owner was proposed; also suggested was provision by the government to permit the tenant farmer to purchase his own land on favorable terms.

Improved workmen's compensation laws were recommended with a request for state funds to assure that the injured workers received the maximum amount of the sums contributed by industry. On immigration, the Report advocated such regulations as would assure rapid assimilation into the American community of immigrants; the Federation also approved the prohibiting of immigration in times of unemployment, and for at least two years after peace had been declared. A system of taxation was suggested that would not unduly burden enterprise, with a progressive tax on incomes, inheritances, and land values held to be the more equitable methods of levying taxes.

Education was advocated which awakens "the mind concerning the application of natural laws and to a conception of independence and progress." It was to be free for all the people, and the "government should exercise advisory supervision over public education and where necessary maintain adequate public education through subsidies without giving to the government power to hamper or interfere with the free development of public education by the several states."

The Report also advocated the abolition of private employment offices. Sanitary and adequate housing were held necessary for the American people, and a program suggested whereby the government was to build

model homes and establish a system of credits whereby workers might borrow money at a low rate of interest and under favorable terms to build their own homes. Credit should also be extended to voluntary non-profit making housing and joint tenancy associations. States and municipalities should be freed from the restrictions preventing their undertaking proper housing projects and should be permitted to engage in other necessary enterprises relating thereto. The erection and maintenance of dwellings where migratory workers may find lodgings and nourishing food during periods of unemployment should be encouraged and supported by municipalities.

The Report argued that the building of public houses was one of the more effective means for relieving unemployment, and that two objectives could be combined, the relief of unemployment and the supplying of public housing to low income groups who would ordinarily be forced to live in slums and inferior homes.

The Report insisted upon the removal of all restrictions upon freedom of speech, press or association. "We insist that all restrictions of freedom of speech, press, public assembly, association and travel be completely removed, individuals and groups being responsible for their utterances. These fundamental rights must be set out with clearness and must not be denied or abridged in any manner."

Unalterable opposition to militarism and to a large standing army was included in the Report. It charged that militarism was a design of tyrants who sought to support their arbitrary authority, and that it was utilized to suppress and enslave other peoples. Moreover, it maintained that large standing armies were a threat to civil liberty, and "the history of every nation demonstrates that as standing armies are enlarged the rule of democracy is lessened or extinguished. Our experience has been that even this citizen soldiery, the militia of our states, has given cause at times for grave apprehension." The Federation declared for the most rapid discharge of soldiers and sailors who had served in the war, and the payment of a monthly salary up to twelve months. It favored legislation which would give the discharged sailors and soldiers ready access to the land, and the government was urged to supply the needed capital for such developments.

On the whole, the Reconstruction Program was a moderate document, which adhered to the traditional views espoused by the A. F. of L. The slight deviation was in advocating government ownership of public utilities, a position that was formerly limited to the advocacy of government ownership of telephone and telegraph lines. The Program was unanimously accepted by the convention. Such acceptance did not, however, indicate that there was unanimity on Federation policy. In fact, opposition to the views of the A. F. of L. on politics and government ownership soon arose. The opposition was made up of two groups: the traditional opponents of the administration, which included Socialists and others who were critical of many of the traditional Federation policies, and the "new opposition" made up of the leaders of unions in the railroad industry but also containing some others. These groups sometimes overlapped, but they could be distinguished from each other in that the "new opposition" was largely made up of those organizations which heretofore had supported the policies of the administration. In addition, the A. F. of L. and other organizations of labor faced a well-organized and well-financed attack from employers.

Joe Hill

One of the important problems in the reconstruction period after World War I was the restoration of civil liberties and the campaign to prevent their further erosion by repressive legislation. The Federation, as its records show, had always spoken out against persecution by governments of political dissidents. In 1915, the A. F. of L. was called upon to help save the life of Joseph Hillstrom, known as Joe Hill. There was more than a minor irony connected with the appeal of Joe Hill. Thomas Mooney, who was given the floor as the representative of the International Workers' Defense League, was soon thereafter himself to face a death sentence following his conviction on a charge of murder resulting from a dynamite explosion during the preparedness day parade in San Francisco.

Mooney was appealing, at the convention of 1915, for aid in behalf of Joe Hill, convicted of the murder of a storekeeper during a holdup of a store outside of Salt Lake City, Utah, during the night of January 14, 1914. It was widely believed that Joe Hill had been "railroaded" to a death sentence because of his efforts to organize the copper miners of Utah into the Industrial Workers of the World. At the time of his arrest, Hill had a bullet wound in his body, which he claimed he had received in an altercation at the home of a woman he was visiting. The case aroused widespread concern, and the Utah Federation of Labor, among others, was convinced that Hill was innocent, and that no substantial proof of his guilt existed.

Gompers appealed to the State Board of Pardons on behalf of the American Federation of Labor: "The sentiments, judgment and desires in the above are earnestly shared by me, and I trust that clemency may be exercised in the interest of justice and humanity."[2] A telegram was also dispatched to the President of the United States and the Swedish Ambassador. President Wilson was urged to use his influence in saving the life of Hill, "particularly when there is so much doubt concerning the case." Neither the pleas of the A. F. of L. nor the urging of the President of the United States was able to win a reprieve from the death sentence. What the incident showed was the willingness of the Federation to protest against and ask for clemency for someone whose conviction was open to question. That he belonged to an organization hostile to the American Federation of Labor, the Industrial Workers of the World, was never raised. The unanimous feeling of the convention was that an effort had to be made to prevent a miscarriage of justice against one whose unpopular views might lead to prejudicial judgment.

TOM MOONEY

In 1916 the American Federation of Labor was called upon to join in the defense of Thomas J. Mooney, who had been convicted of participating in the throwing of a bomb during a preparedness day parade in San Francisco, which resulted in the death of eleven and the wounding of forty spectators. Mooney had been a labor organizer and had aroused the hostility of some local employer groups. He was also closely connected with more radical anarchist elements in San Francisco surrounding *The Blast*, edited by Alexander Berkmen and Robert Minor, who subsequently became a leading Communist publicist.

During 1916 preparedness parades were being organized in many cities as a means of alerting the United States to the need of enlarging and strengthening its military establishment. In many localities, the labor movement was either lukewarm or in opposition to these efforts, and in San Francisco it was decidedly cool to the attempts to arouse interest in a larger army and navy. However, no open hostility was shown to the organizing of a parade to promote military preparedness. During the parade, on July 22, 1916, a bomb was thrown which killed eight and wounded forty. Mooney, Warren K. Billings, and Israel Weinberg of the Jitney Bus Drivers' Union, Edward D. Nolan of the Machinists' Union, and Mooney's wife, Rena, were arrested and charged with the crime. Billings was the first tried, and was sentenced to life imprisonment. Mooney's conviction and death sentence followed. The charges against the others were in the end dismissed.

First to come to the aid of the imprisoned were Mooney's anarchist friends, who revived the International Workers' Defense League. The local labor movement entered the case when it became convinced that the conviction had been obtained by perjured testimony. A demonstration before the American embassy in Petrograd (now Leningrad) on behalf of "Mooni" gave the case national prominence. The issue was brought to the convention of the American Federation of Labor in 1917. After reviewing the evidence, the convention charged that there was a basis for belief under the circumstances "which make it mandatory that they [Mooney and Billings] should be given a new and fair trial, in order that a jury, the composition of which is above suspicion, may pass upon evidence submitted by witnesses whose character warrants credence in their testimony and around whom there hangs no cloud of past viciousness, depravity and attempted subornation of perjury."[3]

The convention of 1917 asked President Wilson to have the case examined, and J. B. Densmore made the investigation. He was convinced that the ends of justice would be served by giving Mooney a new trial. At its meeting in February 1918, the Executive Council thanked President Wilson and at the same time urged the California authorities to act affirmatively upon these recommendations.[4] The A. F. of L. was convinced that "the machinations of the prosecution in the Mooney trial justifies the judgment that he was found guilty on perjured evidence; it is greatly regrettable that the California courts refused to consider this claim which was discovered since that trial." The Council appealed to the governor on the basis that, since the California courts could not go outside of the record in the case, they could not, in the opinion of the Council, take cognizance of the "almost incontrovertible evidence" which "has been discovered since the trial that conviction was had largely upon manufactured and perjured evidence. If the courts cannot or do not take cognizance of these facts, certainly you, as governor of the great

State of California, have the right, the jurisdiction and the power and I trust you will exercise it."[5]

The A. F. of L. also called upon President Wilson and pleaded with him to use his influence to prevent the carrying out of the verdict of execution which faced Mooney. In a letter on behalf of the Council, Gompers appealed to the Secretary of Labor and asked him to prevail upon the President "to go to extraordinary limits to prevent Mooney's execution." The convention of 1918 reiterated its belief that Mooney's conviction had been obtained by perjury, and again asked Governor Stephens to commute his sentence.

The Governor refused, at this time, to take any action to reduce the sentence to a lesser penalty or to make it possible for Mooney to gain a new trial where the charges of perjured testimony could be tested in open court. In July 1918, Gompers again appealed to President Wilson to prevent the execution of Tom Mooney. He informed the President:

From many sections of the country there come to me resolutions, telegrams, in the form of petitions and protests regarding the Mooney case, one cablegram from the Secretary of the Parliamentary Committee of the British Trade Union Congress, the Right Honorable Charles Bowerman, all of them urging, even protesting. I know of no one particular thing that is calculated to do the cause of America and the cause of the allies greater injury than the execution of Tom Mooney. I am exceedingly apprehensive of its consequences if it should be permitted to take place. The Mooney case is now and for months has been an international and political issue, rather than a local or judicial state issue in California, and as the days go on I am sure that the feeling and that issue will become intensified. If Mooney should be executed with the general knowledge or belief that his conviction was based upon manufactured or perjured evidence, and of that there is little or no doubt, I repeat that I am apprehensive of the consequences.[6]

Before his departure for England on a labor mission, Gompers again appealed to Governor Stephens and pleaded for clemency for Mooney, and informed the Governor that there existed a "deep feeling . . . among the workers of France, England, Italy and Russia that a gross miscarriage of justice has taken place in the Mooney trial."[7]

As Mooney had been sentenced to death, commutation of his sentence was the more urgent, and all efforts had been concentrated to win him a reprieve. When this had been accomplished the case of Billings again came into the foreground, and the A. F. of L. was anxious to discover what steps could be taken to bring about the release of both, as the Council was convinced that the two men were innocent. After an investigation by the lawyer retained by the A. F. of L., the Executive Council was informed that, aside from showing possible perjury, no action of a legal nature was possible. It had been suggested to Governor Stephens that he pardon Mooney, indict him for the killing of one of the other eleven victims, and try him again. In the new trial the defense would be on guard against possible perjury, and a fair trial would be given to the defendant. This proposal was rejected by the Governor, and the Executive Council was advised that all legal possibilities had been exhausted, and that until California chose a governor with a different view of this question, nothing could be done.[8]

The convention of 1919 asked for a pardon for Mooney and Billings, and the Executive Council appointed a group of labor leaders in California to wait on the Governor, and convey the views of the Federation to him. After the convention of 1921 had reiterated its earlier views and asked that the two California labor men be pardoned, Gompers wrote to the heads of the international unions advising them of the action "of the convention and to express the hope that you will be helpful in every way within your power and you will keep me advised in regard thereto."[9]

The Federation could, of course, only use persuasion and appeal to the conscience and understanding of the California officials. The latter would not pardon the defendants, and even the appeals of officers of the federal government, including the President of the United States, did little to change their minds. Feeling against the defendants was very strong in employer circles of California and the heads of the state administration were not ready, either because of politics or conviction, to release the prisoners or make it possible for them to gain a new trial.

The Federation had no power to force a new trial; it could only use its voice and its influence in behalf of justice. Much feeling and emotion were aroused by the imprisonment of men whom thousands of union men regarded as innocent. Appeals having failed, advocates of more drastic action appeared on the scene. A number of city centrals, including the Chicago Federation of Labor, endorsed the calling of a general strike unless Mooney was given his freedom. The International Workers Defense League set January 9, 1919, as the date for such a demonstration. A general labor congress was summoned for planning this step and the Chicago Federation of Labor, one of the largest central bodies, was one of the sponsors. In a telegram to Edward Nockles, secretary of the Chicago Federation of Labor, Gompers raised the question whether the Executive Council should not have been consulted before the calling of a general strike was proposed or endorsed. When several other city central labor unions also approved of this congress, the Executive Council declared:

The American Federation of Labor has dealt forcibly and thoroughly with the subject matter urging a new trial for Mooney, and that in accordance with that action the Executive Council has faithfully carried out the instructions of the convention and will continue to the full extent of its ability to urge and insist upon a new and fair trial for Mooney, and the labor movement therefore being properly recorded with reference to the same, the Executive Council has no authority to deal with the subject in any other way than it is doing as per action of the convention. Also that as far as general or sympathetic strikes are concerned all parties are reminded that the authority for ordering strikes rests absolutely and entirely with the International Union whose rules governing the same must be respected. There is not vested in the Executive Council of the American Federation of Labor or any other group, other than the International Unions, the authority to strikes, general or local.[10]

It was neither lack of sympathy nor lack of belief in Mooney's innocence that induced the Executive Council to decry the action of the city central labor councils in this matter, but their usurpation of power and the attempts to foment political strikes. The A. F. of L. had always regarded political strikes as dangerous to the labor movement and likely to arouse strong reactions in the community. Consequently, local or national general strikes were opposed. In addition, international unions were wont to complain if the city centrals induced their locals to violate their contracts and thereby led to the embarrassment of the International Union or to difficulties with employers.[11] Furthermore, the heads of the Federation knew that no demonstration strike would be successful in forcing the authorities of California to release Mooney and Billings, and that a general strike would simply be regarded as a sign of irresponsibility by the non-labor community and make the position of the Federation more difficult. Consequently, appeals for a general strike were looked upon as ill-advised, and experienced labor leaders like Edward Nockles were reproved for endorsing such foolhardy ventures.

POLITICAL PRISONERS

World War I witnessed the conviction of a number of people for violating the espionage law. Eugene Victor Debs, the standard bearer of the Socialist Party in a number of presidential campaigns, William D. Haywood, the head of the Industrial Workers of the World, and many of his associates, Emma Goldman and Alexander Berkman, leading anarchists, and many others had been sentenced to terms in prison. In addition, many were sentenced to prison terms because conscientious objection compelled them to refuse military service.

As the war was drawing to a close, a movement was started to organize a campaign for the release of those imprisoned for violation of the espionage law and for conscientious refusal to serve in the armed services. In the midst of a reception at Chicago, on November 6, 1918, Gompers' services were solicited on behalf of this cause, and "I believe," he told Lucy Robins, "that every man must have his liberty, and that right should be protected above everything else. Yes I will help you. Let Haywood and Goldman come out and comdemn me! It is their personal right."[12]

From the beginning, Gompers favored the release of all convicted for political offenses during the war. However, he warned the promoters of the campaign that resolutions favoring amnesty, if introduced by radical delegates, would inevitably be defeated at the convention of the A. F. of L., and that he was powerless to prevent such unfavorable action. Despite the rejection of an amnesty resolution by the convention of 1919, a representative of the A. F. of L. attended the meeting which established the Central Labor Bodies Conference for Amnesty for Political Prisoners and the Repeal of War-Time Laws. Gompers always felt himself bound by the actions of the conventions of the American Federation of Labor, but he nevertheless arranged for Lucy Robins, Secretary of the Central Labor Bodies Conference for Amnesty, and a representative of the A. F. of L. to confer with the Secretary of War over releasing the conscientious objectors still imprisoned.

In April 1920, a committee of three, representing the A. F. of L., visited Eugene V. Debs, the most famous of the political prisoners. In addition to Lucy Robins, the committee comprised Harry Lang, Labor Editor of the *Jewish Daily Forward* and Jerome Jones, president of the Southern Labor Congress and a leading member of the Southern labor movement. Debs told the delegation to take to Mr. Gompers his regards and added: "Tell Mr. Gompers that I shall never forget to credit him for his efforts to bring about general amnesty."[13]

The convention of 1920 urged "upon the President of the United States, upon the Attorney General of the United States, and the Secretary of War, to make all efforts possible to secure the granting of amnesty to all prisoners whose political beliefs formed the basis of their prosecution, trial and imprisonment."[14] After the convention, President Gompers led a delegation of union officers in a conference with Attorney General Palmer.[15]

President Gompers and Congressman London [who was a Socialist] made a strong and very effective plea for justice and in defense of liberty, basing their arguments upon the rights of freedom of expression and freedom of action. . . . A lengthy discussion took place between President Gompers and Mr. Palmer. Towards the end, Mr. Palmer assured President Gompers that he would do all in his power to help carry out the request made by Labor to release the political prisoners.[16]

After the conference, Gompers wrote to Attorney General Palmer asking him to recommend an amnesty for political prisoners convicted during the war with Germany. "Earnestly hoping," Gompers pleaded, "that you may conclude that it is the most practical, wisest and just course to recommend to the President that he issue a proclamation granting amnesty to political prisoners of the war."[17]

Gompers also informed President Wilson of the meeting with Attorney General Palmer, and conveyed to Wilson the "earnest belief" of Gompers and his associates that the issuance of "a proclamation granting amnesty to the political prisoners . . . would have a most beneficial effect upon a large part of our people, to help allay feelings that have been aroused, and indeed, have a general tranquilizing effect."[18]

As no action was taken, Gompers wrote again to President Wilson before Christmas 1920:

Permit me at this time [he pleaded] when the kindly and considerate spirit cannot but be in men's hearts, to appeal to you in the name of the American labor movement for the performance of an act which I am convinced will meet with the approval of the great majority of our people. I appeal to you for the issuance of a proclamation of amnesty to those political prisoners whose conviction and imprisonment was not because of moral turpitude. Especially do I appeal to you for the granting of a pardon to Eugene V. Debs, now in the Federal Prison at Atlanta, Georgia. During the years that have gone I have had serious differences with Mr. Debs. It is likely that we shall continue to differ. That, however, is beside the point. I never held that Mr. Debs gave voice to any utterance through insincerity or that he was a traitor to his country. His was, I firmly believe, a mistaken conviction, but it was a conviction.

I believe that nothing which it is within your power to do immediately would ease the tension among so many of our people or would so breathe over our country the spirit of peace and good will. A proclamation of amnesty just now would come as a gracious and forebearing act wholly and properly in keeping with the season. In addition, it would be wholly in keeping with the kind of government and the kind of institutions in which we believe and which our people have so lately made such sacrifice to defend. The Montreal convention of the American Federation of Labor, held last June, adopted resolutions urging the granting of amnesty to the prisoners held for political offenses during the war. I believe the convention acted wisely and I am in hearty accord with the thoughts expressed in its action. I need not tell you how loyally and sincerely the conventions of the American Federation of Labor in the years just previous had given their support to the cause of freedom and justice. But the war is ended and the danger has passed. Even those who were most perverse in the advocacy of pacifist views during the war can no longer in the least endanger the safety of the Republic. If the object of the confinement of these prisoners was, as I believe it was, to safeguard the nation, then the object has been achieved. The moral strength of our country, as well as our physical strength, has been amply proven. To open the gates to these prisoners will be no less an example of our moral strength and self-reliance than was their imprisonment in the hour of danger.

Gompers did not ask the release of those who had been charged with offenses involving moral turpitude. Those, he would leave to the normal course of the courts of justice.

But in the case of those who were purely political offenders during the war, as was Mr. Debs, I ask a grant of amnesty, that they may have their freedom and the opportunity to enjoy the life of liberty and justice which our land so richly affords even at times to those who are not worthy of it. Let me say again, that no immediate act of yours would so exemplify the spirit of mercy at this season as the granting of this appeal for amnesty. May I hope this request will find favor in the great heart of a man who has done so much for humanity and who has come to mean so much to those whose faces are turned in hope and aspiration toward the future.[19]

While Gompers always regarded the mandates of the convention as binding upon him, and sought to carry them out to the best of his ability, he was also personally anxious for the release of political prisoners.

When the political prisoners were not released by President Wilson, the Executive Council of the American Federation of Labor turned to the Congress of the United States, where a resolution in favor of amnesty for political prisoners had been introduced. The Council requested a hearing, and Gompers, John P. Sullivan, President of the Central Trades and Labor Council of New York, and Lucy Robins testified as representatives of labor. At the close of the hearings, the witnesses were assured by the chairman of the subcommittee, Senator Sterling, that he would do all in his power to help obtain amnesty for political prisoners. It appeared at the time that amnesty would be proclaimed by the President of the United States, "but President Wilson refused to sign the pardon for many political prisoners, including Mr. Eugene V. Debs, and that was because Mr. Wilson could not be seen in person and, therefore, could not have been fully informed upon the subject as others were."[20]

With the change in administration, Gompers advised that efforts to gain amnesty for political prisoners be renewed. He declared that "labor never gave up a fight for justice and it was our duty to the incoming administration in furtherance of our undertaking." A conference was arranged with President Harding, and Gompers led a large delegation in which the heads of the Building, Metal and Mining Departments, a number of heads of international unions, central bodies, and labor editors conferred with President Harding. Gompers and Congressman London warmly appealed for the release of political prisoners, and they were assured that the cases would be reviewed. Debs wrote "please say to President Gompers and to all members of the American Federation of Labor that we are entirely satisfied with the plea that he and his associates made, and the efforts they put forth in our behalf."[21]

The American Federation of Labor reiterated its views on the subject at its conventions in 1922 and 1923. The work of the American Federation of Labor in

behalf of political prisoners was carried on largely in cooperation with the Central Labor Bodies Conference for the release of political prisoners. In December 1921, President Harding released a group of political prisoners, and it was understood that the remaining prisoners, about forty-five were shortly to be released providing demonstrations were not made on their behalf. Following this the work of the Central Labor Bodies Conference was concluded and we are of the opinion that a discontinuance of the work was proper and justified inasmuch as a full measure of success had been achieved.[22]

The Executive Council believed that demonstrations on behalf of the political prisoners had retarded their release, and the convention of 1922 endorsed continuance of all efforts to effect the release of all remaining political prisoners.

In 1923 the A. F. of L. also appealed on behalf of several Mexican revolutionaries who had been accused and convicted of murder on the Mexican border while "running" arms. Speaking for the Executive Council, Gompers pleaded with Governor Patt Neff, and informed the latter that he had reviewed the cases of these men. Gompers was convinced that "their offence was against the neutrality of the United States." In his view

It was the atmosphere of bitterness that existed along the borderline of Mexico and against the Mexicans at the time of the arrest and trial of these men that really caused their conviction of a crime which was not conclusively proven against any or all of them in such a manner as to merit a life sentence. At the time of their arrest these men were on the point of crossing to the Mexican side of the border line for the purpose of engaging in the general revolutionary movement then going on in Mexico against a government which owed its existence to usurpation of that assassin, Victoriano Huerta. In the course of their pursuit by the Texas authorities, one of the pursuers was killed. The men were tried and convicted of murder and sentenced to life imprisonment. Had it not been for the acute racial bitterness existing at that time along the Texas border, these men would probably have been tried, convicted and sentenced for the real offense committed, and that only; namely, violation of neutrality laws. Happily, today that bitterness has disappeared, and it is hoped, Mr. Governor, that with due regard for the condition that prevailed at the time of the conviction of these men you will give your personal and earnest consideration to the cases of these men, who by reason of said condition are, I am convinced, deserving of your consideration in a way apart from the average appeal for clemency.[23]

In seeking the release of political offenders the American Federation of Labor was carrying out its traditional policies. As Gompers declared in his letter to President Wilson, in many instances he disagreed with the persons involved in these cases, many of whom were his bitter opponents. But on civil rights and the right to free expression the Federation was never guided by the kind of opinions held by those involved in a conflict with the government. For the Federation, the pertinent questions were the rights of individuals and the attempt of the government to suppress legitimate expression of opinion. That such opinions might be undesirable or irresponsible was not the issue. From its defense of the Haymarket defendants to its support of the political prisoners after World War I, the American Federation of Labor always raised its voice in behalf of individual rights and against suppression of unpopular minorities.

SEDITION LAWS

Protection of the civil rights of citizens against legislation to restrict free opinion became another problem after World War I. A sedition bill, known as the Sterling-Graham Bill, was introduced in Congress in 1919. It aroused the strong opposition of the American Federation of Labor. Testifying against the bill, Gompers charged that it could be used to destroy free speech and free assembly, and that "it strikes a deadly blow at legitimate organizations of labor or any other progressive movement for the betterment of the masses which may be opposed by the advocates of privilege and reaction." The bill passed the Senate, and it was again sharply attacked by the representatives of labor when it came before the House, where it was finally permitted to die in committee. At the same time the convention demanded the repeal of the espionage act, enacted to prevent interference with the carrying out of the war. It was under this legislation that many persons were convicted for expressing opposition to the war.[24] The Federation also opposed the enactment of criminal syndicalism laws, aided in having such a law tested in the courts, and sought the repeal of such legislation where it had already been enacted. Because it would constitute an assault upon individual liberty, the Executive Council vigorously opposed a bill for the registration of aliens, introduced in Congress in 1922. The Council charged that

Throughout the bill can be found constant threats of imprisonment, cancellation of naturalization papers and deportation if immigrants do not walk the straight line marked out by the supervisors. Any alien who has become a citizen can have his citizenship taken away and be deported. . . . Strong denunciation of this bill is recommended.[25]

The convention recommended that the Executive Council continue its fight against this objectionable legislation, and in his instructions to the Legislative Committee, Gompers asked the members to "do everything

possible and practicable to carry out the instructions of the convention"
in opposing the legislation for surveillance for aliens.[26]

REFERENCES

1. American Federation of Labor, *Reconstruction Program*, 1919.
2. *Report of Proceedings of Thirty-Fifth Annual Convention of the American Federation of Labor*, 1915, pp. 280, 287, 315.
3. *Report of Proceedings of the Thirty-Seventh Annual Convention of the American Federation of Labor*, 1917, pp. 459-461.
4. Minutes of Executive Council, February 21, 1918; Gompers to Charles A. Knapp, April 24, 1918.
5. Gompers to Governor William D. Stephens, March 25, 1918.
6. Gompers to President Woodrow Wilson, July 19, 1918.
7. Gompers to Governor Stephens, August 10, 1918.
8. Jackson H. Ralston to Executive Council, August 30, 1919.
9. Letter to Paul Scharrenberg, Daniel Murphy, Seth R. Brown, R. L. Enis, and Mike Casey, October 27, 1919; circular letter, August 5, 1921.
10. Minutes of the Executive Council, December 27, 1918.
11. Frank Duffy, secretary of the United Brotherhood of Carpenters and Joiners, to Frank Morrison, July 23, 1919, as an illustration.
12. Lucy Robins, *War Shadows* (New York: Central Labor Bodies Conference for the Release of Political Prisoners, 1922), p. 16.
13. Quoted from the *New York Call*, April 12, 1920, in Robins, *op. cit.*, p. 133. The *Call* was a Socialist daily and hostile to Gompers' policies.
14. *Report of Proceedings of the Fortieth Annual Convention of the American Federation of Labor*, 1920, pp. 865-867.
15. Among them were Frank Morrison, secretary of the A. F. of L.; Joseph Valentine, head of the Molders' Union; Matthew Woll, vice president of the A. F. of L.; the heads of the Building and Metal Trades Departments; William H. Johnstone, president of the Machinists' Union; Thomas A. Flaherty, secretary of the National Federation of Postal Clerks; James P. Noonan, president of the International Brotherhood of Electrical Workers; M. F. Tighe, president of the Amalgamated Association of Iron, Steel and Tin Workers; Congressman London; and Lucy Robins.
16. *Report of Proceedings of the Forty-First Annual Convention of the American Federation of Labor*, 1921, pp. 272-273.
17. Gompers to Attorney General A. Mitchell Palmer, September 20, 1920.
18. Letter to Robins, *op. cit.*, p. 259.
19. Gompers to President Wilson, December 15, 1920.
20. *Report of Proceedings of the Forty-First Annual Convention of the American Federation of Labor*, 1921, pp. 273-274; United States Congress. Senate Committee on the Judiciary. *Amnesty and Pardon for Political Prisoners. Hearing before Sub-Committee, Sixty-Sixth Congress, 3d Session on S. J. No. 171* (Washington: Government Printing Office, 1921), pp. 5-19.
21. Debs to Lucy Robins, May 4, 1921.

22. *Report of Proceedings of the Forty-Second Annual Convention of the American Federation of Labor*, 1922, p. 127.

23. Gompers to Governor Patt M. Neff, July 21, 1923.

24. *Report of Proceedings of the Thirty-Ninth Annual Convention of the American Federation of Labor*, 1919, pp. 101-102, 351-352.

25. *Report of Proceedings of the Forty-Second Annual Convention of the American Federation of Labor*, 1922, pp. 101, 307.

26. Gompers to Legislative Committee, July 28, 1922.

XXV

The Steel Strike, Industrial Conference and Attacks upon Organized Labor

THE STEEL CAMPAIGN

The peacetime sedition and criminal syndicalist bills and the proposed anti-alien legislation were only one aspect of the militant reaction that spread through the country in the years following World War I. Parallel to this reaction was the heightened militancy among workers and their leaders, who were opposing attempts of organized business to destroy many of the labor organizations that had burgeoned in the last five years. The hostile attitude of employers was epitomized by the refusal of the steel industry to recognize its newly-organized workers. Since 1909 the major companies in the steel industry had refused to deal with organized labor. The industry was also the center of anti-union militancy, which it helped to diffuse through the entire economy.

The steel towns were virtually closed to union organizers, and the appearance of a representative of organized labor often meant arrest, imprisonment or forcible expulsion. In May 1917, two organizers of the Amalgamated Asociation of Iron, Steel and Tin Workers were arrested, detained in jail in Gary, Indiana, and then forcibly sent to Chicago.[1] The opposition and power of the industry had steadily weakened the union, and it lacked the resources and stamina to challenge by itself the powerful and militant industrial giants which dominated steel production. Aware of the situation, Gompers had several times over the years suggested to a number of international unions the desirability of a joint campaign in the steel industry, but his suggestions were unheeded.

The Chicago Federation of Labor played a major role in the promotion of the campaign to organize the steel industry in 1918. Led by John Fitzpatrick and Edward Nockles, this central body was the largest and, in many respects, the most important and vigorous of any of the Federation's city central labor unions. Under its leadership the Chicago stockyards and packinghouses had been organized over the strenuous opposition of the employers.

The leaders of the Chicago Federation of Labor now felt that a joint organizing campaign by the respective unions in the steel industry might

385

achieve favorable results. On April 7, 1918, William Z. Foster, a delegate from the Chicago local of the Brotherhood of Railway Carmen, introduced a resolution instructing the delegate to the next convention of the American Federation of Labor to initiate a joint organizing campaign in the steel industry. Foster already had had an interesting career in the radical and labor movements. Starting out as a youthful Socialist, he soon found a place on its left wing, then successively became an active member in the Industrial Workers of the World, a syndicalist, and then a moderately progressive trade unionist, the philosophy and practices of which he now espoused. This phase was not to be of long duration, but Foster was to show himself a resourceful and able leader of trade unionists while he was playing this role.

At the convention of 1918 the executive officers of the American Federation of Labor were formally instructed to call a conference during the convention of all delegates of international unions whose interests were involved in the steel industries, and also the city central bodies and state federations in the steel districts, for the purpose of devising a cooperative organizing program. A preliminary conference, attended by delegates from twenty-one internationals, fourteen city centrals, and seven state federations, was held during the convention. It was decided to embark upon an organizing campaign so as to bring the steel industry, once a pioneer and center of unionism and collective bargaining, into the unionized orbit.

In challenging the great open shop giant, the labor movement was not undertaking an easy task. Yet it was believed that, from the point of view of the receptivity of the workers to the message of organized labor, the time was now most propitious. In addition, the climate of opinion was more favorable to unionism than it had been for a number of years, and some of the labor practices of the steel industry were such as to give the program a strong possibility of success.

On August 1, 1918, Gompers opened a conference of representatives from sixteen international unions.[2] A National Committee for Organizing the Iron and Steel Workers was set up with Gompers as chairman. John Fitzpatrick was appointed vice-chairman, and William Z. Foster, secretary. All organizations represented by delegates donated one hundred dollars, and it was decided that a uniform initiation fee of three dollars be charged, one dollar of which would be contributed to the organizing fund. A headquarters was established, and arrangements for periodical meetings made.[3]

The campaign was an immediate success, and considering the opposition and the basis upon which these workers were organized—the payment of an initiation fee and at least a month's dues—it can be regarded as one of the great organizing feats in American labor history.

Foster, who had been appointed National Secretary, informed Frank P. Walsh that both Gompers and Frank Morrison, who attended his conference on August 1st, had given "the movement the O.K.A."[4] The campaign was immediately successful in Gary, Indiana, and in Chicago, but in the communities along the Monongahela River, Pennsylvania, meetings were suppressed. McKeesport was one of the worst in that regard, and union representatives were not allowed to hold meetings. Upon his return from abroad, Gompers protested to Mayor George Lysle, the suppression of the rights of citizens in McKeesport.[5] Gompers also wrote to John Williams, the head of the Amalgamated Association of Iron, Steel and Tin Workers, urging "a little more aid for a final push to bring the workers into the union." He pointed to the successes in organizing already achieved, and pleaded for all possible assistance to bring the remaining workers into the union fold.[6]

The steel operators did not stand idly before the growing unionization drive which threatened to engulf the entire industry. Workers were discharged for joining a union, and the increasing number of those dismissed for this cause posed a problem for the organizations of labor. To devise methods for dealing with this and other problems the unions called a meeting for Pittsburgh on May 25, 1919. However, before the meeting took place, the officers of the Amalgamated Association of Iron, Steel and Tin Workers were instructed by their convention to seek a separate conference with the heads of the United States Steel Corporation. It did not arouse a favorable reaction from leaders in the industry and Elbert Gray, the chairman of the Board, replied: "As you know, we do not confer, negotiate with, or combat labor unions as such. We stand for the open shop."[7] The action of the Amalgamated was subsequently criticized by Foster, who had not yet entered into the Communist phase of his career. In justifying its action the Amalgamated Association claimed that it had a major stake in the steel industry, while the other unions cooperating in the steel campaign had only a few members in the steel plants. The Amalgamated could not exist without a powerful base in its industry, but the other unions would in the main be basically unaffected by failure, as the major portion of their memberships lay in other industries. If the steel corporations had granted recognition to the Amalgamated there would have been no reason to deny it to the other labor organizations, as the Amalgamated would have bargained for the most important and the largest number of workers in the steel mills. It might therefore be argued that recognition of the Amalgamated would have, in fact, meant recognition for all the unions in the steel industry. Still it cannot be denied that an effort at a separate agreement might have weakened the cohesiveness and unity of the cooperating unions if the major organization work had not already been achieved.

The conference of 583 delegates on May 25th ordered the unions affiliated with the National Committee for Organizing Iron and Steel Workers to seek a bargaining conference with the various steel companies, and a committee was selected.[8] [The committee was composed of Gompers; John Fitzpatrick, the head of the Chicago Federation of Labor and vice chairman of the National Organization; D. J. Davis of the Amalgamated Association of Iron, Steel and Tin Workers; Edward J. Evans of the International Brotherhood of Electrical Workers; William Hannon of the International Association of Machinists; and William Z. Foster of the Brotherhood of Railway Carmen and secretary of the National Committee.]

As chairman of the National Committee, Gompers wrote to Gary, on June 29, 1919, asking him to meet with the above representatives. Gary did not reply, and the National Committee thereupon recommended to the twenty-four cooperating unions that they take a strike vote. On July 20, 1919, representatives of the twenty-four unions met in Pittsburgh, drew up a set of demands, and endorsed the taking of a strike vote. The demands called for the establishment of the right to collective bargaining; reinstatement of the workers discharged for joining the union, with pay for time lost; an eight-hour day; one day's rest in seven; abolition of the twenty-four hour shifts; increases in wages to guarantee an American standard of living; establishment of standard scales of wages in all trades and classifications; double rates of pay for all overtime after eight hours, holidays, and Sundays; check-off of union dues; seniority to be used in reduction and increasing of work force; abolition of physical examination for applicants for employment.

The strike vote gave the National Committee authority to call a walk-out if the steel companies refused to deal with the union. The vote was unmistakably on the side of action, and the committee then called at the offices of Elbert Gary for a conference. It was refused, and the committee was asked to submit its proposals in writing. To a request for a meeting, Gary replied that he did not think the committee was authorized to represent the views of a majority of the employees of the United States Steel Corporation. The committee then proceeded to Washington, where it appeared before the Executive Council. A conference with President Wilson was arranged and Gompers was instructed to accompany the committee to its meeting with the President, where the issues in dispute were presented. Gompers reported that the President was sympathetic with the position of the unions and had declared "that the time had passed when any man should refuse to meet with representatives of his employees" and that he (the President) would do what he could to bring about a meeting of the parties.[9]

President Wilson failed to change the views of the heads of the steel corporations, whose adamant opposition to dealing with an organization of labor was steadily forcing the leaders of the unions to consider a strike. After waiting for some time for word from President Wilson, the National Committee wrote to him, on September 4th, and pointed to the restiveness among the steel workers and to the discharge of many for joining unions which was creating a difficult situation for the heads of the organizations of labor in the industry. On September 9th, the heads of the twenty-four unions and the National Committee again met to consider the situation. President Wilson informed the conference that he was continuing his efforts to bring about a meeting. Most of the leaders did not regard these efforts as sufficiently definite in character to warrant the postponement of strike action, and they made it clear to President Wilson that unless they could guarantee some relief to their victimized members they would be forced to call a walkout. Thereupon President Wilson urged the postponement of the strike until after the forthcoming industrial conference had met.[10] This suggestion was rejected, and the desirability of calling an immediate strike in the steel industry debated. Gompers spoke against such a step, and he gave

instance upon instance of a similar character of national importance to labor and the country, of enthusiasm and impetuosity of the unorganized or newly unionized in driving their movement to destruction, in bringing about disorganization and demoralization to the ranks of the workers for years. Attention was called to the strategic advantage which would accrue from complying with the request of the President and the great disadvantage which would result if the President's request was flouted.

On the other hand, Tighe, Foster, and Fitzpatrick were of the opinion that unless there was some commitment from the steel companies of a willingness to confer with the representatives of the unions, the strike should be called. The heads of three international unions—Johnston of the Machinists, Joseph Valentine of the Molders, and Milton Snellings of the Operating Engineers—voted against the calling of the strike.[11] In fact, Johnston took the same position as Gompers, and argued:

I have given careful thought to the President's message and I do not see how we can afford, in view of the President's appeal to us, through President Gompers, to carry out the program set for September 22nd. I, therefore, wish to be recorded as in favor of complying with the President's request to defer action until after the forthcoming industrial conference.[12]

When the strike was called, Fitzpatrick suggested that a meeting of the Executive Council be called for Pittsburgh, in common with the heads of the twenty-four unions involved, to direct the walkout. This suggestion met with no enthusiasm from the members of the Executive Council except William Green, who was of the opinion that the money and other aid needed by a strike of that magnitude could only be supplied by the Executive Council. The suggestion was, however, rejected.[13] The strike was answered by about 365,000 workers, the largest steel strike in history. The ability of twenty-four unions to organize jointly into the various cooperating unions more than 156,000 workers contradicts the notion that workers could not be organized except through an industrial union. The workers were subsequently divided among the various unions, 70,-926 being turned over to the Amalgamated Association of Iron, Steel and Tin Workers, which received the largest number from the organizing efforts of the National Committee for Organizing Iron and Steel Workers. The more than 156,000 included, however, only those workers from whose initiation fees one dollar was deducted and forwarded to the general office of the National Committee. "It represents approximately fifty to sixty percent of the total number of steel workers organized during the campaign." The National Committee ceased collecting its deduction from the initiation fee early in 1919, and therefore no further record of recruiting of members could be made.[14] It is evident that whatever shortcomings the campaign in the steel industry may have suffered from, it did succeed in organizing several hundred thousand steel workers in the face of the most bitter opposition of the steel industry, supported in virtually every steel community by the courts and the local authorities. The ultimate failure of the strike was not due to lack of unity or support among the strikers or the officers of the unions. In fact, Foster declared before a Congressional Committee that

The steel movement had been carried on according to the strictest trade-union principles. It was overseen by the National Committee, consisting of twenty-four presidents of large international unions. As secretary of this committee I had necessarily worked under the close scrutiny of these men and dozens of their organizers—not to speak of the highest officials of the American Federation of Labor. Yet none of these trade unionists, keen though they be to detect and condemn unusual practices and heresy in the ranks, had found fault with the character of my work.[15]

As the book was written after the strike, when Foster was not on the payroll of the American Federation of Labor and before he had become connected with the Communist apparatus, the statement must be regarded as an accurate account of the nature of the campaign.

On October 6, 1919, several representatives of the National Committee came before the Executive Council to discuss the strike and the methods to support it. Gompers asked the representatives of the various unions what methods they would pursue in supporting their members involved. Tighe was uncertain and pointed to the few members his union had employed in plants not on strike. The head of the Iron Workers' Union offered to donate ten thousand dollars as a beginning; the president of the Coopers and Blacksmiths' union declared that their unions would pay strike benefits. Other unions declared that their unions would pay strike benefits, and some declared their inability to do so. In any event, the financing of the strike through donations and general appeals by the American Federation of Labor was successful, and the commissary and relief organization set by the leaders of the strike were adequate and effective in relieving need.

A more serious problem was, however, facing the strikers and their leaders. The violent repression of meetings and legitimate trade unions activity by the sheriffs, constabulary, and other police authorities was the most serious problem facing the strikers and their leaders. The Executive Council was informed, during the meeting early in October, that unless free speech could be established, the strike would fail.[16] The Executive Council protested, but its protests were without avail.

Members of the National Committee also suggested to the Executive Council then in session that the steel strike be taken up at the President's Industrial Conference. This was agreed to, and the labor delegation, led by Gompers, introduced a resolution which pointed to the steel strike as a source of disturbance of the relations of labor and management. Therefore, the conference was asked to approve the appointment of a committee of six, two from each of the groups represented at the conference—labor, management, and the public—who would seek a settlement of the differences existing between the unions and the employers in the steel industry. At the insistence of Elbert Gary, who was present as a public representative, the resolution was held in abeyance. Gary's opposition to this resolution was on the ground that the Conference was called for the purpose of formulating policies for the future rather than of seeking solutions for problems of the present. It was obviously a refusal to allow any group not under the control of the industry to consider the problem.

Gompers informed Fitzpatrick of the efforts the labor group had made to gain an impartial hearing for the steel workers, and Fitzpatrick was of the "opinion the whole matter was handled in a masterly manner and met with his entire approval."[17]

In the meantime, the steel companies managed to increase their rates of operation. Whereas there had been an estimated 365,000 workers out on strike in the first weeks of the walkout, there were, according to the estimates made by the organizers of the National Committee, slightly below 110,000 out on strike six weeks alter. Consequently, when the National Committee met on December 13th, there was some discussion on the advisability of ending the walkout. James P. Noonan, the head of the International Brotherhood of Electrical Workers, and William

Dobson of the Bricklayers' Union strongly advised against ending the strike, and in the end only the representatives of the Amalgamated Association of Iron, Steel and Tin Workers and the International Union of Operating Engineers voted against its continuance.[18]

The strikers were not only confronted with severe repression, but the press and the steel companies centered their attack upon the presumed radicalism of the strikers, especially upon Foster, whose syndicalist views were dragged out of the past and made a target for attack. As the strike continued the United States Senate appointed a committee to investigate. The committee also trotted out Foster's former views, and Gompers vigorously defended Foster. Believing that Foster had broken unequivocally with his revolutionary past, Gompers argued that he was "entitled to something better than having a mistaken past thrown in his teeth."[19] The strike continued, but the strikers were fighting a losing battle. The increasing rate of operations was mute testimony that the strike was failing, and on January 8th, the National Committee for Organizing Iron and Steel Workers decided to call off the strike. It drew the comment from Tighe that the strike "was not a defeat in any sense," as ultimately the workers would organize.[20] At the end of the month, Foster resigned as secretary of the National Committee, and, according to him, "it was entirely of my own volition." Foster had been bitterly attacked and, as he said,

offered to resign from the conference committee which handled all negotiations concerning the steel strike. But my objections were overruled and I was continued on the committee. Moreover, at any time in the campaign a word from the executive officers of the A. F. of L. would have brought about my resignation. This they were aware of for months before the strike. All of which indicates that the men responsible for the organizations in the movement were satisfied that it was being carried on according to trade-union principles, and also in consideration of the Steel Trust's murderous tactics in the past it was a certainty that if the opposition had not taken the specific form it did, it would have manifested itself in some other way as bad or worse.[21]

Foster admitted that the American Federation of Labor and the affiliated unions supported him during the campaign and the strike, despite Foster's vulnerability from a propaganda point of view. He resigned of his own volition, and the reasons were obviously a desire to lead a movement for the reorganization of the American Federation of Labor.

However, the Amalgamated Association had not been satisfied with some of Foster's activities, and it resigned from the National Committee. J. G. Brown was appointed secretary in Foster's place. Many of the international unions which had cooperated in the steel campaign favored continuance of the effort to organize the steel workers after the unsuccessful strike. They felt some embarrassment at the absence of the Amalgamated Association from the National Committee. At the meeting of the Executive Council, in June 1920, a number of union leaders who had been active in the steel campaign, including Johnston of the Machinists, Noonan of the Electricians, and John Conners of the Switchmen's Union of North America, advised a continuation of the campaign and urged the reaffiliation of the Amalgamated Association of Iron, Steel and Tin Workers with the National Committee. Johnston expressed the view that the Amalgamated Association had withdrawn from the National Committee "because irresponsible men had been appointed by Secretary Foster, in charge of various cities."[22]

Tighe was of the opinion that the problems of his union, as far as the steel industry was concerned, were somewhat different from those of other unions. The unions that had their basic membership in industries other than steel would not be too seriously affected by a loss of a walkout. Moreover, a successful strike would swell their membership, but would not basically change their situation. On the other hand, the Amalgamated, which was essentially a union of steel workers, had to consider that the outcome of any event in the steel industry would seriously affect the union's position. Tighe objected to the organizers of the National Committee concentrating their efforts upon getting workers in organized mills out on strike. Moreover, he also objected to the prolongation of the strike when it seemed apparent that the outcome was certain. His position on this point was based upon the strikers' need to regain their jobs, which would become increasingly difficult if the struck plants succeeded in replacing their striking members. It was the difference over this issue which led to the withdrawal of the Amalgamated from the National Committee.

Another criticism made by Tighe was the insistence of the National Committee that workers as they organized be segregated into separate unions. In his opinion, a "movement of that magnitude should have had only one head. The A. F. of L. should have had entire control of the campaign under the direction of the Executive Council and the Presidents of the international organizations affected."[23] In turn, Foster was critical of several of the cooperating unions, especially the Amalgamated and Operating Engineers, and he was of the opinion that greater unity might have achieved better results. This is doubtful, for whatever limitation craft organization might have, it was not a factor in preventing the organization of hundreds of thousands of workers who were able to force a suspension of the entire industry.

The workers were defeated by the adamant refusal of the steel industry to grant any kind of recognition to the union. The steel magnates would yield neither to the pleas of the President of the United States nor to the pressure of their workers. As a matter of fact, the efforts of the Committee for Industrial Organization to bring the workers of the Little Steel companies into the union in 1937 were defeated by the companies by the use of the same tactics as were used in 1919. It is easy to blame lack of organization, failure to utilize given techniques, the absence of industrial unionism, or the failure of the American Federation of Labor to give adequate support. There was no shortage of finances, although the National Committee was careful in its strike expenditures; the fact is that from November 1919 to January 10, 1920, the A. F. of L. received $418,141.14. At the end of the strike there was a surplus of almost seventy thousand dollars which was turned over to the American Federation of Labor to be held for subsequent organizing campaigns in the steel industry.[24]

The A. F. of L. was anxious to have the campaign in the steel industry resumed, and the convention of 1920 considered a resolution that the Amalgamated Association be asked to rejoin the National Committee. The issue was placed in the hands of the Executive Council, and the unions in the steel industry were called together by the Executive Council on September 14, 1920.[25] The unions involved failed to devise an adequate program, and no attempt to organize the steel industry was made until the 1930's, when the Committee for Industrial Organization took up the fight. The Amalgamated did not itself have the resources, and the other unions in many instances were fighting employer attacks upon their own organizations in their principal jurisdictions. Consequently, an extensive drive to organize one of the more difficult industries, in which a large and heroic strike had just been held, was not placed high on the list by the unions with jurisdictions in that industry.

The steel campaign raised to the forefront one issue that the unions had ignored, the organization of Negro workers. Many strikebreakers were recruited among Negro workers, and the unions were forced to consider that problem. They had been warned that failure to admit Negroes would inevitably lead to their alienation from the labor movement. When the question was discussed by the executive officers some were disinclined to blame the Negro.

FIRST INDUSTRIAL CONFERENCE

The efforts of the labor organizations to reestablish themselves on a major scale in the steel industry ended in failure despite the vast gains in organization and the sacrifices of the steel workers. The steel industry was too powerful and was able to prevent any major breach in the open shop wall the industry had erected around it. The attitude of the dominating groups in business and industry were already revealed at the President's Industrial Conference, called by President Wilson in the early fall of 1919. The selection of a delegation to the Conference also became a source of serious division between the Executive Council and the railroad unions, many of which were affiliated with the American Federation of Labor. On September 3rd, President Wilson requested the American Federation of Labor to appoint fifteen members who would meet with a group appointed by business, and a third by the President "for the purpose of enabling us to work out, if possible, in a genuine spirit of cooperation a practicable method of association based upon a real community of interest which would redound to the welfare of all our people."[26] Wilson was anxious to find "some common ground of agreement and action with regard to the future conduct of industry . . . and to obtain the combined judgment of representative employers, representative employees, and representatives of the general public conversant with these matters." He hoped that there would be a canvass of the tried methods of cooperation between capital and labor so that a genuine spirit of cooperation might be developed.

Upon receipt of the request, Gompers communicated the contents of the letter to the Executive Council, and indicated that some difficulties might arise in the selection of the personnel of the labor representatives. Gompers believed that all members of the Executive Council might wish to serve, yet he noted that some important unions were not represented on the Executive Council. "Then again we ought to have at least one and perhaps two women to make up as part of the delegation, and the railroad brotherhoods, although not affiliated to the American Federation of Labor, because of the importance of the position they occupy in the industrial and transportation fields, should have representation by at least one member."[27]

While the American Federation of Labor was to limit itself to the selection of the labor representatives, Gompers did try to have Franklin Roosevelt selected as a public member. He wrote to Secretary of Labor Wilson telling him: "Both you and I know Mr. Roosevelt and his ability and good qualities," and asked that Wilson use his influence to have Franklin Roosevelt appointed as a public member. This was the only instance in which Gompers recommended that a specific public member be appointed, and he refused suggestions for recommending others, as he did not regard it as altogether proper for him to nominate members of this group. In Roosevelt's case, he and Joseph Valentine, the head of the Molders' Union and a member of the Executive Council, believed that an exception should be made because of his sympathy and for understanding the problems of labor.[28]

As soon as the announcement of the Conference was made, pressure for the appointment of certain individuals, either on the basis of the organization they represented or because they were from certain geographic areas, began. When Gompers offered an appointment as a labor representative to Warren S. Stone, the head of the Brotherhood of Locomotive Engineers, the latter declined on the ground that the railroad unions were not sufficiently represented. Gompers was distressed by the unexpected opposition to his appointments, and he felt that the criticism leveled at him was unfair.[29] On September 23, 1919, the chief executives of the fourteen recognized railroad labor organizations met to consider the selections of representatives of labor for the Conference. It was decided "that this conference go on record as being unwilling to attend or be represented at the Labor Conference called by President Wilson unless the Chief Executives of all recognized labor organizations, both in and out of the American Federation of Labor, are invited to be present." Ten of the unions represented at this conference were affiliates of the American Federation of Labor, and the other four were the operating brotherhoods. A committee of two, B. M. Jewell, the Acting President of the Railway Employees Department, and J. J. Forrester of the Brotherhood of Railway Clerks presented the statement to Gompers, and informed him that the resolution presented to him had been prepared and enacted at the initiative of the ten unions of the railroad industry which were affiliated with the American Federation of Labor.[30]

The railroad unions suggested that the Executive Council call a meeting of the heads of internationals and non-affiliated unions, and that instead of 22 representatives of labor, as planned, approximately 125 should be appointed. Gompers was asked to take this matter up with President Wilson so that the changes in representation requested could be introduced. It was the view of the conference of railway labor organizations that

No conference of the kind proposed, unless it would include the heads of all the recognized organizations, National and International and Brotherhood organizations, affiliated with the American Federation of Labor and the four train service organizations above mentioned, would represent American Labor. And because of this we would not care to trust our interests to anything less.[31]

The proposal that the heads of all of the international unions be appointed as representatives to the Industrial Conference was rejected by Gompers, who questioned the usefulness of such a procedure. He also would not approve the calling of a meeting of the heads of the international unions and the Brotherhoods for consultation during the meetings of the Conference. Gompers regarded this suggestion as "too indefinite" and "did not care to ask the officers of international unions to come to Washington and play the part of call boys." As a result of Gompers' refusal to accept the views of the railroad unions, their representatives voted not to accept membership on the labor delegation. Gompers was especially perturbed about the position of the railway unions that the Executive Council of the American Federation of Labor did not represent the labor movement. In his opinion, the railroad unions "attempted to assume the leadership and spokesmanship of the American Labor Movement in attempting to take away from the conventions of the American Federation of Labor or the Executive Council the authoritative expression of the American Labor Movement in the interim of conventions."

There was also some doubt about the conference in the mind of John L. Lewis. The latter had been appointed after William Green, Secretary of the United Mine Workers and a member of the Executive Council, had offered his place to him. Lewis was, however, dissatisfied with the personnel of the public delegates, and expressed his "lack of confidence in the success of the conference." He had reference mainly to Judge Gary, but Gompers believed that labor, especially the steel workers, might gain some advantage from participating in the meeting despite its limitations.[32]

At the urging of Gompers, the letters were not given to the press by the railroad labor executives. Upon hearing of the differences between the American Federation of Labor and the railroad labor unions, Frank Duffy, a member of the Executive Council, expressed the view that little good would come from the Conference. "You know the committee has neither the power, the right or authority to tie down any organization or anything agreed to nor has the A. F. of L. All that can be done is to use persuasive powers to that end. As far as the Carpenters are concerned, we don't propose to be hampered, limited or restrained in any manner from carrying out our legitimate work as formerly. . . ."[33] Finally, an arrangement was devised whereby the heads of the four railway brotherhoods were appointed as delegates to the Conference as labor members, and Acting President B. M. Jewell of the Railway Employees Department was appointed a public member. The latter appointment was designed to offset the appointment of Gary and Rockefeller as public members.

The conference opened on October 6th, and fifty members representing the three groups were present. Basically they represented the views of labor and management, although there was a large group of public members who presumably were not partisans of any group. As has already been noted, the labor group, which was divided into those selected by Gompers and the representatives of the railway brotherhoods, did not expect much from the conference. On October 14th, the labor group, as was noted above, submitted a resolution under which the differences between management and labor in the steel industry would be submitted to a committee of six, two from each of the major groups in the conference, for adjudication and settlement. In supporting the resolution, Gompers pointed to the great importance of that controversy to both labor and management. Gompers denied that the resolution requested a great concession.

Are we [he argued], at this time, in this year of grace 1919, having driven political autocracy from off the face of the globe, to submit servilely to an industrial autocrat? The time has gone by when any man can say that he is master of all he surveys. Some degree of democracy, some opportunity for fair and full consideration, must be accorded to the workers—the workers not corraled in the plants and under the supervision of the superintendents and foremen and executive officers, but in a place where they can express themselves in their own way and formulate their own grievances, and formulate the remedies and the relief they ask.[34]

Gompers warned that there was a new spirit in the air and that the companies would have to regard it fairly and honorably. Gary finally rose and expressed his approval of "conciliation, cooperation and arbitration whenever practicable without sacrificing principles." He was, however, of

the fixed opinion that the pending strike against the steel industry of this country should not be arbitrated or compromised, nor any action taken by the conference which bears upon that subject. Also that there should be maintained in actual practice, without interruption, the open shop as I understand it; namely, that every man whether he does or does not belong to a labor union, shall have the opportunity to engage in any line of legitimate employment on terms and conditions agreed upon between employee and employer.

Gary expressed his opposition to the limitation of production, and any arrangement which "deprives the workman from receiving the highest wage rates resulting from voluntary and reasonable effort, hinders promotion or advancement in accordance with merit, or otherwise interferes with the freedom of individual action."[35]

The remarks of Gary did not go unchallenged, for as soon as he had finished his statement Gompers was on his feet asking for the floor. After alluding to the unparliamentary irregularity of the procedure that permitted Gary to make a statement on an issue not before the conference, Gompers declared:

As one of those who declared it would be a great pleasure to hear some statement from Judge Gary, . . . I am rather disappointed at the statement that he has made. I did expect, as I think that every one who heard the rumor had the right to expect, that something new was coming forth, to throw some light upon the situation, and perhaps remove some obstacle from the path of our progress. The statement just read by Judge Gary is nothing more or less than the letter he addressed to his subsidiary companies about a month ago, and which has since been made public property, and not either in thought or statement of fact, or in the language employed, is there the slightest variation from that letter.[36]

Gompers pleaded for fairness and understanding, and for the ending of the policy of forcing the strikers to surrender through starvation. Gompers expressed the fear that, in view of the attitude of powerful employer groups, the conference would accomplish little. After a long postponement, the resolution for an investigation and settlement of the steel strike by a committee of six from the conference was rejected, by the votes of the public and employer groups.[37]

The main difference came on the resolution on collective bargaining. The employer group was reluctant to approve any explicit statement endorsing collective bargaining, unless at the same time they endorsed the position of shop councils and similar organizations "where in considering wages and terms and conditions of employment the workmen act as a group from representatives of their own number who meet representatives of the employers for negotiation and the adjustment of the employment relation."[38]

To the employer group, the shop councils or company unions looked promising as a means for development of contentment and efficiency among the labor force of a firm. The employer group contended that the idea of collective bargaining as understood by the labor unions was only of limited use in a manufacturing industry, and the group did not wish to endorse language which might give rise to a misinterpretation of the management point of view.

The employers then submitted a substitute for a resolution on collective bargaining, which had earlier been rejected, in which the right of workers to join unions, shop councils, or other forms of association was recognized, but the "right of the employer to deal with men or groups of men who are not his employees and chosen by and from among them is recognized." This, of course, was no concession to the recognition of the right of workers to join unions, in the sense that the conference would express an obligation upon employers to recognize outside labor unions as collective bargaining agents. An impasse had been reached, and President Wilson was so informed. He thereupon appealed to the conference, urging its members to relent from extreme positions and seek some accommodation for conflicting views.

Despite the President's appeal, no basis for agreement could be found. In fact, the President's letter came at the time when it was evident that the employer group would not concede to labor the right to organize in unions which were uncontrolled by employers. On October 22nd, after the question had been long debated, Gompers introduced the following resolution: "The right of wage earners to organize without discrimination, to bargain collectively, to be represented by representatives of their own choosing in negotiations, and adjustments with employers in respect to wages, hours of work, and relations and conditions of employment is recognized." This resolution was, according to the labor delegates, the test of good faith, and the employer group voted against it. Although it was supported by both the public and labor groups, under the rules of the conference the adoption of a resolution required unanimous consent of all three groups; the labor declaration on collective bargaining was defeated. Thereupon Gompers rose, explained the position of labor, and declared:

You have by your action, the action of the employers' group, legislated us out of this conference. We have nothing further to submit; and with a feeling of regret we have not been enabled with a clear conscience to remain here longer, we have responsibilities to the millions of workers and those dependent upon them, we must fulfill these obligations. Our regret is that the rejection of anything like a fair proposition on our part has occurred. It has been done, and the die is cast.[39]

The conference to all intents and purposes was ended, although the public group decided to remain in session so it could report to the President.

SECOND INDUSTRIAL CONFERENCE

On December 1, 1919, another conference, made up exclusively of public representatives, was held under the chairmanship of Secretary of Labor Wilson. Herbert Hoover was vice chairman. Testifying at one of the sessions, Gompers argued that "there is no really royal road as a solution of the industrial and economic problems of our time. It is a matter of development, a matter of growth." He stressed the undesirability of solving labor disputes by law and by tripartite boards. "What could labor expect in this reactionary period, in this hysteria which is existing in our country if there were a President in the United States to make such appointments as the committee of three representing the public in matters of dispute between workers and employers." Nor was Gompers convinced of the inevitable justice of allowing public opinion to determine labor disputes. He pointed to the following facts:

Public opinion did not concern itself with the long hours of labor of working people; public opinion did not interpose to the eighteen-hour work day of the street and steam railways; did not destroy the sweat shop system; public opinion did not take the breaker boys out of the mines in the anthracite coal region; public opinion did not bring about compulsory education; the limitation of the hours of women and children.

He conceded that strikes should be avoided wherever possible. He believed, however, that they were necessary if more serious social tension is to be eliminated. In his view:

Discontent has been rife in every age of the whole world. How the discontent shall be expressed and manifested is the thing. You will find riots, you will find incipient revolt or general uprisings, in some form or other at various periods of the world's history. [On the other hand], the American Federation of Labor has done more to guide that thought and activity that the spirit of unrest and discontent shall find its natural and rational expression and manifestation, that it shall be loyal to the American Republic, that it shall take its guide and instruction from the spirit of the Declaration of Independence and the Constitution of the United States.[40]

The second industrial conference did not make any major contribution to settling the strained relations then existing between capital and labor.

The guiding thought of the conference has been that the right relationship between employer and employee can be best promoted by the deliberate organization of that relationship. That organization should begin with the plant itself. Its object should be to organize unity of interest and thus to diminish the area of conflict, and supply by organized cooperation between employers and employees the advantages of that human relationship that existed between them when industries were smaller. Such organization should provide for the joint action of managers and employees in dealing with their common interests. It should emphasize the responsibility of managers to know men at least as intimately as they know materials, and the right and duty of employees to have a knowledge of the industry, its processes and policies. Employees need to understand their relation to the joint endeavor so that they may once more have a creative interest in their work.[41]

Based upon this statement, methods for settling disputes, built upon voluntary methods, were advocated. While in the abstract both the right to bargain collectively by the employer and to refuse to bargain on that basis were recognized, the former was asserted as a desirable public policy, but "reliance upon good faith for the enforcement of the bargain" was asserted. The conference dealt with a number of other topics, but its views were not given too much attention by either management or labor.

The Drive for the Open Shop

The failure of labor to gain recognition from the steel industry, and its inability to win the consent of the dominant employer interests for free collective bargaining, indicated that many employers were not willing to accept the labor relations that had developed in many industries during the war. In fact, by the fall of 1920 there was already in existence a well financed and militant drive to reduce the power of labor organizations under the slogan of the "American Plan." The latter was based on the argument that the American Plan of labor relations allowed each worker to determine his own terms of employment with his employer, without the intercession of the business agent or the union. This program received the endorsement of many business organizations, and it made use of the latest devices for forming public opinion. Open shop associations proliferated in many communities, and the single organizations frequently cooperated together on a local, regional, and even national bases. Under the slogans developed in this campaign, many unions found themselves confronted by an aggressive opposition, able frequently to oust the organizations even from well-established and long-held positions. The garment, building, maritime, packinghouse, and even the printing trades' unions felt the furious assault unleashed by anti-union employers.[42]

The Executive Council, meeting in the latter part of November 1920, took cognizance of the widespread attack being then made upon the organizations of labor and decided that energetic action must be taken to combat it. An additional problem then considered was the adverse court decisions which were crippling the ability of labor to resist attack. A meeting of Gompers with the heads of the departments of the A. F. of L. and officers of several labor unions with headquarters in Washington decided to call a conference of international officials for February 23, 1921.[43] The conference, in session for two days, declared that "reactionary employers have joined their might in a campaign which they are pleased to call a campaign for the 'open shop,' which they have been waging vigorously since the signing of the armistice." The statement denounced the use of the injunction in labor disputes, and alluded to the interpretation of the Clayton Act by the courts which had the effect of nullifying the intent of that statute. It warned that the effort to crush labor organizations might also imperil all groups in society, for it endangered the principle of voluntarism. The conference concluded: "The path of progress and constructive peaceful achievement and evolution is laid down by the trade union movement. The road to autocracy, unfreedom and chaos is laid down by its enemies. The choice is now before the country."[44]

The conference of union officers called for public support and recognition of the right of workers to organize into trade unions for the promotion of their interest and protection; the right to engage in collective bargaining through representatives of their own choosing; the right of workers to cease work collectively; and the right to bestow or withhold collectively patronage of any business. In addition, the conference urged the public to support legislation against the issuance of injunctions in labor disputes where such injunctions could not be legally issued in the absence of such disputes; prohibition of immigration for two years; more general utilization of the initiative and referendum in the political affairs of the United States and of the states; abolition of the power of the courts to declare acts of Congress unconstitutional, power which the declaration held to have been usurped; election of judges;

repeal or exemption of labor from the anti-conspiracy laws; and the restoration of the federal employment service. In addition, the statement asked that credit be administered as a public trust in the interest of all of the people, and an investigation of private detective agencies be made by the government.[45]

INJUNCTIONS

The American Federation of Labor was troubled by the increasing attacks upon organized labor, and even more concerned by the hostile court decisions. The A. F. of L. insisted that the decisions in the Duplex Printing Company Case had caused labor to lose the protection which it believed had been granted to organized workers by Section 20 of the Clayton Act, presumably restricting the issuance of injunctions by the federal courts in labor disputes. The A. F. of L. also noted that in the Duplex Printing Company case, the United States Supreme Court held that any effort of the International Association of Machinists to prevent its members from installing presses manufactured by the above company was illegal, because the workers were not in proximate relation as employees to the company whose product was being boycotted. This attitude was held to be unfair and highly prejudicial to labor. In the case involving the Hitchman Coal Company, the Supreme Court held that a labor union could be restrained by the courts from organizing the employees of a company whose workers had signed an agreement, or yellow dog contract, not to join an organization of labor during their employment with the particular company. Such a decision, the Federation feared, would help to keep workers out of unions and prevent the unions from launching any effort to change the status of the unorganized.

In a report to the Executive Council, Gompers called attention to the increasing number of labor injunctions being issued by the courts, and informed the Council that

Scarcely a day passes that does not witness the issuance of an injunction against the workers somewhere in the country, either ordering them to do or ordering them not to do things which they have a lawful right to do. The injunction menace is growing rapidly, not solely because injunctions are being issued with greater frequency but because courts constantly are occupying new ground and constantly widening the scope of their orders so as to make them cover a very widening classification of acts.[46]

Gompers discussed a number of the recent cases in which the courts had severely restricted the activities of the workers engaged in labor disputes with employers. He found that the growing tendency of courts to issue injunctions meant that the unions had to devote an increasing amount of time and money in defending themselves against these restrictions. He suggested that the injunctions be attacked on the ground that they constituted a violation of constitutional rights, in that such orders were based on an implicit assumption that the employer had a property right in the labor of a human being and the good will and patronage of human beings. Injunctions, to be constitutional, must be granted upon the basis of denial or affirmation of certain acts, he pointed out.

The decisions to which Gompers and the other leaders of the American Federation of Labor objected were handed down by the Supreme Court headed by Chief Justice William Howard Taft. The latter had served as a public member of the War Labor Board, and his services there had met with general approval—an approval shared by labor leaders.

However, the American Federation of Labor had, through Gompers, been opposed to the elevation of Taft to the Supreme Court. When reports that he might be appointed were circulated in 1916, Gompers immediately wrote to President Wilson objecting, on the ground that

[As] a federal judge Mr. Taft demonstrated that he is not in harmony with the newer ideals of human freedom and human justice. He established his reputation as a leader in that legal school that holds that employers have a kind of property right in the labor power of their employees. Upon this theory was built up a use of the injunction process that denied to the wage earners their rights as free men and their legal rights under the laws of our country. This injustice to the wage-earners was augmented by unwarranted extension of the application of the writ of injunction and by the fact that in contempt cases growing out of violation of injunctions, the wage-earners were denied the right of trial by jury which was assured under our constitution and laws. Mr. Taft was known as the father of this abuse of the writ of injunction.

Gompers pointed to Taft's opposition to the Clayton Act, and charged that Taft "lacked 'heart-understanding'—an understanding alone which enables the possessor to project himself into the experience, the sorrows, the yearnings of others. Without this quality, justice becomes cold and impersonal—in fact ceases to be justice and deteriorates into legalism."[47] Wilson did not appoint Taft to the Court, and it is not certain that such an appointment was ever contemplated. However, with the change in administration in 1921, President Harding appointed Taft as Chief Justice, where he helped to hand down the majority of decisions which now weighed so heavily upon organized labor.

INJUNCTION IN SHOPMEN'S STRIKE

The temper of the labor movement can best be gauged by the reaction of the Executive Council of the American Federation of Labor to the injunction issued by Judge Wilkerson of the United States District Court, in Chicago, in the railroad shopmen's strike. On September 1, 1922, Attorney General Daugherty applied for an injunction in the Federal District Court of Chicago against the railway shopmen on strike. When the Attorney General left Washington, he announced he was to visit his home in Columbus, Ohio. Instead, he called privately on Judge Wilkerson, a former assistant attorney general and a recent appointee to the district court. Before the subsequent brief hearings in open court, no effort was made to apprize the unions or their officers of the proceedings being started against them. The court, without hearing the representatives of the unions, signed the order drawn by the Attorney General. On the grounds that the defendants were engaged in a conspiracy to obstruct interstate commerce, the court ordered the defendants to refrain from any activity in prosecution of the strike. Among the acts prohibited were the circulation of letters, circulars, telegrams, word-of-mouth information, or any communication through interviews or through printed newspapers which encourage the strike; or the commanding or encouragement of any one to cease work or to enter the service of any railway carrier. The order also restrained the national officers from issuing any instructions, making requests, issuing public statements, or communicating with defendants, or expending any funds on behalf of the walkout.

The unions, through their counsel, challenged the validity and basis of the order issued on the grounds that the strike was lawful; that the court could not carry on a criminal prosecution without a jury trial; and that the order had been obtained by the Attorney General through fraud. After some argument, the court issued a temporary injunction, on September 25th, which in fact modified the extreme character of the first order, for the government made no effort to prevent the continuance of the strike nor efforts on its behalf. Moreover, there was a qualification, a sort of an escape clause, included in the preliminary injunction which did not appear in the restraining order. It read:

But nothing herein contained shall be construed to prohibit the use of the funds or moneys of said labor organizations for any lawful purpose, and nothing contained in this order shall be construed to prohibit the expression of an opinion or argument not intended to aid or encourage the doing of any of the acts herebefore enjoined, or not calculated to maintain or prolong a conspiracy to restrain interstate commerce or the transportation of the mails.

The injunction was held to be a serious threat to labor but, as the United States Supreme Court ruled, in the Pennsylvania case on February 1, 1923, that neither employer nor employee was obligated to obey the decisions of the Railway Labor Board, the unions concluded that this decision meant that the strike of the railway shopmen would therefore be regarded as lawful. Moreover, the unions discovered that it would have involved them in heavy financial expenditures to combat the charges of conspiracy in Judge Wilkerson's court, and in view of the changing conditions, the labor organizations refused to take part in the court proceedings before Judge Wilkerson on May 1, 1923, and ordered their attorneys to withdraw. It was feared, however, that the Wilkerson injunction might serve as a precedent for other judges to follow, and, consequently, the organized labor movement was seriously concerned with the question.

When the restraining order in the shopmen's strike was first issued, many protests were made by labor unions and trades and labor councils, some of which demanded that the American Federation of Labor institute defensive steps against the judicial encroachments. Several demanded that the Executive Council call a general strike as a protest. When one of these declarations was considered, the following resolution was introduced by one of the members: "The Executive Council of the American Federation of Labor has either the right or power to call or advise a general strike. The Executive Council authorizes and directs the communication to the officers of the railroad shopmen on strike that every assistance within its power will be accorded to them, so that they may be victorious in the final result of the contest." This resolution, which stated the historical position of the American Federation of Labor, was not unanimously accepted. An amendment was submitted which further declared: "No suggestion or advising of a general strike [shall be made] until the President shall consult the officers of affiliated international unions."[48] The significance of the amendment is that it implies an endorsement of the general strike if the proper procedure with respect to consultation with the officers of the international unions were followed. In other words, the members who submitted the amendment were not opposed to the use of the general strike weapon when the entire labor movement was threatened; they simply wanted the Executive Council to clear such action with the international unions. This was considerably different from the outright condemnation of the general strike which the Federation had historically espoused. Even more significant, the amendment received three out of nine votes cast, and the motion to lay the original resolution on the table was defeated by a vote of six to two. Finally, the original resolution was enacted by a vote of six to three. As the members did not indicate how they voted, it is not possible to discover which ones favored the use of the extreme measure in the event of a more direct attack upon labor organizations. The event indicates the concern and even the fear with which the attacks upon organized labor in the postwar period were regarded, and the extreme measures of defense some of the leaders thought necessary.

INJUNCTION IN THE COAL STRIKE

The injunction in the railway shopmen's strike was only one of a series which had both threatened and aroused the labor movement. Drastic injunctions had earlier in the postwar period been issued in the bitumi-

nous coal strike of 1919. The Washington agreement covering the bituminous coal fields had been negotiated in the spring of 1918, and was
terminated by the orders of the convention of the United Mine Workers
of America in September 1919. The operators, when presented with the
demands formulated by the convention, argued that the Washington
agreement, made with the union in March, 1918, could not be terminated until March 31, 1920. The claim was based on the clause which
provided that the agreement continue for the duration of the war, but
not exceeding two years from April 1, 1918. The miners insisted that
the cessation of hostilities constituted the ending of the war, while the
operators took the more legalistic view that while the fighting had stopped
the war had not formally ended. Neither the miners nor the officials of
the union were willing to accept such a narrow view. In fact, spreading
strikes throughout the bituminous coal fields were an ominous sign that
dissatisfaction had reached a breaking point.

The convention which met to consider the policies to pursue drew
up a set of demands which included a six-hour day from bank to bank,
and the five-day week; a 60 per cent wage increase for all classes of
labor and for all tonnage, yardage, and dead work; time and one-half
for overtime and double time for Sundays and holidays. The union also
demanded the abolition of the penalty clause, which allowed the operators
to impose a fine of one dollar a day upon all miners engaged in unauthorized strikes. The operators held to their position that the old
contract was still in effect, and rejected the demands of the union. As a
result, a strike was called for November 1, 1919. The response to the
strike order was complete. It was the first major walkout under the
leadership of John L. Lewis, who had assumed the presidency of the
union that year. The government, from the beginning of negotiations, had
taken a hostile attitude towards the miners and, on October 25th, the
government denounced the projected strike. The miners were willing to
negotiate, but the operators were adamant. Two days later, Attorney
General A. Mitchell Palmer asked the Secretary of Labor for copies of
the wage contract, the action of the Fuel Administration in approving the
wage contract, the declaration adopted by the convention of the United
Mine Workers of America at its convention on September 23, 1919, the
names and residences of the officers of the United Mine Workers of
America, the states covered by the union, and other information regarding
the activities of the union.[49] Evidently the Attorney General was preparing to proceed against the strike in the bituminous coal fields even
before it had begun. Moreover, the statement by the President and
Cabinet that the strike was illegal was sharply attacked by President
John L. Lewis of the Miners' Union.

Permit me to say [Lewis wrote to the Secretary of Labor, a former officer of his organization] that the unprecedented and unwarranted action of the Cabinet and the President of the United States in issuing a statement . . . has done more to prevent satisfactory agreement than any other element which has entered into the situation. The President's statement is a fiercely partisan document, because it attacks the intentions of the mine workers without even suggesting that mine operators have brought about this unhappy situation; and further, because threat is made to exercise full force of Government to prevent stoppage of work, without any corresponding threat to exert full force of Government to enforce fair working conditions and a living wage. It is indeed a sad commentary upon principles of square dealing, when the President of the United States and his Cabinet, by unanimous vote, ally themselves with sinister financial interests, which seek to deny justice to Labor, and precipitate our Country into industrial turmoil?

Lewis denied it was unlawful to strike under the laws of the United States, and declared that the "President's statement of October twenty-fifth, nineteen nineteen, threatens invasion of Constitutional and inalienable rights of American citizens; it is a climax of a long series of attempted usurpations of executive power."[50]

As soon as the strike was called, the American Federation of Labor declared its support. The A. F. of L. called attention to the fact that

The mandate of the officers of the United Mine Workers of America was direct from the representatives of the men who at the recent convention decided that unless a substantial improvement in wages and a regulation of the working time were granted the strike order should be issued to take effect November first. President Lewis and his associates had no alternative particularly when the operators left the conference leaving the representatives of the miners alone.[51]

The American Federation of Labor sought to lift some of the burden of responsibility from the head of the United Mine Workers of America who, as has been noted, was directing his first major walkout.

Soon the union and all of organized labor was confronted by a serious problem. Judge Albert B. Anderson of the Federal District Court in Indiana issued, at the request of the Attorney General of the United States, a sweeping restraining order against the United Mine Workers of America, its officers, and members, ordering them to cease all activities tending to encourage the strike in the bituminous coal industry. Upon the publication of the report of the action, Gompers and Secretary Morrison immediately protested to the Attorney General against the intervention of the United States Government in the strike. In a statement to the press, the A. F. of L. declared that it was

inconceivable that a government which is proud of its participation in a great war to liberate suppressed peoples should now undertake to suppress the legitimate aims, hopes and aspirations of a group of its own people. It is still more strange that a nation which may justly be proud of its Abraham Lincoln should now reverse the application of the great truth he enunciated when he said that as between capital and labor, labor should receive first and foremost consideration. The injunction against the United Mine Workers bodes for ill. An injunction of this nature will not prevent the strike—it will not fill the empty stomachs of the miners—it may restrain sane leadership but it will give added strength to unwise counsel and increase bitterness and friction.[52]

Gompers and Morrison decided to call the Executive Council into session to consider the injunction and decide upon the steps to be taken by the A. F. of L. in this situation. When the Executive Council assembled on November 9th, a committee from the United Mine Workers of America, James Lord, Adam Wilkenson, and Edgar Wallace, were present. They informed the Council that the sentiment in the Miners' Union was for ignoring the injunction. Lewis and Green were called on the long distance telephone, and after the question was discussed with them, the Council appointed Gompers, Woll, and Tobin to draw up a report and a statement on the strike. The statement reviewed the causes of the strike, and attributed it to the rising cost of living, and denounced the use of the Lever Act, the law upon which the injunction had been issued, for the purpose of restraining the legitimate activities of labor, and declared that the injunctions against the strike of the coal miners were as "unwarranted as they are unparalleled in the history of our country, and we declare that it is an injustice which not only the workers but all liberty-loving Americans will repudiate and demand redress."[53]

In reply to the statement of the A. F. of L., Attorney General Palmer declared that the strike of the coal miners was in violation of a federal statute, meaning the Lever Act, which regulated the utilization of fuels during wartime. He also assured the labor movement that "nothing that the government had done is intended, or designed, to have any effect upon the recognized rights of labor to organize, to bargain collectively through its unions, and under ordinary industrial conditions, to walk out by concerted action."[54] Palmer reiterated the government's determination to enforce the order against the strikers, which brought forth the statement from the A. F. of L. that the government had pledged, at the time the law was considered by Congress, that it would not be used against workers engaged in a strike or lockout over wages, hours, or other conditions of employment.

After the statements had been issued, Gompers, Woll, and Morrison, as representatives of the American Federation of Labor, conferred with the United States Attorney General. He assured the delegation that he had no desire to injure labor and, as proof of his friendly attitude, Palmer suggested a procedure under which the strike might be settled and the injunction dissolved. Palmers' plan called for (1) the dismissal of the re-straining order and injunction; (2) the calling off of the strike; and (3) the issuance of a call for a conference of representatives of miners and operators. The labor delegation raised the question of the unwillingness of the coal operators to confer, and asked the Attorney General what assurance he could give that they would retreat from their position. Palmer was of the opinion that there would be no question but that the operators would agree to a conference. The labor delegation informed the Attorney General that his proposals would be placed before the officers of the Miners' Union, and asked for assurances that any statement made by Lewis over the telephone, assuming that the wires were tapped, would not be used by the government in proceedings against Lewis. This pro-posal was accepted by the Attorney General. The proposal was presented to Lewis over the long distance telephone, with a stenographer taking down the statements made by Gompers. (Lewis was informed that this procedure was being followed.) When the three conditions were given, Lewis informed Gompers that, once the strike was called off, the operators would be in the saddle, and therefore he could not accept any arrange-ment which would involve the canceling of the strike. When Lewis de-clared his unwillingness to call off the strike, Gompers encouraged him over the telephone: "I may say to you, John, that we did not expect any other answer. We felt, however, that it was necessary to put the question to you and without prejudice and without color and without any sug-gestion of accepting or rejecting it. I wanted to get your best judgment."[55]

The Executive Council felt that the injunction against the coal miners constituted a serious threat to the miners and to all labor. It hoped that the court orders would be disobeyed, and that the issue would be carried to the highest court. The heads of the Miners' Union had consulted with the Executive Council, and the latter's activities were carried on with the approval of the executives of the Miners' Union.

The Council was, however, soon to be surprised, for in the midst of its preparation for a campaign of support of the miners' right to resist an illegal usurpation by the courts, the strike of the bituminous coal miners was called off without the Executive Council of the American Federation of Labor having been informed of this contemplated step. No official action was taken or statement made, but the views of the Executive Council can be surmised by the inclusion of a copy of a news report, on the reaction of some unnamed member of the Council, in the minutes of the meeting of the Executive Council. The following can therefore be regarded as the reaction of the members of the Council:

The news this morning that the miners had decided to call off the strike in compliance with the court order startled many Federation officials. The head of one of the Federation departments on being apprized of the action taken, profanely refused to believe that it was true. Others refused to talk on the subject, but it was evident that they had been taken unaware. The leaders of the Mine Workers' Union, hitherto regarded as radicals, decided to abandon a position declared tenable and just by Mr. Gompers and other leaders of the Federation hitherto regarded as conservatives. Washington is wondering who's who and which is which?[56]

The incident again demonstrates the policy of the Federation on matters which vitally affected the interests of the entire labor movement. It is true that the decision had to be made by Lewis, for it was he and his union which would have had to bear the burden and the penalties of defiance. Yet the heads of the American Federation of Labor had always taken the position that unjust and unconstitutional actions by the judiciary had to be defied, at least until the question had been adjudicated by the higher courts. This was Gompers' position from the beginning in the Buck's Stove and Range Company case, a position he shared with Lewis' predecessor, John Mitchell, and Frank Morrison. There was therefore keen disappointment at the action of the heads of the Miners' Union, especially as it was taken without informing the Executive Council, the leaders in denouncing the action of the government and in rallying labor and public support to the strike.

COURT OF INDUSTRIAL RELATIONS

The enactment of a statute creating a Court of Industrial Relations by the Kansas legislature became another source of difference between the American Federation of Labor and the head of the United Mine Workers of America. During the strike of bituminous coal miners the mines around Pittsburgh, Kansas, had been shut down. The Kansas District, No. 14, was headed by Alexander Howatt, one of the more militant leaders of the union, who had at times clashed with the leaders of the international. At the convention of 1919 Howatt defended the seating of delegates from a group of insurgent locals which had been suspended for supporting an unauthorized strike.

The Governor of Kansas, Henry J. Allen, tried to force a reopening of the mines during the strike, but he was unsuccessful. He thereupon proposed a more permanent solution of the industrial problem. He called the legislature into special session, and at his request, and over the opposition of organized labor, a court of industrial relations was created to administer a system of compulsory arbitration in a number of industries defined as public utilities. The law required the legal incorporation of labor unions so that they could sue and be sued. The term "public utility" was applied not only to the power and transportation industries, but to those producing coal or manufacturing food and clothing. The court, made up of three members, could initiate proceedings upon the petition of an employer, workers, a labor union, or a group of citizens. Decisions made after a hearing and investigation were binding upon both sides. Penalties for refusal to obey the orders of the judges were included. The issue was considered in the report of the Executive Council to the convention of 1920; the law was denounced, and support for those who opposed such laws promised.[57]

The miners of District No. 14, against whom the industrial court law was largely directed, defied the legislation. A protest strike against the law was started, and even though the strike only lasted one day, others followed. For refusing to testify before the Industrial Court, when ordered by a county judge to do so, Howatt and August Dorchy, the District vice president, were sentenced to jail for contempt. The district was in constant turmoil over the attempts to enforce the Industrial Court Law. At this juncture the head of the United Mine Workers of America, John L. Lewis, intervened on the ground that the unauthorized strikes were in violation of the agreement between the union and operators. A dispute over the introduction of mechanical hoists led to a wildcat strike, followed by the suspension of thirty-three locals for violation of contract. Howatt was at the time a political opponent of Lewis and a candidate for vice president of the International Union on the opposition ticket. Lewis suspended Howatt and Dorchy for refusing to desist from violation of the contract, and placed a provisional president in charge of the district. This action led to a bitter internecine struggle, with the Kansas labor movement strongly supporting Howatt, who was regarded as the champion of free labor because of his open defiance of the Industrial Court Law.

This support, coming from the Kansas State Federation of Labor and many of the city central bodies in that State, excited the opposition of John L. Lewis, who requested the American Federation of Labor to prevent its affiliates from encouraging the violation of contract.

In Lewis' opinion, he was enforcing collective agreements, and in aiding Howatt the A. F. of L. affiliates were guilty of violating the principles of the sanctity of contracts espoused by the Federation. Upon hearing Lewis, the Executive Council authorized Gompers to draft an answer to Lewis' plea. In its reply the Council conceded that

There can be no deviation from the settled principles so frequently enunciated and emphasized not only by the Executive Council but by the American Federation of Labor itself, for collective bargaining and the traditional principles that collective bargaining should be faithfully adhered to, and yet, in the case in point, the Executive Council could not disregard the direct instructions of the conventions of the American Federation of Labor upon the situation existing in Kansas, in the fight against the Industrial Court of that state.

Moreover, the Executive Council had denounced the Industrial Court legislation as "an act to establish involuntary servitude for the workers of Kansas," or an "act to protect the financial interests of the owners of public utilities at the expense of their employees." Even more important, in the opinion of the Federation, the law "destroyed the right of collective bargaining, the gateway to industrial peace."

It also called to Lewis' attention the action of the convention of 1921, which commended

the organized workers of Kansas and, particularly the mineworkers and their officers of that state, upon whom the brunt of the battle has fallen, for so courageously opposing this law in the face of injunctions and threats of imprisonment by hostile judges; and thereby preventing this objectionable law becoming operative in the state selected for this legislative experiment and thus fighting the battle for the organized workers of the country.[58]

Lewis was informed that the strike of the Kansas miners, which Lewis claimed was in violation of contract, had been in effect at the time of the A. F. of L. convention and yet the convention had endorsed the resolution unanimously. In fact, both Lewis and Howatt were delegates from the Miners' Union, and neither had spoken on that resolution. Even though Lewis and the Executive Council of the American Federation of Labor may have had coinciding views as to the differentiation between the insistence upon carrying out the principles of collective bargaining and faithful adherence to its conditions, the Council doubted whether one per cent of all the people in Kansas and the United States [would] make such a distinction.[59]

The position of the American Federation of Labor was that the strike against the Industrial Court Law was justifiable, even if it violated contracts. Moreover, any efforts to discourage support by the State Federation of Labor of Kansas or by the city central bodies would lead to an interpretation by the general public that the A. F. of L. was not opposed honestly to the Industrial Court Law. While not explicitly stated, the members of the Executive Council must have been aware that Lewis' eagerness to inflict punishment upon the Kansas miners was not altogether unrelated to the opposition of their leader, Alexander Howatt, to the international administration. Upon the receipt of Gompers' letter, the International Executive Board of the United Mine Workers of America appointed a committee of five to confer with the Executive Council. Gompers, Morrison, Tobin, and Woll were appointed to hear the views of the Miners' Union.

In the meantime, Lewis sought to convince the Council of the desirability of supporting the United Mine Workers of America against its recalcitrant district. He argued that

In the light of historical events relating to the growth and development of the American Federation of Labor and its announced policy in favor of collective bargaining, voluntary agreements between employers and employees, it is difficult for the International Executive Board of the United Mine Workers of America to understand how the President of the American Federation of Labor could, with justification, withhold from an affiliated union, when requested, its moral support through a declaration in favor of collective bargaining, joint agreements, and observance of contracts.

Moreover, Lewis insisted that the question at issue in Kansas was the behavior of a subordinate union of the United Mine Workers of America, and the only issue in dispute was the observance of contracts. Lewis declared that the international office of the United Mine Workers of America was "unrelentingly opposed" to the Kansas Industrial Court Law.

However, in opposing the law, we believe, as reasonable practical men clothed with the responsibility of directing the affairs of the United Mine Workers of America between conventions, that the law cannot be declared unconstitutional, repealed or rendered inoperative by following a senseless or impracticable policy. The avenue open to us through which its validity may be attacked, its repeal brought about or the law rendered inoperative, must first be followed if success is to be attained.[60]

The statement stressed that the International Union was seeking to establish discipline in its ranks, "put down rebellion and compel obedience to the laws of the organization." It deplored the silence of the President and the Executive Council of the American Federation of Labor, who were thereby giving aid to the supporters of violators of the traditional policies of collective bargaining, "contract observance and the supremacy of an affiliated International Union within its conceded jurisdiction." The Executive Council refused to retreat from its position, and would not order the Kansas State Federation of Labor or any central body to end its support of the coal miners who were defying the Industrial Court Law, even when such defiance was in violation of the union agreement. The Executive Council based its decision upon the action of the conventions of 1920 and 1921, which endorsed strong resolutions critical of the Kansas Law.

The same meeting which considered the statement of the committee from the Miners' Union also voted on a resolution on this question submitted by William Green, a member of the Council and Secretary of the United Mine Workers of America:

We, the Executive Council of the American Federation of Labor favor the observance of contracts voluntarily entered into by national and international unions and that it is the declared policy of this Council to cooperate with and to support affiliated international unions in the observance and enforcement of contracts, voluntarily entered into.

Upon the motion of Tobin, action on the resolution was postponed. A subsequent motion on the same question to instruct the state branches and central bodies not to support the striking miners of Kansas was defeated, with only William Green voting in the affirmative.[61] The request for action was in the end withdrawn by Lewis. The Executive Council wanted to avoid any statement that would be used to support the Industrial Court law. The Council was "fully persuaded that the effort to obtain a favorable decision from the judiciary . . . will prove futile and that the only hope for the repeal of that infamous statute lies in the organized action by the workers of Kansas. . . ."

While there were some political elements involved in the controversy between Lewis and the Executive Council, because of Lewis' opposition to Gompers' leadership at the convention of 1921, it is doubtful whether this was a major factor in the Federation's support of Howatt. Even Frank Duffy, the Secretary of the United Brotherhood of Carpenters and Joiners, whose union had supported Lewis for the presidency, voted against him on this issue. Moreover, the Federation would not allow an internal political issue to determine a public policy of the magnitude involved in this question. It was felt that the defeat or nullification by nonobservance of this law was even more important than maintaining the historical position that the observance of contracts was a primary duty of all trade unionists. The feeling of the members of the Executive Council upon this and similar issues can be noted by their reaction to the Wilkerson injunction in the railway shopmen's strike. The belief, evident from a multitude of events, that organized labor was in dire peril from the machinations of an organized and militant employer opposition made the Executive Council reluctant to denounce those who were feeling the brunt of the attack.

REFERENCES

1. John Williams to Gompers, May 2, 1917. Williams was secretary of the Amalgamated Association of Iron, Steel and Tin Workers.
2. John Fitzpatrick, Edward Nockles, Ragnar Johansen of the Chicago Federation of Labor, and Simon O'Donnell, who represented the Chicago Building Trades Council, were present.
3. *Minutes of Conference of Iron and Steel Organizations, held at New Morrison Hotel in Chicago, August 1-2, 1918*
4. William Z. Foster to Frank P. Walsh, July 6, 1918, in the Walsh Collection of the New York Publc Library.
5. *Amalgamated Journal,* December 26, 1918.
6. *Amalgamated Journal,* December 19, 1918.
7. M. F. Tighe to Elbert H. Gary, May 15, 1919; Gary to Tighe, May 20, 1919: William F. Foster, *The Great Steel Strike* (New York: B. W. Huebsch, 1920), pp. 70-72.

8. *Minutes of General Conference of Iron and Steel Industry Organizations Held under Auspices of National Committee for Organizing Iron and Steel Workers*, May 2, 1919.

9. *Minutes of Executive Council of the American Federation of Labor*, August 29, 1919.

10. Fitzpatrick, Hannon, Tighe and Foster to Wilson, September 9, 1919; Tumulty to Gompers, September 10, 1919.

11. Document No. 88, Executive Council Vote Book, September 19, 1919; Foster, *op. cit.*, p. 88, states the vote was unanimous. He is obviously in error, as the Vote Book of the Executive Council shows the above three voted for postponement.

12. William H. Johnston to William Z. Foster, September 12, 1919.

13. Gompers to Tighe, September 12, 1919. The same letter was sent to the heads of the 23 Internationals. Tighe to Gompers, September 12, 1919; Fitzpatrick to Gompers, September 12, 1919; Fitzpatrick, Foster, D. J. Davis, and W. H. Hannon to Johnston, September 17, 1919.

14. *Minutes of National Committee for Organizing Iron and Steel Workers*, April 5, 1920.

15. *Foster, op. cit.*, pp. 152-153.

16. The violence and denial of rights is described in *The Commission of Inquiry, The Interchurch World Movement, Report on the Steel Strike of 1919* (New York: Harcourt, Brace and Howe, 1920).

17. *Minutes of the Executive Council*, October 9, 1919.

18. *Minutes of the National Committee for Organizing Iron and Steel Workers*, December 13-14, 1919.

19. *Amalgamated Journal*, September 26, 1919.

20. *Amalgamated Journal*, January 15, 1920.

21. Foster, *op. cit.*, p. 243.

22. Minutes of the Executive Council, June 14, 1920.

23. *Amalgamated Journal*, May 13, 1920.

24. Minutes of Executive Council, February 23, 1920; *ibid.*, August 1, 1920.

25. Circular letter issued by Executive Council, August 26, 1920.

26. President Woodrow Wilson to Gompers, September 3, 1919.

27. Document 65 of the Executive Councl, November 4, 1919.

28. Gompers to William B. Wilson, September 9, 1919.

29. Gompers to William Green, September 19, 1919.

30. James J. Forrester and B. M. Jewell to Gompers, September 24, 1919.

31. Letter of the heads of fourteen railroad unions to Gompers, September 25, 1919.

32. Document 70 from Gompers to the Executive Council, September 26, 1919.

33. Frank Duffy to Gompers, September 30, 1919.

34. *Proceedings of the First Industrial Conference*, October 6-23, 1919 (Washington: Government Printing Office, 1920), p. 118 contains quote, p. 120.

35. *Ibid.*, p. 221.

36. *Ibid.*, p. 221.

37. *Ibid.*, p. 240.

38. *Ibid.,* p. 242.

39. *Ibid.,* p. 275.

40. Memorandum in the archives of the American Federation of Labor.

41. *Monthly Labor Review,* April 1920, pp. 863-864.

42. Selig Perlman and Philip Taft, *History of Labor in the United States,* 1896-1932 (New York: The Macmillan Company, 1935), Chap., 37.

43. Report to Executive Council, December 30, 1920.

44. *Report of the Proceedings of the Forty-First Annual Convention of the American Federation of Labor,* 1921, p. 61.

45. *Ibid.,* p. 62.

46. Document No. 65, Vote Book, February 8, 1922.

47. Gompers to President Wilson, January 7, 1916.

48. Minutes of Executive Council, September 22, 1922.

49. A. Mitchell Palmer to W. B. Wilson, October 27, 1919, in National Archives.

50. Lewis to W. B. Wilson, October 30, 1919, in National Archives.

51. Statement to the press in A. F. of L. archives.

52. Press release in A. F. of L. archives.

53. Minutes of Executive Council, November 9, 1919. '

54. Minutes of Executive Council, November 11, 1919.

55. Minutes of Executive Council, November 12, 1919.

56. The source of the news report is not given, but it is included in the minutes.

57. *Report of Proceedings of the Fortieth Annual Convention of the American Federation of Labor,* 1920, pp. 378-383, 88-90.

58. *Report of Proceedings of the Forty-first Annual Convention of the American Federation of Labor,* 1921, p. 375.

59. Gompers wrote to Lewis, December 3, 1921: "Whatever you or we may say, the strikes of the miners in Kansas are understood by the workers and people generally as a fight against the industrial court law of that state. Acting upon the whole situation the Executive Council has concluded that the only course we can consistently pursue under the direct and emphatic instructions of the convention of the A. F. of L. is to avoid any public statement which would certainly be interpreted and used to defeat the very purpose of these declarations. In addition, the Executive Council is fully persuaded that the effort to obtain a favorable decision from the judiciary as to the constitutionality of the Kansas Industrial Court Law will prove futile and that the only hope for the repeal of that infamous statute lies in action by the organized workers of Kansas to demonstrate the utter futility of the attempt by law to prevent the strikes and to arouse the consciousness of the people of Kansas to that fact."

60. Statement submitted to the Executive Council by the Committee appointed by the International Executive Board of the United Mine Workers of America, December 9, 1921.

61. Document 42, Vote Book, December 1921; Minutes of Executive Council, February 21, 1922.

XXVI

International Relations

At its first convention in 1881, the Federation of Organized Trades and Labor Unions of the United States and Canada greeted the Parliamentary Committee of the British Trade Union Congress. In 1887, the convention of the American Federation of Labor rejected Gompers' recommendation that the A. F. of L. be represented by two delegates at the international congress planned for the following year. It was deemed "wiser to first unite the labor organizations of America, before trying to unite the workingmen of Europe." P. J. McGuire led the fight against the adoption of the proposal, and he always showed less sympathy for international problems or foreign workers than Gompers and other leaders of the A. F. of L. The convention instead recommended that the "present friendly relations, through correspondence with European trade unions, be encouraged and continued."[1]

In the following year, William Leibknecht invited Gompers to attend an international meeting of labor at Switzerland. Gompers felt obliged to refuse the invitation, and explained that it was the view of the A. F. of L. convention that the American labor movement was not yet sufficiently advanced to permit representation. "You will readily see," he wrote, "that the expression of the convention of the organization is binding upon its president and since no distinction can be made between my position as president and mine individually I am constrained by my sense of duty to decline the honor you wish to confer."[2]

The Executive Council expressed its friendship to the meeting and informed the delegates: "We would be glad to be represented in your body by a delegate of our own, but the work at home requires the active presence of all our available men." The Council declared:

The trade union is the historic and natural form of working class organization. . . . And the conviction is slowly but surely gaining ground that by the organization of the workers upon the basis of their trades and callings and the Federation of the various unions in a grand universal union, with the autonomy of each guaranteed by all, will be found the practical realization of aspiration voiced by our lamented President Abraham Lincoln, in the memorable sentence —"The government of the people, by the people, for the people."[3]

418

The statement further urged the establishment of a permanent bureau which would compile and disseminate statistics and information on trade union questions. While the Executive Council favored the regulation of the hours of labor of children under eighteen years of age, it was "chary of invoking state interference, for . . . [it was] convinced that when the right of free combination is definitely assured, we shall be able to work out our own salvation, as a class, and ultimately achieve that grand transformation for which the whole efforts of ancestors in toil and suffering has been one long and arduous preparation."[4] The statement clearly shows that the leaders of the A. F. of L. were from the beginning reluctant to enter into alliances with organizations other than trade unions. A trade union international, based upon the autonomy of the national sections, was the kind of organization favored by the A. F. of L. in 1888.

In 1889 the Federation was invited to send delegates to the Labor Congress in Paris. The invitation came in the midst of preparation for the first campaign for the eight-hour day, and the leaders believed that this campaign would tax both the energies and the finances of the Federation. Consequently, the A. F. of L. was again forced to refuse the invitation. The sponsors of the congress were informed, however, "that it is not through the want of a fraternal feeling and a recognition of the identity of interest of the workingmen of all countries that we are not represented. Were we prompted by our feelings in the matter I am sure that you would count some of our members among your delegates to the convention."[5]

The desire for international cooperation by the A. F. of L. was based upon a feeling of the identity of interest of the workers of all countries and also upon an idealistic internationalism. Practical considerations, such as the need for devising some method by which the flow of strikebreakers between countries would be reduced, if not completely stopped, also existed. Eleanor Marx Aveling, the daughter of Karl Marx, and Will Thorne had suggested a program for handling the latter problem through an international secretary in each country who would be charged with combating this practice. The proposal made by Aveling and Thorne was, however, limited to an arrangement between England and the United States. While favoring the proposal, there was a feeling by Gompers that it did not go far enough, for it "should be approved and inaugurated not only by one even if by your grand and wonderful organization, but also with practically all of the trade unions of Great Britain and Ireland, Continental Europe, Australia and the American Federation of Labor."[6]

Despite the failure of the A. F. of L. to be represented at the International Labor Congresses, its interest in the international labor movement continued. In greeting the International Labor Congress at Brussels, in 1891, Gompers alluded to the freedom of speech which prevailed within the A. F. of L., freedom which gave to all, whether radicals or conservatives, the right to express their opinions. He also declared that

when the economic movement has sufficiently developed so as to produce a unity of thought on all essentials, . . . a political labor movement will be the result. In fact, there is and cannot be any economic action taken by organized labor unless it has its political and social influence. We in America who enjoy absolute political liberty, have long ago recognized that without economic freedom accomplished by economic organization, political liberty is but a phantasy and a delusion.[7]

In part this letter was directed at the political Socialists, who were in control of the Brussels Congress. Even more, Gompers sought to emphasize a view he held throughout his career, that improvement in the political and social position and well being of labor could be best attained through the strengthening of economic organization.

Gompers and other American labor leaders were on friendly terms with many British Trade Union officers. In 1894, the custom of exchanging fraternal delegates was inaugurated, and Gompers hoped that the extension of such exchanges to the labor movements of Continental European countries might be achieved.

In fact, Gompers sought the approval of the Executive Council in 1896 for the sponsoring by the A. F. of L. of a trade union international. At the same time, he criticized the efforts by political parties in the same direction. Writing for permission to launch his venture, Gompers declared:

Having in mind the previous attempts of conglomerate bodies of labor, middle class men and party politicians have called and held International Congresses under the name of labor which have been failures so far as to impress the workers of the world, and have tended to place the organized labor movement in a most ridiculous attitude before the public, the thought occurred to me that inasmuch as Messers. Strasser and Sullivan, the fraternal delegates of the A. F. of L., are in attendance at the British Union Congress at Edinborough, Scotland, they might use their influence for the purpose of bringing about a tangible, rational, International Trade Union Congress, and I have so cabled our delegates today, requesting them to urge upon the Glasgow Congress to take the initiative in the matter.[8]

Gompers argued that as the A. F. of L. already exchanged fraternal delegates with the British Trades Union Congress, and the German Trade Unions were planning to follow the same practice, it would be desirable "to have this interchange of fraternal visitations extended." Moreover, he believed that "if these fraternal visitations can be conducted successfully, it seemed . . . that they should develop into a holding of bona fide International Trade Congresses every few years, and thus take the place of the fraternal delegations." While the A. F. of L. conventions had taken no action on this question, Gompers deemed it his "duty to request our delegates to make the propositions above indicated." The Executive Council would not accept the plan, and rejected the proposal, with only John B. Lennon, the treasurer, voting to support Gompers.

Gompers' interest in the trade unions of Europe did not slacken. He was most anxious that the leaders of European trade union movements establish viable economic organizations of labor. Answering the leader of the French Typographical Union, who asked his advice on the formation of a national trade union center, Gompers, first criticized a requirement that only unions of five years of uninterrupted existence could affiliate. Such a rule would automatically deprive the newly-formed unions, Gompers argued, from the advantage of affiliation with a national center. Another point emphasized by Gompers was the absolute necessity for building an adequate defense fund. As a first requisite, Gompers advised each union to build up its own funds by a system of adequate dues and assessments. In view of the subsequent history of the French economic movement of labor, the acceptance of this suggestion might have changed the history of the French trade unions, as one of their obvious weaknesses has been their low rate of contributions, and their failure to impress upon their members the need for creating a defense fund.

Gompers also objected to the selection of the governing committees of the projected French Federation of Labor exclusively from the Paris region, as the program contemplated. Instead, he urged that all sections of the country should be represented on the governing board so that the problems and views of all sections of the country would be recognized. He also advised against triennial terms, on the ground that a term of this length was unwise and that officers of a federation should be elected annually. Nor would he approve of rotating secretaries. A secretary should be elected separately from the governing board. Nor did he look kindly on the failure of the French labor movement to reimburse for services. This was the result of an anarchistic bias against paid officers, who presumably would be corrupted by receiving a salary. Gompers was convinced such a scheme does not work in the long run. A worker either neglects the work which provides him with his living or he is forced to slight his union duties; labor organizations just cannot require work over long periods of time without compensation.[9]

In contrast to his relations with labor politicians, Gompers was always ready to exchange experiences with trade unionists and give them whatever advice and aid he could. The A. F. of L. felt closer to the English trade union leaders, both because of the advanced position occupied by the latter and also because the heads of the economic organizations in England and the United States were not separated by a language barrier. Among the English trade unionists of the early century who were closest to the A. F. of L. were Pete Curran, Ben Tillet, Will Thorne, James Sexton, and Issac Mitchell. The latter informed Frank Morrison that he had heard "from all trade unionists that visit the Federation offices that you are a long way ahead of us, in this country."[10] Ben Tillet, a leader of British Trade Unionism and also a Socialist, thought of Gompers after he had toured the United States, "as the old war horse surrounded by those who are too small to value the great soul which every day is giving the world the best that is in him."[11] Aside from the high personal respect many of the English leaders had for Gompers, they also admired the movement which he led.

The A. F. of L.'s interest in the trade union movements of other countries was in part based upon the belief, or at least the hope, that closer relations between the trade union centers of different countries would help to reduce the danger of war. The A. F. of L. convention of 1900 attributed fratricidal wars to commercial competition, the struggle for markets between countries, and the existence of large standing armies. Increasingly, the "preservation of peace in the world devolves more and more upon organized labor, whose voice is ever becoming more potent in the formation of public opinion, that supreme tribunal before which both monarch and merchant must inevitably bow."[12]

In 1905 the A. F. of L. sought to initiate some practical steps towards establishing closer relations with the workers of European countries. In his report to the convention of that year, Gompers declared that American labor could not "be indifferent to the movement and the struggles of peoples of all countries for justice and right."[13] At the suggestion of the Executive Council, the convention approved a program for promoting closer relations between the workers of the United States and European countries. This was to be achieved by an exchange of fraternal delegates and an exchange of union cards of union members traveling between various countries. The Executive Council was instructed to work out a scheme whereby foreign union men in good standing could transfer their membership to unions of their trade in the United States and be exempt from paying another initiation fee. The Executive Council urged international unions to accept this program. However, only twenty-two unions were willing to reply, half of which approved the proposal; the other eleven disapproved.[14]

SWEDISH GENERAL STRIKE

Despite the lack of enthusiasm of most affiliates for the free entry of foreign trade unionists into their ranks, friendly relations between the trade union movements of the continent and the A. F. of L. continued. During the Swedish general strike and lockout in 1909, the Swedish Trade Unions appealed to the A. F. of L. for assistance. The A. F. of L.

convention listened to the Swedish delegation and Gompers, who had been in Europe during the strike, expressed the view that while he had opposed general strikes, he believed that in this instance there

could be no division of opinion that the general strike was justified and deserved the moral and financial support of the workers in every civilized country. When the general strike occurred, my only regret was that it would be so late before I could say a word to my fellow-workers in America that would bring forth some financial response. But late as it is in the strike and general movement, if the American workers will do what they can, in spite of all with which they are confronted, I am satisfied the Swedish contest will come to an end with advantage and honor, and the labor movement of Sweden will be saved to her people.[15]

A special committee, appointed to devise means for aiding the Swedish trade unionists, suggested that the Executive Council appeal to national, international, and local unions for financial aid. Such an appeal was subsequently issued.[16]

INTERNATIONAL SECRETARIAT

In 1901 the European trade union movement established the International Secretariat, a periodical conference of trade union centers. The International was dominated by the German Trade Unions, whose chief, Karl Legien, also headed the International Secretariat. In 1908 the A. F. of L. convention instructed Gompers, who had been appointed as a special representative to the British Trades Union Congress, to attend the international conference of trade unions as a fraternal delegate.

Gompers assured the European trade unionists that the American labor wanted to establish closer relations with the organized workers of the continent. He emphasized "that it must be left to every country to decide its own policy and methods of action." He regretted the hostility shown by some leaders of European workers to the American Federation of Labor, but he believed that if the A. F. of L. were "allowed to work in our own way . . . [it] will soon affiliate with you."[17]

Gompers always insisted upon the need for tolerance of difference in national outlook and tactics. He did not believe that criticism of the labor movement of one country by the organized workers of another promoted international understanding. Consequently, he found the criticism by Léon Jouhaux, the head of the French General Federation of Labor, of the Spanish labor movement undesirable, for such criticism was, in his opinion

calculated to mar rather than harmonize international relations of organized labor. If my opinion were asked, I should express a difference from the tactics and methods of the organization of the working people of Spain, as I might differ from certain phases of the workingmen's movement of other countries; but claiming for the workers of America the right of our activities as judgment dictate, I can only yield to the movements of other countries the right which we ask for ourselves.[18]

Gompers was, in this letter, voicing the historic view of the A. F. of L. The workers of other countries had the right to devise the tactics they believed were the most suitable for themselves. Such differences need not debar the separate movements from cooperation as long as they recognized each others' autonomy. This principle was always followed by the A. F. of L., and the subsequent refusal to join in any alliance containing Communist organizations was based upon the thesis that such organizations were not genuine representatives of the workers but were instead a species of company or government unions.

INTERNATIONAL FEDERATION OF TRADE UNIONS

In 1909 the convention voted to affiliate with the International Secretariat, an annual dues of $561.21 was forwarded to the headquarters of that organization. At the outset, the A. F. of L. proposed the establishment of an international federation of trade unions which would seek to

prevent the workers from one country being induced to emigrate to other countries during periods of industrial depression or when trade disputes exist or are in contemplation; that it shall be the duty of the recognized representatives of the labor movement of the country affected to notify the International Secretary, who in turn shall at once communicate the situation to the representatives of the trade union movement of each country.[19]

James Duncan, the first vice president of the A. F. of L., who was sent as a delegate to the Budapest meeting of the International Secretariat, was instructed to inform the delegates that the A. F. of L. did not favor anti-patriotism, anti-militarism, nor the general strike, which were at the time leading articles of belief of the French General Federation of Labor.

The A. F. of L. also requested that changes in the structure of the International Secretariat be made. Instead of the existing arrangement, whereby the secretaries of the different national trade union centers conferred periodically, the A. F. of L. favored the establishment of an International Federation of Trade Unions, whose chief task would be the prevention of the movement of strikebreakers between countries when strikes existed or were contemplated. In addition, the A. F. of L. asked endorsement of uniform legislation for governing the hours of labor of men and women in dangerous trades, restriction of the labor of children under fourteen years of age, effective laws for improvement of safety in industry, improved sanitary standards, and better housing. The Federation also proposed the publication of a journal or bulletin describing the state of trade, conditions of labor, and progress in welfare legislation.[20]

When Duncan arrived at the conference in Budapest, in August 1911, his right to represent the American labor movement was challenged by William Z. Foster, a delegate from the Industrial Workers of the World. The I. W. W. had applied for affiliation, and questioned the right of the A. F. of L. to represent American trade unionism. The dispute occupied an entire session, and in the end Duncan was seated. Under the rules of the International Secretariat, adopted in 1902, only one national trade union center from a single country could be represented, and the seating of Duncan automatically barred any other group from being represented.

During the debate on the issue, Foster was supported by the French delegation which, at the time, was espousing the doctrine of revolutionary syndicalism. Subsequently, Duncan submitted several proposals designed to prevent a repetition of similar incidents. He proposed that whenever a document assailing the integrity of a national trade union center was received, a copy of the charges was to be forwarded to the official representative of the National Center subjected to criticism. If the accused organization objected to circulation of the document, it would be withheld until the next convention for discussion. Duncan also recommended the transformation of the international conference into an International Trade Union Federation, with the autonomy of each country guaranteed.[21] Duncan's proposals were adopted. The name of the International Secretariat was changed to the International Federation of Trade Unions. Karl Legien, the head of the German Trade Unions, was chosen the first president.

The change in name was made at the convention held in August 1913, in Zurich, Switzerland. George W. Perkins, the head of the Cigar Makers' International Union, represented the United States. He was of the "opinion that the American trade union movement has too long neglected the trade union movement of the world." Perkins believed that the head of the A. F. of L. should always be one of the delegates to the international conventions. What disturbed Perkins was the widespread misunderstanding of the American labor movement by European labor leaders.

Perkins also showed himself a sound observer of the French trade union movement, although not altogether an unsympathetic one:

France is a low dues paying country, which believes in sharp, short strikes, which they are unable to properly finance, and the inevitable result is portrayed by the following signed statement of the secretary: "In 1911 the number of strikes amounted to 1,443, of which 267 succeeded, 613 failed, and 563 were compromised." In one of the strikes which was a failure the secretary apparently took satisfaction in saying that it was "a brilliant proof of the spirit of revolt which existed among the workers."

This attitude did not impress Perkins favorably, but he did praise the efforts of the French trade unions to prevent wars, with "all their destruction, privation, misery, and ruthless slaughter of human life, and sacrifice of human life."[22] Yet Perkins could not avoid noticing that

In France they are lulled into sleep and inactivity on the industrial field by the glamor and cry of a grand revolution, while the present-day necessities and the needs of the workers are being sadly neglected; despite the fact that the leaders there say that a revolution seldom accomplishes lasting results as regards the well-being of the workers, they still cry for the "grand revolution."[23]

The American delegate was critical of revolutionary slogans and the emphasis upon politics then found in many European countries.

THE OUTBREAK OF WORLD WAR I

The next meeting of the International Federation of Trade Unions was scheduled for San Francisco in 1915. It was never held because of the war. The A. F. of L. maintained friendly relations with the German Trade Unions as well as the English, and in 1912 the Executive Council, with three members opposing, voted to invite Legien to tour the United States under the auspices of the Federation. The tour caused some difficulties, for the Socialist Party invited Legien at the same time. It was finally arranged that Legien would make separate tours for each organization. The A. F. of L. rejected any suggestion that the A. F. of L. and the Socialist Party should hold joint meetings.[24]

Legien faced many difficulties which did not confront an American labor leader. For one, there was a careful distinction made in Germany between political and economic organizations, and when the A. F. of L. asked Legien to circulate a resolution endorsing a Naval Holiday, Legien was forced to refuse. He also did not think it advisable to circulate the resolution through the International Federation of Trade Unions. When the war started, Legien assured Gompers that Germany had "done everything possible to preserve peace and to prevent war."[25]

As the war in Europe continued, the A. F. of L. sought to salvage the International Federation of Trade Unions. The convention of 1914 expressed the willingness of the A. F. of L. to call a meeting of the trade union centers of the different countries, at the end of the war, for the purpose of reestablishing fraternal relations. In the meantime, as Germany was a belligerent, a dispute arose over the propriety of continuing the location of the headquarters of the International Federation of Trade Unions within that country. Legien assured Gompers that the International Federation of Trade Unions would not be used to support Germany, but he wanted the headquarters retained in his own country. This view met with the opposition of the French and English Trade Unions which, while not challenging the integrity of Legien, urged that the headquarters be, at least temporarily, transferred to a neutral area. This opinion was shared by Gompers, and when this view was not accepted, the Executive Council, with Vice-President Joseph Valentine dissenting, voted to withhold the per-capita tax from the International Federation of Trade Unions.[26]

The issue of transferring the headquarters of the IFTU had been discussed at a conference of labor parties of the allied nations in London during February, 1915. It was agreed that it would be desirable if the transfer of the headquarters to the then neutral United States could be effected. An objection to this plan was that the United States was not a convenient headquarters for the European trade union movements. In defending the maintenance of the status quo Legien denied that he had engaged in any activity on behalf of the IFTU since the beginning of the war, and he consequently regarded the criticisms as unfair.

Gompers felt, however, that the IFTU could only be saved by shifting its headquarters to a neutral country. He was anxious that the international trade union organization be maintained so that the trade unions of the world would be able to exercise some influence over the eventual making of the peace.

The A. F. of L., in the first years of the war, still clung to its historic pacifism, and the desire of Gompers for a meeting of trade unions simultaneously with the peace conference and in the same city was based upon a hope that the national trade unions might help in the permanent abolition of war. In a letter to W. A. Appleton, Gompers asked

whether the people of Europe will not take the bit in their teeth and declare a moratorium forever and anon, not only for future war projects but of the debt burdens the war entailed. If the war lords and those who stand behind them were given an object lesson of such a character, there is little doubt that it would be the most potent factor to prevent wars of the character that was inaugurated, last year, and which is now being so fiercely and harrowingly waged.[27]

On March 26, 1916, the A. F. of L. consulted the trade union movements of Europe on the desirability of calling a trade union conference on methods for achieving peace simultaneously with the meeting of the peace conference at the end of the war. In the meantime Gompers, acting for the Executive Council, supported the heads of the English and French trade union movements, who were convinced of the necessity for shifting the headquarters of the International Federation of Trade Unions to a neutral country.

J. Oudegeest, the head of the Dutch Federation of Labor, thereupon accused Gompers of trying to destroy the German trade union movement. This was denied, and Gompers insisted that his proposal for transferring the headquarters of the IFTU had no connection with the German trade union movement, and concerned only the

international movement. My position, which has been publicly stated and repeatedly reaffirmed, is that the wage-earners of every country have the right
to work out their own problems in accordance with their own best judgment.
No foreign influence of whatever character has a right to interfere in national
problems and without the consent of those concerned. I have always maintained
the ideal of the sacredness of human rights, individual rights and national rights
and I have never deviated from that ideal. Since the beginning of the European
war, the purpose and policy of the A. F. of L. have been in favor of refraining
from any word or act that would involve us in the European conflict, because
we are convinced that only by maintaining that attitude in spirit and in fact,
can we have any influence to help to bring about peace and be most powerful
to maintain democratic ideals and interests of humanity when the terms of
peace shall be under consideration. It is because I desired above all things
to maintain the International Federation of Trade Unions, as well as the national
movement affiliated with it, free from any association that would engender
racial bitterness and prejudice that grow out of partisan struggles, that the
judgment of the Executive Council of the A. F. of L., including my own, was in
accord with the proposition . . . for the neutralization of the headquarters of
the international federation.[28]

The proposal of the A. F. of L. for the holding of a labor conference
simultaneously and in the same city as the peace conference at the end
of the war was rejected by the other trade union movements. The convention of the A. F. of L., in 1916, then urged the organized labor movements of the warring countries to request their respective governments
that organized labor be given representation on the official commissions to
negotiate peace. The labor movements of neutral countries were also
urged to request their governments to grant labor representation on the
commissions to negotiate peace. It was believed that in this manner the
needs of wage earners would be more effectively presented.

In a statement to the secretaries of the various national trade union
centers, the Executive Council transmitted the views of the A. F. of L.
convention on the ending of war and the achieving of universal peace.
The document had a decided pacifist flavor. The statement called for a
democratically negotiated peace, and the organization of the nations of
the world for peace instead of war. However, the Executive Council
denied that it had any desire to interfere in any way with the nations
engaged in the struggle, and it declared its proposals were motivated by
a desire to serve the interests of lasting peace based upon "justice, freedom, democracy, and humanity."[29]

Clash with Legien

As war came closer to the United States, the American Federation of
Labor became concerned with the defense of the country and Gompers
accepted a place upon the Advisory Committee of the Council of National

Defense. With rising differences between the United States and Germany over submarine warfare threatening to bring about a break between the two countries, Gompers wired to Legien: "Can't you prevail upon German government to avoid break with the United States and thereby prevent universal conflict." No answer was made to this cable, and on the eve of the declaration of war by the United States, Gompers again cabled Legien that the United States could not prevent England from continuing its blockade of Germany, but the "United States must, however, protect its citizens from unlawful and unwarranted destruction of their lives." Legien blamed the threatened extension of the war on the "rejection of Germany's sincere offer of immediate peace negotiations, continuation of cruel starvation war on our women, children and our aged, and our enemies' frankly avowed aims at destruction of Germany."[30]

The telegrams were sent without the explicit approval of the heads of the government of the United States, Wilson refusing to comment when his views were requested. He, however, expressed his gratitude for "the splendid service" after the cablegrams had been sent to Legien. Gompers also appealed to the German Ambassador, Johann Von Bernstoff, against the policies of the German government and urged that efforts be made to settle peacefully all differences between the two countries.[31]

United States in the War

After the entry of the United States into World War I, the A. F. of L. ceased to have any direct relations with the German trade union leaders, but it sought to increase the exchange of visits between American trade unionists and those of allied nations. An invitation by the Swedish Trade Unions, on behalf of those of several other countries, for the A. F. of L. to send delegates to a conference at Berne, Switzerland, scheduled for September 17th, pointed to the division of the international working class by the war, and called upon the trade unions of the world to once "more unite [for] the struggle for the rights and for the protection of workers." It "is a great duty, for the fulfillment of which we must join together in the common cause."[32] The Executive Council regarded this conference as "premature and untimely and can lead to no good purpose. We apprehend that a conference such as is contemplated would rather place obstacles in the way to democratize the institutions of the world and hazard the liberties and opportunities for freedom for all people."[33] The date was subsequently shifted to October 1, 1917, and the call for the meeting issued by the Swiss Federation of Trade Unions.[34]

Stockholm Conference

In the meantime, the trade union conference initiated by the Stockholm meeting of the national trade union centers took place in Berne, Switzerland, in October 1917. No representatives from allied countries were present, but in addition to the German and Austrian movements, the Scandinavian countries, Holland, and Switzerland sent delegates. It was decided to establish a temporary bureau for the International Federation of Trade Unions in Amsterdam. In addition the conference endorsed the social reforms advocated by the labor representatives from allied countries at their meeting in Leeds, England, in July 1916. It was hoped that the program of the Berne conference would influence future social legislation in all countries. Governments which would be represented at the future peace conference were called upon

in accordance with the proposition made some time ago by the President of the A. F. of L., our friend Gompers, to allow a representative of the workers to be present at the peace deliberations, so that the interests of these latter will not be lost sight of, in order that the rights of the workers may be upheld and the enfeebled vitality of the people may be revived after the fearful trials which the nations are now undergoing.[35]

While the war was on, the American Federation of Labor rejected all overtures for a meeting of labor representatives from the United States with those of belligerent countries. In March 1918, the Executive Council sent a delegation of union officers to visit England, and subsequently several other groups were sent to England, France, and Italy. Gompers was also anxious that members of the Executive Council meet the delegations from the labor movements coming to the United States. As he did not feel he had the authority to call the Executive Council into session for this purpose, he asked the members of the Council to give an "expression of their opinion and judgment as to which course to pursue."[36] Even before requesting the Council's views on cooperation with the foreign labor delegation, Gompers called the heads of several unions and departments, stationed in Washington, together, and was advised that the A. F. of L. should show the foreign labor men every possible courtesy. The visits were also useful for establishing friendlier relations between the A. F. of L. and the labor movements of the allied countries.

LONDON MEETING

The A. F. of L. accepted an invitation to attend the inter-allied labor conference at London in September 1918. At this meeting an agreement was reached that as soon as possible after peace was declared in Europe, a conference of the labor representatives of the inter-allied countries and the United States was to be convened at the same place and time as the official peace conference. The French delegates expressed their regret that the American Socialist Party had not received an invitation to the conference, and one of its leaders, Jean Longuet, a grandson of Karl Marx, advocated a reduction in the number of votes of the American delegation. This brought Gompers to his feet with the declaration that

The A. F. of L. represented the American Labor Movement, and yielded not an inch to any other body. . . . They met as representatives of the Labor Movement, and they undertook to confer and agree voluntarily, but it was impossible and impracticable to attempt to override the Labor Movement of any one country, even the smallest country, taking part in the conference. They must have unanimity if they were to come out of the conference with practical results. The majority could not enforce its judgment on the Labor Movement of countries constituting the minority, or cause labor in the minority countries to change its attitude.[37]

Following the debate, the French resolution was defeated and the delegates of the A. F. of L. were given the full vote.

The A. F. of L. submitted a series of proposals in which the war was recognized as the "inevitable conflict between autocratic and democratic institutions"; the contest between the principles of self-development through free institutions and that of arbitrary control of government by groups or individuals for selfish ends. The statement, therefore, declared that it was the determination of the workers of the allied countries to support their governments to the end that the central powers might be defeated. The statement called for an endorsement of the fourteen points issued by President Wilson as a basis for the making of the peace. It then appended a series of demands similar to those submitted to the Berne conference. There was some difference over a number of resolutions, and the delegation from the A. F. of L. was evidently irritated by the constant allusion to "socialism and socialists," for Gompers told the meeting that he "thought it strange that in this conference he so seldom heard the term 'labor.' As the representative of the wage-earners of America he submitted that it would be only right to refer to the workers as workers, and to Socialists as 'Socialists.' "[38]

There was considerable difference of opinion on a number of points, but there was also a desire for compromise. Consequently, on substantive issues the delegates, despite representation from Socialist Parties as well as European trade union centers, were able to agree. On the question of conferring with representatives of the labor and trade unions of the Central Powers, the American delegates sought a declaration that a conference would be held only with those representatives of the Central Powers who were in open revolt against their governments. The proposal was rejected, with only the Americans, Canadians, and a small group representing Italy, voting for the A. F. of L. declaration.[39]

The London conference was made up of representatives of both Socialist political groups and trade unions. In part, the A. F. of L. participated because of the conditions brought on by the war. Subsequently, the Executive Council decided that the representatives of the A. F. of L. should meet with the delegates from other national trade union centers, but would decline to be governed by political parties. At the same time, the Executive Council expressed its desire to aid in establishing a just peace, and to reconstitute "a bona fide international trade union movement."[40]

BERNE CONFERENCE

A delegation, headed by Gompers (and including Daniel Tobin and John Hynes), left for Europe. Upon arrival in London, the American delegation conferred with the Parliamentary Committee of the British Trades Union Congress, and expressed reluctance to meet with the representatives of German trade unionism while the war was still officially in progress. Moreover, the A. F. of L. delegation emphatically refused to meet with representatives of any political party. In addition, the A. F. of L. delegates argued for a meeting in Paris instead of Berne. The objection to the Berne conference expressed by the A. F. of L. delegates was accepted by the Belgians, but Léon Jouhaux, the head of the French delegation, insisted that the responsibility for the war rested on the German government and not on the German people, and therefore opposed severity toward German trade union leaders. Duncan, who expressed the views of the A. F. of L. delegates, was agreeable to a meeting with the representatives of the German trade unions after the signing of the peace treaty, but not before. The Berne conference was, nevertheless, held. The A. F. of L. delegation sent a statement explaining its refusal to attend:

At a labor meeting held in London in September 1918, an agreement was reached that as soon as possible after peace was declared in Europe there should be a conference called of the labor representatives of the inter-allied countries and America, to be convened at the same time and place as the official Peace Conference. A group of men principally interested in their several political parties arranged for a conference at Berne, Switzerland, and at the same time assumed to call, without authority, a labor convention to be held at Berne concurrently with the political convention.[41]

The American delegates would not attend. In this view the American delegation was supported by the Belgian trade union leaders, who through Cornélius Mertens declared their willingness to attend the inter-allied conference but would only discuss with the Germans responsibility for the war and the removal of the secretariat from Germany.[42]

AMSTERDAM CONGRESS

It was decided to hold the conference of delegates from national trade union centers in Amsterdam. It was believed that a visit of a German trade union delegation to Paris, where the peace treaty was being negotiated, might provoke a hostile demonstration. Consequently Amsterdam was chosen instead. In the meantime, the American labor delegation was requested by the Belgian Christian trade unions to intervene on their behalf. The American delegates, holding to their historic policy of noninterference in the affairs of a foreign trade union movement, rejected the request on the ground that they

should not interfere in the contentions of fractional portions of organized labor in the different countries of Europe. . . . With reference to the relationship of the Christian Trade Unions of Belgium or elsewhere in Europe, the A. F. of L., through its delegation, offers its good offices to be helpful in solidifying the labor movements of the countries in order to bring about the general understanding and cohesiveness of action so much desired.[43]

At the Amsterdam conference of trade union centers, on July 25, 1919, Cornélius Mertens of the Belgian delegation protested against the failure of the German trade unions to criticize the conduct of the German government and the army during the war; he was especially bitter against the failure of the German trade unionists to raise their voices against the deportation of Belgian civilians. His criticisms were supported by the A. F. of L. delegates. One of the German delegates, Johannes Sassenbach, declared that German Trade Unions did recognize the "great injustice" done to the Belgian people, but insisted that German trade unionists were not responsible for these acts nor could the German Trade Unions have helped the situation. Subsequently, the statement of Sassenbach was modified by Legien, speaking for the Executive of the German Federation of Trade Unions. Legien maintained "the German workers did all they could to prevent the war. When the war had once broken out, however, they could not do anything else but side with their own country, just like the workers of all other countries did."[44] The question provoked a long debate, and Gompers made a proposal which sharply attacked the conduct of the German Trade Unions. There was a threat from the German delegation that the adoption of Gompers' resolution would compel them to withdraw from the conference. A milder resolution expressing the regret of the German Trade Unions at the conduct of the German troops was finally adopted. After the adoption of the report on the Statement of the German delegation, the old "International" passed into history.

INTERNATIONAL FEDERATION OF TRADE UNIONS

Following the ending of the old International Federation of Trade Unions, ninety-one delegates from fourteen European countries and the United States, representing almost eighteen million trade unionists, met in Amsterdam on July 28, 1919, and formed a new trade union international, the International Federation of Trade Unions. It was made up of legitimate trade unions, and only one national trade union movement in each country was eligible for membership. The International Federation of Trade Unions was empowered to seek a merger of trade union centers wherever a division existed. This was, in fact, an acceptance of the anti-dualism philosophy of the A. F. of L.

On the charter of labor proposed in the peace treaty, a sharp difference of opinion arose between the American delegates and the representatives from several other countries. The committee considering this question found, with Delegate Hynes from the A. F. of L. abstaining, that the charter of labor "did not give full expression of the demands of the working classes of all countries." Gompers attacked the view of the committee, and pointed to his membership on the commission on international labor legislation at Paris, where he had submitted a number of proposals which were defeated by the labor representatives of other countries.

Gompers insisted that the American concept of gradualism meant constant and steady progress toward "justice, freedom and democracy and for universal brotherhood." He therefore offered a substitute that the "International Federation of Trade Union Conference at Amsterdam declares that the labor charter as contained in the Peace Treaty does not give expression to the full demands of the working classes, and urges all the national centers to strive for the complete and early realization of the program of the newly formed international." Despite Gompers' plea, the substitute was defeated by 31 to 20, with only the American and English delegations supporting the proposal.

An undercurrent of bad feeling between the American and German delegations existed. When Gompers objected to a proposal that all national centers be required to accept decisions of an international conference adopted by a majority vote, Legien questioned the integrity of the opposition. In turn, Gompers denounced Legien and declared that this outburst again demonstrated that the Germans were unrepentant about their conduct during the war. The American delegates also objected to decisions favoring socialization, and public demonstrations in behalf of political objectives. W. A. Appleton of the General Labor Federation of England was elected president, much to the satisfaction of the American delegates. In the end Gompers, speaking for the American delegation, made a conciliatory statement. He asked that the American movement be allowed to develop in its own way and with its own views, and he assured the delegates he "would do his best to assist in building up the International."[45]

Gompers had hoped that the A. F. of L. would affiliate with the International Federation of Trade Unions, but there was strong opposition within the Executive Council to such a step. Gompers was always interested in the progress of the trade union movements of other countries, and favored active cooperation between them. When his efforts on behalf of Mexican Labor were commended, Gompers declared that he not only favored the unity of the workers of the Western Hemisphere, but of the workers of all countries for "my international view of unity, fraternity and solidarity is not limited even to Pan America."[46] Not all the leaders of the A. F. of L. were as internationally minded. Several members, Duncan and Tobin among them, were far less enthusiastic about international cooperation, and when the International Federation of Trade Unions called for socialization of the means of production, and for "Down with Reaction and Up with Socialism," the heads of the opponents of international cooperation were strengthened.

Despite his objections, Gompers would have liked to go along and bring American labor closer to the economic organizations of European workers. He wrote to Appleton:

[When] the war was won and the autocratic militaristic attitude of the German government had been defeated, I relented in my resentment toward Germany. With my associates I came to Amsterdam with an open mind to work for the internationality of the cause of labor and to strive for the strong bond of unity and cooperative action in furtherance of the great interests and welfare of the toiling masses of the world.[47]

When the issue of affiliation with the IFTU came before the convention of 1920, the convention referred it to the Executive Council with the suggestion that "self-determination on all political matters" be insisted upon. Had the IFTU made some concessions to the views of the A. F. of L., it is likely that Gompers might have been able to win his colleagues over to cooperating with the IFTU, but the failure to issue a moderate statement on several issues made such a possibility unlikely. European labor was then in a radical phase, with the workers moving quickly to the left and the leadership forced to make concessions to this mood. While the workers of the United States were also passing through a temporary radicalism, the leaders of the Federation were not inclined to make drastic concessions in this direction. Consequently, the breach was widened. Once the war was over and the preliminary conflict between the Germans and the delegates had subsided, Gompers relented in his opposition to Germany.

When the question of affiliation came before the Executive Council in March 1921, it decided to reject affiliation with the International Federation of Trade Unions. The decision was based upon the failure of the IFTU to grant complete autonomy to the national trade union centers, and the issuance of appeals and proclamations by the Management Committee of the IFTU which had committed the organization to a revolutionary policy objectionable to the A. F. of L. In addition, the A. F. of L.

found the system of dues too heavy and burdensome, and it objected to the calls for the socialization of industry made by the IFTU.

Consequently, when the IFTU requested the A. F. of L. to participate in the extraordinary congress, called for November 1921, the A. F. of L. refused.

In declining to affiliate, the Executive Council made a distinction between the views of the various national trade union centers and the IFTU. Under the principle of autonomy, the right of each national trade union center to espouse whatever views it held desirable was recognized; the A. F. of L. assumed no responsibility for such views. It was otherwise with the IFTU. The Executive Council declared:

[We are] most anxious to be part of an international trade union movement. It is our purpose to be helpful to the workers of every country in their purpose to better the lives and work of the toilers wherever they may be. American workers can benefit but little, if at all, by the labor movements of other countries. But yet we shall be glad of the opportunity to cooperate and work with the toilers of all lands to the accomplishment of that end, but in so doing we must decline to be part of a movement which undertakes the destruction of the American labor movement or the overthrow of the democratic government of the Republic of the United States. If such an International Federation of Trade Unions will vouch safe and guarantee the autonomy and independence of the A. F. of L. and make its affiliation possible, we shall join it regardless of the policies and theories for which the various national movements may declare in their own countries.[48]

Despite the plea of C. E. Bowerman, with whom the leaders of the A. F. of L. were on very good terms, the A. F. of L. refused to continue its affiliation with the IFTU. The A. F. of L. had paid four hundred dollars to the IFTU, but this amount was presumably due to the older organization which had ceased to exist. The Executive Council wanted all obligations met, but would make no more financial commitments or retain affiliation with the IFTU. Of course, it was an error on the part of the A. F. of L. leadership to argue that the IFTU had become a revolutionary organization, and several members of the Executive Council knew the European trade union leaders too well to believe that they had suddenly divested themselves of their former trade union beliefs and had become flaming revolutionaries. As Oudegeest argued, the differences between the two organizations were purely semantic.

European workers raised in the Socialist tradition could more easily understand and react to statements employing the language of historic radicalism, and there is more than a grain of truth in the following statement of Oudegeest: "I should like to add here that in all the manifestos which we have issued to the national trade union centers of the various countries we have used the terminology which is current in Europe and which is used by the trade union movement in all countries, in order thereby to exercise as much moral pressure as possible."[49] Certainly there was much to be said for the argument advanced by the secretary of the IFTU, but the A. F. of L., caught in the midst of anti-labor and anti-radical drives in the United States, was reluctant to affiliate with an organization whose views might be misinterpreted by the reactionary forces at home. A considerable number of letters were exchanged between the heads of the two organizations, and the IFTU was anxious to accommodate itself to the views of the Federation. The A. F. of L. would not recede from its position, as it feared the effect of the "meaningless" revolutionary jargon upon American public opinion. Despite the many exchanges, no satisfactory basis for the affiliation of the A. F. of L. with the IFTU could be devised, as each side did not appear to understand the demands and needs of the other.

Gompers, as always, carried out the direction and will of the Executive Council, but he was by no means happy about the severance of the ties between the A. F. of L. and the other democratic trade union centers.

AID TO GERMAN TRADE UNIONS

Late in 1923, Gompers had an opportunity to come to the aid of the German trade union movement. Prior to that time, when he received a letter demanding revenge against the German people, Gompers had advised that the end of the war should have meant the end of differences. While he had had sharp differences with Legien and other German delegates to the Amsterdam conference, he did not forget that the German Trade Unions represented a democratic bastion against injustice and exploitation.

In 1923 the German Trade Unions found themselves in serious financial straits, without sufficient funds to operate the organization, a crisis caused by the inflation then searing the German economy. Neither salaries nor expenses could be paid, and the German Labor Federation appealed for aid to the A. F. of L. Gompers pleaded with the Executive Council to aid the German labor movement, but his suggestion that the Federation seek to raise funds ran into strong opposition. James Duncan, the first vice-president, not only disapproved of the appeal, but asked that his name not be associated with any effort to aid the German Trade Unions. Another member of the Council was quite indignant when the Federation issued an appeal. He charged that "the Executive Council of the Federation is being ignored in many instances and then expected to step forward and endorse and look after any proposition suggested by someone else." The charge, directed at Gompers, was untrue, for Gompers did not issue the appeal without the approval of a majority of members of the Executive Council. There were three votes cast against the proposal, by Duncan,

Fischer and Tobin, and there is evidence that without Gompers' herculean efforts the proposal would have been defeated. Two other members of the Executive Council noted they approved because of Gompers' plea that the American labor movement was obligated to aid the unions of other countries in distress; otherwise, the proposal would have been defeated and the more than $26,000 sent to the German Federation of Labor would not have been raised.[50]

This incident best illustrates Gompers' readiness to aid the trade unions of other countries. In virtually all instances, he urged and worked for closer relations and cooperation with the trade union movements of Europe and England, in whose policies and problems he always showed a lively interest. Within the Federation and the Executive Council there were always some individuals whose views on foreign affairs approached "know nothingism," but, as on all other questions, the issues were fought out in the Council room, and a unanimous decision given to the public. As the executive of the A. F. of L., Gompers was obligated to carry out the decisions of the Executive Council, irrespective of his own views. In relation to foreign labor movements, Gompers always dreamed of the A. F. of L. as a member of a democratic trade union international devoted to advancing the cause of peace, freedom, and the security and welfare of the workers of the world. For a time, the Federation, like the United States, stood aloof from foreign entanglements, but in the end Gompers' vision of the A. F. of L. as a member and leader in the family of international trade unionism was realized.

PEACE CONFERENCE

The delegation from the A. F. of L., headed by Gompers, and made up of four other members of the Executive Council—Duncan, Alpine, Duffy and Green—left the United States for Europe in January 1919. It conferred with the labor delegations of the various allied countries upon its arrival, and defined the attitude of the A. F. of L. toward various questions. While awaiting the meeting of the postwar labor conferences of trade union centers, the American delegates remained in Paris and were in close touch with President Wilson and the American Commission to Negotiate the Peace.

On January 31, 1919, the Commission on International Labor Legislation was appointed, made up of two representatives from each of the Great Powers and five representatives of each of the other powers. Gompers was one of the members of the Commission, and Edward N. Hurley of the United States Shipping Board, the other. The Commission held thirty-five meetings, and drafted a plan for the establishment of a permanent organization for international labor legislation, and elaborated a series of principles touching upon labor matters. The basis for setting up a permanent organization, which subsequently became the International Labor Organization, was the belief that, in order to eliminate international strife, which was to be the main aim of the League of Nations, set up under the peace Treaty, "a remedy for the industrial evils and injustices which mar the present state of society" was necessary. Consequently, it was provided that participation in the ILO was to be a condition of membership of the League of Nations. Provisions for annual conferences and for the governing of the organization were adopted.

When the issue came before the convention of 1919, Andrew Furuseth, the head of the International Seamen's Union, attacked the provisions. He argued that under the covenant

the League of Nations takes jurisdiction over the daily life of the working people throughout the entire world. It says that it deems it its duty and will endeavor to make labor conditions humane and just in nations, members of the League and in the nations with which the League has commercial and industrial relations. That embraces every working man and woman throughout the entire world. If the League has the authority to say the conditions of labor shall be humane and just, there is no possibility to deny that it has the sole right to prescribe what is humane and just. There can be no higher authority anywhere so that whatever is adopted as humane and just by the League will necessarily have to stand as humane and just, regardless of any protest that the working men of any part of the world may feel inclined to lodge against such finding.[51]

Furuseth, moreover, opposed the grant of power to the League of Nations which, he charged, created in fact a "super-legislature." He objected to the handling of labor issues through the treaty power, and it was his view that it could be used as a means to lower labor standards at home. Furuseth was not above appealing to anti-British sentiment, always present at a convention, when he pointed to the twenty-four delegates from the British Empire against four from the United States. He attacked the danger of control of labor conditions by an international legislative body which would eliminate or minimize the control over conditions by the people of the United States, and the overrepresentation of the British Empire on the policy-making boards of the ILO. In all of his arguments, he was appealing to the delegates to support old and established views of the A. F. of L.

Frank McNulty of the International Brotherhood of Electrical Workers introduced an amendment "that nothing in the League of Nations as endorsed by this convention can be construed as denying the right of self-determination and freedom to Ireland." This had reference to a resolution adopted earlier at the convention. Green believed that the amendment was unnecessary, "but if it will satisfy Brother McNulty and his enthusiastic friends I am willing to support it and vote for it."

Green denied the charge that the delegates of the A. F. of L. had agreed to delegate to an international convention all "our sovereignty, all our rights, and all the things for which the American labor movement has stood," as charged by Furuseth. He also explained that Gompers had given all his strength and power to realize the demands of the A. F. of L. at Paris. "It was a most trying experience, an ordeal in my judgment he could not undergo again." Gompers defended the labor provisions, and argued that those were the best the American delegates could obtain. The proposals were endorsed by a vote of 29,909 to 420, with 1830 not voting.

The overwhelming approval of the labor charter does not express entirely the strength of the opposition, as many of the delegates were bitterly opposed to the League of Nations because of the growing isolationism which infected the labor movement as well as the remainder of the community, and especially because of the opposition to England for its treatment of Ireland and the denial of freedom to the latter. The prestige of the American delegation and the desire not to affront Gompers seems, in part at least, to account for the large and overwhelming approval. Whatever may have been the initial doubts and hesitations, the A. F. of L. became a staunch and loyal supporter of the ILO, loyalty and support which have continued to the present.

On June 24th, the Executive Council voted to send a committee to wait upon the President of the United States and urge him to convoke the International Labor Conference scheduled for Washington in October 1919. The Council urged the unions to cooperate so that the conference would be successful. Upon the election of Albert Thomas to the leadership of the International Labor Office, he appealed to the American Federation to cooperate with his organization. Gompers was sympathetic to the ILO and friendly to Thomas; he informed him that the American people had been deceived in the campaign of 1920 when they voted against the League of Nations. He hoped that the disarmament conference would give rise to a real League of Nations so that war might be averted in the future.[52] On occasion, Gompers protested against undue emphasis given by ILO publications to proposals affecting labor not completely endorsed by the A. F. of L. Thomas always showed sympathetic understanding of the attitude of the A. F. of L., and always asked that his position and that of the ILO be understood as trying to allow expression of various views.

REFERENCES

1. *Report of Proceedings of the Second Annual Convention of the American Federation of Labor*, 1887, pp. 26, 29.

2. Gompers to Wilhelm Liebknecht, November 22, 1888.

3. Executive Council to the Officers and Delegates of the Federational Trade

Union Congress in London Assembled from the Executive Council, October 27, 1888.

4. *Ibid.*

5. Gompers to Andre Gily, May 20, 1889.

6. Gompers to Eleanor Aveling and Will Thorne, February 19, 1891.

7. Gompers to International Labor Congress, August 4, 1891.

8. Gompers to the Executive Council, September 18, 1896.

9. Gompers to Auguste Keufer, January 23, 1900.

10. Isaac Mitchell to Frank Morrison, June 13, 1902.

11. Ben Tillet to Gompers, January 4, 1902.

12. *Report of Proceedings of the Twentieth Annual Convention of the American Federation of Labor,* 1900, p. 23.

13. *American Federationist,* December 1905, p. 938.

14. Gompers to Executive Council, September 17, 1906.

15. *Report of Proceedings of the Twenty-Ninth Annual Convention of the American Federation of Labor,* 1909, p. 167.

16. "Appeal for Swedish Workers," Circular issued by the Executive Council of the American Federation of Labor, December 3, 1909.

17. *Sixth International Report of the Trade Union Movement* (Berlin: The General Federation of Trade Unions, 1908), pp. 23-24.

18. Gompers to Karl Legien, December 4, 1909.

19. *Report of Proceedings of the Thirtieth Annual Convention of the American Federation of Labor,* 1910, p. 50.

20. Minutes of the Executive Council, February 20, 1911.

21. *Report of American Federation of Labor Representative at Budapest, Hungary International Trades Convention,* 1911, pp. 16-17.

22. *Report of American Federation of Labor Representative at Congress of International Federation of Trades Unions, Zurich, Switzerland,* 1913, p. 20.

23. *Ibid.,* p. 20.

24. Gompers to Legien, August 27, 1914.

25. Legien to Gompers, August 27, 1914.

26. Vote Book, April 26, 1915; Gompers to Legien, March 4, 1915.

27. Gompers to Appleton, July 1, 1916.

28. Gompers to J. Oudegeest, October 16, 1915.

29. Statement sent to Secretaries of National Trade Union Centers by the Executive Council, December 21, 1916.

30. Gompers to Legien, February 2, 1917; April 2, 1917; Legien to Gompers, February 11, 1917.

31. Joseph Tumulty to Gompers, February 4, 1917; Gompers to Von Bernstoff, February 10, 1917.

32. Invitation to a general international trades union conference from the Landsorganisationen I Sverige, June 8, 1917.

33. Gompers to Lindquist, June 27, 1917.

34. Louis Lorwin, *Labor and Internationalism* (New York: Macmillan Company, 1929), p. 183.

35. Letter to National Trade Union Centers from J. Oudegeest, December 1, 1917.

36. Document No. 10 to Executive Council from Gompers, March 20, 1918.

37. *Proceedings of the Inter-Allied Labor Conference* (Washington: American Federation of Labor, no date), pp. 4-5.

38. *Ibid.*, p. 30.

39. *Ibid.*, pp. 43-47.

40. Gompers to C. E. Bowerman, January 25, 1919.

41. Statement in American Federation of Labor archives.

42. Minutes of the Meeting of Delegates from the American Federation of Labor with the Confederation Generale du Travail and the Belgian Federation of Labor, January 31, 1919.

43. Gompers to E. Van Quaquebeka and J. Roscum, February 19, 1919.

44. Statement submitted to the International Federation of Trade Unions by the German General Federation of Trade Unions, September 26, 1919.

45. *Statement of Preliminary Meeting of International Federation of Trade Unions, July 25-26, 1919; Report of Proceedings of the Fortieth Annual Convention of the American Federation of Labor*, 1920, pp. 131-161.

46. Gompers to Helen Marot, July 13, 1916.

47. Gompers to W. A. Appleton, December 23, 1920.

48. Minutes of the Executive Council of the American Federation of Labor, March 3, 1921.

49. Oudegeest to Gompers, September 29, 1921.

50. Document 134, December 11, 1923; Report to Executive Council, September 11, 1924.

51. *Report of Proceedings of the Thirty-Ninth Annual Convention of the American Federation of Labor*, 1919, p. 400.

52. Albert Thomas to Gompers, May 30, 1922; May 1, 1920, Gompers to Thomas, March 1, 1920; December 30, 1920.

XXVII

Postwar Radicalism

RUSSIA AND THE AMERICAN FEDERATION OF LABOR

The American Federation of Labor, in harmony with its traditional view of opposing anti-democratic governments and defending political prisoners, went on record in 1887 against the extradition treaty then being negotiated with Czarist Russia.[1]

On March 15, 1893, Gompers issued sharp denunciation of the treaty again pending in the United States Senate.

An Extradition Treaty with the greatest tyrant upon the face of the globe— the Russian Czar is about to be consummated by the Government in the name of our people; the fundamental principles engrafted in the Declaration of Independence and the Constitution of the United States are about to become nothing but a relic of our glorious past. By this treaty every Russian patriot seeking to liberate the Russian people from the yoke of despotism, and striving to establish a government of, for and by the people, is to be considered and treated by our government as a common criminal, and as such shall be delivered to the mercies of the Czar and his hangmen. . . . Our protest must be sharp against this attempt to make our Government the safeguard of despotism; our people the consorts and accomplices of the crimes of Czardom; our country, the fugitive slave-trap of the Czar's mercenary hirelings and spies.

Gompers pointed to the horrors of the Yatutsk massacres, the Siberian exiles, the cruelties and oppressions which were the daily concomittant of Czarist despotism. He declared:

[The] Russian people want free speech, free assemblage, free press and elections, suffrage. Shall not all civilized and enlightened nations combine to assist those noble heroes and patriots of Russia, who, in the struggle for these inalienable rights of man, sacrifice their lives? Let the voice of the people be heard in the Senate; let all organized labor raise its thunderous protest against the shameful encroachment of politics upon the moral sense of the people; let us sound the strongest alarm, until our sense of indignation be felt and our voice be heard by the President and his advisors. But to be effective . . . our country must forever remain the asylum and a breathing spot for all who dare brave danger for freedom's sake, and seek refuge from persecution of tyranny and despotism.[2]

443

THE REVOLUTION OF 1905

The revolt of the Russian masses in 1905 was hailed by the A. F. of L. convention, which denounced the massacres by brutal mobs inflamed by reactionary militarists, and congratulated the Russian workers on the success of their movement which "stopped production and supply until freedom and popular government were conceded, and bid them good-speed in their civil and industrial campaign until they shall have instituted in what is now the Russian Empire a representative government under the title of the Republic of Russia."[3] The interest in Russia by the American Federation of Labor continued after the revolt of 1905 had been suppressed. When a political refugee, Jean Pouren, was arrested and held for extradition for crimes he was alleged to have committed during the uprising of 1905, the Executive Council instructed Gompers to use all of his influence to have Pouren released and to have the treaty upon which the arrest was based canceled.[4]

The American Federation of Labor also disapproved the practice of the Russian government in refusing to honor passports of Americans of Jewish descent.[5]

THE REVOLUTION OF 1917

The interest of the American Federation of Labor in Russian affairs was a continuing one. Its concern for Russian problems was undoubtedly influenced by the large number of Russian nationals who were residents of the United States, and thereby keenly aware of the tyranny and oppression of the Czar's government. The A. F. of L. was also concerned with the denial of elementary rights of citizenship to millions of people. It was in keeping with the historic interest of the A. F. of L. for it to congratulate the Provisional government of Russia soon after the overthrow of the Czar.

In a cable, Gompers speaking for the A. F. of L. declared:

We rejoice with Russia's workers in their newly achieved liberty. The splendid proclamations of your provisional government, declared for free speech and press and the right of workers to organize and if necessary to strike for their rights guarantees to Russia's workers opportunities for freedom and progress and assures the New Russia her future greater glory.

This cablegram was either not received or not published, and on behalf of the American Federation of Labor, Gompers cabled another message to the "representatives of working people of Russia."

The Russian workers were told of the warm friendship of American labor, and its rejoicing

at the intelligence, courage and conviction of a people who even while concentrating every effort upon defense, against foreign aggression, have reorganized their own institutions upon principles of freedom and democracy. But it is impossible to achieve the ideal state immediately. When the right foundations have been established, the masses can daily utilize opportunities for progress, more complete justice, and greater liberty. Freedom is achieved in meeting the problem of life and work. It cannot be established by revolution only—it is the product of evolution. Even in the Republic of the United States of America the highest ideals of freedom are incomplete—but we have the will and the opportunity. In the name of America's workers whose watchwords are Justice, Freedom and Humanity we plead that Russia's workers and masses shall maintain what you have already achieved and to practically and rationally solve the problems of today and to safeguard the future from the reactionary forces who would gladly take advantage of your lack of unity to reestablish the old regime of royalty, reaction tyranny and injustice.[6]

At the meeting of the Executive Council, fraternal greetings were sent

to all who have aided in establishing liberty in Russia. We know that liberty means opportunity for the masses especially the workers. The best thought, hopes and support of America's workers are with your efforts to form a government that shall insure the perpetuity of freedom and protect your rights and new found liberty against the insidious forces and agents of reaction and despotism. May we not urge you to build practically and constructively.[7]

In a cablegram to the Workingmen's and Soldiers' Deputies, Gompers called attention to the grave crisis facing the world as a result of Prussian militarism. He assured them that the American labor movement was opposed to punitive indemnities, and expressed approval of the view of the Workers' and Soldiers' Deputies "that the only way in which the German people can bring the war to an early end is by imitating the glorious example of the Russian people, compelling the abdication of Hohenzollerns and the Hapsburgs, and driving the tyrannous nobility, bureaucracy and military castes from power." He was critical of the efforts of the German Socialists to bring about a negotiated peace which would leave the German military caste in control. He assured the Russian workers that "the American Government, the American people, the American labor movement are whole-heartedly with the Russian masses in the great effort to maintain the freedom you have already achieved and to solve the grave problems yet before you."[8]

Ever alert to the desirability of labor representation upon government boards and committees, Gompers, upon learning of a contemplated mission to revolutionary Russia, urged the Secretary of State to appoint a representative of the American Federation of Labor.[9] At the recommendation of the A. F. of L., James Duncan was selected as a member of a commission to Russia which was headed by Elihu Root. Duncan tried, during his trip, to establish relations between the Russian and American labor movements, although he was a representative of the United States government. He addressed the Workers' and Soldiers' Deputies, and sought to encourage the establishment of a democratic labor organization.[10]

THE BOLSHEVIK REVOLUTION

The attitude of the A. F. of L. underwent an immediate change with the overthrow of the Provisional Government by the Bolshevists. From the beginning, the A. F. of L. perceived the Communist regime as a tyranny which had to be fought and opposed. In a memorandum to the American Peace Commission, in March 1919, the delegation from the American Federation of Labor, present at Paris, protested against the favoritism being shown to the Bolsheviks by a number of people attached to the American Peace Delegation.

In the name of a large part of the American people [Gompers wrote] I hereby solemnly and formally warn you against a most dangerous situation. I refer specifically to the policy of favoring both directly and indirectly the Bolshevist, revolutionary and anti-democratic governments which aim to overthrow the democratic governments associated with America in the war and in the formation of the League of Nations. I know as you know that no such policy can bear the light of day before the American people.

Gompers informed the American Peace Delegation that the German General Staff was still in contact with the Bolshevist government of Russia. Moreover, he charged that the German government, headed by a Socialist, was "still managed by the military party and lacks every real quality of democracy." Gompers doubted that the postwar German government would, because of the influence of the military and the general staff, become a bastion of democracy. He believed it was being abetted by the Bolshevist (Communist) government of Russia.

There are now in Paris a number of American citizens [the memorandum declared] who are constantly giving proof that they enjoy the confidence of the administration and of your Commission who constantly and openly express agreement with the Bolsheviki, satisfaction at the success of the Bolsheviki regime and the growth of the movement in other countries—for instance, I may mention in this connection, Mr. Walter Weyl, one of the editors of the *New Republic*, which has urged official recognition of the Bolshevik government and justified and encouraged their attacks upon American troops in Russia; the anarchist, Mr. Lincoln Steffens, whose enthusiasm for the Bolsheviki is so outspoken that we may well believe this to be his primary motive at present. . . . I know that he who today temporizes with Bolshevism or assists those who are helping the Bolshevist cause by agreeing with them are committing an unspeakable crime against civilization itself.[11]

The labor delegates present at Paris were all members of the Executive Council, and they were convinced that President Wilson was not being adequately informed of events. Their memorandum criticized, among others, William Bullitt, then active on behalf of the newly established Communist dictatorship. The labor men were informed that General Tasker Bliss, one of the delegates to the Peace Conference, was much interested in the memorandum sent by Gompers on behalf of the entire labor delegation.

As one looks over the memorandum, it is obvious that it shows an unusual insight into events of the time. First, the dominant position of the German general staff in the future German Republic is already foreseen. Moreover, the American labor delegates were also aware of the connection between the German general staff and the Communist government in Russia. This information had been furnished to Frank Bohn, an American prowar Socialist who was assisting the American labor delegation, by Kurt Eisner, who subsequently headed the revolutionary government in Bavaria. Eisner was a pacifist, and opposed both the right-wing German Socialists, who were cooperating with the militarists in their own countries, and the Communists, with their emphasis upon dictatorship. History has shown that the information was accurate, and could have well been heeded by the American Peace Commission.

In addition the labor delegates, because they started with a clear view of democracy and freedom—which meant for them a pluralistic society, one in which labor is free to pursue, as are other groups, its own interests within the framework of law—were not dazzled by the reports and propaganda which had already begun to pour out of Russia.

RECOGNITION OF SOVIET RUSSIA

Resolutions for the recognition of Soviet Russia, for the lifting of the blockade, and for support to end intervention by outside governments were introduced at the convention of 1920. The resolutions committee and the convention took the position that

The American Federation of Labor is not justified in taking any action which could be construed as an assistance to, or approval of, the Soviet government of Russia as long as that government is based upon the authority which has not been vested in it by a popular representative national assemblage of the Russian people; or so long as it endeavors to create revolutions in the well-established, civilized nations of the world; or so long as it advocates and applies the militarization of labor and prevents the organizing and functioning of trade unions and the maintenance of a free press and free public assemblage.[12]

The resolution adopted in 1920 was more critical of the Soviet Government than the one on the same subject in the previous convention. In 1919 the convention approved of withdrawal of troops from Russia, but endorsement of the Soviet Government was refused until a democratic government was established. As the nature of the Soviet Government became more evident, and its repressive policies better known, the American Federation of Labor took an increasingly hostile position toward that government or its recognition. The feeling that the revolution had been betrayed, and that the hopes for a democratic labor movement had been frustrated by the Bolshevik dictatorship, took possession of the leaders of the American Federation of Labor. They had always opposed dictatorship, and spoken out against oppression and injustice, and saw no reason why they should now remain silent. The views of the A. F. of L. were not approved by a number of liberal journals and journalists, and Gompers, in two articles subsequently published as a pamphlet, quoted from Soviet sources to show the existence of terror, oppression and the denial of the rights of labor.[13]

There was, however, some opposition to the views of the leaders of the American Federation of Labor. It is true that on the issue of recognizing Soviet Russia, the great majority of Socialists and progressives who usually challenged the official view remained silent. Men like Max Hayes, J. Mahlon Barnes, Frank Hayes, and William H. Johnston, who were leading opponents of Federation official policy, did not participate in the debates on the recognition or support of Soviet Russia. Instead, the burden of argument fell upon the delegates from city centrals and state federations, the most prominent being James A. Duncan, the head of the Seattle Labor Council. The enactment of resolutions by one or more conventions did not in this instance, as it never has, put an end to debate.

Demands by a number of affiliates that the A. F. of L. request the American government to recognize and furnish other assistance to the Soviet Government continued. The Chicago Federation of Labor endorsed the calling of a general strike if Russia were invaded. Gompers showed some irritation at this demand. He informed Edward Nockles, secretary of the Chicago Federation of Labor, that the calling of strikes was within the jurisdiction of the international unions, and neither the city centrals nor the American Federation of Labor had authority in this sphere. He also called Nockles' attention to the fact that, in Russia, the workers were denied the most elementary rights, collective bargaining had ceased to exist, and labor was being militarized.

Evidently [Gompers told him], "distance lends enchantment to the view" in this matter as in many others, but the American Federation of Labor has direct, absolute, accurate and authentic information regarding conditions in Russia, the militaristic, autocratic and unjust conditions which are being imposed upon the masses of labor of that unhappy country, for the people [of] which we entertain a deep admiration and for whose emancipation from this autocratic thralldom we must earnestly strive.

Nockles then defended his position by arguing no one knew much about conditions in Soviet Russia, but Gompers refused to concede this. Instead he insisted "the official documents possessed by the American Federation of Labor and upon which the action of the Montreal convention was based, were known to be the official truth about Soviet Russia."[14] Subsequently events demonstrated that Gompers' prescience in this matter was correct. He and the American Federation of Labor had early recognized that a structure of freedom and justice could not be erected upon a slave basis.

The Chicago Federation of Labor was only one of a number of city centrals and local unions which demanded that the A. F. of L. take some action on behalf of Soviet Russia. When the president of the Topeka Industrial Council demanded that the A. F. of L. support recognition of Soviet Russia, Gompers told him:

In Russia the workers are conscripted into the army and into industry. There is no such thing as collective bargaining in Soviet Russia. In fact, no bargain is made. It is compulsion. The workers must work whether they wish or not and must accept wages and working conditions arbitrarily fixed by a military government. It is not possible that the workers of Topeka are anxious that the conditions prevailing in Russia shall be transplanted to the United States.[15]

Even as early as 1920, the leaders of the A. F. of L. showed what appears to have been an uncanny appreciation of the nature of the Soviet state. For the heads of the A. F. of L., the touchstone of a true democratic government was its treatment of labor, and as they watched the behavior of the Soviet government they witnessed continual and increasing restriction being placed upon the worker. To those members of the trade union movement who questioned the position of the A. F. of L., Gompers always sought to present the reasons why the A. F. of L. opposed the recognition of Soviet Russia. To one hostile correspondent Gompers explained:

The Soviet authorities have by decree forbidden organizations of labor to exercise those functions without which labor is powerless. To strike in Russia today is to be guilty of sedition and death. To place the responsibility for Bolshevist injustice and Bolshevik failure to provide for the people of Russia upon the blockade is to fall an easy victim to a misstatement energetically circulated by Bolshevik propagandists. Whatever inconvenience the blockade may have caused the Bolshevik at an early date, it long ago ceased to be a barrier to the importation of whatever the Bolshevik authorities might care to import.[16]

Gompers denied the blockade was responsible for the policies of repression of the Soviet government. Moreover, he questioned the thesis that the resumption of trading relations between them would be of great benefit to the United States, for "the maximum trade that might be expected from Russia even under the full resumption of relations, would be so small as to make no appreciable difference in the condition of

American industries."[17] Even at that time, the argument was made that recognition of the Soviet government would lead to an appreciable increase in trade between the two countries.

The Executive Council reviewed its attitude toward the Soviet Union for the convention of 1921. It severely criticized the intervention of the Soviet government into the affairs of the American labor movement through the Red Labor Union International, and examined the trade argument, then assiduously used by certain pro-Soviet groups. The A. F. of L. again denied that a trade agreement between Soviet Russia and the United States was justifiable either on political or economic grounds. In fact, the A. F. of L. pointed to the poverty of the Soviet and the undesirability of "American trade with that country or of restoring Russian credit so long as the present political and economic system continues." The main argument was, however, directed at the system "of labor compulsion or enslavement." With copious quotations from the records of the Communist Party congresses and official documents, the Executive Council demonstrated that a system of compulsory labor was already being instituted. Moreover, the Executive Council recognized the semantic legerdemain had already been mastered by the Soviet government and its propagandists, so that old and honorable terms were given a new meaning. In its report, the Executive Council declared:

In Soviet Russia the bolshevists are using many words with a new meaning. It has been shown how they sometimes employ the word "democracy" to mean the reverse of what all civilized peoples and the labor movements of the world have hitherto meant by the word. After abolishing all the rights of labor and labor organizations and of cooperatives the bolshevists, nevertheless, continue to apply the term "trade union" and "cooperatives" to the empty shells that remain.[18]

The Executive Council, with substantial documentation, showed that even then, less than five years after the October Revolution, the whole apparatus of rule from above, the denial of the most elementary rights to labor, and the perversion of the functions of trade unions were already well on the way. While these centralized and repressive tendencies reached their perfection under Stalin, they were, as the Executive Council well perceived, an essential and even major part of the Soviet technique of government under Lenin. In fact, in this area, Stalin only improved upon his master, Lenin.[19] Delegate Luigi Antonini of the International Ladies Garment Workers' Union vigorously criticized the report of the Executive Council on Soviet Russia, but it was approved with only four dissenting votes.

At the convention of 1922, there were three resolutions on Soviet Russia presented to the convention. Two were favorable, and one reviewed the policies and practices of the Soviet government and asked for a reaffirmation of the decision of the convention of 1920. This time, majority and minority reports were submitted by the committee considering resolutions dealing with international relations.

The minority report was signed by Max Hayes, an old Socialist and a member of the delegation from the International Typographical Union, and Timothy Healy, head of the International Brotherhood of Stationary Firemen and Oilers. The minority based its plea for approval of recognition of Soviet Russia by the United States Government upon the existence of millions of unemployed in the United States, and the argument that "world peace, which is one of the fondest hopes of the workers, cannot be established while military or economic pressure is used to deprive peoples of self-determination." In addition, Hayes denied the charges that no labor movement existed in Russia; other delegates speaking in favor of the minority report, argued that a revolution could not be suppressed by refusal to recognize. The majority position restated most of the arguments made by the Executive Council in previous reports, and one delegate insisted it was not a question "for the American people to pass upon; it is coming into a trade union convention for the purpose of securing trade union action."[20]

On the same basis, the conventions of the American Federation of Labor had urged the American government not to recognize a government of Mexico which was based upon violence and force, and the same argument was applied in subsequent opposition to the Fascist and Nazi regimes. In other words, when a resolution comes on the floor of the convention of the American Federation of Labor, the issue must be decided on the basis of trade union principles, it was argued. The majority report, critical of the Soviet government and opposing recognition by the United States, was upheld. Resolutions favoring the recognition of Soviet Russia were also introduced at the conventions of 1923 and 1924, but they were largely presented by the same people and the arguments on both sides were much the same.

Recognition does not imply approval, but, as one of the delegates indicated, issues that come before the convention of the A. F. of L. have to be decided on the basis of trade union principles and practices and not upon the needs or exigencies of the United States government. Otherwise, the eloquent denunciations of Czarist tyranny would never have been voiced. For example: the United States might have to recognize and to deal with a government such as Mussolini's, Stalin's or Hitler's, but such recognition would not be an adequate or honorable reason for a convention of the American Federation of Labor to approve such action, if such an issue were brought before it.

ONE BIG UNION

In the postwar period, the American Federation of Labor had to meet the challenge of several radical innovations which for a short time gained considerable following within the ranks. The Federation also faced demands for drastic modifications in its tactics and policies from groups within the movement. The formation of the One Big Union in Canada, and its attempt to gain a following within the United States, created another problem for the A. F. of L., for this was another dual organization which sought to challenge the hegemony of the A. F. of L. over the American labor movement. The One Big Union was organized by 237 delegates in a meeting at Calgary, Alberta, on March 13-15, 1919, with a vice president of the Trades and Labor Congress of Canada acting as chairman. The One Big Union declared that

Realizing that the aims and objects of the labor movement should be improving of the social and economic conditions of society, and the working class in particular, and Whereas, the present system of production for profit and the institution resulting therefrom prevent this being achieved; be it therefore, Resolved, That the aims of labor as represented by this convention are the abolition of the present system of production for profit, and the substitution therefore of production for use, and that a system of propaganda to this end be carried out.

The One Big Union aimed to unite all workers into one large industrial organization, and eliminate all craft divisions in the labor movement. In practice, it had many points in common with the Industrial Workers of the World, which had had, in the period before World War I, some influence in Western Canada where the One Big Union had its inception. To a large extent the One Big Union was an expression of the same dissatisfaction which permeated the labor ranks in the United States. When the Western delegates to the Quebec convention of the Canada Trades and Labour Congress were unable to convince a majority to reorganize the Canadian labor movement on the basis of "modern and scientific organization by industry instead of by craft," they decided to secede and set up their own organization.

A number of affiliates of international unions of the A. F. of L. joined the new organization, and the unions showed concern lest the movement spread across the border. Resistance to secession immediately arose, and the Canadian Trades and Labor Congress, as well as the American Federation of Labor, was alerted to the danger.[21]

In the summer of 1919, the United Brotherhood of Carpenters and Joiners of America protested the action of the Washington Federation of Labor in endorsing the idea of the One Big Union. It was the view of the Carpenters' Union, supported by the Executive Council, that unless the Washington State Federation of Labor withdrew its ballot on this question, its charter should be suspended. The Washington Federation complied with the directions.[22]

In Canada, fear was expressed that the One Big Union might succeed in swallowing the entire trade union movement. "It appeared at certain times as if the international labor movement was doomed to defeat, but thanks to the good sense of the workers, they have rapidly overcome the subtle machinations of those who have been propagating and are propagating those doctrines."[23]

AMALGAMATION

Another source of opposition centered around the "amalgamation movement," based upon a view that industrial unions were the more effective and desirable type of labor organization. Instead of limiting industrial organization to certain industries, the proponents of this view advocated the merging or amalgamation of existing unions into industrial organizations. The leading spokesmen for the program was William Z. Foster, then still operating out of his old bailiwick in Chicago, where he had gained support from the Chicago labor movement.

The Chicago Federation of Labor, under the leadership of Nockles and Fitzpatrick, had always been in the forefront of progressive labor causes, although it had never deviated too far from the traditional attitudes held by the leaders of the A. F. of L. Immediately before and during World War I the Chicago Federation had been instrumental in launching two of the more significant organization drives in American labor history, drives which led to the enrollment of several hundred thousands of unorganized workers into unions.

In the postwar period, the Chicago Federation took a leftward course, which was soon interrupted when a political convention it had sponsored was seized by the already well-disciplined Communist battalions who came representing, on the whole, paper or nonexisting organizations. But for a short period of time, the Chicago Federation of Labor was the spearhead of the movement to challenge the official policy of the American Federation of Labor and many of its international unions. There were city centrals which espoused more radical views, but none possessed the prestige and influence within the general labor movement of the Chicago Federation of Labor. While always known as a progressive city central body, its progressivism usually manifested itself in organizing innovations rather than in sponsoring novel changes within the labor movement.

In March 1922, the Chicago Federation of Labor became embroiled in a dispute with the A. F. of L. over a more important and direct issue:

the structure of the labor movement. Sponsored by Foster, a resolution called upon the Executive Council to summon a conference of international unions for merging the craft and amalgamated unions into industrial organizations. The Executive Council did not receive the resolution until a month after it had been enacted, a somewhat irregular procedure. The hesitancy of the heads of the Chicago Federation of Labor may have been influenced by their knowledge that their proposal would inevitably be rejected by the Council. The Council not only rejected the proposal but pointedly informed the Chicago Federation of Labor that no such conference would be sponsored by the A. F. of L.[24] Gompers was directed to go to Chicago and urge reconsideration of this issue. He carried out his commission, and Foster, while asking for a "good-conduct" recommendation from Gompers, challenged the latter to a debate. Both were refused, and the A. F. of L. also ended its contributions of half of the expenses incurred by the Chicago Federation of Labor. This action was justified by the claim that, in view of the latter's sponsorship of policies that were likely to lead to rebellion and disruption within the labor movement, the Federation was not justified in bearing the financial burden.[25]

The amalgamation movement was also supported by a number of state federations of labor and city central bodies, as well as minority groups within a number of international unions. Its chances of success, aside from some of its questionable sponsors, were not very great. The promoters of the program attempted to solve the structural defects in the labor movement in doctrinaire fashion. Structural adjustments, as the C. I. O. has demonstrated, can only be achieved on the actual organizing level, because they involve the power relations among unions. The adoption of a resolution by a convention of the American Federation of Labor would not compel any international to abandon a part or all of its jurisdiction, nor would it force one to merge with other unions. Consequently, the first phase of the amalgamation movement can be regarded largely as a manifestation of protest and dissatisfaction with the old leadership of the A. F. of L., and would have vanished with the insurgency and militancy of the postwar period.

However, Foster and his Communist followers accelerated the decline of the movement by the use of typical Communist tactics on the political plane. The Chicago Federation of Labor also sought, in the years immediately following the postwar, to mobilize the interest of the trade unions in independent political action. Foster, as a close co-worker of John Fitzpatrick and as a trusted leader of the Chicago Federation of Labor, was naturally allocated a role in this campaign. It was then unknown that Foster had become secretly affiliated with the Communist Party, and was now carrying out in disciplined fashion the dictates of the

Party. In good faith, the Chicago Federation of Labor called for a mobilization of delegates from progressive groups interested in independent political action. Some who were alert to the situation refused the invitation, but the Chicago Federation of Labor, confident of the honesty and good faith of the groups invited, went ahead with its plans.

The meeting, held only because of the prestige of the Chicago Federation of Labor, was taken over by the disciplined delegates sent to the conference by sports clubs, singing societies, local unions, and every other variety of Communist front. The honest trade unionists found themselves out-voted and defeated on every issue. The Communists were in complete control, and set up one of their first "paper" organizations, the Federated Farmer Labor party. The Chicago Federation of Labor thereupon withdrew not only from independent political action, but from the amalgamation movement. A circular was issued declaring that the Chicago Federation of Labor had withdrawn all connections with the movement for amalgamation of trade unions. The circular recited the various steps the Chicago Federation of Labor had taken in this campaign: the enactment of the resolution favoring amalgamation, and its rejection by the Executive Council and by the convention of 1922. Consequently, the Chicago Federation of Labor regarded the issue as closed, and it announced that it no longer would participate in any campaign promoting amalgamation.[26]

SEATTLE CENTRAL LABOR COUNCIL

Progressives, dissatisfied with the policies and management of the American Federation of Labor and many of its unions, found that cooperation with the Communists, whose activities were not yet too well-known, could never be conducted on an honest level. It already was clear that the Communist Party had special interests, and that it would regard the cooperation of other groups as a sort of "marriage of convenience" to be broken whenever it suited its interests. It drove the Chicago Federation of Labor to the right, but the A. F. of L. found itself confronted by "rebellions" in other parts of the country, the most serious in Seattle, at the time a center of radical activity. The difficulty between the American Federation of Labor and the Seattle Central Labor Council began formally in the spring of 1920, when the Council sought to amend its constitution so that it would pass upon the wage contracts of affiliated locals. A protest against the action was registered with the Executive Council, and the Seattle body was informed that the functions of a central labor union "is to support a movement of a local when it is engaged in a dispute or movement approved by the international." It was not, declared the letter, "within the province of a central labor union to veto a duly authorized movement of a local union."[27]

Seattle was not the only city central labor union which showed an inclination to radicalism during this period, although only three others were warned by the Executive Council to conform to the regular policies of the Federation or face revocation of their charters. As a rule, the attention of the Federation was directed towards these recalcitrant units by the protests of affiliated locals or the dissatisfaction of one or more internationals with the conduct of the city central labor unions involved. When a central body, like the one in Seattle, arrogates to itself powers not given to it under the constitution of the American Federation of Labor or its charter, it is inevitable that protests against these policies will be directed to the Executive Council. Even a complaint by a delegate will be carefully scrutinized, if the complaint involves the charge that the city central is intervening outside of its scope or authority.

Subsequently, the Seattle Council sent Hulet C. Wells as a delegate to the Third International, and his report denouncing the American Federation of Labor was received with great applause and ordered printed in the official organ of the Seattle Central Labor Council, the *Seattle Union Record*, with an accompanying recommendation that the report be read by every trade unionist. Thereupon, several locals and internationals requested the Executive Council of the A. F. of L. to intervene. After an investigation, the Seattle central labor body was ordered to give definite proof of its loyalty to the "American Federation of Labor, to abide by decisions of A. F. of L. conventions and to conduct itself in all matters in accord with the laws and principles of the A. F. of L. and the policies declared by it." The Seattle Central Labor Council was ordered to repudiate its endorsement of the Soviet dictatorship and the principles of communism, the Industrial Workers of the World and similar bodies, and, in the future, not to issue credentials of any kind "accrediting any person either as delegate or 'observer to any congress, convention, or gathering of the Red Labor Internationale,' the Communist Internationale or any other body hostile to the American Federation of Labor." It was also ordered to disaffiliate organizations which were not affiliated with bona fide international unions or to the American Federation of Labor, and to have communications from the A. F. of L. read and acted upon by the delegates.

The Seattle Central Labor Council entered a formal denial that its actions were contrary to the principles of the American Federation of Labor, and a special committee was elected to transmit that information to the Executive Council. An exchange of correspondence took place, and finally the Executive Council warned the Seattle body that, unless it were willing to comply with the orders of the A. F. of L., its charter would be revoked. Finally, the Seattle Central Labor Council agreed to accept the stipulations laid down unreservedly.[28]

In fact, the Seattle Central Labor Council soon steered to the right, and in 1925 it expelled six delegates charged with being Communists. The vote was close, 78 to 71, but it indicated that the radical influences which had dominated the central body from World War I, and had led to the calling of the dramatic general strike in 1919, were on the wane. In fact, the Seattle labor movement never again showed the insurgent-type of militancy which characterized it after World War I. It is difficult to account for the changes that had taken place, except to note that the American Federation of Labor never again found it, after 1924, a center of agitation against the policies of the American Federation of Labor.

BUTTE, MONTANA

Butte, Montana, was another center of insurgency against policies of the A. F. of L. In 1923 the Executive Council warned the Silver Bow Trade and Labor Council that it must either conform to the policies of the Federation or face expulsion. Like Seattle, Butte had been for many years a center of turbulent labor activity. Oppositions and dual organizations had burgeoned in that community, and the labor movement of the city was carried along on the wave of dissatisfaction that broke over a number of industries and communities after World War I.

The attention of the Executive Council was directed toward Butte not only because of its espousal of radical policies, but because it sent William F. Dunne, who was known to have Communist affiliations, as a delegate to the convention of 1923. Dunne, who was to edit the *Daily Worker* for a number of years, had been a leading figure in the radical wing of the Butte labor movement during World War I and the years immediately following. His election as a delegate to the convention of the American Federation of Labor was consummated by what is now recognized as a typical tactic pursued by Communists in trade union organizations. Dunne had been reinstated as a member of the Butte local of International Brotherhood of Electrical Workers, and sent as a delegate to the Silver Bow Central Labor Council. It had been arranged that, during the discussion on the sending of a delegate to the convention of the A. F. of L. to be held in Portland in 1923, a certain delegate to the central labor council was to arrive late. Entering the hall the particular delegate addressed the chair and informed the meeting that "inasmuch as Brother Dunne is going to Portland at about time of the opening of the A. F. of L. convention and it will not cost the council anything, I move that credentials be given to Brother Dunne as delegate to represent the Council."[29] It was never ascertained who or what group financed the trip. Dunne was at the time editing the *Butte Bulletin,* a radical labor paper, but he had already moved from his former position as a trade union militant to membership in the Communist Party.

During the discussion of the Federated Press, an investigation of which had been ordered by the convention of 1922, Dunne's right to sit as a delegate was challenged. The Federated Press was organized as a news-gathering agency for left wing labor and radical publications. Initially it had on its governing board of editors trade unionists who, even though they did not always see eye to eye on policy with the heads of the American Federation of Labor, were nevertheless representatives of labor opinion. The Federated Press received substantial aid from the Garland Fund, and soon showed a favoritism to the more radical labor views. Thereupon the American Federation of Labor sought to discover the character of the service given by the Federated Press to its affiliated organizations.

The committee, Matthew Woll, G. W. Perkins, and Chester M. Wright, selected at the direction of the Executive Council, found "that no publication can follow the Federated Press as expressed in its daily service and remain loyal to fundamental principles set up as the standard of constructive trade unionism by the American Federation of Labor."[30] In a letter to the committee the Federated Press acknowledged that the investigation had been fairly conducted, although there were several statements to which objection was made.

During the discussion on the subject Delegate Woll, who was on the investigating committee, declared that the news service of the Federated Press was "not serving labor as it pretends to serve labor. It is not a service that promotes trade unionism as it alleges it intends to promote it." Woll called the convention's attention to the articles attacking the American Federation of Labor and some of the leaders of international unions that had appeared in the *Butte Bulletin*. William Green corroborated these statements, and declared that Dunne's trip to the Pennsylvania coal fields during the strike of 1922 had been financed by the head of the Workers' Party, then the legal front of the Communist movement in the United States. Philip Murray, also representing the United Mine Workers of America, then moved that Dunne's credentials be revoked. Dunne was allowed to defend himself. Dunne admitted that he was a member of the Communist Party, and questioned the moral and intellectual qualifications of his accusers to sit in judgment upon him.

At one point, one of the delegates raised a point of order that the motion to unseat Dunne was not germane to the subject under discussion, and Gompers upheld that contention. After the delegates had upheld the report condemning the Federated Press, the motion by Murray was reintroduced, and it carried by a vote of 27,837 to 108, with 643 not voting. In the third group, among those refraining from voting was the secretary of the Building Trades Department and the head of the Railway Employees Department. This was only the second time, the first in 1895, that a delegate's credentials were revoked by an A. F. of L. convention.[31]

DETROIT FEDERATION OF LABOR

The Detroit Federation of Labor was also cautioned to conform to the policies of the American Federation of Labor. Its leaders suffered the same illusions about the beneficence of the Soviet Government then common to radical and left-wing labor groups in many parts of the world. The points at issue were the sending of delegates to Soviet Russia by the Detroit Federation of Labor, and the encouraging of unions that were not members of the American Federation of Labor. The Detroit Federation of Labor was ordered to "discontinue its practice of furthering revolutionary and dual movements," and the officers of the Detroit Federation of Labor were ordered not to "attend meetings of such movements either officially or unofficially." The job of city central labor union, the Detroit labor body was informed, was to organize the unorganized and show loyalty to the American Federation of Labor.[32]

Martell, the head of the Detroit Federation of Labor, assured the Executive Council that the spirit and letter of the communication would be enforced.

TACOMA, WASHINGTON, AND MINNEAPOLIS, MINNESOTA

The same kind of situation developed in the central labor union at Tacoma, Washington. In this instance again, the Executive Council insisted that the regulations of the A. F. of L. be met or the city central labor union faced the revocation of its charter. In the face of this threat the central labor union agreed to yield. The influence of Communists also arose in the Minneapolis Trades Assembly. This central body was instructed to comply with the directions of the Executive Council. One delegate charged with Communist loyalties was expelled from the Trades Assembly, but only after a long debate. On the rights of officers and members of the American Federation of Labor, the Executive Council declared that an

officer of an organization cannot very well distinguish himself as an individual and any action he may take must necessarily follow it conveys some sort of official sanction. The rights to which a member is entitled are different than those an officer assumes when permitted to represent an organization. There is a moral obligation on the part of the officer to carry the policies of an organization into effect that does not always apply to a member.[33]

While Detroit was at the time a center of the open shop, it is evident that there was a latent and even active radicalism which was to be subsequently an important factor in the industrial and labor life of the community. Under the rigorous pressure exercised, it was not possible to organize the automobile industry, but there were many union men in the city who resented the inability of the workers to come together. When the workers in Minneapolis and Detroit turned to unionism in the 1930's, radical elements exercised a disproportionate share of influence in the new unions. In part it was due to the absence of organization and leaders; in part it was due to the neglect of this area by the older unions. Despite the views generally held, the American Federation of Labor, in contrast to its affiliates, was conscious of the need for organizing some of these unorganized areas.

The desirability of organizing the automobile industry was considered by the Executive Council in 1920. Representatives from the Molders, Metal Polishers, Painters, Blacksmiths, Machinists, Electrical Workers, Upholsterers, and Sheet Metal Workers' unions had met, and discussed a joint organizing program. The Executive Council asked each of these unions to send an organizer into the automobile areas and seek to initiate an organization campaign. The Executive Council was willing to co-operate and send its own organizer into the area. "Referring to the suspension of the Carriage and Wagon Workers' Union, the opinion was expressed that the American Federation of Labor should try to settle these controversies without suspending charters as there is nothing then to limit these organizations to do the things complained against."[34] Nothing came of these attempts, because the American Federation of Labor had no means of compelling its affiliates to conduct organizing campaigns if they were unwilling to do so.

The result of uncertainty, delay, and lack of cooperation was the failure of effort, with the result that the regular unions never established any influence or base in industries such as automobile manufacturing. In consequence the radical groups, which were submerged in the relatively weak general labor movement of the automotive and other centers, were able to come to the surface and gain a preeminent position in the "revolutionary" 1930's.

REFERENCES

1. *Report of Proceedings of the Second Annual Convention of the American Federation of Labor,* 1887, p. 29.

2. Circular letter issued March 15, 1893, in A. F. of L. archives.

3. *Report of Proceedings of the Twenty-Fifth Annual Convention of the American Federation of Labor,* 1905, p. 175.

4. Gompers to President Theodore Roosevelt, September 12, 1908, January 11, 1909.

5. *Report of Proceedings of the Thirty-First Annual Convention of the American Federation of Labor,* 1911, pp. 354-355.

6. Gompers to Chekiji, March 21, 1917, April 2, 1917.

7. Executive Council to Nstcheidge, April 23, 1917.

8. Gompers to Workers' and Soldiers' Deputies, May 6, 1917.

9. Report to Executive Council, May 9, 1917.

10. *Labor Features Russian Revolution,* 1917 (Washington: American Federation of Labor, 1917).

11. Memorandum from the American Labor Delegation to the American Peace Commission. It was undated, but it was acknowledged by H. D. Buckler, March 12, 1919, as having been received the previous day.

12. *Report of Proceedings of the Fortieth Annual Convention of the American Federation of Labor,* 1920, pp. 367-372.

13. Samuel Gompers, *The Truth About Soviet Russia and Bolshevism* (Washington: American Federation of Labor, 1920), is a pamphlet.

14. Edward Nockles to Gompers, September 26, 1920; Gompers to Nockles September 27, 1920, October 1, 1920.

15. Gompers to John C. Schroder, August 20, 1920.

16. Gompers to Julius Selma, June 3, 1921.

17. *Ibid.*

18. *Report of Proceedings of the Forty-First Annual Convention of the American Federation of Labor,* 1921, pp. 91-92.

19. Leonard B. Schapiro, *The Origin of the Communist Autocracy* (Cambridge: Harvard University Press, 1955).

20. *Report of Proceedings of the Forty-Second Annual Convention of the American Federation of Labor,* 1922, p. 427.

21. H. A. Logan, *Trade Unions in Canada* (Toronto: The Macmillan Company of Canada, Limited, 1948), pp. 301-326. A. Farmilo to Gompers, July 10, 1919.

22. Frank Duffy to Gompers, July 25, 1919.

23. *Report of the Proceedings of the Fortieth Annual Convention of the American Federation of Labor,* 1920, pp. 243-244.

24. Minutes of Executive Council, May 20, 1919.

25. Minutes of Executive Council, May 9, 1922; Gompers to John Fitzpatrick, February 24, 1923.

26. Circular from the Chicago Federation of Labor, September 10, 1923.

27. Gompers to James A. Duncan, March 18, 1920.

28. Minutes of Executive Council, May 9, 1922; September 30, 1923; February 19, 1923. Gompers to Duncan, April 21, 1923, May 14, 1923; Gompers to C. W. Doyle, October 27, 1923.

29. Report of C. O. Young to Executive Council, February 9, 1923. Young was an organizer for the American Federation of Labor.

30. *Report of Proceedings of the Forty-Third Annual Convention of the American Federation of Labor,* 1923, pp. 254-256.

31. *Ibid.,* p. 259.

32. Gompers to Frank X. Martell, August 11, 1924.

33. Quotation from Minutes of Executive Council, May 12, 1924; Gompers to Joseph Taylor, August 11, 1924; Taylor to Gompers, September 10, 1924; Paul J. Smith to Gompers, November 5, 1924; Smith to Gompers, November 20, 1924.

34. Minutes of the Executive Council, August 4, 1920.

XXVIII

Government Ownership, Dissatisfaction, and Opposition in the Railroad Unions

Isolation of Railway Brotherhoods

The railroad unions became a focal point of opposition to the traditional policies of the leadership of the A. F. of L. For a short time these organizations were able to challenge the administration headed by Gompers. The railroads had been taken over by the United States Government during World War I and placed under the jurisdiction of William G. McAdoo, Director General of Railroads, who was also Secretary of the Treasury. Instead of showing hostility to organization by railroad workers, the Railroad Administrator ordered all supervisors to cease discriminating against those forming unions and to recognize the organizations of labor for purposes of collective bargaining. This action would have, by itself, lessened the hostility to government intervention in economic affairs which had been an article of faith over the years. Moreover, the unions in the railroad industry affiliated with the A .F. of L. drew closer to the railroad brotherhoods, which had never opposed active participation by government in economic affairs, at least in the affairs of their industry.

The relations between the railway brotherhoods and the American Federation of Labor, while never hostile, oscillated between close cooperation and coolness. In the 1890's, the railway brotherhoods supported the labor provisions of the Erdman Act, which the American Federation of Labor opposed. The latter feared that the freedom of action of the labor unions on the railroads might be imperiled by allowing a government body to intervene in labor disputes. Because of their more direct interest in this area, the railroad brotherhoods felt at the time that the attitude of the American Federation of Labor was not altogether friendly, but the differences did not lead to any permanent rupture in relations between the A. F. of L. and the railroad service unions.

There was throughout the early years some slight resentment on the part of the members of the Executive Council at the failure of the railroad brotherhoods to affiliate with the American Federation of Labor, but in time their abstention was accepted. The jurisdiction of the railroad brotherhoods over their crafts was recognized, and the chartering of dual unions in the railroad service trades was never contemplated. In fact, when several locals of colored trainmen requested a charter from the A. F. of L., the Federation yielded to the objection of the railway brotherhoods and denied them a charter. Over the years, efforts to work out closer cooperation were made. In 1907 the brotherhoods and the A. F. of L. tried to set up a joint committee for the purpose of drawing up legislation limiting the use of the injunction in labor disputes. The conference agreed also to cooperate on other legislation affecting labor, but nothing came of it.[1]

A motion to invite the railroad brotherhoods to affiliate with the American Federation of Labor came before the convention in 1914. There was some opposition to extending a special invitation to these organizations, the opposition being based upon the aloofness and self-isolation of the railroad service unions. Some of the opposition speakers were of the opinion that the Federation had done all that was possible to win the affiliation of the railway service unions. Others, who were members of the shop craft unions on the railroads, were not enthusiastic about extending an invitation, arguing that the railway brotherhoods were not always helpful to members of other railway labor organizations during strikes. In the end, the resolution to extend an invitation was approved by a vote of 149 to 30.[2] It appears that the negative vote was cast by representatives of the railroad unions affiliated with the American Federation of Labor.

World War I

World War I brought the railroad unions of the American Federation of Labor and the railway brotherhoods closer together. The latter organizations seemed for a time to throw off their "isolationist" shells and compete for the leadership of the general labor movement. This was especially true of the Brotherhood of Locomotive Engineers, which, under the leadership of Warren S. Stone, seemed for a time to be a pioneer and innovator in the field of labor tactics and policy. One of Stone's postwar innovations, or at least one of his major activities, was in the field of labor banking. Stone was convinced by Walter F. McCaleb, a professional banker and promoter, of the need for labor to expand its limited horizons by organizing and managing banks. McCaleb also tried to convince the Executive Council, but he failed. The Executive Council would not approve such projects, and the A. F. of L. sought to impress its affiliates that it had "no connection or affiliation with any banking business." Gompers believed that he therefore "could not speak officially or authoritatively regarding any such banks," and he did not regard these schemes as desirable.[3]

AFFILIATION OF RAILWAY BROTHERHOODS

The greater attractiveness of labor banking to the Brotherhood of Loco-motive Engineers, aside from the enthusiasm for such a program by its chief officer, was the experience of the union in the administration of an elaborate insurance program.

To many of its early members the organization's appeal was not necessarily unionism as a protective device, but as an agency supplying insurance in a dangerous industry in which private companies were reluctant to write policies at what appeared to be "bearable" rates. Gradually, the initial attitudes were modified and increasing emphasis was placed upon protective activities, which brought the brotherhoods closer to the general labor movement. This trend was reinforced by the unfavorable experience of the railroad unions with government-promoted arbitration and mediation. As a result, the brotherhoods now found themselves not only closer to other unions in the railroad industry, but more dependent upon the general labor movement for support of their demands. Moreover, most unions in the railroad industry, exclusive of the brotherhoods, were already affiliated with the A. F. of L.

In June 1919, the brotherhoods made application for affiliation with the A. F. of L. On the ground that the Brotherhood of Locomotive Engineers invaded its jurisdiction, the Amalgamated Association of Street and Electric Railway Employees protested the granting of a charter.[4] This objection did not turn out to be a serious obstacle, and an arrangement between the two unions was made clearing the road for the affiliation of the four railway service unions. Before this step could be consummated, the railway brotherhoods withdrew their application for affiliation. In a letter to the Executive Council, Stone explained that the

thing that has caused us to take the step we have is our experience of the last year in trying to cooperate and work in harmony with the American Federation of Labor. During that time, we, as one of the sixteen railroad brotherhoods affiliated and representing a majority of the membership of the organization, the strongest fighting force within the Federation, have been cooperating with these brotherhoods and we note there has not been a single thing we recom-mended that has been approved by the Executive Committee, nor has a single request of the railroad brotherhoods been granted.

Stone was of the opinion that the Executive Council of the A. F. of L. was too powerful, and that affiliates would eventually lose their identity.[5]

What disturbed the railway unions most was the dominant position played by the building trades unions in the affairs of the Federation. According to Stone, the railway unions were numerically the greatest of any group of organizations in the A. F. of L. Yet they felt that both the Executive Council and the policies of the Federation were dominated by the building trades organizations. Another complaint of the railway unions concerned the A. F. of L.'s activity in the settling of jurisdictional disputes among affiliates. It was the view of the railway brotherhoods that too much time was spent by the Federation on this question, and, moreover, "organizations have found themselves subject to decisions reached by others in matters of jurisdiction that solely concerned themselves."[6] While the criticism of the A. F. of L. on the score of its utilizing too much of its time in considering jurisdictional matters may be justified, it must be recognized that the Federation took upon itself this problem only reluctantly.

Gompers was deeply offended at the charge by Stone that "not a single thing" recommended by the railway brotherhoods had been granted." One of the complaints made by Stone was that the A. F. of L. refused to endorse the Plumb Plan of government ownership of the railroads. The Executive Council felt it could not endorse such a program, and it believed that its views would be validated by time. On the other hand, the convention of 1920 did approve government ownership of railroads, sought by the brotherhoods.

Gompers, on behalf of the Council, outlined the various kinds of aid given, from the "hardest kind of a contest against the labor features of the Esch Bill and the Cummins Bill and against the conference report." The letter called attention to the fight made by the A. F. of L. against the criminal features of the Esch-Cummins Law. Gompers called upon Stone to cite a single instance where the A. F. of L. failed to support the railroad brotherhoods in their demands before Congress. Gompers claimed that it was his, Gompers', appearance which "prevailed upon enough members of Congress to vote for the Car Coupling Bill that finally accomplished its passage and enactment," that it was due to the opposition of the A. F. of L. that the compulsory features of the Erdman Act were removed, that the A. F. of L. supported the brotherhoods during the Pullman strike, the Burlington, Ann Arbor, and New York Central strikes, and "in fighting the injunctions of Judges Taft and Ricks and others." He pointed to the effort of the A. F. of L. to secure the enactment of the Adamson Act, and "the effort put forth in helping to secure the agreement of the railroad presidents to the recognition of the eight hour work day, the agreement reached after forty-eight hours of continuous session and struggle."

While ackowledging the militancy of the railroad unions, the A. F. of L. believed Stone was doing "the other militant trade unions in the A. F. of L. a grave injustice and one which would not be taken kindly if they knew of it, for there are many trade unions affiliated to the A. F. of L. whose wages are higher, whose hours of labor are less and whose conditions of employment are better than those of the men engaged in the labor service." What disturbed Gompers was the belief that unions were being dominated by the Executive Council, for which he could find no evidence.

AN ALLIANCE OF RAILWAY UNIONS

Having found affiliation with the A. F. of L. undesirable, the heads of the railway service unions then sought to establish a means of cooperation among the sixteen unions in the railroad industry. At a meeting at the headquarters of the International Association of Machinists in February 1921, it was decided to set up a bureau which would look after the legislative interests of labor. The A. F. of L. had not been invited to send a representative—it was claimed through an oversight. Gompers did not accept the explanation when he learned about the meeting. He charged that a program of this character, which contemplated the setting up of an organization to deal with questions to which the A. F. of L. devoted a good deal of time and effort, was "treason to the A. F. of L." Only after a conference between the Executive Council and William H. Johnston, the head of the International Association of Machinists and a prime mover in this plan, and Senator Robert M. La Follette, did the Council agree to be represented on the committee planning to organize a legislative bureau.[7]

While Johnston, whose union was affiliated with the American Federation of Labor, was not averse to close cooperation with the heads of the A. F. of L., the heads of the railway service brotherhoods were of a different opinion.

On April 12, 1921, the heads of all the railway unions met in the offices of the American Federation of Labor. It was the view of the railway brotherhoods that issues affecting the railways or their workers should be exclusively determined by the unions on the railroads themselves. This was the answer of the railroad unions to a proposal that an offensive and defensive alliance be formed between the railroad unions and the A. F. of L. Gompers had suggested that a joint policy committee be established, upon which the railway brotherhoods would be represented.

The representatives of the A. F. of L. argued that a large number of railroad workers belonged to unions affiliated with the A. F. of L., and that the latter could not detach itself from its interest in railroad legislation. An alliance would not, it was argued, encroach upon the rights of the brotherhoods, and would instead strengthen their legislative position. The service unions found this view unacceptable. W. S. Carter, the head of the Brotherhood of Firemen and Enginemen, speaking on behalf of the four organizations, claimed that mainly the service workers would be affected by Congressional legislation. He, therefore, concluded that a committee with some members representing unions other than the service trades would have the authority to approve or veto legislation which would not concern them directly, and he, as well as the officers of other service unions, disapproved having outsiders determining issues directly affecting their members.

Another officer of one of the service unions, L. E. Sheppard, head of the Order of Railway Conductors, speaking for the heads of all the service unions, believed:

It is difficult at times to make our brothers in the A. F. of L. fully understand our position, and we therefore must respectfully decline to become parties to the complete unification of the different elements in the labor world but hereby pledge ourselves to cooperate and support in every consistent manner any legislation affecting labor generally, and matters aside from railroad legislation we are prepared to follow, almost without reservation, the desire of the A. F. of L. as they shall make them known to us, and we request the engine and train service be given the same consideration by our brothers in the A. F. of L.[8]

The American Federation of Labor would not accept the limitation upon its activities proposed by the railway brotherhoods, as many of its members were employed on the railroads. In addition, the A. F. of L. would not surrender its right, as the spokesman of the largest body of organized workers in the United States, to express an opinion upon important labor legislation. Yet Gompers advised against the creation of a committee to deal with railroad labor legislation, suggested by the Railway Employees Department, a committee opposed by the service brotherhoods. He believed that "pursuing such a course would . . . have offered such an affront to the four brotherhoods that it would be hurtful to the labor movement."[9] In the end, the railroad unions established the Railway Labor Executives Association, upon which the American Federation of Labor is not directly represented but to which its railroad affiliates belong, to watch over the legislative interests of railroad workers in the halls of Congress.

THE PLUMB PLAN

In the immediate period after World War I, the railroad unions, especially the Brotherhood of Locomotive engineers, under the vigorous leadership of Warren S. Stone, sought to gain the leadership of the general labor movement. There was even some mention of the possibility that, once the four brotherhoods had affiliated, Stone would challenge Gompers as a candidate as president of the A. F. of L. The accuracy of such reports could not be verified, as the affiliation of these organizations was never consummated. Yet the vigor and drive of these unions showed them, despite their parochial attitude on issues affecting their own industry, to be desirous of placing themselves at the head of the entire labor movement. While neither the leaders nor the unions could show a record of much interest or aid to workers in their organizing efforts in other industries, the willingness to sponsor new ideas and new methods, some of them of doubtful value, gave to the heads of the brotherhoods a prestige within the general labor movement that they had never before enjoyed. As some of these views ran counter to the traditional attitudes of the American Federation of Labor, the leaders of the brotherhoods could not help becoming aligned with groups hostile to the continuance of the "pure" Gompers tradition in the A. F. of L.

One of the important points of difference developed over the desirability and endorsement of private and public ownership of the railroads. The railroads unions, especially the four service brotherhoods, were in favor of the Plumb Plan of government ownership, sponsored by Glenn E. Plumb.

The Plumb Plan called for the purchase of the railroads by the government at what was defined as their "physical value," or the value at the time the properties were built. No consideration was to be given in setting the price of the properties to reinvestment or market values. The roads were to be purchased through the issuance of special bonds carrying a 4 per cent interest charge, and the amount necessary, according to the Plumb Plan League which sponsored the program, was eighteen billion dollars.

Once the roads had been purchased by the government, the Plumb Plan provided for the setting up of a non-capital operating company to lease the railroad properties. This company would manage and operate the railroads. The leasing and operating company would be governed by a board of directors, made up of fifteen members, five of whom would be elected by the classified employees, five by all the other officials, and five appointed by the President of the United States. The rate-fixing power was to be left undisturbed in the hands of the Interstate Commerce Commission.

As can be seen, the operating and management of the railroads would in fact be virtually placed in the hands of the classified employees and railroad officials. It was also proposed that the railroads would arrange their charges so that at the end of the year they would show net earnings, half of which would be placed in a sinking fund to be used for reinvestment, and the other 50 per cent divided among the classified employees and officers. For the setting of wages and other terms of employment the Board of Directors would appoint, by negotitation with the employees through their duly elected representatives, a central board of wages and working conditions. One half of the members of the latter board would be selected by and from the classified employees and one half by and from the official employees. This board, acting independently or through regional boards, was to have the authority to set wages and working conditions, and the board of directors was to intervene only if the primary board could reach no decision.

For promoting this proposal, the railroad unions organized the Plumb Plan League, with Arthur Wharton, the head of the Railway Employees Department, as president, and J. J. Forrester, the head of the Brotherhood of Railway and Steamship Clerks, as secretary. Gompers, without his consent, was listed as honorary president. The Executive Committee of the League was made up of the officers of the railroad unions, including the four service brotherhoods. Warren S. Stone, the head of the Brotherhood of Locomotive Engineers, informed the Executive Council of the A. F. of L., that irrespective of the latter's position on the question, the brotherhoods would continue to support and promote the Plumb Plan. Moreover, the railroad unions affiliated with the American Federation of Labor supported the same plan. The Executive Council considered the Plumb Plan, and a committee was appointed to report on the question. It refused to endorse or oppose it. During the consideration of the Plan, Gompers objected to the use of his name as one of its supporters. "He insisted that he had never consented to the use of his name, and that he had never agreed to support it."[10]

TRANSPORTATION ACT OF 1920

Instead of a bill sponsored by labor, Congress enacted the Transportation Act of 1920, which the railroad workers and the A. F. of L. bitterly opposed. While the bill was being considered the Executive Council spoke out against its enactment, and declared that its opposition was not predicated upon government control or ownership. It was felt by the Executive Council that "inasmuch as when the railroads were taken over by the government the workers were free men, then when the roads are turned over to the owners for their control the workers should not be handed over manacled and subjected to the tender mercies of the railroad owners." The greatest objections of organized labor were to the labor provisions of the law, which made it difficult for workers to use their economic power. "If normal activities of workers are made unlawful," the Executive Council declared, "no one can tell where it will lead. Other menacing features to labor as well as to the general good are contained in the bill."[11] Nevertheless, the Transportation Act of 1920, or the Esch-Cummins Act, was enacted by Congress.

GOVERNMENT OWNERSHIP

There was united opposition to the Esch-Cummins law, but while far from unanimous, widespread sentiment existed for government ownership of the railroads among the railroads unions, as well as among other organized workers. The question came before the convention of 1920, when a minority report from the resolutions committee, advocating government ownership of the railroads, was presented.

The main argument against the minority view was made by John Frey, the secretary of the resolutions committee. He based his opposition on the ground that endorsement of government ownership would be a reversal of the historic policy of the Federation. He charged that the idea was alien to the United States, and that it had been imported from abroad. Moreover, he argued that it was inadvisable to trust the government to administer economic affairs without encroaching upon the rights of individuals, including labor.

Frank Morrison, the secretary of the American Federation of Labor, supported a contrary view. He argued that this government ownership had been approved by the Reconstruction Program, adopted by the A. F. of L. at its convention of 1919. He also insisted that, as all the railroad unions represented in the convention were

asking that they be assisted in securing "government ownership and the democratic operation of the railroad system and necessary inland waterways," because they believe that no matter what tribulations may come as a result of government ownership, they will fare better than they have in the past and better than they will fare in the future under private ownership. If this proposition was for government ownership and those representing the railroad were here opposing it, then I would consider another proposition; but they are the workers that are interested and they are asking this convention to place them in a position where they can, in their opinion, work to better advantage.

The head of the Machinists' Union, Delegate William H. Johnston, contended that the workers on the railways, and their unions, accomplished more in three years of government control than in twenty-five years of private control. He denied, as did several other delegates, that the endorsement of government ownership meant approval of the Plumb Plan. Gompers opposed the minority report in accordance with his opposition to any extension of the power of government, except under the direct necessity.

The pleas of the opponents of government ownership were unheeded, and the convention endorsed the minority proposal by a vote of 29,159 to 8349, with 1507 not voting.[12]

At the next convention, in 1921, the issue again came before the convention. At the meeting of the Executive Council, in May 1921, Gompers suggested that the Executive Council reiterate approval of government ownership in compliance with the expressed opinion of the preceding convention. During this meeting, Vice President Green's proposal adopted was that

At the Montreal convention of the American Federation of Labor organized labor gave expression to what it believed to be the best solution of the railroad problem. By a decisive majority vote delegates representing the organized labor movement of America decided in favor of government ownership and democratic operation of railroads. This is the latest expression of the American Federation of labor upon this subject. While organized labor is open to the consideration of all serious proposals looking to a settlement of the railroad problem, your Executive Council, responding to the expressed will of the representatives of organized labor, will do what it can to bring about government ownership and democratic operation of railroads. The Executive Council will cooperate with other organizations in carrying into effect the instructions of the Montreal convention.[13]

In pursuance of the decision of the Montreal convention, the Executive Council called a conference of the representatives of the organizations of railroad workers, but the representatives of the four railway service unions asked that the issue of government ownership not be pressed, because of their difficulties in negotiating with the railroad managements. Subsequently, the same view was expressed by the shop craft executives, and the Executive Council refrained from pressing this issue, in compliance with the wishes of those unions most interested. The convention of 1921 also considered the question of government ownership of railroads, and the majority of the resolutions committee again disapproved of this proposal. A minority report endorsing government ownership was again submitted, and it was approved without a roll-call vote.[14]

RAILROAD LABOR BOARD

While the question of government ownership of railroads was settled as far as the A. F. of L. was concerned, the railroad workers were finding the new regime of private ownership difficult and onerous. Under the Transportation Act of 1920, the carriers were returned to their private owners, and a tripartite Railroad Labor Board established to determine labor relations. In fact, the resolution submitted by the railroad unions to the convention of 1922 centered its criticism upon the actions of the Railroad Labor Board, and an amendment endorsing the previous position on government ownership of the railroads was withdrawn at the suggestion of the railroad unions.

The issue of government ownership of railroads ceased to be of much importance, as many of the A. F. of L. unions found themselves confronted by a hostile administration which appeared to be seeking their destruction. Not only were the carriers showing greater vigor in opposing the claims of the unions, but they were demanding sharp reductions in money wages. Some of these demands were imposed upon the workers with the approval of the Railroad Labor Board. The Board formally sanctioned wage reductions, as required by law. The consequence was that the unions and their members were convinced that the Railroad Labor Board was merely a device by which the carriers could impose their will upon their workers. This view was strengthened by the inability of the Railroad Labor Board to compel the roads to obey the requirement that the carriers recognize the legitimate unions of their workers instead of dealing with the company-sponsored organizations. The Board did attempt to compel the carriers to recognize the outside unions, but it was prevented from enforcing its orders by the courts, which held the Board lacked authority.

The Board was also unable to prevent the carriers from farming out some of their work on rolling stock and other equipment to contractors who employed labor at lower rates, which also demonstrated to the labor organizations that the Railroad Labor Board was essentially an instrument for wage deflation. As a result, sentiment for a strike mounted. Even if the officers of the unions involved had sought to prevent a walk-out, it is likely that their views would have been overridden by an aroused membership.

Failure to settle the main differences between the shop craft unions and carriers led to a strike. It began on July 1, 1922, and the hostility of the Railroad Labor Board was quickly apparent. Soon after the beginning of the walkout, the chairman of the Board denounced the strikers and recommended that those who had remained at work form company unions. President Harding also intervened on the side of the carriers, with a declaration that the strike was "against the government."

As the government's hostility toward the strikers became manifest, Gompers requested the Executive Council to authorize a statement in support of the striking shopmen. He was confronted by a minor dilemma because of the failure of the signalmen and maintenance-of-way men, both affiliates of the A. F. of L., to join the other unions on strike. Nevertheless, Gompers criticized President Harding for his statement, and pointed to the disobedience by 92 railroads of 104 decisions of the same Railroad Labor Board. In not a single instance, Gompers declared, were the roads reproved by the President, which was, in his opinion, in sharp contrast with the President's reaction to the strike.

On July 17th the Executive Council denounced the attitude of the Railroad Labor Board, and declared that the stoppage of work could be ended at any moment by the railroads agreeing to negotiations with representatives of their employees. Moreover, the Council charged that

The government by its silence has been a party to the conduct of the railroads in ignoring the awards of the Railroad Labor Board and it must thus stand convicted not only of inconsistency but of bad faith in its present tremendous effort to coerce the railroad workmen into an acceptance of an award that is bitterly unjust and that violates every tradition of American fairness and justice.[15]

When the Railroad Labor Board declared that the unions on strike had forfeited their right to represent the workers on the railroads, the Executive Council labeled it a move to assist reactionary employers "to destroy the voluntary organizations of the workers and to open the door for the establishment of an industrial autocracy in which the workers would be helpless and in which they would be in virtual bondage to the masters of the industrial world." It cited the unequal treatment of workers and their employers by the national administration, and charged that the tribunals and courts which sought to prevent workers from exercising their rights to strike were "undemocratic, that they destroy the peaceful and constructive processes of negotiation and joint agreement, and that they lead only to disturbance of industry replacing negotiation with litigation."[16]

The strikers were, nevertheless, fighting a losing battle. The carriers, aided by the federal government, were managing to restore the services, which had been severely crippled at the beginning of the walkout. On August 19th the Executive Council, at the request of the Railway Employees Department, issued an appeal for financial aid to the strikers. Later in the month the railroads, through their request for an injunction, again forced the Executive Council to denounce the conduct of the government in the strike. On September 1, 1922, Judge James Wilkerson, a federal district judge in Chicago, issued one of the more sweeping injunctions against the striking railroad workers. The injunction was directed against the officers of the Railway Employees' Department, the six shop crafts, whose members were on strike, 120 system federations affiliated with the Railway Employees Department, and attorneys, associates, and members of the strikers. All were forbidden to engage in activities even remotely connected with the walkout. The Executive Council was disturbed by this order, which it felt was in violation of the constitutional rights of the strikers as citizens of the United States. Moreover, in the opinion of the members of the Executive Council, the injunction was in clear violation of the provisions of the Clayton Act.

Whatever may have been the legal merits of the view, the Council regarded this injunction as a grave threat to all organized labor. In a statement approved by all members except James Duncan, the Council declared:

Because we have reverence for law, because we believe that every citizen must be a guardian of the heritage given us by our fathers who fought for and established freedom and democracy, we call upon the workers to resist the establishment of a practice that will destroy the very spirit of freedom and democracy and we call upon the people of America as a whole to protest against these abuses in the exercise of the injunction writ so clearly violative of the constitutional guarantees of the United States.[17]

The strike went on, but it was not successful, for the railroads were able to replace most of the strikers.

The failure of the service trades to honor the picket lines of the shop men doomed the latter to slow defeat. The American Federation of Labor did not have any direct responsibility for the calling of the strike or its management. It was a period when the postwar reaction was in full force, and the government was plainly on the side of employers in their efforts to push back the unions to their less powerful prewar positions.

The A. F. of L. did actively participate in the injunction proceedings, and its counsel assisted those engaged by the shop-craft unions in their arguments and defense of the right of workers to strike on the railroads. In April 1923, the Executive Council directed its attorneys to withdraw from representing the defendants in the cases brought by the government under the terms of the injunction issued by Judge Wilkerson. This step was taken with the approval of the unions directly involved. The action of the A. F. of L. was based upon the decision of the United States Supreme Court in the suit of the Pennsylvania against the Railroad Labor Board, in which the Court held that the decisions of the Board were only moral dicta and could not be legally enforced.

The Executive Council was of the opinion that the decision destroyed the Board's power to prevent strikes and consequently the Federation had no interest in the proceedings. The action of the A. F. of L. embarrassed the government lawyers, who were anxious to try the case, but the withdrawal of the Federation and the union closed the proceedings in the courts.

The strike was finally ended on the basis of a formula proposed by Daniel Willard, president of the Baltimore and Ohio Railroad and a moderate in the matter of unionism. He proposed separate settlements with each railway system. This proposal was accepted by the unions, on condition that strikers would be returned to the seniority and status they held before the strike and that all complaints would be jointly settled. Beginning in the middle of September 1923, a number of roads settled on the basis of the "Willard" formula. While a large number of workers were able to regain their pre-strike status, many others lost their positions as a result of the successful resistance of their roads.

REFERENCES

1. Minutes of conference of representatives of the Brotherhood of Railroad Trainmen, Brotherhood of Locomotive Engineers, Brotherhood of Locomotive

Firemen, and Order of Railroad Conductors with a committee from the Executive Council of the A. F. of L., in archives, June 17, 1907.

2. *Report of Proceedings of the Thirty-Fourth Annual Convention of the American Federation of Labor,* 1914, pp. 338-340.

3. Walter F. McCaleb to Gompers, May 27, 1922; Gompers to Robert Grimshaw, September 8, 1922.

4. Minutes of Executive Council, May 16, 1919.

5. Gompers to Stone, July 23, 1920; Stone to Gompers, August 10, 1920; Stone to Executive Council, June 4, 1920.

6. Warren S. Stone to Frank Morrison, June 10, 1921.

7. Statement to the Executive Council, February 18, 1921; Minutes of the Executive Council, March 2, 1921.

8. Quote from L. E. Sheppard to Gompers, April 20, 1921; W. S. Carter to Gompers, April 28, 1921; Gompers to Carter, May 21, 1921.

9. Minutes of Executive Council, June 6, 1921.

10. Report of Plumb Plan to the Executive Council (Unpublished). Minutes of Executive Council, August 30, 1919.

11. Executive Council to President Wilson, February 24, 1919.

12. *Report of Proceedings of the Fortieth Annual Convention of the American Federation of Labor,* 1920, pp. 399-420.

13. Minutes of Executive Council, May 9, 1921.

14. *Report of Proceedings of Forty-First Annual Convention of the American Federation of Labor,* 1921, p. 371.

15. Document 107, Executive Council Vote Book, July 13, 1922; Statement of Executive Council, July 17, 1922; *Washington Star,* July 15, 1922.

16. Vote Book, July 13, 1922.

17. Minutes of Executive Council, September 7, 1922.

XXIX

Political Problems

Differences over political action made their appearance within the labor movement in the postwar period. In fact, the war experience, added to the growing importance of government in the economic field, made many labor organizations formerly lukewarm to political activity more deeply interested in and actively concerned with politics. The position of the A. F. of L. leadership on politics had been changing over time. While the A. F. of L. would not accept independent political action as desirable, the attention and expenditure of energy spent upon political activity greatly changed over the years. At the beginning, the interest of the American Federation of Labor was in lobbying for legislation favorable to labor, and avoiding any direct participation in politics.

This view could not altogether be followed, and the American Federation of Labor found itself, against its wishes, propelled into more active political participation. Even while the American Federation of Labor was disclaiming any support of third or independent parties, local unions, central bodies, and even state federations might support Socialist or labor candidates. In communities such as Milwaukee, Wisconsin, where the Socialists were strongly entrenched and where they had a fighting chance for election, the entire labor movement normally supported the Socialist Party. In fact, the American Federation of Labor officially endorsed, at least once, the election of Victor Berger, the first Socialist Congressman.

The rise of the Non-Partisan League in North Dakota in 1915 and its successful election of a governor, stimulated interest in a new type of third party politics. Although the Non-Partisan League advocated organized campaigns within the old party primaries, so as to elect government representatives favorable to the farmers' interests, its failure to win in the Republican primaries in the neighboring state of Minnesota gave an impetus to the third party movement in that state.

The rising sentiment for a labor or farmer-labor party was recognized by the Executive Council. Gompers, addressing a meeting of trade union officials, affirmed that in New York City and several other communities the labor movement, speaking through the central labor councils, had endorsed a labor party. Gompers reviewed the history of labor-party movements in the United States, and touched upon the political activities of labor on the continent and in England. He declared that it "is not true, as some carping critics allege, that the American Federation of Labor is a non-political organization. As a matter of fact, the workers of the United States and the organized labor movement act voluntarily in the exercise of their political right and power."[1] It was Gompers' contention, in this speech as elsewhere, that labor legislation could not be adequately promoted if a labor party were supported, for there would no longer be any basis for appeal for relief to the old parties.

Nevertheless, the attitude of Congress toward the demands of labor, and the broad dissatisfaction existing among the rank and file, led to a constant rise in the sentiment for independent political activity by labor. Early in 1919 the Chicago Federation of Labor established a labor party, and ran its president for mayor. In the fall of the same year, a referendum on the formation of a labor party was decided upon by the Indiana State Federation of Labor. Powerful support for this tendency also appeared among the railroad unions. The "progressive" farmers' organizations, chafing at the failure of the Congress to grant them relief, appeared before the Executive Council in October 1919, and suggested the calling of a conference of national and international unions and farmers' organizations for the purpose of devising a common legislative policy. The chief promoters of this "unified" program were Warren S. Stone of the Brotherhood of Locomotive Engineers, James J. Forrester of the Brotherhood of Railroad Signalmen, and George P. Hampton of the "progressive" farmers' organizations. The Executive Council thereupon called the conference for December 13, 1919.

FARMER LABOR PARTIES

In the meantime, a national farmer-labor conference was scheduled for Chicago on November 21-22, 1919. Stone and Forrester had requested of the Executive Council that Gompers be authorized to attend this meeting. Gompers expressed some misgivings about the possible trend of such an all-inclusive gathering, but at the urging of Stone and Forrester it was agreed that he attend. When it was subsequently announced that the Chicago conference would form a labor party, Gompers asked the Executive Council to reconsider its decision. In response to Gompers' wishes the Executive Council authorized him to refrain from attending the meeting if he believed it was in the interest of the American Federation of Labor to follow such a policy.[2] Nevertheless the Chicago Conference carried out its plan and formed an American Labor Party.

The meeting called by the A. F. of L. Executive Council met on December 13, 1919. It was attended by representatives of international unions, and by delegates from the railway brotherhoods and farmers' organizations. A statement, "Labor's Grievances," was issued, denouncing the attitude of the steel industry toward recognizing the union in its plants, and criticizing the employer members of the President's Industrial Conference. The conference regarded as the paramount question of the time the "perversion and the abuse of the writ of injunction and the necessity for full and adequate protection of the voluntary associations of wage earners organized not for profit." It pointed to the extension of the labor injunction, and "whereas they were formerly of a prohibitive character they had been enlarged to include mandatory orders whereby men have been compelled to do specific things which they have a lawful right to refuse to do."

The conference also criticized the rising cost of living and demanded that labor be given a share in the rising productivity of industry. The statement declared that the labor movement was "fully cognizant of the efforts of powerful interests to reduce its influence and cripple the organizations of workers. They seek to reduce wages and thus lower the standard of living." The conference also called for the ratification of the peace treaty, and lauded the labor draft convention of the treaty.[3]

The conference resented the efforts of the opponents of unionism to "classify the men and women of Labor with those groups which have nothing in common with the constructive purposes and high ideals, and with the fundamental principles of our country."

In keeping with the suggestions of the December conference, and also with traditional A. F. of L. policy, the Executive Council considered the participation of the Federation in the presidential campaign of 1920. In accordance with the instructions of the Executive Council, Gompers appointed the heads of the Building Trades, Metal Trades, Mining, Railway Employees, and Union Label Trades departments as the National Non-Partisan Committee of the American Federation of Labor, to conduct labor's campaign.

An executive committee of Gompers, Morrison and O'Connell was appointed to direct all activities.

In the meantime, the political policy of the American Federation of Labor came under increasing attack from within the labor movement. In Indiana, a conference of delegates from local unions, despite the warning of Daniel Tobin, the treasurer of the A. F. of L. and head of the Teamsters' Union, voted to establish a Labor Party. Gompers thereupon wrote to William Mitch, the head of the Indiana District of the United Mine Workers of America and a leader in the Indiana Labor Party, that

The effect of a separate political labor party can only be disastrous to the wage earners of our country and to the interests of all forward looking people. The votes that would go to a labor party candidate, would, in the absence of such candidate, go to the best man in the field. In no case would he be an enemy of labor. There can be no hope for success of labor party candidates. The effect, therefore, of a political labor party will be to defeat our friends and to elect our enemies. Labor can look upon the formation of a political labor party only as an act detrimental to the interests of labor and exactly in line with that which is most ardently desired by those who seek to oppress labor.[4]

Other groups were also expressing opposition to the traditional political policies of the A. F. of L. The head of the Detroit Federation of Labor came out for a labor party. It was Gompers' opinion that only a few of the approximately forty thousand locals of the unions of the American Federation of Labor favored a third party, and he did not believe that the sentiment for this novel policy was sufficiently widespread to warrant what was, for him, a dangerous experiment. The railroad unions, while not yet going all the way toward endorsing an independent political party or candidate of labor, set up the National Campaign Committee of the Sixteen Associated Recognized Standard Railroad Labor Organizations. This group urged members of the railroad unions to combine into local campaign committees and cooperate with the A. F. of L. and farmers' organizations. The National Campaign Committee was instructed to study the legislative records as prepared by the four transportation unions and the A. F. of L. and draw up a statement which could be used by the local bodies during the campaign.

The records of members of Congress were divided into groups: congressmen whose records were of a character who deserved the unequivocal support of labor; those whose records were mainly favorable but who had been wrong on some major issues; those with records sufficiently unfavorable to labor as to justify outright opposition.[5] One of the main targets of the efforts of the railroad unions was the defeat of the supporters of the Esch-Cummins (Railroad Transportation) law, which Congress had enacted in the last days of the Democratic administration.

Differences with the Railroad Unions

Differences between the American Federation of Labor and the railroad unions over political action were on the increase. The American Federation of Labor, while entertaining no illusions about the real attitude of members of Congress to organized labor, approached political questions largely from the historical and pragmatic points of view. The railroad unions believed that they, more than the rest of the labor movement, had a tremendous stake in the kind of administration in control of the government. To a greater extent than perhaps other industries, their members were at this time subject to government regulation and control. Consequently, they sought to devise methods by which they could exercise more direct influence upon Congressional opinion and Congressional action.

In June 1921, a group of leaders of railroad unions met in the office of Senator La Follette; Gompers and Morrison were invited to attend. It was decided to establish a People's Legislative Service which would provide aid to Congressmen. A request for Morrison's participation on the executive committee was made, but Gompers was at first opposed, because he regarded the new venture as one which encroached upon the authority of the American Federation of Labor in the political arena. Gompers' attitude aroused the anger of William Johnston, the head of the Machinists' Union. The latter's position was that "when Senators call for help I am willing to give that help. All the wisdom of the labor movement is not in the Executive Council of the A. F. of L., and if the A. F. of L. is not represented as such, a great many of the nationals and internationals will be represented."[6] The A. F. of L. would not join.

The progressives, led by the railroad unions, continued to widen their political activity despite the reluctance of the Executive Council to follow their lead. The convention of the American Federation of Labor in 1921 voted to continue the Non-Partisan Political Campaign committee on a permanent basis. In the meantime, the railroad unions decided to call a large-scale political conference in February 1922. Gompers and other representatives of the Federation were invited to attend.[7] The Executive Council rejected the invitation, but it did take a step in a new direction when it voted, by eight to one, to participate in the primaries of that year. The Council voted to appeal for contributions; Duffy of the Carpenters' Union opposed both proposals.[8] In a dispatch to all central labor unions and state federations, the American Federation of Labor Non-Partisan Political Campaign Committee urged organized labor that "wherever necessary Labor should place candidates in the field. This should be done where the candidates on both dominant party tickets are unfriendly to our cause."[9]

At the same time, the Executive Council expressed its satisfaction at the absence of an independent political movement, which the Council believed would only interfere with the effectiveness of the A. F. of L.'s nonpartisan policy. The position of the Executive Council was supported unanimously by the convention of 1922. During the Congressional campaign of 1922, a Farmer-Labor Party in Washington nominated James A. Duncan, a leader of the Seattle Central Labor Council, as candidate for United States Senator. When he was endorsed by the Seattle Central Labor Council, Gompers was of the opinion that the Council violated the policy of the American Federation of Labor. However, nothing was done to compel a reversal of the endorsement. Gompers himself pleaded for support of the Democratic candidate, Clarence Dill. He pointed to the possibilities, shown to have been correct, of defeating the incumbent Republican, Miles Poindexter, labeled by Gompers as an extreme reactionary and anti-labor senator.[10]

CONFERENCE FOR PROGRESSIVE POLITICAL ACTION

The dissatisfaction with the old parties was widespread even among many traditional unions. Those in the railroad industry, whose special problems were not being handled satisfactorily by the administration, were among the more active seekers for a new political alignment. Sparked largely by the railroad unions, the Conference for Progressive Political Action was formed in February 1922. The Socialist Party was allowed to affiliate. Acceptance of the membership of the Socialist Party in a body dominated by trade unions was in itself a major change, even though many unions had always been more favorably inclined toward the Socialist Party than the American Federation of Labor. At the meeting of the Conference for Progressive Political Action a half-way policy was devised, in that Socialist and labor candidates were to be supported in the Congressional elections when they had a chance for victory; otherwise the policy of supporting favorable candidates in the primaries of the old parties was to be followed. A national committee, upon which each major group was represented, was chosen to direct policy.

Following the Congressional elections of 1922, the Conference rejected the immediate formation of a labor party by a rather narrow vote of 64 to 52. A legislative program was drawn up, calling for the repeal of the Esch-Cummins law, increased taxation of large incomes and inheritances, support of the bill to increase the value of farm products, a soldiers' bonus, amnesty for political prisoners, safeguards for civil liberties, the abolition of the use of the injunction in labor disputes, and the abrogation of the right of the courts to declare laws of Congress unconstitutional.

The American Federation of Labor watched these developments and, for a time, failed to take any steps to change its own traditional political policy.

In 1923 several resolutions endorsing a farmer-labor party were presented to the convention. Endorsement was refused and the formation of such parties rejected by a vote of 25,066 to 1895, with 1628 not voting.[11] Sentiment for a third party movement was nevertheless on the increase, largely because the two old parties had failed to meet even the minimum demands of organized labor. The outlook for a farmer-labor party also seemed to many labor people more propitious. With the election in Minnesota of Henrik Shipstead to the United States Senate, in 1922, the united front of progressive farmers and militant labor had achieved its first statewide victory. The Farmer-Labor Party which had gained the victory was formed largely as a result of the farmers' failure to capture the "old party" primaries—a tactic which the farmers had, at one time, successfully utilized. To many the experience in Minnesota foreshadowed a basic change in the political tactics of all labor.

COMMUNIST INFILTRATION

While the heads of the Farmer-Labor Party showed considerable knowledge and sophistication when dealing with events in Minnesota, they did not exhibit too much understanding of problems and personalities in the labor movement of the country at large. In the hope of launching a national movement, the Minnesota Farmer-Labor Party summoned a national convention for St. Paul, Minnesota, on June 17, 1924. Inexperienced in national labor matters, the leaders were unaware of the plans of the Communists to seize control of their enterprise, as they had earlier of a similar effort directed by the Chicago Federation of Labor. Even though the American Federation of Labor was not concerned, it believed that the affiliation of honest and unsuspecting unions in an enterprise manipulated by the Communists would be to the disadvantage of all labor. As a result, the National Non-Partisan Political Campaign Committee issued a warning circular that there was available

dependable information that those who are planning the St. Paul conference and who intend to direct its work are the group of international communists who . . . are sowing seeds of dissension and revolutionary propaganda wherever they can obtain an opportunity. This group works through professional radicals and such well meaning agents it can deceive.[12]

They called upon "progressive farmers and trade unionists to abandon the Farmer-Labor Party for the time being and to support by every honorable means the laws, principles and policies of the American Federation of Labor Non-Partisan Political Campaign." The American Federation of Labor had, however, an even more direct and significant role in spiking the attempts of the American Communists to place themselves at the head of the third party movement. As soon as the intentions of the Communists became known, Gompers called a meeting of progressive Senators, Congressmen, and labor men. He warned the meeting of the danger of affiliation with the St. Paul conference, which Gompers was convinced would be a Communist trap. "My purpose was that those men should save themselves, and that further Senator La Follette, [who] was to be the leader of the Progressive movement if there is to be any Progressive movement, should not be crucified by the Communists." After the discussion, which lasted all evening, Gompers reported:

I said "The Senator must be made acquainted with this situation and save himself and save whatever there is of a Progressive movement, political, economic, industrial or agricultural. I will issue a circular letter to organized labor of the country. I will assume the responsibility of advising them of the trap that has been laid for them by this St. Paul meeting. I will withhold the issuance of that circular letter Senator if La Follette will take a stand in repudiating this gang." I wanted him to have this opportunity to disentangle himself from that gang whoever they might be. That famous letter he wrote, you remember. I had Secretary Morrison give him the information, to go to him to save him—not only his political career but the country and the movement of labor and the farmers.[13]

TRADITIONAL POLICY

In the meantime, the Executive Council continued its traditional nonpartisan political policy: it submitted to both political parties a statement of its demands. It requested the repeal of the labor clauses of the Transportation Act of 1920 and the "enactment of legislation that will afford opportunity for the voluntary organizations of management and employees to deal with problems of industrial relations." It asked for legislation to protect free labor against the competition of goods produced in prisons, a program of public works to relieve unemployment, full rehabilitation for those injured in the World War, adequate compensation and classification for government employees, and more comprehensive laws to govern compensation of workers injured in industrial accidents where such workers were not covered by state laws. Repeal of the Volstead law and the enactment of legislation to permit the manufacture and sale of beer not containing more than 2.75 percent alcohol were also advocated. The statement declared "for the maintenance of freedom of speech, press, assemblage and association. We oppose any regulation to restrict these fundamental rights, believing that individuals and groups should be responsible for their acts and utterances. We oppose conscription as a military measure for defensive war and oppose all proposals to initiate compulsory labor under whatever guise."

A committee from the Executive Council appeared before the Platform Committee of the national Republican Party, and was given ten minutes in which to present its case. The convention rejected virtually all of the demands of the American Federation of Labor. The Non-Partisan Political Campaign Committee also appeared before the Democratic convention, and although its representatives were more satisfied with the hearing they received, the demands were rejected.

LA FOLLETTE ENDORSED

At its meeting to decide a policy for the Presidential campaign of 1924, the Executive Council faced a dilemma. Strong opposition was expressed by several members to the Republican candidates, especially Charles Dawes, the nominee for vice president. The latter was regarded as highly objectionable in that he had publicly favored anti-unionism. A statement drawn up by Gompers, Morrison, O'Connell, and Woll pointed to the failure of both parties to furnish any relief to labor. There remained the candidacies of Robert La Follette and Burton K. Wheeler, and an endorsement would in fact mean a change in historic policy.

Gompers, who had been seriously ill, mindful of the importance of the issues confronting the Federation, came to the meeting. He took the lead and criticized the Republican and Democratic platforms and the candidates nominated.

I was against them [he declared] and made up my mind if it takes the last bit of energy I have to put it in the campaign for La Follette. The situation is entirely different from the previous campaigns. Here we have practically no choice, one is no nearer to us than the other. You look at the platforms of 1908, 1912, 1916 and you will find nothing in any of them in the platforms of 1924. The Republican convention, they have got hold of the boodle and where they cannot make excuses they have not said a thing. The Democrats say they want honesty. There must be something more than honesty—something more than an indictment of crooks. Here is something where we may help. It is at least a protest and perhaps something better.

Tobin moved an amendment that La Follette and Wheeler be endorsed by name, to which both Green and Duncan objected. Green was active in Democratic politics, and Duncan believed that the endorsement violated traditional political policy. He was not opposed to the candidacy of La Follette. Faced with the possibility that the amendment of Tobin would not receive unanimous support from the Executive Council, and that Green and Duncan would oppose an endorsement of the La Follette-Wheeler ticket, Gompers asked Tobin to withdraw his amendment, as "there is no other construction that can be placed on that document than the feeling that La Follette and Wheeler deserve the support of the masses between the others—Davis and Coolidge, Dawes and Bryan." After Gompers had explained his position, Ryan, who had seconded Tobin's motion that La Follette and Wheeler be endorsed by name, agreed to the withdrawal of the motion when he was assured by Gompers that the statement of the Executive Council was an "endorsement of La Follette."[14]

In the statement on the national campaign, the Council emphasized that it did not approve the views of all the groups supporting La Follette. It took the position that in approving the records of the independent candidates, it did not identify the American Federation of Labor "with an independent party movement or a third party, nor can it be so construed as support for such a party group or movement, except as such action accords with our non-partisan policy."[15]

The action of the Executive Council was protested by William B. Wilson, who had been Secretary of Labor in the Cabinet of President

Wilson and a former officer of the United Mine Workers of America. Wilson claimed that Davis was the author of Section 6 of the Clayton Act, and had always been favorable to organized labor. At the instructions of the Executive Council, Gompers wrote:

The Executive Council appreciates your advice regarding the early struggle and career of Mr. Davis. It likewise weighed in the balance his labor utterances and courses, associations and training. We are confident that our judgment and action are well founded. . . . We have not overlooked your reference to Senator La Follette and we are glad, you may be sure, that you have no "antagonism toward" him. You will not fail to remember that among the many constructive legislative achievements of Senator La Follette the Seamen's Act stands out as a beacon light. It was this great piece of legislation which, in the language of our mutual friend, Andrew Furuseth, "made the last of bondsmen free." We recall no instance in which Senator La Follette has hesitated to give faithful service in futherance of legislation supported by our movement.[16]

The Federation did not modify its position during the campaign. While the Executive Council was overwhelmingly for La Follette and Wheeler, it limited its statement because of the opposition of two members of the Council. The Council had always felt that revealing a division in the ranks of the Council not only weakened its pronouncements, but created difficulties for individual members because of possible pressure being exercised upon them. However, there was no doubt in the minds of the members, especially Gompers, Tobin, Morrison, and Ryan, that their support of La Follette was the proper course, although the break with the traditional policy of avoiding third parties was undoubtedly difficult for them.

The La Follette-Wheeler ticket was spearheaded by the railway unions. They were, however, not concerned with the same problems, nor was their attitude on politics similar to those of many people and organizations supporting a labor or farmer-labor party. The railway unions, whose representatives met in Cleveland, Ohio, on November 9, 1924, after the election, discussed future political tactics. On the motion of Bert Jewell, the head of the Railway Employees Department, it was decided to oppose the formation of a third party. This proposal was unanimously adopted by the representatives of twenty unions present, and a committee was appointed to visit Senator La Follette to inform him of the action taken. Warren S. Stone, the head of the Brotherhood of Locomotive Engineers, and L. E. Sheppard of the Order of Railroad Conductors both expressed the view that the Conference for Progressive Political Action had been taken over by politicians, and unless the railroad unions again took control they would be compelled to drop out.[17]

The results of the election of 1924 were, from the point of view of the unions, unfavorable to the policy of independent political action. Although the independent ticket polled almost five million votes, the failure to carry more than Senator La Follette's home state, Wisconsin, foreclosed any continuation of the movement. In contrast to those interested in long-term political alignments, the unions, including the railroad unions, were interested in immediate results. When the Conference for Progressive Political Action met on February 25, 1925, the unions, in accordance with their earlier plans, withdrew. This left the traditional proponents of third parties in full control. They, however, did not have sufficient following to continue the movement, with the result that independent political action as a significant force within the labor movement expired, not to be revived even in the subsequent depression of the 1930's.

THE DEATH OF GOMPERS

The statement made by Gompers that he had left his sick bed to propose an endorsement of La Follette was not mere rhetoric. At the meeting of the Executive Council on October 2nd, the question of his illness and medical expenses was discussed, and the Council voted to pay the bills. Gompers refused to accept reimbursement, and declared that, with his salary and the amount in his possession as a result of the sale of two lots which had been purchased some years ago, he had been able to meet all obligations incurred in connection with his illness, that he was not in debt and that so long as this was the case he would not present any bills for doctors, nurses, hospitals, etc.

Several members of the Council then expressed the view that Gompers should be repaid for all of his medical expenses as he suffered his illness in his line of duty, and that the Federation should be financially responsible. Moreover, several argued that it was necessary to pay the medical expenses so that Gompers would utilize all the available medical services for conserving his health, and thereby "preserve for the labor movement the inestimable value of his services." Gompers would not yield, and

persisted in his declination to accept reimbursement for expenses incurred on account of his illness, and stated that if the motion would be adopted they would have it upon the minutes for all time but he would not even then avail himself of it. He expressed his deep appreciation of the thoughtfulness and kindness of the members of the Executive Council throughout his illness as well as that of the office employees.[18]

Gompers never fully recovered from his illness, but he resumed his duties and, despite the dangers involved, insisted upon attending the meeting of the Pan-American Labor Federation. He became ill, and was rushed across the border. He died on December 3, 1924, on American soil.

After the funeral services a successor had to be named. Under the constitution, the secretary who succeeds the president when the latter resigns or dies in office, must call a meeting within six days to elect a successor. The Council met on December 13, and when nominations were requested, Vice President Duncan, who had served since the 1890's, expressed the view that it was customary for the first vice president to succeed the president; that he had held the vice presidential office a long time, and that he had given a great deal of service to the movement.

Duncan, who became one of Gompers' closest co-workers, had supported McBride for president in the 1890's, but he had worked in harness for many years, and had not only helped to hammer out the Federation's views on most questions, but had been of great service to many individual unions and to the labor movement. Duncan felt "it is an honor that is due to me from this Council to make me the successor of President Gompers until the next convention." The Council would not, however, yield to sentiment, for no one could guarantee what might happen at a convention once Duncan had been elected to the office.

Thomas Rickert nominated William Green, and James Wilson of the Pattern Makers' League seconded the nomination. Martin Ryan of the Brotherhood of Railway Carmen spoke on behalf of Duncan. Daniel Tobin expressed the view that Green represented the most powerful union in the United States, and that the Council could not ignore this fact in naming its selection. Woll then seconded the nomination of Green, who was elected with both Green and Duncan not voting.[19] It marked a new chapter in the life of the A. F. of L.

Except for one year in its history, the hand of Gompers had guided the movement. Now it would be absent from the steering wheel, and other men would have to devise solutions to the issues and problems that would confront the Federation.

REFERENCES

1. Gompers, Samuel, *Should a Labor Party Be Formed* (Washington: American Federation of Labor, 1919), p. 13.

2. Vote Book, November 13, 1919.

3. *Report of Proceedings of the Fortieth Annual Convention of the American Federation of Labor*, 1920, pp. 63-78.

4. Minutes of Executive Council, February 23, 1920; Gompers to William Mitch, February 19, 1920.

5. Circular issued by the sixteen standard railroad unions.

6. Minutes of the Executive Council, June 6, 1921.

7. Minutes of the Executive Council, February 24, 1922.

8. Document No. 83, March 17, 1922.

9. *Report of Proceedings of the Forty-Second Annual Convention of the American Federation of Labor*, 1922, p. 79.

10. Gompers to James A. Duncan, August 7, 1922; October 23, 1922.

11. *Report of Proceedings of the Forty-Third Annual Convention of the American Federation of Labor*, 1923, pp. 282-291.

12. Circular letter issued by National Non-Partisan Political Committee, May 28, 1919.

13. Minutes of the Executive Council, August 4, 1924.

14. Minutes of the Executive Council, August 2, 1924.

15. *Report of Proceedings of the Forty-Fourth Annual Convention of the American Federation of Labor*, 1924, p. 174.

16. William B. Wilson to Gompers, August 2, 1924; Gompers to Wilson, August 6, 1924.

17. Minutes of Executive Council, November 24, 1924.

18. Minutes of Executive Council, October 2, 1924.

19. Minutes of Executive Council, December 13, 1924.

Index

Adamson Act, 465
affiliates, autonomy of, 90, 163
  intervention in affairs of, 163-182
  structure of, xv
AFL, A. F. of L., *see* American Federation of Labor
Age, The, 314
Alarm, 64
Allen, Henry J., 411
Alpine, John R., 209, 335, 438
Altgeld, John P., 66, 77
Amalgamated Association of Iron and Steel Workers of America, 7, 10, 14, 31, 52, 56, 80, 85, 135, 136, 237, 272 ff.
Amalgamated Association of Iron, Steel and Tin Workers, 335, 385, 387, 390, 392
Amalgamated Association of Street Railway Employees, 102, 464
Amalgamated Clothing Workers of America, 180, 181-182
Amalgamated Labor Union of Terre Haute, 8
Amalgamated Meat Cutters and Butcher Workmen, 169
Amalgamated Society of Carpenters and Joiners, 57, 185, 203
  see also Carpenters and Joiners' National Union; United Brotherhood of Carpenters and Joiners of America
Amalgamated Society of Engineers, 156, 202
Amalgamated Wood Workers' International Union, 205, 250
amalgamation, of related trades, 202-205
amalgamation movement, 201, 453-455
Amalgamation of International Trades Unions, Special Committee on, 7
American Agents' Association, 167, 168
American Alliance for Labor and Democracy, 358-360
American Bridge Company, 275
American Federation of Catholic Societies, 337

American Federationist, The, 127, 252, 263, 265, 268
American Federation of Labor (AFL or A. F. of L.):
  aid to German Trade Unions, 437-438
  aid to local and national unions, 48-51
  aid to United Mine Workers, 137
  anarchism and, xvi
  annual income, first year, 52
  assessments and defense funds, 113-114
  assessments for needy affiliates, xii
  assessments for United Textile Workers, 251
  attacked by Debs, 155
  autonomy as basic principle of, 39-40
  autonomy vs. jurisdictional disputes, 213
  becomes regarded as U.S. trade union central federation, 57
  beginnings of, 1-18
  Bill of Grievances, 294
  Catholic influence in, 336
  central defense fund, 120
  changes during and after World War I, 362-368
  changes within, 233-259
  changing political tactics, 295-298
  changing political views, post World War I, 476 ff.
  charges against Knights of Labor prior to first convention, 32
  charter requirements, 57
  Chinese immigration question and, 302-305
  Church cooperation and, 334-340
  civil rights extension and, xix
  coal mines and, 137-140; *see also* coal miners; United Mine Workers
  Commission of Industrial Relations, 286-287
  conferences with Knights of Labor, 40-42
  consolidation of scattered locals, 45-46
  conventions, *see* Conventions, AFL
  declares inability to bind affiliates, 90

489